Israel's Academic Arena

Pinhas Haliwa

Israel's Academic Arena

The Colleges and University Extensions Revolution

PETER LANG

Bibliographic Information published by the Deutsche Nationalbibliothek
The Deutsche Nationalbibliothek lists this publication in the Deutsche Nationalbibliografie; detailed bibliographic data is available online at http://dnb.d-nb.de.

Library of Congress Cataloging-in-Publication Data
A CIP catalog record for this book has been applied for at the Library of Congress.

This publication has been supported by the Ashkelon Academic College.

Ashkelon Academic College

The Hebrew edition was published by Tel Aviv University, Dor Ledor – Studies in the History of Jewish Education in Israel and the Diaspora – The Prof. Arieh Lewy Series of Monographs XXXVII/2021.

Translated by: Yael Meilijson Nachumi.
Cover illustration : © Goldmund/istock.com.

ISBN 978-3-631-83707-8 (Print)
E-ISBN 978-3-631-85496-9 (E-PDF)
E-ISBN 978-3-631-85497-6 (EPUB)
DOI 10.3726/b18425

PETER LANG
Open

Peter Lang – Berlin · Bern · Bruxelles · New York · Oxford · Warszawa · Wien

This publication has been peer reviewed.

www.peterlang.com

Preface

In the past 25 years Israel's Higher Education System has changed beyond recognition. From a monolithic system comprising academic universities, it evolved into a binary one with two main types of educational institutions – Universities and a diverse range of Academic Colleges that are widely spread and include technological institutions, colleges of art, education and general colleges offering academic degrees in a wide range of disciplines.

The greatest change took place in the mid 1990s as a result of a number of political and social pressures which ultimately led to the removal of obstacles that prevented the system's development. Interestingly, the Council for Higher Education (hereinafter, the CHE), which is the official authority for higher education in Israel, did not initiate the change. Rather, it responded to the growing public demand which for years had remained unanswered. Public pressure, converted into political pressure, finally led the CHE to embrace the long-awaited change. The CHE's programs towards expanding the system in order to make room for the growing demand was met by academic campuses which were by then very much prepared for the transition, having operated for years through regional and technological Colleges spread throughout the country. The early deployment of these campuses was made possible through Local and Regional Councils throughout the country that contributed greatly to the establishment of these local institutions as Post-Secondary Colleges. In turn, the Extension model, that had facilitated the integration of academic education in these colleges, can be attributed to Bar Ilan University, which in the 1960s introduced the American College Extension model in Israel. This model, originating at Christian academic institutions in the USA and imported to Israel by the founders of Bar Ilan University, became a paragon among leaders of Israel's Regional Colleges which until the 1970s had been limited to serving as vocational Post-Secondary education institutions. When the CHE was petitioned to enhance Israel's higher education system in response to growing demand, it identified five colleges operating under the auspices of Bar Ilan University which already offered academic studies towards an undergraduate degree granted by Bar Ilan. One of these, Ariel College, ultimately achieved university status and became Ariel University.

Bar Ilan University's Extensions in the north and south of the country facilitated the matriculation of hundreds of students when the gates to higher education were still largely shut to many. This encouraged other universities to establish academic study forums outside their main campus, leading to the development of Regional Colleges that operated under the academic auspices of one of the country's established universities, alongside additional vocational studies offered.

The religious and social vision promoted by Bar Ilan University's founders, that led to the establishment of three Extensions and two auspices colleges in peripheral regions, was adopted by the CHE in the mid 1990s and became its new social vision. The Regional Colleges model, offering academic studies under a university's auspices, led to the academic recognition of dozens of colleges throughout the country.

This book outlines the developments that led to the revolution in Israel's Higher Education System and the ways in which the program to expand the system was implemented. Had the increased demand for higher education been met? Is higher education today accessible to new populations proportionately to their percentage in the general population? And finally, assuming that reducing social gaps in accessibility to higher education may lead to increased social mobility, the book discusses whether the expansion of the academic system had in fact contributed to reduced social gaps in Israeli society as a whole?

I wish to thank everyone who has supported me in the publication of this book. First and foremost to my colleagues and fellow members of the College Board of Directors – Prof. Shlomo Grossman, President of the College and Chairperson of the Planning and Budgeting Committee, for his valuable input on the Israeli Colleges system in general and the Ashkelon College in particular; Prof. Shimon Sharvit, the College Rector and Prof. Yuval Dror, who encouraged me to publish this book.

A special thanks to my wife and children for their continuous support and encouragement throughout this journey, even when research and writing hours took over precious family time.

Pinhas Haliwa

Table of Contents

List of Figures

List of Tables

Introduction

The beginning of the twenty first century has seen a major transformation in Israeli higher education, the center of which had been the establishment of new academic colleges, the academization of Regional Colleges spread throughout the country, and the transformation of Extensions of established universities into independent academic institutions. As of the end of the 1980s and more in the 1990s, decision makers at the Council for Higher Education (CHE) strived to address the growing public demand for higher education. Among Israel's senior and more recently founded universities, Bar Ilan University was a pioneer in the establishment of academic Extensions far from its main campus in Ramat Gan – a central Israeli city located next to Tel Aviv. Less than a decade after inaugurating its main campus in Ramat Gan in 1955, being the first Israeli university to be inaugurated following the establishment of the State in 1948, during the 1960s Bar Ilan University founded three Extensions in the country's southern and northern peripheral areas. This process continued into the 1980s and 1990s. In the mid 1980s the university extended its academic auspices also to the Ariel Regional College in Judea and Samaria, which later became Israel's ninth university (Ariel University), and to the Western Galilee Regional College in the mid 1990s.

Global developments in higher education and its perception as a tool for social and professional advancement did not remain unnoticed in Israel. The first signs of growing demand for higher education in Israel could be noted as of the end of the 1970s and beginning of the 1980s, with this trend enhanced with the *Aliyah* (immigration) waves of the 1990s. Finally, the continuously growing demand led the CHE to initiate planning operations so as to address this growing need. Although proposals for increasing accessibility to higher education had been deliberated at the CHE as far back as the beginning of the 1970s, comprehensive planning resources were allocated to the matter only by the beginning of the 1990s. The change in the CHE's policy included a renewed planning of Israel's Higher Education system: The addition of new institutions, upgrading of existing ones from general education colleges to academic colleges and the change of status of Bar Ilan University's Extensions into academic colleges. By the end of the 1990s, global changes in education that had greatly influenced Israel's higher education system led Bar Ilan University's management to seriously contemplate whether to continue the Extensions' affiliation to the university. In their new status as colleges, the former Extensions had now integrated in the CHE's academic system expansion program. This expanded accessibility to higher education, which consequently led to a proliferation of academic institutions and a growing competition for State budgets and academic prestige as well as the aspiration to be considered in the same lines as all other universities both locally and globally, ultimately led the university to define new and different targets than those originally envisioned by its founders.

The CHE's program for enhanced accessibility to higher education in the beginning of the 1990s included Regional Colleges that operated under the auspices of Israeli universities, but did not include Regional Colleges operating under the auspices of Bar Ilan University which at the time amounted to 45 % of the country's general Regional Colleges. The program's second phase – which began towards the end of the 1990s and lasted until the first years of the new millennium – did include Bar Ilan University's Extensions as a further stage of development of the country's higher education system. Ultimately, the Extensions' integration in the national system led to a change in their status – from institutions operating under the academic auspices of their parent university and as an integral part of it, to independent academic colleges that are part of a new academic system aiming to fulfill a social-national mission.[1]

Thus, the university's decision to establish Extensions in the 1960s significantly influenced the present map of the country's academic institutions.

The Global Development of Higher Education: Causes and Implications

The twentieth century gave rise to an educational revolution throughout the world. In the first half of the century, elementary education in the west became common, and in its second half, upon their release from colonial chains, third world countries followed suit. However, Secondary and Tertiary education remained restricted to exclusive and elitist parts of the population, and only in the 1950s did high school education also start to become widespread. Today high school education is widely available in most countries.

Table 1 presents changes in primary, secondary and higher education over a 120 year period: 1870–1980.

---

1 The following colleges embarked upon the process of transitioning from operating under the auspices of the university to becoming fully independent: Kinneret College, Ashkelon College, Western Galilee College and Zefat College. This process was completed only recently, in the 2019/20 academic year.

Tab. 1: Percentage of students of the relevant age group in primary, secondary and higher education in selected countries and in Israel

	Primary education				Secondary education				Higher education			
Country	**1870–1910**	**1920–1940**	**1950–1970**	**1970–1980**	**1870–1910**	**1920–1940**	**1950–1970**	**1970–1980**	**1870–1910**	**1920–1940**	**1950–1970**	**1970–1980**
USA	91 %	90 %	86 %	99 %	3 %	21 %	33 %	99 %	3 %	10 %	36 %	57 %
Austria	62 %	78 %	74 %	87 %	2 %	5 %	11 %	74 %	1 %	4 %	7 %	24 %
Italy	37 %	54 %	56 %	100 %	1 %	3 %	25 %	73 %	1 %	2 %	9 %	27 %
UK	62 %	81 %	65 %	96 %	–	6 %	43 %	78 %	–	1 %	5 %	20 %
Belgium	57 %	73 %	70 %	97 %	2 %	5 %	22 %	89 %	1 %	2 %	7 %	25 %
Germany	74 %	75 %	69 %	–	3 %	7 %	20 %	–	1 %	2 %	7 %	28 %
Denmark	62 %	66 %	68 %	97 %	–	8 %	22 %	100 %	–	2 %	9 %	29 %
Netherlands	68 %	74 %	65 %	94 %	1 %	6 %	22 %	82 %	1 %	2 %	7 %	30 %
Norway	66 %	73 %	70 %	100 %	3 %	6 %	24 %	97 %	1 %	2 %	7 %	26 %
France	82 %	74 %	70 %	100 %	2 %	5 %	29 %	79 %	1 %	3 %	12 %	25 %
Sweden	70 %	63 %	61 %	97 %	3 %	7 %	28 %	86 %	1 %	2 %	10 %	37 %
Switzerland	79 %	78 %	78 %	–	3 %	6 %	8 %	–	1 %	2 %	5 %	18 %
Israel[a]	–	–	98 %	95 %	–	–	56 %	72 %	–	–	20 %	26 %

[a] For further information on the development of the Israeli Education System see Chapter 1 – The Development of Higher Education in Israel.
Data: Yogev, 1992: 8

Higher Education was the final stage of development in global educational systems in the second half of the twentieth century. Until the mid-1950s the proportion of students in institutions of higher education in most European countries was 2 %–3 % among 18–23 year olds, except for the USA, where it reached 16 %. A global change in perceptions towards higher education and its goals can be noted only as of the second half of the twentieth century and since then higher education is consumed by masses. As can be seen in Table 2, Recent data from 2018 continue to point to an expansion of higher education in OECD countries.[2]

2 The Organization For Economic Co-operation and Development (OECD) started out as an economic organization working in parallel to NATO to help implement the Marshall Plan for Europe's economic recovery following World War II. Later the organization was joined by countries outside Europe and in 1961 gained its current name. The OECD currently includes 34 member countries accounting for over 60 percent of the worlds' GDP. Member countries share common values that include Democracy and a free market economy.

Tab. 2: Holders of an academic education aged 25–64 in OECD countries in 2009 and 2018

Country	Percentage of holders of an academic education	
	2009	2018
Norway	34 %	48 %
USA	30 %	48 %
Netherlands	28 %	47 %
Israel	28 %	48 %
Iceland	28 %	47 %
Denmark	25 %	47 %
New Zealand	25 %	44 %
Canada	25 %	61 %
Korea	24 %	49 %
Australia	26 %	51 %
Japan	25 %	56 %
UK	26 %	51 %
Sweden	24 %	48 %
Estonia	22 %	44 %
Switzerland	21 %	51 %
Finland	22 %	41 %
Ireland	20 %	56 %
Russian	20 %	41 %
Spain	20 %	44 %
Poland	21 %	44 %
Luxembourg	17 %	55 %
Hungary	19 %	31 %
France	17 %	47 %
Germany	16 %	32 %
Greece	17 %	43 %
Belgium	17 %	47 %
Portugal	13 %	35 %
Slovakia	13 %	37 %
Italy	14 %	28 %
Slovenia	12 %	41 %
Estonia	23 %	44 %
Chile	17 %	34 %

Source: OECD, A1.1a (2009) Education at a Glance and Education at Glance (2019) A1.2 http://www.oecd.org/education/education-at-a-glance-19991487.htm/?refcode=20190209ig, retrieved 1 March 20

The past two and a half decades have seen extensive reforms and changes in Western countries' higher education systems (Volansky, 2005; Yogev, 1992, 2008; Menachem, Tamir and Shavit, 2008; Trow, 2004), expressed first and foremost in an expansion and massification of higher education. The second aspect relates to institutional changes to higher education – a diversification in the types of institutions that resulted in stratification of the systems; and the third aspect pertains to changes in the relationship between the State and the market and between them and higher education. The Globalization process, which led to a liberalization of markets and privatization of corporations as part of the competitive framework of the global market, also led to new expectations from research institutions (Menachem, Tamir and Shavit, 2008). Moreover, the recognition of the role of higher education and research as generators of prosperity in the globalization era has led to an emphasis on the creation of useful and practical knowledge at universities and a massive inflow of people striving to acquire an academi8c degree (Valimaa, 1999). This trend contributed to a reexamination of the role of the State in funding higher education.

The Evolution of Higher Education: Social Aspects

According to Volansky (2005), until the mid-1950s the relatively low proportion of students attending higher education could be explained by two main causes: The first is the belief that universities' main mission is scientific research; and the second the perception of universities as institutions dedicated to training society's elites. According to scholars such as Havighurst (1989), Morrison (1998), Collins (1979) and Dore (1976), in order to preserve their status, elite groups blocked the gates to higher education by developing their own screening tests, thereby maintaining their status for a long period of time. These researchers believe that historically the education acquired by these groups was intended to serve as a tool in their management of the State – both politically and economically. The Higher Education System functioned at the time as an incubator for training the elites (Morrison, 1998) and therefore was perceived by investigators as a lever of reproduction of the existing social structure (Havighurst, 1989). This situation, as can be seen from the tables, has changed, with current data pointing to a global trend in which higher education is no longer exclusively utilized by the elites, but is much more widespread and largely perceived as a universal right rather than the privilege of an elite minority.

The culmination of this trend has led many investigators to assess that in the twenty first century the value of an undergraduate degree is normatively equal to that of a high school diploma in the twentieth century, based on the assumption that when a product becomes available to the masses, its value decreases (Allene & Allene, 2003). The relatively quick proliferation of higher education became known in the 1970s as the "Massification of Higher Education" (Trow, 1974), a term resulting from higher education becoming increasingly universal and the increasing importance of academic degrees in modern society. According to these and other studies, over the past thirty years higher education has gained a number of additional roles other than the training of professionals or researchers. In line with Valimaa's explanation mentioned above, Trow (2004) explained that in recent years higher education is filling increasingly central functions in areas such as economics, governance, the military and social justice. In the USA as well as in many European countries, higher education is considered a means for realizing the full potential of one's talents and capabilities towards achieving social mobility. From an occupational perspective, modern society has become a "Credential Society" – a term coined by American Sociologist Randall Collins – with diplomas becoming more and more influential in the availability of desirable work as well as a high income and status. According to this approach, the proliferation of higher education resulted in a "credential inflation" in the labor market (Dore, 1976; Collins, 1979).

Such expanded accessibility to higher education has inundated institutions with masses of students, leading to the establishment of new institutions and an excess of holders of an undergraduate degree. As a result, people are expected to present academic diplomas even for positions which do not required academic certification at all. The question today in most Western countries is not for whom is higher education intended, but rather what are the means to making it accessible to all, resulting from the demands of modern economies and as part of the principles of justice and social equality, as shall be illustrated below. The underlying assumption is that higher education needs to be available to all those who possess the qualifications and abilities to study (Tonks, 1999). However, the global expansion of higher education is accompanied by a range of different opinions as to its social objectives and missions. Opinions differ mostly over the question whether higher education in its current format of screening candidates while ensuring institutional stratification contributes to the reduction of social gaps between the center and periphery in each society, or whether it maintains these gaps and perpetuates them, in which case the expansion of higher education is in fact an illusion.

To understand the roles and objectives of higher education, we need to first understand the reasons for its global proliferation since the 1950s. As this is a global phenomenon, explanations raised by Sociologists, mainly from the USA and France, are true for every Western society. The proliferation of higher education as a global phenomenon was broadly studied by John Meyer and his colleagues (Meyer et al., 1977) who concluded that there is no single "objective" or empirical explanation for the global proliferation of higher education. However, the phenomenon gained many theoretical explanations in this and other more recent studies. Some researchers trace back the process to the principles endowed to democratic societies by the French Revolution (1789). According to this explanation, principles such as equality, liberty and civil rights were very slowly assimilated over the years, finally becoming ingrained in democratic consciousness following World War II (Cohen, 2001). Common to all sociological theories and specifically those pertaining to the Sociology of Education, is the explanation of a long chain, with each link relying on certain assumptions regarding the social structure, leading to certain processes that in turn lead to an educational process, the result of which is the proliferation of education. Israeli researcher Abraham Yogev summarized the sociological theories in this area into a framework consisting of three main explanations from which most models and theories are derived (Yogev, 1992): (1) Functional-Systemic Explanations; (2) Marxist Conflictual Explanations; and (3) Weberian Conflictual Explanations.

The conflictual explanations (2, 3) are interrelated and can be seen as a continuum. These include Marxist and neo-Marxist explanations, both of which point to a tension in society, resulting mainly from tensions between strong groups to relatively weaker ones.

Functional-Systemic Explanations

Functional-Systemic explanations, just like any functionalistic argument, rely on the assumption that every human society strives to achieve internal unity and tirelessly acts to fulfill all its needs in order to achieve its most important goal – the proper functioning of society. This permanent and continuous action is influenced by social, technological and other factors. Society works to adjust its needs and available tools to achieve its goals, based on which it is given the right to change and to direct its demands to all individuals comprising it in order to provide the tools required for maintaining social cohesion. Within this prototype, a number of models were developed to explain the proliferation of higher education as a global phenomenon.

The **Modernization** or **Industrialization** model was developed in the 1950s and 1960s through an underlying assumption that technological changes in the economy raised the need for professionals possessing specific expertise needed in order to cope with the needs of the new economy. In industrialized society, a person's occupation becomes a central axis for class stratification, linking between the investment made in human capital and its returns. Based on this model, a growing reliance on learners' abilities and less on their ascription background results in a reduction in importance of background factors, meaning that social advancement would be achieved based on ones' educational achievements (Lenski, 1996).

Educational systems in industrialized societies have an important and crucial role – to expand on all levels so as to address the growing need for skilled and specialized workers. Industrialized society's reliance on education and training systems is an important component on the path to social equality. Learners' expertise defines their status while the influence of their social-ascription background is reduced or disappears. Social mobility is influenced by educational and vocational diplomas and therefore a person's social belonging is in his or her own hands (Yogev, 1992). The implementation of this requisite began through the process of socialization for work through the education system. According to this theoretical framework, the expansion of higher education was a direct response to the demands of industrialized society which prefers the most talented, without considering their social status. These requisites effected the educational system in the initial stages of education, which resulted in the development of secondary education, followed by the next link in the chain of change – higher education. The social outcome that accompanies the expansion of higher education means more opportunities for acquiring professional skills and a better chance for social mobility and equality (Parsons, 1970).

In contrast, the **Systemic Model** emphasizes the nation State's institutionalization process, especially in Europe. In the nation State social requirements focus on the establishment of a common national culture. This aim is achieved by developing a national education system that is able to implement national values and unity in early educational stages. The education system in the Nation State has an important social role on which the State relies, resulting in the development of national education networks which enhance the circulation of education among the general population. The expansion of primary and secondary education within these national networks leads to an increased awareness for higher education and ultimately a process of acquiring professional skills which facilitates social mobility and reduces social gaps.

Marxist Conflictual Explanations

Marxist explanations rely on the basic assumption of the existence of social classes across society and their struggle over the country's resources. This struggle, in turn, creates constant social conflict and confrontation which eventually leads to the expansion of higher education. There are two separate neo-Marxist models and one theory for explaining the expansion of higher education:

The **Class Conflict Model** – at the foundation of this model is the assumption that there are two classes: A capitalist class and a working class. The struggle between them is for social resources, and it is never resolved, but causes gradual changes in the status of each, with the working class aspiring to bite into the pie of the capitalist class. One of the changes that results from this interclass struggle, a result of a compromise between the sides, is an interclass agreement to open the gates of higher education to all. While according to its basic approach the capitalist class perceives higher education as the prerogative of the elites, the interclass struggle leads to the opening of the gates of higher education to the working class as well. This results in growing demand, and consequently a growing supply of institutions offering higher education.

The Class Coercion Model – according to this model only the capitalist class is able to organize into a powerful class, and it ensures that its interests are developed in order to preserve its continued class-based control. As the capitalist class controls, according to Carl Marx, the "superstructure", which includes the education system, it is able to expand it while creating a social myth of meritocracy – an ideology in which social placement is based on performance and achievements. Justification relies on the existence of "objective" barriers such as admission exams to institutions of higher education. These exams are seen as artificial barriers serving the higher classes in order to preserve their status and block the lower classes from acquiring higher education.

The Maximally Maintained Inequality (MMI) Theory – the expansion of the academic system would not necessarily result in a reduction of gaps and equality in education until the higher classes reach a point of saturation in their education level. The reason for this is that the chances of the higher classes to utilize opportunities for their professional advancement are higher than those of the lower classes (Raftery & Hout, 1993). According to this theory, the more affluent classes are more aware of the range of opportunities offered by the newly expanded academic system and moreover they are in a better position to take advantage of these opportunities than the lower classes. The higher classes would be able to take advantage of opportunities to acquire their education in prestigious institutions charging a high tuition, while the lower classes, consisting of residents of the social periphery, will tend to study in less prestigious and less sought after institutions. The quotas in the prestigious institutions would be reserved for the higher classes and largely blocked to the lower classes, thereby maintaining the same social gaps despite the expansion of higher education.

Weberian Conflictual Explanations

Explanations according to this approach rely on the work of Max Weber, who while acknowledging the importance of diffused cultural processes resulting from social change, also recognizes the existence of conflicting interests between social groups leading to social stratification. According to Weber, human history is a type of battlefield between value systems. The success of one system as opposed to the failure of another is in many cases the result of the systems' adjustment to a changing external reality and the ability to allocate them a comprehensive social validity. This phenomenon is society's attempt to attach rationality to changing processes.

This type of explanation can be found in two neo-Marxist theories on the expansion of the Higher Education System: Collins' theory of **The Credential Society**, by which despite the competition between different groups over society's available resources, the process does not necessarily lead to confrontation. Rather, competition is seen as leading the credential society to a consensus of sorts between groups. This consensus is a solution for a possible confrontation between them, resulting from a struggle over society's resources. Although low status groups in society do not have access to society's resources as much as do the higher classes, there is general consensus that education credentials are a tool for advancement in the work force. This approach creates a certain vagueness as to the existence or non-existence of a conflict between the classes, while ignoring the strong impact of the State on the expansion of Higher Education. This inherent vagueness is enhanced in neo-Marxist theories such as the Credential Society, in which the State represents capitalist interests. Collins points to the formation of prestigious professional status groups, defining boundaries and preventing penetration of "outsiders" from lower status groups. The means for defining the boundaries of the group is raising academic prerequisites for entering prestigious professions. The social result is the expansion of higher education in society, but in turn it also prevents lower status groups from significantly penetrating prestigious professions, thereby gaining a higher social status (Collins, 1979).

According to French social scientist Pierre Bourdieu's **Field Theory** ('Champ') on the modern aspects of the struggle between the classes, the lower class is sophistically exploited by the ruling class with the aid of science and the media. Based on this theory, modern society is comprised of "fields" or institutionalized social arenas operating according to well established internal rules. Similarly to physical forces, fields are social arenas imbued by unending power struggles in which, willingly or not, people spend most of their lives. Everything one does is an outcome of the field in which he or she spend most of their life (Weitmann, 2002). The "field" is the area created around the people and institutions organizing around a common central occupation, which could be real estate, rock music, professional tennis, high-end fashion, or any other occupation. While each field is unique in that it is organized around a specified occupation, the methods of gaining the fields' capital are similar. Education, higher education and science are a "field", just like any other space in society. And similarly to any other field, the field of science and education has its own history, rules of struggle and aims.

The unique interests of each field cannot be reduced to general interest, but include a struggle over the legitimate definition of the field's operation. Each field has similar characteristics, such as the struggle between "seniors" and "juniors", between those with years of experience and those that have only recently joined. In each such field, struggles for a monopoly over capital take place according to predetermined rules. The structure of each field is defined based on the balance of powers between its members and the struggle taking place within it. In a given power relations situation, each field is inhabited by its seniors, who hold the monopoly over its capital and act to maintain the capital distribution structure, thereby strategizing to preserve the functional and hierarchical structure in the field. In turn, the "Juniors" entering the field have very little of its capital and tend to adopt strategies aimed at undermining the existing order. However, their undermining itself is founded upon the field's predefined and accepted rules of conduct. Young entrants are forced to pay "entrance fees" to prove their recognition of the rules of the game, including cooptation-based selection and acceptance processes. Despite the fact that the new joiners adopt strategies that undermine the existing situation, the fear that they would be rejected forces them to restrict their undermining initiatives to certain limits, meaning that the revolutions taking place do not undermine the very existence or the foundations of the field. While the results of this struggle that takes place according to accepted rules may lead to an internal change in the field, it also prevents a paradigmatic change and thus contributes to the reproduction of the field in its existing structure for many years ahead.

Based on this theory, in the field of higher education and science, as in any other field, there is a struggle that is defined by its structure of powers: The old universities and those that control them wish to preserve the existing structure in order to uphold their monopoly over the field's capital, which includes financial and cultural resources. The cultural resources act as a monopoly in influencing society and its culture, for instance through educational means such as admission exams to higher education institutions. Compared to the older institutions, the new and younger agents, be they institutions or new populations wishing to fight for some of the field's capital, are forced to adopt undermining strategies within limited, predefined areas. This means that any change achieved by the new institutions cannot be revolutionary if they wish to gain the recognition of the senior members of the field – i.e., universities and their representatives. Therefore, the transformation achieved by the education system is an internal one, which does not undermine the foundations of the structure of the field but maintains the existing hierarchical structure in the higher education system.

In the extremities of Bourdieu's theory, the field of intelligence includes a phenomenon he calls 'Sociodicé', or "Racism of Intelligence". According to Bourdieu there are various forms of racism, as the number of groups feeling the need to justify their current existence. The racism of intelligence is the most sophisticated form of racism because contrary to regular, extrovert racism, this form of racism cannot be identified. The racism of intelligence is the racism of the ruling class, whose reproduction depends in part on the transfer of cultural capital. Through the racism of intelligence, the ruling class aims to create a "theodicy", or "justification of the law" – justifying their privilege to control the social order for which they are responsible. They feel and also make sure that others feel, that they belong to a higher essence and therefore the racism of intelligence is theodicy, or a form of social justification characteristic of the ruling class, whose power relies on credentials. These credentials replace, according to Bourdieu, old world credentials such as titles of nobility and property deeds (Bourdieu, 2005). The existence of a class struggle in modern society is upheld through the ruling culture, which is the culture of the ruling classes that hold a monopoly over social concepts and mental talent. This monopoly becomes an allegedly scientific discourse aimed at justifying the racism of intelligence, which in turn is permitted because science represents the ruling form of legitimate discourse. The ruling class, believing it is based on science, turns to science for establishing its rule. Discrimination in society is based on "intelligence", which is assessed by the education system and specifically within the field of psychology, which in itself is a product of the social factors that determine the racism of intelligence. Educational classification is a form of social discrimination legitimized and confirmed by science. Exams that assess early social training predetermine the result of examinees whose social background has not been established culturally and educationally. By this form of discrimination, class distinctions become distinctions in intelligence. Through educational classification and with the support of science[3] intellectuals experience these contradictions without signs of any special unease, as explained

3 Contrary to Bourdieu, Howard Gardner believes that current methods for evaluating intelligence do not allow assessment of a person's ability to acquire knowledge in different areas, such as musical talent or the ability to learn a foreign language. According to Gardner, the problem is not the testing method, but the way in which we think about intellect and intelligence. See: Gardner, 1995: 91–93.

by Bourdieu: "Those who claim the existence of a monopoly of thought about the social world do not at all intend for anyone to think of them in sociological terms" (Bourdieu, 2005).

Recent studies on equal opportunities and higher education have shown that there are still demographic and Socioeconomic barriers to acquiring a higher education. Many factors affect the level of education acquired by the individual beyond his or her personal attributes, including standard of living, Socioeconomic status, place of residence, parental involvement and parents' level of education (Hans-Vaughn, 2004). Thus, young adults from peripheral areas generally achieve lower academic results than their peers living in the center. Parents' country of origin, family size, income and sector are all factors which are also highly influential on the education of the young generation (Horn & Bobbitt, 2000). The level of education of both parents also effects children's' education. When at least one parent holds an academic degree, this fact has a greater influence on the education of the second generation than both parents without an academic education. It was found that the expectations of students whose parents have no academic education are lower than among those whose parents have an academic education (Hans-Vaughn, 2004). In addition, a relationship was found between disadvantaged economic background and the selection of field of study and institution: students who are first generation to academic education are more apprehensive of studying far from their family's home. This in turn effects the types of institution in which they choose to study.

The Expansion of Higher Education: Institutional Aspects

The expansion of higher education through the opening of its gates to wider populations and the expanding of the academic system had widespread implications also in the nature and behavior of the institutions themselves. While the older universities compete with each other on funding, donations, outstanding students, excellent faculty members and academic ranking, the system's expansion forces them to collaborate in research and teaching, for the benefit of all sides. The evolving relationships between the old universities and the new institutions includes a competition over students and State funding, which has increased in all countries due to the growing number of institutes and students. In this struggle the older institutions adopted a tactic of segregation and differentiation so as to maintain their position and historical status. A similar struggle exists between the new institutions themselves, over students, senior faculty and State and private resources. This struggle is further aggravated through competition between public and private institutions whose financial management is free of national regulation, and therefore their ability to employ faculty members is higher. The competition and pressures asserted on the system challenges sacred traditions and principles in the old academic world, and each institution works hard to ensure its own status and power within the system.

The professional literature presents opposing opinions as to the system's expansion and diversification. Some see such expansion as a blessing for research and science, while others view it as an uncontrolled process that creates a false impression and therefore, rather than being a blessing, the expansion undermines the system's normal operation. Those perceiving the expansion as a blessing adopt an essentially functional approach, expressed in the "diversity" school. On the other hand, those who are opposed to it take an essentially conflictual approach, expressed in the "stratification" approach. Researchers working within the diversity approach view the development of a wide and diverse range of higher education institutions as a process that contributes to institutions, to science and to social equality. According to this approach, the justification for the existence of different institutions is in their contribution to consumer diversity, which in turn addresses the diverse needs of the economy and of populations that did not find their place in traditional universities.

The new institutions operating alongside the old ones attract new sectors which did not take part in the Higher Education System in the past. The establishment of these new institutions enhanced general awareness to higher education among the lower classes by offering an opportunity to achieve qualifications and contributing to promoting the social status of these classes. Such higher education system serves social society and its diverse needs as it adjusts itself to a society characterized by social diversity (Meek et al., 1996; Hurtado, 1999). Proponents of this approach believe that the expansion process of the past two decades, which is still underway, leads both the institutions and the Higher Education System itself towards a period of important transitions which will deeply affect science and research. These transitions can be noted over the past decades on the global, national and institutional levels (Guri-Rosenblit, 2005).

The Global Dimension

Affected by globalization and the growing pressures on the academic system following its substantial expansion, the old and new academic institutions undergo changes expressed in a growing openness and abandonment of the alienated historical "Ivory Tower" of higher education. This diversity can be noted in new research methods, diverse funding sources and the attempt to achieve global uniformity in the language of research and teaching. One example of this can be found in the reform that has taken place in Europe following "The Bologna Process" (Bologna University, 1988), which culminated in the drafting of a "Magna Charta Universitatum", A document signed by 430 Rectors and heads of universities throughout Europe, with the aim of increasing collaboration between Europe's universities and establishing mutual recognition (Guri-Rosenblit, 2005). According to the agreement, students taking courses in any of the participating universities would be accredited in all other universities and would be able to finish their degree in any of them. This resulted in an increased efficiency of the academic system, increased mobility of students throughout the continent and a growing and more diverse body of students and researchers. According to the diversity approach, an increased diversity of the academic system on the national level influenced the ties between all types of institutions with similar ones on the global level: Teacher-training institutions and colleges training technicians and practical engineers would collaborate with their counterparts in other countries and join international organizations which would contribute to their development and to the level of teaching offered.

Another example of the global aspect is the expansion and diversification of the higher education system in Asia, Eastern Europe and the Persian Gulf region through foreign universities, mostly American ones, who opened Extensions in these regions. The foreign universities brought with them a western "fragrance" and soon became international institutions functioning within a global network. Within such networks there soon evolved a global competition for attracting senior faculty members and researchers and gaining academic prestige. These Extensions of established American universities attract researchers and scholars from around the world, mostly in areas that are at the forefront of advanced knowledge, while in comparison weaker universities loose researchers every year in a "Human capital flight".

The push for differentiation and prestige can be noted in the global system through world university ratings published in London and in Shanghai, ranking the top 500 universities in the world. Although the American weekly magazine *U.S. News and World Report* has for years been publishing a rating of top American universities, the global rating is relatively new and is a result of the expansion of the system and the globalization of the academic world (Rabinowitz, 2009). According to researchers, all of these steps will increase the number of students applying for academic studies at universities, which in turn would further develop research and increase the chances of scientific and social progress (Trow, 2004).

The National Dimension

Researchers point to a number of specific countries that revolutionized their Higher Education System following the system's expansion and the globalization process.

Australia – until 1988 there were 18 universities and over 100 colleges and Post-Secondary education institutions in Australia. In 1987 the Minister of Labor published a document entitled "Green Pages",[4] which outlined a change in the binary structure that had been ingrained for many years, consisting of a clear distinction between universities and colleges. The purpose of the reform document was to reduce institutional diversification and create a unified national system by making research a national priority, increasing external funding for research and teaching a larger variety of disciplines such as Applied Sciences, Computer Science, Technology, Business Administration and other disciplines that can potentially contribute to economic growth. The reform's implementation reduced the horizontal and vertical diversification of higher education in Australia and led some of its existing institutions to merge, thereby creating a 39 universities structure. Despite this national initiative, however, over the past decades three groups of universities having similar attributes and goals organized to establish their differentiation from the others. In 1999, a coalition of eight leading Australian universities founded "The Group of Eight" (Go8). Another coalition of the time included five universities focusing on applied study and research fields and a third group of relatively new universities established a partnership aimed at strengthening their status and gaining a larger share of the national allocation of funds. These organizations, formed despite the national plan to promote the system's unity, attest to the pressing need for diverse institutions for diverse purposes, both for horizontal diversification, such as in the case of old research universities vs. new ones, and for vertical diversification such as in the organization of leading research universities compared to others.

Japan – Until April 2004 Japan's universities were operated and closely monitored by the country's Ministry of Education. University employees including academic faculty members were employed by the State, a fact that did not allow university heads to independently manage their institutions, and moreover for many years outdated curriculums were used, which did not fit the requirements of the evolving economy. Pressures by Japanese corporations and the diminishing reputation of the country's universities led to a reform that provided managerial flexibility to the universities' managements and release from tight State supervision. The direct result was an annulment of the old employment status of university employees and a newfound freedom in the drafting of updated curriculums.

---

4 From: The status of higher education and research universities in Israel: Warning signs and policy directions, the Committee of the "Bashaar" Association (Academic Community for Israeli Society), led by Y. Yurtner, 2004.

In April 2004, the State's employment of university employees was cancelled and each individual institution became the employer of its staff. The main purpose of the reform had been to implement change in the managerial level so as to diversify the types of available institutions of higher education in the country and to provide universities operational freedom to create new and creative curriculums beneficiary to the Japanese economy. Such change was possible in Japan because the growing demand for higher education led to the system's expansion and in turn to a different view of the changing needs of the economy. The changes that followed the system's expansion led to the creation of new programs and to institutions embarking upon a new start following a period of local economic recession (Guri-Rosenblit, 2005).

The Institutional Dimension

The Bologna Process and the global expansion of the academic system pushed senior institutions to redefine their goals and methods of operation. Leading universities invest extensive efforts and resources in positioning themselves as a 'World Class University' (Altbach, 2004). The prestige of these institutions relies on leading resources, excelling students and a world-renowned academic faculty. Such institutions tend to differentiate themselves from new institutions who are yet to prove their academic and scientific potential.

The impact of this expansion process and globalization is not limited to the repositioning of institutions, but leads them to the creation of common academic standards designed to improve the relationship between the academic institution and society, alongside the aim for its integration in national and international systems. There are many examples for this change in the level of institutional positioning, in many countries including Israel. Universities across the USA collaborate in research and in the accreditation process for students between institutions, including non-academic ones such as Community Colleges. Such collaboration consists of universities recognizing courses and preparatory programs completed by students at Community Colleges even though they are not academic institutions. A unique example of this new collaboration model which increases the efficiency of participating institutions is the reform conducted by the Swiss Federal Institute of Technology in Lausanne (EPFL). An example of a change at the institutional level: The institute, that operated 12 Departments of Technology, replaced them by five multidisciplinary schools and established collaboration agreements with additional institutions such as the University of Lausanne that offered programs in the Humanities. The Institute offered technology courses to students of the university, and the university offered the institute's students courses in the Humanities. This initiative attracted students of advanced degrees to the institute, and in 12 years the EPFL doubled its number of students studying for advanced degrees.

While the diversification approach views the presence of institutional hierarchy as a marginal process of diversification serving a wide range of populations and needs, according to the Stratification approach institutional hierarchy is a central factor in the creation of a stratified system (Tiechler, 1988). Uncontrolled and unstandardized expansion leads to unequal competition between the different institutions and therefore not only does it not result in positive social change, but it further deepens social differences and Class stratification. From an institutional perspective this approach views the competition for students, both in the private and the public (supervised) systems, as a process that leads to a priori discrimination. While the public systems operate under public supervision and budgeting, the private ones have no such limitations, and under such competition the public institutions don't stand a chance.

Such competition leads to a hierarchical stratification of the institutions, and a functional differentiation that grants more power to the strong and further weakens the new and the weak. While the expansion also leads to the establishment of new institutions with diverse interests and management methods so as to address a wide range of educational and social needs, the budgetary limitations of the public system, which is forced to cope with more and more institutions, does not leave room for equality. The result is predetermined – the establishment of new educational institutions competing over the same population, using unequal tools such as the lack of research budgets, results in the creation of second class institutions and a differentiation process which forces the senior institutions to invest in excellence and academic achievements in order to maintain their hegemonic status. In doing so, of course, they leave the new institutions far behind. Thus, two types of institutions are created: the first, prestigious ones that attract the elites, and the second serving the lower classes. Researchers from this school of thought (for instance Ben-David, 1972; Farnum, 1990) have identified this differentiation process in American Elite universities such as Harvard, Yale, Princeton and Columbia. In recent years, these universities, which started off as institutions serving the descendants of local elites, began to emphasize academic excellence due to the need to compete for students with the newer universities. The result of this competition was a stratification between the Elite universities and the others, the formers' successful in attracting higher achieving students compared to those attending the newer institutions. A similar process occurred in England – where universities such as Cambridge and Oxford, which had historically served the descendants of British nobility, began to compete with new universities founded in the cities towards the end of the Victorian period (Jones, 1988), and with the polytechnic colleges,[5] which later gained academic status. This inequality leaves the new institutions with no standing chance and establishes a basic stratification in the system, that is gradually legitimized by the supervision bodies, as was the case in England when the Higher Education Funding Council for England, which funds the country's universities, adopted a funding method that is based on institutions' research and teaching capabilities (Watson, 1999). Based on the stratification approach, the chances of the new institutions to succeed in their academic mission is significantly lower than that of the more senior institutions, which hold all the tools for success. In a comparison between the evolvement of the higher education system in the England, Australia, Japan, France and Holland, Teichler (1988) concluded that all higher education systems in these countries are stratified from an institutional perspective. A further explanation for this stratification process was proposed by Vallimaa, who argued that institutional stratification is a result of confrontations between the State, that strives for diversity so as to enable equal opportunities, and the public bodies supervising the Higher Education System, controlled by old institutions or affected by their interests. While the result of this confrontation is indeed a more diverse system, the more diversity is implemented, it also becomes more and more stratified (Vallimaa, 1999).

5 Following reforms in the structure of the British Higher Education System led by British governments and specifically the Thatcher administration, many technological colleges became universities of technological professions.

1 The Development of Higher Education in Israel: Causes and Implications

The expansion of higher education in Israel is largely similar to that of Western European countries. It occurred as a culmination of the process that led to the expansion of the education system and created the last layer that followed the expansion of primary and secondary education. As seen in the tables presented above, in the beginning of the 1950s Primary education became widespread, followed by Secondary education as a result of legislation: the Compulsory Education Law legislated in 1949, and the 1953 State Education law which led to the State taking over all forms of education available in the country at that time. As all other Zionist initiatives, the development of all levels of the education system was perceived as an inseparable part of the Jewish Revival ideology and was widely affected by it (Bolotin, Shavit & Ayalon, 2002).

Historical Background

The Jewish "*Yishuv*" (Jewish community of pre-State Israel) viewed the establishment of an education system as a means for realizing the homeland for the Jewish people as promised in the 1917 Balfour Declaration. During the period of the British Mandate for Palestine (1920–1948), the Jewish education system in the region was owned by the Zionist Organization and its institutions. With the growth of the Jewish population, the education system grew steadily, and in 1920/1921 it numbered 135 institutions, 523 teachers and about 13,000 children. A further 3,000 children attended dozens of other institutions, including as the Haredi (Ultra-Orthodox Jewish) education system and the Alliance Israélite Universelle private schools. In 1984, with the establishment of the State of Israel, the number of students multiplied by 6.5 (Dror, 2008).

The education system inherited by the State upon its establishment can be divided into three different educational streams, distinguishable both ideologically and politically: The Zionist-Religious "Mizrachi" stream accounted for 18 % of all preschools during the British Mandate, 27 % of Primary schools and 10 % of High schools. The Zionist-Socialist "Labor" stream accounted for 37 % of preschools, 23 % of Primary schools and only 3 % of High schools, while 45 % of preschools belonged to the "general" stream, meaning the general-Zionist, as well as 49 % of Primary schools and 87 % of High schools (Dror, 2007: 1–5). The mostly Ashkenazi (Jews originating from Eastern Europe) Anti-Zionist Haredi education was not included in the "*Yishuv*" educational streams.

Each of the streams offered a separate curriculum, held separate education conferences and published separate educational texts and journals. The Kibbutz education system's curriculum emphasized an interdisciplinary learning approach as well as personal and group studies, while the "general" stream offered a "classic" education at its High schools: the Hebrew Gymnasium in Tel Aviv, Haifa and Jerusalem.

The State's education system was largely formed during the first two decades of its existence, predominantly as a continuation of the system established during the pre-State "*Yishuv*" period. Each educational stream used its own methods and emphasized different areas in its curriculum. With the constantly growing number of Jewish immigrants *("Olim")* arriving in Israel, the needs of the existing education system continued to change and expand. The system now had to cope with the absorption of hundreds of thousands of new Jewish immigrants from Arab countries and from Eastern Europe, and to adjust itself to a constantly changing reality. The first step in this direction was the legislation of the Compulsory Education Law in 1949, followed by the 1953 State Education law which unified the separate educational streams under a single system. While in practice each of the three streams continued to remain separate under their old names, the new legislation brought the entire education system under the wings of the State's authority and supervision. The State education system consolidated the general secular education and the Zionist Organization stream; the State-religious education was the successor of the "Mizrachi" stream, and the Haredi stream persisted in its independence.

Until the beginning of the 1960s the Israeli education system upheld a uniform and centralized "formal equality" policy that aims for a nationalist education based on the Zionist-Ashkenazi method of education. The ideological education streams inherited by the State operated according to the ideologies of movements that originated in Eastern Europe and their educational work was targeted and adjusted to the needs of the new immigrants the their children. The *Yishuv* educational policy, that had persisted into the first years of the State, caused significant gaps between the local population and the new immigrants of the 1950s and 1960s because it did not suit the expanding size of the system that increased 6.5 times during that period. During the 1960s this policy led to a large proportion of students being classified as "disadvantaged" *(Teunei tipuach)*. In the Primary education system their proportion reached approx. 60 %, leading to a high dropout rate among students from disadvantaged areas and to a selection process in High school admission.[6] These deepening social gaps led to a policy of compensatory education

6 For further information on the importance of the reform and the conditions that preceded it, see: Dror, 2006: 35–59.

in an attempt at affirmative action for disadvantaged populations, especially children of *Olim* from Arab countries. The integration reform was the second stage of attempts to reduce existing gaps in the education system (Levi, 2006). Zalman Aran, Minister of Education at the time, who had held the position intermittently between 1956 and 1970, undertook the task of reducing the gaps and increasing educational continuity, which ultimately led to a reform in the education system and to a certain extent to educational and social integration. According to Dror, the most important event in the history of Education in the State of Israel was the reform introduced in the education system during the 1960s, which essentially involved the implementation of six-year primary schools followed by three-year Junior high schools and High schools. Compulsory education was extended until the end of Junior high so as to allow disadvantaged populations a better chance to reach High school. The aim of the reform was social integration through education, in the same way in which the heads of the Council for Higher Education (CHE) viewed the increased accessibility to Higher education in the 1980s and 1990s as a tool for reducing social gaps.

The third, fourth and fifth decades of education in the State of Israel were marked by continued integration and an emphasis on the autonomy of teachers and schools. In the 1970s and 1980s many new initiatives aimed to solidify integration, including the implementation of comprehensive programs for improving academic achievements. The Ministry of Education established the 'Shahar' (Hebrew acronym for Education and Welfare Services) Division, and projects were launched to strengthen disadvantaged municipalities, including "the Holistic Project" that took place in 30 municipalities; and 'Project Renewal' – a joint program of the government of Israel and the Jewish Agency for Israel for rehabilitation of around 70 distressed neighborhoods. During the same period academic institutions initiated special programs and differential teaching methods in heterogenic classrooms to assist students in coping with the difficulties that resulted from the gaps in the education system. All of these activities since the onset of the reform in the education system and integration led to the outcome that can be seen in Tab. 1, showing that the global education revolution of the twentieth century did not skip the Israeli system: Between the years 1950 and 1970, 98 % of all children of relevant ages attended Primary education. At the same period 56 % of all children of relevant ages attended Secondary education, with this number increasing to 72 % in 1979–1980. As was the case in all Western countries, Primary and Secondary education in Israel became common and widespread.

Higher education remained the last layer of the education system that did not grow in parallel to the population and to the needs of society and the economy. The history of Post-Secondary and Higher education in Israel was to some extent similar to that of Primary and Secondary education: Teachers' training was divided by ideological streams. Until 1920 there were two teacher-training institutions in Israel: The Lewinski Seminary for Teachers in Yafo and the Hebrew Seminary for Teachers in Jerusalem. The two institutions belonged to the general education stream. Higher education included three institutions: The Hebrew University of Jerusalem; The Technion – Israel Institute of Technology in Haifa; and the Weizmann Institute in Rehovot (founded in 1944 as the Hebrew University Institute for Agriculture Studies, and later the Ziv Institute).

The main Zionist principles towards the establishment of the State, renewal of the Hebrew language and revival of Jewish culture also included a vision of academic institutions that will serve as an international Jewish center of research and science serving the needs of the Jewish people settling in its country and signifying the image of the modern Jew. Testimonies of initiatives for the development of the Higher education system in Israel date as far back as the nineteenth century, from Rabbi Zvi Hermann Schapira's call in 1882–1888 to found a university that will be a center for the theoretical and practical culture of the Jewish people, to the work of "The Democratic Faction" – a group of young Zionist intellectuals aiming to promote Jewish culture and the academic education of young Jews in Europe, which eventually led to the decision to establish a University in Jerusalem (Zelechowski, 2013: 203–235).

The decision to establish a Hebrew University in Jerusalem also included a vision for an institute of technology in Haifa, but the paths of the two institutions were separated very early on. The Zionist plan developed in 1902 by Zionist leaders Martin Buber, Berthold Feiwel & Chaim Weizmann included the establishment of a "Jewish School of Higher Learning" as part of the future Jewish university, with the Technion being but one non-central aspect of this plan.[7] Dr. Paul Nathan, founder and head of the non-Zionist "Relief Society of German Jews" ("Ezra") preceded the Zionist movement and began the establishment of a Post-Secondary technical school, a "Technicom" for training practical engineers in the Central European and specifically German tradition, based on the "Technische Hochschule" model (Kirsch, 2014). In 1909 a special association was founded for this purpose and in 1912 works commenced for the construction of the "Technicom" at the Hadar Carmel neighborhood in Haifa and next to it the "Hebrew Reali School of Haifa" was founded. The War of the Languages that started a year later as well as World War I led to the collapse of the "Ezra"

7 Buber, Feiwel & Weizmann, 1968.

network and preparations for the construction of the "Technicom" were stopped. After the war, the "Technicom" buildings were sold to the Zionist Administration, which decided to proceed with the establishment of the technical school and The Hebrew Technion was official inaugurated in 1925. Only in 1931 was the Technion recognized as an independent academic institution, independently of the "Reali" school (Dror, 2007: 182–183).

The establishment of academic institutions in Israel such as the Technicon was accompanied by material disputes within the Zionist movement itself, which was influenced in this regard by global academic traditions. Decision makers had three models to look to: The Central European model (which was predominantly German), the British model and the American model. Chaim Weizmann (biochemist, President of the Zionist Organization and later first President of the State of Israel) was influenced by the German model, but when the British occupied the region and he joined the British Academy, the British model became the most influential, and Weizmann aimed to develop an integrated future model: A Jewish university, or as it was called in Zionist circles "The Jewish College", that would also include a Technion for technological disciplines. Weizmann supported interim technological training in Haifa in order to serve the practical needs of the Jewish settlement. Achad Ha'am (Zionist leader and founder of cultural Zionism) supported Weizmann's position, emphasizing the importance of a gradual process of establishing a Jewish university, consisting at first of the establishment of small research institutes of Jewish studies, Humanities and Social Sciences, and only later the development of teaching disciplines and the establishment of the Technion. Revisionist Zionist leader Zeev Jabotinsky, who had been influenced by the American model, proposed to establish a research and teaching university that would offer scientific and practical technology studies.

Much was written on the history of the Hebrew University. The first essay was written in the 1930s by the university's faculty member Prof. Joseph Klausner. In his essay Klausner reviewed the origins of the idea of founding a Jewish university and summarized the University's seven first years. A review of the history of the Hebrew University was published in three volumes: The first, edited by Shaul Katz and Michael Heyd was published in 1977; the second, edited by Hagit Levski in 2005, and the third, also by the same editor, in 2009. These extensive volumes expose the process of establishing the university, its development and foundation in the pre-State Jewish *Yishuv*, in the State of Israel, and through to the new millennium. It began with Zvi Hermann Schapira's call for the foundation of a Jewish university. His call did not go unanswered and in 1913 the 11th Zionist Congress voted for the establishment of a university in Jerusalem, in which the teaching language would be Hebrew. In July 1924 the Zionist Movement obtained a permit from the British authorities to lay a cornerstone for the University, and the gates of the new institution were officially opened at Mt. Scopus in 1925.

The Technion and the Hebrew University were owned by the Zionist Organization until they became independent institutions. In all ongoing dilemmas involving the debate between the global role of Higher education and the imperative to address the needs of the State in the making, the national need took precedence: In its first years the Technion focused on training practical engineers, and only after four years of study its graduates were granted the degree of "Engineer". From 1931 to 1950, under the management of Shlomo Kaplanski, the Technion invested in deepening academic research and began to establish its reputation as a world renowned academic institution (Dror, 1996: 330–357).

The Weizmann Institute was founded in 1934 as a research institute which at first was called the Ziv Institute, in memory of Daniel Ziv, son of Lord Israel Ziv and Rivka Ziv founders of the famous British retail chain Marks and Spencer. The initiative for the Institute's establishment was led by Haim Weizmann, and its aim was to conduct research in the area of chemical processes for the development of fertilizers that would enable cultivation of crops in dry soil, as well as in the area of chemical processes for the Israeli chemical industry. Zionist activists from the USA headed by Meyer Weisgal raised funds to enable the institute's expansion and its name was changed to "the Weizmann Institute of Science". In 1946 the cornerstone for the new institute was laid, and in 1949 its first building was inaugurated. These pioneering institutions were the cornerstones of Higher education in Israel, even after the establishment of the State.

Later in the book we will discuss the establishment of Bar Ilan University (founded in 1955) and the religious-social ideology of its founders. Tel Aviv university was established in 1956. The city of Tel Aviv, that was less impacted by the War of Independence than Jerusalem, quickly grew to become the country's central commercial and cultural metropolis. The ongoing waves of immigration doubled its population and in 1961 the city became home to nearly 700,000 people. Its meteoric growth and unique character as a commercial and cultural center increased the demand for Higher education in Tel Aviv, rather than in Jerusalem, where studies required travel and housing expenses and therefore making it significantly difficult for those who had to travel from Tel Aviv to Jerusalem to study. The Tel Aviv Municipality, headed by Mayor Haim Levanon, undertook the initiative to establish a university in Tel Aviv and in 1953 decided on the foundation of a university institute of Natural Sciences, which was to become the foundation for the future university.[8] The management of the Hebrew University, fearing competition from the newly founded academic institute in Tel Aviv, appointed a committee to investigate the questions that were raised following the possibility that the idea of the establishment of a university in Tel Aviv would be realized, and decided to take upon itself the academic responsibility for the institute to be founded in Tel Aviv. One of the members of the committee, Dr. Joshua Prawer, submitted to the Rector and President of the Hebrew University a document entitled: "The establishment of a university Extension in Tel Aviv". Prawer assumed that such an institution would be established with or without the support of the Hebrew University, due to the size and pace of growth of the city of Tel Aviv (Cohen, 2002). According to the program recommended by Prawer, within five years, an institution named "The Hebrew University of Tel Aviv" would be established in Tel Aviv, funded by the city's Municipality. The institution would only offer undergraduate studies in the Faculty of Humanities, and any continued studies would be held at the Hebrew University. While the Hebrew University's management delayed the plan, the Tel Aviv Municipality continued to promote it and in 1954 founded the Institute of Jewish Culture, focusing on Jewish studies. Despite the Hebrew University's efforts to curb the establishment of an independent university in Tel Aviv, the Tel Aviv municipality announced the establishment of the Tel Aviv University by merging between the Institute of Natural Sciences, the Institute of Jewish Culture and the private college of Law and Economy that operated in the city since 1935 into a single institution (Gross, 2008).

Backed by the processes taking place in the country's Higher Education System since the establishment of the State, the government decided to intervene and in May 1956 Minister of Education Zalman Aran appointed a committee led by then Governor of the Bank of Israel David Horwitz to examine the field of Higher Education in Israel. According to its letter of appointment, the committee was requested to examine the condition of Israel's Institutions of Higher Education (Cohen, 2002). Ten months following its appointment, the committee submitted a report specifying the urgent need to expand accessibility to higher education so as to promote the assimilation of exiles and cultures (the 'melting pot' metaphor). The committee recommended that educational institutions be established near students' places of residence, so as to facilitate accessibility. The result came rather quickly, and two additional universities were founded, in the north and the south of the country. The idea to establish a university in the southern Negev region began to unfold back in 1961 as an initiative by David Tuviyahu, the first Mayor

8 Cohen, 2002.

of the southern city of Beer Sheva. The idea had been initiated in conversations with David Ben Gurion, Israel's Prime Minister at the time, and with Levi Eshkol who became Prime Minister in 1963. Eshkol appointed a committee headed by Prof. Efraim Katzir, and in consultation with Prof. Ernst David Bergmann, studies were established at Beer Sheva on behalf of the Weizmann Institute of Science and the Hebrew University. In 1963 the Ottoman Association was established with the aim of founding a university in Beer Sheva, to be entitled "The Institute of Higher Education in the Negev".[9] In 1969 the government decided to establish a university in Beer Sheva, which was inaugurated in 1970 in a similar process to that of Tel Aviv university and the University of Haifa. The Beer Sheva University made its first steps as an institute of higher education under the joint auspices of the Hebrew University of Jerusalem, the Technion and the Weizmann Institute of Science (Klein, 1998; Yogev & Shapira, 1992).

The University of Haifa was founded through a gradual process that began in 1952 with an initiative of the Haifa municipality that had decided to found a Post-Secondary education College for adult education. The school operated under the auspices of the People's Education Center (the Buber Center) at the Hebrew University. A committee on behalf of the university led by Prof. Joshua Prawer recommended that the Hebrew University's management establish a university institution in the city of Haifa, that would be based on the activities already taking place at the College. The Haifa Municipality funded the operation and the Hebrew University provided its auspices through an academic counselor based on campus. The aim of the new campus was to train a reserve of teachers for high schools in the northern region, but the city's leaders and university counselors aimed that the institution would become a real university. In 1969 an agreement was signed between the municipality and the institutions to offer undergraduate and graduate studies, and in 1972 the CHE recognized the academic institution as an independent university (Dror, 1997). The main period of establishment of Israel's universities ended with the establishment of the Open University in 1973, although it became authorized to grant undergraduate degrees only later, in 1980.

The rise in the number of universities from the 1950s to the 1970s expressed the growing demand for higher education throughout the country. This demand continued to grow with the growing numbers of new immigrants after the early 1970s. The immigration of the 1970s from the USSR, the wave of immigration from the same region in the early 1990s and economic-social developments in Israel and the Western world all created a growing demand for Higher education.

---

9 Ben Gurion University Archive: http://in.bgu.ac.il/aranne/Pages/Tuv.aspx Retrieved March 1, 2020.

Table 3 presents the rise in the number of students in Institutions of higher education as of the establishment of the State until 2019. As can be noted, the percentage of students in the higher education system has gradually grown in significant numbers:

Tab. 3: Number of Students in 1984– 2018/19 (excluding the Open University)

Year	Number of students	Population size (thousands)	% of Students
1948	1,600	1,059.0 (in 1949)	0.16
1958	9,000	2,000.1	0.45
1970	35,000	2,974.0	1.12
1980	54,480	3,677.7	1.48
1990	76,000	4,660.2	1.63
2000	180,229	6,289.2	2.86
2004	199,000	6,689.7 (in 2003)	2.974
2007	208,046	6,990.7 (at the end of 2005)	2.976
2010	237,747	7,965,000 (at the end of 2010)	2.984
2013	257,145	7,984,500	3.220
2019	268,355	9,092,000	2.951

Source: Stav, 2009; CHE website – A collection of data towards the 2010/11 academic year; Central Bureau of Statistics Table 1: Students in Higher education institutions by degree and institution type; 2010 and 2013 data from the Israel Statistical Annual 2013, number 64 table 2.1. 2019 data from: Central Bureau of Statistics Website, Table A – students by academic degree and institutions – 2009/10 and 2018/19; Higher Education in Israel – Selected date for the 2018–2019 academic year. Retrieved March 2, 2020.

As will be seen in later chapters, the 1990s were breakthrough years leading to a structural transformation of the Higher Education System. The immigration waves and growing number of students eligible for a high school diploma pushed the CHE to develop extensive absorption programs and increase the number of Institutions of Higher Education during the 1990s. The extensive rise in the number of students in the mid 1990s and beginning of the new millennium in parallel to a deceleration in the demand for higher education compared to the beginning of the 1990s, caused the CHE to decide to stabilize the number of students, allowing for a moderate growth based on a predefined higher education budget.

Structure of Israel's Research Institutes

Since the establishment of the first institutes in Israel at the beginning of the twentieth century through to the 1950s, most academic institutions in Israel were based on the European/German model, which relied mainly on Wilhelm von Humboldt's 1810 modern university model – a research-based university that integrates between teaching and research and emphasizes full academic freedom in these two areas. The belief that scientific research is a powerful component that would ensure the excellence and future of the State of Israel beyond its size and financial strength dictated the nature of Israel's higher education institutions until the 1950s. This construct became well established in Israel for a number of reasons:

a. The initiators of the plan to establish the first Jewish university in Israel – Buber, Feiwel & Weizmann, were influenced by the German research universities and the technological Post-Secondary education institutions in Germany and Central Europe.
b. Most teachers who immigrated to Israel in the 1920s and 1930s came from Germany and Central Europe.
c. Early on, the Technion and the Hebrew University established academic ties with Central European academic and technological institutions and were influenced by them.

Only during the British occupation of the area did the British model gradually infiltrate, giving emphasis to the teaching component. This influence resulted from a number of reasons:

a. The Zionist Administration convened in central London and was influenced by British culture.
b. Large quantities of research equipment was sent to the country from the UK following the occupation.
c. Weizmann, one of the leaders of the Zionist movement, joined the British Academy back in 1904.
d. At first, close ties were established between the British authorities and the Jewish *Yishuv*, leading to collaboration in a wide range of areas, including British consent for the establishment of the Hebrew University and the laying of its cornerstone in 1924.

The American model was nearly unknown in the region during the first half of the twentieth century and its influence on the structure of universities in Israel began to be noticeable only following the Second World War. The American institutions, that attempted to learn from the German model began to replace the German model during the second half of the century. Their influence on institutions in Israel grew as of 1950, for a number of reasons:

a. The academic system developed substantially following World War II due to America's growing global influence.
b. Beginning in 1950, many American teachers arrived in Israel, including senior academic faculty members. One of the most prominent of them was Alexander Dushkin, who greatly influenced the teaching methods used at Israel's universities. Dushkin was the head of a committee for reform and change of the teaching organization at the university and was the recipient of the Israel Prize for Education in 1968.[10]
c. Israeli academic faculty members continued their education in the USA in the 1960s and upon their return brought with them American influence.
d. An ongoing academic and research collaboration was established between faculty members and academic institutions in Israel and their counterparts in the USA.

The American model, integrating basic research, applied research and teaching, filled the place of the German model, with the USA quickly becoming a world science center following World War II. This model succeeded in integrating the accessibility of education for the masses with the need to position the most prestigious research universities at the forefront of scientific development (Kirsch, 2014). The research orientation of Israel Universities was strongly established in the beginning of the twentieth century through the influence of the German model and continued with the influence of the American model until the beginning of the 1990s, but without expanding academic accessibility for the masses. This structure in Israeli research institutions was expressed in a number of areas:

a. **The mix of students** – the number of students studying for advanced degrees at universities, as noted by the Chairperson of the CHE's Planning and Budgeting Committee (Hereinafter: PBC), should be one third to half of the total number of students studying at the institution (Lev Zion, 2001).
b. **Scientific Excellence** – a research institution is required to maintain scientific excellence and work towards its acquisition. Its role is to create knowledge on

---

10 Dushkin immigrated to Israel in 1919 but returned to the USA, finally settling in Israel in 1934. He completed his academic degrees in the USA including the degree of Rabbi which he achieved from the American Rabbinical Seminary. For more information on his educational and academic work, see: Iram, 1977.

a global level, to develop knowledge centers and scientific infrastructures and to train Israel's future scientists.

c. **Evaluation tools** – research institutions are in a constant state of evaluation. They are evaluated based on the amount of knowledge created and its usability.

Until now, this structure of research universities in Israel situated the country at the forefront of international knowledge. In recent years Israel has been ranked third in the world in the number of scientific publications per capita. In Citation Indices for technological fields the ratio Israel/World was the highest in 1999–2003 (Kirsch, 2010). Israel is ranked 13th in the world in the number of Nobel Prize Winners per capita (1.20 per million) and first in a number of indices of international collaboration. However, many still believe that Israel's full scientific potential is yet to be realized, mostly due to a budgetary shortage compared to other research institutions in the world – such as in the UK and the USA (Lev Zion, 2001).

During the universities' first years, their role was multi-faceted: Promoting knowledge, education and training of national leadership in all area, developing new technologies, training engineers and scientists and forming the foundation of Israeli culture. As of 1931, when the Technion began its process of deepening academic research, and until the 1970s, the academic system remained the exclusive provider of Higher education in Israel, with an orientation towards research and a close integration between teaching and research activities (The Shochat Committee, 2007). From this research-based uniform model, the Higher Education System in Israel transitioned to a binary (dual) one, that was based on the Californian model according to which universities should include research and teaching and their undergraduate students should not exceed 10 %, while colleges' role is to focus on teaching undergraduate students. The binary model, informally adopted in Israel as of the beginning of the 1980s and formally at the beginning of the 1990s, aimed to address the growing demand for education, which became noticeable during the 1980s. The adoption of the binary model was a result of the radical reform in the Higher education system, that had transformed it into a dichotomous system (Soen, 2004). According to researchers, this system operates in two main directions: The first consists of research universities, mainly expected to cover the system's 'autonomous functions' (Trow, 1970), consisting of the provision of 'high culture' and the promotion of science through research; while the second includes Colleges whose role is to cover 'popular functions' (ibid.). According to this model, all research resources are concentrated at universities, while colleges provide high level professional knowledge and train future students of advanced studies. The principle adoption of the binary systemic model became reality with the approval of the academization plan for academic colleges, accepted by the CHE in 1994 as a response for the growing demand, and which had in turn led to today's dramatic expansion of Israel's Higher Education System.

Reasons for the Growing Demand for Higher Education

According to data published by the Council for Higher Education's Planning and Budgeting Committee (PBC), a number of factors impacted the substantial growth in demand for Higher education from the mid 1980s to the mid 1990s:

a. **A rise in the number of 18 year olds** – in the mid 1980s there were 73,000 18 year olds in Israel. by the mid 1990s this number rose to 103,000 – a 41 % growth rate. The reason for this growth is an increase in births as well as the immigration from the former USSR that occurred during the relevant period (Lev Zion, 2001).
b. **Increase in the number of students eligible for a high school diploma –** In the 1986/87 school year, this number reached 28,100 students, growing in 1995/96 to 47,600 – a 69.3 % growth rate. The eligibility rates of some of these students from age 18 onwards during that period rose from 36.7 % to 46.9 %. While the rate of success in exams remained stable, there was a rise in the total number of examinees, some of whom were 18.
c. **A rise in the number of students attending pre-academic preparatory programs (*Mechinot*)**– the number of students in these programs rose from 6,000 in 1990 to 10,800 in 1997 – an 80 % growth. Among all students of pre-academic preparatory programs in Israel in 1997, 50.1 % studied at Mechinot that are affiliated with colleges.
d. **New populations in the pool of undergraduate degree candidates** – the rise in this category resulted from the large immigration wave from the former USSR as well as from populations that were underrepresented in the past in Higher education due to their lower Socioeconomic status. In 1991 the number of candidates in this category was 25,985, and in 1992 this number grew to 27,816 candidates. Most of this increase is accounted for by the immigrants from the former USSR. This growth trend increased in 1997, reaching 32,924 candidates, mostly due to local demand.
e. **An increase in the number of institutions offering undergraduate degrees –** the number of institutions offering undergraduate degrees rose from eight universities in 1970 to 35 institutions in 1990 and 65 in 2007 (PBC, 1996/7; PBC, 2006/7).

f. **Development of curriculums** – Practical curriculums were developed, mainly in the fields of technology, management and communication. These programs created demand by a public whose approach to Higher education is instrumental (Lev Zion, 2001).

The growing demand for Higher education and the system's expansion led to impressive comparative results: Compared to OECD countries Israel ranks high on all indices of accessibility to Higher education: The percentage of candidates accepted to undergraduate studies in 2007 was 57 % compared to the 56 % OECD average. Israel is at the top end in terms of the number of people possessing a Post-Secondary education – 48 % of people aged 25–34, compared to the 44 % OECD average.[11]

Through an analysis of the range of opinions available in the professional literature (Volanski, 2005; Menachem, Tamir & Shavit, 2008; Kirsch, 2010), the process of expansion of Higher education in Israel can be divided into four central periods:

a. **1924–1955: The first academies and the evolution of the Jerusalem hegemony**

During this period the first academies of the Jewish people were founded. The establishment of the Hebrew University and the Technion in the mid 1920s became possible thanks to a close collaboration between the Jewish Pre-State *Yishuv* and global Jewry. While the seeds of the first academic Jewish institution were planted long before the existence of a Zionist Jewish *Yishuv* in Israel, these seeds sprouted only 40 years later. The plan to found the Technion also originated many years before the establishment of the State, but it embarked upon its scientific-research path only as of the 1930s. After the establishment of these two academic research institutions, they began to develop national goals and aims for training leading professionals and researchers. In the absence of suitable governmental mechanisms for coping with the realization of these goals, this period was characterized by a process of self regulation by the first institutions themselves, under a hegemony of the Hebrew University which determined the academic levels of high schools and held a monopoly over academic degrees and admission requirements for academic studies. The academic-scientific field was evaluated based on the university's decision. An example of this hegemony which in some cases gained official statutory status can be found in the Israel Bar Association

11 Source: OECD Education at a Glance, 2019: Table A1.2., http://www.oecd.org/education/education-at-a-glance-9991487.htm/?refcode=20190209ig Retrieved 1 March 2020.

Law of 1961, of which article 24 defines the required higher legal education recognized under this law:

(1) A graduate of a law faculty of an institution or of a college in Israel, recognized under the Council for Higher Education Law, 5718 – 1958, as an institution of higher education;
(2) A law graduate of an institution abroad recognized (for the purposes of this provision) by the Hebrew University of Jerusalem, as an institution of higher education; or a person who has studied at such an institution and has passed examinations to an extent that, in the opinion of the Hebrew University of Jerusalem, he may suitably be regarded as granting him a higher legal education.

The development of the two first institutions was gradual, both in terms of the number of students and the topics taught; however, as of the establishment of the State in 1948 they were supported by the government and received substantial budgets in order to promote research in Israel and provide suitable solutions for the demand for higher education among the country's constantly growing population.

b. 1955–1973: The number of Israel universities is increased and a monolithic Higher Education System emerges

This period can be defined as the foundation period of Israel's research universities, that together with the Hebrew University and the Technion formed the scientific basis of the State of Israel. The country's research institutions were founded in two waves: The first in the 1950s with the establishment of Bar Ilan University in 1955 followed by Tel Aviv University in 1956. The Ziv research Institute founded in 1934 led to the establishment of the Weizmann Institute of Science in 1944, and as of 1958 it became one of the institutions certified to train students for advanced degrees in the Natural Sciences. The first wave was concluded with the legislation of the CHE Law in 1958 and the conclusion of the self regulatory period of the institutions. The second wave began in the 1960s. The institutions established in this wave were, as mentioned earlier, the Ben Gurion University of the Negev and the University of Haifa. Both institutions were founded following the legislation of the Council for Higher Education (CHE) Law which defined a continued self-regulating regime under State supervision (Menachem, Tamir & Shavit, 2008).

Alongside the research institutions, Bar Ilan University's Extensions were founded one after the other as of the mid 1960s. The Ashkelon Extension was founded in 1965; The Jordan Valley Extension – in mid-1958; and the Zefat Extension in September of the same year. The Extensions operated as integral parts of Bar Ilan University, offering academic studies in locations geographically distant from the country's largest academic campuses.

c. 1973–1993: The onset of dramatic changes – the transition from a monolithic to a binary system (based on two educational systems – colleges and universities)

This period is characterized by dramatic changes to Israel's Higher Education System. The academic structure that operated based on a classic-European approach, and the American one which replaced it over the years, both view the role of institutes of Higher education as institutions purely dedicated to scientific research. This approach began to change following global changes and the parallel growing demand among Israeli population. Initial attempts to expand the country's Higher Education System date as far back as the 1970s when then Minister of Education Yigal Alon appointed a committee led by Prof. Yurtner (more on this later) to examine the feasibility of establishing an academic institution in the Galilee. Initial discussions were held at the CHE at the beginning of the 1970s and lasted over a decade. During those years the idea to establish non-university institutions was examined, with the aim of addressing the growing demand for higher education as well as providing trained professionals for the developing economy. Also in this period the Higher Education System evolved in three main stages:

1. **Academic accreditation of non-university institutions of higher education** – institutions that provided academic education in Israel but were not accredited, and others founded during the 1970s, gradually gained official accreditation by the CHE. Some of these senior institutions include the Rubin Academy of Music & Dance in Jerusalem founded in 1947 and recognized in 1974 as an academic institution granting undergraduate degrees. Another such institution is the Bezalel Academy of Art and Design which was founded in 1906 as an art school and in 1973 was accredited as an academic institution eligible to grant undergraduate degrees. Following the accreditation of these institutions, further non-university institutions were gradually recognized and accredited: The Jerusalem College of Technology was recognized in 1977; the Shenkar College of Engineering, Design and Art in 1979; and the Ruppin College was accredited and certified in a process that commenced in 1975 and ended with its accreditation in 1980 (Volanski, 2005).
2. **Academic accreditation of teacher-training institutions** – this process took place during the 1970s and 1980s when the CHE gave teacher-training seminars the accreditation to grant a B.A in Education. These institutions included the David Yellin College – 1979; The Jerusalem College for Girls – 1979; the Beit Berl College – 1981; the Wingate College for Physical Education – 1984; the Levinsky College of Education – 1986; the Kibbutzim College – 1988l; Oranim College – 1990; and "Ort Israel" College for training teachers of Technology – 1991 (Volanski, 2005).

3. **Accreditation of Regional Colleges and Bar Ilan's Extensions as Public Colleges** – the Regional Colleges that operated at first as Post-Secondary education institutions and began, one after the other, offering academic curriculums, were accredited as Public Colleges during this period. Twelve Regional Colleges began operating under the Ministry of Education's newly established Regional Colleges Division. In 1991 the Ministry of Education recognized Bar Ilan University's academic Extensions at Ashkelon in the south and Zefat (Safed) in the north as Public Regional Colleges. The Jordan Valley Extension, which had operated as a college since the early 1970s, already belonged to the system of Regional Colleges and therefore did not require special accreditation.

d. **1993 and onwards: The formal establishment of a binary Higher Education System**

This period is unique in that formal decisions reached during this period dramatically impacted the character of Israel's Higher Education System. For the first time, the system's expansion was regulated by a master-plan submitted to the CHE in December 1993 by Prof. Amnon Rubinstein, then Minister of Education and Chairperson of the CHE. The plan included the academization of colleges in three different categories: Regional Colleges operating as general vocational institutions that also offered an academic curriculum under the auspices of a university; a group of 12 teacher-training colleges added to the existing teacher-training colleges certified to grant B.Ed degrees in the 1980s; and technological colleges that were granted academic independence under the master-plan. At the end of 1994 the technological colleges, most of which were dedicated to training practical engineers and technicians, were permitted to offer academic studies towards a B.Tech degree: The Ort Bruada College in Karmiel was the first to be certified to offer students a B.Tech degree. Later on, further colleges were included under this category: The Holon Institute of Technology which began offering undergraduate degrees by the end of the 1990s; The College of Judea & Samaria; The Jerusalem College of Technology; and The Ruppin Academic Center. All in all, by the first years of the new millennium there were nine technological colleges in Israel, including the older technological colleges such as Shenkar and Bezalel.

Among the Regional Colleges operating under the Ministry of Education's Colleges Division, in 1993 three colleges were selected to be the first to undergo the academization process. Towards the end of the 1990s until the beginning of 2001 each of the 12 Regional Colleges were offered to join the academization process and thus to operate under the CHE/PBC. Bar Ilan University's Extensions, belonging to the Division as Regional Colleges, began joining the process in 2001: The Ashkelon Extension began its academization process in 2003, followed by the Jordan Valley Extension and then the Zefat Extension in 2007.

A further expansion not included in the CHE's master-plan was a result of an external initiative – The establishment of Non-Publicly Funded Academic Colleges, which did not receive any governmental funding. More than anything else, the opening of these colleges marked the final collapse of the barriers of national supervision on Higher education, its regulation and planning. The first signs of this process can be found at the College of Management, which was the first to create such precedence in Israel's Higher Education System. At the end of the 1980s its management succeeded in convincing the CHE to allow them to offer undergraduate studies in Business Administration and Accounting. The CHE, believing that in these areas the universities are training more graduates than are needed in the market and that there is therefore no justification for governmental funding of these areas of study, accepted the request of the College of Management and granted it the necessary accreditation to offer undergraduate degrees without public funding. In doing this the CHE established a precedence for the inauguration of Non-Publicly Funded studies in highly demand professions meaning that the State has no incentive to allocate further budgets for these areas. This precedence resulted in a dramatic transition to private initiatives, through two stages of legislation:

The first stage, that paved the way for extensive Non-Publicly Funded studies was the amendment to the Bar Association Law approved by the Knesset in 1989, which allowed graduates of non-academic institutions to take examinations for admission to the Israel Bar Association. Under this amendment, a number of law schools were added to Israel's Higher Education System, which later became non-publicly funded academic institutions. Among the first institutions to operate under this framework were the Interdisciplinary Center, the Netanya College, the Hod Hasharon College of Law and Science and the Ramat Gan College. The amendment to the law gradually led to a more extensive privatization of institutions of Higher education aiming to address the needs of students that could afford to pay high tuitions (Menachem, Tamir and Shavit, 2008).

The second stage is known as "the Internationalization of Higher education". In the beginning of the 1990s Israel was inundated by Extensions of foreign universities offering academic degrees of universities abroad, mostly from the USA and UK, but also from Eastern Europe and South Africa.[12] For years the CHE was unsure how to deal with these institutions, and after various legal debates and consultations the CHE Law was amended to include the 11th amendment to the law regarding Supervision of Foreign University Extensions. The law came into force in February 1998, defining the terms for the continued operation of foreign

12 These included the Extension of Manchester University from the UK, which became the Ono College, the college of the USA-based Touro College which became the Lander Institute of Jerusalem, and the Derby University Extension which became the Or Yehuda College.

Extensions in Israel. When the terms for their continued operation were met, these Extensions joined in an indirect and unplanned manner the list of Higher education institutions in Israel, becoming a further layer of Non-Publicly Funded institutions within Israel's Higher education system.

The Binary System in Israel

The Higher education landscape began to transform, and a binary system comprised of two main Extensions started to take over as of beginning of the new millennium (The Shochat Committee, 2007). Diversity is among the most prominent characteristics of this system. In recent years the number of institutions of Higher education permitted to grant academic degrees has grown and diversified, and these can be identified according to two central differentiating categories: Research institutions and non-research institutions. But they can also be classified according to their topics of specialization, such as institutions offering technological undergraduate degrees, undergraduate and graduate degrees in teaching, or in the Arts. Table 4 presents changes in this area from the 1980s until 2014 – classified into five groups, with a stabilization noted in the number of institutions in 2019:

Tab. 4: Institutions of higher education in Israel between the years 1990– 2019

Institution type	Number of institutions in 1989/90	Number of institutions in 1999/00	Number of institutions in 2006/07	Number of institutions in 2013/14	Number of institutions in 2018/19
Universities	8	8	8	9	9
Non-Research institutions:					
General Academic Colleges	5	7	12	20	20
Teacher-training Colleges	7	22	27	22	21
Non-Publicly Funded Colleges	1	7	9	16	11
Regional Colleges under the Auspices of Universities	12	7	3	0 (Included in the number of general colleges)	0
Total academic institutions	35	57 62.8 %+	65 14 %+	67 3 %+	61[a]

a Amendment 11 to the CHE Law gradually led to the closing of colleges that were Extensions of foreign universities despite their conversion into Israeli institutions such as the Lander Institute and the Or Yehuda College. Other colleges were closed mainly as a result of the decline in law studies, such as the Carmel Academic College, and others.
Source: The Council for Higher Education Website, list of institutions – May 2014. Retrieved July 22, 2014. 2019 data from: CHE website, list of institutions – March 2020. Retrieved March 2, 2020.

Another attribute of the binary system is the ongoing rise in the number of students in both types of institutions, that one side cannot overshadow the other, at least in terms of the number of students. The old system that enrolled all students in research institutions has cleared the way for a system that develops in a way that most of the increase in undergraduates students is gradually but steadily transferred to colleges, while the universities grow in advanced degrees. Table 5 illustrates the formation of this binary system over the course of three decades: The first decade, 1990–2000 marked an increase in the number of undergraduate students at colleges, reaching a 16.9 % annual average, while the parallel increase at universities had been 2 % only. The second decade – 2000–2010 marked a deceleration of the growth, and with a 9.9 % annual average at colleges and only 0.2 % at universities. This pace of growth at the colleges decelerated during the years 2004–2019, reaching an annual average of 8.5 %. As of the previous decade a decline can be noted in the pace of growth also at academic colleges, with the number of students reaching 94,515 in 2013, a growth of 3.1 % compared to 2002. This deceleration trend in the pace of growth continues into 2019, as can be seen from the data in Tab. 6.

Tab. 5: Students at Universities and Colleges 1989/90–2018/19

Year	Total number (Not including Open University)	Universities	Percentage	Academic Colleges	Percentage	Academic Colleges of Education	Percentage	Open University
1989/90 1989/90	75,487	67,201	89	3,668	4.86	4,618	6.1	13,007
1999/00 1999/00	170,953	112,987	66	33,709	19.7	24,257	14.2	32,661
2009/10 2009/10	243,858	123,964	50.8	91,569	37.5	28,325	11.6	43,051
2011/12 2011/12	258,693	125,546	48.5	101,822	39.4	31,325	12.1	41,441
2012/13 2012/13	262,938	125,058	47.5	105,716	40.2	32,164	12.2	42,760
2018/19 2019	268,355	125,286	46.7	107,456	40.0	35,613	13.3	48,000

Source: Statistical Abstract of Israel 2013, number 64, table number 8.54. Open University data – from the CHE website: http://che.org.il/?page_id=6802, Table 7. Retrieved July 22, 2014. 2019 data from: Higher education in Israel – Data in anticipation of the opening of the 2018/19 academic year, table A students by degree and by institution – 2009/10 and 2018/19. Retrieved March 2, 2020.

Tab. 6: Number of undergraduate students by institution type – 1989/90–2018/19

	Total absolute number	Total – percentages	Universities – main campus	Academic programs under the auspices of universities	Academic Colleges	Teacher-training Colleges
1989/90	55,250	100	85.0	–	6.4	8.6
1994/5	86,320	100	72.8	4.5	10.9	11.7
1999/2000	126,800	100	52.7	5.7	26.3	15.2
2004/05	155,900	100	44.8	5.5	35.3	14.4
2009/10	178,400	100	37.2	4.8	46.7	11.3
2010/11	186,160	100	36.3	4.6	47.7	11.4
2002	188,255	100	35.2	4.4	48.7	11.7
2013	190,810	100	34.7	4.1	49.5	11.7
2013/14	192,710	100	33.9	3.7	50.0	12.3
2019	193,996	100	38.2	Included in the Academic Colleges	47.4	14.3

Source: The Council for Higher Education – Collection of data towards the opening of the academic year 2013/2014, 10 October 2014. Source for 2018/19: Central Bureau of Statistics (CBS), Higher education in Israel – Selected Data for the 2018/19 academic year, on the occasion of the start of the academic year, Table A – Students by academic degree and institution – 2009/2010 and 2018/19. The rise in the number of university students results from the allocation of the Ariel Academic College to the Universities' budget.

Looking at the number of undergraduate students we find that in recent years this number is constantly on the rise in colleges and in decline at universities. The number of undergraduate students at all non-university institutions has crossed 60 %, reaching 66 % in the 2014 academic year, compared to 34 % at universities (CHE, 2014). Although in 2018/19 the numbers of students at the Ariel Academic College were included in the count of students studying at universities, still the number of undergraduate students at colleges exceeds 61 % of the total number of undergraduate students in Israel.

Figure 1 illustrates the change in the structure of the academic system in Israel and the transition of students from undergraduate studies at universities to academic colleges.

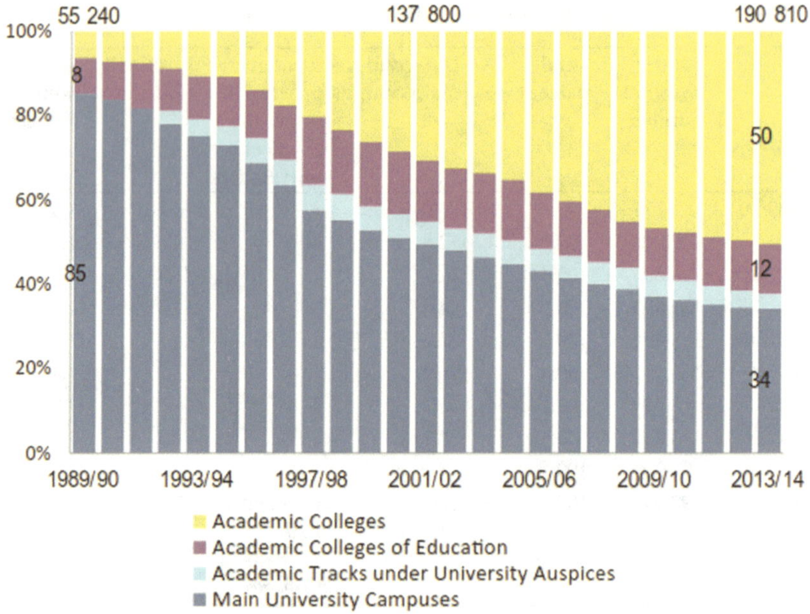

Fig. 1: Undergraduate Students in the Higher Education System by institution type, 1989/90 – 2013/14

The Evolution of Higher Education in Israel: Social and Institutional Aspects

Researchers differ in their opinions as to the ways in which the expansion of higher education has affected the structure of Israeli society, as well as the social and institutional aspects of the phenomenon, which are reciprocal and integrated in one another. However, all researchers agree that with the establishment of the State, Israeli society has changed dramatically and quickly. in the transition from the Pre-State *Yishuv* period to the State, professional considerations, economic orientation and professional and managerial positions overcame partisan and ideological ones (Eisenstadt, 1973). This process led to professional specialization and a flocking to the education system that was perceived in the world and in Israel as able to carry out professional and social change. However, researchers believe that modernization processes that took place in Israel led to an accelerated democratization in the primary and secondary education systems, while higher education remained caught within the hegemony of its Ashkenazi founders who acted to maintain their position and strength within the system (Shavit and Kraus, 1992; Yogev and Shapira, 1992)

The literature focuses on the effect of higher education on Israeli society, both in terms of its accessibility and in terms of the question of distributive justice, which can be evaluated by the level of entry of the systems' graduates into the job market. A review of this literature exposes a number of explanations ranging between two central approaches in Sociology: According to the conflictual approach, the expansion of higher education in Israel is identified with a class conflict, with the expansion of higher education in its current format being perceived as a compromise rather than an ideal situation. Proponents of this approach point to the class conflict between the old "Ashkenazi" class and the "Mizrachim" – Israelis of Middle Eastern and North African descent, relatively newer immigrants, generally of lower status and residing in geographically peripheral areas. According to the Functional approach, the system's expansion is a result of structural-social changes in the newly forming Israeli society, taking place in parallel to a similar global process of expansion of higher education, which influences the process and contributes to its formation.

Similarly to our global review, the national review will also examine the social effects of the phenomenon and its influence on the structure of the Israeli academic system.

The Social Aspect

According to the Conflict approach, the class conflict began back in the pre-State period – the *Yishuv* – when social classes developed and various points of view were consolidated regarding higher education and the correct way to achieve social order. According to one approach, the aim was to establish a bourgeois-capitalist social order in which higher education is a means for developing an individualistic and international career based on competition and initiative. This approach, developed at the Hebrew University, contested with the socialist approach of the political leadership of the *Yishuv*, by which a socialist, service-based social order is needed, emphasizing the individual's contribution to the collective (Cohen, 2001). While this approach was founded on a socialist world view aspiring for equality, it also expressed, to a large extent, an approach of a "serving elite" (Lissak, 1996). These opposing world views led by the Hebrew University on one side and the *Yishuv*'s political leadership on the other, were on a cultural collision course (Shapira, 1997), with one opposing the global purpose of higher education as it does not advance equality and the needs of the *Yishuv*, while proponents of the other approach alleging that only through science and global research would Israel be able to cope with the challenges ahead. For example, the practical implications of the first approach led the *Yishuv*'s educational leadership in the years leading to the establishment of the State, to develop vocational curriculums at Kibbutzim high schools, which did not track their graduates towards a Bagrut (high school matriculation) diploma (Cohen, 2006).

Others who studied the education system believe that the Israeli education system during its *Yishuv* formative years had been based on central-European models. During that period the European education system had been elitist, with only a small proportion of European youths attending high school. High schools in Israeli cities, as opposed to those at Kibbutzim, were built in the image of central-European Gymnasiums. Academic requirements in these schools were high, the goal being to prepare students for Bagrut exams. Mizrachi immigrants had a hard time integrating into this strict system and many of those who attended these schools in the post-State era did not do well in their studies. Consequently, these students were encouraged in various ways to attend vocational schools, where academic requirements were low. This approach was based on the assumption that vocational studies are suitable for weaker students (Svirski, 1990; Shavit, 1992). The expansion of vocational education led to two changes whose implications remained visible as late as the beginning of the 1990s: The number of students enrolled in technological/vocational schools increased from 2002 students in 1984 to 70,681 in 1980. This figure continued to grow, reaching its peak of 115,224 students in 2000. This trend began to change only in 2008, when the number of students in technological/vocational schools decreased to 87,415.[13] In parallel, all ethnic groups showed an increase in the percentage of high school students, with the gap between the different groups gradually closing. However, the gap in the percentage of students eligible for a Bagrut diploma was maintained, as well as among students continuing to Post-Secondary education (Nahon, 1987; Shavit, 1992).

According to the Credential Society theory, the expansion of higher education in Israel is part of a global trend of Primary education system expansion in the 1950s and 1960s, and of the Secondary and Post-Secondary education systems in the 1970s and 1980s. The requirement within Israeli society, as in all industrialized countries for skilled and professional workers created a huge demand and led to the expansion of all levels of education. This, in turn, to a large extent, led to Israeli society becoming a "Credential society", where educational diplomas are a primary criteria in occupational positioning. This credentialing principle had been prevalent in the dominant Ashkenazi group even before the arrival of Mizrachi immigrants in the 1950s (Yogev and Shapira, 1992; Yogev, 2008). According to

13 From: Dagan, 2013: 92.

Randall Collins, who coined the term "Credential Society" in 1979, the main interest of professional status groups in the USA had been to protect the group from the penetration of newcomers. Researchers identified a similar phenomenon in Israel, when the old Ashkenazi status group acted to protect its position and the boundaries of its establishments in the high levels of the higher education system. These researchers believe that the democratization of modern society in Israel is expressed only in the primary and secondary education systems, while higher education remained under the control of the old educated class, that continued to place barriers at its gates (Shavit and Kraus, 1992). These barriers were expressed in education diplomas defined as admission criteria although they were not available to most lower classes and new immigrants. Studies have shown that while education served as a central criteria for job placement for the Ashkenazi population, for immigrants from Middle Eastern countries, who lacked certification, or whose diplomas were not recognized, further criteria were introduced, such as "IQ". This requirement gradually diminished as the new immigrants from Arab countries began integrating in education and vocational training in line with the Credential Society concept (Yogev and Shapira, 1992).

The establishment of the Credential Society was identified by Uri Cohen in his study on the admissions policy of the Hebrew University during the pre-State *Yishuv* period and the first decade of the State of Israel. According to Cohen, the management of the Hebrew University took a dominant part in the structuring of a new Israeli identity – the "Credential Society" culture. The university management created "rates and gates" aimed at regulating and supervising outputs and resources in the new society. At the center of this principle was the need to protect the boundaries of the old elitist groups from penetration of newcomers. During the first years to the establishment of the State, the Hebrew University held a monopoly not only over academic degrees but also for the terms of admission into the country's universities. The approach of the senior academics of the Hebrew University formed the country's education policy, perceiving science and technology as a top interest of the State, ensuring the growth and cohesion of the new society. This approach pushed aside the fact that the ruling class formed around "the old Ashkenazi" academics, who in the 1950s became central actors in the formation of a class and ethnicity based order and the establishment of a new class awareness, including prerequisites for quick social mobility among members of this class compared to others (Cohen, 2001, 2006). This monopoly began with the University's close supervision on high schools levels as of the 1930s until the establishment of the State in 1948. This type of control also enabled the regulation of human resources to an academic institution, with the gates of regulation changing as needed in order to absorb Ashkenazi immigrants that arrived during the

1950s immigration waves. Following the establishment of the State, the Hebrew University's admissions policy had changed with the introduction of rules that encouraged the admission of second generation Ashkenazi Israelis and new immigrants by lowering admission terms into the Hebrew University, thereby enabling the formation of a separate ethnic group that differed from the group of "newcomers". Justification for this step originated from the old group sensing a cultural threat from the newcomers, and thereby acted to redistribute university admission priorities. For the university, this was a correct, just and social step, considering the personal contribution of group members and the country's needs. The establishment of a Credential Society enabled senior groups having ethnic characteristics to present itself as a non-ethnic group, nurturing the illusion that the expansion of higher education would lead to social equality. Based on the Credential Society theory, the real purpose of the diploma is to serve as a barrier blocking the way of the lower classes to controlling positions, as a method of reproducing the social structure they are protecting. The lower classes, unable to cope with the requirements of admission exams to higher education and prestigious schools, find themselves outside the Credentialing game (Shavit, 1992).

The modernization of industrialization model, based on the functional approach, attributes the growth of the education systems in general and in higher education in particular to technological changes in industrialized economies such as Israel. The needs of the industrialized market led to a preference of the skilled while ignoring social class. Volansky believes that in the Israeli economy the academic system should provide equal opportunities for acquiring professional skills that would lead to social mobility. Higher education and professional skills are the key to reducing gaps in modern society. Skills are also essential throughout occupational careers (as an ongoing process). Volansky believes that the results of the educational revolution of the 1990s point to the great impact of higher education on class equality. The revolution in Israel's academic system and the opening of the gates of education through colleges transformed a number of indices indicative of the reduction of social gaps. Public colleges that for many years functioned as Regional Colleges was the most prominent example of the affinity of higher education to the periphery. These colleges brought higher education to distant geographical areas in a period in which nearly all learning centers were in Jerusalem and Tel Aviv (Volansky, 2010).

To assess whether the gaps in higher education were reduced in recent years since the establishment of Academic Colleges, I present data based on two central measures used for examining the status of social gaps in higher education: the number of students in the geographic periphery, and the ratio between the number of students living in lower social-economic clusters compared to all students.

Based on recent data published by the CHE for the 2018/19 academic year we see a clear trend of expansion of accessibility for higher education among populations living in peripheral regions and among disadvantaged populations. About 25 % of all undergraduate students studied in 2018/19 in institutions located in the Northern and Southern districts; 9.7 % in the Northern district, and 14.6 % in the Southern one, compared to 8.7 % who studied in the same district in 1989/90, as can be seen from the data presented in Table 7.

Tab. 7: Undergraduate Students by institution district, 1989/90, 1999/00, 2018/19

	1989/90	1999/00	2018/19
Total absolute numbers	55,250	126,900	190,650
Total – percentages	100.0	100.0	100.0
Jerusalem	22.7	15.5	13.9
North	–	5.3	9.7
Haifa	21.7	17.9	12.1
Center	4.1	15.9	17.9
Tel Aviv	8.42	31.5	31.9
South	8.7	13.9	14.6

Source: The Council for Higher Education – Collection of data towards the opening of the academic year 2019/2020, 3 March 2020.

According to the second measure we see a clear trend of expansion of higher education among students coming from towns ranked very low in the social-economic clusters (2–1 and 3–4). In the 5–6 Socioeconomic cluster we also see a trend of stabilization in the number of students following the change in classification to cities, while in the highest cluster (9–10) a decline is noted relatively to their proportion among all undergraduate students.

Tab. 8: Number of Undergraduate Students by Socioeconomic Cluster of the town where the students completed 12th grade during the years 2009–2019

Year of study	Total Percentage	Cluster 1–2	Cluster 3–4	Cluster 5–6	Cluster 7–8	Cluster 9–10
2009	100	3.4 %	18.0 %	37.1 %	38.1 %	3.5 %
2017	100	7.5 %	20.7 %	25.5 %	40.7 %	2.7 %
2018	100	7.9 %	21.1 %	25.2 %	40.7 %	2.7 %
2019	100	8.3 %	21.3 %	24.6 %	40.0 %	2.7 %

Source: 2019 data from: CBS, Statistical Abstract of Israel 2019. 2017–2019 data from: CHE, Collection of data towards the opening of the academic year 2019/2020. The data does not include Open University and Education Colleges students.

The data presented in Table 8 points to a rise in the number of undergraduate students among students residing at disadvantaged towns belonging to Socioeconomic clusters 1–4. The proportion of students from towns classified at the two highest social clusters declined in comparison to the total number of undergraduate students, and the proportion of public colleges in this increase exceeds that of the private ones. If we link this data to the rise in the number of students in the south and north districts – whose proportion before the change was substantially low, we find that accessibility to higher education had increased, with colleges filling the role attributed to them, as can be seen from Table 9.

Tab. 9: Number of Undergraduate Students at public and private academic colleges, by institution type and Socioeconomic Cluster of the town where student completed 12th grade during the years 2000–2018

		Total absolute numbers	Total Percentage	Cluster 1–2	Cluster 3–4	Cluster 5–6	Cluster 7–8	Cluster 9–10
Colleges funded by PBC (Including programs under the auspices of a university)	1999/00	17,422	100	2.5 %	12.6 %	32.8 %	37.2 %	14.8 %
	2004	32,233	100	3.0 %	24.8 %	27.8 %	42.0 %	2.4 %
	2011/12	62,100	100	4.0 %	20.1 %	45.5 %	24.2 %	2.4 %
	2012/13	63.655	100	6.9 %	21.2 %	48.2 %	16.9 %	4.7 %
	2019	56,530	100	9.7 %	23.7 %	30.8 %	31.3 %	1.9 %
Non-Publicly Funded Colleges	1999/00	15,828	100	0.8 %	8.9 %	23.4 %	43.9 %	23.0 %
	2004	18,853	100	% 1.5	14.3 %	18.8 %	61.3 %	4.1 %
	2011/12	37,857	100	3.1 %	15.1 %	36.1 %	37.9 %	4.3 %
	2012/13	38,730	100	3.6 %	17.3 %	43.9 %	23.9 %	8.3 %
	2019	34,195	100	7.2 %	19.6 %	22.7 %	43.6 %	2.5 %

Source: The Council for Higher Education – Collection of data towards the opening of the academic year 2013/2014, 10 October 2013.
CBS: Academic Colleges, Jerusalem, 2006, Table 6. Not including Open University and Education Colleges students. Collection of data towards the opening of the academic year 2017–2018. CHE. The data does not include Open University and Education Colleges students.

The data reinforces the general trend outlined above, that the number of undergraduate students from disadvantaged towns and peripheral districts has been gradually increasing. Among students from the 1–2 Socioeconomic cluster attending public colleges we note an increase of 7.2 % between 2000 and 2018. An even higher increase of 10.8 % can be noted during the same period among students from towns belonging to the 3–4 Socioeconomic clusters. Non-Publicly Funded private Colleges also play an important role in the expansion of accessibility to higher education among disadvantaged populations. The increase among these populations during the period reviewed among Socioeconomic clusters 1–2 amounted to 6.4 % and in the 3–4 clusters 10.7 %. Although the increase noted during the examined period is not substantial, it does point to a clear trend, especially considering the fact that the examined period was marked by a significant general decline in the number of undergraduate students in all institutions, as shown above. Moreover, the proportion of students coming from towns classified in the two highest social clusters declines in comparison to the total number of undergraduate students in private colleges, thereby pointing to their increased contribution to the expanded accessibility to higher education among relatively disadvantaged populations or those for which higher education had not been accessible in the past, such as the Haredi (Ultra-Orthodox Jewish) and Arab populations.

In addition to the above, Volansky pointed to occupation and salary as indices of the yield of higher education leading to reduced social gaps: The average salary for holder of an academic degree in 2007 was ₪12,672, while that of non-academic workers was ₪7,374 on average. The number of unemployed among holders of a academic degree was 1/8 compared to 7/8 among non-academics. CBS 2014 publications reinforce this – the average salary of workers in the professional service sector, science and technology reached ₪12,573.[14] Comparative OECD data for 2019 also point to the same trend – the likelihood of holders of a high school diploma and above to find employment exceeds that of candidates who have not completed high school. The employment rate of holders of a high school education is 18 % higher and the employment rate of holders of an academic education is 28 % higher than of candidates without a high school diploma.[15]

A similar conclusion arises from a study published by the Taub Center in 2009, showing that the proportion of holders of academic degrees in Israel doubled in 2008 compared to 1995, and that despite the increase in the number of holders of an undergraduate degree, their income did not decrease. Compared to the population of holders of academic degrees, the economic status of those who do not hold such degree has deteriorated, as their leverage in the labor market was

14 CBS public announcement: average salary for Israeli employees in April 2014 [6 July 2014], figure 7.

15 Kortiokov, D. (2012). Higher education in Israel and OECD countries: A comparative perspective: Analysis of the OECD Report, Education at a Glance. Tel Aviv: The National Union of Israeli Students, Research & Policy Department.

undermined due to competition with the growing number of academics (Bar, Haim, Blank and Shavit, 2009).

2017 OECD publications on occupation continue to point to a higher likelihood of finding a job by holders of a higher education (84 % compared to 74 % for those who do not possess such education). Moreover, holders of a higher education earn on average 56 % more than those who do not hold such education.[16] 2019 data point to a similar ratio of 85 % employed among those holding a higher education compared to 76 % among those who do not. Holders of a higher education among the 25–34 age group earn 38 % more than those who do not have a higher education among the same age group, and among the 45–54 age group, holders or a higher education earn 70 % more than those who do not hold such an education among the same age group.[17]

Accessibility as a Key for the Establishment of a New Mizrachi[18] Middle Class in Israel

A different perspective on the influence of accessibility to higher education on the social structure can be seen in the work of social researchers Uri Cohen and Nissim Leon (2008). According to them, the emergence of the nation State had been fraught with revolutionary transformations following the development of new social constructs that differ from traditional dichotomies. Such process of transformation includes a structural change that gave rise to the formation of a new middle class. Not a revolutionary class aiming to seize economic and social change with power, such as in the case of the Black Panthers of the 1970s,[19] but a middle class looking towards a horizon of social mobility. The identifying attributes of this class are expressed in its geographical horizon – a redesign of the peripheral geographic space and its transformation into a new and attractive

16 Education At a glance 2017: OECD indicators. Executive Summary, p. 25: https://www.hm.ee/sites/default/files/eag2017_eng.pdf Retrieved 1 March 2020.

17 Education At a glance 2019: OECD indicators. Executive Summary, p. 24: http://www.oecd.org/education/education-at-a-glance-9991487.htm/?refcode=20190209ig Retrieved 1 March 2020.

18 "Mizrachi/m" (or Sephardic) refers to Jews of Oriental, North African, or Middle Eastern origin, as opposed to "Ashkenazi/m", referring to Jews of European origin.

19 The Black Panthers were an Israeli protest movement of second-generation Jewish immigrants from North Africa and Middle Eastern countries and one of the first organizations in Israel striving for social justice for Sephardi and Mizrachi Jews. The movement had been inspired by the African-American Black Panther organization.

center. These researchers point to the demographic transformation of the city of Yavne and the town of Gan Yavne as an example of a transformation of a peripheral space into an attractive area for affluent populations. The second trend in the formation of a new middle class can be noted in a growing accessibility to higher education through colleges. In addition to professional opportunities, this change also has cultural importance. The establishment of colleges created knowledge centers in which residents of peripheral areas not only acquire higher education but also an awareness of the ability of higher education to serve as a key to social mobility. The colleges revolution is by nature a cultural one, as it facilitates a completely new "class horizon" to the one available to the Mizrachi "muscle proletariat". Higher education becomes an accessible virtue identified with local culture, which over time evolves to represent the world of knowledge as a source of class mobility and integration in the country's middle class. From a multi-generational perspective, even if a college undergraduate degree is less prestigious than the one offered by universities, the cultural impact on second generations to parents with an undergraduate degree is substantial. To illustrate their position, and as can be seen in Table 10, Cohen and Leon point to the substantial rise in the number of recipients of graduate degrees among students of Asian-African descent between 1984/5 and 2003/4.

Tab. 10: Recipients of University degrees in Israel by ethnic origin

Country of origin	**Undergraduate degree**			**Graduate degree**			**PhD**		
	1984/5	**1994/5**	**2006/7**	**1984/5**	**1994/5**	**2006/7**	**1989/90**	**2005/6**	**2006/7**
Israel	16.5 %	31.8 %	43.1 %	11.6 %	27.6 %	36.1 %	12.3	32.6	34.1
Asia-Africa	24.3 %	27.4 %	25.2 %	14.0 %	23.2 %	27.1 %	14.9	16.3	18.3
Europe-America	59.2 %	40.8 %	37.9 %	74.4 %	49.2 %	40.9 %	72.8	51.1	47.6
Total percentage	100 %	100 %	100 %	100 %	100 %	100 %	100	100	100
Total numbers	8,113	13,154	18,176	2,140	3,767	9,328	450	1209	1288

Source: Cohen and Leon, 2008: 83–101. PhD data from: CBS, Recipients of degrees from institutions of higher education, 2006/7, table 11.

While the data on recipients of an undergraduate degree among the Mizrachi population is stable over the past twenty years and even shows a certain decline, the number of recipients of a graduate degree among this population has nearly doubled. The absolute number has multiplied by more than eight times – from 300 to nearly equal to the general proportion. This trend has also affected the number of PhD students among Mizrachim: In the 1990 academic year, the proportion of PhD students among Mizrachim was 14.9 % compared to 72.8 % among Israeli of European/American descent. In the 2006 academic year it increased to 16.3 % and in 2007 it reached 18.3 %. The data points to the formation of a new Mizrachi middle class that views education as promoting class mobility. The second generation of this class will view higher education as an accepted means for professional promotion and social mobility.

Comparative data in 2009 OECD reports point to a clear mobility trend in the participation patterns of students who are their families' first generation in higher education. The likelihood of a young person from an OECD country (aged 20–34) with parents having a high school education or less to attend academic studies is only 0.44. Comparatively, the likelihood of a young person with academic parents to attend higher education are nearly double – 1.9. In OECD countries, about two thirds of youths with at least one parent with an academic degree are expected to obtain an academic degree. Only one of every five youths among families with parents who do not have an academic degree are expected to obtain an academic degree themselves.[20] This trend was further reinforced in a study on the impact of accessibility to higher education among young adults from peripheral areas, in which it was found that students from families in which at least one parent has an academic education have a higher likelihood to integrate in Israel's Higher Education System. It was found that 76 % of students having at least one parent with a higher education continue to academic studies, compared to 61 % among youths whose parents do not have an academic education (Feniger, Ayalon & Mcdossi, 2013).

Later studies further reinforce the class horizon theory and the relationship between parents' education and academic studies. Position papers published by the CBS in 2015[21] and 2018[22] also show a strong generational impact on higher education. Most parents (77 %) want their children to acquire a higher education. This percentage steadily grows the more educated the parents: 84 % of parents with an undergraduate degree and 86 % of parents with a graduate degree or PhD want their children to have a higher education. In fact, we find a positive relationship between these parental aspirations and the data on higher education in Israel – the higher the education of the parents, the higher proportion of academic degrees among the second generation. There is a positive relationship

20 OECD Education at a Glance, 2012: 105

21 Dobrin, N. (2015). Equal Opportunities in Education: Demographic and Socioeconomic Barriers. Jerusalem: Central Bureau of Statistics.

22 Dror-Cohen, S. (2019). Collection of data from the 2018 Social Survey, Intergenerational mobility: Education, Occupation and changes in the level of religiousness, published on 29 October 2019.

between parents' education and income. The proportion of the population with a higher income is higher among those whose father has an academic degree and relatively lower among those whose father has not completed high school.

The relationship between education and income as a factor in the selection of a field of study, was found in a study that examined the fields of study chosen by students who are their families' first generation to academic studies. The study findings show that first generation to academic studies whose parents are well-off financially tend to study more lucrative areas compared to their peers whose parents are not (Ayalon, 2018).

The Institutional Aspect

The social stratification theory discusses the effect of the expansion of the higher education system on institutional stratification as a decisive factor. The results of institutional stratification impacts the social structure of the institution and of society for generations to come. Studies on Israeli society that rely on the stratification perspective tend to ascribe the generational reproduction of inequality to structural barriers which forestalled entry into higher education among the second generation of 1950 and 1960 immigrants, reducing their likelihood of obtaining an academic profession, and as a result effecting their earning capacity and their chances of mobility between social classes (Svirski, 1995). Proponents of this approach believe that these barriers that result in most of the lower class population and residents of Israel's periphery not acquiring an academic degree are not to be found at the gates of universities, but in earlier stages of education. Israel's fifty years of education policy led to the discrimination of disadvantaged groups and reinforced their status. The path of these groups, which populated mainly Israel's geographic peripheries, had been blocked from acquiring equal education because their teaches were less skilled and an emphasis was given in their schools to a vocational rather than academic curriculum, which usually did not lead to a 'Bagrut' matriculation, meaning that their path was blocked at an early stage. A further obstruction to those that overcame the Nagrut obstacle was met at the gates of the universities in the form of the various admission exams such as the psychometric exam and increasing admission requirements. Curriculums established by the same education system defined the future of students in Development towns[23] and other peripheral regions, leading them to professions and employment types prevalent among the lower classes in global populations (Svirsky and Svirsky, 1997; Shavit, 1990).

23 Development towns were new settlements built in Israel during the 1950s in order to provide permanent housing for a large influx of Jewish immigrants from Arab

According to other studies published at the start of the millennium, the absence of liberalization in primary and secondary education as well as the child's family background jointly impact orientations toward higher education and the perpetuation of social gaps. The effect of liberalization in the higher education system on equal opportunities depends on the opening positions of each group and the extent of satiation of the elites. Liberalization in higher education will not contribute to equal opportunities but to the preservation and even expansion of inequality, unless liberalization and equal opportunities are embarked upon in parallel to the liberalization of Israel's school system. Researchers concluded that the effect of social background in the selection of field of study during the first years of education is stronger than that of liberalization in the higher education system (Bolotin, Shavit & Ayalon, 2002). Others have argued that Development towns are situated in an inferior position compared to other urban areas in Israel, but this fact does not explain the inferiority of their residents. The disadvantaged social and economic composition of these towns also results from selective migration, resulting in stronger individuals tending to leave the area and weaker ones to stay. While the level of schools in the periphery is indeed a preliminary obstruction, a large part of the reasons for the gaps are beyond schools' control. The family's social background has a very strong impact on field of study selection, as well as on continued academic studies (Adler, Levine and Shavit, 2003).

Recent studies continue to strengthen the argument that high school curriculums still have a very strong impact on continued studies in the higher education system. Students who choose to study scientific curriculums in school will go on to study at leading research universities, while those who select vocational studies or humanities will continue to colleges. Moreover, it was found that students taking scientific curriculums and belonging to the higher classes will tend to study at leading research universities, and less so at knowledge acquisition universities (Yogev, 2008). This preference can be also noted in the selection of fields of study: Disciplines that are in high demand such as law, business, technology and architecture will be preferred over teaching, humanities and the arts. Students from established families will compete for places in highly desired disciplines within the Elite universities, and only afterwards at the knowledge acquisition universities. Within colleges there is a preference for desired professions first at the private colleges, followed by the public ones (Yogev, Livne, Glosman & Ayalon, 2008). These studies clearly show a strong affinity between high school

countries, Holocaust survivors from Europe and other new immigrants who arrived to the newly established State of Israel.

and higher education, relying mostly on the Bagrut matriculation. Graduates of socially established schools remain with the necessary levels of freedom to select out of a larger number of places to study within the higher education system (Ayalon & Addi-Raccah, 2008).

The Expansion of Higher Education and its Impact on the Structure of Israel's Academic System

The expansion of higher education in Israel also affected the structure of the country's academic system and its scientific achievements. Here too some researchers rely their hypotheses on the stratification theory, while others on various other theories. According to both opinions, the academic system in Israel underwent a substantial change from monolithic to binary structure, towards the gradual establishment of a dichotomous classification of types of institutions of higher education. According to one approach, this process would lead to equal opportunities in higher education (Guri-Rosenblit, 1996, 1999), and to a reduction of social gaps in Israeli society (Volansky, 2010). According to the second approach, the present binary structure leads to discrimination and even to the illusion that such a system can reduce social gaps and provide equal opportunities for a better society (Svirsky and Svirsky, 1997; Sherman, 1996). From a systemic viewpoint, some believe that the system's expansion and its growing accessibility have impacted its quality, and in many areas this resulted in a reduction in the level of achievements. This argument relies on the CHE committees that examined the quality of curricula over the past five years in various academic institutions in the country. The diminished quality results from a decline in investment in research equipment and in the distribution of State budgets to a system that has expanded beyond the country's needs. Even when the proportion of growth in the number of institutions does not require government funds, the emergence of many institutions that focused on undergraduate degrees, including Extensions of foreign universities with relatively low admission requirements, resulted in the system's proliferation, especially in undergraduate degrees in the humanities (Gal-Nur, 2009).

Proponents of the **Social Stratification Theory** view the expansion of higher education in Israel as a process that created institutional stratification, with research institutions – universities – positioned at the top, most prestigious stratum, enjoying research budgets and elaborate academic facilities, while at the bottom stratum are the new institutions, mainly consisting of public colleges including teacher-training colleges and engineering/technical colleges. The inferiority of the new institutions, and most of all the public colleges, results from their main role being teaching rather than research. According to this approach, the absence of research work in the foundations of the new institutions undermines their chances of ever reaching an equal status as the more senior institutions, and moreover undermines the level of teaching that had been defined by the ruling class as their main purpose (Ackermann et al., 1985; Yogev, 2000; Svirsky & Svirsky, 1997; Svirsky, 1995; Shai et al., 2002; Sherman, 1996). According to these researchers, the stratification process that occurred in Israel was legitimized by regulatory bodies: The CHE and its budgeting body, the PBC, which had officially defined the system as stratified.

Universities were defined as the system's "first stratum", compared to colleges, which were defined as its "second stratum" (PBC, 1997). Moreover, both the first and the second strata are stratified – between the universities themselves, as well as between colleges. Stratification between colleges distinguishes between private colleges offering studies in highly desired disciplines, and public colleges offering less desired areas of study, catering to lower classes and the less financially affluent population (Yogev, 2008). This stratification impedes the ability to reduce gaps by opening the gates to higher education in view of the fact that public colleges positioned at the bottom of the hierarchy carry the social role of reducing these gaps (Svirsky, Conor-Attias, & Abu Khala, 2010). Proponents of this approach argue that the geographic deployment of public colleges and their accessibility to lower and less established classes, results in a social division that perpetuates class inequality and social gaps, as can be seen from the data to be presented by these studies, which will be shown later on. They further argue that Israel's higher education system can be described in pyramidal form, with the universities located at the top of the pyramid, where they enjoy public research budgets and diverse curriculums. Below them are the private colleges offering programs in professions perceived by students as prestigious such as Law, Accounting, Business Administration and Psychology. After them in the pyramid are the public colleges that offer less prestigious disciplines such as social sciences, teacher-training and technological professions. At the bottom of the pyramid are Post-Secondary institutions offering vocational diplomas such as practical engineering and certification studies that are not recognized and not supervised by the CHE (Dagan-Buzaglo, 2007). Ayalon (2006) found that population groups characterized by low levels of participation in universities, such as residents of peripheral areas, the Arab sector, and to a certain extent also Jews of Asian and African descent, integrate mainly in Regional Colleges and in teacher-training colleges. In general, the higher the prestige of the academic institution, the lower the proportion of Jews of Asian and African descent, residents of peripheral areas and the Arab sector studying in it. Study findings also point to a significant level of inequality in areas of study among residents of the country's center and periphery within the Regional Colleges. It appears that residents of central regions studying at Regional Colleges tend to select highly desired programs, while residents of the periphery tend to focus on social sciences and business administration. Conversely, it appears that private colleges, most of which are located at the center, contribute to the lowering of ethnic inequality in higher education as the percentage of Mizrachim in these institutions is high.

This form of stratification has, therefore, a two-way influence that creates class inequality: although the new institutions aim to be similar to the older ones so as to attract students, their attempt is destined to failure as they lack the ability to be similar to universities due to gaps in academic facilities, budgets and senior academic faculty. On the part of the students, in both types of institutions they are classified by their achievements and academic ability. The senior institutions attract students with high academic abilities and a suitable social background, while the new institutions attract students from a more disadvantaged background and comparatively lower abilities. The senior institutions aspire to distinguish themselves from the new ones, leading to a dichotomy in the system, which despite its expansion in recent years and despite economic and occupational growth, a significant overlap remains between ethnicity and individual Socioeconomic achievements (Shavit-Kraus, 1992; Schafferman, 2007). According to these researchers, this type of stratification perpetuates the education system's shortcomings in setting separate education programs and preventing disadvantaged populations from continuing to higher education.

According to conflict theories, although colleges did lead to the lowering of academic barriers to admission to higher education, existing relationships between financial ability and accessibility to higher education remain, with the financial classification enhancing the cultural one and undermining the chances of candidates from the periphery to be accepted to prestigious programs, which remain blocked to them as they had been in the past. Moreover, systemic stratification led these researchers to predict a deterioration in the social condition due to the rise of private colleges which further increased the gap through their financial ability to recruit senior academic faculty members and attract students with financial means. With the growing number of private colleges, more and more prestigious professions are blocked to candidates from the social periphery, even at private colleges. Table 11 describes this stratification in the higher education system, perpetuating the class inequality and undermining the changes of the lower classes to reduce existing gaps.

Tab. 11: Undergraduate students at universities and academic colleges by gender, religion, ethnic origin and budgeting source, 1999/00, 2003/4

Religion and ethnic origin	**1999/00**				**2003/04**			
	Universities	**Academic Colleges Budgeting source**			**universities**	**Academic Colleges Budgeting source**		
		Total	**Public**	**Private**		**Total**	**Public**	**Private**
Total absolute – numbers	74,194	33,250	17,422	15,828	78,561	51,086	32,233	18,853
Percentage	100	100	100	100	100	100	100	100
Men	43.5 %	56.2	60.4	51.6	44.1	55.2	57.2	51.8
Women	56.5 %	43.8	39.6	46.4	55.9	44.8	42.8	48.2
Jews and others	91.0 %	93.9	93.8	94.7	90.2	94.8	94.6	95.3
Arabs	9.0 %	6.1	6.2	5.3	9.8	5.2	5.5	4.7
Jewish ethnicity:								
Israel	36.1	37.1	33.5	40.9	41.6	39.3	36.5	45
Asia-Africa	24.9	30.2	30.4	30.0	22.4	28.6	28.6	28.5
Europe-America	38.9	32.7	36.1	29.1	36	32.1	35.2	26.6

Source: Dagan-Buzaglo, 2007. Note: Since the option to specify country of origin was revoked, it is no longer possible to classify students by ethnic origin.

The data points to a preference for affluent populations in admission to universities or private colleges offering programs in highly demanded fields, while public colleges are more prevalent among the less affluent classes. A further reinforcement of this position can be found in Table 12.

Tab. 12: Students at academic colleges by district of residence and budgeting source, 1995/6, 1999/00, 2003/04, 2016/17

District of residence	1995/6	1999/2000	2003/04			2016/17		
			Budgeting source			Budgeting source		
			Total	Public	Private	Total:	Public	Private
Total absolute – numbers	13,538	33,250	51,086	32,233	18,853	88,916	54,890	34,026
Percentage	100	100	100	100	100	100	100	100
Jerusalem	9.1 %	7.4 %	7.0 %	8.2 %	4.5 %	9.5 %	10.7 %	7.6 %
North	6.8 %	12.6 %	13.8 %	17.2 %	6.8 %	18.0 %	%23.9	8.4 %
Haifa	6.5 %	11.1 %	10.6 %	11.8 %	8.1 %	9.3 %	10.1 %	8.1 %
Center	26.5 %	29.5 %	29.0 %	24.3 %	39.0 %	26.1 %	19.0 %	37.9 %
Tel Aviv	44.9 %	27.6 %	21.9 %	16.7 %	32.7 %	17.7 %	12.3 %	25.8 %
South	4.3 %	9.0 %	13.6 %	16.7 %	7.1 %	15.3 %	19.3 %	8.7 %
Judea, Samaria and the Gaza Strip	1.9 %	2.8 %	4.1 %	5.2 %	1.9 %	4.0 %	4.2 %	3.7 %

Source: CBS, 2006, table 12, pg. 21. 2016/17 data from: CBS, table 2.30 Students by Degree, District of residence, District of study and institution type, 2016/17.

According to this data, the population of central Israel takes advantage of the opportunity to study prestigious professions such as Law, Business Administration and Computer Science at private colleges, while public colleges, which are nearly devoid of free professions, serve a higher proportion of residents of peripheral areas. A social situation report published by Adva Center still points to stable gaps in higher education in 2008/09:

a. The proportion of students aged 20–29 who are residents of affluent Jewish towns and studied for an undergraduate degree at a university was 10.1 %. This rate was double the parallel one in Arab towns – 4.8 %, while at Development Towns it was 6.0 %. A social situation report published by Adva Center in 2016 points to a similar conclusion: The proportion of students in the same age group who are residents of affluent Jewish towns and studied for an undergraduate degree at a university was 11 %. This rate continued to be double the parallel one in Arab towns – 5.4 %; and in Development Towns – 5.3 %. These gaps also remain stable in the 2018 report published by Adva Center (Svirsky & Conor-Attias, 2017).

b. Despite the fact that the goals defined by the State for public colleges was to open opportunities to residents of Israel's periphery, the data for 2002/03 and onwards point to gaps between residents of affluent towns and those of the country's Development towns: The proportion of students in colleges in 2008/09 among residents of affluent towns in the same age group was 10.6 % and in Development towns 6.4 %. While the proportion of students studying in colleges among resident of Development towns increased from 3.8 % in 2002/03 to 6.4 %, still the gap between them and residents of affluent towns remained intact (Svirsky, Conor-Attias, & Abu Khala, 2010). The 2016 situation report points to a continuation of this trend: The proportion of students in colleges in 2016/7 among residents of affluent towns in the same age group was 10.5 % and in Development towns 7.2 %. While the proportion of students studying in colleges among resident of Development towns increased, still the gap between them and residents of affluent towns remained intact (Svirsky & Conor-Attias, 2017).

The data supports the approach that accessibility to higher education in Israel has in fact not expanded and that in practice social gaps remain intact and maybe are even aggravated due to the competition between institutions. Based on this theory, the center will remain central and the periphery will remain peripheral.

Even in the 2018 report, Adva Center researchers continue to point to a substantial gap in participation in higher education in Israel. Students commencing their studies at institutions of higher education are not equality representative of the different groups in Israeli society. The highest proportion of students commencing academic studies is among the Jewish population cohort residing in towns belonging to the high Socioeconomic clusters who had studied an academic program in high school, while the lowest participation rates were noted among the Arab population coming from towns belonging to the lower Socioeconomic clusters (Svirsky, Conor-Attias, & Liberman, 2018). In 2011 only 14 % of the Arab population had attended academic studies, compared to 33.5 % of the Jewish population (Svirsky, Conor-Attias, & Ophir, 2013). Although in 2017 the proportion of Arab students in that age group was on the rise, according to these researchers the gap between Arab and Jewish towns is still substantial. A follow-up on high school graduates in 2009 who continued to academic studies in 2017 (meaning within eight years) shows a proportion of 26.3 % among that age groups in the Arab population, and 37.7 % among the Jewish population (Svirsky, Conor-Attias, & Liberman, 2018).

These findings, however, did not include Arab students studying at the Open University or at teacher-training colleges. The data does not distinguish between students in private colleges, those in public ones, or students at academic colleges under the academic auspices of a university, and these were included in the group of university students. Moreover, we do not have precise data regarding Israeli Arab students studying in academic institutions in Arab countries. The absence of such data leads, in my opinion, to an imprecise situation report regarding the proportion of Arabs attending academic studies in Israel.

In addition, a review of the number of Arab students in 2016/17–2017/18 points to a changing trend, as shown in Figure 2.

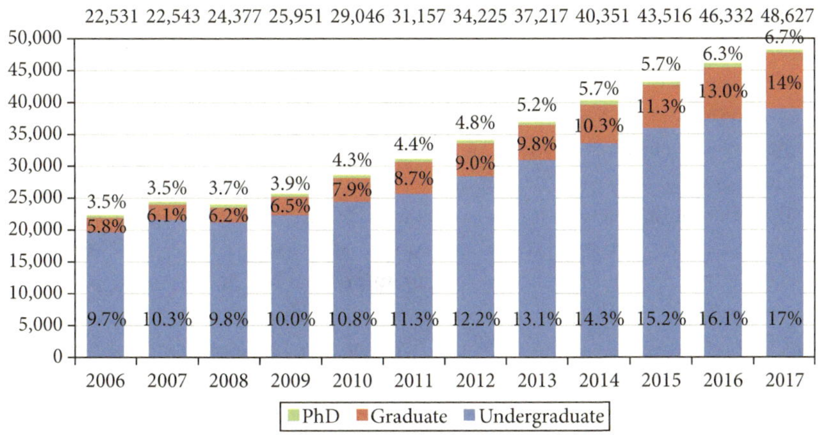

Fig. 2 : The number of Arab students in all degrees, 2006/07–2017/18

Source: CBS website – Collection of data towards the opening of the academic year 2018/19, Retrieved 8 March 2, 2020. Note: percentages pertain to the proportion of Arab students of all students in the same degree level.

In the 1990s the number of Arab students increased from 7 % in 1995/96 to 10 % in 1999/00. As of 1999/00 the deceleration in applications to academic studies also affected the Arab students, whose percentage in 2012/13 was only 13 %. In 2017/18 Arab students accounted to 15.0 % of all students in Israel's higher education system. Most of the increase in the proportion of Arab students was at universities, teacher-training colleges and academic colleges under the auspices of universities, located near their places of residence. A significant rise can be noted among Arab women. During the 1990s women accounted to only 40 % of Arab students, increasing to 66 % in 2012/13.

Inequality in Access to Higher Education among Young Adults from Established Areas and Those from Less Established Ones

Studies held after the change in Israel's higher education system point to inequality between social groups in admission to higher education despite the expansion of the academic system in general. Researchers distinguish between two dimensions of inequality: Vertical inequality and horizontal inequality. The vertical inequality is expressed in continued education and the attainment of degrees, while horizontal inequality expresses differences between different types of certificates at the same level of education, such as between diplomas obtained from more prestigious institutions compared to those from less prestigious ones and differences between areas of study. In a research report on the accessibility to higher education among young adults from Israel's social periphery, Feniger, Ayalon and Mcdossi (2013) point to the following: despite the dramatic expansion of Israel's higher education system in the past two decades, there are still substantial and notable social gaps both in the vertical and horizontal dimensions of inequality. On the vertical dimension, young adults born to the long standing Jewish population, having similar backgrounds and achievements in their Bargut high school matriculation and Psychometric exam, still participate in higher education at higher proportions compared to young adults from the country's social periphery. This gap is even wider in comparison to the Arab sector. The researchers find a further gap between young adults whose parents have a higher education and those whose parents do not. On the horizontal dimension, a gap was found between dominant groups in Israeli society and groups belonging to the country's social periphery. Immigrants from the former Soviet Union have a higher likelihood to attend academic studies in programs leading to higher incomes compared to young adults from Mizrachi origin, Arabs, Jews of Ethiopian descent and even young adults from a mixed Ashkenazi-Mizrachi descent.

Further horizontal inequality can be found in the gaps showing higher income for university graduates compared to graduates of colleges (Shwed & Shavit, 2006). Ayalon, Yogev and others have shown that the social profile of students of desired fields at colleges is similar to that of university students. Students from discriminated groups due to class, nationality or ethnic origin, utilize the expansion of the higher education system but take part in less prestigious programs (Ayalon & Yogev, 2005; Getz & Dar 2007).

A later study pointed to the willingness of students from the periphery to compromise in their choice of field of study, as long as it would grant them a job at the end of their studies, more so than those living in the center of the country. 10 %–15 % of students in the periphery made such a compromise compared to 40 %–45 % of students from the center who chose their field of study due to their interest in it and not only based on the likelihood to find a job. Hence, students from the center of Israel tend to show more interest in their field of study while students from the periphery tend to select a field that would ensure they find a job, rather than basing their choice on their personal interest in the field. In fact, according to these researchers, Israel's overall social inequality is closely linked to inequality in accessibility to higher education and a report on inequality in access to higher education cannot ignore economic inequality (Ben Haim & Shavit, 2018). Thus, gaps are also maintained later in life. Another relevant study addresses the situation in which the fact that employers are faced with applicants coming from a wide variety of institutions has led to the adoption of a graduates quality ranking approach that not only examines graduates' field of study, but also the institution in which they studied. Prestigious institutions are perceived by employers as not only teaching but also educating and better preparing for employment (Barzilay-Shacham & Yaish, 2015).

According to other researchers, the core of inequality is in the education system which in their opinion is built as a pyramid – with the number of participants in each level diminishing towards the top. The top echelon, representing the proportion of university students, amount to only a third of the relevant age cohort. Even when data point to an increase in the number of high school graduates from less affluent towns who are eligible for a Bagrut matriculation diploma, a gap remains between those eligible for a Bagrut diploma that facilitates entry to academic studies, and one that does not. Such inequality has implications on earnings and consequently also on social mobility. Researchers found a relationship between earning horizon and chosen major in high school. Students who have chosen to major in a scientific area were more likely to be accepted to higher education programs leading to a high income, such as engineering and the exact sciences, compared to students who majored in high school in the social sciences and education (Feniger, Ayalon & Mcdossi, 2013; Biggeri, Bini & Grilli, 2001; Davies & Guppy, 1997; Gerber & Schaefer, 2004). Thus, researchers believe that geographical inequality in higher education begins in the local education system (Svirsky & Conor-Attias, 2017). The data affected by the education pyramid reinforce this approach, also according to 2014/15 and 2018 data (Svirsky, Conor-Attias, & Liberman, 2018).

The key, therefore, to a more equal society, is according to these researchers the education system, and the change must begin in Primary and Secondary education. the expansion of higher education was achieved, according to this approach, in a way that reproduces the differential structure of opportunities that already exists in the Primary and Secondary education system. The expansion did not lead to an increased level of equality in terms of accessibility to higher education. While the Non-Publicly Funded Academic Colleges lowered barriers such as the Psychometric score as an admission requirement, in parallel the relationship between financial ability and accessibility to higher education remained intact (Dagan-Buzaglo, 2007).

Stratification at the Top Echelon

According to Yogev (2000), proponents of the stratification approach focus on the institutional stratification which mainly occurs between universities and colleges, while ignoring stratification within universities. He classifies three universities – the Hebrew University, Tel Aviv and the Technion – as elite institutions aiming for theoretical and scientific excellence, while Ben Gurion university, Bar Ilan and Haifa are classified as Target Universities, two of which aim to bring higher education to the periphery (Ben Gurion and Haifa), and one – Bar Ilan – to the religious-traditional population. Signs of this type of stratification can be noted, according to Yogev, in the growth and development of universities in recent years: while Target Universities absorbed most of the 1990s demand, the Elite universities increased their numbers of advanced degree students. Central Bureau of Statistics data in Figure 3 point to this trend.

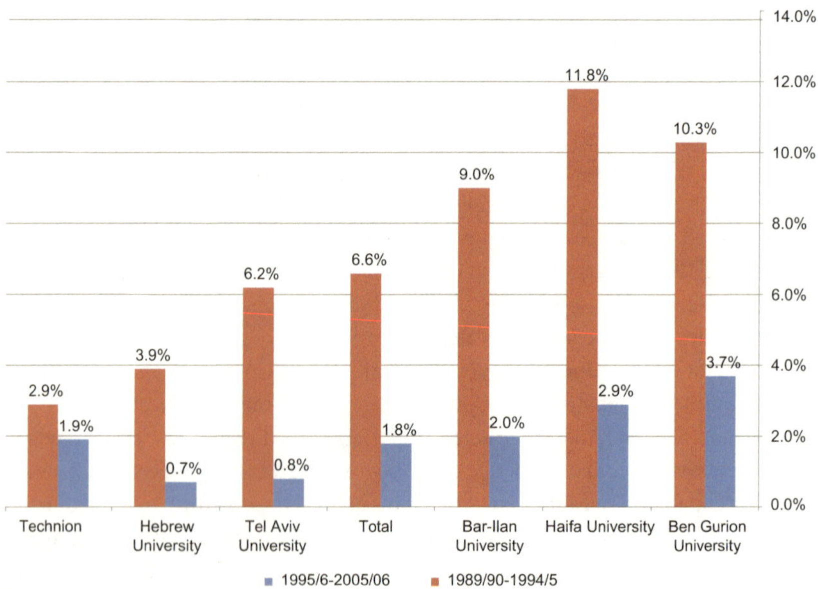

Fig. 3 : Increase in the number of university students 1989/90–2005/06
Source: Aharoni & Biham, 2008.

The data on the number of students of advanced degrees shows a clear preference forElite universities where the number of students of advanced degrees has for many years been higher than its parallel at Target Universities. Although the gaps were reduced in 2005/06, Yogev believed that this trend is ongoing, as can be seen in Tables 13 and 14.

Tab. 13: Number of Graduate students in 1989–2007

Years	Total	The Hebrew University	Technion	Tel Aviv University	Bar Ilan University	Haifa University	Ben Gurion University	Weizmann Institute
1989/90	16,155	4,717	1,949	5,443	1,930	1,105	824	187
1999/00	30,454	6,409	2,775	9,346	4,352	3,231	4,128	213
2006/07	33,817	6,887	2,812	9,070	5,831	4,964	3,982	271
2008/09	34,336	6,383	2,774	8,984	6,072	5,339	4,526	288

Source: CBS (2010). Higher Education in Israel 2007/08 Table 2.5, pg.143. CBS 2008/09 data, Higher Education in Israel 2008/09, Table 2.11.

Tab. 14: Number of PhD students 1989–2009

Years	Total	The Hebrew University	Technion	The Aviv University	Bar Ilan University	Haifa University	Ben Gurion University	Weizmann Institute
1989/90	3,764	1375	438	852	407	83	148	461
1999/00	6,647	2099	643	1447	882	389	611	576
2006/07	9,972	2698	925	2069	1667	898	999	706
2008/09	10,272	2609	877	2173	1751	978	1176	708

Source: CBS (2010). Higher Education in Israel 2007/08, table 2.5, University students by Degree, Gender and Institution, pg. 143. CBS 2008/09 data, Higher Education in Israel 2008/09, Table 2.12.

In 1990, 73.5 % of all students of advanced degrees in Israel attended the Hebrew University, Tel Aviv or the Technion. Despite a certain decline in 2005/06 and in 2008/09, these three institutions still teach over 53 % of all students of advanced degrees in Israel.

Data from a national survey of first year students at colleges and universities point to the existence of socio-demographic variables reinforcing the argument of university stratification and its relationship to Israeli society's inequality in accessibility to higher education (Yogev, 2008). Yogev argues (2000, 2008) that the academic stratification of Elite universities also affects their social stratification. Socio-demographic variables examined over the course of a decade point to a relationship between student population and the academic stratification of Elite universities. It was found that the relative proportion of Mizrachi students is higher than expected at each of the three Target Universities, while their number is lower than expected at Elite universities. The proportion of older students (over 35 years old) at the Target Universities is higher than expected – a fact that can be explained by the need to study to achieve job promotion or a professional career, rather than as typical research students. The proportion of women is also high at the Target Universities, and this fact is true also for Ben Gurion University which is comparable to the Technion as a quarter of its students study engineering. Yogev's explanation may point to the tendency among women to study at a later age, after childbirth, aiming for occupational promotion or an academic career. Another interesting point is the relatively high number of Target university students whose parents' incomes are comparatively low, and of students whose parents' education is relatively lower than those of similar backgrounds studying at Elite universities (Yogev, 2008). Although differences between students at the two types of institutions are not high, they are, nevertheless, statistically significant. Yogev's suggested explanations for these differences in students populations are as follows:

1. Attitudes towards higher education – Students at Target Universities tend to consider practical and professional considerations in selecting their field of study.
2. Target Universities attract larger populations from the periphery and therefore their student population is characterized by a generally less affluent social background.
3. The reputation of Target Universities is well known – institutions whose academic requirements are lower than those of the Elite universities and which attract more students from less affluent Socioeconomic backgrounds (Yogev, 2008).

I have examined Yogev's thesis a decade after it was published and found that it does not withstand the test of time in the new reality that evolved as a result of the colleges revolution. During the 2018/9 academic year, only 33 % of all students of advanced degrees studied at universities defined by Yogev as research universities – while an identical number (32.7 %) studied at institutions defined as Target Universities. The remaining graduate degree students attended colleges.[24]

Israeli Universities in World Universities Rankings

In world universities rankings Israel's three Elite universities are ranked among the world's top 200 universities while its Target Universities are ranked lower. The world rankings rely on a number of accepted benchmarks such as quality of teaching,

24 CHE, Collection of data towards the opening of the academic year 2018/19.

quality of academic faculty, academic outputs and quality of research in relation to the size of the institution. There are many and diverse rankings, but there is generally a high statistical correlation between then, so that specific criteria do not substantially change the results. Accordingly, the best university is ranked in more than one ranking, as is the worst one (Kirsch, 2010). Following are the rankings of Israel's Elite universities in two well-known international rankings:

THES – Time Higher Education Supplement[25]
ARUW – The Institute of Higher Education, Shanghai[26]

According to the THES, the Hebrew University, the Tel Aviv University and the Technion were ranked in recent years among the world's top 200 universities, and in some years the Hebrew University was ranked among the first 100. Table 15 presents the ranking for 2004–2013.

Tab. 15: Ranking of Israeli Universities in the general ranking of the top 200 universities (THES), 2004–2013

	2004	2005	2006	2007	2008	2009	2011/2012	2013/2014
The Hebrew University	93	77	119	128	93	102	121	191
Tel Aviv University	90	188	147	151	114	114	166	199
The Technion	158	194	158	231	109	132	201–225	201–225
Weizmann Institute								

Source: Kirsch, 2010: 37. 2011 – 2014 ranking from: http://www.timeshighereducation.co.uk/world-university-rankings/2013-14/world ranking

In the ARWU ranking Israel's Elite universities are better rated than in the THES ranking. As shown in Table 16, in the general ranking of the past five years, these universities were ranked among the top 150 universities in the world, led by the Hebrew University which during those years ranked among the top 65.

25 A global ranking of universities, published by a weekly magazine based in London that has been reporting news and issues related to higher education since 2004. The ranking is based on many indexes, from teaching environment to innovation and inputs of research in industry.

26 This global ranking of universities was first published in June 2003 by the Center for World-Class Universities (CWCU) under the auspices of the Academic School of Education of Jiao Tong University, Shanghai, China.

Tab. 16: Ranking of Israeli Universities in the general ranking of the top 200 universities (ARWU), 2004–2013

Institution/year	2004	2007	2010	2013
Jerusalem	90	64	72	59
Tel Aviv	101–152	102–150	101–150	101–150
Weitzman Institute	101–152	102–150	101–150	92
The Technion	202–301	102–150	101–150	77

Source: http://www.shanghairanking.com/ARWU2013.html, retrieved on 23 July 2014.

When examining rankings in specific areas, we see that these universities achieve impressive positions, as can be seen in Table 17.

Tab. 17: Ranking of Israeli Universities in the general ranking of the top 200 universities (ARWU), 2004–2009

University/ Discipline	Mathematics	Physics	Chemistry	Computer Sciences	Economics	Natural Sciences and Mathematics	Social Sciences
The Hebrew University	51–77	51–77	76–101	25	51–75	53–76	52–75
Tel Aviv University	25	78–104	76–101	29	51–75	77–101	52–75
The Technion	51–77	–	51–75	17	–	40	–

Source: Kirsch, 2010: 38.

As can be seen in Table 18, this trend continues in 2010–2013:

Tab. 18: Ranking of Israeli Universities in the general ranking of the top 200 universities (ARWU), 2010–2013

Discipline/Institution	Jerusalem		Technion		Tel Aviv		Weizmann Institute	
	2010	2013	2010	2013	2010	2013	2010	2013
Mathematics	51–76	17	51–75	51–77	26	33	–	–
Physics	51–75	76–100		151–200	76–100	101–150	51–75	51–77
Chemistry		101–150	51–75	38		101–150	51–75	76–100
Computer Sciences	21	28	15	18	31	44	12	23
Economics and Business Administration	44	76–100			78–100	76–100		
Natural Sciences and Mathematics	51–75	53–76	51–75	38	76–100	76–100	46	51–75
Engineering and Technology		78–100	38	46		101–150		

Source: http://www.shanghairanking.com/ARWU2013.html, retrieved on 23 July 2014.

Compared to the relatively high ranking of Elite universities, Bar Ilan University was ranked above 301 in the 2009–2013 ARWU and Ben Gurion was ranked 304 in 2004 and 2013, and above 2000 in 2007 and 2010. The University of Haifa was ranked 467 in the list of academic institutions.[27]

Compared to the change in the proportion of advanced degree students in research universities in 2019, which does not support Yogev's thesis, the international ranking still ranks research universities higher than other universities. In the general 2019 ARWU ranking, the Technion was ranked 85th, Jerusalem between 150–201 and Tel Aviv 151–200. Bar Ilan, Ben Gurion and Haifa were ranked between 401 and 500.[28] In the 2019 ranking by professions, the Technion, Tel Aviv and Jerusalem are still ranked relatively high compared to Bar Ilan, Haifa and Ben Gurion.

Proponents of the **Diversity Approach** perceive the expansion of higher education in Israel, as in the world, as a positive process for society and for the academic system as it creates institutional diversity that allows a wide range of populations to attend higher education. Institutional diversity provides the economy and society with all its professional needs, which in turn further develop based on many social factors, expanding the circle of students of advanced degrees (Guri-Rosenblit, 1996, 1999). Diversity is also apparent in the types of institutions of higher education and the type of students attending them. Types of students are generally determined based on their academic-professional goals. Diversity is not in students' level of academic ability, but in their choice of field of study and type of study program. The diversity of institutions and programs enables each candidate to find his or her place according to their professional inclination and academic ability. The fact that universities are located at the top of the pyramid as research institutions contributes to the expansion of science and research, as the new institutions would enhance the country's potential pool of researchers, thereby increasing the system's chances of coping with scientific challenges and global competition in a globalized world. Proponents of this approach believe that the stratification approach ignores the need of the Israel economy, which according to them requires the existence of institutions with diverse goals for diverse needs, as in any other modern society. The diversity needed for Israel's economy and society is expressed in its types of colleges: Colleges training for the teaching professions and offering undergraduate and graduate degrees in Education, technological colleges training professionals for emerging technological needs – in High Tech as well as in Low Tech, engineering training colleges, professional colleges training practical engineers, art colleges, and others (Volansky, 2010)

27 http://www.shanghairanking.com/ARWU2013.html, Retrieved 23 July 2014.

28 http://www.shanghairanking.com/ARWU2018.html, Retrieved 9 March 20.

When examining the data on students in 2019 we see a significant effect of the expansion of accessibility to higher education on the entire academic system. In 2019 the number of undergraduate students in colleges multiplied many times over: In 1990 there were 8,286 students in colleges, while in 2019 their number soared to 116,263. When graduate studies came to be offered at colleges in 1999, a total of 413 graduate students studied at these institutions, while in 2019 their number grew to 22,866. This meteoric increase impacted graduate and PhD studies throughout the academic system and led to a significant increase in advanced university degrees over the past decade.[29]

The Test of Compensation in the Labor Market

To address the question of the impact of higher education on distributive justice between social classes, researchers examined the effect of changes in the higher education system on equal opportunities in the work force, and whether the expanded accessibility to higher education creates a differentiation in the income and occupational prestige of university graduates compared to graduates of the new institutions – public and private colleges.

According to Benrnardi and Ballarino, 2012 the expansion of higher education may lead to three possible scenarios in terms of the value of education in the labor market:

1. The Best-off scenario – The expansion of higher education leads to a reduction in educational inequality, and the labor market mobilizes accordingly to absorb the graduates.
2. The Trade-off scenario – The expansion of higher education does in fact reduce inequality in higher education, but the labor market does not expand accordingly and the result is an inflation of candidates with a higher education and the value of education is eroded.
3. The Worst-off scenario – The expansion of higher education leads to an increase in inequality, as the strongest classes take advantage of the expanded accessibility to higher education due to their high awareness to the higher value of education compared to the weaker classes, and inequality in higher education is reinforced. Meanwhile, the market does not expand accordingly, and the stronger classes take advantage of the small number of employment opportunities available (Benrnardi & Ballarino, 2012).

29 CHE. Statistical data files on Higher education in Israel, Table 5 and Table 6. Retrieved March 9, 2020.

A study by Bar Haim, Blank and Shavit (2009) led to a number of conclusions on the relationship between the expansion of higher education during the years 1995–2008 and the labor market:

1. The expansion of higher education must be accompanied by a policy compensating disadvantaged populations, for instance by investing in the education system in disadvantaged areas, a longer school day, financial support, individual one on one teaching support and smaller classes.
2. The attractiveness of certain professions diminished in the absence of a parallel expansion of these professions in response to the expansion of higher education in the same areas.
3. Despite its first and second conclusions, the study does point to the existing value of higher education compared to employees who do not possess one (ibid: 14–15).

Another aspect of the expansion of higher education and its effect on the test of change in the labor market is the question of the effect of institutional stratification on the level of income among graduates of the entire academic system. In a study that examined differences in earnings between graduates of Israeli colleges compared to universities, 2,542 students were interviewed in a representative sample of universities and colleges and it was found that graduates of public colleges earn less than their peers who graduated from universities and private colleges. Yossi Shavit, one of the researchers, provided the following explanations:

1. Private colleges attract affluent populations whose ability to integrate in the work force yields higher incomes than that of students at public colleges.
2. Universities and private colleges offer studies in prestigious areas, while professions with a lower professional prestige are studied at public colleges (based on accepted global rankings, areas of study offered at the public colleges were ranked 51 of 100, while areas of study offered at universities were ranked 62.5 of 100).[30]

A further study that examined the differences in the quality of higher education between universities and colleges based on the level of compensation in the labor market reached similar conclusions – that graduates of academic colleges earn in the first year after graduating with a bachelor degree approx. 20 %–30 % less than university graduates in areas such as economics, accounting, law, computer Sciences and engineering. The study further shows that graduates of bachelor degrees from colleges generally come from a more disadvantaged Socioeconomic

30 Tamara Traubman, "Students at colleges were not surprised: University graduates earn more", Haaretz, 22 March, 2006.

background compared to university graduates, and that their educational achievements are also lower compared to university graduates. Graduates of private colleges are similar in their background to university graduates (excluding educational data), while in terms of background graduates of public colleges (such as parents' education and income) are relatively disadvantaged compared to graduates of private colleges. The researchers concluded that public colleges did in fact increase the accessibility of the lower classes to the higher education system, but apparently also deepened quality gaps between universities and colleges (Zusman, Furman, Kaplan & Romanov, 2006).

A recent study by researchers from the Bank of Israel's Research Division points to a reduction in the earning gap between graduates of colleges and universities and in particular research universities. In 2018 the gap between university graduates and graduates of public colleges was 10 %. This gap has been further reduced and according to recent data is currently only 6 %–7 % compared to graduates of private colleges where highly demanded professions are taught, including Law and Accounting. This recent data supports the conclusions of researchers investigating the field throughout the world. Most studies point to a gap of 0 %–20 % between graduates of selective institutions compared to other institutions, with the gap never exceeding 10 % outside the United States (Ahdut, Gutman, Zusman, Lipiner & Maayan, 2018).

The Establishment of Extensions and Their Integration in the Council for Higher Education's System of Public Colleges

The idea to establish Extensions was part of the general ideology that guided the founders of Bar Ilan University, whose idea to establish an academic-religious institution originated from an aim to influence the religious image of the State of Israel. The way to achieve this central goal was influenced by two models: That of the Christian academic institutions in the USA, and the principle of autonomy in education – a model adopted during the *Yishuv* pre-State period, and which continued to exist after the establishment of the State and until today. The principles of the two models served as a guideline both in the idea of the establishment of the university and in the later establishment of its Extensions. The idea to establish Extensions was developed from a unique approach consisting of an ideological synthesis of religious and social goals. These two integrated goals form the basis of the model of Christian academic institutions in the USA as well as of the principles of the autonomy in education.

The establishment of the Extensions followed two main stages: The foundation stage, which involved a strong ideological drive and religious fervor and therefore led to an attempt at a paradigmatic transformation in the academic field; while the second stage was characterized by an undermining strategy and proceeded according to acceptable rules in the academic field. This transition stems from the acceptance of governance and a willing subordination to regulation following the university's official accreditation three years after its establishment in 1958 and following the legislation of the CHE Law later that year. This subordination led to a toning down of the religious and social aspirations of the university's founders and the setting aside of the ambitious idea of a multi-campus university with a central campus and Extensions throughout the country. This strategic change led to a gradual abandonment of the idea of the Extensions, leaving a number of small academic Extensions (at Ashkelon, Zefat and the Jordan Valley) devoid of a suitable academic foundation. These Extensions continued to operate in this format until the beginning of the 1990s. Table 19 presents the foundation and the disconnection periods. The first Extensions were established in 1965–1968, and the gradual disconnection process began in 1990. At the time of writing these lines, the process of fully disconnecting from the parent university is still underway.

Tab. 19: The Extensions' foundation and disconnection period

Foundation and establishment 1965–1990			**The disconnection period 1990–2014**		
1965–1968	**1968–1972**	**1972–1990**	**1990–1999**	**2000–2003**	**2003–2014**
The establishment of the first Extensions	The attempt to establish the idea of a nation-wide university	The Struggle for the existence of the Extensions	The Extensions as Regional Colleges – **The organizational disconnection**	The Extensions as colleges under academic auspices	The Extensions as Academic Colleges – **The Academic disconnection**

Changes in higher education policies led to a disconnection between the Extensions and their parent university and ultimately to their integration in the country's system of academic colleges as part of the expansion of accessibility to higher education:

1. Amendment number 3 to the CHE's Law, legislated in 1972, prohibited the establishment of centers outside the main campus without the CHE's approval, and in doing so accelerated the end of the religious-social initiatives of Bar Ilan University's founders.

2. The fact that the PBC did not recognize the Extensions as budgeted institutions burdened the universities' budgets and served as catalyst to the initiative of the university's Rector and president in the mid 1980s to transfer the administrative responsibility of the Extensions from the university to the government, while leaving the university with only academic responsibility.
3. The expansion of higher education in the world and later in Israel led to a dramatic turning point in Israel's academic field. The management of the founding university had to cope with the transition to a binary system that created a regulative distinction (as instructed by the CHE) between the university and its Extensions. This distinction positioned the university on the same side as other universities in Israel in its need to compete with colleges for budgets and students.
4. The further amendment to the 1958 CHE Law, known as the Colleges Amendment (revision 10) in the 1990s and transferring of the handling of colleges including the university's Extensions to the government (hence, to the CHE) completely transformed Israel's higher education system and increased the number of institutions competing for a share of the budget. The Extensions switched to the other side of the system, becoming new institutions competing in parallel to the parent university over State budgets that gradually diminish from one year to the next.
5. The policy that was agreed upon by the university management consisted of an abandonment of the founders' path (mainly the policies dictated by the university's founder Pinkhos Churgin) and instead focusing on a practical approach that considers only the benefit of the university. The priorities of the university's leaders gradually changed – with the advancement of research and scientific excellence positioned at the top of the ladder, in an aim to compete over academic and scientific capital and differentiate itself from the new institutions, as can be explained by Bourdieu's Field Theory on which I will elaborate later.

While Bar Ilan University decided to abandon its Extensions for the reasons described above, there is no ignoring a single clear fact – that the initiative of Bar Ilan's founders during the 1960s to establish Extensions in other parts of the country made a lasting and decisive impact on Israel's academic system as it evolved in the 1990s. Towards the end of the 1990s, the CHE, that had to cope with a growing demand for higher education, identified Post-Secondary institutions ready for operation throughout the country. These institutions offered academic studies under the auspices of Israeli universities, and the CHE added them to the national effort to address the growing demand for higher education in the 1990s. Eleven Regional Colleges taught academic courses under the auspices of universities, including five colleges that operated under the academic auspices of Bar Ilan University. The three Extensions established in the 1960s served as a model for Post-Secondary institutions established by Regional Councils, and all of them joined (a small number of them are currently in their last stages of joining) the system of academic colleges and they are nearing the end of the process of obtaining full academic independence.

It is difficult to imaging Israel's higher Education system without the initiative of Bar Ilan's founders in the 1960s. This initiative led to permanent changes in the academic field and effected Post-Secondary institutions that imitated the founders and offered academic studies in a similar format. Such were the Jordan Valley and Tel Chai Colleges in the north of the country, which in the 1970s seeked the academic auspices of the University of Haifa. In the mid 1970s the Sapir and Achva Colleges adopted a similar method, joining the list of colleges offering eclectic studies under the auspices of Ben Gurion University, with further attempts made with Tel Aviv University and the Hebrew University in the 1980s, which will be discussed in later chapters.

Conclusions

The expansion of higher education is a result of the expansion of the education system in the West in the first half of the twentieth century. This universal phenomenon also affected Israel, whose academic system steadily expanded and gradually opened its gates as of the 1980s and onwards. In view of the growing demand for higher education in parallel to the country's growing population following the immigration wave of the 1990s, heads of the academic system were forced to provide solutions for the huge demand for higher education and for the requirements of the modern economy. The country's academic system which up to the 1990s functioned as a monolithic system having a research-based orientation, modeled first according to the German-European mode and as of the 1950s, according to the American model, transformed into a binary system operating via two main arms: Research universities and non-research institutions of higher education – Colleges. During the 1990s the CHE identified an infrastructure of Regional Colleges that taught academic courses under the auspices of universities, and was therefore very easily able to include 11 such colleges in the national program. The Regional Colleges, including the Bar Ilan University Extensions were incorporated into the academic level, with the clear goal of becoming teaching institutions without research activities.

The definition of the academic-institutional system according to these two models led to dichotomous opinions among researchers in the field: Opinions differ between those who view the system's expansion as a blessing for Israel's academy and society in general, and those who perceive the expansion of the system in this format as a reproduction of the previous condition or the development of a "second class" academic education. The fear of a diminishing level of higher education in Israel was discussed in all frameworks pertaining to the system's regulation (PBC and mostly CHE) since the approval of the master plan for colleges. Although everyone acknowledges the necessity of the colleges, opinions differ as to the method of their development and the relationship between them and universities. The main role allocated to colleges in the master plan was the expansion of accessibility and community roles, for instance by offering further professional training. However, their fast evolvement and the binding ties between teaching and research lead to disagreements as to their development directions and place in the system in relation to research universities.

Developments in higher education in recent years, and mostly between 2010 and 2014, point to gradual changes in the academic approach to colleges. In a document prepared by PBC Chairperson Prof. Manuel Trachtenberg in anticipation of the discussion on the status of the Ariel Academic College, he pointed to a problematic dichotomy in the structure of higher education in Israel and the need to pave the way to a new structure that would address the many needs of higher education in the country. According to Prof. Trachtenberg, the dichotomous model is anachronistic and needs to be revised as soon as possible. This conclusion stems from the many roles of the academic system. Institutions of higher education are required to fulfill a number of roles including expanding accessibility to higher education, developing advanced technologies, training professionals and creating knowledge. These roles cannot be realized if colleges are defined as non-research institutions. An academic institution aiming to position itself at the forefront of technology and knowledge would find it difficult to evolve under limiting conditions. Moreover, colleges are led by senior researchers who have developed their careers at universities. Therefore the PBC's Chairperson determined in his letter that the dichotomous model of universities with colleges alongside them is not optimal and moreover may hinder the system's development:

> A further complex of institutions should be considered alongside universities and colleges, as is customary in many countries around the world. To facilitate the discussion by relying on existing terms, we can refer to these newly defined institutions as "University centers".[31]

Heads of colleges feared that the absence of research in colleges would lead to their being classified as "second class" institutions of higher education. This fear

31 Letter from the PBC's Chairperson to the Chairperson of the Judea and Samaria CHE, 15 July 2012.

was most worrying for their academic faculty members who embarked on a struggle to obtain identical employment conditions as their colleagues at universities. Although they did not succeed in obtaining completely equal terms of employment as university faculty members, this was an important step on the path to achieve the changes hoped for by the heads of the colleges and their academic faculties.

In 2012 a collective agreement was signed between the PBC, faculty organizations and the colleges, consisting of the regulating bodies indirectly recognizing the importance of research at the colleges. A financial compensation mechanism was developed for colleges, granting indirect legitimation for conducting research at colleges through an institutional research committee allocating research funding to the institution's permanent academic faculty members. These research grants are not personal as at universities, but determined by an institutional committee following a review of the researcher's application and based on the availability of funds. This is an important change that attests to the rise in the status of colleges. They are no longer only teaching institutions, but institutions of higher education with diverse roles. In recent years (2018–2020) the CHE has been assessing the most suitable ratio between the different tasks allocated to each institution – the role of colleges in relation to the role of universities defined as research institutions. The CHE has formed a committee participated by representatives of universities and academic colleges with the aim of drafting a treaty that would define the roles of the institutions and the relationships between them. It seems that an interim institution – a "University center" as coined by Trachtenberg, or another name – positioned between the universities and the rest of the colleges, is no longer on the CHE's agenda, but rather the opening of opportunities to colleges meeting the necessary conditions, to teach and offer advanced research degrees, including PhD's. Such approval was granted in 2020 to the Interdisciplinary Center Herzliya, which has already opened its PhD program for the 2020/21 academic year.

Chapter 2 Bar Ilan University: Establishment and Formative Years

Historical Background

A discussion on the establishment of the Extensions in the 1960s until their integration in Israel's academy in the mid 1990s requires an understanding of the goals that accompanied the establishment of Bar Ilan University, as well as more recent developments (2010–2015) during which the university's image has largely been formed as a research institution. The roots of the idea of founding a religious university in Israel can be found in the religious ideology of the "Mizrachi" political movement as had evolved within the social reality of the Pre-State *Yishuv* in Israel and the needs that arose immediately following the establishment of the State of Israel in 1948. As stated, in the Pre-State era, there were three institutions of higher education: The Technion as an institute of technology, the Hebrew University that aimed to be an international Jewish center of science and research (Ben David, 1985), and the Weizmann Institute of Science established as a modern research institute through private initiative in 1934. These institutions, founded in the Pre-State era, continued to function independently without governmental supervision after the establishment of the State. However, as their dependence on State budgets grew, in parallel to the growing public demand for higher education, demands began to be voiced to regulate their relationship with the State. The imminent State supervision evoked fears regarding the undermining of academic freedoms and intervention in the institutions' management. However, governmental intervention was in fact necessary in order to address the growing demand for higher education, which continued to grow in the 1950s following waves of immigration from Eastern Europe and the Middle East. this state of affairs led, as already mentioned, to the decision of Minister of Education at the time Zalman Aran to appoint a special committee led by Governor of the Bank of Israel David Horwitz, to investigate the situation of Higher Education in Israel and the pros and cons in government funding. About nine months after it had been appointed, the committee submitted its report to the minister, with the following conclusions:

a. The three old institutions do not provide the country's needs for trained personnel. In particular, the committee stressed the significant importance of developing the sociological structure of the population and its geographical dispersal.

b. The body of students studying at the Hebrew University and the Technion is predominantly comprised of a narrow stratum of the old *Yishuv*. Under such circumstances, integration of exiles and of cultures in Israel will not be possible.
c. The establishment of an academic leadership among *Olim* (new immigrants) is a necessity of the State's social structure.
d. A recommendation to appoint a special council to supervise academic institutions and their relationships with the government.

The committee's recommendations to increase the number of students beyond those studying at the Hebrew University and the Technion required more institutions of higher education and strengthening the relationship and coordination between the old institutions and the new ones to be established. The committee further recommended appointing a special independent council to supervise the institutions and their budgets so as to prevent political involvement in their management and in the budgets allocated to higher education.[32] This recommendation was in fact legislated, and in the following year the Council for Higher Education Law, 5718–1958 was legislated by the Knesset. Immediately after its legislation the Council for Higher Education began to operate.

Despite the fact that as shall be explained below the council ignored its existence, Bar Ilan University, founded by private foreign initiative, opened its gates in 1955 and began operating as an non-State, Non-Publicly Funded religious university three years prior to the legislation of the law and two years prior to the publication of the Horwitz Committee recommendations.

The necessity for a further academic institution and the general need to increase the overall number of academic institutions in the country, as concluded by the committee, became apparent in the pre-State era and strengthened after the establishment of the State. Such need was first raised in 1947 among a group of religious academics and the idea gained the support of leaders of religious Zionism in Israel and globally: Rabbi Yitzhak HaLevi Herzog, Chief Rabbi of Israel, Rabbi Meir Bar-Ilan President of the World Mizrachi movement, and many others (Ben Yosef, 1967). However, the first to raise the idea for public discussion was Rabbi Binyamin (Yehoshua Radler-Feldman-Hatalmi).[33] In 1949 he published a series

32 Bar Ilan University Archive, container 1031, file 13; Horwitz Committee Report, 26 Adar 'A' 5717, 27 February, 1957. The committee was appointed on 22 May, 1956.

33 Writer, journalist and public figure. Founded the "Hatzofe" newspaper and translated most of the writings of Theodor Herzl.

of articles in religious publications, where he expressed his fear as to the fate of the many students attending the country's only university at the time (the Hebrew University), among them many religious students. In his article titled "In anticipation of the second million, in anticipation of the second university", he wrote:

> Will one university be enough? Of course not. Would it be possible to quickly establish a second university? Of course not. Is now the time, on the occasion of the 25th anniversary of the first Hebrew University, to begin to consider this matter? Of course. (Ben Yosef, ibid.).

While Rabbi Binyamin evoked the public's awareness to this need in Israel, the idea was shaped outside the geographic borders of the State – in the United States. The yearning of religious Zionism in the USA to take part in the building of the nation and the State alongside secular Zionism, led to a strong push for the realization of the idea to establish a religious university in Israel. The idea first emerged in the 1950s as part of the religious-nationalist world view of the global "Mizrachi" Religious-Zionist movement. The movement, founded as part of the World Zionist Organization in 1902, was a response of orthodox Jewry to the secularity of the Zionist movement and the struggle to focus Zionist activates on the political arena rather than education and culture. When Zionism began to show its involvement in education, an internal controversy arose within Orthodox Jewry as to the question whether to seek involvement in matters of education and culture, or to refrain from such involvement. This controversy, referred to as "The struggle for culture" (Don Yechiya, 2001), led to the establishment of the Religious Zionist movement – the "Mizrachi". The fear of a rift in the Zionist movement led to a compromise achieved during the 1902 Zionist Convention in Minsk. The compromise stipulated the principle of autonomy in education, by which education be autonomous, meaning that each camp would manage its own education system independently and based on its own ideology. This decision led in practice to a division between religious education and its various streams, and secular education and its individual streams. It commenced in the *Yishuv* in 1920 and continued following the establishment of the State and until 1953.[34] In fact, even now Israel's education system operates through three distinct national systems: The national education (divided in itself into Jewish, Arab, Druse and Bedouin education), the National-religious education, and the Ultra-Orthodox (Haredi) education and its various sub-systems. The Ashkenazi Haredi education, which is the independent educational Extension of Agudat

34 For a historical background of the development of Israel's education system, see: Dror, 2007: 182–183.

Yisrael (ultra-Orthodox Jewish political party), was not included in the Zionist education system, and upon the establishment of the State was institutionalized as a further education stream as instructed by Israel's first Prime Minister David Ben Gurion – for partisan reasons and in line with his nationalistic world view (Tzameret, 1997).

The Struggle of the Religious Camp for Education and the Establishment of Bar Ilan University

While the decision on the principle of autonomy in education prevented a rift in the Zionist movement, the struggle for education continued for decades in the Jewish pre-State *Yishuv* as well as following the establishment of the State. Don Yechiya (2001) characterized the social structure during the *Yishuv* period according to Val R. Lorwin's definition of 'Segmented Pluralism'(ibid.), by which society is divided into sub-cultures or ideologically distinct political camps, each with its own autonomous education system and political party. Under such social condition leaders of the country's political elites aimed to achieve a state of regularization, or as coined by Arend Lijphart – 'politics of accommodation' aimed at maintaining mutual existence and avoiding harsh confrontations in the Jewish camp in general and the Zionist one in particular. Despite the wish to maintain national unity, all political camps were well aware of the fact that education is the most important tool in the process of forming the country's social patterns. Therefore, the struggle in this area was long and tempestuous, reaching its peak between the years 1949 and 1952, with the large wave of Jewish immigration from Arab countries. It was clear that the struggle for education will not only determine the character of the country but also the future of its political parties, and therefore, as explained by Don Yechiya, the educational crisis can be defined as a 'systemic crisis', a term coined by Scott C. Flanagan (ibid.). Changes in Israel's population blend threatened to undermine the status quo and the regularization rules that were upheld by leaders of the country's political camps as to the question of the education of the children of the *Olim* (new immigrants) and its division according to the relative presence of the country's leading ideological movements. In 1951 the ratio between the number of *Olim* from Arab countries and those from Europe and America changed significantly: 71 % of all *Olim* during that year came from Arab countries, compared to 29 % from Europe and America, with new immigrants amounting to 40 % of the country's general population. This change, according to Don Yechiya (2008), affected the existing arrangements in two main ways:

1. The change in the ratio between *Olim* from Arab countries and from the West put an end to the status quo principle in education, by which the division into educational streams was determined according to the size of the educating stream and the ideological belonging of the *Olim* to a certain stream or political party comprising the *Yishuv*.
2. The social-cultural composition of the *Olim* from Arab countries, many of whom had no Western education nor political background or inclination, did not enable a partisan division as had been the custom until then. The lack of political belonging, the absence of an awareness of local politics and the lack of formal Western education created a dependence of these *Olim* on the establishment, while also making them convenient subjects of competition between parties and education streams for their political support.

The far reaching control of the Mapai[35] Political party over the country's governmental establishments and immigration absorption institutions served to distance between *Olim* and the religious camp, as Mapai's people in the absorbing establishment took advantage of their influence to instill non-religious education among the *Olim*. At first leaders of the religious camp protested, but realizing that their protests are to no avail, they moved their struggle to the press, where it was widely publicized both in Israel and in Jewish communities in Europe and the USA, leading to the "Mizrachi" leaders in the United States to threaten to damage "Magbit" operations in the USA. Following this protest, in January 1950 the government decided to form a Public inquiry commission on the matter of education at the *Olim* camps (Hacohen, 2005).

The establishment of the State did not transform the education polemic or the official positions of the parties (with the exception of the addition of Agudat Israel's independent education stream), but added a further aspect to the polemic: Proponents of the national approach argued that the establishment of the State required transferring the authority on educational matters in a centralized manner to the State. Others, who viewed education as a potential area in which to preserve and even enhance their political power, thought that it should remain in the hands of the individual ideological streams at the Zionist movement. As did others, the religious parties presented a position that combined ideological principles and partisan ones. Their leaders believed that the ability to ensure the right to a religious education is stipulated upon the existence of an autonomous religious education system managed by the religious public and its

35 Mapai, a democratic socialist political party in Israel, was the dominant force in Israeli politics until its merger into the modern-day Israeli Labor Party in 1968.

institutions. The transition to an independent State resulted in an era marked by trends of both change and continuity (Levi, 2006). The Compulsory Education Law (1949) marked this change in the very fact of the subjugation of education to the law of the State, while the continuity trend can be noted in the State Education Law (1953). This law in fact expressed the education system's conversion from one segregated education system (Zionist), to another (National). The country's education streams expressed the ideologies of movements originating in Eastern Europe and therefore only expressing the needs of European Jews. The needs of immigrants from Arab countries were not reflected in the pre-State era nor after its establishment and therefore ideological segregation in Zionist education concealed the existence of an ethnic segregation. Rather than concealing the problems, the State Education Law exposed them. The understanding between Mapai and the "Mizrachi" paved the way to an agreement on the State Education Law, by which the "religiousness" of the *Olim* from Arab countries automatically allocated their children to the National-religious education stream. Education in the new State exhibited religious and ethnic segregation in both Primary and Secondary education.

The segregation approach accommodated the approach of the "Mizrachi" leaders in the United States – the founders of Bar Ilan university: While being exposed to the ongoing struggle over the religious education of the religious *Olim* in Israel and to the importance of the principle of autonomy in educating the religious sector, they were also exposed to the impact of religious academic institutions in the USA on education and on curbing the spreading of secularism in the USA. As shall be seen later in this book, "Mizrachi" leaders aspired to reproduce this ability in Israel with the establishment of an independent religious-academic institution that would continue the sequence of autonomous education also in academia, based on the model of the Christian academic institutions in the USA. The big immigration wave of Jews from Arab countries to Israel and Mapai's attempts to force them into a secular education system only increased the need to act in the field of education in the same way in which religious academic institutions did in the USA among immigrants in the 1950s. More on this relationship will be discussed later on.

The Establishment of Bar Ilan University: In Practice

In 1922 the religious-Zionist movement split in two. from the main movement, the "Mizrachi", a sister movement called "Hapoel HaMizrachi" set out on a different route. The leaders of the new movement aimed to emphasize socialist values and the importance of manual labor as a prerequisite to a new life of freedom and redemption. The new movement cooperated with the Zionist-Socialist Labor movement, and as early as the 1930s a group of young men from "Hapoel HaMizrachi" left their Yeshiva studies to join the socialist mission of agricultural labor in Israel's fields. Contrary to "Hapoel HaMizrachi", the "Mizrachi" movement viewed education as the main expression of its Zionist way, and therefore focused its activities in this area (Don Yechiya, 2001). This focus also resulted from the success of the secular Zionist ideology in the mid 1940s and beginning of the 1950s. The establishment of the State, the War of Independence and the harsh consequences of the Holocaust, led to a secular wave in the Jewish world – a situation that caused great worry among Jewish religious leaders throughout the world. Ultra-Orthodox (Haredi) groups, large parts of which were murdered in the Holocaust, responded by creating their own segregated worlds, while the leaders of the "Mizrachi" religious-Zionist movement decided to increase their involvement in the affairs of the newly established country (Klein, 1998). The Zionist Project, which in the 1950s was entirely in secular hands, did not leave many options to the global "Mizrachi" movement but to operate in the field of education in response to the secular wave. The origins of this trend can be identified in the 1905 decision to open the "Tachkemoni" school in Jaffa, after religious-Zionist leaders realized that the Hebrew Gymnasium in Jaffa is secular. In later years the "Mizrachi" movement founded the "Tachkemoni" network of schools, followed by the better known "Yavne" educational network which has operated ever since in Israel and in Jewish communities around the world. The idea of the establishment of Bar Ilan University was also developed as an alternative or counterweight to the Hebrew University, which in many ways marked the secular-nationalist Zionist revival (Klein, 2006), as well as expanding the principle of autonomy in education also to higher education, rather than limiting it to Primary and Secondary education. The expansion of this principle to higher education provided an academic alternative to religious youths in Israel who did not want to be exposed to academic approaches that are not in line with the religious approaches of the "Mizrachi" movement.

The decision on the foundation of the university was received during the "Mizrachi" convention held in November 1950 in the USA, and it was named after one of the "Mizrachi" leaders of the beginning of the century – Rabbi Meir Bar Ilan. The ideology that led to the idea to establish the university included religious, social and national ideals. The founders defined two main aims for the university: To bridge between the State of Israel and the Diaspora and to serve as a framework for activities in the area of higher education in Israel – an alternative for religious youths interested in academic studies, ultimately aiming to create an echelon of educated religious Jews who would make an impact on Israeli society in the new State. From a social perspective, the university's founders set a mission of improving the quality of life of the country's citizens and integrating between its various types of populations (Rackman, 1988). According to the "Mizrachi" leaders in the USA, a religious involvement and impact is needed in the process of forming society in Israel, and they perceived education and science as high-impact areas.

This approach by the "Mizrachi" corresponds with Bourdieu's Field Theory and the roles of the intellectual in society (2005). According to this explanation, the Mizrachi movement did not perceive the figure of the intellectual as an autonomous personality operating in a purely academic framework, but rather as a personality that accumulates cultural capital due to its position in the autonomous field of academics in order to convert it in the public sphere and thus to acquire the right for social involvement and impact. According to this theory, their aspirations for social involvement were the Mizrachi's motivation to act in the academic field in order to obtain the cultural capital needed for influencing the character of Israeli society. Within this field, they believed they would be able to cope with the country's senior intellectuals who have already earned the social capital needed for social involvement. The attempts made by the Mizrachi in the USA to join the academic field in Israel resulted from their aim to fight for ownership over the intellectual assets of the field, the right to construct a new reality and to take part in the general struggle of Israel's religious camp over the country's education.

Two years following the decision to establish a religious university in Israel, the Mizrachi elected the university's first President – Prof. Pinkhos Churgin, who had led the Mizrachi in the USA since 1949. Although he was not the first to formulate the idea of a religious university, his religious-Zionist approach and educational orientation added a religious-Zionist fervor to the idea, and from the moment he was elected President, the idea of the establishment of the university became his life's work. His remaining years until his death in 1958 were tirelessly dedicated to the realization of the idea and its implementation (Ben Yosef, 1967). Churgin's first step on his mission for the establishment of the university was to meet with David Ben Gurion, Israel's Prime Minister at the time, to inform him of the Mizrachi's aspiration to establish a religious university in Israel (Rachman, 1988). In July 1955, about three years following the decision to establish the university, its cornerstone was laid in the city of Ramat Gan. That year Churgin immigrated to Israel and headed the university. The first academic year was opened in September 1955, with the completion of the construction of the first buildings. Prof. Churgin, as did others in religious-Zionist circles, perceived Israel's revival as more than a mere political event. The establishment of the State was perceived in religious Zionism as the beginning of a realization of the eternal destiny of the people of Israel in their historical land (Klein, 1998). Churgin, who had been a teacher and educator in America, believed in the centrality of education (Liff, 1988) and viewed the university as a mechanism that would contribute to the formation of the character of the State more than any other means. In his opening remarks in the conference during which the two Mizrachi movements were unified in 1956,[36] he described the importance of education for the State and for the Mizrachi movements:

> The realization of our ideals depends on our success in education. As I have said time and again, it is not my intention to imply that other activities, whether in settlement of the land or in the field of economics are of any less importance than activities in the field of education. Nevertheless, everyone admits that if we fail to act properly in the educational direction of our young generation, we will gain no benefit from advances in the areas of economy or settlement.[37]

The aim of his remarks was to bring the two Mizrachi movements closer together in order to unify forces towards the religious struggle over the character of the State. This unification increased the extent of activities of both movements in the area of education. One of the results of the unification was the official establishment of the Bnei Akiva Yeshiva and the "Hesder" (arrangement) Yeshivas that followed, although the first Yeshiva was established by Rabbi Neriya at Kfar Haroe back in 1940.

In articles published in local and foreign press and in many interviews, Churgin expressed his educational creed and the Mizrachi's hopes for the religious university:

> We aim to educate a generation who will be religious by spirit and imbued with an understanding of the most crucial goals of the State and of the individual within such State. Bar Ilan University will emphasize the humanism, the good social concepts and the principles of elevated life [. . .] The establishment (of Bar Ilan University) was preceded by a national religious aspiration as well as a general educational one. . . This new academic institution will aim to nurture the young generation educated in Israel, filled with creativity and a love for the entire nation in Israel and abroad. . . A generation who knows its Torah and studies it, walks in the footsteps of past generations and in the light of the revival of the people in its land, a generation healthy and pure of spirit, free of hate

36 In 1956 the "HaMizrachi" and "Hapoel HaMizrachi" were unified to form the National Religious Party (NRP).

37 Bar Ilan University Archive, container 1458, file 209. Opening remarks by Prof. Churgin at the merger convention between "the Mizrachi" and "HaPoel HaMizrachi", 20 June, 1956.

> complexes, tolerant and recognizing its affection towards the homeland, the people and humanity (Ben Yosef, 1967).

In his introductory remarks for the university's Student body annual publication, the publication of which he perceived as a milestone in the development of the idea to found a religious university, he wrote: "I am filled with hope that this annual publication of the student body will also serve as a suitable stage towards the realization of country and people".[38] Churgin's idealist-romantic approach on the foundation of the nation and his awareness of the power of academy among the religious-nationalist public in the USA (Shalmon, 1998/1999), led him to perceive the university as a religious and social agent of change, able to impact the building of the nation and its society (Katzburg, 1981). In the cornerstone ceremony Churgin also illustrated the social aims of the institution:

> This institution will stand as a symbol of the basic internal unity of man. . .Its doors will be open to every person of able mind. . .No student shall be turned away because of economic strictures.[39]

At their first meeting with the Minister of Education, the university's leaders reiterated their social goal: "We have set a principle from which we shall not stir, for we cannot lock our doors to students lacking in suitable means who are eligible, based on our strictest requirements, to join the university".[40]

According to Bourdieu's Field Theory, the tasks allocated by the founders of the university for the religious institution challenged the acceptable rules of conduct in Israel's academic field, thereby enabling the founders' behavior in the 1950s as a Subversive Strategy towards Paradigmatic Change. During that period the Israeli academic field was controlled by the country's two senior academic institutions: The Technion and the Hebrew University. Since the establishment of the State these two institutions enjoyed State budgets and moreover the character and nature of Israeli academy was formed during those years based on the policies implemented by the heads of these two institutions, and most of all by the leaders of the Hebrew University. Israel's academic system operated during those years under a purely research orientation based on the European-German

---

38 In: Bar Ilan, Year Book on Jewish Studies and Humanities, Bar Ilan University, volume D-E (book of the Decade) 1955–1965: 2.

39 In: P. Churgin (editor), Vision and Legacy: Selected works and writings of his life and legacy. Ramat Gan: Bar Ilan University: 15–13; Churgin's speech at the Cornerstone ceremony, 26 July, 1953.

40 Bar Ilan University Archive, container 1046, file 122. Letter from the university management to the Minister of Education, dated 28 November 1957.

university model and its successor the American research university (Kirsch, 2014; Klein, 2004; Shenhar-Elroy, 2005). The diversity presented by the founders of Bar Ilan University upon entering the academic field was extensive, and moreover unacceptable in the field, and therefore their actions cannot be characterized as those embarked upon by newcomers wishing to enter a field according to its accepted rules. Moreover, this diversity cannot be characterized as an expression of Subversive Strategy of "young adults" or "newcomers". This diversity was made apparent in a number of aspects: The first, the new university model with which the founders attempted to penetrate the academic field was influenced by American models, both the religious-Christian universities model and the College model, while the other, and more substantial, pertains to its religious-social purpose and aims which were not a deliberate part of the existing Israeli universities: The university raised the banner of science and research as its leading principle, as is the accepted practice in the European-German model and its American successor. However, first and foremost it defined its religious and social roles, and only afterwards its scientific and research ones, for instance – the dissemination of the Torah and Jewish tradition based on Torah and science, in parallel to a close involvement in the building of the land out of a sense of mission and the realization of the vision of the prophets as to the revival of the people and the land of Israel (Ben Yosef, 1967; Klein, 1998; Schwartz, 2013).

The religious university was destined, according to their vision, to produce a perfectly educated Israeli who is dedicated to the idea of national revival, but also who would hold ties to his Jewish past, to the vision of the return to Zion, and to universal science (Ben Yosef, 1967; Klein, 1998). In addition to these challenges, the religious university will also be a source of attraction to young Jewish people from around the world and a bridge between the State of Israel and the Diaspora, by attracting students from abroad as well as by sending faculty members to the Diaspora to disseminate the teachings of the Torah. All this would be achieved through an organizational structure which in itself was uncommon in the academic field – the American college structure, aimed at emphasizing an educational rather than research-based orientation.

To realize their religious goals while challenging the rules of the academic field and still being recognized as an academic institution, the founders avoided requesting support from the State and its institutions so as not to operate under limitations of national regulatory bodies. In the first three years of its existence the university did not require any State budgets and was operated solely based on donations collected from world Jewry with the support of the global "Mizrachi" women who collected funds among American and British Jews, which also served towards the construction of the campus and its maintenance (Rackman, 1988).

College or University: Adjusting the Structure of the Institution to Its Tasks

As aforesaid, the founders of Bar Ilan University envisioned the university according to the model of the American college, whose roles included similarities to the first Catholic universities of the United States (Klein, 2004). According to this model, the envisioned institution was according to its founders an educating institution rather than solely a place of transmittal of knowledge, as is the case in research universities, which is why some view this institution type as similar to the model of the university of the middle Ages (Shwartz, 2013).

The "Mizrachi" leaders believed that the present need requires training of professional teaching staff and of educated individuals for managerial positions. Thus, the research university model did not correspond with the goals set for it by its founders. Moreover, they saw great importance in the attractiveness of the new institution in the eyes of Jewish youths around the world, and the college model had an advantage due to its teaching method that enabled a closer relationship between students and teachers. Such advantage, according to the founders, could result in a sympathy among students towards the institution's ideology and its goals. As an educator whose academic education originated in American and Jewish institutions, Churgin believed that the method of operation of the American institutions, and most of all colleges, is suitable for a number of reasons:

a. This format facilitates the training of educated religious persons according to the State's needs, as a human foundation that would bridge between Torah and "Derech Eretz" (the way of the land).
b. The present need requires practical, and not only theoretical training. As an institution that educates rather than only extending knowledge, this model was suited to the important task of training suitable personnel to fill senior positions in the State service and in teaching, so that the religious Zionist approach would permeate society through public opinion agents such as teachers and various levels of public servants.
c. The teaching method at the American college facilitates closer relationships between teachers and students, as opposed to the relatively distant teaching method at universities. The character of such an institution would encourage the absorption of many students from the USA (Gross, 2006), thereby fulfilling a further aspiration of the founders – to form a bridge to the Jews of the diaspora by offering an academic institution that would be attractive to Jewish youths throughout the world, and especially in America.

The similarities between religious academic institutions in the USA and Bar Ilan University, at least in its early years, has led me to follow the operational method of Catholic and Protestant academic institutions in the USA and to compare them to those of Bar Ilan University at the time of its establishment.

The College Model: Chronicles of Higher Education in the USA

The initial steps towards a Higher Education System in northern American took place in the seventeenth century, at a time in which most of the east coast was under British colonial rule. The first colleges on the east coast were replicas of Oxford and Cambridge. The end of the British rule (1766) and the Civil War (1861–1865) led to both qualitative and quantitative changes in North American colleges. In parallel, during that period, Germanic-style colleges became much more prevalent in the region. Many students from the USA studied in Germany, and upon their return influenced the character of American academies, most of all the independent ones. At the same time, colleges began to break free from the auspices of their British counterparts with the establishment of State Colleges as well as private initiatives by various American churches (Mizrachi, 1994). In the beginning of the millennium there were about 4,200 institutions of higher education operating in the USA, with over 15 million students: 2,500 private institutions with 3.5 million students; and about 900 religious institutions with 1.5 million students, supported by 23 individual Christian communities, each belonging to a separate founding or supporting church. The largest group of these institutions is the Catholic one. Catholic institutions in the USA offer the entire range of disciplines and professions taught at institutes of higher education: 4 medical schools, 28 law schools, 18 engineering schools, 18 nursing schools, 177 schools of education and teachers' training, and 16 schools for women. These Catholic institutions offer the entire range of academic degrees, and include four research universities (James, 2013).

The historical reasons for the relationship between the academic institutions and their adoptive religious communities in the United States date back to the aspirations of the first settlers to establish religious communities founded on Christian faith, morality and spirituality. The educational approach of the first Christian settlers in the United States was that education and moral development should be removed from the hands of parents to the educating and teaching institutions, thereby leading to the need to support these institutions and supervise their work. This conviction pushed Christian communities to also support Post-Secondary education institutions in order to influence the development of young adults. This religious mission increased and strengthened with the expansion of secularism in American society in the 1950s and 1960s.

To assess the similarities between the religious academic institutions in the United States and Bar Ilan University in its formative years I will examine the characteristics of the Catholic and Protestant academic institutions in the United States based on the literature in the field (Mizrachi, 1994; Klein, 2004; Tippens, 2013; James, 2013; Schweitzer, 2013).

Attributes of Catholic Academic Institutions in the USA According to James (2013) and Klein (2004)

a. The academic institution, whether a university or college, belongs to a recognized Church
b. The institution employs faculty members who are experts in teaching religion
c. The institution's daily operation corresponds with a religious life style
d. The institution offers religious studies as part of its academic curriculum

The supervision over religious obligations and style of the supported institution is overseen by a religious Senate (established in 1892) that functioned as an external supervisory board whose role was to grant an initial accreditation to supported academic institutions. Supervision included an examination of the moral level of administrative and academic faculty, approval of syllabi and supervision of the religious life style at the campus.

The following external changes affected the religious conduct of these institutions in the 1950s and 1960s:

a. The Federal Government's decision to offer scholarships to veteran soldiers resulted in an indirect influence of the Federal Government also on private institutions, including the Catholic ones, wishing to attract candidates.
b. The availability of public funding for buildings and research and funding of special programs for veteran soldiers led to a rise in the number of students, and the institutions required public funding for construction, which resulted in the direct influence of the Federal government on their operation.
c. Technological developments and growing access to new information required specialization and the acquisition of knowledge by both academic and administrative faculty members.
d. The rise in the number of students in higher education in general and at private and religious institutions in particular, resulted in a fierce competition over students, which pushed institutions to encourage excellence among their academic faculty in teaching as well as in research. Achieving the new goals required the institutions' managements to encourage their administrative and academic

faculty to achieve professional advancement based on universal rules of academic promotion, namely: acquiring advanced degrees, research and publications.

Over time, this process of change led to an academic uniformity across institutions, and the religious-Catholic nature of the institutions gradually faded.

Attributes of the Protestant Academic Institution in the United States, According to Tippens and Schweitzer

According to Tippens (2013), the seeds of change and reformation in Christianity first appeared in the Christian academic institutions about 100 years before they were accepted. Ideas of reformation were first raised by Christian scholars trained in the Christian universities such as John Wycliffe (1330–1384), who served as Professor of Philosophy at Oxford University and was the first to translate the Bible into English, believing in the exclusive authenticity of the commands of the Bible. He believed in the need for reform within the Catholic Church, that would commence with a direct knowledge of God's commandments. He was declared a heretic and his writings were banned. However, in Protestantism he is seen as the precursor to the Protestant Reformation. His student, Jan Hus (1369–1415) served as Rector of the University of Prague. Like his teacher he preached for a return to the sources of the scriptures, and despite his being a priest he was burnt at the stake in 1451 for heresy and preaching for changes in the Catholic Church. Following the first precursors of the reform, the reformation movement was led by Marthin Luther, a German Augustinian Priest who served as Professor of Theology at the University of Wittenberg in Germany. This in contrast to the situation in Germany, where the Protestant movement did not see the need to establish religious academic institutions (Schweitzer, 2013). In the United States the symbiotic relationship between Protestantism and academia found its outlet in the establishment of academic institutions, for a number of reasons that are at the foundation of the Protestant institution:

a. The Protestant faith is committed to the ideal of Priesthood for all its followers, not only of the Catholic Church. This ideal required the proper training of educated priests.
b. Protestantism values a meticulous understanding of the scriptures, which explains why linguistics became a discipline that requires specialization and an acquisition of specific language and cultural skills.
c. Language and rational discourse became symbols of Protestantism.
d. As the privatization of the institutions grew, so did the need for support from religious institutions at institutions of higher education, as part of the mission to improve moral standards among educated youths.

All the above led to the establishment of academic institutions aimed at training clergymen who would then educate the young generation to a Christian life style. These basic goals marked the nature of these institutions not as research or science centers, but as centers dedicated to the advancement of moral behaviors and community work (Mizrachi, 1994; Tippens, 2013).

In his paper on religion and academics in Israel, Klein (2004) notes the attributes and milestones in the development of American universities in general and Catholic ones in particular, according to studies by researchers in the field (Belbington, 1992; Dahrendorf, 1995; Gleason 1967; Greeley, 1969; Hassenger, 1967; Marsden & Longgield, 1992; Marsden, 1992; Marsden, 1992a; Marsden, 1994; Reiss, 1967). He identified three main common attributes to religious academic institutions in the United States and Bar Ilan University:

1. The target population and the religious mission;
2. The educational purpose;
3. Adjustment and change of purpose.

Analysis of the Common Attributes Identified by Klein (2004) and Their Application to the Case of Bar Ilan University

1. **The Target Population and the religious mission**
   1.1. The religious universities in the United States
   These universities were established from within the heart of the Christian Church on behalf of working and low class immigrants seeking a suitable path for Socioeconomic mobility. The Catholic universities were the first to offer these groups such a solution. The founders of the religious universities were concerned at the accelerated secularization of American society and attempted via the universities to save religious faith.
   1.2. Bar Ilan University
   According to one of the university's first publications: "The root and the purpose of Bar Ilan, are of a religious nature. The university was founded and managed by the Mizrachi Histadrut in America, but Bar Ilan's roles and aspirations are beyond partisan matters or matters pertaining to any specific Jewish group".[41] And in another publication: "Upon its establishment the university define its a basic goal – to educate a generation of culture and science scholars, who will also be knowledgeable in the *Torah*

41 Bar Ilan University Archive, container 1458, file 203. Publication in anticipation of the inauguration of the first buildings on 7 August 1955.

> and Jewish faith, maintaining and continuing the tradition of Israel and its culture.[42]

Given that, according to Klein, Bar Ilan University was not founded by a religious organization as were the Christian institutions of the United States, we can nevertheless see certain similarities between the underlying motivation among Christian communities to establish institutions of higher education and the work of the "Mizrachi" movement in the USA, in its aspiration to influence society in Israel rather than leaving the Zionist mission solely in the hands of the secular Zionist movement. Concerns about the secularity of the founding Zionist generation and their influence on the character of the State motivated the "Mizrachi" leaders in the USA to increase their work in the field of education so as to enhance their impact on Israeli society (Katzburg, 1981). This aim was strengthened by the large immigration waves from Arab countries and Eastern Europe in the 1950s and the expected influence of secular Zionism on these immigrants. Here too the "Mizrachi" leaders acted similarly to American religious institutions in the 1950s among new immigrants to the USA.

In many interviews to local and Jewish press in America (Ben Yosef, 1988), Churgin expressed his concern of the secularity of the Holy Land and did not conceal his intensions and the hope he felt in the establishment of the new university. In his speech on the occasion of the laying of a cornerstone for the university's first buildings on 26 July 1953, Churgin defined the purpose of the new institution, as follows:

> This institution, in which Jewish learning and the *Torah* of Israel will be studied together with all the latest findings in the field of human research, will symbolize the unbounded strength and limitless understanding of Judaism, and will stand as a living monument to the return of Jewry to its place of origin and source of its greatest glory.[43]

To achieve the religious aspirations of the new institution while avoiding national limitations, its founders refrained from seeking any State support. Churgin and others invested extensive efforts in raising needed financing from eminent community members in the USA, Britain and Canada. This was a joint effort led by the "Mizrachi" leaders and the women of the "Mizrachi" in the USA. Churgin

---

42 Bar Ilan University Archive, container 1046, file 126. Published on 21 June 1956.

43 Churgin's full speech, entitled 'Bridge to the Future', can be found in: Bernstein, A. Z. (1988). The man and his literary legacy. In: P. Churgin (Ed.), Vision and legacy: Selected works and writings of his life and legacy (pp. 16–21). Ramat Gan: Bar Ilan University.

made many fundraising trips in Britain and the USA, and in his passionate letters described the religious goals to be achieved through the university:

> Our dear friends who tirelessly and faithfully work towards achieving the great idea of this project, see in their minds eyes the great buildings being built one after the other and their hearts flutter with joy and happiness for having succeeded in a short time to prove to many the strength of our faith in our aspirations and our hopes to transform our holy and free land into a land to be proud of.[44]

2. **The educational purpose**
   2.1. The religious universities in the United States
   The founders of the Catholic universities in the United States viewed the university first and foremost as an educational institution, and only then as a research center and a place in which professional skills are acquired (Klein, 2004; Mizrachi, 1994).
   2.2. Bar Ilan University
   Various researchers have noted that during the university's formative years, learning and teaching were more dominant than research, which began to assume a stronger role in recent years (Klein, 2004, 2006; Schwartz, 2006, 2013). The emergence of the group who nurtured the educational orientation of the institution was a result of the goals set by the founders, their professional backgrounds and the needs of the country at the time. Churgin, as well as his successor and partner Prof. Rabbi Joseph H. Lookstein, had their academic origins in the field of education and their professional views were based on this profession. Rabbi Lookstein also had a rich educational history as President of the "Rabbinical Council of America and among the founders of the Hebrew Teacher-training College for Girls. Rabbi Lookstein worked together with the university's management in Israel to strengthen its educational-pedagogic side (Katzburg, 1979).

This educational-religious line initiated by Churgin continued to be the prominent line among other leading figures in the university's management: Haim-Moshe Shapira,[45] who served for fifteen years as Chairperson of its Board of Trustees and throughout his life struggled for the advancement of religious education in Israel

44 Religious Zionism Archive, 025, file symbol 15, date of certificate – 23 August 1954. Letter from Prof. Churgin to Rabbi M. Shmidman, New Jersey, USA, 23 August 1954.

45 The political leader of Religious-Zionism and its representative in the Israeli government: Minister of Immigration and Ministry of Health in the temporary government and a minister in Israel's governments between the years 1949–1952.

(Burg, 1972; Bar, 1972), viewed the university as a means for instilling religious values and nurturing them with care in order to form an intellectual center for education and fulfillment of a Jewish religious life (Bar, 1972; Don Yechiya, 2004).

Even at a time in which the university's identity and direction were contended and it was necessary to choose between academic independence and the realization of the institution's religious and national goals, not one of the founders retreated from their obligation to upholding the university's pedagogical-religious role to model the character of Israeli society. Moreover, even Prof. Baruch Kurzweil, considered a leader of the academic independence line and one of the first teachers at the university, viewed the university's religious mission as important and crucial, alongside its academic development. The 'new Israelism' worried him even more than the danger to Judaism in the diaspora, because of the possibility that it would serve as an opening for the evolvement of a new type of Jew able to ignore his Judaism without morality or conscience, as he wrote: "Only methodical, fundamental, religious and scientific education can create the change we aim for" (Kurzweil, 1967).

These goals dictated the initial strong establishment of Jewish Studies alongside pedagogy in order to train teachers for all levels of education in the country and to create agents of social change who would disseminate the religious-nationalist approach and its values (Katzburg, 1981). Various fields of Judaism gained a special status at the Faculty of Jewish Studies, including Talmud, Bible, Jewish Thought and Israel Studies. Jewish Studies were obligatory even for students who were not studying towards a degree in Jewish Studies.[46]

3. **Adjustment and change of purpose**

   3.1 The religious universities in the United States

   Transitions in American society following World War II led to an over emphasis on liberalism and universalism and a de-legitimation of sectoral education. The Catholic university model had to cope with these universal changes, while also contesting with the growing strength of the Protestant university, creating an interim model between secular and Catholic universities (Klein, 2004). Two main changes affected the religious universities at the United States: The first resulted from social aspirations for openness, liberalism and universalism. According to proponents of the industrialization or modernization theories, professional needs of the

46 This obligation still constitutes over 20 % of all obligatory courses required of undergraduate students to complete their degree: Eight yearly hours in Talmud, four in bible studies and two in Jewish History or Jewish Thought.

industrialized economy and the need for specialization, professionalization and academization generate social changes which in turn encouraged educational institutions to train professionals as a prerequisite for achieving social mobility. The second change involves the opening of the gates of higher education after the Second World War to social classes other than the economic or social elites. World War II and the Cold War that followed led to the strengthening of democratic values, humanism and human dignity. These changes in American society increased the need for liberalization. Protestantism was the first to mobilize for change, transitioning from being strictly religious and academic to becoming a social and moral phenomenon. In turn, the Catholic universities were left with no choice but to adjust to the demands of society in general and of the academic field in particular, leading to a transition from a pedagogic-religious orientation to a more research-based one.

3.2. Bar Ilan University

In a similar transition to the one experienced by religious universities in the United States, Bar Ilan University underwent a two-stage process of change and adjustment of aims: the first stage began in the mid 1950s when the university gained official accreditation and public budgets comparable to those of the Hebrew University, the Technion and Tel Aviv University. While the official accreditation did lead to financial stability, the university's level of independence as a religious institution having religious and social aims was reduced, and its founders now had to function within the rules dictated by the Israeli supervisory body – the Council for Higher Education (CHE). Religious faith and social aims were set aside in order to leave room for coping with budgetary issues and official accreditation. The second stage was part of the many changes that took place in Israel's academic field since the 1980s. The founding generation, who had been fully committed to their religious-social beliefs, was replaced by second generation leadership, who found itself struggling on two fronts: Achieving full recognition of the university as an academic institution from Israel's senior academics, while in parallel coping with the substantial rise in demand for higher education and the wave of immigration of the 1990s. The gates of higher education which were opened to the general public led to a proliferation of academic institutions and a division of the national budget to a larger number of institutions. This changes of recent years (which are still underway) led to research institutions aiming to differentiate themselves in order to create a bi-polar system comprised of Research vs. teaching institutions (Kave, 2001). Prof. Moshe Kave, President of Bar Ilan University and also Chairperson of the Committee of University Heads of Israel ("VERA"),[47] led the process of differentiation of universities from all other academic institutions. The origins of this process, that was accelerated recently, was identified by researchers in the struggle over the future of Bar Ilan University as a religious institution and an operational tool in the hands of religious Zionism, with its peak point being at the start of the millennium (Klein, 2004, 2006; Schwartz, 2006). Researchers pointed to significant changes in recent years in two central identifying characteristics of Bar Ilan University: On the academic level, transition from a teaching-based university to a research university in order to compete for prestige and research budgets with the country's other universities. According to Schwartz (2006): "On the ideological level, we see a transition from a metaphysical and theological destination to a social, practical and pragmatic one".[48]

The Struggle for Recognition of the Academic Field

The university model envisioned by the founders of Bar Ilan University differed from the European university model represented by the Hebrew University until the 1950s and was closer to the model of the first American universities, which Bar Ilan's founders were highly familiar with. In 1950, the Hebrew University also initiated a change in the structure of degrees to correspond with the American model. This was also published in the first information leaflets for students:

> The acceptable methods in institutions of higher education in Anglo-Saxon countries and their curriculums are parallel to those common in American universities, with the addition of Jewish Studies. Upon its establishment in 1955, a 4-year program was inaugurated, granting its graduates a B.A degree [. . .] In line with the university's doctrine, each student is obligated to take courses in Jewish and Israel Studies, regardless of their major.[49]

47 The Committee of University Heads of Israel is comprised of seven members representing Israel's universities (with the exception of the Open University). The Chairperson of the forum, one of the Presidents of the member universities, is appointed for a single term. VERA is a highly influential body representing the interests of Israeli universities.

48 Schwartz, 2006: 63.

49 Bar Ilan University Archive, container 1046, file 122. Students Information leaflet, 21 June, 1956.

A reinforcement of Bar Ilan's religious model can also be found in its admission requirements, which gives preference to candidate knowledgeable in Talmudic studies.[50] In its choice of resembling the American religious model was also the hope of succeeding where the first universities of the United States succeeded, with another American model also held in high esteem – the Yeshiva University[51] – a model for advanced Jewish studies.

According to Bourdieu, there are two possible struggles between new and old in the same field: Attempts by newcomers to create a paradigmatic change in the field, or a struggle of newcomers against the older establishment according to the accepted rules of the field, including rules of admission in order to create a further struggle from within. The entrance ticket to the struggle is in fact an agreement as to its basic rules. The struggle at the entrance to the academic field is for the right to construct reality within and outside the field, to teach students and to grant degrees. Following the struggle of admission, the second struggle is over hierarchy and status in the field, aimed at gaining more influence in and outside the field, including the political sphere and through it to the public, or in our case, to the developing Israeli public sphere. In his book 'Homo Academicus' (1984) Bourdieu argues that not national politics determines the fate of the academic man, but rather his academic status forges his place in the political map, thereby enhancing his ability to influence both the political map and the academic system. Bourdieu used his own example to show how he protected the autonomy of the intellectual field, while on the other hand also intervened in the public sphere, utilizing as much weight as possible in academic research in an attack against globalization, capitalism and neo-liberal ideology. Similarly, the founders of Bar Ilan University and the Zionist-religious movement saw it as a political means (Schwartz, 2006) through which they could transform the religious character of society in Israel. The question is whether the aim for a change originating in the academic field functions within an acceptable strategy or constitutes a struggle towards paradigmatic change?

We can identify both strategies in the founders' initiatives: at first they strived for a paradigmatic change, and when it proved unsuccessful they assumed a more accepted strategy with a higher likelihood to success: During the formative stage

50 Ibid.

51 Yeshiva University is a private research university in New York City. Its curriculum is based on the integration model of modern American orthodoxy, namely "*Torah* and Science". All its academic programs include Jewish Studies.

the founders adopted a Subversive Strategy that strived to transform the accepted rules of the field, which can be seen from their following moves:

a. The university's founders defined religious goals for the institution, in an aim to achieve social change and only then academic goals. The combination of religious-social goals with academic ones was not acceptable among the senior representatives of the field as openly declared goals in the country's academic field (Gross, 2008; Klein, 1998, 2006).
b. The accepted organizational model in the field was the European-German model, replaced in 1950 by the American model with an academic structure that is more research-based than educational-pedagogical. This model was defined by the senior representatives of the field and those whose control over it was uncontested – the Hebrew University. The model chosen by the founders of Bar Ilan University challenged the model that had been prevalent in Israel for 25 years. Bar Ilan's founders preferred the model of the American religious university over the accepted model at the time in Israel's academic field.
c. The curricular structure proposed by Bar Ilan's founders consisted of four years of study and obligatory Jewish studies (approx. 20 % of the entire degree scope) for all students of the university. Such requirements and general obligations were not common in academic curriculums in Israel (excluding Engineering studies, which also required four years).
d. National accreditation was not sought after at first, as it had the potential to undermine the chances to realize religious and social aims which were outside the accepted scope of institutions of higher education. Undertaking the burden of official State recognition through budgeting required subordination to regulation and a gradual separation from all non-academic aims.

The religious and social aims that marked a struggle for transforming social order in the field and undermining the dominance of its senior actors, resulted in these senior actors completely ignoring the academic work of the founders of the university in the beginning of the 1950s, as can be seen from the Horowitz Commission report as well as in the response of the Hebrew University to the intensions of the "Mizrachi". The management of the Hebrew University believed that the new institution would be "an American island" in Israel. that it would enhance "Americanism" but would not be an academic institution according to their definition. Representatives of the Hebrew University did not participate in Bar Ilan's opening ceremony and moreover showed no interest in the work being done at Ramat Gan.[52]

---

52 Bar Ilan University Archive, container 1458, file 206; The University Journal, 1970.

According to Gross (2008), the Hebrew University, as the unchallenged controller of the academic field, focused its struggles on the intentions of Tel Aviv's Municipality to establish an academic institution, rather than on Bar Ilan University which had already opened in Ramat Gan. The struggle of the Hebrew University against Tel Aviv's intentions was conducted according to the acceptable rules of the field, namely, the more senior representatives doing their best to prevent newcomers from entering the field and obtaining the right to enjoy a part of the cultural and material capital of the field. As was expected, Tel Aviv's intentions worried the leaders of the Hebrew University, who voiced common arguments of rejection such as the fear of lowering the level of academic studies in Israel and a division of resources that would weaken the Hebrew University. So as to not completely reject the ability to study in a big city such as Tel Aviv, the leaders of the field agreed to see it as an Extension of the Hebrew University, offering undergraduate studies only. Compared to Jerusalem's apprehensions towards the intentions of the founders of Tel Aviv University, the work done by the founders of Bar Ilan University did not worry them, simply because this new institution had not officially requested an "entry ticket" into the academic field. In their view the new institution operated within a narrow ethnic framework of religious Zionism, making do with offering undergraduate degrees. Gross (2008) believes that Jerusalem failed to pay sufficient attention to Churgin's letter to the editor of "Haaretz" daily newspaper published on 4 August 1953, in which he clearly outlined his intention to establish a university that would be based on the American model.

Using Bourdieu's theory, the heads of the Hebrew University perceived the work of Bar-Ilan's founders as a struggle outside the accepted rules of the field (unlike Tel Aviv), and therefore at first the struggle between senior actors and newcomers did not take place at all, as the newcomers were not seen by the senior actors as having requested entry into their field. The struggle remains in the political field, in which the private initiative originating from outside the State is seen as a foreign initiative that does not concur with official State procedures. This opposition was led by Prof. Ben Zion Dinur, Minister of Education during the years 1951–1955.[53] Although the struggle took place in the political field, Dinur's

53 Dinur was born in Ukrain in 1884. His family belonged to the Chabad Orthodox Jewish Hasidic dynasty and he was ordained as Rabbi at the age of 18. He studied in many Yeshivas in Eastern Europe, showed great interest in Zionism and became an avid Zionist. Studied at universities in Germany and Russian and immigrated to Israel in 1921. In the first Knesset he served as Knesset member on behalf of Mapai, filling a position reserved for intellectuals identifying with the party's ideology. In the third

opposition, as a professor at the Hebrew University, can also be seen as an expression of the first seeds of opposition among senior actors in the academic field. His opposition relied on two main reasons: The first material and the other more technical. His first fear was, as expected, from the expected competition with the Hebrew University over budgetary and academic resources. The technical fear was interpreted as lack of justification for a further academic institution in such a small country as was Israel in the beginning of the 1950s. The material opposition on behalf of the senior actors of the field was led by a fear of competition over material resources with the Hebrew University, as was alleged in the case of Tel Aviv. However, Dinur's opposition to Bar Ilan University resulted from his perception of its struggle as paradigmatic, both due to his personal and professional views and due to his being a part of the Hebrew University. He believed that the secularization of the Jewish messianism by Zionism has led to the establishment of the State of Israel (Ben Sasson, 1967). The Hebrew University was to him the spiritual climax of the Jewish Settlement in Israel and of the nation's national revival, while Bar Ilan University stood in contrast to his personal beliefs, for a number of reasons: It was founded as a private initiative by a religious group from outside Israel with the aim of reinforcing the Jewish foundation of the nation's revival and establishing reciprocal ties between Israel and the diaspora. According to Dinur, all these reasons were in complete opposition to the accepted rules in the wider academic field, which had been integrated in the renewing statehood and in this case also in modern Judaism, Zionism and the idea of national revival in the land of Israel.

The national opposition even threatened to revoke the principle consent granted by the Jewish National Fund to allocate a plot of land for Bar Ilan University, if the government grants its agreement. A government discussion was held as to the question whether the act of allocating the land would in fact constitute as an indirect recognition of Bar Ilan University. A decision could not be reached during the first government discussion on the matter, and it was delayed. Only threats by the President of the global "Mizrachi" movement that the government's opposition would dampen Israel's relations with American Jewry, and the fact that the Mayors of the cities of Tel Aviv and Ramat Gan agreed to allocate land for Bar Ilan University, eventually led to the government's consent. According to the decision dated 2 March 1952:

Knesset he was appointed Minister of Education, a position which he held between the years 1951–1955.

a. It (the government) does not oppose the allocation of a site in Ramat Gan towards the construction of a Yeshiva-University.
b. This decision does not constitute a recognition of the need for a second university nor a direct or indirect ratification of further fundraising for the institution to be established by the Mizrachi (Ben Yosef, 1967).

The text of the decision strongly reflects general opinion towards the establishment of a further university. When the founders' intentions were understood as aiming to establish a Yeshiva-University which does not pertain, according to Dinur's approach, to the academic field, the opposition softened. However, when founders' intentions were perceived as aiming to establish a university, the opposition was firm, as this was seen as a struggle towards a paradigmatic change in the field. Even if the founders' intentions are perceived as aiming for social change through the political field, the decision conceals an opposition motivated by a secular world view characteristic of a type of struggle against those wishing to undermine the hegemony of the senior actors in the political field who represent a secular Zionist approach. An emphasis of the institution's name points to the nature of the opposition: Although it was not called a Yeshiva-University, and its founders had no intention to call it so, the name "Yeshiva-University" coined by Dinur stuck to it. It seems he had used that name for the two reasons that he represented: From a national and political aspect, for him the name "Yeshiva" represented the historical Jew of the diaspora, that does not belong to the world of Dinur's new Jewish reality, not in the academic field and not in the political one. From an academic perspective, as one of the senior actors of the field, Dinur expressed his great doubt in the ability of a university to uphold a religious value-system while being committed to independent academic research.

The second stage of opposition commenced with the State's recognition of the needs of Bar Ilan University and its budgeting (1958) and the establishment of the Council for Higher Education in 1958. At this stage, when the university's accreditation was no longer at the mercy of any specific governmental committee, an overt opposition emerged from the direction of the senior actors of the field, that was based on State regulation rules that had become the accepted rules of the field. The university's founders understood they must accept the rules of the field, and so in their first meeting with the members of the temporary Council for Higher Education they clearly stated their intent to establish a university based on the American model, rather than an American college or Yeshiva-University, as Dinur had attempted to attribute to them. At this stage they withdrew from their original aim to operate independently from any governmental rule in order to implement their religious and social aims, which is also why they had conceded State budgets.

After budgetary accreditation had been obtained, the Hebrew University acted as can be expected of senior actors in the field, and moreover from those holding a monopoly over it: Their opposition was now centered on academic rules, and the aim to disqualify Bar Ilan's accreditation focused on arguments regarding the university's failure to meet accepted academic rules, such as its ability to operate according to a religious and academic value-system (Klein, 1998, 2006), or its ability to accept students without discriminating based on their level of religiousness. In the next stages of the struggle within the CHE, worries were voiced as to whether the new university should be granted the right to offer graduate studies without requiring a prolonged trial period as had been the custom with the country's first universities. Bar Ilan University's struggle ended with its victory, due to national reasons and the practical needs of Israeli society.[54] From this point onwards the continued struggle within the academic field centered on the hierarchy in the field, prestige and academic status, as described by Bourdieu in his Fields Theory. Churgin expressed this opposition towards Bar Ilan University in one of the university's first publications:

> This may be seen as a paradox, but in the State of Israel a university aiming not only to teach and instruct research students but also to educate on Jewish and humanistic ideals that have accompanied the People of Israel for generations, has a far more difficult time in achieving its aims than a parallel institution in the diaspora (Churgin, 1967–1968: 5–7).

Another type of opposition came from the Jewish Ultra-Orthodox (Haredi) sector. Despite the fact that the founders had no intention to approach this field and did not perceive it as relevant, the Haredi world nevertheless embarked upon a type of struggle that originated from their fear of a paradigmatic change in the religious field. The Haredi community in Israel viewed the new religious university as an incarnation of the Jewish Reform movement. Haredi leaders feared that the establishment of a religious university in Israel would influence the young generation, who would see in it an opening for the secularism represented by the State's founders, and that this would result in a reduction in the number of Yeshiva students (Ben Yosef, 1967). This opposition, although not very strong, was met by Churgin's appeasing response, alleging that the university does not replace or compete with any Yeshiva or other religious institution. Moreover, he argued, its establishment would only serve to enhance the love for one's fellow Jews and for the *Torah*. Churgin's response stemmed mostly from his particular strategy that is characteristic of those who did not see themselves as "young" or new in

54 For more about the struggle and accreditation see: Klein, 2006.

the Haredi field, and was directed mostly towards the academic field rather than towards the religious-Haredi establishment itself.

The Transition from Subversive Strategy Aiming to Achieve Paradigmatic Change, to Subversive Strategy Based on Accepted Academic Rules

The onset of the change in the founders' position could be noted in the method of presenting the institution's aims to the temporary higher education committee appointed to examine the status of higher education in Israel towards the end of the 1950s. In their responses to the committee members we see a transition to the adoption of a subversive Strategy, but one that would be acceptable within the academic field, while retreating from aspirations for paradigmatic change. In a position paper prepared for the meeting with the committee, the founders wrote:

> Bar Ilan University was founded by Americans and is being built in Ramat Gan (next to Tel Aviv), Israel, thanks to funds donated in the USA. The organization of the university, the buildings and plans, were all prepared by American academics [. . .] As had been the practice at the first universities of America, Bar Ilan's roots and its purpose have a religious character. The university was founded and is managed by the Mizrachi Histadrut in America, but Bar Ilan's roles and aspirations are beyond partisan matters or those pertaining to any specific Jewish group. Bar Ilan was the Hebrew surname of the esteemed leader Rabbi Meir Berlin of blessed memory, and the university is named after him and in his memory. . . he was also the President of the Rabbi Isaac Elchanan Yeshiva, which later became Yeshiva University[55]

In response to material questions asked by committee members such as: "Why is the institution called a university in its formative years?" And "If the aim is to educate religious scholars, why not Rabbis?" the answers point to the eminent change and attempt to work according to accepted rules. Despite the fact that, for reasons explained above, Churgin tended towards the college model, he emphasized that the new institution must hold the name "university", just like the Hebrew University when it was founded, as well as Brandeis university in the USA.[56] As to the institution's religious aspirations, it was explained that the

55 Bar Ilan University Archive, container 1458, file 203. The management's message in anticipation of the university cornerstone laying ceremony on 7 August 1955.

56 Ibid. Brandeis is a private university founded in 1948 in Massachusetts, USA. The university was named after the Jewish judge Louis Brandeis, who was the first Jewish USA Supreme Court Judge. In 2006, half of its students were Jewish. A vast majority of its donors are Jewish, and it was headed by Jewish presidents including an Israeli born in Haifa – Yehuda Reinhertz.

demand for religious leadership of students does not in any way undermine the universal value of an academic institution. Any academic institution is entitled to its own requirements, provided that these are required of all candidates, without prejudice. On the other hand they noted that also non-Jewish students are accepted, in which case the requirement to take Talmud and Bible courses is waived. As to the question on rabbinical ordainment studies, Churgin responded that this was not the intention at any stage of the planning of the university:

> Bar Ilan university cannot take upon itself to educate rabbis on behalf of Israel, as the special requirements of rabbis in Israel are highly intensive and therefore the candidate must dedicate all his time to Talmudic studies, leaving no time for general curriculums.[57]

Churgin's initial aim to create a foundation for religious and professional academic education, had not been accepted over the years, with the main reasons being the following:

1. **A process of moderation in religious-nationalist aspirations within the struggle for paradigmatic change** – the need for national accreditation resulted from budgetary concerns and entailed the recognition of the senior actors of the field due to the Hebrew University's hegemony both within the academic field and in its extensive influence on the government on matters pertaining to the field. Moreover, since from its onset the university had aimed to integrate in the same field as other academic institutions in Israel rather than within either the religious-Zionist or the Haredi sectors, it had to moderate its positions towards entering its relevant field. The aspirations of the university's senior faculty members during its formative years as well as State pressures to fit into the Hebrew University's employment model also ultimately led Bar Ilan's development towards the path of becoming a competitor of the Hebrew University.
2. **Growth and Development of the Academic system in Israel and the world** – A gradual acceptance of the rules of the academic field was a result of an overall acceptance of growth and development processes within the structure of higher education, and differences between the structure of higher education in Israel

57 Ibid, container 1458, file 210. Protocol of one of the meetings of the Committee for Higher Education held on 3 September, 1956, prior to the establishment of the Council for Higher Education. Bar Ilan's management, headed by Prof. Churgin and Dr. Bilubluzki appeared before the committee to present the university and its aims towards obtaining accreditation as an institution eligible for national budgets. Committee members included minister Yosef Burg, who also served on the university's board of trustees, and it was headed, as mentioned, by David Horwitz, at the time Governor of the Bank of Israel.

and in the United States (Katzburg, 1981). In the American model, professional graduate studies follow undergraduate college studies, while in Israel as early as the 1960s professional undergraduate studies were introduced in a number of fields in the Social Sciences, such as Law, Accounting and Social Work, and the new university could not ignore these trends. moreover, the changes in the economy and its professional needs pushed the university's founders to change and adjust, in the spirit of theories of industrialization and modernization.

The Process of Formation of the Academic Religious Model: An Overview of Comparative Analysis

As mentioned above, the choice of an academic-religious model was influenced by the American Catholic and Protestant institutions. I will, therefore, summarize the common characteristics of the American Christian institutions and Bar Ilan University in Israel:

1. **Pedagogic goals.**
2. **Institutional orientation** – an emphasis of educational-pedagogic aspects, more than scientific-research ones.
3. **Belonging to a supporting religious body** – the religious institutions in the United States belonged to Churches that supported them.

During its formative stage, Bar Ilan University belonged to the global "Mizrachi" movement who supported it both directly and indirectly through likeminded philanthropists throughout the world. The unification of the two movements – the "Mizrachi" and "HaPoel HaMizrachi" – which led to the establishment of the National Religious Party (NRP) political party, increased the support of the new movement at the university. This support was apparent in the stages of acquiring national accreditation, and for many years in the corridors of power. A large part of the university's Board came from the global "Mizrachi" movement and were among the leaders of the NRP in Israel. Until the 1980s NRP ministers took part in the management of the university, serving as members on its Board, for instance minister Haim-Moshe Shapira, of whom Yosef Burg said: "He was the man who paved the road for an active governmental support of the development of Bar Ilan University."[58] Burg himself also served for many years on the

58 Burg, Y. (1971). Eulogy for Minister Shapira, in the book Haim-Moshe Shapira (1902–1970), edited by Haim Ze'ev Hirschberg, Ramat Gan, 33. Burg was among the leaders of the religious-Zionist movement, the National Religious Party (NRP), a Knesset Member and Minister in Israel's governments for 40 years.

university's management boards. Zevulun Hammer, Israel's Minister of Education for three terms, was also a member of the university's Board for many years. Zerach Warhaftig[59] was Chairperson of the university's Board until the 1990s.

4. **A characteristic religious life style** – similarly to the religious universities of the United States, Bar Ilan University was also characterized by a religious life style:
   4.1. The university's statute defines its religious nature and religious-academic goals in promoting "learning and research in all Extensions of the *Torah* and science in the spirit of Jewish religion and tradition".[60] Accordingly, the university upholds a religious life style, which includes a campus Rabbi, steps taken to increase Jewish identity, and an appropriate dress code during studies in general and during religious studies in particular.
   4.2. While Bar Ilan University does not offer Rabbinical ordainment programs, it nevertheless requires all its students to take various Jewish Studies courses in all of the following areas of study: Bible, Talmud and Jewish Thought. This obligation resulted in an extensive scope of courses offered in Jewish Studies, and required the recruiting of faculty members whose main areas of specialization are Jewish Studies and religion.
   4.3. In its main campus, the university offers traditional study programs such as the Institute of Advanced Torah Studies – "The Kolel" for men and the Women's College for Tora Studies where students study *Torah* in the morning, and academic courses in the afternoon.
5. **Reinforcement of a rational discourse on religion** – While Klein (2008) found many similarities to Catholic institutions, I believe that many can also be found with Protestant institutions in the United States. Bar Ilan University sees itself (even today) as providing a bridge between religious and non-religious people in Israel. This bridge was built on pillars of wisdom and science and a strengthening of the rational understanding of the Bible and its commandments, similarly to Protestant institutions. Protestantism aimed to use rationalism to return Christianity to its origins, and Bar Ilan University functions in the same way. The university recruited heads of Jewish Studies Departments from universities in the

59 Israel politician and jurist, among the leaders of the Mizrachi and the NRP religious-Zionist party. Knesset Member from the first to the ninth Knesset. Minister of Religions between the years 1961–1974.

60 Bar Ilan University Archive, container 1046, file 122, "Bar Ilan University Association" Regulations, as registered at the Ministry of Interior on 29 September 1968.

USA, Belgium, England and Canada, so as to deepen the study of Jewish heritage using an academic language that would be accepted by Israel's non-religious elite.

6. **Adjustment and change of aims** – similarly to the American institutions, Bar Ilan University was influenced by the changes that took place in the Academic system both globally and locally. The need for professional adjustments to suite the requirements of the Israeli economy, as explained by proponents of the industrialization-modernization school of thought and the Credential Society theory; the need for recognition by senior actors of the field according to Bourdieu's thesis; and the expansion of higher education; forced the second generation of the university's management to reexamine its academic and social path. The change took place in stages:
    6.1. A retreat from the college or Yeshiva-university model – this retreat was one of the first stages, occurring in the beginning of the 1970s, but whose seeds can be found as far back as the appearance of the university's leaders before the temporary higher education committee. The college model was unsuited to the Israeli style for two main reasons: Undergraduate studies take four years, compared to three years at the rest of the universities in Israel and the influence of industrialized society and Credential Society demanding specialization and expertise as an entrance ticket to the work force led Israel's universities to offer practical and specialized undergraduate curriculums, as opposed to American institutions where specialization begins in graduate studies. Such specialized studies included Accounting and Law.
    6.2. A retreat from the independent university idea – the university's founders aimed to operate within higher education in a way that would be free of governmental influence so as to realize their social and religious aims. This idea encountered financial difficulties as early as the second year to the university's existence, and the first application for State funding was made in November 1957 when the university's general secretary and Chairperson of its Finance Committee applied to Zalman Aran, Minister of Education at the time, with the following request:

> Following the university's fast development we have reached a point in which we must request the government's support in order to maintain and further develop the institution [. . .] "We have set a principle from which we shall not stir, for we cannot lock our doors to students lacking in suitable means who are eligible, based on our strictest requirements, to join the university".[61]

61 Ibid, container 1046, file 122, Letter dated 28 November 1957.

The request for State support marks the beginning of the end of the founders' non-academic ideas that they aimed to implement in an independent manner. With the legislation of the Council for Higher Education Law in 1958, the university was included under the CHE's regulatory supervision. It should be noted however that not only developmental problems but also social ones led to the decision to request governmental support.

6.3. The university's founders did not seek legitimation in the Yeshivas world, but in the academic one, which they perceived as the relevant field for their work, and therefore over the years they had to accept the rules of the academic field, as defined by its senior actors – in this case – the Hebrew University. An example for this can be found in the demand of Bar Ilan's faculty members for their employment terms to be identical to those of their colleagues at the Hebrew University.

6.4. A global trend – the real competition over the capital of the academic field takes place in research. This competition was greatly enhanced with the expansion of the academic system that commenced in the 1990s. Institutions had to differentiate themselves from the new non-research institutions so as to be eligible for larger resources and appropriately position themselves in a globalized era. The academic rules of the game pushed Bar Ilan University to a single line with all other universities in Israel, especially in terms of a growing adoption of the European-German model that emphasizes research over pedagogy.

Conclusions

The first seeds of the idea to establish a religious-academic institution in Israel sprouted in an ideological-religious field, the first stages of which can be dated back to the establishment of the religious-Zionist movement in 1902. Religious-Zionism saw education as a highly powerful tool which it could operate in Jewish communities around the world. Its aim to integrate in the Zionist project in Israel rather than leaving it in secular hands led the "Mizrachi" movement in the USA to initiate the establishment of a religious academic institution that would educate a generation of scholars who would serve as public opinion agents, and in this way the "Mizrachi" would leave its mark on the development of society in Israel. The question why did the Mizrachi leaders choose the academic field has two main answers:

1. The Mizrachi leaders acquired their academic education in American institutions, which provided them with a model of inspiration for the success

of their educational and religious activities, especially among new immigrants of the 1950s. The Mizrachi leaders aimed to use this model to reproduce the success of these institutions, in Israel. They also had a good practical example for a successful integration between academics and a traditional Jewish institution, in the Yeshiva-University of New York.

2. The field of education, chosen as the core of religious-Zionist work since the movement was founded, remained without a Zionist parallel in Israel, after the Mizrachi's sister movement "Hapoel HaMizrachi" decided to take part in the practical building of the country through agricultural settlements and socialist values as a religious-Zionist way of life. The "Mizrachi", whose educational activities were mostly outside Israel, chose education as its practical expression of building the country, and following its involvement in Primary and Secondary education, academia was chosen as a suitable project to cope with 1950s reality in Israel, In essence, the "Mizrachi" adopted the idea of autonomy in higher education, in a similar process to that which took place in formal education: Its origins can be found in the consent of the elites to accept a regulatory regime and its culmination in the State Education Law which regulated segregation through legislation. Thus, the Mizrachi's initiatives in the field of higher education began from a need to provide religious students a protective religious academic framework, continued with the acknowledgment of the elites in government as a result of the NRP's support and ended with a legal and national recognition (by court ruling) of religious segregation in higher education.

These responses shed light on the way in which Bar Ilan University developed as a religious academic institution in Israel, from its formation to recent years, through a period in which the country's academic system transitioned from monolithic to binary structure. The university's formation still influences its social, religious and scientific goals, and even the changes in the aims it has set for itself since its establishment.

The development of its image as an institution of educational-pedagogic literacy can also be ascribed to the model of the religious universities in the United States, but no less so to the character of its founders in the 1950s and 1960s. Prof. Churgin was a Rabbi and educator whose education had been acquired in American and Jewish teaching institutions. His successor Rabi Lookstein was among the leaders of Jewish Orthodoxy in the United States and a founder of a college for Jewish female teachers. The partners of the "Mizrachi" in Israel were all educators: The first, Haim Moshe Shapira, was the Chairperson of the University's Board, was an avid warrior for religious education in Israel. He viewed the university not only as an institution of higher education, but as one whose top obligation is to provide religious values in order to create a spiritual center for the realization of Jewish heritage and laws. Other members of the Board were educators as well, including ministers Yosef Burg, Zevulun Hammer and others. The common professional background uniting them all was education, and they made their professional impact on the university during its formative years.

As part of the same ideology on which the university was founded, and mostly with the influence of the religious academic institutions of the United States, about a decade following the university's establishment it began to open Extensions. The first Extension was established in Ashkelon in 1965, followed by others in the north of the country: The Zemach Extension and the Zefat Extension, both in 1968. The older Extensions were joined in the beginning of the 1980s by Ariel College and the Western Galilee College in 1995. Both did not join as regular Extensions, but under a slightly different format of collaboration. while the older Extensions were founded as an initiative of Bar Ilan University and through its funding, the later ones operated as independent institutions under the university's academic auspices.

Chapter 3 Establishing the University's Religious and Social Mission

The Institution's Mission as Expressed in its Regulations

The religious-social goals which according to the university's founders were the core of its uniqueness and aim, had been implemented in the regulations drafted upon its establishment. The university was officially founded in August 1954, through a Corporation established by the Mizrachi Histadrut of America. The corporation's regulations point to the religious aspirations at the core of its operations. In the first part of the regulations, research is described as a means for achieving religious aspirations, which are presented as superior:

> 3.a) To organize, institutionalize, establish, fund, equip, hold and manage a university. . .in order to promote learning and research in all areas of science in the spirit of the Torah and Jewish tradition.
>
> b) To annex or Extension to this university some other institution in Israel or outside it having similar roles.[62]

The aim to expand, which existed from the university's formative stage, despite strong opposition to the new institution (Gross, 2008; Klein, 1988, 2006), points to very different organizational aspirations than those common in Israel's academic field at the time. In one of the leaflets published by the university's management for the academic year 1978/79, the Extensions were defined as Chapters: "Extensions are Chapters of Bar Ilan University, located outside the Ramat Gan campus and offering university courses. The Extensions are an integral part of the university".[63]

This section of the regulations includes directives that are at the core of the idea to establish a different type of university that would operate through a central campus and chapters deployed throughout the country, so as to increase its influence even if the institution would not be accepted by the country's existing academic field.

---

62 Bar Ilan University Archive, container 1031, file 8. The Corporation's articles of incorporation: "Bar Ilan University, established by the Mizrachi Histadrut of America" on 5 August, 1954. Addendum 1.

63 Ibid, container 753, file 285. Leaflet containing answers to fifty questions about the Bar Ilan Extensions – Ashkelon, Jordan Valley, Zefat – 1978/79 academic year.

In the section on membership in the founding body it is stated that the Board is the institution's highest authority, and its roles include:

> 4.a) To recommend to the Mizrachi Histadrut of America, candidates for any available or new position at the "Board of trustees" (ibid).

Following the national accreditation of the university's budget after three years of operation, and in order to gain an entrance ticker to the academic field, the university's management was required, as part of the rules of the academic field, to officially establish an Association, rather than formally belonging to a political movement, as had been the case in the regulations of the founding Corporation. The Board of trustees appointed a mobilization team entrusted with the establishment of the new Association entitled "Bar Ilan University". The university's regulations were officially ratified by the Ministry of Interior on 29 September 1968, and the new regulations mentioned no official affinity to the Mizrachi movement. In the statute's interpretations clause, the institution's affinity to the America Corporation was mentioned, including its full title, here too with no mention of any affinity to a political body: "The Bar Ilan University in Israel under a charter granted to it by the university of the State of New York".

The concept of religious and social activities was stipulated both directly and indirectly in the section pertaining to the authorities of the Association, which were redefined as follows (articles 3 and 4):

> 3. To uphold, promote, maintain and manage the university with the aim of nurturing and promoting learning and research in all areas of *Torah* and science in the spirit of Jewish laws and traditions.
> 4. In order to promote its aims, the Association shall be authorized to carry out and perform the following activities and acts…
> 4. e) to annex, to join, to affiliate, to be affiliated with, to merge and collaborate with other institutions of education and higher education, in Israel or abroad.[64]

I wish to focus on two statements made in the founding regulations of the two types of official forms of incorporation and the difference between them:

a. The 1954 Corporation's regulations clearly and explicitly marked the university's political affiliation to the "Mizrachi" movement in America and later in Israel, leading us to the conclusion that the university's religious aims were formed by an Israeli and Jewish-American political body. In practice, the Mizrachi movement in America was the university's highest authority during

64 Ibid, container 1046, file 122. The Bar Ilan University Association Regulations as registered at the Ministry of Interior on 29 September 1968.

its formative years, until its reorganization as an Association in 1968. This authority also defined membership in the organizing body and the ability to be employed by the university.

The practical affinity to the "Mizrachi" movement in Israel and the USA was maintained in the new Association's regulations of 1968, although the formal affinity to the "Mizrachi" movement in America was removed from the regulations. An addendum to the regulations stating the names of the university's 14 founders included eight of the leaders of the movement in America: Joseph Lookstein – President of the University (a representative role devoid of operational authorities, consisting primarily of raising funds and representing the university); Ludwig Jesselson, Philip Stoelman,[65] Rabbi Zambrovski,[66] Rabbi Lieberman and others. Five others belonged to the National Religious Party (the NRP) in Israel: Three ministers in office: Haim Shapira, Minister of the Interior at the time of foundation of the Association; Zerach Warhaftig, Minister of Religions; Yosef Burg, Minister of Welfare; Shlomo Ben Meir, Deputy Minister of the Interior and Knesset Member on behalf of the NRP; Michael Hasani. The political control of the "Mizrachi" movement in American and the NRP in Israel remained intact, although not officially declared.

b. The regulations of both the Corporation and the Association clearly show the founders' intentions to operate within areas that had been out of the ordinary in the academic field at the time. Any matter that could have promoted its religious aims was potentially ratified in the regulations. The most prominent change in the corporation's regulations can be noted in articles 4 (d) and 4 (e) pertaining to the university's aspirations to spread geographically and organizationally in order to promote the implementation of its goals. Article

65 Ludwig Jesselson and Philip Stoelman, Jewish American philanthropists who donated extensively to Bar Ilan university in its formative years. Ludwig financially supported the establishment of the university's Institute of Advanced Torah Studies, which is named after him. Both were granted an honorary PhD from the university. Jesselson in 1973, and Stoelman in 1980.

66 Rabbi Zemach Menachem Zambrovski was one of the leaders of the World Mizrachi movement and among the founders of the Mossad HaRav Kook ("Rabbi Kook Institute") publishing house. He was involved in the settlement of central religious disputes that rocked the Jewish world in the USA and in Israel, including the question of who is a Jew and the question of autopsies. In 1973 the university granted him an honorary PhD.

4.d defines the following authorities: "to organize, establish, uphold, finance and manage the university and its auxiliary institutions".

Article 4 (e) did not limit the university to annex or affiliate existing institutions, as had been defined in the Corporation's regulations of 1954, but rather grants it, as per the Association's regulations of 1968, the authority "to annex, to join, to affiliate, to be affiliated with...". The term to be affiliated with means to create Chapters branching off existing operations; this and article 4 (d) regulating the existence of auxiliary institutions, point to the emphasis made in the new regulations following the actual establishment of chapters – Extensions and the affiliation with both new and existing institutions, such as in the case of the Jordan Valley College, as shall be shown later in this book. This type of operation through "Extensions" as a long term plan was defined in the Board's decisions of 29 June 1971 that had paved the way to the practical implementation of the university's social-religious vision. Among other matters, the Board agreed that it would discuss proposals presented on the matter of the Extensions, such as the examination of steps towards the establishment of an Institute of Advanced Torah Studies which will fulfill the university's Jewish role in the world. To this end it was decided that a global Council would be founded on behalf of Bar Ilan, its role being to maintain the university's close ties with the young generation of the Jewish world. Dr. Yosef Burg was elected chairperson of the Council. During the same meeting long term academic aspects were also examined, and it was agreed that a plan would be prepared towards the establishment of a Medical School. This decision has only recently began to be put into practice, based on the CHE's decision of 12 January 2010, by which Bar Ilan University is permitted to submit a plan for the establishment of a Medical school. The Board' regulations and guidelines for the university's statute defined the university's areas of operation, which includes religious-social and academic goals.

Establishing the Institution's Mission as Expressed in its Management's Policies

I have found reinforcement for the university's religious-social mission approach in the words of its Board members at a number of meetings held throughout the 1960s. Members of the Board, some of whom also represented the NRP political party in the Knesset and government, often expressed the founders' aspirations to deepen the university's involvement and social impact among the Israeli and Jewish public, on four dimensions:

a. The legislative dimension
b. The pedagogic dimension
c. The social dimension – reducing social gaps
d. The Jewish dimension – involvement in the Jewish world using religion as a unifying force

The founders' aspirations were implemented in practice in the following ways:

A. **The legislative dimension** – the aim had been to generate involvement in legislative procedures, mainly in the legislation of basic laws towards the possibility of the establishment of an Israeli constitution. The argument raised at Board meetings involved "the need for the university to deal with legislative matters in order to apply the laws of the *Torah* as the law of the State".[67] The tendency to promote the concept of a State relying on the *Torah*, at least on a declarative level, had been prevalent in religious Zionism since the establishment of the State (Cohen, 1998). However, during the early years the university's leaders viewed it as a politicized academy. The term expressed the founders' aspirations to integrate, through the university, in all wakes of life of the State, and to promote the realization of their religious goals under an academic mantel. More often than not, however, its religious goals determined the university's missions. For instance, the reasoning for the establishment of the university's law school was to train jurists who would initiate a transformation in the understanding of Jewish law and its assimilation in the law of the State; while the reasoning for the establishment of the School of Education had been to train teachers who would transform public opinion and the social and political image of the State.

Members of the Board, which included Ministers in offices, acted to assimilate Jewish law in the country's legislative body as well as in academia: Minister of Interior Haim Moshe Shapira also served for 15 years as Chairperson of the university's Board. His successor was the Minister of Religious affairs, Dr. Zerach Warhaftig, who was a jurist by education and a leading legislator at the Knesset (Warhaftig, 1988; Goldberg, 2001: 295–332; Yinon, 2001). Dr. Yosef Burg and

---

67 Bar Ilan University Archive, container 1088, file 338. The university's Board protocol dated 12 January 1967. The demand to intervene in legislative matters was presented in the protocol under the title: "National roles". The title included a list of topics which the university should aspire to be involve in beyond its tasks as an academic institution. Aspirations in the area of legislation, education and the relations with the Jews of the diaspora were mentioned.

others were among the founders of the university and of Israel's Parliament – the Knesset. All were involved in countless legislative processes throughout the NRP's participation in Israel's governments, leaving their mark in terms of Jewish law on the State of Israel's book of laws. Following are a few examples.

According to the Foundations of Law act of 1980 that replaced Article 46 of the Palestine Order in Council, Israel's heritage is defined as a legal source of reference. The Hours of Work and Rest Law of 1951, regulating Jewish holidays as recognized days of rest, as well as work laws and many financial laws of the State, were influenced by legal arrangements originating from Jewish law, and all these legislations involved members of the university's Board and NRP Knesset Members (Racover, 1989). As mentioned, Dr. Warhaftig had also been closely involved in these legislations. In his book "A Constitution for Israel" he listed three ways to assimilate Jewish law in the laws of the State: (a) through legislation; (b) through its inculcation in the ruling; (c) through research and study, thereby influencing legislators and judges. Having headed the university's Board for many years, I can say that his third statement had been the basis for the idea to establish the university's Law School. The academic support for the legislative operation was formed following the Board' decision to establish the Law School, whose main aim was to promote the study of Jewish Law in anticipation of its integration in the laws of the State. At the Board' meeting held on 21 February 1968, Minister Warhaftig reported on the discussions of the committee chaired by him which had been appointed to discuss the foundation of a Faculty of Law. In its decision to establish a Faculty of Law, the committee wrote: "It was agreed to recommend to the managerial institutions of Bar Ilan University to establish a Faculty of Law, together with an Institute for the study of Jewish Law, with the aim of training religious jurists".[68]

Following prolonged discussions and deliberations as to the necessity of a Faculty of Law, Warhaftig's position was accepted, and the Faculty of Law was inaugurated in 1970. An Expression of Bar Ilan's special role in the field of Jewish law can be found in a review by then Minister of Justice Yaacov Shimshon Shapira on his ministry's legislative work:

> We do not have an abundance of personnel for this matter. I think that in two or three years we will have a more substantial group of people from the Faculty of Law of Bar Ilan University, as following my suggestion and by their initiative they maintain their Faculty of Law in small numbers, preferring to accept students who are already learned in Jewish law (Racover, 1989).

68 Ibid, container 1088, file 338. Protocol of Board meeting held on 2 February 1968.

Even when the Supreme Court was asked to rule on the question of the existence of discrimination in accepting Yeshiva graduates to the university's Faculty of Law, the judges acknowledged the existence of a purely academic preference resulting from the openly declared aims of the Faculty of Law, or in the words of Judge Shilo:

> The discrimination – and such does exist – is a preference stemming from purely academic reasons. It is practical and even desirable, as it serves the general and declared aim of the Faculty of Law at Bar Ilan University, namely: revival of Jewish law by training jurists who are well versed in the *Halacha* [Jewish law] and in General law and conducting research in both fields. The Faculty's curriculum will focus on the practical study and research of Jewish law.[69]

B. **The Pedagogic dimension and training of educators** – members of the Board, who, as mentioned, were among the leaders of the religious-Zionist camp, viewed education as a powerful tool for disseminating *Torah* and science, with the aim of educating the next generations in the same spirit. Contrary to discussions on the establishment of a Faculty of Law, during which opposing voices were also heard, everyone involved agreed that the field of education is crucial in order to train teachers in the spirit of *Torah* and science, who will then train generations of youths in the path of the religious-Zionist movement. The national-religious stream of education which became more and more established under the leadership of the NRP political party, gave it widespread governmental authorities in this area: In 1953 national-religious education accounted for 24.5 % of all national and Haredi education in Israel, with the number rising to 28.8 % by 1972 (Neuberger, 1994). The national-religious education generated a wide range of academic activities for training teachers in the religious sector. In its initial discussions on the matter, the Board raised the question of how essential is the university's teacher-training unit alongside the Department of Education. Arguments in favor were public, pedagogic and most of all religious:

> Religious education in Israel will most probably face a dilemma following the educational reform.[70] The 9th grade will enter the State education system. Religious education will have to decide whether it will continue to train

---

69 Supreme Court 131/81 Moshe Dover vs. The Council for Higher Education, verdict 35 (4), 263, 268–269 (1981).

70 The integration reform was initiated in 1968 following large waves of immigration and the resulting gaps created in the education system between Israeli children and new immigrants. The reform centered on increasing the number of children continuing onto High school and Bagrut matriculation, reduction of educational and social gaps as maintained by the gaps in education. As explained by Yuval Dror, the national-religious

> teachers for these institutions and moreover will be required to meet schedule requirements and emerging pressures. However, there is a danger that if a clear answer is not provided, different frameworks will emerge, which will direct religious education to unwanted paths [. . .] The university's reasoning: If we don't do this side by side with the university, general developments will lead to the emergence of similar educational frameworks. As a religious university we would not want to forego the training of teachers [. . .] The advantage: A religious population will flock to the university.[71]

The fear expressed by members of the Board at the meeting is reminiscent of the fears among the religious-Zionist camp as to the influence and even coercion of secular education on new immigrants from Arab countries who arrived in Israel in 1949–1951.

It seems that there had been broad agreement on the question of education between the political approach of the leaders of the religious camp, and the academic-religious aspect presented in this regard. Eventually it was decided to establish a teacher-training unit that would cope with the planned reform in national education, and it became a teacher-training unit within the university's Department of Education, as it is to this day. In many Board discussions the importance of education and training of religious-Zionist teachers throughout the country was discussed time and again, and it was agreed that this matter is crucial, even if the university would be required to initiate the establishment of a religious teachers seminar. The importance that the Board ascribed to the training of teachers corresponded with the academic religious approach of the religious institutions in the United States. In the two types of institution, teachers were seen as agents of social and religious change, given the role of influencing future generations.

C. **The social dimension**[72] – we learn of the aims and concerns of the university's management to work to achieve social equality and reduction of social gaps

---

education stream in Israel opposed the reform for a number of reasons: A fear of increasing the number of disadvantaged students and a violation of the fragile inter-ethnic fabric because most religious-Zionist population comes from eastern origins ("Mizrachim"); Differences in the level of observance of Jewish laws among Ashkenazim and Mizrachim, most of which are observant (traditional); and the large geographic dispersal of students in this sector which may cause parents to simply send their children to the nearest school (Dror, 2006).

71 Bar Ilan University Archive, container 1088, file 338. Protocol of Board meeting held on 26 September 1968.

72 It is surprising that in a new book on the future of a religious university: The destiny of a religious university, edited by Yaacov Iram, Yehuda Friedlander and Shimon Ohayun

from the founders' declarations and the goals they defined for the university's Extensions project, which began to take form with the establishment of the first Extension in Ashkelon in 1965. The university's social message was voiced by its founder in his speech during the campus' cornerstone ceremony:

This institution will stand as a symbol of the basic internal unity of man. . .no student shall be turned away because of economic strictures.

(Churgin, 1988).

The social goal was emphasized in the first letter from the university's Finance Committee chair and General Secretary to the Minister of Education at the time, Zalman Aran, when the university's management conceded to financial pressures and applied for State support for the first time. In the letter, the social aspirations of the institution's leaders was expressed as follows: "(not to) lock our doors to students lacking in suitable means who are eligible, based on our strictest requirements".[73] During the 1960s, minister Haim Moshe Shapira – Chairperson of the Board, focused on the difficulties among Sephardi's to pay tuition, and he acted to increase the number of scholarships offered so as to allow these students the opportunity to integrate in key positions in their regions (Bar, 1972: 4). This sensitivity to the social task was expressed in a follow-up publication of the number of students of Sephardic descent ("Mizrachim") in the university's journal: A report in the 1967 journal noted the university's general growth and expansion, with an emphasis on the part of Mizrachim in this growth. In that year 2,731

(2013), printed by Bar Ilan University, which is a collection of articles written by the university's senior leaders, I could not find any reference to the university's prominent social operations – namely, its peripheral Extensions. Even when the writers did discuss the university's social or community operations in the past or present, no reference was made to its Extensions. This shortcoming is especially noted in the words of Prof. Dov Schwartz and Prof Zemira Mevarech. Even when Prof. Mevarech noted the university's contribution to the community, detailing projects such as the Discussion Program, opening of the Jewish Bookshelf, the Responsa Project and other special projects for students, the university's greatest social project – both in terms of its scope and its contribution – was not mentioned: the bringing of academic education s to the periphery through academic Extensions. The lack of consideration of the Extensions' activities is also noted in previous studies on higher education, especially those by Menachem Klein.

73 Bar Ilan University Archive, container 1046, file 122. Letter from the Chairperson of the Board, Hollander, and the university's General Secretary, Baruch Unterman, to Minister of Education Zalman Aran, dated 28 November 1957.

students attended the main campus, of which 460 were Mizrachim – 16.8 % of all students.[74] In comparison, the proportion of students of Asian-African descent among all university students in the country during the 1965/66 academic year was 11.9 %, and in 1974/75 it was 14.7 %. From a speech by then Vice President of the USA Hubert Humphrey in a ceremony in which he was granted an honorary PhD from the university, we can learn the extent in which the university's social policy was clear to all those who were familiar with its founders:

> During these past years it followed the principle that learning is not separate from daily life, but is an inseparable part of it. In addition to the study of the historical legacy of Jewish thought and spirit, the university dedicated itself to Israel's current problems, and especially to the absorption of new immigrants from Africa and Asia, which, as Prime Minister Levi Eshkol noted, are "the greatest concern of our generation". (Ibid, University Archive).

In the first discussion on the conclusions of the committee appointed to examine the operation of the Ashkelon Extension, and with an aim of convincing the members of the Board to grant it a permanent status, the University's President Dr. Lookstein noted that "many [students] of Sephardic descent participate in the course at Ashkelon" and he believes that "there is a good chance that the students will continue their studies at Bar Ilan".[75] In preliminary reports issued by the Extensions Manager to the university management, a reporting routine was established, by which a special emphasis was given to the number of Sephardic students at the Extensions compared to the main campus. A special example of the management's sensitivity to the number of Sephardic students at the Extensions can be found in a 1967 correspondence between the Extensions Manager and the Chairperson of the Board. According to the first report: "Sephardi or Yemenite – 37 %. Ashkenazi – 63 %" (Ibid). The number of Sephardic students highly disappointed the Chairperson of the Board, who responded: "I believe this requires a more fundamental analysis. I was convinced that in the development areas including Ashkelon, the percentage of Sephardic students should have been higher." (Ibid). This response forced the Extensions Manager to reexamine the data, and he explained in a further letter that a review of the number of students among the locals points to 42 % of Sephardi descent if not including the number of students coming from nearby Kibbutzim (with predominantly Ashkenazi populations). Later on he described his educational-social aims which more than

---

74 Bar Ilan University Archive, container 1458, file 206. University journal, 1967.

75 Ibid, container 1088, file 338. Board' Protocol, 21 February 1968.

anything expressed the aspirations of the university's management in light of the condition of Israel's social periphery in the 1960s:

> In any event we must remember that most of the population in the south is among the Sephardi group, and most of their youths do not finish high school or teachers' seminar, as do most Ashkenazi youth [. . .] There is no doubt that an increased popularity of Secondary and Higher education among the Sephardi ethnic group would raise their proportion in our university, both in Ashkelon and in Ramat Gan.[76]

We can learn of the relationship between the university's religious-social goals and those of the religious-Zionist camp and the importance of the principle of autonomy in education and in higher education, from the words of Minister Burg at a meeting of the University's Board: "It should be noted that in our university there is a relatively large number of Sephardic students and we see this fact as the fruit of the national-religious education in which the NRP invests great efforts." (Ibid). In the same discussion the Extensions Manager noted with satisfaction the progress of university courses at Ashkelon, in which there is a large number of Sephardic students.

During the 1960s the university's management defined a number of methods of operation aimed at realizing the institution's social goals:

1. Reducing the gap between the number of Sephardic students and those of Ashkenazi ethnicity.
2. Increasing the number of academics among the Mizrachim to integrate in government and education.
3. Offering preparatory courses towards full academic studies in peripheral areas.

The transition from the declarative stage to the practical was expressed in the decision to expand to northern and southern peripheral regions and to gradually establishing Extensions of the university that with time would integrate in the university's master-plan, as shall be further outlined in the next chapters.

D. The Jewish dimension – the relationship with global Jewish communities was highly important to the members of the Board, perceived by the founders as a Jewish-religious and national goal of increasing the relationship with the Jewish world so as to increase immigration to Israel and, no less importantly, to contribute to the cultural level of global Jewry. This concern was primarily expressed in improving the prestige of world Jewry by studying its cultural and disseminating its accumulated knowledge. The practical expression of the

76 Ibid. Letter from Dr. Tuvia Bar Ilan to the Board, 2 March 1966.

realization of this mission can be identified in the Board' decision to establish a **Global Council** for Bar Ilan, to be led by Minister Burg.[77] The council's role was to bring young Jewish people from around the globe to study at the university in special programs to be taught in English, such as summer seminars and exchange programs with Yeshiva university.

The religious and social goals defined by the university management, which were not common in the structure of other academic institutions in the country (that were based on the European-Germanic model and later the American one), express a position which Bourdieu would have defined as a strategy initiated by "newcomers" in a process of undermining the accepted paradigm of the field. The emerging organizational structure and preparations for implementing the university's many non-academic missions points to the institution's fundamental aim to block secularism so as to change the rules of the game in the academic field. Such change would be achieved by acquiring the field's cultural capital, and through it influencing the development of society in Israel. The decision of the "Mizrachi" movement in the USA to join the struggle of the religious-Zionist camp in the field of education also attests to the intentions of the university's leaders during those years.

The university's main campus in Ramat Gan could not contain the entire scope of the university's social and religious tasks during its first years of existence. Ten years following its establishment, the university's founders initiated a widespread plan towards the foundation of Extensions throughout the country. The expansion of the university's operation through the Extensions was a preliminary stage towards the implementation of a new organizational structure that would correspond with the realization of the institution's religious and social aims in the country's periphery – considered convenient ground for religious operations.

77 Ibid, container 1046, file 122. Board decisions, 29 June 1971.

Chapter 4 The Multi-Campus University Model and the Establishment of the First Extensions

Objectives

The idea to establish Extensions a decade after the university's foundation – while it is struggling for the State's recognition – relies on the principles of the religious-Zionist ideology and the vision of the university's founder Prof. Churgin.[78] The aspiration to open university Extensions in the Negev (south of Israel) and the Galilee (North) was a part of this greater ideology. Based on this approach, the idea of the Extensions had three main aims:

A. **The religious aim** – the founders perceived the Extensions as a further pillar in their religious agenda to disseminate Jewish religion and tradition in emerging Israeli society. The Extensions served as a long arm or extension able to reduce the time needed for disseminating *Torah* and science and establishing the University's general impact on society in Israel. We can see quite a few similarities in the methods adopted by the university's founders and those used by founders of the religious academies in the USA. The founders of the religious universities in the United States feared the growing secularity of American society and the strong influence of modernism and materialism on society at large; the founders of Bar Ilan University – the leaders of the "Mizrachi" in the United States – also feared the strong influence of Israel's secular leadership on the formation of its society. They chose education as an effective area of operation through which they would be able to intervene in the formation of the image of Israeli society. In the United States, as in Israel, the founders of religious institutions directed their attention towards new immigrants who were yet influenced by the secularity of society in their new country. In both cases immigrants were the target of educational activities aimed at blocking secularity, reinforcing religious values and gradually influencing society at large. The motivating force among many immigrants from Arab countries was a return to Zion for religious aspirations, and most of them were either religious or traditional. These immigrants were generally not politically inclined and were not familiar with Israel's political system.

78 Ibid, container 1458, file 206. University journal, 1970.

The university's founders and the religious sector realized the huge potential in religious academic activities among these immigrants and its impact on society and the religious sector in general, and therefore acted mainly among their younger generations, through which they hoped to promote the concept of the religious intellectual combining religion and science. According to this religious approach, the locations of the first Extensions were chosen based on concentrations of these relevant populations in the country's southern and northern peripheries. In the south the first Extension was established at Ashkelon in 1965; in the north, the Zefat Extension in 1968, and in 1968 the Jordan Valley Extension that was to attract both the religious and traditional residents of Tiberias and members of the religious Kibbutzim of the Beit She'an Valley.[79]

B. **The Social-Political aim** – similarly to the religious universities of the United States at the time of their establishment, also in Israel we see further social aspirations alongside the religious ones – aspirations that encouraged the founders to utilize higher education in order to promote equal opportunities in the acquisition of higher education. The founders believed that this aim can be achieved through Extensions located in peripheral regions which will serve as a means for reducing existing social gaps, some of which date back to the first years of Statehood. Here too the university founders responded similarly to their counterparts in the United States: The new immigrants arriving in the USA in the nineteenth century and the beginning of the twentieth century searched for ways in which to increase their chances of integrating successfully in their new society. Higher education, according to Collins' Credential Society theory, is perceived as an entrance ticket to the world of employment and a tool for achieving social mobility according to Industrialization or Modernization theories. The founders of religious universities in the United States were motivated by social justice values and saw the promotion of academic studies among new immigrants as a potential for change that would lead to their successful integration in American society. The "Mizrachi" leaders in the United States were exposed to these beliefs and goals, and followed suit in the establishment of remote Extensions in an aim to shorten the process of change, taking advantage of the wave that began with the establishment of the

---

79 The Zefat Extension obtained the approval of the university's Board in its meeting held on 26 September 1968. The Jordan Valley Extension was not approved by the Board as were Ashkelon and Zefat, and instead an agreement for provision of academic services was signed with it on 12 August 1989. As an initial investment was not needed, the Board was not required to provide its approval.

country's religious university. The Mizrachi also had its image to consider: As opposed to its sister movement "HaPoel Hamizrachi" which was perceived as a socialist workers movement (Neuberger, 1997), The "Mizrachi" was perceived in the Israeli public as bourgeois. Its exposure to American values of freedom and equality encouraged it to change this image, and the concept of Extensions in peripheral regions served as a long awaited opportunity to implement such change.

From an academic-religious aspect, this work aimed at social equality positioned Bar Ilan University in one line with the social activities of the American religious academies. In the 1960s Israel's geographic periphery was located far from the country's educational and science centers as well as from knowledge-based employment opportunities, and therefore the initiative to establish academic centers in these regions gave the university a social image as the bearer of the flag of social reform, as indeed can be noted from the words of the Vice-President of the United States, mentioned earlier. The physical distance from learning centers made it difficult for residents of the country's periphery to take part in academic studies, due to financial difficulties entailed in studying far from home, but no less due to the emotional difficulties which led to alienation and distancing. The establishment of the Extensions among these population was perceived by the founders as a special contribution to social stability in the periphery with the hope that this would lead to a more meaningful process of their integration in society, through diplomas of education, as was also aspired by the founders of the religious academies of the United States. According to Schwartz (2006: 71): "Bar Ilan's sense of mission was among the factors that led to the adoption of colleges in the periphery and providing them with its academic support. The university's massive academic support of the colleges at Ariel, Ashkelon, the Western Galilee, Jordan Valley and Zefat was perceived as a national calling". Mevarech (2006: 123) also pointed to the importance of the national mission that Bar Ilan had set for itself at the Extensions: "Approaching the periphery was an unusual step at the time. Bar Ilan was the first and for many years the only university to do so [. . .] In the name of equality Bar Ilan was the first and until recently the only university to establish Extensions in provincial towns".

The composition of the university's management which included both academic and political leaders contributed to the integration of political considerations with social and religious ones. This leadership viewed the establishment of Extensions in Development towns and in predominantly religious areas as a convenient opportunity ensuring religious and political success more than any parallel activity in the Country's predominantly secular center. Such political motivations also indirectly contributed to the achievement of the academic goal of obtaining recognition from the senior actors of the academic field: They hoped that the process of recognition would commence with a social acceptance that would lead to an increase in the numbers of students at the institution, followed by national accreditation, and finally – the recognition of the senior actors of the field. An enhanced social influence could potentially promote the university to an important position that cannot be overlooked. This struggle consisted of "newcomers" struggling to integrate in the field so as to attain some of its cultural capital, thereby influencing society at large, as described by Bourdieu. Moreover, politically the idea of approaching underdeveloped regions of the country had been was convenient for the NRP, who during the period between 1949 and 1981 had amassed significant influence in areas whose populations were predominantly less affluent and originating from oriental and North African descent (Don Yechiya, 1990). Its influence even exceeded its electoral strength in these areas: while the electoral power determined its holding in local government, its power within these local authorities was larger than its actual electoral power. The NRP had a strong influence and practical control over the national-religious education system, which in Development towns was even more prominent than the national one. At the religious councils the NRP's power exceeded its political strength. Neuberger (1994) presented three examples of this power held by the NRP, all pointing to its comprehensive control over religious services in all religious councils throughout the country until the mid 1980s, and especially at Development towns: In Kiryat Gat the NRP had two representatives at the city council, but in the religious council it had five. In Jerusalem the NRP's representation in the city's religious council was three times as strong as its representation in the city council itself. In Petach Tikva it had seven representatives in the religious council compared to three in the city council. These examples point to the NRP's control over government mechanisms pertaining to religious services and education, which apply to all citizens (Don Yechiya, 1989). An analysis of the NRP's downfall in the 1981 elections also shows that its electoral strength in Development towns was large compared to its strength in affluent towns and cities, and the background to its political downfall, from which it failed to recover until today, was the ethnic split (Don Yechiya, 1990; Friedman, 1982).

The national accreditation and with it financial support from the State were achieved through the direct assistance of representative of the religious sector in the government, after three years of operation, as can be seen form Burg's eulogy to Minister Haim Moshe Shapira, Chairperson of the "Mizrachi" in Israel: "He was the man who paved the way for governmental support of the development of

Bar Ilan University".[80] His words attest to the strong connection between the political strength of the religious camp and recognition of the university's social and academic roles. Therefore, as the political power of the NRP and its part in the government grew, so did the university begin to enjoy a better position which led to its further development, and indirectly also to a recognition of the senior actors of the field in its work. As we will see below, the fact that Zvulun Hammer was Minister of Education and Chairperson of the CHE directly supported the transfer of the Extensions' budgets from the university to the Ministry of Education – a decision that resulted in a significant alleviation in the university's investment and cleared the road for the Extensions' independence.

C. **The National aim** – the founders' religious-social ideology influenced their national perceptions. From a review of many discussions in meetings held by the university management we see that the establishment of the Extensions led, among other things, to an aspiration to increase the university's hold on Israeli society, not only as an academic institution but as one having long term impacts on political and social processes. In the protocol of the Board meeting dated 12 January 1967, members emphasized its national roles, stating that:

> The university holds the role of being a leading factor in the fulfillment of national tasks in all areas of life - all the more so in a country that is still being built physically and socially and is surrounded by enemies. A religious university in a "**Jewish State** in the making" has further special roles [. . .] that the university would deal with constitutional matters in order to apply Jewish laws within State law [. . .] The importance of our educational work is both in terms of schools and for work abroad. A further relevant role is the nurturing of the cultural level of Jews in the Diaspora.[81]

Klein (1998: 17–18) notes that the university's founders, and most of all Churgin, viewed the foundation of the State as a first step in the realization of the classical vision of the Prophets. According to Churgin's approach, the return to Zion is first and foremost national, and then universal. The university is destined to form a bridge between the State of Israel and the Diaspora by bringing students from abroad to study at the university and return as teachers to Jewish communities around the world. The values on which any university is built, correspond, according to Churgin, with the values of the *Torah* and with the revival of the people of Israel in their land, and all these components together lead to harmony.

---

80 Bar Ilan, Haim-Moshe Shapira Book (1902–1970), edited by Haim Ze'ev Hirschberg, with the participation of M. Bar, Y. Don, L. Woller, Ramat Gan 1972, pg. 33.

81 Bar Ilan University Archive, container 1088, file 338. Board meeting Protocol, 12 January 1967.

This approach, as mentioned before, led to the establishment of the Teachers' training unit and the Faculty of Law, but the founders also viewed the university as a bridge between the State and world Jewry, utilizing religion as a connecting factor. This task was perceived by them as a national mission aimed at strengthening ties with the Jewish world and bringing more Jews to Israel, but no less important, this task also resulted from an aim to ensure the cultural level of Jews in the Diaspora. To implement this idea the university's management positioned the Zefat Extension, as shall be further illustrated, as a point of attraction for hundreds of young religious Jews from around the world. The idea was that international students would be attracted by the unique mystical learning experience offered at Zefat. A further national target that Churgin marked was to revive, via the university, the glory of Jewish culture and its wisdom, in the eyes of the world. It was clear to him that the success of such a mission must pass through the accepted academic path, whose rules he knew well from the USA. In order to achieve this he travelled extensively around the world to recruit prominent Jewish scientists to teach at the new institution as local faculty and guest speakers so as to contribute to the strengthening of the university's academic status. The establishment of Extensions in different areas of the country increased the university's attractiveness to potential faculty, as there was now a wider range of possibilities on offer for employment closer to home. The Extensions were also presented as an option for guest lecturers from abroad to teach during the summer or to local academic faculty members interested in teaching outside campus.

The Multi-Campus University Structure and its Adjustment to Social Objectives

The idea of the Extensions led in the beginning of the 1970s to exposing the university's bigger plan – defining its status as a **Multi-Campus University**. The ideological foundation for this new structural concept can be found in the Corporation's regulations, and later in those of the Association, both of which define the need to establish Chapters for the university. The idea of the Chapters further evolved in the 1960s into Extensions, requiring a more comprehensive academic response which was expressed in the decision to develop suitable academic facilities. For this the university needed State support, a fact which was presented to the State's authorities as a general plan when conditions were right.

The idea was initially presented to the committee appointed by Minister of Education and Deputy Prime Minister at the time Yigal Alon in his role as Chairperson of the CHE, to examine the existence of an academic institution in the north. The committee's report was submitted to the Minister and to the CHE on 26 July 1971. The committee was established following Bar Ilan's request for approval to establish a university campus at Zefat. The committee was appointed on 14 April, 1971. It was headed by Prof. Yehushua Yurtner, and its members included: Dr. M. Avidor, General DiRector of the National Academy of Science and former General Manager of the Ministry of Education and the Jewish Agency; Arnon Gafni, DiRector-General of the Treasury; Shlomo Derech of the Kibbutz HaMeuchad movement; Prof. Shlomo (Seymour) Fuchs, Manager of the Hebrew University's School of Education; Prof. Asher Peres from the Technion; and Dr. Avner Chai Shaki, Deputy Minister of Education and Culture. In his presentation to the minister, the university's Rector Prof. Harel-Fish explained the plan for the establishment of such a campus:

> [In this campus] it would be possible to fulfill all undergraduate requirements through nine departments [. . .] The plan for the establishment of a second Bar Ilan campus is expected, therefore, to solve some of the general problem of the absorption of students from abroad [. . .] There is no need to expand on the national implications of the establishment of an institution of higher education at the Upper Galilee region.[82]

The committee hearings were attended by heads of institutions in the region, heads of local councils and representatives of Bar Ilan University. The university's delegation included the former Rector Harel-Fish, the new Rector Prof. Kadari, the Manager of the Extensions Dr. Tuvia Bar Ilan and three Deans. This high ranking delegation attested to the fact that the university saw great importance in the development of the idea of Extensions, as part of a large and comprehensive organizational plan, its central principles being:

a. Bar Ilan University aims to establish itself as a national multi-campus university comprised of a number of campuses including Zefat. According to the plan, the main campus would not be big, and will operate alongside additional campuses spread throughout the country. The argumentation in favor of a relatively small main campus was defined at the committee meeting as a "pedagogic decision" aimed at distributing pedagogic work between a number of campuses.
b. According to the multi-campus plan, each Extension has a unique purpose: The university's intentions for the Zefat Extension were disclosed at the Yurtner Committee: According to the plan, the Extension at Zefat was destined to serve as a special campus attracting young religious Jews from abroad

82 Ibid, container 474, file 247. Letter from the university management to the Minister of Education, 24 January 1971.

seeking a holy and mystical Jewish experience, due to the city's unique Jewish character as a Kabbalistic center. The academic emphasis at the Zefat campus would be Jewish studies.

c. Some of the academic faculty would arrive from Bar Ilan, working part time at Zefat. Alongside these part time faculty members, the institution's full time faculty members would be expected to live in Zefat.
d. The university would establish dorms to be used by local students and those coming from abroad, mostly New York.
e. At first the university will offer nine departments at its Zefat campus: Bible, Literature, History, Political Science, Economics, Psychology, Education, English and Talmud.
f. The university's management intends to invest in Zefat three to five million dollars in the construction of permanent buildings.[83]

The argumentations raised by university's representatives include goals that combine religious and social principles, in addition to the academic ones:

A. **Fear of undermining the university's religious character** – until the 1970s non-religious students avoided Bar Ilan University, but since that time the campus gradually diversified, with more and more non-religious students filling its classrooms. The fear of secularization of the campus and loss of the university's religious nature worried its management for many years, with this fear growing in line with the increase in the number of students attending the main campus. One of the central goals of a multi-campus structure was to cope with the danger entailed in the university's religious nature following a significant rise in the number of non-religious students, residents of the Metropolitan Area of Tel Aviv (Gush Dan), at the main campus. The Yom Kippur War and the pressures asserted by the CHE on academic institutions to accept two classes in a single year, further increased the number of non-religious students, and the problem had to be urgently dealt with. The hope of the university's management to attract religious candidates was not realized in full, as these also applied to the Hebrew University and to the High Yeshivas. The fear of losing the religious character of the campus was discussed at the Board meeting held on 12 June 1975. Dr. Yinon, Chairperson of the Admissions Committee, presented information as to the number of non-religious students, and to clarify it was agreed that graduates of non-religious

83 Archive of the Council for Higher Education, The Y. Yurtner Committee discussing Bar Ilan University's plan to establish at university campus in Zefat, 26 July 1971.

schools will be considered as non-religious. According to Yinon, in 1975 the number of new non-religious students accepted exceeded the number of religious candidates. Prof. Albeck, Chairperson of the Admissions Committee until then, noted that until the Yom Kippur war in 1973, 65 %–75 % of all students on campus were religious. After the war this figure changed and the non-religious students became the majority. This fact worried the members of the board to such extent, that members were asked not to mentioned the number of non-religious students in public and to also refrain from mentioning them in meeting protocols, fearing that such information becoming common knowledge would harm the university's image as a religious institution. The idea of Extensions and a multi-campus structure were the solution of the beginning of the 1970s: Academic campuses at areas populated by predominantly religious or traditional populations that settled in the country's northern and southern peripheries serving as a counter-weight to the penetration of non-religious populations to the university. Keeping the central campus small and opening additional ones in the midst of traditional-religious communities may contribute to the university's ability to maintain its religious character. However, fears continued to grow among members of the board, who would not wait for the implementation of the multi-campus idea. While the plan was being considered, the Board appointed a "Committee for examining the religious atmosphere at Bar Ilan".[84] The committee, headed by the Rector Prof. Sprecher, soon presented its practical recommendations which were brought before the Board on 12 June, 1975. The proposed solution was presented through two alternatives: (a) Seclusion, dedicating the university to an exclusively religious public; (b) The university's continued development as a religious institution, while persisting in the implementation of the goals defined by its founders, aimed at enhancing its influence among the Israeli public and the formation of the religious image of Israeli society. Until the founders' goals are implemented, the committee recommended the following:

1. Appointment of a special committee to examine ways to collaborate with religious high schools and Yeshivas.
2. Initiation of lectures by university faculty members at religious schools.
3. Maintaining ties with graduates and recruiting them for marketing the university among the religious public.

---

84 Bar Ilan University Archive, container 1088, file 338. Board' Protocol,12 June, 1975.

4. Financial incentives to young women in national service for studying at the university or its Extensions
5. A recommendation that had already been implemented was the establishment of an Institute of Advanced Torah Studies at the main campus.
6. Appointing a campus Rabbi who would be dedicated to holding religious activities on campus, such as study Sabbath, and others. Back in the 1960s the Board raised the requirement to appoint a '*Mashgiach*' (spiritual supervisor) to supervise the religious character of the university's main campus.[85] The appointment of a campus Rabbi had been a continuation of this requirement.

The Board unanimously accepted the committee's recommendations and authorized the committee members to continue discussing further ways to mitigate the damage to the university's religious character. It was agreed that further recommendations or a more comprehensive plan would be discussed by the Board. Later on, additional recommendations were implemented, such as: the establishment of a college for women – the "Metivta" college for training female rabbinical pleaders; a general obligation to study advanced Jewish Studies for all students at the university; and enhancing Jewish Identity in a range of ways including publication of a page on the Weekly Torah portion and Torah seminar days.

B. **Realization of social aims** – The multi-campus university structure was well suited for the implementation of the university's social sims, especially in terms of practical presence in peripheral areas yearning for access to higher education.[86]
C. **A functional uniqueness to each campus** – The discussions held at the committee appointed to examine the establishment of an academic institution in the north, exposed Zefat's special role in the plan. In the overall plan, Zefat was pinpointed as an Extension also intended for foreign students coming to Israel to specialize in Jewish Studies. As we shall see later on, the founders made a point of dedicating a different academic identity to each Extension in each area.

---

85 Ibid, The university's Board protocol, 12 January 1967. Proposal by Rabbi Zambrovski, member of the global Board.

86 Ibid.

The willingness of the university's delegation to invest huge sums of money (in 1970 figures) in permanent buildings leaves us with no doubt as to the intentions of the leaders of the university at the time: to establish a multi-campus university, whose main aims would be academic, religious and social.

First Steps Towards Implementation of the Multi-Campus University Program

The first step in implementing the idea of the Extensions was initiated by the university's Rector in the 1960s Prof. Avrom Saltman. In 1964 Prof. Saltman appointed Dr. Tuvia Bar Ilan as the Senate's envoy to identify suitable locations in Israel in which to establish Extensions. Dr. Bar Ilan examined recommended locations mainly based on region. According to the university's policy, the idea was to identify locations in peripheral areas where there are populations of religious or traditional new immigrants, as can be noted from one of Dr. Bar Ilan's letters: "We do our best to assist Development towns and far off towns in obtaining a minimum of higher education. Towns closer to the centers of higher education can and should make do with the existing [institutions]".[87]

After a potential peripheral location was identified, the second criteria was examined – the willingness of the local municipality or existing institution to collaborate by providing organizational or financial support. A final criteria was to measure the potential of students in the area, based on two variables:

1. **High school education** – the prevalence of high school education at the intended region.
2. **Candidates' potential as having social influence in the region** – areas where there was a higher concentration of sectors characterized as social change agents, such as teachers or public service employees, were preferred over less socially and publicly active areas. Due to the importance of this criteria from a religious-social aspect, it gained precedence even when the high school level education was unsatisfactory.

As mentioned, the definition of a region as social or geographical periphery populated by Sephardic Jews was a primary and decisive prerequisite, but during the relevant years there was a high correlation between all requisites: The regional aspect also determined the presence of ethnic, social and political relevance,

87 Ibid. Letter from Dr. Tuvia Bar Ilan to the management of "Hasharon" school in Raanana, dated 11 October 1966.

and therefore the idea of establishing Extensions in peripheral areas integrated between religious, social, academic and political aspirations:

1. **The religious aspiration** – The Extensions were the university's extended arm aimed at disseminating the religious-Zionist approach of the "Mizrachi", which consisted of the integration of *Torah* and Science. This approach matched that of the Protestant academic institutions in the United States, that had acted to enhance the religious-rational discourse.
2. **The social aspiration** – The university's leaders believed that the success of the Extensions would result in a reduction of social gaps through social mobility that facilitates higher education, as explained by proponents of the "Modernization" theory. The reinforcement of both religion and science among religious scholars who would later integrate in key governmental positions in these regions, would increase the influence of religion on the character of the State, while also extracting them from a life of low pay and a low social status.
3. **The academic aspiration** – from an institutional perspective, the idea of the Extensions was intended to lead to the university's general expansion in a short period of time, with the intention of deepening its influence among the Israeli public in general and in the academic field in particular, in line with Bourdieu's Field Theory.
4. **The political aspiration** – I learned of this particular aspiration from the words of the NRP's leaders as documented in protocols of the university's Board in the 1960s and 1980s, as shall be further detailed later on. This aspiration relies on the NRP's political position at Development towns and others populated by Mizrachim. The Party's far reaching representation and official authorities gave it the confidence to operate in peripheral areas, so as to further solidify its holding in those areas. Although the inclinations of NRP leaders to operate in Development towns were political in nature, they also included social motivations, as can be seen in the words of NRP ministers Shapira (Burg, 1972), Hammer and Burg. During one of the university's Board meetings minister Burg presented the direct relationship between the struggle over religious education in Primary and Secondary schools, and academic studies, and the social implications derived from them: "It should be noted that in our university there is a relatively large number of Sephardic students and we see this fact as the fruit of the national-religious education in which the NRP invests great efforts".[88]

88 Ibid, Board meeting Protocol, 12 January, 1967.

At another meeting Zevulun Hammer expressed his clear cut opposition to undermining the Extensions, and in doing so also expressed his political opinion in this matter: "The Project of the Extensions is among the university's greatest and most important projects educationally and in terms of mission. Undermining the Extensions in the current state of the economy and the population distribution in the country would result in the lower classes to be the first and foremost to be harmed by the budgetary cuts".[89] In his eulogy to NRP Chairperson Haim-Moshe Shapira, Minister of Finance Pinchas Sapir praised Minister Shapira's work for religious education in general and for Bar Ilan University in particular: "Thanks to his vigor and hard work the national-religious education system, from preschool to the secondary Yeshivas and Bar Ilan University has expanded and prospered".[90]

From the perspective of the residents of those regions, the connection with the NRP was more natural than a connection to other religious parties such as the ultra-Orthodox Agudat Israel or Poalei Agudat Israel. The NRP was for them a religious-sub-culture. Mizrachim were able to easily and without a sense of loss of identity adopt the NRP's approach in areas close to their hearts, such as the use of a Sephardi accent in prayers and in the study of the *Torah*, and as a bridge between religion, tradition and modern culture (Friedman, 1982). Ten to twelve seats in each Knesset election until 1981 were testimony to the electoral stability of the NRP among Mizrachim in these towns. Its steep decline in the 10th Knesset elections (1981) was an expression of an ethnic split (Don Yechiya, 1990) rather than an ideological one, as declared by Friedman (1982). The NRP shrunk nearly everywhere, but its downfall was most decisive in areas where most of the population consisted of Mizrachim and underprivileged communities (Don Yechiya, 1990). Entire Chapters of the party transferred their votes in this election to the "Tami" Mizrachi-dominated political party (Friednman, 1982).

The First Steps in the South of Israel in 1965 and Outlining the Stages of Operation

Dr. Bar Ilan's search in the South of the country began in the beginning of 1965. He visited the cities of Beer Sheva, Kiryat Malachi, Kiryat Gat, Ashkelon, Ashdod, Ofakim and the Shafir and Nahal Sorek Regional Councils.[91] Following his first

89 Ibid, container 753, file 285. Board meeting Protocol, 30 January 1975.

90 Bar Ilan, Haim-Moshe Shapira Book, 1902–1970, pg. 25.

91 Bar Ilan University Archive, container 1088, file 338. Dr. Bar Ilan's letter to Harman Hollander, Acting Chairperson of the Board, 2 March 1966.

search expedition he presented the Rector with a report that included general observations, local data and recommendations. His general observation was that wherever he visited he was met with enthusiasm and a willingness to work with the university to promote the idea. His recommendations to the Rector included stages in the process of development of the Extensions which were to become an important part of the university's multi-campus structure program. In the following section I discuss the outline proposed by Dr. Bar Ilan for each stage in the process of development of a potential location for an Extension, the principles of which would have implications on students as well as faculty members:

1. **A peoples' university** – this preliminary definition pointed to the university's cautious progress through local academic lectures on current affairs, Judaism and culture, aimed at disseminating *Torah* and science to all interested. Recommending this cautious step was aimed, according to Dr. Bar Ilan, at examining the level of local interest and understanding the region's true potential in order to avoid investing huge sums in infrastructures if there is no likelihood for success. This cautiousness resulted from financial difficulties which were already felt in the university's operations by the mid 1950s following the abandonment of the pretentious idea to operate as an independent university without regulative limitations that reduce its religious and social freedom. These difficulties and the disappointment from the level of donations had led the university, as mentioned, in mid 1958 to regulatory subjugation, which was legislated that same year. This new status had implications on both students and faculty:
   A. **Students** – studies were offered to the general public without prerequisites or acceptance thresholds, and therefore no academic accreditation was granted to students. Lectures were available to the public, and students were not required to pay tuition.
   B. **Lecturers** – as these lectures were not bound by a yearly or semester-based academic structure, payment was given to lecturers per lecture, and not as part of their position at the main campus. This way no foundation was developed towards a permanent faculty. However, as the purpose of the lectures was ideological and their organizes strived to attract large number of participants, the most senior lecturers from the different departments were sent to provide the first few lectures, in order to present the institution at its best. This fact was noted in the following letter from Dr. Bar Ilan to the Rector: "I wish to emphasize the last thing being that the lecturing

skill is more important in this case than academic achievements alone, and the reason is clear".[92]

In this regards there was great importance to exposing the university to a large number of students in order to identify from within them those having potential for comprehensive academic studies. Success in this category was measured based on a large number of students, estimated at dozens of students attending two to four lectures every week. In his letter to the university's Rector on 9 June 1965, the Manager of the Extensions noted that the budget that had been approved by the Board for this task is 3,000 Israeli liras. It was agreed that studies would commence in the summer or fall, and only in three locations. The result was a small number of lectures which therefore resulted in exposure to only a small number of listeners.

2. **University courses** – the success of the first stage was the basis for examining the second, in which the university would hold academic courses at the new site. At this stage studies were offered under an academic framework with similar curriculums as in the main campus. The implications of this definition on students and faculty were as follows:

   A. Students were not required to meet the admission requirements of the main campus, and were therefore also not registered as students of the university. However, the courses were recognized in retrospect as academic points eligible towards a degree, if the student was later accepted for studies at the main campus.
   B. Faculty – as the courses were defined as external and transient, their teaching was not considered an integral part of the lecturer's position at the main campus, and the payment was per individual lecture, based on the teaching unit tariff defined by the PBC for Adjunct lecturers. Despite the transience of the appointment, this type of employment pointed to great potential and a serious intent of the university's management to hold regular studies at the new locations towards the establishment of a full blown Extension as part of the university's multi-campus plan.

The success of this stage was measured according to actual demand for a large number of courses and was based on the actual number of students registering

92 Ibid. In his first letter to Prof. Saltman the Rector of the university on 9 June 1965, after having undertaken to assess extra-university courses, Dr. Bar Ilan presented a list of terms describing a pre-Extension condition.

for each course. At this stage, the existence of 4–8 courses, each with about 15 students, was considered a success and a good basis for the future (Ibid.).

3. **University Extension** – the success of the second stage and further accumulated conditions in addition to the ideological ones, such as collaboration of the local authority and a physical infrastructure, led after two to three years to the establishment of a university Extension seen as an integral part of the university. A direct annual budget was allocated by the university towards the operation of the new Extension. Tuition was paid directly to the university, and accepted applicants were considered students of the university for all intents and purposes. This definition was a decisive stage towards the site's integration in the multi-campus university plan.

The implications of this definition for students and faculty were as follows:

A. **Students** were admitted based on criteria defined at the main campus. The students at the Extension were required to submit their applications to the main campus, and immediately following their official acceptance were defined as students of the university. The entire curriculum at the Extension was approved in advance, and students accumulated academic credits similarly to any other student at the main campus. The main difference between students attending the main campus and those studying at the Extension was the smaller selection of departments offered at the Extension compared to the main campus, and the fact that the curriculum at the Extension was limited to two years, with all students required to complete their third year at the main campus.

B. **Faculty** – their work at the Extension was a part of their position at the main campus, and included all the benefits granted to faculty members employed only at the main campus. Contrary to the previous two stages, the number of students and courses grew significantly during the Extension stage and required the recruiting of faculty members and their placement according to well-regulated comprehensive planning. The need to plan in advance and the relatively large number of courses made planning very difficult during the first years. Often Dr. Bar Ilan would apply to the religious and social ideology of faculty members to convince them to travel to teach at the Extensions. There were also objective difficulties at the main campus due to a shortage of teachers at certain departments. This difficulty impacted the decision to open additional areas of study at the Extensions as well as the academic level of the lecturers. When there was no other choice, lecturers with only a Graduate degree were sent to the Extensions, contrary to what had been originally declared.

The success of this stage was measured based on demand for courses rather than the total number of students at the Extension. Under this framework an attempt was made to offer programs based on departments which gradually developed a full year 1 curriculum, adding year 2 courses according to the level of success of year 1. In an aim to promote the regular operation of the Extension, faculty positions were allocated in advance according to a departmental index, and marketing efforts were invested in attracting students accordingly.

During the first years of operation of an Extension, a general, widely accepted Social Sciences curriculum was prepared. The curriculum relied on introductory courses and basic courses in Jewish Studies. The aim of this structure was to examine the efficiency of the operation of the Extension and its suitable scope. While generally the mix of courses on offer was aimed at assessing the Extension's attractiveness and defining an index for offering a permanent and non-eclectic program, at least for years 1 and 2, on the other hand demand for a specific program also provided an opportunity to assess the university's ability to operate in farther areas. The success of a certain field of study at an Extension was related to the university's teaching capacity at the main campus in the 1960s and the beginning of the 1970s. The university's likelihood to succeed at the Extensions was influenced by the relative success of the department at the main campus and the willingness of faculty members to take part in this special initiative. The task of recruiting faculty to teach at the Extensions was not an easy one, and still the university did not withdraw from its expansive plan to operate remote campuses throughout the country.

The difficulty in recruiting faculty members to teach at the Extensions resulted from three main reasons: The first was the physical distance between the center of the country and the Extensions, and this is true in many cases also in the case of Ashkelon which is the closest Extension to the main campus.[93] The second reason was the general shortage in teachers in many areas of study during the university's first years of existence. The university's management was willing to employ only religious faculty. As these were relatively few in Israel, the university's President would often travel abroad to recruit Jewish scholars from universities in the USA, UK and Canada.

93 As an Extension Manager in the mid 1980's I realized that for many senior faculty members that I tried to recruit, the distance to Ashkelon was perceived as far as the distance between center and periphery. Often I had to describe the actual distance in great detail, just to convince candidates who had perceived it to be twice as far and even more so.

The third reason was the fact that senior and sought after lecturers were working full time at the main campus and either had no time left, or saw no reason to travel long distances to teach at the Extensions. Moreover, senior faculty members did not teach at the Extensions during the first years as advanced courses and seminars were still not offered at the time. The result was that in many cases teachers at the Extensions were there because they had not been offered a full time position at the main campus; others who were not sufficiently involved in research and therefore were not eligible for a permanent tenure at the main campus or their employment was not assured; and junior faculty members who had just completed their Graduate degree and were studying towards their PhD and needed a job.

4. **University campus** – to describe this structure I will use the presentation of the university's position at the Jortner Committee and the Rector's letter to the Minister of Education in July 1971. Based on these documents, the third stage consists of upgrading the Extension to one of a number of campuses within a national, multi-campus university. The clear advantage of this stage is in its large number of departments on offer and the existence of a full undergraduate curriculum, without needing the main campus. A full undergraduate program outside the university's campus required the prior approval of the CHE. The implications of this stage on students and faculty were as follows:

    a. **Students** – this structure offers a significant advantage to students as it allows them to begin and complete their entire undergraduate studies at their local university campus, compared to the previous Extension status that had them traveling to the main campus in their second year, and sometimes even to complete their first full year. Completion of studies at the regional campus granted students the same degree they would have achieved at the main campus. The proposed program submitted to the minister included a large variety of courses and full academization outside the center. Socially this framework offered all the advantages of bringing academic studies to the periphery, as it would save students the travel time to the main campus and all other expenses entailed in studying there.
    b. **Faculty** – this structure did not significantly affect teachers' terms of employment, and moreover it enabled the addition of positions and mobilizing teachers between campuses throughout the country, or employment near the faculty member's place of residence. The difficulties in recruiting faculty members are equal to those in the previous structure of Extensions.

This format did not reach fruition and therefore we cannot examine its success. As shall be detailed later on, the implementation of the university's plan was blocked in a legislative process in line with the Jortner Committee's recommendations.

Launching of Extra-University Activities at Ashkelon, Based on Dr. Bar Ilan's Instructions

We learn of Dr. Bar Ilan's impressions of the responses of the heads of local councils he had met with and his thoughts on his mission on behalf of the university, from his letter to the Rector upon completing his southern journey: "I can generally say that our university's aim to carry out pioneering work in the intellectual field was received with enthusiasm in each and every place. We were promised real and tangible support".[94]

The first attempt to hold studies based on the "people's university" model took place at Ashdod, but it was destined to failure after only a few lectures. The only reason for the failure of this attempt was defined as "religious" after the university management had been informed that Sabbath desecration activities were held at same location. Dr. Bar Ilan continued to search for a place in other cities including Beer Sheva, Ashkelon and Kiryat Gat. Beer Sheva was ranked high as a suitable location for an Extension due to its size and the fact that it is considered the "Capital of the Negev", and due to the relatively large number of faculty members living in its vicinity. In his letter, Dr. Bar Ilan stated the following:

> The only place in which these courses (academic courses) can be considered is Beer Sheva. The city is willing to give us every possible support and if we establish an Extension there it would be very willingly accepted. It should be noted that now and then courses in Physical Chemistry were offered by the Technion, and courses in Biology by the "Negev Research Institute". It is crucial that a final decision is reached in the near future so as to enable us to prepare a detailed plan for the first two years (Ibid).

Contrary to the plans made by Bar Ilan University, that year (1965) the government prepared a program towards establishing a university in Beer Sheva as part of its plans to develop the Negev region. The "Negev Research Institute" that had already operated in the city and other local operations by the Technion were used as the basis for the establishment of the planned university. These plans, of course, put an end to Dr. Bar Ilan's aspirations for an Extension in Beer Sheva. However, in Ashkelon he found a sympathetic ear and a willingness for generous support from the Mayor of Ashkelon at the time, Rehavia Adivi, including the allocation of a temporary location, the promise for the construction of a campus in future, allocation of personnel and an annual budget covering the university's special expenses. The Mayor's willingness to collaborate sealed the fate of the academy in Ashkelon, and in 1965 the university management voted for the first time in favor of the establishment of studies outside

---

94 Bar Ilan University Archive, container 1088, file 338. Dr. Bar Ilan's letter to the Rector, 9 June 1965.

the main campus – to be located Ashkelon. The support promised and the building allocated increased Dr. Bar Ilan's confidence in the venture and he recommended that the university's management skip the first stage and go on to establishing "university courses" at Ashkelon – the second stage. From Dr. Bar Ilan's letters to the university's CEO we can learn of the position of the Ashkelon municipality:

> I am pleased to enclosed herewith the letter of undertaking signed by Rehavia Adivi, Mayor of Ashkelon. As you will see, the sum of 3,000 Lira for the current year and 12,500 for the coming year, are considerable amounts. . . kindly write a letter of thanks to Mr. Adivi. In addition I am pleased to invite you to the graduation ceremony at Ashkelon. . . all the leading persons of the city will be present.[95]

In a further letter to the university's President, Dr. Bar Ilan wrote: "I am pleased to inform you that the Mayor of Ashkelon has increased the annual allowance for the current fiscal year to 2,500 Lira, and promised a sum of 25,000 Lira for the following fiscal year, as a sign of utmost appreciation and partnership".[96] Despite the fact that at this stage studies were eclectically held towards the accumulation of academic credits, this year can nevertheless be see as the first year of operation of the Ashkelon Extension, which later became the Ashkelon Regional College. This finding is opposed to reports by which the Ashkelon College was among the last to be opened, and that it was preceded by the Zefat and Jordan Valley Colleges. These reports did not distinguish between the establishment of an academic Extension and that of a college as a Post-Secondary education institution, such as the other Regional Colleges had been.[97]

While the aim of the other Extensions had been to offer vocational rather than academic studies, Bar Ilan's Extensions in Ashkelon and Zefat were established only for academic purposes and during their formative years did not offer other types of studies. A second significant distinction is that all other institutions, which later became Regional Colleges, were the initiative of Regional Councils led by Kibbuzim and Moshavim in the region, and their first and foremost aim was to provide vocational training to their members. The Extensions at Ashkelon and Zefat, founded as an initiative of Bar Ilan University, offered exclusively academic studies.

---

95 Ibid, container 747, file 247. Dr. Bar Ilan's letter to the Rector, 1 July, 1966.

96 Ibid, Letter from Dr. Bar Ilan to the President of the university, 12 February 1968.

97 See: Volansky, 2005: 133; Iram, 1996: 291–301. Even in Kirsch's (2010) comprehensive review the establishment of the colleges was not reviewed in a precise chronological manner.

Very soon, the success of the Ashkelon Extension became apparent: by its second year its number of students was 195, with 25 academic courses offered. Success was also expressed in the fact that the university appointed a committee to assess the studies at Ashkelon in order to grant it status of an Extension. In 1966, the committee recommended acknowledging the academic courses offered at Ashkelon as an Extension of the university, based on the good relations with the Ashkelon municipality and its promises for further investments, as well as on academic success, as can be seen from the committee's report:

> The committee declares with satisfaction that the courses held at Ashkelon for the past 2 years and three months have proven their worth. Teachers report commendable academic achievements that do not fall short of those of Ramat Gan, a strong motivation for progress and success and a high bar of studies. The committee recommends an expansion of the courses to the point of a full blown small college, with an independent campus and a real university atmosphere.[98]

Appointment of a Manager for the Extensions

The commencement of operations at Ashkelon in the framework of "university courses" forced the university management to appoint a person responsible on its behalf to oversee the operation. Eventually a Manager of the Extensions was appointed to managed the Extensions from his office at the university. The person selected for the role was Dr. Tuvia Bar Ilan, who had already contributed significantly to the implementation of the idea of Extensions at peripheral areas. This role was added to his other positions at the university. The position of Manager of the Extensions was not documented in writing in those years, and in practice included a number of tasks:

1. Identifying faculty members to take part in the university's mission in the periphery.
2. Preparing a curriculum suited to the needs of the Extension as well as to the university's policy.
3. Establishing relationships with the local authority and raising local funds for the Extension.
4. Advertising and marketing the studies offered at the Extensions and registering students at the university.

98 Bar Ilan University archive, Report of the committee reviewing university courses at Ashkelon, 19 December 1967.

Upgrading Available Options at Ashkelon

The university's initial initiative was met with enthusiasm at Ashkelon and the surrounding region. The number of students grew from one year to the next, as did the number of courses. In the first years six courses were offered; in the second year this number doubled and in the third year a total of 50 courses were offered. In its third year there were 200 students studying at the institution, a 75 % increase compared to the first year. Following the first trial year, the university's Board appointed, at Dr. Bar Ilan's recommendation, a committee to examine the level of courses offered at Ashkelon so as to consider moving on to the third stage of operation. The committee's composition points to the high importance allocated by the Board to promoting the idea of the Extensions. Committee members arriving at Ashkelon included the university Rector, its CEO, manager of external academic courses and members of the Board. When the first class had graduated, the committee prepared a list of recommendations for changing the status of academic studies offered at Ashkelon, as well as general rules for studies held outside the main campus. These rules served later on as threshold conditions for examining the opening of other Extensions in the 1960s: The committee recommended upgrading studies at Ashkelon to Extension level, and even: "An entire small college, with an independent campus and a real university atmosphere".[99] The curriculum was based on two full years at Ashkelon and a third year at the university campus.

1. The topics taught should express the needs of the region. These needs were assessed based on the size of the teaching population and public service personnel. In addition to the importance of these populations as public opinion agents, that specific period in time also dictated the need to promote the training of teachers and public service personnel for the following reasons:

Teachers in Israel – in the 1960s the demand for teachers in the country had grown substantially in line with the growing population and consequently the growing number of schools quickly built to address the needs of the education system. Many schools felt the shortage of graduates of teaching seminaries, and therefore the Ministry of Education began to certify teachers through alternative paths and accelerated "internal" procedures. These certified teachers were potential

99 Bar Ilan University Archive, container 747, file 247. Report of the committee reviewing university courses at Ashkelon, submitted to the Chairperson of the Board minister Haim-Moshe Shapira, on 1 January 1968. The report was signed by the members of the committee: Matityahu Adler, the CEO of the university; Alfonso Zabah, member of the Board; Mordechai Haim Stern, member of the Board; Tuvia Bar Ilan, Manager of the Extensions; and the Rector Prof. Avrom Saltman.

candidates for a teachers' training department. The purpose of such department would be to provide them with vocational training for the teaching profession.

Public service personnel – this sector too was targeted by the university for similar reasons, most of which was due to the growing population as well as specific demand for civil servants in peripheral regions. This position of the university's founders can be noted in protocols of Board meetings as well as letters sent by the Manager of the Extensions to the university's management. The following can be found in the protocol of the Board meeting held on 12 January 1967:

> Among our students is a substantial number of students of Sephardic descent. After completing their studies they will surely fill influential positions within their public, including public service positions and at the local authority [. . .] [It is important] to take note of this fact and attract young adults of Sephardic descent to study Political Science and Public Administration. To this end we must develop these departments to a high level.[100]

In a letter from the Manager of the Extensions to the university Rector dated 9 June 1965, Dr. Bar Ilan emphasized the importance of offering courses in the area of Public Administration: "I know that Mr. Hollander believes differently and also mentioned more than once that we must teach Public Administration at Development Towns in order to elevate the level of local officials".[101]

Other needs of the region were derived from the unique location of the intended Extension. At Zefat, the founders believed, there is a need for academic training in the area of Jewish Studies, due to the city's unique Jewish character. At Zemach located in the Jordan Valley, there was a high demand for Economics and Business Administration. The local demand resulted from the needs of the people of the area, and the university accommodated these needs. At Ashkelon demand arose among local government officials and bankers wishing to obtain academic training.

2. The committee recommended opening certificate courses granting a vocational diploma so as to create an academic incentive for local residents to study, in addition to the academic credits from academic courses.
3. The committee demanded that an "academic atmosphere in general, and a religious academic one in particular" be ensured. "The committee emphasizes that Bar Ilan University's unique character as a religious university must be protected at all costs, by setting clear and binding rules of conduct."[102]

---

100 Ibid, container 1088, file 338.

101 Ibid.

102 Ibid, first letter containing the committee's report, sent to the Chairperson of the Board minister Haim-Moshe Shapira, on 19 December 1967.

The university's Board discussed the committee's report on 21 February 1968 and accepted the recommendation to acknowledge "university courses" at Ashkelon as a university Extension. The decision followed a social discussion during which the social considerations at the foundation of the special operation of the Extensions were discussed. Dr. Burg praised the figures pointing to the relatively high number of students of Sephardic descent studying at the campus and discussed the ways in which this trend may be further enhanced at the Extensions.

The 1967/68 academic year was the first in which a pre-structured curriculum was offered, during the evenings throughout the week. Students were presented with a list of courses, and each students was requested to select courses to be taken during the school year. The list also included the number of hours of study and weekly hours of each course. Table 20 describes the first schedule of courses at the Ashkelon Extension, its scope and the topics offered during the academic year 1967/68:

Tab. 20: The first curriculum presented by Bar Ilan University in its first Extension

Field of study	Title of course	Weekly hours	Day	Hours
Jewish Studies: Bible	Book of Psalms	2	Sun.	19:00–21:00
	Ugaritic	1	Sun.	18:00–19:00
	Biblical grammar	1	Sun.	17:00–18:00
Talmud	Selected laws of the Halacha	2	Tues.	19:00–21:00
	Topics from the Sanhedrin tractate	2	Tues.	17:00–19:00
Jewish history	History of the Jews in Israel	2	Wed.	17:00–19:00
Languages & Literature	English – Preparatory course	4	Sun. Tues.	17:00–19:00 17:00–19:00
	Advanced preparatory course	2	Tues.	19:00–21:00
Hebrew Literature	Selected Chapters	2	Wed.	17:00–19:00
	Comparative Literature	2	Wed.	19:00–21:00
Social Sciences & Humanities: General History	Europe 1848–1918	2	Thurs.	17:00–19:00
	Europe 1918–1960	2	Thurs.	19:00–21:00
Psychology	Foundations of Psychology	2	Thurs.	19:00–21:00
	Introduction to Psychology Lab	3	Thurs.	19:00–22:00
	Introduction to Personality Psychology	1	Thurs.	16:00–17:00
Sociology	Introduction to Sociology	3	Mon.	17:00–20:00

Tab. 20: Continued

Field of study	Title of course	Weekly hours	Day	Hours
	Comparative Research of Institutions	1	Mon.	20:00–21:00
Economics	Introduction to Economics	3	Sun.	17:00–20:00
	Introduction to General Accounting	3	Sun.	17:00–21:00
	Price Theory	4	Sun. Wed.	17:00–19:00 17:00–19:00
Education	Theory of Education	2	Mon.	19:00–21:00
	Psychology of Education	2	Mon.	17:00–19:00
Natural Sciences and Mathematics	Introduction to Mathematics	3	Tues.	16:00–19:00
	Statistics	4	Tues. Thurs.	19:00–21:00 19:00–21:00

Data from the Ashkelon College Archive, file 1968. Registration form for the 1968 academic year.

The program was therefore proposed in a partial and eclectic manner, included different areas and offered night classes only. It did not include a proposal for regulated studies in a certain area, nor a full academic year. The method of presenting the courses was aimed at examining areas of interest instead of expanding its offering towards the establishment of a comprehensive program consisting of full academic years.

Steps Taken up North: 1965–1968

To complete the university's development plan, Dr. Bar Ilan searched the north of the country for a suitable location. Ashkelon's success story had reached the north and Dr. Bar Ilan's initial contact was with the municipal leaders of the city of Zefat. Discussions were held towards the possibility of offering university courses at the city. While he was examining options at Zefat, in 1968 the university management was contacted by the Jordan Valley Regional Council.

Jordan Valley Regional Council's Initiative

The initiative of the Jordan Valley Regional Council to open an Extension of a religious university in their area stemmed from two main reasons. The first was the decision of the Union of the Kibbutzim and of Groups to allow Kibbutz members, young and old, including graduates of "Nahal" groups, to attend academic studies. This decision followed many years of ideological opposition to academic studies at Kibbutzim (Cohen, 2001). In the first decades of the State of Israel, this opposition even led to Kibbutz high schools (excluding the religious Kibbutz movement) adopting a curriculum that does not include Bagrut matriculation exams, so as to prevent high school graduates from Kibbutzim to continue to academic studies that were perceived as threatening the Kibbutz' social structure, the fear being that such studies may push young adults to abandon the Kibbutz.

The decision to allow Kibbutz members to obtain a high school diploma and even continue to Post-Secondary education laid the foundation for the establishment of four Kibbutz Movement colleges: At the Jordan Valley – the "Zemach" Post-Secondary school; at Tel Chai – the Tel-Hai College established under the academic auspices of Tel Aviv University (and as of the mid 1970s – of University of Haifa); At kibbutz Mizra – "Ohel Sara" under the auspices of University of Haifa from the start; and at the Menashe region – the Hadera-Menashe College, under the academic auspices of Tel Aviv University.[103]

The second reason was the competition between the Kibbutzim and peripheral towns and cities of the same region. Each wanted to open an academic institution within its vicinity. The long standing social rift between the Kibbutzim and the cities of the periphery in the 1960s only increased their competition over each academic institution in Israel. After Tel Aviv University gave its auspices to Tel-Chai College, the race was on and the management of the Jordan Valley School of Post-Secondary education urged the heads of the Regional Council to take advantage of Bar Ilan University's initiative to establish an Extension in the north, and negotiate with the university towards the establishment of such an Extension at the Jordan Valley. Thus, in this case the university was approached by the locals, and not vice versa. The university's management did not remain indifferent to their initiative, seeing it as an opportunity for spreading *Torah* and science, in line with its religious-social ideology. In a surprising and unplanned turn of events, the Kibbutzim of the Jordan Valley region found themselves in the arms of a religious university, a fact that they were willing to overlook, just so as not to lag behind Tel-Chai College. The competition between the Kibbutzim and the cities of the Galilee, and other unexpected moves, at least on the part of the founders, led, of all places, to Bar Ilan University's religious and social initiative settling at the Jordan Valley Regional Council, which was comprised of the Kibbutzim of the

---

103 The 1990 State Comptroller and ombudsman's report, a review of institutions of Higher Education, University of Haifa, auspices of academic programs at Regional Colleges: 259–271.

valley, and whose members were very far from the spiritual and social world view of the university's founders.

During those years, the university's management ascribed great importance to its dissemination among diverse population sectors, and therefore responded positively to the approach by the Jordan Valley Regional Council, even though it did not initially plan to operate in that region. In retrospect, the relationship also gained a social justification and not only a religious one when the university's management identified the potential of enrolling students from Tiberias and Beit She'an, cities whose population was predominantly Sephardic, as well as members of the religious Kibbutzim of the Beit She'an Valley Regional Council. The secular Kibbutz members were not a target of the university in the first place, but the emerging relationship with them corresponded with the university's religious aspiration to distribute *Torah* and science in an academic manner. in this regard we can see similarities between Bar Ilan University's aspirations at the Jordan Valley and the Protestant academies of the United States. In both cases great importance was attributed to a rational discourse on issues of religion and bible, in addition to the importance of accessibility to disadvantaged populations, such as at Development towns.

For local residents, the strange connection between the Kibbutzim and Bar Ilan University ignited diverse responses, as can be seen from a number of articles published in "Haaretz" newspaper as of the beginning of the 1970s. In one of them, entitled: "Service rather than mission", the writer, Atalla Manzur (23 March, 1975), presents two different opinions: The first is the university's penetration as a mission – its goal being to disseminate *Torah* among the secular Kibbutzim population. Proponents of this position were surprised to see religious-Zionist operations at the place of burial of the founders of the Labor Movement at Kibbutz Kinneret of all places. The other position was represented by Yona Rosen, deputy Chairperson of the council. He did not view the university's work as missionary, but rather as a social step taken by the university's management, contrary to other universities that tended to hide in their academic ivory towers and are unaware of the needs of the periphery: "The people of Bar Ilan, contrary to the common practice at other academic institutions in Israel, have not enclosed themselves in an ivory tower. They feel that the existence of the university's Extensions at Ashkelon, Zefat, Afula and the Jordan Valley is a matter of calling".

Deputy Chairperson of the Local Council and College Coordinator Menachem Daniv listed the advantages of the relationship with Bar Ilan. According to him, the university's faculty members were in no way missionary and lessons in Jewish Studies were all conducted on an academic level, with no involvement of the theological aspect of the subject matter. It is important to note that the university's entry to the Jordan Valley Regional Council was made possible following an abatement in the secular rebellion of the region's Kibbutzim. In this context Daniv noted that as early as the 1970s magnificent synagogues were built in a number of Kibbutzim including his own Kibbutz Maagan, and that about half of the members of his Kibbutz fasted on Yom Kippur (Day of Atonement).[104]

Even though the original initiative had been of locals, the operation of the academic program was partially funded by the university, in contrast to Tel Aviv University that provided the Tel Chai College with academic auspices in return for full payment. The level of appreciation of the management of the local college towards their relationship with Bar Ilan can be seen from one of Daniv's letters to the CEO of the university: "I wish to take this opportunity to again reiterate our gratitude and appreciation to the university for its admirable work and extensive support to the development of university studies at the Regional College of the Jordan Valley".[105]

Initial Steps at the Jordan Valley

Following a short round of negotiations in mid 1968 between the university's president and the head of the Jordan Valley Regional Council and after the signing of an agreement between the parties, the university's first "university courses" at the north were opened at the Regional Council's Post-Secondary Education School. The initial format of the courses at the Jordan Valley was similar to that of Ashkelon, and here too there was no need for the trial "People's University" stage, as the local authority had promised financial and physical support. However, the agreement with the Jordan Valley Regional Council differed from the agreement with Ashkelon, for a number of reasons: At Ashkelon the university initiated, founded and operated the new institution, and therefore a contractual agreement was not required. However, at the Jordan Valley the university supplied, pursuant to local demand, courses for an existing institution. Thus, vocational courses were held alongside the academic ones. Courses were managed by the local management of the Jordan Valley institution, rather than by the university – as was the case at the Ashkelon Extension. The university management sent teachers and supervised the teaching level, but at this stage did not perceive the institution as

---

104 For more information on the collision between different values at the Kibbutzim see: Brandeis, 2007.

105 Bar Ilan University Archive, container 753, file 285. Letter from Daniv to Matityahu Adler, the university's CEO, 2 April 1971.

an integral part of the university according to the multi-campus approach, and therefore the Board's approval of university courses at the Jordan Valley was not required, while it had been required at Ashkelon.[106]

Upgrading the Status of the Jordan Valley Institution to an Extension

In retrospect, the development of the Jordan Valley operations were stipulated upon an enhanced involvement of the peripheral population of the area: The cities of Tiberias and Beit She'an, and the religious Kibbutzim. Towards the Senate meeting held on 4 January 1970, Dr. Bar Ilan prepared a review of the topic, including a request for recognizing university courses at the Jordan Valley as an Extension. Contrary to the case of Ashkelon, he requested that the status of the Jordan Valley institution be upgraded only after two years (in 1972). Based on the data presented, the scope of activities at the Jordan Valley at the time was small, and consisted of courses offered in four Departments: Psychology, Education, Literature and History. As the courses were purchased from the university, there was no need to report the number of students, and therefore there is no available data as to the extent of demand during the first years. However, the Manager of the Extensions was satisfied that the courses are attracting local students, and that most of them are full. In his report he emphasized the potential of the religious Kibbutzim of the areas, as well as that of Tiberias and Beit She'an. In his recommendations he stipulated the fulfillment of the full potential of these areas in an upgrading of the status of the Extension, and to this end he proposed granting it the status of Extension only in 1972, following an assessment of the ability to implement such potential. His fundamental request to upgrade academic activities at the Jordan Valley to Extension status was accepted, but its effectiveness was to be approved subject to increasing the number of students from the target populations defined by the university's management for Extensions, meaning residents of peripheral areas and the religious population of the region. Four months following the Senate hearing, Dr. Bar Ilan reported the following to the Rector: "I am presently pressuring the people of the region to expand the activities in a way that would serve the Beit She'an Valley, the city of Beit She'an and the city of Tiberias [. . .] It should be added that also the (number

106 Jordan Valley College Archive, Bar Ilan University file. The agreement between Bar Ilan University and Jordan Valley Regional Council Post-Secondary Education School, 12 August, 1968.

of) religious students from the Kibbutzim of the Beit She'an Valley is constantly on the rise every year".[107]

In a report towards the implementation of the decision to upgrade activities, Dr. Bar Ilan noted the following regarding the developments and fulfillment of the university's social and religious aims:

> Only three years ago we began recognizing university courses offered by our faculty members at the college. We started with about 10 registered students. A year ago this number increased to 30, and this year to 127. It should be noted that a significant number of students come from the Beit She'an Valley (34) and from the cities of Beit She'an and Tiberias (37). It appears that this too is a significant turn in the right direction.[108]

Beyond his own efforts, Dr. Bar Ilan attributed this success to two changes that occurred at the time: The Ministry of Education decided to fund most of teachers' expenses towards academic studies; and the Union of the Kibbutzim and of Groups decided to support Kibbutz members wishing to attend academic studies, contrary to the previous ideology of the Kibbutz movement.

In practice, and as will be further explained below, the decision to grant the status of Extension to the academic activities at the Jordan Valley in 1972 was reached mainly in response to the university's struggle against the amendment to the CHE Law accepted that year, prohibiting the opening of Extensions. According to the provisions of the amendment to the law, the prohibition applies in retrospect to Extensions or existing extra-university activities. Following extensive pressures by the university's management, a transitory provision was added, by which the university, as the main party impacted by the retroactive application of the amendment, would issue a request for post factum approval of existing Extensions. The university, that had planned to use its Extensions to develop into a multi-campus structure, was left with no other alternative but to upgrade its existing centers of operation in order to be able to apply the provisions of the amendment to them. As the amendment initiated by the CHE in 1972 did not permit the opening of new Extensions, the university defined the academic activities taking place at the Jordan Valley as an Extension, although in practice it differed from the Extensions at Ashkelon and Zefat, as shall be explained in the Chapter discussing legislative amendments.

---

107 Bar Ilan University Archive, container 753, file 285. Dr. Bar Ilan's letter to the Rector, 6 April 1970.

108 Ibid, Extensions Status Report for 1972, 6 November 1972.

Onset of Academic Activities at Zefat

The task of identifying a suitable location for an Extension at the northern region focused from the start on Zefat due to its high status among the religious public, many of whom were Mizrachim. The initiative came from the university, but it immediately became mutual. The university's representatives – Tuvia Bar Ilan and its CEO Matityahu Adler met with the Mayor of Zefat in the beginning of 1968, after the latter had expressed his enthusiasm towards the possibility of holding academic studies at the city, and offered financial support. Dr. Bar Ilan's letter to the acting Rector Prof. Yehoshua Shechter, points to the competition that existed between towns in the area which all wanted to collaborate with the university. Having apologized for the premature publications by the city's leaders, Dr. Bar Ilan noted that: "It seems that the enthusiasm of local leadership and the information they had read on Ashkelon's catalogue were enough so as to release certain news items to the local media, through which the information reached editors of newspapers in Tel Aviv and Jerusalem [. . .] I do hope that the matter of Zefat will be discussed at the upcoming Senate meeting."[109]

The Board discussion on the request made by the municipality of Zefat was held on 26 September 1968. According to the meeting protocol, the decision to open courses in Zefat, as in Ashkelon, was based mostly on religious and social considerations. The collaboration of the Zefat Municipality and its financial support encouraged the Senate to approve "university courses" at Zefat, skipping over the required trial stage. Prof. Shechter informed Dr. Bar Ilan of the Senate's decision, which included the following rules of operation:

a. The format of studies would be identical to the one at Ashkelon
b. The administrative and organizational rules will be identical to those set at Ashkelon, and not to those at Zemach
c. The activity at Zefat will be supervised by the same Academic Council appointed at Ashkelon

Towards the end of his letter Prof. Shechter emphasized the nature of the Zefat initiative: "I greatly admire your work for the dissemination of knowledge by the university at the most remote corners of the land and I wish you success and satisfaction".[110]

109 Ibid, container 747, file 247. Dr. Bar Ilan's letter to the Rector, 21 June 1968.
110 Ibid, container 1088, file 338. Letter from the acting Rector Prof. Yehoshua Shechter to Dr. Tuvia Bar Ilan, 24 July 1968.

On 23 October 1968 the first courses were opened in a festive ceremony participated by the Mayor and the city's eminent persons, as well as university leaders.

The Ashkelon and Zefat Extensions were operated directly by the university through the work of Tuvia Bar Ilan. These Extensions were added to the university's development plan and became an integral part of it. In the two locations plans were made for raising further funds through friends associations. The purpose of the associations was to further develop the university's remote campuses in Israel. The aim of their first manager, as had been often expressed at the Senate, was that the Ashkelon and Zefat campuses would serve as the university's location for special summer activities, including professional courses, not necessarily academic; academic summer courses to enable students to complete their credits also during the summer; a place for young Jewish people visiting Israel to study; and advanced learning for teachers.[111]

Upgrading the Status of the Zefat Institution to an Extension

From its onset, a wide range of courses were offered at Zefat. The university's founders' preference for Zefat and the support provided by the municipality encouraged the university to offer courses in diverse areas including Bible, Education, Psychology and Political Science. The short distance between Zefat and the Jordan Valley contributed to the logistic efficiency of operating the two centers. Teachers were taken by organized shuttle from Bar Ilan, a fact that required coordinating the days and times of courses as well as the schedules of teachers who taught courses in both Extensions.

In a report prepared by Dr. Bar Ilan towards a Senate hearing he reviewed the activities taking place at Zefat, the high demand for courses and the high potential of students at the center. He directed management's attention to two main populations: employees of local authorities and teachers. In another review submitted by Dr. Bar Ilan to the Rector, he noted his apprehension at the ongoing competition with the Kiryat Shmona municipality and with Tel Chai, which had jointly applied to Tel Aviv University in a request to open academic courses at Tel Chai, in addition to the small number of courses already offered there. In an attempt to win the race and realize the religious and social potential at Zefat and its surrounding area, Dr. Bar Ilan recommended granting Zefat the status of an Extension which would offer a full curriculum for the first two of the three undergraduate years. In this way he hoped to overcome all competitors. In a statement

111 Ibid, from a report submitted by Dr. Bar Ilan to the Senate on 4 January 1970.

prepared towards the senate hearing of 4 January 1970 on the status of the Zefat Extension he recommended granting Zefat the status of Extension as early as 1971, about two years into the inauguration of university courses there. During the hearing Dr. Bar Ilan recommended that the Jordan Valley center be granted Extension status a year after Zefat, even though courses there commenced only a few months before they had in Zefat. This points to a preference of Zefat over the Jordan Valley, for the following reasons: The Jordan Valley center was not considered an Extension from the onset, as it was the result of a local initiative which, as explained above, integrated well with the idea of Extensions, but in retrospect.

A reinforcement of this approach can be found in a letter from the Rector of the university to the Ministry of Education on 24 January 1971 – about a year following the recognition of Zefat as an Extension of the university. In his letter the Rector outlined the university's plan to become a national, multi-campus academic institution.[112] The first university campus to take part in this plan is the Zefat campus. In practice the establishment of a university campus was the fourth stage in the development of an educational institution. This stage, at least from a planning perspective, was achieved only by the Zefat Extension. The amendment to the law and the Jortner Committee's recommendations led to a material transformation in the university's plans, as shall be described in the following chapters.

The Uniqueness of Each Extension in the Eyes of its Founders

In the first stage of their establishment, the university's leaders attempted to determine a unique aim for each Extension, which integrated in Bar Ilan University's fundamental religious and social aims. A review of the protocols of the university's Board meetings of the 1960s shows that each Extension had been allocated an unofficial designation:

A. **The Zefat Extension** – as already mentioned, the location of the Extension was influenced from Zefat's religious and spiritual image among the religious population and the fact that it was populated mostly by Jewish new immigrants from Arab countries. However, its uniqueness in the overall project of the Extensions was a result of its being a Kabbalistic center. Bar Ilan's management hoped that the northern Extension would attract young Jews from abroad seeking an atmosphere of holiness and Jewish mysticism, a fact

112 Ibid, container 474, file 247. According to the letter, the Rector's proposal included full undergraduate studies at Zefat.

that would also be suited for summer studies and workshops for the entire teaching faculty of the university during the summer months.[113]

B. **The Ahskelon Extension** – located within a predominantly Sephardi and Yemenite neighborhood, the Ashkelon Extension was designated to serve as the founders' spearhead in their mission to reduce social gaps in higher education.[114]

C. **The Jordan Valley Extension** – as explained earlier, the establishment of the Extension at the Jordan Valley was not a result of an initiative by the university's management, but when the academic activities at Zemach were proven successful and the place had been recognized as an Extension, two aims were defined for it in retrospect, suited to the specific activities taking place at the Extension and well integrated in the ideology of the university's religious leadership: First – the Extension's proximity to the region's Development towns – Tiberias and Beit Shean, and to the religious Kibbutzim (originating in the "Hapoel HaMizrachi" movement), was suited to Bar Ilan's social aims; and second – its geographic location in the center of secular Zionism provided an opportunity to train the workers of the country's non-religious agricultural sector. This offered the university management a sense of belonging and participation in building the holy land.[115] The basis of the religious-Zionist mission was the aim to form a bridge between 'the new Israelism' and the Jewish religion, as did the Protestant academies in the United States.

---

113 As can be seen from reports presented by Bar Ilan University representatives appearing before the Jortner Committee.

114 Bar Ilan University Archive, container 1088, file 338. Protocol of the Board meeting held on 8 August 1973. In Dr. Tuvia Bar Ilan's presentation to the members of the Board he identifies Ashkelon as an Extension whose majority of students are Sephardic Jews and therefore he assumes that the funding for the campus will come either from affluent Sephardic Jews in the Diaspora or from Jewish communities for whom the social issue is central, such as the South African Jewish community. In Dr. Bar Ilan's letter to the Secretary of the Jewish Federation of South Africa on 25 March 1968 he notes that the Ashkelon Extension promotes the city's population, most of whom are immigrants from North Africa, and that therefore a third of the students at the Extension come from North African descent. Moreover, he proudly pointed to the Extension's social mission: We are instrumental in creating a homogeneous and intellectual nation. Ashkelon College Archive, file 1968.

115 Bar Ilan University Archive, container 474, file 247. A periodical review by Dr. Bar Ilan to the members of the university Board, 1972.

A Local Perspective

From the viewpoint of the mayors of the municipalities in which Extensions were established, the partnership with Bar Ilan provided a unique opportunity to present the local education system as one that offers education from preschool to university.[116] The relationships established between the managers of the Ashkelon and Zefat Extensions and their respective mayors were influenced by a mutual enthusiasm that was part of the spirit of pioneering vision characteristic of the first years of the State. This enthusiasm for the university's integration in their vicinity pushed away the need to delve into an understanding of the goals of the university's management and their plans. In fact, official agreements between the university and the municipalities of Ashkelon and Zefat were only signed in the mid 1980s. Until then the work was based on complete trust between the parties and letter correspondences.[117] The opening of the Zefat Extension was accepted on an ideological basis without a clear undertaking by the municipality, as can also be seen from the Board's decision and the summation made by the Chairperson of the Board, Minister Shapira: "Interested in strengthening the spiritual aspect at Zefat".[118]

The above points to the parties' willingness to "do" the work, with less emphasis given to formal-bureaucratic contractual aspects. Despite the enthusiasm of the respective mayors and their willingness to support the Extension in any way they can, the actual management of the institution was exclusively in the hands of the university, and it did not share its academic plans with the local leaders. Municipality officials were not aware of the role and designation allocated to each Extension in the university's master plan.[119] They were guided by the social-cultural effect of an academic institution in the periphery, having clear advantages for a number of reasons:

---

116 From interviews with Moshe Yanai, Vice President of Education at the Ashkelon Municipality as of the mid 1970's until today. As part of his job, Yanai was responsible for the relationship with Bar Ilan University on all matters pertaining to the Ashkelon Extension.

117 The letters were presented as part of a description of the university's success at Ashkelon. These letters point to the special relationship between the Mayor and the Manager of the Extensions, a relationship based on complete mutual trust. This can be noted from the Manager of the Extensions's letter to the Rector on 12 February 1968, as well as from the report of the committee examining the courses offered at Ashkelon, 19 December 1967.

118 Bar Ilan University Archive, container 1088, file 338. Protocol of the Board meeting held on 26 September 1968.

119 By the mid 1970's The university's unilateral management led to local repercussions, with local enthusiasm being replaced by new aspirations that contrasted with those of the university's management, as shall be explained later in this chapter.

a. The presence of an Extension in the city would result in a growth in the city's population through local and foreign immigration. In a letter from the Mayor of Ashkelon Aharon Haiby to the Rector of the university he described this aspect of the Extension's contribution to the city: "The contribution of the Bar Ilan Extension is not limited to the acquisition of education, but can be evaluated on the basis of its important role in preparing an academic reserve of local residents who continue to hold close ties to their region rather than abandoning it, and influenced the development of the population, especially in the field of education".[120]
b. The presence of an Extension in the city would provide training for a local teaching force, thereby increasing the likelihood of success of local children in the primary and secondary education systems. A high level of education would attract an educated population to the city.
c. An academic Extension would contribute to commercial and economic growth thanks to the arrival to the city of students from the entire region. For generations local mayors have seen the presence of an academic institution in their municipalities as an important stage in the level of services offered to local residents (Rosen and Razin, 2004: 20, 48–49).
d. In the eyes of the city's leaders, the success of an academic Extension would evolve the existing institution, ultimately leading to the establishment of a university or at least another institution of higher education in the city.[121]

The Jortner Committee Report sheds light on the social aspect that interested the municipal leaders at the Galilee region in general and those of the city of Zefat in particular. Committee hearings were attended by the Mayors of Zefat and Tiberias, the heads of the Ma'ale HaGalil and Upper Galilee Regional Councils, and representatives of the Tel Chai and Jordan Valley colleges. They noted the importance of the social and public perception of an academic institution in the Galilee:

a. Overly social aspect: solving the higher education problem of underprivileged local residents
b. Improving the cultural level of local residents
c. Providing training and academic education to local teachers
d. Preventing human capital flight from the region

120 Ashkelon College Archive, file 1974. Letter from the Mayor to the Rector, 26 December, 1974.

121 Ashkelon College Archive, file 1974. Letter from the Mayor to the Rector, 26 December, 1974. The Mayor believed that the Extension would form the basis for the establishment of a daughter-university that would serve the entire region.

e. Attracting intellectuals and academic teaching faculty from other areas in Israel and abroad to these regions
f. Increasing the overall number of residents of the Galilee.[122]

The reasoning presented by the municipal leaders of Zefat pointed to their high level of agreement with the university management and left no doubt as to their intent to establish an Extension in their city. They praised the social considerations while not failing to also attend to the religious ones:

a. As did Bar Ilan's representatives, the Mayor of Zefat emphasized the natural and historical attributes of the city as a Kabbalistic center – attributes which offer the city an advantage in the development of a campus that would offer academic studies as well as a spiritual center, in line with the plan devised by Bar Ilan University.
b. The Mayor reinforced the university's plan to utilize the city's religious uniqueness in Judaism in order to attract young Jewish people around the world to come to Zefat to study academic courses and Kabbalah. The Mayor informed the committee members that he will immediately provide a building to be used for studies and student dormitories at a low cost.[123]

Despite the financial difficulties encountered by the Zefat municipality in the 1960s, the Mayor acceded to the university's proposal and promised partial participation in the institution's financial expenses. In parallel, attempts were made to establish a Friends Association that would raise donations towards the further development of the Extension.

The municipal leaders in the country's southern region viewed the idea of Extensions in much the same way. In the 1960s the Mayor of Ashkelon was the first to warmly receive Dr. Bar Ilan, the university's emissary, and even undertook to fund some of the university's expenses, in addition to the administrative support given.[124] By the beginning of the 1970s, the enthusiasm of Ashkelon's municipal leaders led to their decision to allocate a site for the construction of a new campus, and that year a process commenced towards raising the funds required for construction. In total the cities of Zefat and Ashkelon promised a budget of 45,000

122 CHE Archive, Bar Ilan University file. The Jortner Committee Report, p. 14.

123 Ibid. The Mayor of Zefat, his deputy and the manager of the municipality's Department of Education appeared before the Committee, stating their conviction that Zefat is suitable for housing an academic institution, and emphasizing that they intend to allocate accommodations for students from Israel and abroad, as well as classrooms. The Zefat college still houses the same buildings today.

124 Bar Ilan University Archive, container 747, file 247. Letter from Dr. Bar Ilan to the university's President Dr. H.J Lookstein, 12 February, 1968.

Lira, from a total expenditure of 312,000 Lira in 1970 – 14.4 % of the university's total expenditure for the operation of its Extensions.[125] during the 1990s, municipal leaders had a number of reasons to accept the Extensions with open arms:

A. Bar Ilan University was the only university to establish Extensions at distant peripheral areas of its own initiative and under its administrative responsibility. At Ashkelon and Zefat the intent had been to establish Extensions that would form an integral part of the university, and it assumed full academic and financial responsibility over their operation. Until the end of the 1980s the university did not receive any PBC budgets for its students at the Extensions. According to the PBC's position, eclectic studies do no justify budgeting for students at the Extensions and therefore they were not included in the number of students that granted the university access to PBC budgets. Moreover, the university's demand for a special budget for the operation of the Extensions was also declined. Nevertheless, the university continued with these operations for ideological reasons. While it did receive funding for students from the Extensions when they arrived at the main campus to complete their studies, this fact did not influence the university's decision to continue operating the Extensions. Practically, the PBC was unable to prevent the budgeting of students coming from Extensions to continue their studies at the main campus, as these students were included in the list of university students budgeted according to a F.T.E (Full Time Equivalent) index.[126]
B. The local authority was invited to financially support the Extension not as a partner in its operation, but as an encouraging and supporting bystander.
C. Contrary to the university, who viewed the Extensions as an integral part of itself, the locals saw the Extension as a promise for the future development of an independent academic institution, with the establishment of universities in Tel Aviv, Beer Sheva and Haifa being a source of inspiration as of the early 1970s. This local position can be noted from a letter written by the Deputy Manager of the Extensions in 1974: "Based on Mr. Haiby's own words I understand he sees our Extension as no more than a transitional stage".[127]

The university's management was aware of this situation and therefore kept the management of the Extension in its own hands. This can be noted from a

125 Ibid. Dr. Bar-Ilan's review on the Extensions in his letter to the Rector Prof. Harel-Fish, 27 March, 1970.

126 Full time tuition format based on which the institution is eligible for PBC funding.

127 Ibid, container 753, file 285. Letter from the Deputy Manager of the Extensions Dr. David Koliv to the Rector of the university on 4 April, 1974.

discussion at the university's Board in August 1973. The Manager of the Extensions presented this collision between approaches as a crucial problem:

> If we allow the Ashkelon Municipality to take upon itself the entire funding of the building and make do with merely providing academic auspices, we may eventually find ourselves in a situation in which the municipality demands us, under pressure from non-religious parties, to remove our auspices from the Extension so as to transform it into a municipal university. However, if we take an active part in funding the construction of the building, it [the building] will be registered under our name.[128]

These thoughts describe a latent struggle between the local municipal leaders and the founders of the Extensions at the university, which can be characterized as a center-periphery dichotomy as defined by Lissak and Horowitz (1990). The opening of the Extensions by the university, in the absence of any active local partnership or operational responsibility, positioned the university as the exclusive patrons of the Extension. This patronage is characteristic of the center's approach towards the periphery. According to Lissak and Horowitz, the center is perceived by the periphery as possessing institutional and modal meaning. It represents, interprets and refines values and rules of conduct ascribed formal and informal legitimacy by its recipients, who therefore remain loyal to the center and its authority. However, despite this loyalty, the periphery is alienated from the center and unable to penetrate it though it constantly yearns to take part in the center's activities and gain a place within it. Moreover, societal changes may lead to a decline in the periphery's willingness to accede to the demands of the center and the wish to become closer to it.

Until the mid-1970s the university was perceived by locals as an academic center and its actions were legitimized without intervention. The university, on its part, dictated the topics of lecturers given at the Extension, the courses taught, their scope which was determined based on the supply of courses offered at the campus, and the level of teachers, and all this only after the requirements of the main campus had been met. The locals had no part in the development of the character of the Extension nor in its academic path. Social changes that followed the ethnic struggle of the 1970s as well as the Yom Kippur War, led to the onset of a transitional era in terms of perceptions in the periphery, and a growing aspiration to take part in decision making. Among municipal leaders, Extensions were increasingly seen as an initial stage towards the establishment of an independent academic institution, which is the reason for their willingness to give the Extension as much as they could. This covert struggle, like others between center and periphery, was reaffirmed following Israel's political upheaval of 1977 which allocated increased accessibility to the central government and allowed municipal leaders a different

128 Ibid, container 1088, file 338. Protocol of the Board meeting held on 8 August, 1973.

view of their relationship with the center. Rather than patronage, this relationship was now diverted to taking part in political power struggles aimed at promoting their localities in different areas, including higher education.

This struggle accumulated further social implications through the influence of modernization on the emerging Israeli society, as can be explained by the Industrialization or Modernization theories and Collins' Credential Society theory. According to the Industrialization theory, an industrialized society prefers skilled people, who have acquired an education suited to advanced industry. Proponents of the Credential Society theory among Israeli researchers believe that Israel has been a credential society since the 1960s and that this fact did not skip the country's geographical periphery, whose leaders noted the need to give preference to education and training in their regions so as to promote the skills and capabilities of their residents. The sense among peripheral municipal leaders was that local higher education is an essential means for reducing gaps between them and the center, and that only through such means would members of the periphery be able to achieve public and economic positions of power and penetrate the structures of central government.

Central Bureau of Statistics 1950–1970 data point to gaps in higher education between the country's center and its north and south regions, as described in Table 12, and between Jews of Ashkenazi descent and those born in Israel and Mizrachim, as described in Table 21.

Tab. 21: Jewish University Students, by ethnicity and degree, 1965/66–1974/75

	1965/66	1970/71	1974/75
Total:			
Ashkenazim	78.4	76.4	67.7
Mizrachim	11.9	13.7	14.7
Born in Israel	6.6	7.0	6.7
Undergraduate degree			
Ashkenazim	79.2	75.8	67.9
Mizrachim	**12.6**	**14.9**	**16.6**
Born in Israel	7.0	7.3	7.2
Graduate degree			
Ashkenazim	72.3	78.8	72.1
Mizrachim	**8.2**	**10.0**	**9.8**
Born in Israel	5.1	6.5	5.6
PhD			
Ashkenazim	81.0	77.9	60.8
Mizrachim	**6.4**	**7.6**	**6.7**
Born in Israel	4.0	5.4	3.2

In: Svirski & Svisrki, 1997: 18. Remarks: "Asheknazim" and "Mizrachim" – born abroad and born in Israel whose father was born abroad; "Born in Israel" – born in Israel whose father was born in Israel.

The Mayors of Ashkelon and Zefat viewed Bar-Ilan's initiative not only as an opportunity to reduce social gaps in education, but also as a good opportunity to promote their regions, and therefore agreed to all of the university's terms, despite their financial situation.

The reasons behind the decisions of the municipal leaders at the Jordan Valley were different, mostly due to the different approaches of the Kibbutzim to higher education during the State's formative years. The pioneering approach, that had defined agricultural work and manufacturing as a topmost value, still influenced Kibbutzim in the mid 1960s, a time in which higher education was still perceived as opposed to their pioneering values. The positions of the leaders of the Jordan Valley Kibbutzim towards the university's initiative can be divided into two stages:

In the first stage, the university's integration at the Zemach Post-Secondary Education School was perceived as a way to professionally upgrade the school, whose main aim had been to provide professional training to members of Kibbutzim within the municipal jurisdiction of the local council, in areas of agriculture and agricultural industry. However, this aim changed after a short while following changes in approaches within the Kibbutz movement towards higher education in the beginning of the 1970s. The second stage began with this change in approaches towards higher education in general. No more alienation towards higher education and a complete focus on the settlement of the land, as had been the case in the pre-State era and the first decades of the State, but a growing need for encouraging higher education as a means for personal, social and even ideological advancement. These goals sanctified the means, even if the means consisted of a religious university that viewed the dissemination of Jewish doctrine as its topmost goal.

This newfound attraction among members of Kibbutzim towards higher education and professional training can be noted in Central Bureau of Statistics data presented in the Jortner Committee's Report (1971): The number of students of higher education among residents of the north was relatively small: 1.1 % of the total population of the area. Comparatively, the proportion of students in the entire country that year was 1.7 % of the population. Of 1,099 students residents of the north studying at universities throughout the country that year, 429 (39 %) were members of the Kibbutzim of the northern district.[129]

129 CHE archive, Bar Ilan University Extensions file. The Jortner Committee Report, 1971.

Chapter 5 The Council for Higher Education's Struggle against the Multi-Campus University Model

The plan to establish a multi-campus university in Israel in the beginning of the 1970s was blocked from two directions: The Jortner Committee (1971) rejected the university's request to establish a university campus at Zefat; and the 1972 amendment to the CHE Law prohibited the establishment of centers outside the main campus without the CHE's approval. In the following sections I discuss the far reaching implications of each of these two directions.

The Jortner Committee Recommendations

The committee was established following Bar Ilan University's plan to establish a university campus in Zefat, but in its list of aims the committee stated that it intends: "To examine the need for a university institution in the Galilee; what is the forecasted demand for such an institution; what is the likelihood for recruiting permanent faculty members; what would be its nature and its uniqueness".[130]

The composition of committee members represented, to a certain extent, the senior actors operating in Israel's academic field: The Chairperson of the Committee – Prof. Jortner – a senior faculty member at Tel Aviv University, who started his career at the Hebrew University; Dr. Avidor – CEO of the Ministry of Education during Ben-Zion Dinur's term in office, and at the time of the committee's work manager of the Israeli Academy of Sciences; Prof Fuchs – head of the Hebrew University's School of Education; and Prof Asher Peres – from the Technion. Another member, Arnon Gafni, represented the Ministry of Finance; and a further member was the representative of the Kibbutz Ha'Meuchad movement – S. Derech. Only Dr. Yigal Shaki, Deputy to Minister of Education Yigal Alon, was closer in his world view to Bar Ilan University's religious-social positions. From the balance of powers in the committee it was clear that Bar Ilan University, representing a subversive strategy in the field, is perceived as a threat and as striving for paradigmatic change. The committee examined the available data from the Galilee and the positions of the local leadership. The data was presented to the committee by representatives of the CHE, of the institutions

130 CHE archive, Bar Ilan University Extensions file. The Jortner Committee Report, 1971.

that operated in the Galilee in the beginning of the 1970s and of the Ministry of Finance. In addition, the committee summoned representatives of all relevant parties active in the field of education at the Galilee: Managers of institutions of Post-Secondary education; the Mayors of Zefat and Tiberias; heads of local municipalities in the region; and representatives of Bar Ilan University, that had already been active for three years in the Galilee through its Extensions at Zefat and the Jordan Valley. Following three months of work the committee submitted its conclusions and recommendations to the Minister of Education. Below I discuss those conclusions and recommendations that are relevant to the work done by Bar Ilan University in the region:

1. "The committee believes that any new university must have the option to develop into an independent institution which is not part of another university".[131] In this conclusion the committee rejected any possibility of linking between the new institution at the Galilee and Bar Ilan University.
2. "The committee believes, that no university in the Galilee or elsewhere in the country should be established on the basis of bringing students from abroad" (ibid). This conclusion stood in clear opposition to the approach presented by Bar Ilan's representatives, who aimed for the Zefat Extension to rely on Jewish students from abroad.
3. "The success of a university depends first and foremost on the level of its teachers. The young universities encounter extensive difficulties in obtaining good teachers in general, and ones willing to settle in the area in particular" (ibid). This conclusion too was detrimental to Bar Ilan University, whose representatives notified the committee that they are able to secure a fixed and permanent faculty for the institution that would operate as a university campus.
4. "The committee believes that a university institution in the Galilee, if founded, must at first be managed under the auspices of a number of recognized academic institutions" (ibid).

In its recommendations section, the committee made the following recommendations:

1. "The committee recommends the establishment of an academic institution in Zefat".
2. "The institution will commence operating in 1973, after the Council for Higher Education institutes academic auspices for this institution by two or three universities (the Hebrew University, Tel Aviv University and Bar Ilan University)

131 Ibid. 15.

> [...] Despite Bar Ilan University's important contribution to higher education in Zefat, the committee does not recommend that the auspices for the institution be given only to this university" (ibid).

These recommendations were made despite Bar Ilan University's important contribution at the north and despite the fact that the institution is destined to operate, as recommended by the committee, from the same buildings in which it had operated for three years as an Extension of Bar Ilan University.

The CHE dedicated two meetings to the report (21 December 1971, 25 January 1972). Bar Ilan University's representatives who were invited to the first meeting expressed their discontent at the committee's recommendations and even accused its members of subjectivism and unprofessionalism. The Rector demanded that the committee present its explanations, mostly those leading to the decision not to retain full responsibility in the hands of Bar Ilan. He also protested as to the fact that the committee did not see fit to describe the hard work done by Bar-Ilan in Zefat, at a time in which no other university expressed any interest in the area. He declared that despite the committee's recommendations the university will continue to operate the Zefat Extension as it had in the past, even in the absence of State support. He emphasized the university's commitment to the religious aspects of the Extension and declared that it would continue to maintain the religious-cultural nature of the Extension and will not collaborate with other universities. The Rector's anger and his struggle against the committee's report attest to the subversive paradigmatic strategy implemented by the university during those years.

Upon conclusion of its discussions on the matter, the secretary of the CHE informed the Rector that the university's request to establish a university campus at Zefat has been denied. The CHE even expressed a more radical approach towards Bar-Ilan than had been expressed in the committee's report, informing the university that it prefers to approve the establishment of an academic institution in the Galilee under the auspices of an academic committee, thereby rejecting the Jortner committee's recommendation for joint auspices to include Tel Aviv university, the Hebrew University and Bar-Ilan.[132]

To conclude the committee's recommendations, not only that Bar Ilan University's request to establish a university campus at Zefat was rejected, but the committee members aimed to block its continued operations at Zefat and the Jordan Valley. The university's continued presence only at the Jordan Valley would

132 Ibid, Protocol of the meeting of the fourth council number 3 (51), 25 January 1972.

have created financial burdens beyond those that it had agreed to undertake when it decided to open the Extension.

In retrospect we can conclude that had the CHE accepted the committee's recommendations in full, Bar Ilan University would have had to cease its operations at Zefat and the Jordan Valley in the beginning of the 1970s, and the map of Israel's academic colleges as defined in 2000 would have changed accordingly. The struggle within the committee's arena is an example of the struggle of a field's senior actors against newcomers, especially when the newcomers adopt a subversive strategy which strives to establish a paradigmatic change in the field. The rejection of the university's request forced it to continue its attempts of acceptances into the field, until it would finally agree to undertake the field's accepted rules of conduct.

Amendment Number 3 to the CHE Law and the Struggle over the Legal Status of the Extensions

The Council for Higher Education Law, legislated in 1958, did not include provisions as to the legal status of university Extensions and did not determine legal arrangements as to any extra-university operations. This lacuna in the law enabled Bar Ilan university to operate in the 1960s until 1972 without legal limitation. And yet, with the legislation of the CHE law, a new and different situation emerged, which deviated from the one which the university's management had encountered in its year of establishment: The subordination of the institutions of higher education to the law and its derived national arrangements, positioned all institutions under a uniform regulatory framework supervising every step they made, even if such step was not specifically regulated by the law. While the establishment of Extensions was a type of activity not defined by the law, the fact that the university had been subject to the 1958 law was also relevant to the Extensions, which together with the university entered under the wings of State regulation. The plans of the university's management to establish a university campus in Zefat to correspond with stage four in the evolution of Extensions, required an official application to the CHE, as opposed to the initiative of opening Extensions corresponding with stage three of the evolution.

The CHE responded on two fronts, both aimed at thwarting the university's plan: The Jortner Committee discussed above, and in parallel the CHE's legal advisors were busy drafting the amendment to the CHE law aimed at blocking the ability, which until then had been permitted, to open Extensions. Also on this front the university's position was problematic: among the 25 members of the third CHE, 12 were members of the senior faculty of the Hebrew University including Prof. Benjamin Akzin,[133] Prof. Ya'akov Katz,[134] Prof. Ephraim Urbach,[135] Prof. I. Sciaky; and five members of the Technion, including Prof. Asher Peres,[136] Prof. R. Shalon, Prof. Ollendorff[137] and Prof. Shneior Lifson.[138] Each of the new universities, Bar-Ilan and Tel Aviv had a single representative. The committee further included five public figures including Minster of Education Yigal Alon, a representative of the Kibbutz HaMeuchad, David Horwitz former Governor of the Bank of Israel, and Yaacov Dori who had been President of the Technion (1951–1965). From the letter of response to Bar-Ilan's application to establish a university campus at Zefat we learn of the CHE's secretary's sense of discomfort at the lacuna in the law and the university's conduct on the matter of Extensions:

> On 24 January 1972 Bar Ilan University issued a request to the Council for Higher Education to establish a university campus at Zefat. At the time the law did not required the council's approval for opening a university institution, but it was known that the CHE had been preparing an amendment proposal to the Council for Higher Education Law, one of the aims of which was to require such an approval by law. The council, as was its custom, appointed a committee to examined Bar Ilan's request. The committee recommended opening university studies at Zefat under the auspices of two or three universities. When the council discussed the committee's recommendations, the Knesset had already approved amendment number 3 to the CHE law, by which the opening of a new academic institution requires a permit from the Council for Higher Education.[139]

133 Benjamin Akzin, Political Science Professor at the Hebrew University. Among the founders of the University of Haifa and its Rector, 1967 recipient of the Israel Prize for law.

134 Prof. Jacob Katz, a historian and sociologist, recipient of the Israel Prize for Jewish Studies, Rector of the Hebrew University between the years 1969 and 1972, member of the CHE in 1961–1971.

135 Prof. Ephraim Urbach, Scholar and researcher of Judaism. President of the Israeli National Academy of Science 1980–1986, recipient of the Israel Prize for Judaism in 1955.

136 Asher Peres, Physicist, professor at the Technion, winner of the Rothschild price for Physics in 2004.

137 Prof. Franz Ollendorff from the Technion, recipient of the Israel prize for exact sciences in 1954.

138 Shneior Lifson, physicist, professor at the Technion, recipient of the Israel prize for Life Science in 1969, among the founders of the Open University and the Scientific Manager of the Weitzman Institute in 1963–1967.

139 Bar Ilan University Archive, container 474, file 247. Letter from the CHE Secretary to the Rector, 21 August, 1972.

The amendment to the law not only threatened the expansion of the Extensions project, but also endangered the continued operation of the existing Extensions already operating at Zefat, Ashkelon and the Jordan Valley, as can be seen in the new article 21a(b) to the law: "As to this article, it makes no difference whether the institution was opened or established by an institution of higher education, whether as an Extension or Chapter or in any other way".[140]

This legal situation left the university with the dilemma of choosing one of the following two alternatives: Submitting to the dictates of the amendment to the law as worded, and in doing so in fact accepting the dictates of the senior actors of the academic field, or struggling for its religious-social ideology while changing its subversive strategy from aiming for a paradigmatic change to aiming to achieve change within the framework of the accepted rules in the field, by acting to minimized the application of the amendment and making due with an official acknowledgment of the existing Extensions, and maybe also of those for which the planning had already been completed on the way to their inauguration.

Although Tel Aviv University extended its academic auspices to a number of courses at Tel Chai College, the amendment to the law did not threaten it as its involvement at Tel Chai was minor and insubstantial, and moreover was a result of a local initiative, with the university being asked to provide academic auspices only to a number of specific courses. Tel Aviv was not asked to take part in any managerial or organizational tasks or responsibilities, and its work at Tel Chai was not tied to any ideology. Conversely, Bar Ilan University had been the initiator of its involvement in the region, and moreover had directly operated the courses offered at Zefat. Also at the Jordan Valley the university had managerial responsibility over the operation of the college. Thus, the CHE's initiatives aimed at blocking Bar Ilan University's expansion can be seen as an attempt to curb its operations and conform it to the accepted style within the academic field. This intention of the CHE can be deducted from correspondences between the Council's Secretary and the Rector of Bar Ilan University. In one of the letters from the Secretary to the Rector, when the latter had alleged that the new version of the law does not apply to existing Extensions, the Secretary clarified the CHE's intentions:

> The accreditation granted at the time to Bar Ilan University was given to the institution in Ramat Gan following an evaluation process by the Council for Higher Education. Bar Ilan University's Extensions are not an integral part of the university, but in fact new institutions of higher education, offering parallel courses to those offered at Ramat Gan.

140 Council for Higher Education Law, 1958.

> The accreditation granted by the Council for Higher Education to Bar Ilan University does not authorize the university to open institutions of higher education at any other site. Article 21a(b) to the law clearly stipulates that an institution of higher education, whether recognized by the CHE or not, intending to open an Extension, must obtain the Council's approval. The transitional order requires an institution founded prior to amendment number 3 to the law to submit a request for permit within 90 days following the inception of the law.[141]

As can be expected, when the CHE's intension to retroactively apply article 21a(b) to existing Extensions had been exposed, the university's management seeked legal counsel.

The Struggle for More Extensions

While it was waiting for a legal opinion, during the first years of the 1970s the university received new applications for opening Extensions, following its success in the north and the south. The south was no longer a possibility and the request by the municipality of Kiryat Gat to establish a "Peoples' University" was rejected due to the success of the Ashkelon Extension. The existing two Extensions at the north were gaining a reputation and a growing number of students, leaving no room for an additional attempt. The other requests that arrived during those years came from the cities of Netanya, Afula and Nahariya, all of which were not defined as peripheral. However, and despite the fact that these cities did not meet the criteria set in the 1960s and the legal limitations hovering over the entire project, a certain change can be noted in the university's policy at that time, consisting of a tendency to act quickly so as to take advantage of the momentum before the entire idea of Extensions is brought to an end – even if this means operating in non-peripheral cities. This change of policy and drive to create reality from the ground up, was reinforced by religious considerations and an aspiration to further increase the university's impact within the Israeli public so as to hasten its recognition by the senior actors of the academic field. The applications received from these cities were not rejected as had been the application from the municipality of Raanana in the 1960s. In these cities the university's management identified a potential for training additional public opinion agents in the fields of education and public service, areas which it perceived as higher important. The religious aim for spreading *Torah* and science among this public was stronger than all other considerations, and therefore a decision was made that the university would

141 Bar Ilan University Archive, container 474, file 247. Letter from the Secretary of the CHE, 21 August 1972.

operate in these cities, despite their being central. The first courses for teachers began in the summer, while the university's management was still awaiting the opinion of its legal advisor.

The opinion was finally presented to the Rector on 10 April 1972 and it distinguished between the existing Extensions and the planned ones such as Afula, Netanya and Nahariya. As to the Extensions at Zefat, Ashkelon and the Jordan Valley, the legal advisor Adv. Meron recommended submitting a request to the CHE for an operating permit, as was required in the amendment to the law. As to the new Extensions discussed in his opinion as a current case, he recommended their operation under a non-binding framework, or in his exact words: "The study of *Torah* for its own sake".[142] Based on this opinion the Rector decided to postpone publishing the notification regarding preparations for opening Extensions at Afula and Netanya until a permit has been granted, as noted in his letter to the Mayor of Afula:

> I received the legal opinion of Bar Ilan University's legal advisor following our latest meeting regarding the Extension at Afula, and therefore I have to ask you to wait with the publication of the opening of Bar Ilan's Extension until a permit is received from the Minister of Education, Chairperson of the CHE, as according to article 21 to the latest amendment to the CHE Law, a university must obtain a permit for every Extension it opens, if it intends to offer academic credit points to students studying there. There is no need for a permit, if studies are held only for the sake of studying.[143]

About three weeks after the university's Rector delayed the publication and after a discussion at the university's Board, he informed that he has removed his request to delay publication of the preparations for opening extra-university studies for teachers at Afula and Netanya. The hopes of the Board members relied on the current need for training teachers, and the hope that the education system and its responsible Minister, who is also the head of the CHE, would permit such a specific operation. The training of teachers was essential following the integration reform legislated by the Knesset in 1968 and which began to be implemented only in the beginning of the 1970s. The leaders of the national-religious education system were opposed to the new reform, fearing that it would further weaken the religious education system as it is most active among less affluent populations. It can also be assumed that the establishment of the University of Haifa, that began as a teachers' training department, presumably due to the shortage of teachers

142 Ibid. Adv. Meron's letter to Prof. Kadari, 10 April 1972.

143 Ibid, container 753, file 285. Letter from the Rector to Mayor of Afula Shimon Schori, dated 20 April 1972.

in the north, encouraged Bar-Ilan's management to approach the population of teachers in that region. Over time, the inauguration of such extra-university activities in these cities would become a fact, and if the timing was right – even an Extension. In the Rector's letter to one of the mayors of these cities he was decisive in his position to act against the CHE's decision, while also implementing caution so as not to risk the university being extracted from the activities. To illustrate his position, following is an extract of one of his letters:

> I am hereby glad to inform you that the university's management has decided at its meeting held on 16 May 1972 to remove the delay of publicizing the preparations towards opening an Extension of Bar Ilan University at Afula in the academic year 1973, provided that you would be willing to ensure, prior to implementing the above, the municipality's official commitment to pay the university a sum of 100,000 Liras to cover the municipality's part in the expenses of the Extension.[144]

The wording of the letter and the decision of the Board point to the intent to establish a different relationship than that which existed at the previously established Extensions. Although in his letter the Rector referred to the planned operations at Afula and Netanya as "Extensions", in many of Dr. Bar Ilan's reports he made a point of referring to these special operations as "external courses", and they were based on a relationship having no resemblance to the older Extensions. The many differences included the prerequisites defined prior to the university granting its consent:

a. The initiative for operations at Netanya, Afula and Nahariya came from local residents or a national institution such as the Teacher-training Unit at the Ministry of Education, as was the case at Afula and contrary to the university's initiatives at Ashkelon or Zefat.
b. The activity was limited and defined as intended for training of specific target populations. Defining teachers and public service employees as target populations points to the religious purpose that directed the university's decision to operate in these cities, as opposed to the Extensions at the north and in Ashkelon where studies were offered to local residents with no sectoral division. The religious consideration in these cases defined a purpose by which the university hoped to disseminate through teachers a world view integrating *Torah* and science.

---

144 Ibid. Letter from the Rector to the Mayor of Netanya Oved Ben Ami, 17 May 1972.

c. In each of these cities the local authority committed to cover all expenses in advance, based on a predefined quota of students.
d. Studies were not semester-based, but rather scheduled during teachers' summer vacation or between holidays, and based on the university's ability to provide an available teaching staff for this task.

In another letter from the Rector to the Secretary of the Council for Higher Education, Prof. Kadari described a more moderate approach which can be seen as a retreat from his previous position. He made a clear distinction between the activities at the central cities, and those taking place at Ashkelon, Zefat and the Jordan Valley:

> As to Afula, the university consented to the demands of the Teachers' Advanced Learning Department at the Ministry of Education, and took upon itself to provide the required courses for such advanced learning studies, at Afula. During the holidays these courses will be given at Nahariya [...] As to Netanya: The university will be willing to assume academic responsibility for courses in Jewish Studies, which the Netanya municipality will organize as part of its plans for Post-Secondary Education in the city. Here too, the initiative and funding come from the Netanya municipality.[145]

Conversely, the CHE's determination left no room for discussing interpretations to the law also in the matter of the existing Extensions, and therefore the university's management, realizing that the struggle for converting the new locations into Extensions is futile, accepted the demand of the Secretary of the CHE from 24 May 1972, and submitted all data pertaining to the existing Extensions in order to obtain a permit for their continued operation by law.[146] In his application he did not ignore the rest of the new and planned locations, making due with presenting them as centers offering advanced training courses for teachers during special times, in the hope that they will be defined as a national requirement and therefore be able to remain as teacher-training centers.

As to the existing Extensions, the university did not despair from continuing with its interpretive struggle on the lawfulness of the amendment's application, even after the request for permit was made. The Rector approached the Secretary of the CHE in a letter of clarification, requesting to revise his previous letter to the minister. According to the letter, he agrees to the interpretation applying the amendment to the existing Extensions, for two main reasons:

---

145 Ibid. Container 474, file 247. Letter from the Rector, Prof. Kadari, to the Secretary of the Council for Higher Education, S. Bendor, 1 June 1972.

146 Ibid. Letter from the Rector to the Minister of Education, 10 April 1972.

1. The existing Extensions cannot be defined according to the terms of the law. They are not a "Chapter", "Institution", "Representative", but remote classes of the main campus, and as he wrote:

> The clarification pertains to Bar Ilan's "Extensions" that have been active for the past number of years at Ashkelon, Zefat and the Jordan Valley College: These Extensions cannot be described in the same terms as defined by the amendment to the Council for Higher Education law of 28 January 1972. They are not Institutions, nor Chapters, Representatives, etc., of Bar Ilan University, but local extensions for certain courses offered at the university's various Departments, and instead of offering them in one of the classrooms at Ramat Gan, they are held at one of the aforementioned locations.[147]

2. The amendment should not be retroactively applied to the existing Extensions, just as no modern legal system would apply a law in retrospect, unless explicitly stipulated. In any event, these Extensions have been operating for a number of years before the amendment to the CHE law came into force, meaning that when the university received official accreditation, it included the Extensions (ibid).

For the university's management, as long as the Jortner committee recommendations were not published, the struggle for the amendment's influence on the existing Extensions may have affected the struggle for sustaining a campus at Zefat. The definition of the Zefat campus as an Extension would require the Jortner committee to change its definition of the activity taking place at Zefat, and if the committee would recommend Bar Ilan University for the task, the path would then be cleared for the establishment of a university campus and a multi-campus structure.

To conclude, the Jortner Committee's recommendation to reject the university's request and the initiated amendment to the CHE law left no doubt as to the CHE's intentions, as representing, at the time, the senior actors of the academic field, to block Bar Ilan's expansion and to force it to conform to the accepted rules of the field. The realization of a multi-campus university vision, which was anomalous at the time in the academic field, seemed farther than ever. Left with no other choice, the university conceded to maintaining its Extensions in their current formation.

147 Ibid. Letter from the Rector to the Secretary of the CHE, 1 June 1972.

Chapter 6 Establishing the Official Status of the Extensions

The 1960s introduced extensive initiatives and pioneering work. Having assessed the feasibility of establishing an Extension, in the 1970s the university's management moved on to its implementation. In general, the steps taken towards establishing Extensions focused on two main tasks:

a. Drafting of long term agreements between the university and the local authority
b. Defining the desirable scope of academic activities for each Extension

Drafting Contractual Agreements

In the beginning of the 1970s the university held extra-campus activities at three locations which its Board had officially defined as Extensions. At three other locations – Afula, Netanya and Nahariya, special programs were held for teachers. The university decided to struggle to obtain a permit for its future Extensions in order to integrate them into its general structure and this aim was expressed in its types of agreements or arrangements with local authorities. The correspondences and agreements signed in the 1960s and 1970s point to three main measures for assessing the university's approach towards each new site:

1. **Initiative** – so as to assess the nature of the relationship between the university and the locals, and especially the future of the place, an examination is needed of the source of the initiative for establishing studies at the new location: Whether the activity had been initiated by the university or by the local authority.
2. **Expense** – whether the question of operational expenses was a prerequisite for commencing activities at the site, or was this was not a decisive consideration.
3. **Location and target population** – was the intended location part of the country's geographic periphery, and did the local population adhere to the university's religious aims.

Activities at Afula, Netanya and Nahariya will be examined in comparison to Ashkelon, Zefat and the Jordan Valley, based on these measures.

1. **Initiative** – the initiative for establishing academic courses at Afula, Netanya and Nahariya came from their respective local authorities: the university was approached by the municipalities' departments of Education, sometimes via

the Ministry of Education. At Ashkelon and Zefat the university made the initial contact. At the Jordan Valley the local initiative was readily accepted by the university due to its timing and the conformance between it and the founders' religious-Zionist ideology.

2. **Expense** – the initiators at Afula, Netanya and Nahariya committed to cover all of the university's financial costs prior to initiating studies at the new location. The initiating local authority organized a suitable site for classes and ensured its ongoing maintenance. The budget came directly from the authority or through the Ministry of Education. In contrast, at Ashkelon and Zefat the measure of expense was not a decisive factor in the decision to hold studies at the new site, and despite the disadvantages of the distanced activities at the Extension, the university perceived the new location as an integral part of its own establishment. At the Jordan Valley a special formula was developed, by which three parties would be responsible for covering operational expenses: The students, the local authority through the Post-Secondary School, and the university, that had agreed to fund part of the cost. Despite differences in this measure between Ashkelon and Zefat, the activity at the Jordan Valley differs from all other cities in which activities had been stipulated upon the prerequisite that all expenses would be covered.
3. **Location and target population** – studies at Afula, Netanya and Nahariya were not intended for the general public, but for a predefined public comprised mostly of teachers who are residents of the area or civil servants whose training was a prerequisite for their job promotion. At Ashkelon, Zefat and the Jordan Valley, courses were open to the general public in the area, and as a result the variety of courses was much larger and more varied. Ashkelon, Zefat and the Jordan Valley were defined as peripheral areas, while Afula, Netanya and Nahariya were considered affluent areas whose residents had a higher level of accessibility to existing academic institutions.

The formal agreements at Afula, Netanya and Nahariya were achieved through letter correspondences between the university's management and the local authority. These letters show that the university did not see these cities as areas justifying investment in social activities of a nature, as opposed to areas that had been selected in advance as locations for Extensions. In a report submitted in 1973 by the coordinator of academic activities outside the main campus, activities are differentiated between the type of activity held at Afula and Netanya, and the one taking place in Ashkelon, Zefat and the Jordan Valley:

> University courses are held at Afula ins response to a request by the municipality and the Ministry of Education. The purpose of the courses is to provide further studies for teachers working in the area [. . .] Expenses are funded by the Ministry of Education & Culture. At Netanya we began this year to offer university courses in Jewish Studies [. . .] The Netanya municipality is funding the cost of these courses. The Extension at Ashkelon was established 8 years ago [. . .] At the Jordan Valley the university's Extension operates under the Regional College [. . .] at the Zefat Extension.[148]

To conclude, based on contractual measures, it appears that a location defined as an Extension in the first place, is seen to have been initiated by the university, with the university's willingness to cover all or part of the cost, and with the definition of social or religious aims for the campus, suited to the area and its population. Operations at Afula, Netanya and Nahariya did not meet the criteria defined by the university's management for an Extension, and therefore it was easier for the university to distance itself from these sites, especially in a reality of accumulating difficulties. In practice, courses in these cities were given only during the years 1972–1979, and were stopped for two main reasons:

1. The amendment to the CHE law and the Council's insistence on not including activities in the new cities in the permit granted for the older Extensions – all these caused the university's management to realize that they had better invest their energies in strengthening the Extensions at Zefat, Ashkelon and the Jordan Valley. Moreover, the contractual measures point to the existence of a temporary, goal-based relationship, targeted at a special population. The social and peripheral criteria did not apply to these locations.
2. The Ministry of Education, which the university's management relied on when establishing operations in these areas, decided that the existence of an Extension near Afula would lead to undesirable competition to the nearby Ohel Sara college. The population of teachers' was therefore not referred to Bar Ilan University as the Minister of Education had been opposed to the university's activities at Afula and Nahariya.[149]

Activities at Afula were officially terminated in the Rector's letter to the CHE Secretary:

> We regret to hear that "our Extension" in Afula was also included in publications regarding registration to Bar Ilan University's Extensions. We have instructed that these publications, which included Afula among Bar Ilan University's Extensions, are

---

148 Ibid, container 753, file 285. A report to the Board from the Manager of the Extensions, 17 May 1972.

149 Ibid. 1972–1979 Review.

> immediately stopped [. . .] If we cannot receive a temporary permit for 1975, we are prepared to immediately cease preparations for these studies.[150]

The Agreement with the Jordan Valley Compared to the Relationships with the Ashkelon and Zefat Extensions

As can be concluded from the three aforementioned measures regarding the existing Extensions, the differences in the agreements with each points to the university's different intentions at Ashkelon and Zefat compared to the Jordan Valley. The Zefat and Ashkelon Extensions conformed with the three measures: Initiative, expense and periphery. However, at the Jordan Valley these measures were not fulfilled and the method of the agreement there points to the difference between this Extension and the ones at Ashkelon and Zefat: Despite the fact that the Jordan Valley Extension was not the first to be established, the first agreement between the university and any of the Extensions was the one signed in 1968 with the "Jordan Valley Regional Council School for Post-Secondary Education". The existence of a first agreement in the 1960s with the Jordan Valley of all places was not accidental and points to a basic different in the nature of the university's relationship with the Jordan Valley Extension compared to its relationship with the Extensions at Ashkelon and Zefat. A comparison between the wording of the agreement with the Jordan Valley Extension and those signed with Zefat and Ashkelon in the beginning of the 1980s shows clear differences between them.

The Agreement with the Jordan Valley

The agreement includes only five clauses, the essence of which is as follows:

1. "Bar Ilan University **will provide** (the emphasis is mine) teachers to the Post-Secondary school in Jewish Studies and Social Studies or in other areas, according to its ability".
2. "Bar Ilan University will cover the cost of these courses up to two thirds of the academic salaries to be paid and two thirds travel expenses. The remaining third will be covered in full by the Post-Secondary School".[151]

The agreement does not cover the methods of operation or development of university studies at the site. Moreover, it does not define the site as an Extension

150 Ibid. Letter from the Rector to Dr. Bazil Herman Secretary of the CHE, 4 March 1974.

151 Jordan Valley College archive, agreement dated 12 August 1968.

or a future Extension. It's wording leaves the management of the school in the hands of the locals and creates a special pattern of communication which differs from the one established with Netanya and Afula, where the entire cost had been covered by the locals, and the one established with Ashkelon and Zefat, where the university covered the entire cost. The school with whom the agreement was signed held other studies in parallel, and paid the university the remaining one third after collecting students' tuition fees. However, the tuition itself was collected by the university – which left a certain responsibility in its hands – similarly to the situation at Ashkelon and Zefat.

The Agreements with the Municipalities of Zefat and Ashkelon

Contrary to the situation at the Jordan Valley, the agreements between the university and the Ashkelon and Zefat municipalities were signed, as aforesaid, only in the mid 1980s and consisted of a different framework than the agreement signed with the Jordan Valley.

The essence of the agreement with the two municipalities:

1. The agreements, conducted following many years of operation of the Extensions at Ashkelon and Zefat (14–16 years), open with a declaration of the existence of an Extension in the city.
2. The university has full responsibility over the management and supervision of studies, which are an inseparable part of the main campus. Teachers at the Extension were selected from the departments at the main campus and allocated to the different courses by the university's administrator of Extensions. The actual management of the Extensions or courses was performed by a manager appointed by the university and who worked from his office at the main campus.
3. The university collects tuition directly from the students.
4. The local authority will allocate a suitable and appropriate facility for holding academic studies, which will be available to the university for the purpose of holding such studies. It was also stipulated that the university will have no proprietary or quasi-proprietary right over the facilities it receives for this purpose.
5. As the study facility remains in the hands of the local authority, it is also responsible for its maintenance. In the agreement with the Ashkelon municipality, the municipality undertook to provide: "Maintenance of the wing (within an existing school) including cleaning services and water and electricity repairs".[152]

152 Ashkelon College Archive, file 1984. The Agreement with Bar Ilan University, 1 February 1984, contract number 2215.

6. Wherever an Extension is operated, the local authority will fund the salaries of a secretary and librarian who will work part time and will be professionally managed by the Manager of the Extensions, who will regularly visit the site.

An analysis of the agreements and correspondences that preceded the university's operations at Zemach, Zefat and Ashkelon, points to five measures for examining the different contracting methods:

1. **The timing of the Agreement** – the fact that contractual agreements were prepared and signed with Zefat and Ashkelon only in the mid 1980s, 14–16 years following commencement of the operations, points to the fact that the work done in Ashkelon and Zefat was pioneering and ideological by nature. The university's establishment of operations at the Jordan Valley was stipulated upon the signing of an agreement from the onset. Here, therefore, we find a 'normal' method of contracting, mutually agreed upon by all parties.
2. **Formalization** – the commencement of the university's operations at the Jordan Valley was, as explained above, stipulated upon the existence of an arrangement regulating the relationship between the university and the local authority. Conversely, the activities at Ashkelon and Zefat was initiated by the university, rather than being stipulated upon the existence of a specific agreement. The Parties made do with a general declaration of intents and the goodwill of the local authority towards the allocation of a suitable temporary site for holding academic activities.
3. **Type of contract** – the Extensions at Ashkelon and Zefat were considered an integral part of the university's campus, a fact that determined the scope and nature of academic activities taking place at those sites, while the activities at the Jordan Valley were determined under a service provision agreement.
4. **Operational responsibility** – at the Jordan Valley the university provided lecturers and academic accreditation, while the local Post-Secondary school covered the university's expenses as stipulated in the agreement between the Parties. The local school, which had existed prior to the university's arrival at the site, operated as a Post-Secondary education institution, offering both academic and non-academic activities. The local administrators remained responsible for managing the school and all its activities. In contrast, at Ashkelon and Zefat the university had full operational responsibility. It was the only partly responsible for covering the site's expenses, just as it was similarly responsible at the main campus: The university paid the lecturers' salaries and directly collected tuition from all students; academic courses were held during the evening at an existing school which was available in the afternoons and evenings. The local authority took care of the schools' maintenance as part of its routine

maintenance of the city's schools. Even when the local authority did allocate financial support to the university, it was done on the basis of goodwill only, and not as a prerequisite for the university's operation at the site. Thus, during the initiation stage, the university's founders made do with a local willingness to collaborate, and the opening of the Extension was not stipulated upon receiving specific financial support.

5. **The site** – at the Jordan Valley studies were held at the same building of the local authority's Post-Secondary school, where other Post-Secondary education studies were held in parallel, with the university's activities being a part of the Post-Secondary studies offered at the school. This academic activity is still held at the same site today, as it had for over forty years. At Zefat and Ashkelon courses were held at the school after hours. Many letters exchanged between the university and the mayors of the local authorities in the 1960s and beginning of the 1970s attest to the temporariness of the sites and the intent of local authorities to eventually hold the activities in existing permanent buildings which would serve the university in the long term and even be awarded to it as an asset. Moreover, plans were being developed in both cities towards the establishment of a university campus: The local authority locates a site, and the university raises donations for this purpose.[153]

Defining the Scope and Contents of Academic Activities at the Extensions

The same general program was applied to all Extensions, which had been based on the study topics offered at the main campus in Ramat Gan, adjusted to the facilities available at each site. In 1956 – a year following the university's establishment – the following topics were taught at the main campus:

1. **Jewish Studies:** Bible, Talmud, Aggada and Midrash, Jewish History and Hebrew Literature.
2. **Natural Sciences and Mathematics:** Biology, Chemistry, Physics and Mathematics.
3. **Social Sciences:** Philosophy, Psychology, Sociology, Political Science, Economics and Education.
4. **Languages and Literature:** Hebrew, Arabic, English, French, Spanish, Greek and Latin.

153 As presented by Bar Ilan's delegation at the Jortner Committee hearings.

In the absence of suitable academic facilities for teaching Natural or Exact sciences (Hard Science), and mostly due to lack of laboratories, studies at the Extensions focused on Jewish Studies, Social Studies and Humanities. In the first years the main body of students the Extensions included teachers, public service employees and bank clerks. The schedule was adapted to their needs, meaning that studies took place in the afternoons and evenings. Between 1965 and 1968 the same topics were offered at each of the first three Extensions: Education, Economics, Sociology, Hebrew grammar, General History, Psychology, Talmud and History of Israel.[154]

Studies were offered in a general rather than Departmental structure. Two to four elective and introductory courses in each area of Social Sciences were offered, but courses were not sufficient for completed a full academic year. The program enabled students to accumulate credit points towards a degree or for continuing education remuneration, with the option to continue their studies at the main campus. In the beginning of 1970, when the Manager of the Extensions became convinced that the time has come to upgrade the offerings at the three Extensions, a detailed plan for their development was presented to the Senate for approval. The plan included a substantial change in the Extensions' operation. According to Dr. Bar Ilan's plan, the university would offer full undergraduate studies for years 1 and 2, with the third year being completed at the main campus in Ramat Gan. Dr. Bar Ilan's presentation included a forecast of future demand at each Extension, as well as a recommendation to reduce the number of courses on offer so as to focus academic attention on highly demanded areas of study for which a full annual curriculum would be offered.

Table 22 presents the limited program proposed by the Manager of the Extensions in order to focus the resources of each Extension on the most highly demanded areas, thereby increasing the likelihood of providing a full curriculum for the first two years of study.

154 Bar Ilan University Archive, container 1458, file 206. University journal, 1968.

Tab. 22: Departments at the Extensions in 1965–1970 and the list of discontinued courses

Areas of study	**Ashkelon 1965–68**	**Zefat 1968**	**Jordan Valley 1968**	**Ashkelon 1970**	**Zefat 1970**	**Jordan Valley 1970**
Talmud	√	–	–	–	–	–
Hebrew grammar	√	√	–	–	–	–
Bible	√	–	–	√	√	–
Sociology	√	√	–	–	–	–
Education	√	√	√	√	√	√
Psychology	√	√	√	√	√	√
Economy	√	√	–	√	–	–
Political Science	–	–	–	–	√	–
History	√	√	√	√	–	√
Literature	–	–	√	–	√	√

Data from Bar Ilan University's Archive, container 753, file 285. Extensions Manager's report, 17 May 1972.

In the forecast of future demand prepared by Dr. Bar-Ilan for each of the Extensions, he expected a growth rate of 38 % to 50 %, despite the difficulties ahead, of which he had also warned:

1. **Locating suitable academic faculty members** – difficulties in convincing senior academic personnel to agree to travel to remote Extensions. His apprehensions grew when senior lecturers were required for teaching advanced courses and he emphasized that this difficulty had prevented the opening of full programs at the Extensions. For highly demanded fields such as Psychology, only introductory courses were offered at the Extensions. The difficulty in obtaining senior lecturers lowered the likelihood of opening new departments, while others remained open at the Extensions but offered only an eclectic list of courses.
2. **Second and third year studies** – difficulty to operate a program while relying on a small number of courses, which did not enable a significant growth in the number of students. Students who wished to complete their undergraduate obligations within a reasonable time had to travel to the Ramat Gan campus after their first year at the Extension in order to complete their first year obligations towards continuing on to year 2 and 3.
3. **The format of operation** of the Extensions in the afternoon and evenings made it difficult to attract young students who wanted to complete their studies in three years as was customary in other academic institutions. This format brought the same type of students to the three Extensions: Teachers, civil servants, employees of local authorities and bank clerks wishing to gain professional and job advancement.

Dr. Bar Ilan's plan was partly realized. About two years after commencing academic courses at Zefat and the Jordan Valley, these campuses were recognized as Extensions of the university. Hours of study were increased and a larger number of mandatory courses were offered in the Social Sciences. Table 23 presents the number of hours and courses offered at the first Extensions in the 1970s:

Tab. 23: Number of academic hours offered at each Extension by field of study, 1972–1979

Field of study	Ashkelon			Zefat			Jordan Valley		
	1972	1973	1979	1972	1973	1979	1972	1973	1979
	Weekly hours	Weekly hours	Weekly hours	Weekly hours	Weekly hours	Weekly hours	Weekly hours	Weekly hours	Weekly hours
Bible	10		4	8		4	8		8
Talmud	8		4	4		4	4		4
History of Israel	6		4	4		4	4		8
Jewish Philosophy	4		4	4		–	–		–
General History	4		4	6		4	4		–
Hebrew grammar	2		4	2		–	4		8
Hebrew Literature	4		4	4		4	6		8
English	12		8	8		8	8		8
Psychology	6		–	8		4	4		8
Economy	20		12	8		8	7		19
Political Science	–		–	4		8	–		2
Education	10		8	8		8	4		8
Geography	–		8	–		–	–		–
Mathematics/ Statistics	8		–	8		–	8		–
Sociology	–		4	–		4	–		6
Social Work	–		–	–		4	–		–
Total Courses	56	52	35	38	36	29	30	49	42

Data from Bar Ilan University's Archive, container 753, file 285. Informational leaflet published by Dr. Bar Ilan, "Answers to fifty questions about the Extensions", academic year 1978–79. The data does not include the centers at Afula and Nahariya, which were seen at the time as only temporary.

Although less courses were being offered at each Extension, Table 24 shows the constant growth in the total number of students between 1965–1973.

Tab. 24: Number of students at the Extensions 1965–1973

Extension	Number of students			
	1965	**1970**	**1972**	**1973**
Ashkelon	76	180	234	280
Zefat	–	80	136	165
Jordan Valley	–	30	242	300 *

Data from Bar Ilan University's Archive, container No 753, file No 285. Extensions Activity Report, 6 November 1972.

Note: The number of students includes "free listeners" not required to present a high school matriculation diploma. Studies granted credit points to be accumulated towards a degree, but these students were not classified as degree students unless they met the admission requirements for free listeners. This status was especially prominent at the Jordan Valley Extension, in which most students came from the Kibbutzim of the area, following the change in the position of the Kibbutzim Movement towards academic studies. As in the past many Kibbutz members completed their high school studies without Bagrut matriculation exams, they tended to take part in academic studies as free listeners.

An analysis of the mix of students in 1971 confirms that their numbers did in fact increase every year, but not necessarily the number of degree students – as most of the growth resulted from continuing education students and free listeners who raised the total number of students at each Extension from one year to the next. Table 25 shows the proportion of undergraduate students at each Extension.

Tab. 25: Students at the Extensions – 1971/72 academic year

Place of study	Undergraduate students	Continued education courses for teachers, preschool teachers and nurses	Free listeners and certification studies	Total	Credit towards a degree	Number of students continuing At the university campus	Number of graduates
Ashkelon	94	133	49	276	34	50	10
Zefat	57	65	4	126	45	10	2
Jordan Valley	61	72	133	266	23	2	–
Total	212	270	186	668	31.7	62	12

Source: Bar Ilan University Archive, container 753, file 285. Extensions Activity Report, 6 November 1972.

In sum, the three measures for determining the university's intent point to the existence of differences even between the Jordan Valley Extension and the Zefat and Ashkelon ones. Zefat and Ashkelon were intended to be Extensions from the start, and form a part of an organizational structure led by religious and social aspirations. To this end the university undertook the financial and operational burdens of these Extensions. Even when the fate of the multi-campus plan was unclear, the university hoped to established campuses at these cities, to function as its sub-campuses and serve as teaching centers during the year and for continuing education programs during summer vacation. The university's activities at the Jordan Valley had not been preplanned or included in its future organizational structure. The university never proposed to contribute towards building a future campus at the site. The center's existence as an Extension was determined in retrospect, mainly as a result of the CHE's struggle against Bar Ilan University's expansion plans and its plans for a multi-campus organizational structure. When it seemed that the chances of expanding the Extensions program were lost, the university realized the importance of maintaining its existing operations, and as a result the Jordan Valley Extension, which had been initially coincidentally opened, officially became an Extension – five years after its establishment – while the Extension at Zefat and Ashkelon were recognized three years after they began their operation. The decision to recognize the Jordan Valley Extension had been a decisive factor in its becoming a part of Israel's landscape of academic colleges in the 1990s.

Solidifying Academic Activities at the Older Extensions

Realizing that it is unable to expand its extra-university activities and that the realization of the multi-campus idea is seeming farther than even, during the mid-1970s the university began to adopt an increasingly realistic and less pretentious policy. The university's management began transitioning from the stage of examining the level of demand for studies at the three Extensions, to the second stage aimed and establishing their status as its remote campuses. After the first stage and the rise in demand, the university was forced to transition to a more responsible stage, in which it was required to address growing demands, mostly for regular academic studies that would enable students to complete their mandatory requirements for the first years of their degree. This trend corresponded with the university's main purpose in the beginning of the 1970s, that the Extensions would form an important pillar in its plan for a multi-campus university. As this idea slowly became a distant dream, a more modest idea gradually took its place, by which the existing Extensions would become so called sub-campuses of the main campus. This intent can be noted from steps taken by the university's management in the early 1970s:

1. **The Legal foundation for the Extensions** – the Rector's petition to the Minister of Education in April 1972, following the amendment to the law, to grant the university a permit to operate at Zefat, Ashkelon and the Jordan Valley, points to the intent of the university's management to regulate the legal status of the Extensions to remove all legal obstacles preventing the university from continuing with their development.
2. **Establishment of the Extension at the north** – in a letter from the Rector of Bar Ilan University to Minister of Education Yigal Alon on 24 January 1971, the university requested approval for establishing the Zefat Campus at substantial financial investment. The main sources of funding came from philanthropists with ties to the university. The construction plan included student dormitories and the absorption of Jewish students from abroad. It was further proposed that full curriculums would be offered in nine Departments.
3. **Establishment of the Extension in the south** – in a meeting of the university's Board of Trustees in 1972 (decision number 18) it was agreed that the Rector and Dr. Bar Ilan would be entrusted with the task of preparing an action plan towards the construction of a campus at Ashkelon. The assumption of the plan's developers was that the funding for the project would come from Sephardi Jewry in the diaspora. This assumption relied on the fact that Ashkelon's population was mostly comprised of new immigrants from North Africa and Yemen, and therefore it would be easy to convince Jewish Sephardi philanthropists to contribute to such goal. The municipality, which took an active role in the project, identified a 100 dunams potential site that had been allocated for the construction of an education campus, the center of which would be the university Extension. The municipality offered a budget of 300,000 Lira to implement the plan, and the university was required to allocate most of the funds needed for construction. At the university's Board meeting held on 8 August 1973 it was agreed that the university would finance the construction together with the municipality, and in return the municipality would be required to solidify its long term relationship with the university.[155]

A short while later the municipality began to promote an architectural plan for the construction of the campus, and joint efforts were made to identify funding sources. The Manager of the Extensions led these initiatives at Ashkelon and Zefat, investing extensive efforts in promoting the university's plans in both

155 Bar Ilan University Archive, container 1088, file No 338. Protocol of the Board meeting held on 8 August, 1973.

cities. His efforts to accelerate the planning works at Ashkelon were fruitful, and on 3 September 1976 the Mayor called a meeting towards the construction of a building for the Ashkelon Extension. The guidelines for the planning were provided by the Manager of the Extensions and the manager of the municipality's Education Department.[156] In guidelines to planners it was noted that in 1976, about ten years following the establishment of the Extension, there are 300 students at the center, taking a total of 35 courses, all during the afternoon and evening. The planners were required to consider the expected growth in the number of students following construction of the first buildings and the transition to morning studies. Estimates pointed to 800 students within three to four years. The mix of buildings planned consists of an operational concept of a remote campus containing basic facilities which may enable a certain level of organizational independence: Management building, library, student dormitories and a restaurant. However, the Extensions were required to be completely dependent on the main campus for academic management.

4. **Struggle for a monopoly over the idea of Extensions** – Vigorous work by the university's management in the 1970s pointed to its strong conviction to maintain its monopoly over the idea of Extensions. initiatives involving academic auspices began to take form nearby to Bar Ilan's existing Extensions, for instance at the Sha'ar Hanegev Regional Council near the Ashkelon Extension, and at the vocational Tel Chai College in the north, located near the Zefat and Jordan Valley Extensions. This development led to a decisive response on the part of the university's management, as can be seen in correspondence between the Manager of the Extensions at Bar Ilan University and the Chairperson of the Regional Colleges Committee at the Council for Higher Education, Prof. A.M Meir of the Hebrew University. In his letters to Prof. Meir, the Manager of the Extensions attempted to remove the threat that he believed was emerging in the south: "The Negev College must not offer university courses". Prof. Meir saw his role of Chairperson of the Colleges Committee as a tool for the development of colleges which would increase accessibility to higher education in the periphery, and consequently rejected Dr. Bar Ilan's demand. In his response he wrote:

> I must disagree with your statement that "The Negev College must not offer university courses". This is not my opinion, nor does it correspond with the aims of the committee which I am Chairing. There is, by the way, no reason why competition between

156 Ashkelon College Archive, file 1976. Plan for Bar Ilan University's Extension and Teachers' College, Ashkelon, 10 September 1976.

> institutions should not exist. The question is only the nature of such competition and the way in which it is enforced.[157]

The university's Rector also joined the struggle against the new initiatives in the north and the south. He rejected the solution offered by the Chairperson of the CHE's Colleges Committee by which all institutions will mutually recognize courses taken outside the main campus. From the Rector's letter we see that the university's Senate, after discussing this request, completely rejected it. As to the actual struggle, the Rector wrote:

> As to the actual problems raised in your two memorandums and your attempts to prevent duplicities, I wish to note that the Sha'ar Hanegev College was only founded two years ago, many years after our Extension at Ashkelon. Had this college not been opened, there would not have been any duplicity issue.[158]

The university's management, as the first to have formulated the idea of Extensions with religious and social goals, viewed activities by other universities as trainsient, devoid of an ideological foundation and motivated solely by the aim to increase their number of students. Conversely, it perceived its own work as a national calling, while the actions taken by Ben Gurion and Tel Aviv Universities were perceived as devoid of any social-ideological purpose and therefore they saw no common basis for collaborations with other universities in the periphery. Attempts by the Chairperson of the Colleges Committee at the CHE to establish a system of mutual recognition between the Zefat Extension and the Tel Chai in the north, and between the Ashkelon Extension and the Sh'ar Hanegev College in the south, proved to be futile. A document compiled by the CHE in 1977 defining mutual recognition procedures did not reach fruition either, and each institution continued to operate independently towards establishing its presence in the area.

Ben Gurion University's actions can be seen as the expected behavior of a Target University, as defined by Yogev. While the three other universities – the Hebrew University, Tel Aviv and the Technion – are perceived by Yogev as Elite institutions aiming for scientific excellence, he defined Ben Gurion University, Bar Ilan and Haifa as Target Universities aimed at bringing higher education to the periphery, as had been done by Bar Ilan University for its target religious and traditional population (Yogev, 2000). According to this explanation, Ben Gurion's activities at the Sh'ar Hanegev Regional Council near Sderot was part of its social

---

157 CHE Archive, Bar Ilan University file. Letter from Prof. A.M Meir to Dr. Bar Ilan, 12 March 1978.

158 Ashkelon College Archive, file 1978. Letter from the Rector to Prof. A.M. Meir, 8 January 1978.

mission. As an institution operating in the capital city of the Negev region, established in the south so as to develop this area of the country, its social mission is embedded in the very idea of its foundation. However, Bar Ilan's social activities through the unique idea of Extensions remains unnoticed by Yogev. As I have shown until now, Bar Ilan University had been active in the social field for years before the other Target Universities, and the latter, even when they did join, did not perceive their extra-university activities as Extensions, but as specific, time-limited activities, as shall be shown later on.

Chapter 7 Difficulties in the Extensions' Operation and the Struggle for Their Continued Existence

Amendment number 3 to the CHE Law and the rejection of the university's request to open a university campus in Zefat were important turning points in the future of the Extensions. The legal obstacles brought a quicker end to the university's plans to expand through sub-campuses. The university decided to stop promoting the multi-campus idea and the idea of sub-campuses, for fear of damaging its relationship with the CHE. In January 1974 the university's Senate convened to discuss the future of the Extensions, and finally agreed to freeze plans for constructing the Ashkelon campus.[159] Ten months later, the Rector, Prof. Kadari informed the Mayors of Ashkelon, Zefat and the Jordan Valley that due to budget reductions, the university would only be able to continue operating the local Extensions if suitable funding is found.[160] The purpose of the letters was to push the municipalities to assist the university, and in a letter of clarification to the Manager of the Extensions the Rector clarified that the intention is not to close the Extensions, but to minimize their operations. In their defense, the Manager of the Extensions presented financial statements showing that the deficit amounted to only 1.4 % of the university's overall budget in 1978. He further noted that 800 students from the Extensions had completed their degree at the main campus, and a further 250 had been studying at the main campus at the time.[161] Table 26 presents the scope of financial operations at each Extension and the deficit accumulated by each, as presented by Dr. Bar Ilan.

159 Bar Ilan University Archive, container 753, file 285. Letter from the Rector to the Chairperson of the Board, 20 January 1974.

160 Ibid. The Rector's letters to the Mayors of Ashkelon and Zefat and to the Manager of the Jordan Valley College. All letters are dated 29 October 1974.

161 Ibid. Report of the Manager of the Extensions, 1974–1975.

Tab. 26: Financial operations at the three Extensions in 1978

Type of expense/ Extension	Ashkelon	Zefat	Jordan Valley
Number of students	300	120	320
Expenses: Academic faculty	322,902 Lira (11 positions)	201,816 Lira (7 positions)	217,368 Lira (7 positions)
Library	8,000 Lira	6,000 Lira	– (Expense incurred by the college)
Taxis	–	30,000 Lira	30,000 Lira
Income: Tuition	180,000	72,000 Lira	148,420 Lira
Deficit	150,902 Lira	165,816 Lira	98,948 Lira

Source: Bar Ilan University Archive, container 753, file 285. Estimate of expenses and income at the university's Extensions, 1975.

The accumulated deficit in all three Extensions in the 1978 academic year reached 633,034 Lira. Following deduction of the grants received from the local authorities, the deficit amounted to 256,307 Lira.[162]

Dr. Bar Ilan approached the university's CEO and the members of the Board, requesting that they convince the Rector to moderate his position. Consequently, and as shall be seen later on, the members of the Board, among them leaders of the NRP political party, were resourceful in supporting the Extensions. However, signs of the founders' fading religious and ideological enthusiasm began to take their toll during that period. The multi-campus idea was deferred, and with it the management's plan to raise donations and obtain State support. The university was exposed to growing financial difficulties, for the following reasons:

1. **Lack of designated State budget** – in the first years studies at the Extensions did not require special academic facilities as they were held in the afternoons and consisted of a partial and eclectic curriculum, a fact that explains why throughout the first 15 years of their operation the PBC refused to budget them, alleging that such a framework does not justify funding the students. Moreover, the university's demand for a special budget for the operation of the Extensions was also declined. Therefore, the university received funding for students from Extensions only when they arrived at the main campus to

162 The budget of the Ashkelon, Zefat and Jordan Valley Extensions amounted to 1.4 % of the university's 1975 budget, as specified by Dr. Bar Ilan in his report to the Rector on 8 April 1975. Bar Ilan University Archive, container 753, file 285.

complete their studies. Payment for these students was received as part of the overall budgeting of students at the university and based on the F.T.E (Full Time Equivalent) index. This policy by the PBC was based on its 1960s and 1970s policy of refraining from encouraging the existence of Bar Ilan's Extensions. An explicit expression of this policy was given by the PBC's Chairperson, Prof. Yaacov Ziv,[163] in his letter to the Rector of Bar Ilan University in 1987:

a. The PBC encourages academic activities in the periphery, with a preference for Regional Colleges.
b. A demand will not be made to close existing Extensions, but the PBC will not encourage the opening of new ones or the expansion of activities at existing ones.
c. The PBC will not allocate further special budgets to the Extensions [. . .] As to the existence of pre-academic preparatory studies at Zefat and Ashkelon, we do not oppose these activities, provided that the funding that had been promised to you covers the expenses.[164]

This policy had put an end to expanding the number of Extensions and mounted further difficulties to the continued existence of the existing ones, the result being that by the beginning of the 1980s the university was faced with the following dilemma: While on the one hand the demand for higher education in Israel grew, and could be addressed through the Extensions, maybe even changing the CHE's perception towards them, on the other hand the fact that the university continued with the same limited operation allowed it flexibility in their remote management with a small academic and administrative staff and a single manager for all three Extensions. The university's management knew that a transition to a full academic curriculum, at least for years 1 and 2 as presented by Dr. Bar Ilan, required further academic faculty to become involved, as well as the appointment of a separate manager for each Extension and overall supervision by the university. Such a step entailed a further burden on the university's finances with the PBC remaining out of the picture and taking no financial responsibility over the Extensions. Not even the 1977 political upheaval, that had raised political awareness among residents of the country's periphery to their electoral strength and their rights, led to any change to the CHE's social position. Even the appointment of a member of the

---

163 Yaacov Ziv, a professor at the Technion, two time recipient of the Israel Security award and recipient of the Israel Prize for Exact Sciences in 1993. President of the National Academy of Science and Chairperson of the PBC in 1991–1994.

164 CHE archive, Bar Ilan University Extensions file. Letter from the PBC Chairperson to Prof. Krausz, the university's Rector, 31 March 1987.

university's Board – Zevulun Hammer, as Minister of Education and Culture in 1977 did not bring the university State budgets which would have alleviated some of the financial burden entailed in the continuing operation of the Extensions. Historically, the CHE perceived the Extensions as part of Bar Ilan University in terms of their funding and their operation. Accordingly, they were not even included in the CHE's discussions on the expansion of accessibility to higher education in the 1970s and 1980s. The CHE's policy on the matter of expanding accessibility to higher education during these years considered Regional Colleges as potential institutions for expanding the accessibility, while the Extensions were excluded from such potential. All applications by the university and by the Extensions to the Minister were responded by his staff as follows: "The Council for Higher Education views the Ashkelon Extension of Bar Ilan University as an integral part of the University. The Extension is included in the university's budget".[165]

2. **Termination of municipal support** – as opposed to the Jordan Valley Extension which acquired most of its courses from the university, thereby reducing its deficits, the direct operation of the Extensions at Zefat and Ashkelon led the university to financial deficits which inflated substantially by the beginning of the 1980s. The understandings reached between the university's management and the local authorities in the 1960s became more and more obsolete as the financial situation of the local authorities worsened and the basic needs of their residents grew. Countless petitions made by the university's leaders to the Mayors asking for support in the maintenance of the Extension under their jurisdiction were to no avail. Left with no other recourse, the university's Rector pointed his arrows directly at the local mayors. Only following struggles by the political members of the management such as Dr. Alfonso Zabah, Asher Ochayon and Dr. Haim Cherki to hold back the threat to cut the Extensions' budget, did the Rector admit that "Publications in the press were deliberately inserted by us, so as to prove that we would not be able to operate the Extensions without local support".[166] Attempts by members of the university's management and public officials in the beginning of the 1980s to initiate the establishment of an Association for nurturing higher education in development areas did not lead to a solution of the financial problem, and the

---

165 Ibid. Letter from the Secretary of the CHE Abraham Ben Yaacov to the manager of the Center for Post-Secondary Education at the Ministry of Education, 4 November 1975.

166 Bar Ilan University Archive, container 753, file 285. Protocol of the Board meeting held on 30 January 1975.

Extensions' operating deficits continued to grow. At the time the local municipalities believed that the responsibility for budgeting the Extensions should be allocated to national authorities. However, attempts by the mayor of Ashkelon to convince the Ministry of Interior to allocate budgets for the Extension were unsuccessful. In his letter to the Mayor of Ashkelon, the manager of the Administration of Local Authorities responded: "The Ministry of Interior does not budget universities. At the most it recognizes the municipality's expenses when calculating grants to the municipality. Therefore, the Ashkelon municipality is the party responsible for supporting the university's Extension".[167]

3. **A new dilemma: invest in developing the Extensions or the main campus?** As operations at the main campus grew and expanded, the university's management was faced with a new dilemma, destined to accompany them for many years until the university's official separation from the Extensions in 2001: whether to invest most of its financial and human resources at the main campus, developing research capabilities, or remaining dedicated to the religious and social aims served by the Extensions. The university's management knew very well that the number of hours taught at each Extension would have to grow in order to further develop the Extensions, but this would require enhanced financial expenditure and organizationally require students to commit to full two year studies. This dilemma was added to the question of the university's identity and its commitment to become a research institution, as already discussed by Menachem Klein in his studies about the university (Klein, 1998; Klein, 2004: 201–253; Klein, 2006: 23–61). Would a continued devotion to the university's social and religious aims determine its pace of development and identity, or will its commitment to developing research and science – similarly to any other academic institution in the world – define its identity and designation. The more the university's commitment to research and science grew, and the stronger the voices calling for its scientific independence, its management grew more and more committed to developing the main campus at the expense of the university's religious-social aims. While this process deepened, there was a growing sense of the Extensions becoming a financial burden on the university's development (Schwartz, 2006). First signs of this trend can be noted as early as the beginning of 1975, at Board discussions on the topic of the university's budget for that year. The dilemma was whether to continue investing in the Extensions, knowing that such

167 Ashkelon College Archive, file 1985. Letter from the Manager of the Training Division at the ministry of Labor to the Mayor, 3 October 1985.

investment would be, at least partially, at the expense of further developing the main campus. While university leaders promoted its academic development, representatives of the NRP religious political movement in its Board – Knesset Member Hammer, Minister Burg and Minister Hazani – struggled against the idea to cut the budget of the Extensions, which they perceived as a religious-social and political project of the highest importance. This approach was voiced at Board meetings by Hammer and others:

> I have been informed that the budgetary plans are expected to impact the Zefat and Ashkelon Extensions. This surprises me, as the project of the Extensions is among the university's greatest and most important projects both academically and in terms of the mission behind it. Undermining the Extensions in the current state of the economy and the country's existing population distribution would result in the lower classes being the first and foremost to be harmed by the budgetary cuts. The Extensions are the university's heritage assets which should not be touched whenever the need arises for budgetary cuts.[168]

The politicians were able to thwart the idea of cutting the Extensions' budgets, and Minister Hazani reiterated that: "The official position regarding the Extensions is to be seen as a warning". The Board sent a message to the CHE and especially to the local authorities at which the Extensions operated, to assist the university in their operation. The Rector, Prof Fisch, concluded the discussion with the following words: "The Extensions are a highly important operation, having a relatively low cost compared to its huge benefit".[169] This "huge benefit" involved the social and public image which was also used to raise donations from rich Sephardi donors such as Dahan and Assraf from the USA and Alphonso Sabag from Israel.

4. **Loss of the monopoly over extra-university studies at the periphery** – Until the latter part of the 1970s Bar Ilan University held the exclusive initiative for holding extra-university studies. However, this monopoly gradually began to diminish with the entry of Tel Aviv University, Ben Gurion and Haifa to this area of operation. As mentioned earlier, these universities granted academic auspices to institutions that operated near Bar Ilan University's Extensions: In the north Tel Aviv University gave its auspices to the Tel Chai Regional College,

---

168 Bar Ilan University Archive, container 753, file 285. Board meeting protocol, 30 January 1975. This is an example of the different designations of the Extensions: The political leadership in the university's Board saw their social-political importance, while the academic leadership also saw their social-academic roles.

169 Ibid. Minister Hazani's remarks during the Board meeting; ibid, the Rector, Prof. Fisch's remarks.

while the University of Haifa gave its auspices to the Yezreel Valley Regional College. In the south Ben Gurion University gave its auspices to the Sapir Regional College located not far from Ashkelon. These universities had no intention of establishing Extensions in these areas, and therefore the CHE's approval was not required for their operation, as stipulated in amendment 3 to the CHE law. Granting academic auspices required no special preparations, as the entire initiative originated from the Regional Colleges themselves. Students taking academic courses at these Regional Colleges enjoyed a retroactive accreditation of their studies at the colleges following their acceptance for studies at the university campus. Despite the limitations of this process, Bar Ilan's management knew from past experience that such limited operations may in future become an Extension, especially if pressures are increased due to the growing need to increase the accessibility of new populations to higher education. The discomfort felt by the university's Board towards these activities can be noted from the response of the Manager of the Extensions in his progress report to the Rector. Dr. Bar Ilan estimated that operations at the Jordan Valley would not be undermined and may even expand. However, he also estimated that problems may arise at Zefat due to the growing competition and efforts invested by the city of Kiryat Shmona towards developing academic studies at nearby Tel Chai. Dramatically, and so as to encourage the Board to respond to Tel Aviv University's move, he even suggested considering the future of the Zefat Extension if the government would not prevent the opening of further Extensions in the north:

> I believe we will have to close the Extension there, despite our significant achievements of the past two years. There is a war between us and Tel Aviv University on this matter, and at the end of the day I believe that we should not forsake our position.[170]

In the south Dr. Bar Ilan demanded the intervention of the CHE's Committee for Regional Colleges so as to ensure that the Negev College, which began in 1976 to offer academic courses by Ben Gurion University, would stop holding any academic activities. The university's Rector joined him in this struggle, applying to the Chairperson of the CHE's Committee for Regional Colleges and asking him to use his authority to stop Ben Gurion University from operating at Sapir College. The Rector's reasoning focused on Bar Ilan University's rights as the first university to operate in the periphery, and the fears that the uniqueness of its project be undermined: "I wish to note that the Sha'ar Hanegev College was only founded

---

170 Ibid, container 474, file 247. Letter from Dr. Bar Ilan to Professor Harel-Fisch, the university's Rector, 6 April 1970.

as a college two years ago, many years after our Extension at Ashkelon. Had this college not been opened, there would not have been any duplicity issue".[171]

Attempts by Prof. A.M Meir, Chairperson of the CHE's Committee for Regional Colleges, to establish a collaboration between the Sha'ar Hanegev (Sapir) College and the Ashkelon Extension were, as mentioned earlier, unsuccessful, and the university's Senate rejected his proposal for mutual recognition between the two institutions. Prof. Meir's response to the university's opposition expressed the CHE's position in terms of Bar Ilan's monopoly and the need to increase accessibility to higher education in remote regions. Although the change in the CHE's position did not involve the establishment of new Extensions similarly to Bar Ilan's existing one, Bar Ilan's social uniqueness in the periphery had been undermined, as explained by the Rector (ibid.): "I believe that the Negev College provides services to a different population than the Extension at Ashkelon and I have no doubt in the College's necessity, including its academic track".

5. **A new generation** – the financial and logistic obstacles of the 1980s were not new and their impact was already felt in the mid 1970s, but the initial period of ideological enthusiasm shadowed financial and operational difficulties. The university's founders thwarted any attempt to undermine the Extensions for either financial or logistic reasons. The impact of these difficulties began taking its toll in the beginning of the 1980s when the founding generation was replaced by a second generation leadership. The new leadership operated within a different academic reality: The university had been officially accredited in the beginning of the 1970s, the multi-campus university idea was permanently removed from management's agenda and the main campus expanded as a result of a substantial increase in the number of students. The commitment for a balanced financial management and academic competition with the country's other universities were first on the agenda of the new managers. The PBC's preference for supporting universities teaching at Regional Colleges rather than at Extensions positioned the financial problem at the top of the agenda of the university's leaders in its discussions about the Extensions. The ideal of shaping the religious image of Israeli society became less realistic in view of the difficult financial situation. The new generation managers realized that the university carries a great financial burden in order to fulfill its social and religious aims in the periphery and they believed that this task should be borne by the State. An expression of this conviction can be found in

171 Ashkelon College Archive, file 1978, letter from the Rector to the Chairperson of the CHE's Regional Colleges Committee, 8 January 1978.

the Rector's letter to the Minister of Education, 23 September 1990: "I wish to note that in the past the Board considered closing the university's Extensions due to the budgetary problem. Only our ambitions to build a just society and shape the image of Israeli society prevented it until now".[172]

6. **The passing of Dr. Bar Ilan** – Dr. Bar Ilan struggled tirelessly for the realization of the religious and social aims represented by the Extensions. Since their establishment he worked hard to obtain budgets, allocate academic faculty and increase the number of courses offered at the Extensions. His death in June 1979 was a hard blow to the Extensions, which consequently remained for over a year with no manager to struggle on their behalf. Dr. Bar Ilan's status as one of the university's founders and the son of Rabbi Meir (Berlin) Bar Ilan, in whose memory the university was named, enhanced his authority to struggle against any decision which may have harmed the Extensions. After his death the Extensions were measured according to their financial stability, and consequently their operations gradually diminished, the most tangible expression of which can be noted in the termination of his plan for two full years studies at the Extensions. This meant continued eclectic studies, but these in turn did not attract young students who wished to study regularly within a predefined curriculum. The continued operation of a limited program which did not facilitate the completion of credits for years 1 and 2 even in topics that had already been taught at the Extensions, undermined their attractiveness among young adults. The transition to full studies, at least during the first two undergraduate years, as had been envisioned by Dr. Bar Ilan, would have generated an expansion process, leading to recruiting lecturers, expanding academic facilities, attracting students and increasing administrative staff – with the implications being an increase in the gravitational force of studies, as can be seen at universities.

172 Ibid, file 1990. Letter from the Rector to the Minister of Education, 23 September 1990.

Chapter 8 Ideological Renewal: Extensions as a Social Model

The Social Lobby for the Extensions

Despite the difficulties noted, the Extensions continued to operate, but in a way that while justifying their existence, did not contribute to their further development. More and more voices were heard at the university's management calling to close down the Extensions due to financial and operational difficulties and the fact that the PBC consistently ignored their needs. Others, led by senior Board member Alfonso Zabah, supported their expansion. Among supporters were public figures members of the Board of Trustees, Asher Ochayon, Head of the Department of Sephardi Communities at the World Zionist Organization, and NRP (National Religious Party) members who joined the struggle – all committed to leading a strong front that prevented budgetary cuts to the Extensions. They also struggled to further expand the Extensions' operations. This social lobby aimed to be a new driving force that would lead to the realization of social and national aims, and not necessarily religious ones. Members of the lobby believed that the university should emphasize its social designation and the national mission fulfilled by the Extensions in Israel's southern and northern peripheries. This message gained special meaning following the 1977 political upheaval and the greatest fund raising initiative in the Jewish world until then towards of the rehabilitation of developing neighborhoods. The university's management, far from ignoring the social message, was quick to support these steps alongside the social lobby in the university's Board of Trustees. This social atmosphere marked the opening of a new era for the Extensions. The new generation of university leaders, considering the budgetary issues of the time, had placed the Extensions under danger of closing, but the existential crisis led the university's management in search of alternatives for the PBC's lack of support, which would assure the continued operation of the Extensions. Their social message marks a transition between two periods of operation of the Extensions:

1. The foundation period – characterized by a religious-ideological fervor, similarly to the fervor that characterized the founders of the religious universities in the United States and the behaviors of "newcomers" wishing to undermine the hegemony of the field so as to obtain its cultural capital.
2. The second period – began in 1980 and consisted of a new representation of the Extensions based on a social model devoid of religious aspirations. The timing

of the change is not accidental, and was a result of the social transformations that took place in Israel following the 1977 political upheaval (Eisenstadt, 2004). The awakening of ethnic struggles and sense of deprivation among Mizrachim living in the periphery, took their toll on the country's religious nationalist party in the 1981 elections for the country's 10th Knesset. The NRP, who had in the past succeeded in gaining the political support of religious new immigrants, had lost half its political power, with its most notable decline noted in development towns and areas heavily populated by Mizrachim (Don Yechiya, 1990; Friednman, 1982). In such times the social message proposed by the lobby members gave hope to the university's leadership, who became convinced that indeed the continued existence of the Extensions is among the central interests of the university and the religious camp, both towards the university's Sephardi donors and Israel's social and political leadership. The university's inclination towards the lobby's social approach can be noted in the approaches of its leaders in the beginning of the 1980s. For instance, the university's Rector Prof. Rackman was quoted as having said the following during a meeting held in Ashkelon: "Bar Ilan University's great contribution to this project [has been] a blessing to the Extensions project and its role in reducing social gaps in Israel". At the same meeting the Chairperson of the Board Dr. Zerach Warhaftig said: "I see the Extensions as a tool for bringing academic education to remote places", and his fellow Board member and long term Knesset member on behalf of the NRP, Abraham Melamed[173] noted that: "I see the Extensions as a part of the effort towards solving the country's social problems".[174]

The new policy and pressures asserted by the social lobby led the university on its new path, the first stage of which had resulted in two important decisions involving the Extensions:

1. **The establishment of a steering committee for Extensions as part of the Senate committees** – the university's central committee decided to appoint a social steering committee for the Extensions, its purpose being to advise the university's management regarding possible methods of operation and to identify sources of support for funding the Extensions. The committee's

173 Politician and NRP Knesset member in the 1970's and 1980's, among the founders of the "Mizrachi" movement and the Nir Ezion religious cooperative agricultural settlement.

174 Bar Ilan University Archive, container 753, file 285. Protocol of the Public Council Committee for academic education in Development towns, 29 December 1982.

composition was selected based on the new policy: Alfonso Zabah was appointed as Chairperson of the Steering Committee. Its members were social activists coming from a wide range of local organizations, including Dan Moreno, Deputy Director of Finance at the National Insurance Institute, Ministry of Justice legal assistance unit head Jorpan Claude Nidam, Dr. Haim Cherki, who had been active at the Department of Sephardi Communities at the World Zionist Organization, and Asher Ochayon, Head of the Department of Sephardi Communities at the World Zionist Organization. These activists were dedicated to support the university in promoting the social aims of its Extensions.

2. **Establishment of a public committee for nurturing academic education in development areas** – the university's management responded to the initiative of the social lobby in the establishment of a "Public council for nurturing higher education in development areas". The council included the Chairperson of the Board of Bar Ilan University – Dr. Zerach Warhaftig, heads of the university in the beginning of the 1980s – the President Prof. Rackman, the Rector Prof. Eckstein, the CEO David Altman, Knesset member Abraham Melamed; Mayors of Tiberias, Ashkelon and Zefat; and public figures from the university's social lobby. The first task of the public committee was to establish an Association dedicated to nurturing higher education in development areas, consisting of the members of the public committee. Among the aims specified in its statute:

> To care for and act towards the reduction of higher education gaps in developing areas. To support and assist Bar Ilan's Extensions in developing areas in Israel in any possible way. To act to reduce educational and social gaps [. . .] To raise donations for these operations in Israel and abroad. All the above would be carried out and implemented via Bar Ilan University's Extensions.[175]

The following was decided during the council's first meeting held at Ashkelon in January 1983:

1. A small committee would be appointed, comprising of a number of members of the public committee
2. A scholarships fund would be established for students at the Extensions
3. Efforts would be made to secure national resources towards the construction of a campus for the Ashkelon Extension

---

175 Ibid, container 753, file 285. Statute of the Association for nurturing higher education in development areas, article 3, b, c, e.

4. The feasibility of establishing a union of towns for higher education at the periphery would be examined[176]

According to the decisions reached at Ashkelon, the university renewed its petitions to the Minister of Education, in the hope that his close familiarity with the Extensions and his support as a member of the university's Board in their social mission would lead to a change in the PBC's policy towards them. The letter from the university's CEO in March 1983 illustrates the university's policy change:

> For many years the university perceived this mission as a national task, knowing that the acquisition of higher education serves all walks of society [. . .] The hardships of our times has made it increasingly difficult for the university to continue to carry the burden and it was about to inform that it is unable to continue to provide academic education outside of campus due to the huge budgetary difficulties entailed in such a program. However, Public figures, Knesset members and heads of local councils protested against Bar Ilan's intentions to cease providing this service and consequently dedicated their efforts to continue to hold these operations through an Association - the Public Committee for Academic Education in Development Areas. It is astounding and surprising to find that national institutions are mounting objections and obstacles [. . .] We believe that national public bodies should reconsider the project's future and continued operation.[177]

According to the council's work agenda, each member was allocated tasks based on his area of specialization and public influence. Heads of local councils were also recruited for the task, approaching Government ministries that support local government such as the Ministry of Education and the Local government administration at the Ministry of Interior.

While the council's work focused on public and political lobbying and the allocation of public resources, the Steering Committee acted within the academic system, allocating administrative and academic funds for the Extensions' operation. In its first meetings, the council encouraged the university's management to take a number of essential steps for promoting the Extensions:

1. Appoint a Manager of the Extensions to replace Dr. Tuvia Bar Ilan, about a year after his death. The President of the university accepted the recommendation of the members of the Steering Committee and appointed Dr. Moshe Berreby who had made Aliyah for social and Zionist reasons and had been

176 Ibid. Protocol of the Public Council Committee for academic education in development towns, 29 December 1982.

177 Ibid. Altman's letter to Minister of Education Zevulun Hammer, 24 March 1983.

employed at Bar Ilan University as a professor of Statistics. This appointment was a result of the university's new social policy.
2. Approach the university's Sephardi donors, requesting donations towards improving the deficient educational facilities at the Extensions.
3. Appoint local managers for the Zefat and Ashkelon Extensions – their role being to follow the university's policy, serving as the operational arm of the Manager of the Extensions.[178] The decision to accelerate these appointments was made in part due to the fact that the number of students at the Extensions in the beginning of the 1980s was very small, and the committee members realized that without increasing the number of students, no development plan for the Extensions would be feasible. This is why the local managers' work during these early stages focused on marketing so as to increase the number of students.

The first decisions were being implemented and the social aims began to take shape:

1. The entry of Dr. Berreby into the role of Manager of the Extensions led to an acceleration of the work taking place at the three Extensions. Upon his leaving for sabbatical two years after accepting the appointment, his substitute Dr. (later Professor) Haim Gaziel from the School of Education continued working with the same drive and conviction to further implement the university's mission. The work focused, as aforesaid, on the social mission. Dr. Gaziel continued communicating with the local authorities in in order to improve the physical infrastructure of the Extensions, making them more suitable for academic studies. Moreover, he petitioned the Mayors to allocate suitable buildings. A Friends Association was founded at each of the cities in which an Extension was located, comprised of both locals and university representatives. Its aim was to recruit as many local forces as possible in favor of the local Extension. Upon his return from sabbatical Dr. Berreby drafted operating agreements with the Ashkelon and Zefat municipalities, through which the relationship between the local authority and the university was regulated for the first time.

178 As explained earlier, the Jordan Valley Extension operated independently in terms of administration, and its manager was the manager of the Post-Secondary education institution in which the academic Extension resided. The manager was appointed by the Regional Council and the university had no involvement in the management of the institution.

2. The vigorous work of members of the Steering Committee and their insistence on their social message proved successful, and an initial foreign donation of $50,000 was received for each Extension. The donation was dedicated to improving academic facilities at the Extensions, and in 1989 the first computer laboratories were installed at each of the Extensions.
3. Although a permanent arrangement for managers' salaries was not found, two Extension managers were appointed – at Ashkelon and Zefat, and their employment was temporarily arranged through the local Association that had been established in order to further develop the local Extension. The fact that managers were appointed at Ashkelon and Zefat quickly led to a rise in the number of students. The importance of appointing a manager for the Extensions' development during that period was described in Dr. Berreby's letter to the Ashkelon municipality: "I must note that our experience at Zefat and Zemach has proven beyond doubt that an active and responsible manager is able to achieve significant change".[179]

The University and the Local Authorities: First Signs of a Center-Periphery Struggle

Contrary to the vigorous work of the university's internal Steering Committee and its success stories, the Public Council did not see the fruit of its hard work, as all its members' petitions to governmental bodies came to nothing. For instance, attempts by the University's CEO to directly approach the Minister of Education Zevulun Hammer in order to obtain budgets for the Extensions' operation, were blocked by the PBC, which continued to reiterate its position that the Extensions are an inseparable part of Bar Ilan University and therefore are not eligible for a separate budget.[180] This position of the PBC was present also in responses to the approaches made by various Mayors to the Minister of Interior and to the Local Authorities Administration in the mid 1980s. In all cases the answer was the same: "The Ministry of Interior informed the authorities that education in general, and higher education in particular, are outside its jurisdiction, and therefore it is the local authority who is responsible for supporting the Extensions".[181]

179 Ashkelon College Archive, file 1980. Letter from Dr. Berreby to the Education Department Manager at Ashkelon Municipality, 4 December 1985.

180 CHE archive, Bar Ilan University Extensions file. Letter from the PBC Chairperson to the Rector, 31 March 1987.

181 Ashkelon College Archive, file 1985. Letter to the Mayor from the Training Division Manager, 3 October 1985.

The Public Council's failure in the public-political arena as well as financially, gradually led to its ceasing to exist, nearly two years following its establishment. The university remained the only body carrying the operational and financial burden of the Extensions at Zefat and Ashkelon. To reduce its expenses as well as to avoid closing down the Extensions, as had been suggested at the university, the Steering Committee initiated an application to the local authorities, demanding an operational agreement that would regulate their mutual relationship. In February 1984 agreements were signed with the Municipality of Zefat and the Municipality of Ashkelon, stipulating the responsibilities of each of the Parties in the operational expenses of the local Extension. It was agreed that the authority would cover some administrative costs, such as the salary of a secretary, the salary of a janitor, ongoing maintenance costs of the building – usually a local school – and the salary of the manager. The University's part focused on the academic operation of the institution: faculty members' salaries, a library and ongoing costs incurred by academic management. The university collected tuition from students through payment vouchers.

The agreements marked a new era in the relationship between the university and the local authorities: No longer the initiative of a single entrepreneur motivated by religious-social fervor, but parties having common social interests who have joined forces, each for its own reasons, in operating a local academic institution. An expression of this change in the relationship between the parties can be noted in a letter from the Manager of the Extensions to the Manager of the Education Department at the Ashkelon Municipality: "So as to avoid misunderstandings between us in future, I suggest that before we move to the next building, we prepare a contract to be signed by me and by you".[182] A short time later a contract was sent, resonating the new relationship: "The contract must outline the proper relationship between our two institutions, for the benefit of the students studying at the Extension and that of the residents of the district of Ashkelon".[183]

The formal relationship which emerged from the contractual agreements also had implications. Contrary to the relationship during the foundation period, any violation of the agreement caused tensions in the relationship between the parties. Attempts by the Ashkelon Municipality to evade its obligations to the Extension often resulted in harsh responses on the part of the Manager of the Extensions. In one of his letters to the Mayor he warned: "As you know, we are

182 Ibid, file 1983, Letter from Dr. Berreby to Moshe Yanai, 10 November 1983.

183 Ibid, letter from the Manager of the Extensions to the Manager of the Municipality's Education Department, 4 December 1983.

unwanted sub-tenants at the Tagar School [. . .] If the municipality does not act soon to solve the two most urgent issues: A suitable building for the Extension and a suitable library, the university will consider its next steps, including closing the Extension".[184] The Rector of the university also wrote: "I was informed by Dr. Berreby, the Manager of the Extensions, that the physical situation at Ashkelon is unbearable and that the school does not meet the terms of the contract signed between the Ashkelon municipality and Bar Ilan University in this regard".[185]

Although at that stage the CHE did not see itself as a party in the Extensions project, the Chairperson of the colleges committee at the CHE, Prof. Yaacov Rand from the School of Education at Bar Ilan University, joined the struggle, taking the university's side. In its letter to the Mayor of Ashkelon he demanded that the municipality fulfill its obligations as per its agreement with Bar Ilan University: "Bar Ilan University insists on full implementation of all parts of the agreement signed between the Municipality and the University".[186] The Municipalities of Zefat and Ashkelon, who had their own budgetary difficulties, could not invest the financial expenditure necessary for operating a local Extension, and therefore in collaboration with the university established local associations to operate the Extension and cover the municipality's obligations towards the university. According to their approach, the local association would offer additional courses, such as occupational training, continued education programs and certification studies, thereby generating an income which would be directed towards funding the academic expenses. The authorities' lack of motivation to financially support the local Extension expressed an atmosphere which had been voiced from time to time over the years, but until then did not find a practical pipeline. This approach was motivated by three main considerations:

1. **Budgetary priority** – the mayors were committed to the formal education system of their jurisdiction: Preschools, primary schools, secondary education and informal education. They were not as committed to higher education at the Extension. The education system supported by the State was given precedence in municipal budgets, while the activities at the Extension, which was not supported by the State, was not. The expenses of the operation of the

184 Ibid, Letter from Dr. Haim Gaziel to the Mayor of Ashkelon, 7 February, 1983.

185 Ibid, file 1984. Letter from Prof. Albeck to the Mayor, 9 October 1984.

186 Ibid, file 1985. Letter from Prof. Rand, Chairperson of the Sub-Committee, to the Mayor, 29 April, 1985.

Extension were not included in the budgets of the Zefat and Ashkelon municipalities in the 1980s, and in practice they were neglected.

2. **Lack of control** – as opposed to the local authority's control over the formal education system including its scope, contents and influence, the Extensions were directly operated by the university with no involvement of the local authority – not in scope, not in contents, and even not in admission requisites. This state of affairs caused alienation on the part of the local authorities, and beyond general willingness to have an Extension in the city in the 1980s, there was no actual practical support by the local authority.
3. **Center-Periphery Struggles** – first signs of a Center-Periphery Struggle could already be noted in the second half of the 1970s. Municipal leaders were not satisfied with the ongoing operation of the Extension, but wanted to see it as an academic institution that aspires for independence and offers local residents both academic and vocational studies. The university, which controlled the operation of the Extensions, did not always operate according to local needs, but according to its available pool of lecturers and areas of study that could be most easily managed remotely. These usually included departments which did not require laboratories or extensive databases and educational facilities. Moreover, the demand for higher education, which continued to grow since the beginning of the 1970s, pushed the CHE to examine ways to further expand accessibility to higher education in Israel. The municipal leaders, aware of such discussions, urged the university to expand the offerings of the Extension so as to be able to address growing demands or alternatively to be included in the CHE's emerging plans to increase accessibility. The demand for higher education in the 1980s was also noted in the local election campaigns at Zefat and Ashkelon. The younger local population demanded increased academic opportunities at the Extension, thereby raising awareness among municipal leaders to the benefit of having an Extension in their city. This can be noted from a letter from the Chairperson of the Student Body at Ashkelon to the Manager of the Department of Education at the municipality:

> Enclosed is a schedule of courses offered at the Extension in 1984. It appears that the curriculum is very meager, and does not address the needs of students at the Extension. There is a sense that the curriculum was put together so as to meet the most minimal requirements for the Extension's continued operation. The shortage in courses should be noted in particular. There is no General History, and only one course in the History of Israel. I kindly ask for your immediate intervention with the person responsible for the Extension or the Rector of the university to urgently add courses in General History and Education. If additional hours are not added, I am afraid that the Extension would soon

> cease to exist, in which case we would lose a university institution that has contributed greatly to the city and its students.[187]

Following pressures asserted on the university is was agreed that: "The manager of the Extension (at Ashkelon) will open additional courses. These courses will be targeted towards diverse populations and will also include non-academic courses (such as preschool assistants training, and more)".[188]

So as to be able to reap the fruit of success during their term, the young politicians urged the university to increase the Extension's scope of operations. The duration of long term planning towards a suitable academic institution was to their detriment, and therefore the intent was to take advantage of the full potential of the Extension as it is. Signs of this trend could be noted as early as the mid 1970s: Aharon Nachmias, the new Mayor of Zefat at the time, pressurized the university to choose this direction.[189] Aharon Haiby, the Mayor of Ashkelon, did not hesitate to examine other possibilities which may replace Bar Ilan University. He approached the Ministry of Education requesting to include Ashkelon in plans to establish colleges such as the one at Sha'ar Hanegev. However, in parallel he also urged the university to further develop the Extension and avoid further budgetary cuts. In one of his letters to the Rector he demanded the following:

> In our opinion Bar Ilan University should see its mission beyond the narrow role of an academic institution, as it has a Jewish pioneering duty to bring values of education and culture to the new Israel and to development areas. Therefore, we find it difficult to accept your explanation that from the university's annual budget of hundreds of millions of Lira you saw fit to begin budgetary cuts with our single prized possession – the Ashkelon Extension.[190]

The harmony and enthusiasm of the foundation years were replaced by demands and resolute tones. In his first meetings with the university's representatives, the Mayor of Ashkelon stipulated the allocation of land designated for the new campus as per the university's agreement, upon the transferring of entire faculties to Ashkelon. In a statement submitted to the Senate by Dr. Koliv (substituting for Dr. Bar Ilan who at the time had been on sabbatical), he argued that the Mayor of

---

187 Ibid, file 1983, Letter from the Chairperson of the Student Body to the Manager of the Department of Education, 31 March, 1983.

188 Ibid, Protocol of the Bar Ilan Extension Friends Association, 6 November, 1983.

189 Zefat College Archive, file 1974. Letter from David Koliv to Aharon Nachmias, Mayor of Zefat, 26 February 1974.

190 Ashkelon College Archive, file 1974. Letter from the Mayor to the Rector, 26 December, 1974.

Ashkelon "sees our Extension as nothing more than a transitory stage". According to Dr. Koliv, "The Mayor's plans and the university's plans are two parallel lines that will never meet".[191] About six months later the Mayor wrote to the Rector: "I believe that in the near future we will establish at Ashkelon a daughter-university on the foundations of today's Extension".[192] In parallel he approached the Minister of Education at the time, Aharon Yadlin, requesting support for the Ashkelon Extension, or alternatively approval for the establishment of a Regional College at the city, which would also offer practical engineering studies:

> I will assist as much as I can in ensuring the continued operation of Bar Ilan University's Extension at Ashkelon, and I have already discussed the matter with the Council for Higher Education's Planning and Budgeting Committee.
> The matter of the School of Practical Engineering requires a joint evaluation with the authorized persons at the Ministry of Labor and Ort Education Network. This evaluation should be performed with positive intentions.
> In view of the fact that I have decided that the Bar Ilan University Extension at Ashkelon should continue its operations, I believe the decision on the matter of the Regional College can be postponed for the time being.[193]

The minister's response had been influenced by the CHE's position, by which the Extension was a part of the university. As to the Mayor's request to establish a Regional College in the city, the CHE's Secretary responded as follows:

> The Council for Higher Education views Bar Ilan University's Ashkelon Extension as an inseparable part of the university… The planned college was an initiative of the Sha'ar Hanegev Regional Council and the other local councils who issued a request to the Council for Higher Education to be recognized as an institution of higher education – an Accredited College… Only following the council's discussion will I be able to inform you of its position.[194]

Following the letter from the CHE Secretary, a similar letter was issued by the Manager of the Post-Secondary Education Center at the Ministry of Education:

---

191 Bar Ilan University Archive, container 753, file 285. Dr. Koliv's letter to the Rector, 4 April, 1974.

192 Ashkelon College Archive, file 1974. Letter from the Mayor of Ashkelon, Aharon Haiby, to the Rector, Prof. Kadari, 26 December, 1974.

193 Ibid, file 1975, Letter from the Minister of Education to the Mayor of Ashkelon, 30 July, 1975.

194 Ibid. Letter from the CHE's Secretary, Abraham Ben Yaacov, to Mordechai Peled, Manager of the Post-Secondary Education Center at the Ministry of Education and Culture, 4 November 1975.

> A Sub-Committee of the Council for Higher Education, chaired by Prof. Alexandra Polyakov-Mayber will soon submit its recommendations to the Council General Assembly regarding all Regional Colleges in the country [. . .] Meaning that the matter is still under "*sub judice*" on the part of the Council for Higher Education [. . .] I suggest that the formal status of the Extension be identical to that of the Extension at the Jordan Valley College in Zemach. Bar Ilan University should take the initiative in this regard.[195]

These power struggles, typical of center-periphery classifications, increased and subdued alternately during the 1970s and 1980s. To a significant extent, the changes of personnel and the growing demand for higher education determined fluctuations in these activities and influenced Bar Ilan University's relationships with the authorities. While the development of the Extension was affected by these struggles, the dependence of the local authorities on State institutions in agreeing to an alternative to the Extension, left then with no choice, and the relationship between the Parties fluctuated between a willingness to support the university and the Extension, and an aim to establish a multi-faceted academic institution at the city, one that they would be able to influence.

To conclude this chapter in is important to note that the 1960s were characterized by a pioneering fervor both on the part of the local authorities, and the university's founders. Wherever a university representative would visit, he was met with great enthusiasm and the willingness to assist the university in realizing its social ideology. Financial difficulties at the Zefat and Ashkelon municipalities did not stop this level of support, as the potential entailed in the existence of an Extension in their city overshadowed financial difficulties. The growing demand for higher education in the mid 1970s and the initial discussions at the CHE as to ways to expand the academic system, led Mayors to pressurize the university's management to further develop the Extension. The 1977 political upheaval gradually led to a growing involvement in the situation. Their increasing accessibility to central government and the knowledge that they are able to make a difference encouraged the Mayors to act to establish a college in their city, through State funding. So as not to lose the momentum and the general awareness to the periphery, they urged the university to further develop the Extension.

---

195 Ibid. Letter from Mordechai Peled, Manager of the Post-Secondary Education Center at the Ministry of Education to the Mayor of Ashkelon Aharon Haiby, 5 November 1975.

Chapter 9 The Extensions as Regional Colleges and an Enhanced Accessibility to Higher Education in the 1990s

Regional Colleges: From Post-Secondary Schools to Regional Colleges

In parallel to Bar Ilan's operations in the periphery, the country's growing Post-Secondary education system further expanded through Regional Colleges originally founded as Post-Secondary schools and used as cultural centers, professional education and vocational training centers in diverse areas (Volanski, 2005; Kirsch, 2010). In his latest review on higher education, Kirsch (2010) does not distinguish between the development of Regional Colleges and that of Extensions. However, Regional Colleges, as opposed to Extensions, evolved from Post-Secondary education institutions offering non-academic training for professionals in various fields needed by the local economy, as well as adult education, and were not eligible for State budgets.[196] The initiative for the establishment of colleges came from local politicians, Regional Councils, Kibbutzim and local councils, wishing to provide professional and recreational solutions for their local population. Gradually the managements of these institutions were joined by representatives of other towns in the area, but even then, the management of the Regional Colleges remained in the hands of the initiating Regional Council. A turning point towards the end of the 1970s and the beginning of the 1980s transformed the identity of the Regional Colleges: an academic program under the academic auspices of the country's research universities was added to the Post-Secondary and professional programs. The relationship between the universities and the Regional Colleges during those years was formed following the initiative of the colleges and with no national guidance. Students attending Regional Colleges were able to select courses from an eclectic list, and had to complete most of their degree at the main campus of the respective university. During the period of academic auspices,

---

196 This description does not correspond with the development of Regional Colleges which were originally established as Extensions of Bar Ilan University, and which are the subject of this book. In his research, Kirsch refers to the Regional Colleges as a single unit, which is not the case: The establishment of Bar Ilan's Extensions and their operation is nothing like the process of development of the other Regional Colleges which began as Post-Secondary education institutions.

Regional Colleges were not recognized as part of the list of academic institutions supported by the CHE or the PBC. However, the fact that the universities had academic responsibility over the courses taught at the colleges forced them to operate the colleges just as they would any other academic program. The universities were required to pre-approve the academic programs offered at the Regional Colleges under their auspices and to ensure that their level does not fall from that offered at the main campus.

The Extensions as a Source of Inspiration for Academic Activity at the Regional Colleges

Bar Ilan's work outside its main campus was the only example of extra-university studies in Israel. It was a source of inspiration to local municipal leaders and managers of Regional Colleges in the north and south who strived to enhance the attractiveness of their institutions among potential candidates in the beginning of the 1970s. Bar Ilan University's Manager of the Extensions saw this new phenomenon as an unfair competition as in his view it was not ideology-driven, as were Bar Ilan's initiatives, and therefore he did his best to struggle against it, especially when these new operations backed by other universities were located near Bar Ilan's Extensions, as was the case at Tel Chai in the north and Sha'ar Hanegev in the south. The joint initiative of the municipality of Kiryat Shmona and Tel Chai college to request that Tel Aviv University grant its academic auspices for academic studies at Tel Chai, was met in 1970 by a harsh response from Dr. Bar Ilan. He suggested that the university's management take all available means to block Tel Aviv University's operations in the north, to the point of threatening to cease Bar Ilan's operations at Zefat. With the same insistence he responded in 1976 to the initiative of the Sha'ar Hanegev Regional Council to open academic courses at the Sha'ar Hanegev College, under the auspices of Ben Gurion University.

However, the growing demand for higher education in the periphery and mounting pressures by the heads of Regional Councils and colleges overcame Dr. Bar Ilan's resistance, and in 1970 limited academic activities were launched by additional universities in the north, and in later years expanded to the south as well. The ideas implemented by the founders of Bar Ilan University in their first Extensions, served in the 1970s as a source of inspiration for local initiatives by heads of local councils and managers of Regional Colleges, who approached other universities, requesting to hold extra-university studies at their colleges. This inspiration influenced both the methods of operation and the scope of the initiatives. For example, the agreement between Bar Ilan and the Jordan Valley was studied and served as an example for the local council in discussions with the

University of Haifa.[197] Five years following the opening of Bar Ilan's first Extension at Ashkelon and two years following the establishment of two further Extensions, other universities began holding academic studies outside their main campuses, as listed below:

1. Tel Aviv University was the first to follow Bar Ilan in holding academic studies under its auspices outside its campus. In 1970 it agreed to the request of Kiryat Shmona Municipality and Tel Chai Regional Council and granted its auspices to academic courses at Tel Chai College. This relationship lasted for four years until 1974.
2. In January 1973 the University of Haifa agreed to operate academic courses at the Yezreel Valley Regional College. In the 1974/75 academic year, the Tel Chai College joined this program, following termination of its relationship with Tel Aviv University.
3. In 1976 Ben Gurion University launched academic courses at the Sha'ar Hanegev College, and later also included in its program the Eilat College and the Achva College at Beer Tuvia Regional Council.
4. Towards the end of the 1990s the Hebrew University opened a Jewish Studies Extension in Rehovot, which operated for two years and closed.
5. The Open University attempted to establish learning centers at Regional Colleges. Such a center was inaugurated in 1976 at the Yezreel Valley Regional College, in addition to the auspices of the University of Haifa, and later on also at the Western Galilee College and additional locations.

Table 27 lists the colleges that offered academic courses under the auspices of Israeli universities as of the 1970s to the 1980s, including Bar Ilan's Extensions.

197 Interview with Yoram Raz, CEO of the Yezreel Valley Regional College, 17 August, 2009.

Tab. 27: List of institutions under academic auspices 1970–1990

	Name of Institution	Year of Establishment
Academic auspices of Ben Gurion University:		
	Eilat College[a]	**1980**
	Achva College	**1971**
	Sha'ar Hanegev College	**1976**
Academic auspices of Haifa University:		
	Tel Chai College	**1969**
	Yezreel Valley College	**1976**
	Western Galilee College[b]	**1972**
Academic auspices of Tel Aviv University:		
	Hadera-Menashe College[c]	**1982**
Academic auspices of Bar Ilan University:		
	Zefat College	**1968**
	Jordan Valley College	**1968**
	Ashkelon College	**1965**
	Ariel College	**1982**

[a]The college became part of Ben Gurion University in 2002, and its college status was canceled.
[b]In the mid 1990's the Western Galilee College joined the colleges operating under the academic auspices of Bar Ilan University, following the CHE's recommendation.
[c]In 1997 the college transitioned from the academic auspices of Tel Aviv University to that of the University of Haifa. The college was closed in 1998.

Extensions and Local Colleges: Similarities and Differences in Their Relationships with the Universities

Despite all the extra-university activities it appears that between 1970 and 1980 there was nothing resembling Bar Ilan's Extensions project. To prove this I will analyze the agreements signed between all parties based on the four measures presented in the Chapter on Bar Ilan's agreements with its Extensions in the beginning of the 1970s.

The nature of the agreement between Bar Ilan and its Extensions differed from the other agreements. The agreements signed in the beginning of the 1970s between the University of Haifa and the Tel Chai and Yezreel Valley Colleges, and the one signed between the Open University and the Yezreel Valley College were auspices agreements. At no stage did the other universities consider defining their operations outside their main campus as an Extension, or perceiving a certain location as an integral part of the university, as had been Bar Ilan's approach towards its Extensions at Zefat and Ashkelon. The relationship between the parties had been limited to the granting of academic auspices to academic courses offered at the college. In this context the agreement between the University of Haifa and the Open University and the Yezreel Valley College is similar in its nature to the agreement between Bar Ilan and the Jordan Valley, but despite similarities between the agreements, this agreement also includes significant differences originating from the different approach of the founders of Bar Ilan's Extensions, and not necessarily from the practical approach of the heads of the Jordan Valley Regional Council.

The agreements between the University of Haifa and the Yezreel Valley College and later also Tel Chai, were limited to a predefined period, and their contents attest to the university's intention to offer courses without undertaking the responsibility entailed in their operation, as shall be further explained below in the presentation of the various measures. The agreements stipulated a clear organizational and administrative separation between the parties, while the agreement between Bar Ilan University and the Jordan Valley College did not stipulate such clear division. Moreover, it did not limit the period of the agreement between the parties nor did it imply any reservations from joint responsibility for the management of courses and their contents. Bar Ilan University, who saw in each Extension a basis for realizing its religious and social mission, insisted on holding courses in Jewish Studies even at the Jordan Valley, covering part of their operating costs. Conversely, the agreement between the University of Haifa and the Yezreel Valley College emphasized each party's independence and the complete separation between management and academic auspices.

An expression of the above can be found in the first clauses of the agreement between the University of Haifa and the Yezreel Valley:

> Whereas the University of Haifa wishes to promote higher education in the north [. . .] by encouraging the relationship with Regional Colleges and schools for girls, and the Yezreel Valley College at "Ohel Sara" wishes to obtain the academic auspices of the University of Haifa [. . .] the university and the college have agreed on the integration of academic studies at the college under the university of Haifa's auspices according to the terms defined below: [. . .] This agreement is for three years as of its day of signing. However, each party is entitled to cancel it even before termination of three years.[198]

198 Yezreel Valley College archive. The auspices agreement between the College and the University of Haifa, 23 January 1973.

Tel Chai College signed a similar agreement when it had accepted the auspices of the University of Haifa after Tel Aviv University ceased its operation at the college, and the agreement between the Open University and other Regional Colleges for the opening of study centers.[199] These agreements underline the differences between Bar Ilan's approach to the idea of Extensions and the approaches held by other universities that gave their academic auspices to colleges in the 1970s and 1980s, which I assess based on four central measures:

1. **Initiative** – The opening of Extensions at Ashkelon and Zefat was the result of a unique initiative by Bar Ilan University as part of its future master plan. As opposed to these Extensions, the Extension at the Jordan Valley was initiated by the heads of the Jordan Valley Regional Council, but this initiative nonetheless corresponded with Bar Ilan University's plans and its general intent to open Extensions in the north. This mix of intents can be described using a well-known Hebrew proverb: "The cow wants to nurse more than the calf wants to suckle".

Conversely, agreements with Tel Aviv, Ben Gurion and Haifa Universities were initiated by representatives of the Regional Colleges themselves, whether the college management or the heads of the Regional Councils in which they operated. The universities were invited to hold partial studies, offering academic auspices for specific courses, and beyond that were not required any further responsibility. This fact was a basic tenet of the agreements and the foundation to the universities' consent to take part in the initiative.

2. **Time** – Bar Ilan University viewed its Extensions as an integral part of itself and an important pillar in its future master plan, and therefore at no stage was there talk of a time limited agreement. Although the relationship with the Jordan Valley was different in its essence than the one established with Ashkelon and Zefat, the unlimited aspect of the agreement with the Jordan Valley attests to a clear intent that the Jordan Valley would in future become an Extension. And indeed, after one year of operating, the Extensions project had also incorporated the Jordan Valley (accreditation was achieved in retrospect). Contrary to Bar Ilan, the other universities did not view their academic activity outside their campus as a long term academic or social aim. These time-limited agreements came in response to requests from the periphery, and formed a way to contribute to a different social image for the universities, as

199 Ibid. The auspices agreement between the College and the Open University, 26 March 1976.

opposed to the image of alienated scholars sitting in their ivory towers, and the operations outside of campus were destined to be limited in time.

3. **Operations** – this measure expresses the fact that Bar Ilan perceived its work as a mission, while the other universities did not. Bar Ilan initiated and directly managed the Extensions at Ashkelon and Zefat. At the Jordan Valley it also had some responsibility over operations. Bar Ilan's Manager of the Extensions was also responsible for the operation of studies at the Jordan Valley, and moreover he often determined the scope of the courses and areas of study available at the Extensions, as well as at the Jordan Valley. This direct operating responsibility also meant that Bar Ilan was responsible for financial expenses: Bar Ilan carried most of the expense on its own, as well as the responsibility. For this reason it had appointed its own Manager of the Extensions. This responsibility required taking note of educational facilities, which were also under the university's responsibility. For instance: The books and teaching aids at all Extensions including the Jordan Valley were university property. The university raised donations to cover expenses and upgrade academic facilities.

Conversely, the limited responsibility of the other universities to academic matters only, had been a material component of their agreements with the colleges and a prerequisite of the relationship between the parties. The Regional Colleges, which, as already mentioned, had originally been Post-Secondary schools offering advanced learning programs and vocational studies organized by local councils,[200] operated within their council's area of jurisdiction and enjoyed its facilities. In the absence of a legal limitation to use the title "college", as opposed to "university" which could not be used without authorization, they adopted the name "college", thereby opening their scope to additional activities such as practical engineering studies, vocational studies and academic studies for credits as is the practice at Community Colleges in the USA.[201] During the first stages of their operation, academic courses had been their missing link, and therefore an

200 State Comptroller's report on institutions of higher education, auspices over academic programs at Regional Colleges, 1990. The report reviewed the academic programs at Tel Chai and Yezreel Valley Colleges and in general praised the academic programs in the north.

201 Community colleges in California. Graduates of these colleges may continue on to university undergraduate studies, with the courses they have completed at the community college being recognized as long as they are suited to the degree requirements. From a lecture by Martin Trow given at a conference on the role of colleges in the expansion of higher education in Israel– lessons learned from the American experience, 8 April 2003, U.S. Israel Education Foundation, Tel Aviv, 2004: pg. 35 –39.

important pillar of their development. Academic studies under the auspices of universities extended their aura to the rest of the activities offered at the college, thereby raising its status in the eyes of the local population, which began viewing the colleges as a natural place for academic studies, even when these were only partial. The administrative staff of the college was responsible for the operation of academic studies and the relationship with students. The university who gave its auspices, however, instructed college management on how to hold the courses, but did not appoint a manager or any type of administration to supervise the extra-university studies. The managers of Regional Colleges managed each university department individually.

4. **Exclusivity** – this measure points to a material difference between the Extensions at Ashkelon and Zefat and the one at the Jordan Valley, and to substantial similarities between it and the Regional Colleges. The Ashkelon and Zefat Extensions, which were founded and operated by Bar Ilan University, offered exclusively academic courses. At the Jordan Valley Extension and the Regional Colleges, however, other studies were also held, with academic courses added in the 1970s and 1980s amounting to only a small part of their activities. Among Bar Ilan's agreements, its relationship with the Jordan Valley is closer in its format to the relationships established between other universities and the Regional Colleges, but Bar Ilan's relationship with its Extensions at Ashkelon and Zefat emphasizes, as already mentioned, the fact of their being an inseparable part of the university.

Academic Programs at Regional Colleges: Admission Policy

From their early days it had been the policy among Israeli universities to only accept candidates meeting high admission requirements. This policy influenced high school curriculum in the Pre-State era, and even more so after its establishment. Before Bagrut matriculation exams were instituted, universities set their admission requirements for high school graduates based on entrance exams. This policy was not changed, despite the fact that in the early days of Statehood only about 10 % of each year attended high school (Brandes, 1996), and they tended to come from a high socioeconomic background and achieved high academic results (Shmida, 1987). Table 28 shows the number of students each year since the establishment of the State, and the annual growth rate in two different periods: The monolithic system era and the binary one. The changes in admission policies in the 1990s and the proliferation of institutions of higher education led to a notable change as of the mid 1990s.

Tab. 28: Number of students in institutions of higher education during the years: 1948/49–2007/08 and the average annual growth rate

Academic year	Number of students at universities	Growth rate Annual/ Average	Number of students in other institutions	Total	Annual growth rate
1948/49	1,635				
1959/60	9,275	17.1 %			
1964/65	18,064	14.3 %			
1969/70	35,374	14.4 %			
1974/75	49,849	7.1 %			
1979/80	54,480	1.8 %			
1984/85	61,155	2.3 %			
1985/86	62,360	2.0 %			
1986/87	63,500	1.8 %			
1987/88	64,190	1.1 %			
1988/89	65,080	1.4 %			
1989/90	67,750	4.1 %			
1990/91	71,190	5.1 %			
1991/92	78,640	10.5 %			
1992/93	84,990	8.1 %			
1993/94	91,480	7.6 %			
1994/95	96,600	5.6 %			
1995/96	101,700	5.3 %	23,747	125,447	
1997/8	109,130	7.3 %	41,108	150,238	19.7 %
1999/00	112,920	3.4 %	53,257	166,177	10.6 %
2001/2	118,283	4.7 %	61,936	180,219	8.45 %
2005/6	121,680	2.8 %	87,519	209,199	16.0 %
2008/09	120,098	0.1 %	100,372	220,470	5.4 %
2009/10	123,965	0.3 %	113,782	237,747	1.33 %
2010/11	125,059	0.8 %	120,660	245,719	0.6 %
2011/12	125,574	0.04 %	127,214	252,788	0.54 %
2012/13	124,957	0.1 %	132,188	257,145	0.4 %

Source: CBS, Students at institutions of higher education by degree and institution type, table1: http://che.org.il/?page_id=6802, Retrieved 28 July 2014.

The data presented in Table 28 point to the tangible change that took place in accessibility to higher education, following the approval of the CHE's plan for the system's expansion through colleges. Until then universities' admission policies positioned the education system, particularly the secondary one, between two different aims – equality and excellence – which tugged at it in opposing directions. On the one hand, the system aspired to provide knowledge as a common basis for all graduates of the education system, while on the other hand it aspired to instill learning skills so as to nurture excellence towards higher education. Towards the end of the 1950s and onwards, the Bagrut matriculation exams served as an entrance ticket to universities, and in the 1970s, under pressure of university leaders, the transition was made to a system of credit points, so as to address the universities' demands for further expressing personal qualifications and abilities. In the beginning of the 1980s, the value of this tool diminished due to a general decline in the level of teaching at high schools and a decline in the level of Bagrut examinations. Therefore, a new measurement tool was added – the Psychometric exams.

The nature of the relationship between the universities and Regional Colleges to which they gave their academic auspices led to a dilemma in the general education system: Equal opportunities or excellence. By the 1980s it was clear to universities that by entering extra-academic activities they would have to modify the terms of admission of college students to the university, for a number of reasons:

1. In most cases academic studies at Regional Colleges began as an accumulation of academic credits and not as full undergraduate degree studies. While in this state of affairs the final admission remained in the university's hands, the terms of admission to academic courses at colleges were relatively low, and a successful outcome in these courses generally paved the way to acceptance to the university that had granted its academic auspices to the courses.
2. The potential number of students in the south and the north of the country was too small to provide the necessary number of students for local institutions. During the establishment of the State in 1948 the overall population in the north and south regions of the country amounted to only 19 % of the country's population. Despite the growing population, in 2006 the two regions together still amounted to only 31 % of the country's total population.[202] The number of high school graduates eligible for a Bagrut diploma in these regions in the 1960s and 1970s was substantially lower that the parallel number in the center of the country. In his 1999 annual report, the State Comptroller examined the situation in the south, finding, among other issues, low percentages in all educational measures compared to other cities in the country. Table 20 describes the poor condition of the country's Development towns in the field of education until the end of the 1990s:

202 The CBS (2008). Sixty years – a Statistical Perspective. Nurit Yafe (editor), Statistical 80.

Tab. 29: Educational data on Development towns in the South

The item examined	Southern Development towns	Affluent cities	Large cities
12th grade students 17–18 years of age	71.1 %	95.3 %	80.4 %
Participated in Bagrut exams	37.3 %	84.8 %	56.6 %
Eligible for Bagrut diploma	20.9 %	72.1 %	46.1 %
Commenced academic studies within seven years after completing high school	7.6 %	45.4 %	27.0 %

Source: State Comptroller's report (1999). Higher education in Development towns. Annual report number 50 (b). 71–95.

In the 1970s these figures led to a leniency on the part of the universities granting their academic auspices to Regional Colleges, as they had been requested to accept any student meeting minimum requirements, such as a Bargut diploma or equivalent, so as to achieve the minimal number of students necessary for operating the college.

3. The Geographic location of colleges within the jurisdiction of Regional Councils resulted in a clear ideological motivation to serve the Kibbutzim population, which until the 1970s had been generally comprised of high school graduates without a Bagrut diploma (Cohen, 2001). This led to a challenge for universities to allow these high school graduates to study at colleges and accumulate academic credits. The colleges, on their part, aimed to serve their nearby population, including unqualified teachers, army and police officers and civil servants who aspired for promotion, but due to time and financial constraints as well as geographic distance, postponed their studies.

Under these circumstances, the colleges managements placed the matter of admission terms to academic studies at the colleges as a top priority in their agreements with universities. The agreements between the universities and the Regional Colleges stipulated special admission terms at colleges, as opposed to those implemented at the universities' main campuses. The first agreement signed between a university and a Post-Secondary institution was the agreement between Bar Ilan University and the Jordan Valley College. It was signed in 1968, and stipulated special admission terms. In the agreement the parties made allowances for admission terms of candidates from specific populations, which each of the parties had the interest of promoting. The certified teachers held teaching positions, but were not graduates of teaching seminars; the IDF officers were high school graduates without a Bagrut Diploma; as were high school graduates of the kibbutzim in the 1960s and 1970s. The founders of Bar Ilan University saw these teachers, civil servants and officers as public opinion agents and encouraged their admission to academic studies. While high school graduates from Kibbutzim lacked a Bagrut diploma, they were natural candidates for Regional Colleges. With the growing demand for studies at the Extension, the university was faced with a dilemma: while the number of students at the Extension was a central measure of its success (the more students enrolled, the more academic activities could be offered), the rising number of students and the flexible admission terms essential meant two levels of admission for the same university – one for the Extension, and another for the main campus. In fact, students at the Extension enjoyed a situation akin to affirmative action, when applying later on for studies at the main campus.[203] Moreover, lowering the university's admission requirements may have undermined its chances of promoting research and scientific excellence. Despite this dilemma, Bar Ilan University and the Jordan Valley College defined special admission terms to specific populations, as shall be detailed below:

1. "An accredited teacher with 12 years of teaching experience or experience at management/supervision of education institutions [...] and who is at least 35 years of age, the admissions committee and the status committee will discuss his or her admission".
2. "A senior IDF officer in permanent service, whose rank is at least Major, would be accepted according to the same terms as in Chapter 5 a (teachers)".
3. A candidate who has worked for at least 12 years in a certain professional area (for instance, agriculture), has shown knowledge in his area of work, and is at least 35 years of age, would be admitted based on the terms stipulated in chapter 5a (teachers), provided that he or she specializes in a field of study that is related to his or her area of work and also provided that his or her basic education is equivalent to 11 years of systematic education.

---

203 The term affirmative action is well-known in the USA, where for years it had been among the most complex and disputed topics in the country's legal and political discourse. The U.S. Supreme Court ruled in a number of cases that in principle affirmative action in education does not violate the 14th amendment to the constitution, only if it is carried out in a certain manner, without defining specific quotas for minorities, and for a predefined period. The Israeli Supreme Court ruled that authorities are permitted to use affirmative action, mainly in filling public positions, in favor of disadvantaged groups in Israeli society. The Civil Service Commission defines four main groups which should be suitably represented by way of affirmative action: Women, minorities, Jews of Ethiopian origin, and disabled persons.

4. “A student who does not have a Bagrut diploma, but that his general education is equivalent to that of a high school education [. . .] may still be accepted as an audit student, with all regular obligations and rights applying. In such case, the student, when transitioning to full studies at Bar Ilan University, would have to commit to passing during his first year of studies at Ramat Gan, Bagrut exams in two topics and completing all other Bagrut requirements during the second year”.[204]

Similarly to the agreement between Bar Ilan University and the Jordan Valley College, the University of Haifa also stipulated in a special addendum to its agreement with the Yezreel Valley and Tel Chai, flexible admission terms for candidates who do not meet the university’s regular terms of admission. All options included a “conditional” program regulating the transition to full admission. A “conditional” admittance category was defined for the following five populations of candidates:

1. Candidates without a Bagrut diploma:
   1.1. High school graduates of schools in the Kibbutzim.
   1.2. High school graduates at development towns, with a high school diploma but no Bagrut.
   1.3. High school graduates from Moshavim, with a high school diploma but no Bagrut.
   1.4. Druze students with a Syrian diploma.
2. Candidates with a partial Bagrut diploma would be accepted for one year “on probation” and will complete their Bagrut during their first year of studies at the college.
3. New immigrant (*Olim*) candidates will be admitted to a special preparatory year for *Olim*.
4. Older candidates without a Bagrut diploma will be admitted “on probation” based on their personal credentials.
5. Experienced teachers will be accepted to certification studies which do not grant an academic degree.[205]

---

204 Yezreel Valley College archive. The agreement between and Jordan Valley Regional Council Post-Secondary Education School and Bar Ilan University, 12 August, 1968.

205 Yezreel Valley College archive. Agreement on the integration of academic studies at the Yezreel Valley College under the auspices of the University of Haifa, 23 January 1973, and addendum to the agreement between the University of Haifa and Tel Chai College for the 1974/5 academic year.

Ben Gurion University, which commenced its extra-university activities at Sha'ar Hanegev only towards the end of the 1970s, offered only a limited program, and therefore did not draft agreements with Sapir College or defined admission terms until the 1990s.[206]

As mentioned, the decision to teach outside the main camps required special attention to potential candidate populations. This required joint consultations with the college so as to define admission terms suitable to the background of local candidates. Special attention was given to the population of teachers, older students, new immigrants and kibbutz high school graduates who had not studied a curriculum that grants a Bagrut diploma.

Conclusions

The special admission policy corresponded with Bar Ilan University's social and religious missions – as seen in the religious academic institutions in the USA – and its political ones – as promoted by its religious-Zionist political leaders. All this was linked to the university's general struggle against the senior actors of the academic field, towards obtaining its accreditation. As to the other universities, their extra-university activities matches Yovev's (2000) definition of Target Universities – designated for northern and southern populations. Tel Aviv University is different in the fact that its operations in the area lasted only a few years. The universities of Haifa and Ben Gurion, although they did not initiate the activities, could not ignore the needs of disadvantaged populations, as this would have labeled them with the ivory tower image that followed the Hebrew University, an image which they had struggled to be free of throughout their process of entrance into the field. The accreditation of these universities was entirely in the hands of the senior actors of the field, in Jerusalem.

The test of time attests to the different intent of Bar Ilan compared to the other universities: The University of Haifa's external activities commenced about five years after those of Bar Ilan, and ended following the academic independence of the Yezreel Valley and Tel Chai Colleges. Ben Gurion University continued its relationship with Achva College until 2014 with the CHE's encouragement, as until that time conditions had not matured at that college for academic independence. The relationship with Sapir college is a minimal one, resulting from national considerations that have nothing to do with academics. Bar Ilan University continued

206 Interview with the College CEO Dr. Nachmi Paz, 8 July 2010.

with full academic responsibility over its three Extensions at Ashkelon, Zefat and the Jordan Valley until 2003. When Ashkelon and Kinneret College (aka Jordan Valley College) gained academic independence in 2003, the parties continued their relationships by mutual agreement.

Chapter 10 The CHE's Initial Responses to Initiatives by Universities and Colleges

As already mentioned, Bar Ilan's plans for a campus at the northern town of Zefat led in 1971 to the establishment of the Jortner Committee. The Committee's official name attests to its purpose: "The committee on behalf of the Council for Higher Education for discussing Bar Ilan University's plans for a university campus at Zefat".[207] In practice, however, the committee examined the general idea of an academic institution at the Galilee, and not necessarily Bar Ilan's specific initiative. In the beginning of the 1970s, growing demand for higher education and demands voiced by local leaders for increasing its accessibility led the CHE, headed by Ministers of Education – Yigal Alon between the years 1969–1974, and Aharon Yadlin in 1974–1977, to examine ways of expanding accessibility to higher education in general, and to technological and vocational education such as teaching and practical engineering, in particular. Amendment number 3 to the CHE law prohibited, as aforesaid, the establishment of Extensions or chapters of existing universities without the CHE's approval. The amendment to the law blocked Bar Ilan's aspirations to open further Extensions across the country, and gave the CHE the necessary time and authority to examine the situation without worrying about steps being taken in parallel. During the early 1970s the CHE held many discussions on ways to expand accessibility, appointing a range of committees who discussed the status and roles of institutions that may join the country's academic and Post-Secondary education system.

The Lifson Committee

Although the Jorner Committee's recommendations were not accepted, it was the first to determine the necessity of an academic institution in the Galilee and recognize the need for accessible higher education for remote populations. Following the Jortner Committee, the CHE appointed another committee headed by Prof. Shneior Lifson from the Technion, to examine way of expanding the academic system. Committee members included: Professors Ephraim A. Urbach, Yehushua

207 CHE archive, Bar Ilan University Extensions file. The Jortner Committee Report, 26 July 1971: 1.

Jurtner and Haim Barkai from the Hebrew University; Prof. A. Saltman from Bar Ilan; Rachel Shalon from the Technion; and Prof. Gabriel Cohen from Tel Aviv University and Labor Party Knesset Member. The committee's report was submitted for a preliminary discussion at the CHE in May 1971. At the discussions voices were heard in favor of expanding Post-Secondary education as a means for deploying the population throughout the country, encouraging education in border settlements and Development towns, and most of all among Mizrachi Jews. Alongside the CHE's aim to expand accessibility to higher education, some of its members raised concerns as to the academic level of the degree to be given by colleges, while others discussing the need to establish a "National Senate"[208] responsible for the academic level taught at colleges who are not under the academic auspices of a university.

As can be seen from the committee's discussions, according to most CHE and committee members, a college is a general or professional institution dedicated to training teachers and vocational studies. There was no mention of an academic institution as was already common in other countries, nor of the basic right to grant a recognized academic degree. Their firm academic position was that only a university is authorized to grant an academic degree. The positions voiced during the meeting, represented by senior actors of the academic field from the Hebrew University and the Technion, reaffirm the conclusions of Raftery and Hout (1993). These researchers rely on the Maximally Maintained Inequality (MMI) hypothesis to show that education expansion would not necessarily lead to a decline in inequalities in higher education, as the most advantaged socioeconomic group would only permit higher education for all, as in our case, after the saturation point has been reached. The lower socioeconomic groups or residents of the social periphery would have to make do with less prestigious institutions, while prestigious institutions would still be reserved to the advantaged group and will be blocked to lower socioeconomic classes, thereby maintaining existing gaps, despite the illusion of equality created by the system's expansion. Clearly, this academic view point was presented as concern for the country's level of education, but concealed typical elitist positions, which were common among the senior actors of the academic field that strived to protect – as shown in Bourdieu's Field Theory – their continued possession of the field's cultural capital. A request made by Prof. Yaacov Katz, member of the CHE, towards the interim summation of the discussion, illustrates this approach: "Prof. Katz requested that it be noted

208 Ibid. Minutes of meetings of CHE meeting number 18, 4 May 1971.

in the protocol that he does not see this summation as an approval for a college to grant an academic degree".[209]

The interim summation also corresponded with the Maximally Maintained Inequality (MMI) hypothesis: Members emphasized that the institutions discussed will not grant academic degrees. Moreover, it is clear that this possibility was not even considered. Upon conclusion of the discussions, the CHE decided to accept a number of the Lifson Committee's recommendations, as follows:

1. Encourage the establishment of regional and community colleges, as well as colleges for teachers and other professions.
2. Promote the establishment of a "National Colleges Administration" at the CHE – a forum that would review the matter of colleges until the CHE's permanent policy on the matter would be established.
3. Examine an experimental plan to hold studies at Regional Colleges as part of the Open University, following its establishment.

Despite their intent to encourage the establishment of colleges, CHE members would not discuss the right of a new institution to grant any academic degree. The aim that had been concealed in the decision to link between the colleges and the Open University – that at the time had still not been founded – resulted from a dual approach towards the Open University as an institution that is entitled "university" and therefore authorized to grant undergraduate degrees, and yet it is limited to undergraduate degrees and therefore does not compete with the other universities represented by the CHE members.[210] Despite this position the Lifson Committee's recommendations did influence the institutions operating at the time, and these took advantage of the momentum to promote their expansion plans. In the early years of the 1970s heads of 30 colleges presented their applications for graduate courses. This led to apprehensions among CHE members, and a review of their positions shows their attempts to avoid opening the gates of higher education and maintain the hegemony of the universities. The most pragmatic members were willing to examine the possibility to authorize these degrees on the condition that they by clearly distinguished from degrees offered at universities. Yigal Alon, at the time Minister of Education as well as the Chairperson of the CHE, opposed differentiating between degrees, with the exception of the distinction between the university degree and the degree in Education

209 Ibid: 2.

210 Ibid, Protocol of the CHE meeting number 18, 4 May 1971: 2.

(eventually known as a B.Ed – the undergraduate degree in Education), granted by Teachers Colleges.

Establishment of The Colleges Administration at the CHE

The CHE's decision to adopt the recommendations of the Lifson Committee led to the establishment of a forum dedicated to examining applications received from colleges. The forum was established as part of the CHE, with Prof. Lifson appointed as its Chair. The forum's authorities included:

1. Issue recommendations to the CHE and the Minister on methods for future development of academic Post-Secondary education.
2. Propose to the CHE amendments to the law in order to adjust it to colleges.
3. Issue recommendations to the CHE on permitting the establishment of a college type institution, or affirm it while granting accreditation and authorization to use certain titles.
4. The center is authorized to appoint committees to examine the programs offered by new institutions.

At the CHE's 16th meeting the forum defined the preliminary characteristics of a college eligible for granting a graduate degree, without discussing the type and nature of such degree:

1. The college would not be involved in research, and will offer a high level of teaching.
2. The college should promote areas of study which have not been suitably handled at the universities, alongside regular programs.
3. The college should offer studies at remote locations so as to enable suitable academic education.

In addition, a distinction was made between three main types of colleges:

1. Technological Colleges.
2. Teacher-training Colleges.
3. Multi-disciplinary Colleges.[211]

211 Ibid. Council meeting number 16, 24 April 1973: 4.

The Struggle over the Type of Degree to be Granted at Colleges

Disagreements over the type of degree to be granted were long and ongoing between members of the CHE and the Colleges Administration. The compromise that emerged at one of the meetings was to recommend an interim degree between high school and university degree: A.A – Associate of Arts. The purpose of distinguishing between the two was to maintain the prestige of the university degree and the elitist institution granting it, while permitting other institutions that would grant less prestigious degrees so as to create an impression of openness and accessibility to higher education, which in practice would be a lower education. Naturally, the acceptance of this position would have led to universities continuing to teach the upper classes, while the new institutions would teach the lower classes. This elitist approach had been prevalent in the Western world until the mid-1950s. According to this approach, universities served as an incubator for training the elites (Morrison,1998) and a lever for reproduction of the social structure (Havighurst, 1989). From this perspective, the position of CHE members in 1971–1974 was no longer considered valid in the Western world.

Despite the fact that the decision regarding two types of degrees had been accepted at the CHE by a majority of members, other raised doubts as to the effectiveness of such a degree in the labor market. One of the proposals raised was to grant a degree following two years at a college – which would be recognized by universities and bestow the student with academic credit for continued studies at the university, similarly to the accreditation granted by the University of California to students of Community Colleges. However, the social danger entailed in discrimination in higher education was not left out of the discussion. The fear of social unrest, which had already taken its toll at the time in the social struggle led by the Black Panthers movement in 1971 – all these and other protests in later years led Ministers of Education to promote a more moderate position than the one voiced by those who blatantly opposed opening the gates of higher education.

Signs of moderation can be noted in another proposal raised at the time: To separate between the discussion on the opening of a new institution (with a permit to teach undergraduate courses) and the decision on the type of degree to be granted by the institution. The purpose of this distinction was to delay the CHE's decision, but it also attested to the mounting public pressure on the CHE – from the Minister, who is also Chairperson of the CHE's and from the heads of local authorities and politicians. This decision led to a situation in which the members of the CHE, while promoting accessibility to higher education, in practice did not settle on the question of the degree and retained the elitist system intact (the period between granting the permit and the actual accreditation and certification may last up to three years).

The discussion was concluded with the decision that the Chairperson of the Colleges Administration would prepare a review for continued discussions in future CHE meetings. The period between 1971 and 1974 saw ongoing disputes among CHE members between those who supported opening the gates of education, albeit in a non-equal manner, and those who opposed such steps, fearing degradation of the academic degree and an inflation in the number of academic institutions. Even the most adamant supporters for opening the gates of higher education agreed that the approval of undergraduate degrees should be stipulated upon meeting all academic criteria. A clear proponent of the opinion that the gates of higher education should not be opened to all was member of the CHE at the time, Supreme Court judge Moshe Landau: "I see the academization of Post-Secondary education a phenomenon that is not positive. We should beware of academic inflation as any inflation results in devaluation. Therefore, we must withstand the pressures of institutions aiming to inch their way towards an academic degree". A less adamant opinion but still an elitist one was voiced by Prof. Don Patinkin, President of the Hebrew University: "The existing degree should remain, but differences must be clear in the values of the degrees, and a minimum line should be determined in granting a B.A degrees. But certainly it is not possible to achieve an Equal B.A at all institutions and in all disciplines".[212]

In another discussion, Prof. Poliakov, member of the CHE from the Hebrew University, noted that: "It is necessary to distinguish between university education and higher education [...] There is no other recourse but to create a new degree which would not be mixed with the university degree".[213]

The CHE's strict position in the 1970s on the question of the degree increased the pressure on the council. In all discussions on ways to expand the academic system, Ministers of Education Yigal Alon and Aharon Yadlin after him presented their support of the opening of the gates of education as a result of the mounting public and social pressure from heads of local councils and politicians. An expression of the tension between the two positions can be found in the words of Minister of Education Aharon Yadlin during one of the CHE's meetings on the matter:

> We cannot ignore the democratic revolution in which we are living and the need to provide recurring opportunities for studies and therefore to open an alternative path in

212 Ibid, CHE meeting protocol number 16, 24 April 1973, and number 17, 8 May 1973.
213 Ibid, Protocol of the CHE meeting number 23, July 1974.

> smaller and less expensive institutions, with modest pretensions. The academic higher education in Israel should break free from its tendency for monopolies.[214]

The applications from colleges awaiting the CHE's decision, and on the other hand the apprehensions among CHE members towards the degradation of the degree and the system's inundation by institutions which may become mini-universities, made reaching a practical decision very difficult, and so partial and non-innovative solutions continued to be raised at CHE meetings. An example for such a partial solution that continued to be raised following the Lifson Committee's recommendations, was the idea of linking between colleges and the Open university, or the name by which it was referred to in CHE meetings at the time – "University for all". The approval for its establishment was granted in 1973 (it was certified to grant a degree in 1980), following two years of discussions, and immediately a practical proposal was raised to link between it and colleges. While some colleges did establish a certain relationship with the Open University, it was not enough to provide a full solution that would be suited to peripheral regions.

The discussion at the CHE's 17th meeting pointed to a certain progress on the topic of the degree, as can be seen from the decisions reached at that meeting:

1. The Council does not accept the proposal to create a degree lower than B.A. It does not oppose approval of a graduate degree in general education, provided that the academic level is suitable.
2. If the establishment of academic colleges is approved, they would be entitled to teach courses towards a B.A degree or at least to grant academic credit points recognized by institutions of higher education. It was also agreed that only a college offering 50 % of courses to be recognized for academic credit points would be entitled to be called a college.
3. The Colleges Administration will examine the possibility to collaborate with the Open University when it is opened.

It was further decided that that the discussion on the status of the graduate degree would be held in the following meeting. The decision not to allow colleges to offer a degree lower than a B.A marked progress compared to opinions voiced in previous discussions. A review of the opinions voiced during many meetings points to a change in members' opinions, although this change was a gradual one, occurring over a period of six or seven years.

---

214 Ibid, Protocol of the CHE meeting number 26, 19 November 1974.

The Extensions as a Recommended Model

A surprising turning point in the CHE's position on the matter of Regional Colleges can be found in its 26th meeting protocol. The meeting was opened by the CHE's Chairperson and Israel's Minister of Education at the time Aharon Yadlin, with a historic review of all discussions and proposals raised on the matter of the colleges until then, and the need to implement the decisions. Finally, Yadlin described his position on the issue of higher education in general, and colleges in particular:

> I have said in the past that in my opinion there is no room for new universities in Israel in the near future, but that this fact requires opening alternative paths towards a higher education, even an academic one in the form of colleges [. . .] Education should include three levels: (a) Post-Secondary education leading to a diploma (accredited teacher, practical engineer, nurse, accountant, etc. . .); (b) A college granting undergraduate degrees; (C) The multi-staged university. As to the training of teachers – this is an applicative interdisciplinary area [. . .] Their degree can be a B.A in teaching, but also a B.Ed may be granted [. . .] As to the technological colleges – the possibility that a technological college would lead to a degree such as a B.Sc. should not be ignored [. . .] As to the academic Regional Colleges, these would offer the first stages of academic studies in the various disciplines, but the end of the degree (the third year) would be at the universities. The academic Regional Colleges would be adopted by a university and operate as their Extensions.

Following a long discussion with opposing and supporting opinions voiced, the minister concluded: "The realistic solution for Regional Colleges is university auspices and the universities should be convinced to do so and adopt the colleges in their geographic vicinity".[215]

About ten years following the establishment of Bar Ilan's first Extension at Ashkelon and following many discussions at the CHE, the council's members concluded that a system of Extensions would be the best way to promote higher education in the country's geographic periphery and to reduce social gaps. The CHE's conclusion arrived very late, and only following strong social struggles of Mizrachim and mounting demands for higher education among the population. Bar Ilan's founders were aware of these struggles as far back as the 1950s, at the time of the establishment of the university, thanks to their social and religious viewpoint, which had been learned from methods used by the Christian religious academic of the United States. The change in the CHE's position is all the more

215 Ibid, Protocol of CHE meeting number 26, 19 November 1974.

surprising in view of its persistent struggle against the idea of the Extensions and its blocking of Bar Ilan's plans through amendment 3 to the CHE law in 1971.

The minister asked the members of the CHE to assist him in convincing the leaderships of the universities to adopt this model. At the end of the discussion the CHE again reiterated its position that there is no room for a further university in Israel in the coming years. To refute the apprehensions of university leaders, the minister noted that the accreditation of colleges under the CHE law would not lead to their becoming a university, as universities teach undergraduate, graduate and post-graduate students, as well as being involved in research.

The CHE recognized the need to provide Post-Secondary education in peripheral areas and saw the Regional Colleges as a means to provide this service. To implement this task, the CHE approached the Ministry of Education, requesting a national mapping of Regional Colleges, and the idea of the Extensions received a further ratification:

> The Council for Higher Education expressed its wish that universities would provide academic auspices to academic programs at colleges, so that students would be able to commence academic studies at colleges and complete their degree at a university. The Council for Higher Education appoints its Chairperson to discuss the matter with the Heads of the Higher Education Institutions Committee.[216]

The CHE dedicated most of this meeting to examining the possibility of holding academic studies at Regional Colleges under the auspices of universities. For this purpose, heads of all universities were summoned to the meeting. Bar Ilan University's Rector, Prof. Menachem-Zvi Kadari, who was closely familiar with the matter of studies outside the main campus, supported this opportunity, which corresponded with the university's policy. However, the heads of the older institutions – the Hebrew University and the Technion – behaved as senior actors in the field, expressing their apprehension at the scattering of national budgets. They called the CHE to beware of degrading the academic degree and nurturing illusions among the disadvantaged. The heads of the newer institutions – the Universities of Haifa and Ben Gurion – were willing to settle for granting their auspices for acquiring credits only, but not for entire degrees.

The principles developed by the Lifson Committee and the final report presented by the Colleges Administration served as guidelines in other CHE discussions regarding colleges in the 1970s. Guidelines included priorities in decision making based on the policy led by the Chairperson of the CHE and Minister of Education at the time Aharon Yadlin, who as early as the 23rd meeting of the CHE expressed

216 Ibid, Protocol of the CHE meeting number 26, 19 November 1974.

his opinion that "It is necessary to encourage colleges offering a practical education and training professionals". As to Regional Colleges, the minister proposed that they would not grant a degree but credits towards one, which would then be recognized by universities. To prevent unwanted proliferation of universities, each should be limited to a relationship with only two colleges.[217]

Opening the Gates of Higher Education through Professional Colleges

In the first half of the 1970s the CHE attempted to reach practical decisions based on a list of priorities defined by the minister, the principles of which were disclosed to the CHE members in a memorandum dated 16 February 1975, that included a review of all decisions reached by the CHE on the topic of colleges until that point. The memorandum makes a clear distinction between a college authorized to grant an academic undergraduate degree and therefore destined to be defined under the CHE law as an "Accredited college" or an "Academic college", and a Post-Secondary college which is not authorized to grant an academic degree.

The authorized colleges would be permitted, based on their areas of specialization, to define the undergraduate degree to be granted by them as "Bachelor of Accredited College" – with the addition of the specific area of specialization. For instance: B.Mus (Bachelor of musical disciplines) or B.Ed (Bachelor of Education) and at the technological colleges – B.Tech (Bachelor of technology). It was further defined that graduates would be able to continue to advanced studies subject to meeting the terms of admission and following completion of the universities' specific requirements. This accreditation program pertained to three types of institutions:

1. Institutions mainly focusing on art or other professions not offered at universities. The first of these was the Rubin Academy of Music & Dance in Jerusalem, founded in 1947. In 1971 it was granted the CHE's permit to offer "academic studies in non-university institutions", and in 1974 was accredited as an institution of higher education. The Bezalel Academy of Art and Design, founded in 1906, was the second to join this category and in 1973 was recognized as an academic institution eligible for granting undergraduate degrees. In 1975 the Ruppin College was granted a similar permit, followed by the Shenkar School of Textile in 1976 and the Jerusalem College of Technology for the religious sector in 1977.

217 Ibid, Protocol of the Committee meeting, 23 July, 1974.

2. The Teachers' Training institutions started off as Seminaries and gradually underwent an academization process, at the end of which, in the 1970s and 1980s, they gained a permit and accreditation as institutions of higher education for granting a B.Ed degree (Volansky, 2005). These were considered by the CHE to be professional institutions, which the labor market requires, and not as competitors to universities.
3. Regional Colleges defined as multi-disciplinary The academic future of this group remained in the hands of the universities. Despite the decision to allow them to obtain the academic auspices of a university or become an Extension of one, this could not be seen as a path that would ensure the academic future of the Regional Colleges as its success was completely dependent upon the good will of the universities. Realizing this, the colleges applied to the CHE, requesting to be granted a permit to offer their own undergraduate programs, similarly to the first group. it was clear in all discussions held on the matter that they would join the emerging arrangements for the expansion of the academic system, both due to their being experienced institutions and due to their geographic location and their ability to provide solutions to residents of the geographic periphery. However, the CHE's list of priorities pushed the final decision as to their academic future to a later stage. The Regional Colleges were essentially shoved aside at the time, for two main reasons:

   A. The operation of academic programs under the auspices of universities was a temporary arrangement that marked openness and accessibility of higher education to the periphery, and therefore the CHE members did not see any reason for haste in solving the problem of the Regional Colleges.
   B. The implementation of academic programs under the auspices of a university left the future of their academic development entirely in the hands of the university granting its auspices. Whenever the university would perceive colleges as competitors, it would have the tools to curb such competition from its onset. Contrary to Regional Colleges, the professional colleges did not threaten the universities, that did not view them as competitors at all, and therefore it was easier for the CHE members to reach practical decisions in their regard.

Consequently, the CHE rejected requests by Regional Colleges to grant them permits to offer undergraduate degrees, and the proposal to establish collaborations between them and the Open Universities were raised again towards the end of the 1970s. However, the lack of satisfaction among managers of Regional Colleges and local politicians pushed the CHE Chairperson, Minister of Education Aharon Yadlin, to appoint a Sub-Committee to examine ways for their promotion and to submit its practical recommendations to the CHE.[218] Prof. A Poliakov, who had previously expressed her opinion on the issue of the colleges and expansion of the accessibility to higher education was appointed Chairperson of the committee. On the matter of the Regional Colleges she argued that: "Regional Colleges were unjustly treated by removing them from the definition of 'academic college'. They are not Extensions of a university, only operate under its auspices, and will therefore encounter administrative difficulties".[219] On the diversification of the academic system she said: "There is room in the country for institutions who would offer higher education knowledge without being universities. If we create institutions under such status, we would reduce the flow of people to universities".[220]

Poliakov Committee

The 38th meeting of the CHE in 1976 was dedicated to a discussion on the Poliakov report. The committee was appointed to examine whether Regional Colleges can be defined as "Accredited Colleges", as determined by the CHE in its decisions regarding professional and technological colleges – decisions that had led to their accreditation as institutions of higher education. Committee members relied on the Lifson Committee recommendations and the accreditation criteria later developed by the CHE. Before preparing its report, the committee visited four Regional Councils: The Eilat, Menashe, Sha'ar Hanegev and Tel Chai colleges, and in two others after writing most of its report. Committee members were surprised to find that these colleges did not meet the criteria defined by the CHE in its previous discussions, including percentage of academic courses and the level of educational facilities, and were defined by the committee's Chairperson as universities' evening schools. The Chairperson of the committee expressed her conclusions following her visits to the colleges in a way that leaves no doubt as to her position:

> We did not find institutions which can be referred to as "colleges". In fact we found universities' evening schools. In addition, two such institutions with evening classes which do not belong to universities: The Menashe and the Eilat colleges… All of the colleges

218 Ibid, Protocol of the CHE meeting number 38, 9 March 1976.
219 Ibid, Protocol of the CHE meeting number 28, 21 January 1975.
220 Ibid.

> [we have visited] are not equipped to complete the undergraduate studies as "Accredited college", because their libraries are not suitably equipped.[221]

Although they praised the efforts invested by universities and the colleges' contribution to the regions in which they operate, committee members did not agree to accepting them as candidates for accreditation. The committee did not find suitable facilities necessary for full academic studies: not a suitable library nor appropriate budget for the development of such library. Lecturers came from the university, and their work at the college was deemed secondary to their main work at the university. The range of courses did not arrange into a regulated degree curriculum and did not even enrich students' education. However, despite the committee's reliance on these findings, its members did not agree as to the solutions. Due to the conflicts of opinions, the Chairperson suggested that the CHE be presented with two alternatives for discussion and solution. The first, "Contractual university auspices" and the second – the majority's opinion – "establishment of a separate authority to manage colleges":

1. **Contractual university auspices:** Committee members' lack of satisfaction at the way in which academic courses were managed at colleges, led them to the conclusion that "university auspices" should become a formal status aimed at regulating academic studies at colleges, for the benefit of their students. Based on the committee's recommendation, the CHE would form an auspices agreement with the universities. The agreement would include the following terms:

   A. Regional Colleges would be called Extensions of a university.
   B. Students studying academic courses would be university students.
   C. The university would define the admission terms, and would discuss admission or rejection of candidates to the college.
   D. The university would have full responsibility over the contents and academic level of the academic courses.

The committee presented the Hadera-Manashe College as a case study for a problematic relationship between a university and a college. The Menashe College, who had been granted academic auspices by Tel Aviv University, lost these auspices following a unilateral decision of the university, which left the college with no way of protecting itself or its students. The absence of a binding auspices agreement stipulating methods of protecting the college from the arbitrary decisions of the university exposes the college and its students to unreasonable risks.

221 Ibid, Protocol of the CHE meeting number 38, 9 March 1976, Poliakov Committee Report.

Therefore, the granting of auspices should include clear conditions such as a schedule, rules for terminating the auspices, and a transitional period. The Eilat College, whose substantial distance from the center impacts its ability to create ties with any of the universities, remains without an academic horizon or governmental support. Only an agreement between the CHE and the universities would assure the level and stability of universities' academic auspices. Having said that, committee members believed that if the matter of university auspices would be regulated in an agreement and responsibility for colleges would be transferred to universities, this would lead to a higher education model which does not correspond with the CHE's decisions, or with most of them. In line with this position, before presenting her second solution, the Committee Chairperson described the current incongruence between this model and the CHE's decisions on the matter of colleges:

A. The education offered by universities in the auspices model is no different than that offered by universities in their main campus, while the purpose of college studies is to offer a wide and different scope of education for regional residents, mainly consisting of areas of study not available at universities.
B. Studies at the colleges under the auspices of universities would be more costly than those offered at the universities themselves: lecturers would arrive from the university and earn a regular university salary plus travel and idle time, and studies would be held in small study groups, which would increase the relative cost of each student compared to studies held at the main university campus.
C. The auspices model would reduce the ability to absorb young lecturers or returning Israeli lecturers from abroad, as positions at the Regional Colleges would be filled by the university's own lecturers.
D. The auspices model leads to an absurd situation in which candidates who cannot afford to study at a university due to its distance or financial difficulties, would choose to study in an institution close to their homes rather than at a university. This absurdity is presented by Prof. Poliakov as a preference of colleges over universities for impractical reasons. In her opinion colleges should offer a different education than that offered by universities, while the proposed model created a situation in which colleges are selected due to a lack of choice, and is therefore undesirable.

2. **Establishment of a separate authority for managing colleges:** A majority of committee members believed that Regional Colleges should remain

independent institutions operating under the full supervision of a national authority within the CHE or the Ministry of Education, whose role would be to ensure the level of colleges. Such an authority would assist in directing colleges' academic programs, identify teaching faculty for them, handle professional promotions of academic faculty and deal with all other academic aspects of the college management. The proposal included the option that a single lecturer would be employed by more than one college, so as to ensure full time employment.

A long term aim of such an authority would be to promote the development of colleges towards a situation in which each college would be able to grant its own undergraduate degree. According to this proposal, colleges that had operated under the auspices of a university would also be able to gradually join the authority's system, gradually disconnect from the university and commence a process that would prepare them to offer their own undergraduate degree. According to the committee's conclusions, the authority would be authorized to confirm that a certain college would grant a degree following four years of studies and would be able to enroll students who have studied at auspices colleges and wish to complete their studies at a college certified to grant them an undergraduate degree instead of the degree granted by the auspices university that is farther from their place of residence. The college degree would be recognized for salary purposes, but would be open for evaluation and refereeing by universities in case the student applies for graduate studies.

Through its proposal to establish a separate authority, committee members attempted to cope with the disadvantages of the first proposal:

A. The high cost of studies under the auspices model and the inability of new faculty members to join.
B. Avoidance of complete dependence on the will of the university granting its auspices, which is liable to abandon the college at will, as had happened at the Hadera-Menashe College.

Committee members, who had been aware of the problem caused by Tel Aviv University at the Hadera-Menashe College, realized that universities' arbitrary behavior is liable to put the stability of a college and the future of its students at risk.

During the discussion at the CHE on the Poliakov Committee's proposals, the option was discussed for the Open University to become the center of colleges, which would in turn serve as its remote campuses. This proposal corresponds with the 1971 Lifson Committee recommendations, and at the same meeting was supported by Prof. Lifson and other committee members, but the proposal was ultimately rejected under the assumption that conditions have not ripened to impose such a task on the Open University, which had only just started operating, and its level of stability and success in Israel was yet unclear.

The Establishment of the CHE Colleges Committee

The Poliakov committee recommendations remained largely undecided: The Open University had yet to reach a sufficiently high operative level to undertake the operation of remote academic centers. The establishment of a separate authority was not being promoted, and in the meantime the CHE decided that in view of the complexity of the solution required for colleges, a permanent committee would be established within the CHE on the matter of colleges, whose role would be to follow their development, suggest solutions for their further growth and periodically report to the CHE of further directions. The members of the committee included CHE and PBC (Planning and Budgeting Committee) members. In May 1981, PBC member, Prof. Nehemia Lev Zion,[222] further to the CHE's request, submitted a comprehensive report on the current status of colleges and recommendations as to their continued operation. He reviewed the rationale for holding academic studies at colleges and ways of developing them. The main principles of his report were as follows:

1. Colleges have an existing administrative, organizational, physical and budgetary system that facilitates academic activities under a university's academic responsibility.
2. The PBC does not see Regional Colleges as precursors of institutions of higher education.
3. Students attending academic programs at Regional Colleges are students of the university granting its auspices, for all matters and purposes.
4. The university granting its auspices is authorized to operate academic studies at colleges only in areas taught at the main campus.

222 Prof. Lev Zion served as Dean of the Faculty of Humanities at the Hebrew University in 1978; Headed the Ben-Zvi Institute and was President of the Open University 1987–1992; Headed the Van Leer Institute in 1994–1997 and was Chairperson of the PBC in 1997–2002.

5. The teaching faculty would be selected from among the university's faculty, and the curriculum and admission terms would be fully controlled by the university.
6. Students attending academic programs at colleges would be able to complete their two first undergraduate years, and will complete their third year at the main campus of the university granting its auspices to the college.
7. The PBC's budget for academic programs would be allocated only through the university, with no direct relationship between the PBC/CHE and the colleges.
8. Most colleges were founded by Regional Councils. However, a clear trend can be noted, by which a growing number of college students come from development towns, moshavim and Arab and Druze villages. The idea to hold academic studies at Regional Colleges is led by the aspiration to develop higher education in areas distant from the country's academic centers with the hope in future to see them well established in their regions. The gradual development of colleges would result in recruitment of local lecturers which currently are not able to find employment at universities, and will increase the number of students in higher education. The aim of this mode of operation was to ensure that the level of academic faculty accepted according to the university's rules is maintained, as well as that of students, which are also admitted based on university terms of admission.

In October 1981 the CHE appointed a new Colleges Committee headed by Prof. Lev Zion. The committee included representatives of the universities, and of the Department of Culture and Art at the Ministry of Education and Culture, that had been responsible for the administration of colleges at the Ministry. Following are the roles defined for the committee:

1. Ensure that teaching at colleges would be the responsibility of the universities granting their auspices.
2. Assist in the relationships between universities and Regional Colleges.
3. Approve the budget which the department allocates for the operation of the academic programs, regardless of budgets received by universities for their responsibility for academic programs at colleges.[223]

223 State Comptroller's report (1990), Auspices on academic programs at Regional Colleges. The academic programs of Tel Chai and Yezreel Valley Colleges were examined.

Overview of the CHE/PBC's Position

Until the end of the 1980s the position of the PBC and the CHE on the issue of Regional Colleges expressed the main conclusions of all the committees that examined the possibility to expand the higher education system in response to the growing demand in Israel and in the entire Western world. During this period, the position voiced by the CHE was that the universities would absorb any demand, and there is no need for a second layer of institutions of higher education, for fear of a decline in the level of the degree.[224] This position expressed a conservative atmosphere and European approach by which only a research university should supply the demand for higher education. During this period the CHE ascribed to one of the world's three most prevalent approaches: (a) Higher education is a matter for the social elites – an approach that had been prevalent in Europe up to World War II; (b) A completely opposing approach by which higher education should be open to a very wide group, with screening taking place during rather than before studies – an approach still practiced in France; (c) An Anglo-American approach by which there is no single gate for higher education but various gates, to which each person enters according to his or her relative height.[225] As mentioned, until the end of the 1980s the CHE's position included a screening method that relies on a single entrance gate. This approach perceived the needs of higher education from the perspective of universities, and therefore approaches towards colleges pertained to programs offered by universities at colleges. As to the colleges' own programs, the CHE's position towards the end of the 1980s was as follows:

1. The academic programs at Regional Colleges are important mainly socially, in the fact that they facilitate the admission of many students residents of development towns and remote areas into higher education.
2. The academic programs at the Regional Colleges would be partial, not exceeding two academic years, during which students would accumulate credits towards their degree. The third year would be studied at the main

224 Rubinstein, 2004 – from a collection of lectures published by the U.S. Israel Education Foundation. Prof. Amnon Rubinstein, former Minister of Education, presented the CHE's decision of 1 January 1989, by which all students applying for higher education would be accepted to universities. This decision was accepted nearly unanimously.

225 From a lecture by Martin Trow given at a conference on the role of colleges in the expansion of higher education in Israel– lessons learned from the American experience, 8 April 2003, U.S. Israel Education Foundation, Tel Aviv. Trow, 2004: 35–39.

campus of the university granting its auspices. This way a suitable academic level would be maintained.

3. Colleges are yet to utilize their full potential for recruiting students and academic faculty having suitable qualifications in their region.
4. The PBC will act to open academic studies at Regional Colleges and will ensure that a suitable level of studies is maintained through the universities.
5. The PBC has always and still aims to develop academic programs at colleges through the Open University.
6. Until the option for studies at the colleges through the Open University can be realized, the PBC/CHE will maintain direct financial and academic ties with the university granting its auspices rather than with the managements of the colleges themselves, in all matters pertaining to the academic program.

Chapter 11 Bar Ilan's Extensions and Their Positioning within the CHE's Plans

While the CHE identified the concept of auspices for academic studies outside of campus (an idea that had been at the basis of Bar Ilan's Extensions) as a solution for the matter of Regional Colleges, its plans did not include Bar Ilan's Extensions – Ashkelon and Zefat – as these did not operate as Regional Colleges. The CHE/PBC did not directly recognize them and did not encourage their continued existence. Deliberations as to the continued development of this educational path were dedicated entirely to the Regional College model. This position was presented by PBC Chairperson Yaacov Ziv in his letter to the Rector of Bar Ilan University, Prof. Ernest Krausz:

> The PBC encourages academic activities in the periphery, with a preference for Regional Colleges. A demand will not be made to close existing Extensions, but the PBC will not encourage the opening of new Extensions, or the expansion of activities at existing ones. The PBC will not allocate further special budgets to the Extensions [. . .] As to the existence of pre-academic preparatory studies at the Zefat and Ashkelon Extensions, we do not oppose these activities, provided that the funding that had been promised to you covers the expenses.[226]

This position which solidified over the 1980s, also defined the CHE/PBC's position regarding Bar Ilan University's existing Extensions. Although this position gave the university full authority for the management of academic programs, Bar Ilan's plans during the 1960s and 1970s to establish further campuses as Extensions of the university seemed unreasonable for a number of reasons:

1. **Planning difficulties:** The Extensions, similarly to colleges, were limited to the accumulation of academic credits equivalent to a maximum of two academic years, with students moving to the main campus in their second or third year. This solution led to extreme overloads at the university and undermined its ability to plan the scope of courses for students from the Extensions in the last years of their studies. These planning difficulties focused on the inability to forecast the number of continuing students and the number of advanced courses, especially in the third year. The structural decentralization of the university's work as planned for its multi-campus structure had not

226 CHE archive, Bar Ilan University Extensions file. Letter from PBC Chairperson, Prof. Yaacov Ziv to the Rector of Bar Ilan, 31 March 1987.

been realized, and the situation mounted operational difficulties on the main campus.

2. **Budgetary difficulties:** Similarly to Regional Colleges, the Extensions were not eligible for a regular PBC budget. However, the colleges were generally more financially independent than the Extensions. This independence was expressed in the Regional Colleges' ability to expand their academic activities through the university under which the college operates. Such expansion would have been encouraged and supported by the PBC, as per its policy. A further expression of the independence of Regional Colleges was their ability to collect tuition from students, which was not part of the Extensions' responsibilities. The authority to directly collect tuition had implications both on the institution's independent position towards its students as well as its ability to plan the extent of its academic activities to a certain level of independence. At the Extensions, expansion was limited by the PBC and tuition was paid directly to the university. Special expenses for operating the Extensions were not covered by the PBC and relied on the benevolence of the university, which continued to operate the Extensions at a growing deficit despite the PBC's policy, but meanwhile did not expand their operations due to the PBC's policy and the growing deficit incurred by the university due to their operation. Operations under deficit was also the share of the Regional Colleges, mostly due to the fact that the number of students at these institutions did not suffice for balanced budgetary operations.[227]

The PBC's, which had further solidified its position over the years, encouraged the existence of academic programs at Regional Colleges. This position enabled it to fulfill its national obligation without delving too deeply into the situation. Management and direct responsibility remained in the hands of the college, with the Ministry of Education, the universities and the CHE supervising without assuming direct responsibility even if social need required them to do so. Unlike the colleges, the Extensions, which were part of Bar Ilan University, operated indirectly according to the regulatory rules that applied to the universities, without being officially required to do so. For instance, the student quota defined for all universities included the students of the Extensions as they were included in Bar Ilan's quota, while the students of the Regional Colleges were not included in the quotas of the universities granting them academic auspices. The budgeting of educational facilities for the university did not include the Extensions, and

227 State Comptroller's report (1999), Auspices on academic programs at Regional Colleges: 270.

therefore the allocation of budgets for such facilities at an Extension was paid for entirely by the university, while academic facilities at Regional Colleges were not a component of the agreement between the universities and the Regional Colleges under their auspices. This policy, however, did not discourage Bar Ilan, and it did not withdraw from its intent to continue holding on to the Extensions due to their essential social and religious nature. However, the budgetary burden forced the university's management to refrain from further developing the Extensions, and it searched for ways to continue operating them and even expanding their operations in a way that would be accepted by national authorities.

Expanding the Extensions Project: Extensions as Regional Colleges

The CHE's firm position against the existence of Extensions and its clear preference for Regional Colleges led Bar Ilan to realize it must act according to the rules of the game defined by the CHE. On one hand it refused to relinquish its aspirations to hold studies at the periphery and to disseminate the university's religious and social vision, while on the other hand this aspiration led to financial difficulties entailed in the continued operation of the Extensions. As opposed to other universities granting their auspices to Regional Colleges without undertaking any financial responsibility for their operation, Bar Ilan University continued to persist with its social mission despite accumulating a heavy annual deficit in the mid 1970s due to its operation of the Extensions, estimated at about half a million Liras, amounting to about 2 % of the university's budget in those years. As aforesaid, although religious enthusiasm declined, the university's management continue to search for ways to preserve its Extensions, with the social message guiding its path. This social message, having spearheaded the struggle over the continued operation of the Extensions, corresponded with the political atmosphere of the time, as well as the CHE's policy and the growing need to invest in the periphery. However, the Extensions were no longer among the university's top priorities as they had been in the days of the multi-campus university plans. The abandonment of the multi-campus idea required directing all resources to the main campus, towards its physical and academic development. If in the 1960s the university's management viewed its religious-social mission as the pinnacle of its operation, in the 1980s the development of the main campus became the center of attention. Although the development of the Extensions was not completely abandoned, management felt that in view of the fact that the social issue is the country's most pressing need, sooner or later the Extensions would become a national priority and the university would gain State support. The growing demand for higher education in Israel in general and at the periphery in particular and the CHE's policy to encourage academic activities at Regional Colleges encouraged the university to act in line with the rules of the game of the academic field, which were, as always, dictated by the senior members of the field – the CHE – whose leaders made a clear distinction between types of institutions destined to serve the system in the 1980s, up to the point in which the CHE would defined the term "academic college" under the CHE law. To ensure that these terms are clear to the reader, following is a list of useful definitions:

1. **Extension**
   An academic institution that is an integral part of a recognized university and holds academic studies on behalf of that university only. No other types of studies are held at Extensions, contrary to Regional Colleges. Academic studies are operated directly by the university. The Extension's income and expenditures are managed directly by the university. Two such Extensions operated in Israel in the 1980s: Zefat and Ashkelon.
2. **Regional College**
   The first Regional Colleges in Israel were initiated by their respective Regional Councils, in order to address the professional needs of residents of local Kibbutzim and Moshavim. In the beginning of the 1970s academic courses were added to the vocational studies offered at the colleges, granting academic credits at a university which would recognize them in retrospect.
3. **Academic Programs at Regional Colleges**
   A university's academic program held at a Regional College towards academic credits for up to two years of academic studies. Students taking part in these programs cannot complete their degree at the college and so in their final year they attend the institution granting the college its academic auspices. This type of program was encouraged by the CHE in the 1980s and 1990s to address the growing demand for higher education in remote regions. Courses in the academic program were managed by the college, with the university's approval. As opposed to studies towards accumulation of credits, in the academic program the college and the university aimed to offer more diverse academic studies, offering a full program for the first and second years. Studies at the academic program required enrollment at the university and admittance according to the terms defined by the university for the academic program held at the college. Courses taken for credit did not require registration to the university or meeting terms of admission.

Bar Ilan University's Academic Auspices to the College of Judea and Samaria (CJS)

Since the opening of its latest Extension in 1968 and as a result of the ban on opening new ones following amendment number 3 to the CHE law, towards the end of the 1980s the Extensions project encountered a new turning point, this time in the form of the academic programs promoted by the CHE at Regional Colleges. This new direction gave new life to the old model of Extensions, which had become exceedingly difficult to promote. Some of Bar Ilan's leaders, who believed that new ways should be examined for achieving the university's religious-social ideology, saw in this new model of operation an opportunity to regain the ability to implement the university's religious and social goals which had been the underlying foundation of the Extensions. On this backdrop, in the beginning of the 1980s an opportunity occurred with the request of Benny Katzover and Zvi Slonim of the university to extend its academic auspices to the new colleges founded at Kdumim and Ariel. Despite the fact that the initiative did not originate from the university's management, and that its initiators also included faculty members from the Hebrew University and Tel Aviv, including Prof. Yosef Ben Shlomo – a settler in Samaria and one of the leaders of the settlement movement – the initiators saw Bar Ilan University and its management as the natural academic institution for implementing the idea of establishing an academic college in Samaria. The religious approach of the university and its management, and the ideological-religious proximity between the university's leaders and the settlers' leaders, led in the 1980s to a natural connection that enabled the university to hop on board the project.[228]

The establishment of the college in Samaria began during the period of the peace agreement with Egypt and the evacuation of Yamit. The initiators' intent had been to establish an educational center for settlers in Judea and Samaria, which would focus on Israel studies and geography. The college initially included two study centers: One at the settlement of Kdumim, where theoretical studies

228 Ariel college, or as it was initially called – the College of Judea & Samaria, had never been an Extension of Bar Ilan University, as noted by Dana Zalikowski (2013). From its onset it had operated as a college receiving academic auspices for academic programs from Bar Ilan University (and also from the Hebrew University for Agricultural studies, until this fact was published in the media and was stopped). See above definitions on the distinction between Extensions and Colleges under academic auspices.

were held, and the other in Ariel, for technological disciplines, mainly computer studies at various levels. The relationship between the management of the college and Bar Ilan University was initiated by Prof. Yizhak Levin, who had served as Chairperson of the university's Extensions Committee in the beginning of the 1980s and was among the founders of the College of Judea & Samaria. In his letter dated 1 December 1982 to the CEO of the Ministry of Science, Prof. Levin proposed a gradual plan for the development of the college, the optimal stage being its accreditation as one of Bar Ilan University's Extensions:

> I have been handling the idea raised by Zvi Slonim and Benny Katzover for the establishment of an Extension of Bar Ilan University at the Kdumin settlement in Samaria. The matter has been positively discussed at the Extensions Committee [. . .] The general trend in these discussions has been that although the university has been affirmative towards the idea, it is still too early on to discuss an Extension.[229]

The CHE/PBC's decisive opposition to the opening of further Extensions was clear to decision makers at Bar Ilan, and despite their wish to support the college, Prof. Levin's letter points to an extreme wariness and an attempt to act according to the CHE's rules, while still recognizing the College of Judea & Samaria as an Extension. To achieve this aim without risking the CHE's opposition, he proposed the following gradual plan:

1. The founders would work to establish a suitable physical facility for an academic college at Kdumim.
2. After the establishment of any type of studies at the college, the institution would be required to include academic courses, without the university's formal accreditation. such accreditation would be achieved gradually, the first stage being individual recognition of courses based on their academic level, to be achieved though Bar Ilan University's academic faculty and others from other universities, who would teach just as they would the same courses at university campuses.
3. All academic studies would be retroactively accredited on an individual basis when students arrive at campus to complete their undergraduate degree. According to this method, students would receive academic credits for all

229 Bar Ilan University Archive, container 753, file 285. Letter from Prof. Levin to the CEO of the Ministry of Science and Development, 1 December 1982.

their studies at the College of Judea & Samaria, similarly to students at the Extensions, but without the establishment of an Extension being declared.
4. The final stage of the establishment of a dependent academic institution would be reached with the university granting formal accreditation to the colleges as academic Extensions.

For the sake of caution and so as to avoid violating the guidelines of the CHE/PBC, it was clear to Prof. Levin that such accreditation of the colleges as Extensions would be internal – meaning that the university, or its unit dedicated to accrediting prior courses, would recognize the studies achieved by a student coming from the College of Judea & Samaria, just as it would recognize the achievements of a student coming from the university's other Extensions. The accreditation of lecturers and annual curricula would be achieved through the planning and follow up forum, as is the custom for annual curricula of all Extensions. However, externally the accreditation would be granted to the academic program of the college, just as had been done by other universities at the time.

The university's caution in its relationship with the College of Judea and Samaria can be noted from the correspondence between its CEO David Altman and Zvi Slonim, Manager of the Samaria community center, following publications in the media giving the impression that Bar Ilan University has established a new Extension at Samaria. In Zvi Slonim's letter of apology he denied any relationship to the publications and the resulting damage which may have been caused to the university: "I never declared that we are an Extension of Bar Ilan University, I never declared that we have been recognized by it [. . .] The management of the College of Judea & Samaria has no connection to these publications".[230] However, despite these denials the central committee of the university's senate approved the request of the College of Judea & Samaria to recognize studies held at the college and the continued studies of its students at the university.[231]

However, the management of the college at Judea and Samaria did not make do with its successful relationship with Bar Ilan University, but continued with its efforts to expand by attempting to also recruit the Hebrew University. It approached the Hebrew University, requesting its academic auspices for an Agricultural studies program, which did not exist at Bar Ilan and was necessary for expanding the knowledge of settlers aiming to develop agriculture in the

230 Ibid. Letter from Zvi Slonim, Manager of the Samaria community center, to David Altman, CEO of Bar Ilan University, 6 December 1982.
231 Ibid. Letter from Prof. Krausz, Rector of Bar Ilan University, to Knesset member Yigal Cohen-Orgad, Chairperson of the College of Judea & Samaria, 19 November 1987.

region. The relationship between the college management and that of the Hebrew University serves as a further case study for Bar Ilan University's unique approach towards the concept of distributing knowledge through Extensions, which differs from that of all other universities in Israel.

Although faculty members from the Hebrew University were among the founders of the college at Judea and Samaria, and although its management agreed to provide consulting services in the field of agricultural studies, the Hebrew University rejected the request of the college to grant it academic auspices, and made do with providing consulting services through its Faculty of Agriculture at Rehovot. The different responses of the managements of Bar Ilan and the Hebrew University to inquiries from the media point to their different approaches. In response to a question from "Haaretz" daily newspaper, Prof. Hanoch Gutfreund, Rector of the Hebrew University, said the following: "The Standing Committee of the Senate discussed the request and decided against it. We have decided not to grant our auspices but allowed the Faculty of Agriculture at Rehovot to advise the College on Agricultural matters". In response to the question whether the reason for not granting the university auspices is political, he answered: "I don't know whether there had been disagreements at that meeting and whether political questions were raised in this context. I must say that the Hebrew University could not have avoided offering consulting services as we are the only university with a Faculty of Agriculture".

Contrary to Prof. Gutfreund's self-defending response, the response given by Prof. Harvey Babkofh, Bar Ilan University's representative, to the same question from Haaretz newspaper, points to a clear social-religious approach:

> There is growing demand in Israel for general education, from a wide population. The idea of Regional Colleges was developed for this purpose. The college at Judea and Samaria fulfills this need [. . .] It is no different, in our opinion, from other Regional Colleges, to which we and other universities in the country provide our auspices, such as colleges at Zefat, Ashkelon, Tel Chai and others.[232]

The collaboration between Bar Ilan University and the College of Judea & Samaria expresses their joint interests and goals. From the viewpoint of the college founders, the relationship with a university and the existence of an academic program at the college were essential for the realization of its comprehensive vision, which was the establishment of an independent academic institution which would attract young and older people living in Samaria and others who will come to the area, thereby increasing the total number of settlers in the region. From

232 Melman, Yossi. The Settlers' College, Haaretz, 1 November 1991.

the university's viewpoint, granting academic auspices to the college breathed fresh air into the Extensions project that had largely stagnated due to budgetary constraints as well as the CHE/PBC's struggle against the idea. The establishment of an academic program at the college gave the university a new opportunity to realize the aspirations of its founders to enhance its religious-social impact through academic studies in the periphery. "Operations at remote locations have been a religious and social aim in the 1960s, and the opportunity to work in Judea and Samaria fulfilled a religious and social ideal in the second half of the 1980s".[233]

The auspices granted by the university to the college at Judea and Samaria and the appointment of Yigal Cohen Orgad, former Minister of Finance, as Chairperson of the College in 1985, contributed significantly to its academic development. The relationship between the parties grew stronger towards the end of the 1980s, in parallel to the expansion of the college's fundamental aims: No longer an institution serving the settlers community but a college aiming to attract new settlers arriving in Samaria from the entire country and even from other countries. To achieve these aims, from the first days of the college it included dormitories, a transportation system and extensive efforts invested in improving its access roads, alongside the expansion of collaboration with the university.[234]

Extensions or Auspices: The Transition in the Status of Extensions in the beginning of the 1990s

The inclusion of the College of Judea & Samaria in Bar Ilan University's list of Extensions as a college rather than an Extension relying on university budgets, and on the other hand the CHE's instructions not to open new university Extensions, quickly led the university's leaders to identify the great potential in this new type of relationship. For the university, this path, developed with the CHE's encouragement as a current need and social solution, created a further opportunity to act in the periphery without entailing further financial expenses. The university's academic patronage as expressed in the auspices model gave it full control over the nature and scope of studies without any resulting managerial, organizational or budgetary responsibility, as had been the case in the Extensions model. The special relationship with the Jordan Valley College, where the university operated an Extension, had been closer to the model of the Extensions of Zefat or Ashkelon

233 Interview with Prof. Harvey Babkofh, head of the Colleges Administration at Bar Ilan University, on 17 August 2009.

234 For more on the establishment of the College of Judea & Samaria, see: Zalikowski, 2013.

more than to the auspices model. The differences between the types of operation – Extension, auspices, and Extension within the college, will be evaluated using managerial tools:

1. **Operating model: "Extension" Vs. "Extension within a College"**
   A. **Managerial rules:** The Ashkelon and Zefat Extensions were directly operated by the university, with no other studies held at the sites except for the university's academic studies. Despite this distinction we have seen that the university defined its relationship with the Jordan Valley College as an Extension. This was first and foremost due to timing, and in addition it is also safe to say that its characteristics are similar to those of an Extension. In what way? The academic studies at the college were operated as an organic unit of the university, completely unrelated to other study units operating at the same site. The academic and administrative rules of the Extensions at Zefat and Ashkelon were also applied to the Jordan Valley Extension. Managerial decisions remained under the university's exclusive authority, including the cost of tuition, scope of studies each year, terms of admission, suspension from studies and accreditation of previous studies.
   B. **Budgetary management:** As opposed to the Extensions at Ashkelon and Zefat, who were operated fully by Bar Ilan University, the Jordan Valley Extension was operated under a financial arrangement that left most financial responsibilities in the hands of the college, and only a small part with the university. But despite the difference between it and the Ashkelon and Zefat Extensions, the university participated in the costs of the Jordan Valley Extension for the operation of academic courses and Jewish Studies, due to the university's religious aspiration to expose the area of Jewish Studies to growing numbers of students, from a scientific and rational perspective. Moreover, it was in the university's best interest to offer more courses in Jewish Studies than the college had requested, so as to provide full time employment to lecturers employed at the Jordan Valley and at Zefat, in addition to their work at the main campus.
2. **Operating model: Auspices College**
   A. **Managerial rules:** The academic courses within an existing college are operated by the college management, as an organizationally and financially independent institution. The college management defined the scope of academic studies each year based on its forecasts and planning; employed lecturers and determined their salaries and extent of employment.

Lecturers normally also filled other teaching positions at the college and the university did not intervene in the management or scope of studies.

B. **Budgetary management:** In view of the fact that the academic activities remained under the college's full responsibility, it also covered the entire financial expense entailed in academic studies, including payment to the university for its academic auspices. The university's management was not involved in any way in the general balance of academic activities. It provided an academic service and was fully compensated for it.

Table 30 offers a comparison of management types by four basic managerial rules.

Tab. 30: Differing types of operations: Extension and Auspices College

Managerial tool	Influencing factor		
	Zefat/Ashkelon	**Jordan Valley**	**Judea and Samaria**
Uniform academic Managerial rules	Defined and operated by Bar Ilan University	Defined and operated by Bar Ilan University	Defined and operated by Bar Ilan University
Budgetary management	Bar Ilan University	Combined: Bar Ilan University and Jordan Valley College	Independent
Scope of activity	Bar Ilan University	Combined: Bar Ilan University and Jordan Valley College	Independent
Academic management	Bar Ilan University	Bar Ilan University	Combined: Bar Ilan University and Judea and Samaria
Academic responsibility	Bar Ilan University	Bar Ilan University	Bar Ilan University

The managerial potential entailed in the new relationship established between Bar Ilan University and the College of Judea & Samaria led the university's management to transform its method of operating its Extensions. No longer operating under deficit as per the founders' historical model, but a strive to change the status of the historical Extensions from being operated by the university to becoming independent Regional Colleges, both organizationally and in terms of budget. While this change forced the university's management to part with the historical operating model that granted it exclusive managerial authority, it also included a solution for its constantly growing budgetary deficit, while still retaining the university's academic patronage.

The historical turning point in the university's position as to the method of managing its Extensions was led by Prof. Zvi Arad, who had been appointed Rector in 1989. Upon commencing his tenure he set the following priorities in obtaining the goals that in retrospect affected the Extensions: The first goal was increasing the university's budget, and the second – maintaining its special character. After being appointed Rector he wrote the following to all faculty members: "As Rector I have set a goal for myself to promote a number of topics that seem important to me. I wish to maintain the special religious nature of the university and continue in the path paved by the university's founders".[235]

As mentioned above, the achievement of these two goals influenced the future of the Extensions: The university's religious character and the social ideology of its founders formed the ideological basis for the establishment of the Extensions in the 1960s. The path paved by the founders to disseminate *Torah* and science motivated the university's management to expand to the country's social and geographical periphery. In addition to these aims, the new Rector was closely familiar with the Extensions due to his previous position as Chairperson of the university's Extensions Committee in 1985–1989. In that position he often had to struggle against attempts by his predecessor, Prof. Michael Elbak[236] to shut down the Extensions that by that time had accumulated a deficit of seven to eight million shekels.[237] Despite this position his new role as Rector required a different approach to the university's budget and he soon found himself in a difficult dilemma: Increasing the Extensions' budget would also increase the university's deficit resulting from their operation, while on the other hand freezing their development despite growing public demand for academic education in the 1990s may lead to their liquidation. The changes in the CHE's position on the matter of Regional Colleges and the rise in demand for higher education that began taking its toll in the 1990s urged the Rector to take two different but complementary paths of action to solve the dilemma:

1. **Transferring the budget of the Extensions to the State** The operating model which the Rector saw at the College of Judea & Samaria and the ban on opening further Extensions led him to conclude that for the benefit of both the university and the Extensions, the Extensions' budget must be transferred to a State authority. The advantages in transferring budgetary responsibility to the State would be felt by both sides. In the 1990s the university faced extensive academic and research challenges

235 Ashkelon College Archive, file 1989. Letter from the Rector to the faculty of the university and the Extensions, 11 October 1989.

236 The university's Rector from 1982 to 1985.

237 Interview with Prof. Zvi Arad, 18 December 2007. Arad served as Rector of Bar Ilan University from 1989 to 1993, and as President of the university from 1993 to 1996.

in the competition over prestige and academic status with the country's other universities, and the growing budgetary deficit due to the operation of the Extensions made it increasingly difficult to cope with these challenges. The Extensions, whose academic operations were stalled due to lack of budget and means for coping with the demand for higher education in the 1990s, were now faced with a new opportunity for changing their status following the CHE's new policy and its plans to expand accessibility to academic studies in the periphery. The Rector concluded that a change in the formal status of the Extensions and their transition to becoming Regional Colleges would contribute to their prosperity while freeing the university from the budgetary burden of their direct operation. The transfer of responsibility to a governmental ministry would lead the Extensions to obtaining an organizationally and financially independent status, and their managements would be able to promote their operation as independent Regional Colleges. Under this formula the university would remain exclusively responsible for academic studies at the college, thereby maintaining its religious and social aims in the periphery. According to this method of operation, the founders' aspiration to bring the religious academy to the periphery would continue to exist through the granting of academic auspices to the colleges.

Being experienced on the matter of Extensions, Prof Arad supported the opinion that in transferring responsibility to a national authority the university is leading the Extensions to a more responsible position, by which their managements would be encouraged to attract more students and undertake operational responsibility suited to local needs. According to this approach, local managements would be required to operate similarly to any other academic institution in Israel, both in terms of its income derived from the number of students and donations, as well as in terms of their responsibility for expenses derived from employing academic and administrative faculty as well as the institution's maintenance. Such responsibility would create a commitment for success as the institution would not continue to rely on the university's remote management, which for years had to define the scope of operations in each Extension according to financial constraints.

2. **Increasing the Extensions' educational activities and responsibilities:** the first step, aimed, as aforesaid, to disconnect the Extensions from the university's budget, was bold and far reaching, and also entailed significant risks. Its success depended on the success of the local management to increase the number of students and the scope of courses offered. For the first time, local managements were required to stand at the helm and steer the ship without the university's financial support and succeed within a short period of

time where the university had not managed in many years. The scope of academic and financial activities of the Extensions at the beginning of the 1990s was not promising for two main reasons:

A. **Format of studies:** As aforesaid, until the 1980s the university offered only a very limited program at its Extensions. The programs offered were eclectic, and the courses available each year did not fulfill even the first year's obligations in any single department. At the end of their first year at the Extension diligent students had to travel to the main campus to complete their first full year so as to pass on to the second academic year. This situation prevented students from joining an annual program, meaning that a curriculum suitable to students' needs was not available.
B. **Student population:** Since their establishment, the Extensions attracted students that combined work with evening studies. Most of them were older students employed at places of work close to their homes: Teachers, bank clerks and civil servants. At Ashkelon and Zefat nursing students at the local school for nurses took part of their studies at the Extension. Army officers serving at the IDF's northern command at Zefat and at the Gaza strip took their first academic courses at the Ashkelon and Zefat Extensions. The selection of courses was eclectic, with students accumulating between four to eight academic hours every year before moving on to advanced courses, at which point they had to transfer to Bar Ilan's main campus. The younger population of students, who generally aspire to complete their studies as soon as possible and find work, did not tend to choose the Extensions as their place of study. The few ones who did take their first steps at the Extensions quickly transitioned to the university's main campus in their second year. This format did not allow management to present a growth in its number of students, a requirement which was a central prerequisite for the success of any Extension. The result of the limited curriculum and the population that elected to study under this format was a institution type that in those years served as a transitory station for the university's campus. Even when the efforts by the new management of the Extensions bore fruit and the number of year 1 students increased, the total number of students at the Extension was still low as a result of the transfer of existing students every year to the main campus.

Prof. Arad, who had been aware of this problem in his role of Chairperson of the Extensions, understood that improving the Extensions' financial and academic status requires a fundamental change in its format of studies. Concerns among the managers of the Extensions as to the budgetary separation from the university led him to implement a corresponding process, and for the first time since the establishment of the Extensions, they were able to offer their students a full undergraduate degree by Bar Ilan University. These innovations – the transition of budgetary responsibility to the State and the implementation of a full curriculum at the Extensions – had been the core of Prof. Arad's work plan.

The Struggle for a National Budget for the Extensions

The CHE's policy, which encouraged academic programs at Regional Colleges, and Zvulun Hammer's return to the position of Minister of Education, encouraged Prof. Arad to act to obtain his goals by directly contacting the minister, and by applying to the heads of the CHE and the PBC:

A. **Working with the Ministry of Education:** Yitzhak Shamir's government was in office in the years 1990–1992. The Minister of Education was once again the NRP's representative, Zvulun Hammer. For many years Hammer was a member of Bar Ilan University's Board, and often expressed his wholehearted support of the continued operation of the Extensions. He struggled against any attempt to cut their budgets and urged to increase their scope of operation due to their social importance and contribution to the periphery, which had been the NRP's political stronghold. Prof. Arad proposed to the Minister of Education that the time has come to recognize the university's Extensions as Regional Colleges to be operated as new units under the ministry's annual budget. An expression of the Rector's pressure on the Ministry of Education can be found in his letter to the Minister on 23 September 1990:

> Despite the importance of the Extensions for the development of the Galilee, the Negev and Judea and Samaria, until now governmental support has not been extended to the Extensions, and they are dependent upon the university's budget as an intolerable and unjust burden.[238]

Following the Rector's letter and requests by the Ministry of Education, the CEO of the CHE/PBC responded as follows:

238 Ashkelon College Archive, file 1990. Letter from the Rector to the Minister of Education, 23 September, 1990.

> The matter of the Extensions at Bar Ilan University is highly problematic. We have held conversations on the matter with Prof. Arad and with the Minister of Education and Culture and have proposed that the Extensions [...] would become Regional Colleges and would be managed, as is customary, by the Ministry of Education and Culture, while the academic programs under the university's responsibility would also be handled, as is customary, by the Council for Higher Education's Sub-Committee for Colleges [...] Moreover, in a budgetary agreement with the university last year Prof. Arad emphasized that as of 1990 the Extensions would not be budgeted by Bar Ilan University and would be operated as Regional Colleges.[239]

Prof. Arad did not make do with his application to the minister, but added the political power of the mayors of Ashkelon and Zefat in order to assert further political pressure on the minister and his top management. The mayors were convinced that changing the status of the Extension in their city would result in its prosperity and establishment as an independent institution and decided to take their own initiatives to achieve the goal set by Prof. Arad. However, their final goal was different than the university's: contrary to the Rector's position, aiming for a budgetary alleviation for the university, the mayors realized that they are faced with an opportunity to promote a process which may begin by achieving budgetary independence but may eventually lead to an institutional and academic one. Initially, the Extension's separation from the university's budget and its establishment as an independent Association would offer it independence also in other educational directions which had not been possible under the university's framework, such as practical engineering studies, certificate programs and preparatory studies for completing education. Second, its academic success and increase in the number of students would in future require a different approach to its partial independence. The budgetary change initiated by Prof. Arad seemed, therefore, to the mayors and the managers of the institutions as having potential for a far reaching transformation, and they took an active part in the realization of his plan. An example of the type of letters sent by the mayors of Ashkelon and Zefat following the Rector's initiative can be found in the following extract of a letter from the mayor of Ashkelon to Dan Sharon, at the time CEO of the Ministry of Education:

> Bar Ilan University's Extension at Ashkelon was founded about 29 years ago and has been continuously active since then, with hundreds of academic graduates from Ashkelon and

239 Archive of the Council for Higher Education, Bar Ilan University file. Letter from Guri Zilca, CEO of the CHE/PBC to Ms. Zelig at the office of the Minister of Education and Culture, 22 October 1990.

> the region - young and older students who if not for the Extension would have had no opportunity to acquire academic education. Over the past five years, the Extension at Ashkelon served as a Post-Secondary education center in many areas – in both academic and preparatory studies for completing education; in this regard and for all intents and purposes the Extension operates as a college [. . .] We believe it is both justified and necessary to grant it college status.[240]

About a month later he again issued a letter to the Minister of Education Zvulun Hammer: "Further to my letter to the CEO of the Ministry of Education [. . .] I would be thankful if you would agree to meet me for a conversation at the Knesset or your office at the Ministry of Education on the matter of granting the status of college to Bar Ilan University's Extension at Ashkelon".[241] The struggle between center and periphery, whose first signs could be noted since the mid 1970s, reached during these years a practical window of opportunities in which the mayors were able to implement a move that would lead to the establishment of an academic institution in the city or the area without depending upon the university and its dictates. The Rector of the university also believed that budgetary concerns make such step a necessity, but contrary to the mayors he also believed that the risk of separating from the Extension is slim in view of the financial and academic resources entailed in the establishment of a new academic institution.

B. **Lobbying with the CHE/PBC:** The promotion of academic programs at Regional Colleges was led and inspired by the CHE as part of preparations for addressing the growing demand for higher education in the country. In all internal discussions held at the CHE in the 1970s and 1980s the conclusions was clear: The supply of institutions should be increased so as to address growing demand. Prof. Arad's aims corresponded with the CHE/PBC's position for a number of reasons:

   1. The long term opposition to the existence of the university Extensions model could lead to its successful conclusion. The Extensions model was foreign to Israel's academic field, predominantly because only Bar Ilan University had adopted such a model. Moreover, the foreignness of the model was opposed to the research-oriented academic model of the European-German approach, and that of the American one that took its place. As already noted, Bar Ilan University, that had been founded in the USA, brought with it an American

240 Ashkelon College Archive, file 1990. Letter dated 22 May, 1990.
241 Ibid. Letter dated 24 June, 1990.

managerial orientation that was based on the model of the religious academies in the United States, and this included the concept of Extensions. For the first time since the establishment of the Extensions, the CHE was able to consensually eradicate the concept of Extensions and instead present them as national institutions operating under its policy.

2. The transformation in the Extensions' status and their establishment as Regional Colleges offering an academic program would add to the country's Higher Education System two new institutions and increase the supply of academic programs at the periphery. The inclusion of the two institutions did not require significant national investment, as would have been the case had the government decided to establish two new institutions at Ashkelon and Zefat, rather than using the existing ones.
3. The operation of the Extensions as colleges would result in their direct supervision by the CHE/PBC without the involvement of Bar Ilan University, ensuring conformance with the CHE/PBC's regulatory rules both directly and via the Ministry of Education.

An expression of this general approach by the CHE was expressed in discussions between the CHE/PBC's CEO and the Minister of Education following the university's request to change the status of the Extensions to colleges:

> The matter of the Extensions at Bar Ilan University is highly problematic. We have held conversations on the matter with Prof. Arad and with the Minister of Education and Culture and have proposed that the Extensions would become Regional Colleges and would be managed, as is customary, by the Ministry of Education and Culture, while the academic programs under the university's responsibility would also be handled by the Council for Higher Education's Sub-Committee for Colleges [...] As long as Bar Ilan University handles academic programs at remote Extensions, this directly creates a budgetary burden on the university, which it would not be able to carry in the long term.[242]

Following consultations with all relevant position holders at his office and at the CHE and after obtaining their recommendations, the Minister of Education decided to grant the Ashkelon and Zefat Extensions the status of Regional College budgeted by the Ministry of Education. For him this step also included an appreciation of Bar Ilan University's work in the periphery and an understanding of its resulting budgetary distress. In the certificate of accreditation granted to the Zefat and Ashkelon Extensions, their new identity was defined as "Regional College

242 CHE archive, Bar Ilan University Extensions file. Letter from Guri Zilca, CEO of the CHE/PBC to Ms. Nurith Zelig at the office of the Minister of Education and Culture, 22 October 1990.

recognized by the Ministry of Education and Culture under the auspices of Bar Ilan University".[243]

To properly prepare for handling the Extensions and other Regional Colleges, the Ministry of Education established a Colleges Unit next to its Division for Training Teaching Personnel, whose role would be to supervise existing Regional Colleges and new ones to be added, in preparation for absorbing the growing demand for higher education in Israel and their budgeting. Initially the unit published rules of accreditation and support and declared its accreditation of 12 Regional Colleges from Tel Chai in the north to Eilat in the south.[244] The responsibilities of the new unit were limited to budgeting the academic program, and academic supervision was provided by the CHE's Colleges Sub-Committee. In a circular distributed by Abraham Scheinfeld, Manager of the Colleges Unit, upon entering his position, he lists the roles of the colleges and the authorities of the new unit:[245]

1. The colleges would aim to increase the number of undergraduate students among the target population in their areas of operation at cities and development towns, Kibbutzim, Moshavim, communal settlements, and more.
2. The colleges will aim to provide their students with adult education and higher education.
3. The colleges will aim to develop unique programs suited to local needs in the areas of society and economics.
4. The colleges will not be involved in research, and will focus on teaching.
5. The colleges will recruit local teaching staff who will form the initial core of the local academic faculty. The Ministry of Education's working assumption was that the development of a local academic faculty in the area would accelerate the academic development of the college, which would in turn contribute to the development of the region.

---

243 The certificates were presented on the 6th of January, 1991. On the 6th of February 1991 Bar Ilan University held a ceremony in which it declared the Ministry of Education's accreditation of the Ashkelon and Zefat Extensions as Regional Colleges. The ceremony was held in the presence of Minister of Education Zvulun Hammer.

244 Ashkelon College Archive, file 1991. Circular published by the Colleges Division on 30 April 1991, in which it declares recognition of the Regional Colleges Tel Chai, Yezreel Valley, Jordan Valley, Zefat, Eilat, Sha'ar Hanegev, Ashkelon, Judea and Samaria, Beit Berl, Western Galilee and Achva.

245 Ashkelon College Archive, file 1991. Circular of the Cultural Administration at the Regional Colleges Unit, 30 April 1991.

Rules Governing the Ministry of Education's Support of Regional Colleges

The distributed circular defined the following rules:

1. Support would only be granted to academic programs in recognized Regional Colleges.
2. The colleges will be recognized public institutions.
3. Academic programs would be budgeted according to the number of students in each course.
4. Support will include a library and transportation for students and teachers to overcome the physical distance between the colleges and the towns in the area, and will encourage the development of a local teaching staff.

The manager's circular published by the Ministry of Education, outlining the rules of support and accreditation, also included the following:

> The aim of the academic programs at the Regional Colleges is to allow a growing number of students to complete an undergraduate degree, thereby addressing the national need to increase the number of places of study within the higher education system. The academic degree will be granted by one of the universities giving their auspices [. . .] and would be recognized by the Council for Higher Education.[246]

The new status of the university's Extensions and the establishment of the Colleges Unit at the Ministry of Education ended 26 years of the university's initiative, management and budgeting. The new tasks defined for the Extensions were based on national need and were part of a national program for addressing the demand for higher education. However, the university had still not relinquished its academic assets at the Extensions, and their academic dependence on the university remained absolute. The university's efforts were now directed towards developing the academic character of the Extensions as independent Regional Colleges. The university's academic responsibility led to new and crucial challenges for its Extensions, and albeit being devoid of financial risk compared to the past, the future of the Extensions was still very much dependent upon the university's success.

The first goal of transferring the Extensions to Stage budgeting was achieved, and the Rector proceeded to implement his plan to ensure the stability of the budgetary separation process and enable the future establishment of an institution of higher education under academic auspices.

---

246 Ibid.

Increasing the Extensions' Academic Scope and Responsibility

To ensure the success of the first stage it was essential to fundamentally change the format of studies at the three Extensions. In this regard Prof. Arad accepted the position of the Extensions' managers: Pinhas Haliwa (Ashkelon), Hebron Trabelci (Zefat) and Israel Elkabetz (Jordan Valley) and commenced the process of approving a full undergraduate curriculum at the Extensions. The initial idea was presented to the university's central committee, and in its meeting on 25 June 1990 it was decided to accept the Rector's proposal and approve the appointment of a committee of experts who would propose an agreed plan for the university's approval. The fundamental principles defined by the central committee are included in the Rector's letter to his advisor Prof. Shlomo Yehuda,[247] who headed the committee:

> I wish to propose a committee appointed to prepare a Bachelor of General Studies (BGS) program at the Extensions according to the decision of the central committee [. . .] I wish to include in the committee a representative of the Open University so as to develop an agreed program. It was agreed that, as part of the requirements for A BGS degree, the university would recognize the Open University's courses to be agreed upon, up to 14 (weekly) hours.[248]

In his letter to the Extensions Managers, Prof Arad reiterated the principles of the program and the aims of the accompanying committee:

> An accompanying committee would be established in order to propose a curriculum and a detailed operating plan. The program will commence at Zefat and the Jordan Valley (combined program), with the participation of the Open University. Students would be able to complete their entire BGS studies at the Extension.[249]

An examination of the principles points to the extreme caution implemented by Prof. Arad to ensure the success of the program among students. The aim of the proposal was to enable students to combine Open University courses, which would be recognized in retrospect by the university. The assumption was that such as solution would make it easier for students to complete their degree requirements if they would be able to study in their free time. For the colleges the possibility to include Open University courses was aimed at

---

247 Psychology Professor at Bar Ilan. Was appointed as a member of the Senate.

248 Ashkelon College Archive, file 1990. Letter from Prof. Zvi Arad to Prof. Shlomo Yehuda, 1 July 1990.

249 Ibid. Extract from a letter from the Rector Prof. Zvi Arad to the managers of the Extensions and the Mayors, 25 June 1990.

facilitating their planning and the financial expense of operating 14 weekly hours (7 annual courses) to be recognized by the Open University. These hours would be deducted from the total expenditure for operating a full curriculum. The proposal to open the program in the first stage at the two northern Extensions was intended to increase the chances of its success in its first year. The geographic proximity between the two colleges would facilitate recruiting lecturers for the program and their mobility from the center to the north. A single transportation service for both colleges would assist in logistics and provide faculty members with more work hours as they would be employed at the two colleges. However, the opening of the program at Ashkelon, which functioned as the single Extension in the south, would require increasing the number of teachers and their partial employment at a single institution.

The Report of the Committee for Evaluation of General B.A Studies (BGS) at the Extensions

The committee appointed by the Rector for developing the program included three senior faculty members at Bar Ilan's Faculty of Social Sciences: Prof. Yossi Hudra from the Department of Sociology, Prof. Simcha Feldblum from the Department of Talmudic Studies, Prof. Shlomo Yehuda from the Department of Psychology and the Manager of the Extensions Dr. Moshe Berreby from the Department of Economics. The committee was headed by Prof. Shlomo Yehuda, who served as advisor to the Rector.

Having examined its options according to the procedures of the Council for Higher Education and having visited the Extensions and examined the needs of their students, the committee set the foundation for a full BA program at the Extensions, focusing on Social Sciences and Jewish Studies, and provided the following recommendations:

1. **A new Bachelor of General Studies degree (BGS) program** at the Jordan Valley College and the Zefat Extension, to be considered for this purpose as a single academic unit.
2. **Curriculum:** The BGS program will not replace existing programs but add to them. The committee decided that the program would be somewhat different than the one offered in Social Sciences and Jewish Studies.

The Faculty of Jewish Studies: Initially it was decided to adopt the structure of the combined Jewish Studies Department and diversify the number of possible combinations of departments.
The Faculty of Social Sciences would offer the following three programs:

A. Education – Educational management or Foundations of Education
B. Economics – Business Administration
C. Israel Studies – Tourism

In each of these three programs students would be required to attend 20–24 annual hours (40 – 48 semester hours) in their selected major and 8–12 hours in another department at the same faculty, completing the remaining hours to 64 annual hours (128 semester hours) at the university, as is customary.

3. **Admission terms:** The admission terms will be as defined by the university's Extensions Committee and will not be lower than the university's minimal terms of admission. The committee recommends forming a special planning and follow up forum dedicated to academic supervision of the BGS curriculum at the Extensions.
4. **Administrative faculty:** The committee decided that an Academic Manager would be appointed for the program on behalf of the Rector. The committee recommended that the academic manager be positioned at the Zefat Extension and would work academically and administratively under the Manager of the Extensions.
5. **Academic faculty:** The operation of the three proposed program tracks required the addition of at least six to seven positions. Each of the tracks in the program required 12–14 positions.
6. **Budget for libraries:** The committee required allocating an annual budget for readers and reference books of at least $10,000.[250]

Equipped with the committee's report and the approval of the university's central committee, Prof. Arad contacted the PBC's Chairperson Prof. Yaacov Ziv, requesting the CHE/PBC's approval for the program[251] and the Minister of Education requesting that he approve a special budget for this purpose. In his letter to the minister he again reiterated the importance of the Extensions to the country and particularly to its periphery and the need to strengthen them:

> Despite the importance of the Extensions for the development of the Galilee, the Negev and Judea and Samaria, until now governmental support has not been allocated, and they are dependent upon the university's budget as an intolerable and unjust burden. The Extensions brought progress and higher education to remote areas and made an important contribution to Israeli society. It is important to recall that the Extensions provide

250 Ashkelon College Archive, file 1990. Committee's report submitted to the Rector in June 1990.

251 Ibid. Letter from Prof. Arad to Prof. Ziv, 5 November 1990. In its meeting on 11 September 1990 the central committee of the Senate approved the program.

> higher education in areas where there are no universities, bringing higher education to a population we all aspire to nurture, so as to prevent social gaps. I am convinced that with an annual budget of $2 million it would be possible to expand the Extensions to include 2,000 students (500 in each Extension). We are willing to undertake the organizational burden, academic supervision and the operation of the program in its entirety, if the budgetary solution is found. I have found a sympathetic ear for the idea among Ministers and Knesset Members from different parties, but without your decisive support I don't see how we would be able to make our plans a reality. I wish to note that in the past the Board considered closing the university's Extensions due to the budgetary problem and only ambitions to build a just society and shape the image of Israeli society prevented it until now.[252]

The Ministry of Education's accreditation of the Extensions as Regional Colleges, received in November 1990, solved the budgetary problem of the Extensions in general, as well as that of the implementation of a complete degree program. The process was completed with the granting of the program's academic approval by the Council for Higher Education.[253]

Organizational Structure of the Regional College

The latest changes including the budgeting of the Extensions by the Ministry of Education required their managements to transition to a legal structure that would express their financial and administrative independence. In 1990, the Ashkelon and Zefat Extensions, until then operated by the university, registered for the first time as an Association under the academic auspices of Bar Ilan University. The Extensions' organizational structure relied on the existence of academic and administrative authorities at the college, such as a Board of Trustees, Managing Board, Academic Council and professional committees on behalf of the Academic Council. According to the new structure, the college would be headed by a public or professional figure. The administrative structure would be operated by divisions: An academic studies division, a Post-Secondary studies Division and a financial division. The college would have a statute defining the responsibilities of each division and ensuring first and foremost the independence of its academic program. The structure presented by the Colleges Unit at the Ministry of Education is presented in Figure 4:

---

252 Ibid. Letter from the Rector to the Minister of Education, 23 September 1990.

253 Ibid. Letter from Perahia Bachar, Deputy Secretary of the Council for Higher Education, 16 June 1992.

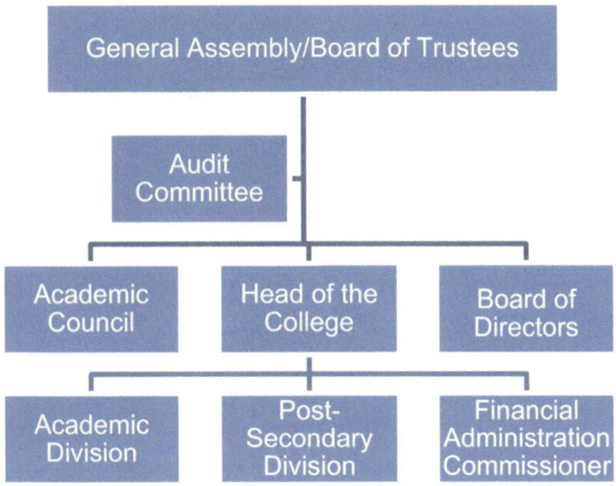

Fig. 4: General structure of Regional Colleges

Senior position holders:

1. Head of the College
2. Chairperson of the Board of Trustees
3. Chairperson of the Board
4. Chairperson of the Academic Council

Role of the Board of Trustees:

1. To approve the appointment of senior positions: Chairperson of the Board, Chairperson of the Academic Council, Chairperson of the Audit Committee, Head of the College.
2. To approve multi-annual budgets.
3. To approve the audited annual financial balance.

Role of the Board:

1. Any authority vested in it under the Associations Law.
2. Responsible for the financial management of the college.
3. To approve the establishment of new academic units.

Role of the Academic Council:

1. Maintain and promote the level of teaching.
2. Recommend the establishment of academic and other departments.
3. Academic supervision over all programs taught at the college.
4. Appointment of appointments committees and any other committee promoting studies and teaching.

Role of the Head of the College:

1. Responsible for managing the college.
2. Responsible for the budgetary management of the college.
3. Appoints all other positions which are not under the authority of the other bodies.[254]

Extensions as Regional Colleges and Their Positioning within Bar Ilan University's Academic Structure

The formal approval of the BGS program at the Council for Higher Education marked for Prof. Arad the successful conclusion of the two initiatives that had led to the university's budgetary separation from its historical Extensions. For him, the transition of the Extensions' budget to the Ministry of Education's responsibility and approval of the BGS program by the CHE served as a solution to the Extensions' plight and an end to the university's financial burden. From a sense of huge satisfaction he informed the Managers of the Extensions of the CHE's decision:

> I must note, with a sense of satisfaction, that the extensive efforts that we invested in the development of the Extensions have proven hugely successful. I have no doubt that the BGS program will contribute to the development and promotion of the Regional Colleges that are so important for the university and for the State of Israel.[255]

This solution, which originated from practical, financial considerations, led to a new approach towards the Extensions than had originally been defined by their founders:

A. This had been a turning point for the Extensions, positioning them outside the university's organizational structure: The Extensions as Regional Colleges became external to the university, institutions which from now on procure academic services, and as any other external institution receiving a service, they are committed to pay for them. If until now they had been a financial burden on the university, from now on they have become a source of income to cover the university's deficit accumulated due to its extra-campus activities. An expression of this approach of the university's management can be found in the Rector's letter to the Manager of the Extensions Dr. Berreby and to the Mayors

254 Association of Regional Colleges Archive, file 1997. Master plan – Regional Colleges, Development trends, Characteristics and Planning, 1998–2003. Submitted by Eli Israeli to the management of the Israeli Association of Regional Colleges.

255 Ashkelon College Archive, Bar Ilan, 1992. Letter from the Rector to the College Manager, 25 June, 1992.

of Ashkelon, Zefat and the Jordan Valley. However, despite efforts invested in the approval of the full BGS curriculum at the Extensions, Prof. Arad stipulated the opening of the program upon covering all of the university's expenses for its operation,[256] and only after the budgetary clause for the program's operating costs was assured, and after the Extensions' budgets had been assured by the Ministry of Education's budget, did Prof. Arad proceed to define the principles on which the relationship between the institutions would be established, in order to ensure what he believed was the plan's proper operation.

B. The new principles of operation defined by Prof. Arad relied on the new understanding that the Extensions in their new format are external institutions to the university rather than being an integral part of it as in the past. The relationship between the sides does not lay any budgetary or organizational responsibilities on the university, only academic ones. According to the new principles, there is a clear separation between the direct management of the college and the university's academic responsibility which is devoid of financial risks. This division between the parties determined the responsibility of each, as follows:

1. The university's responsibility:
   A. Appointment of lecturers for academic programs at the colleges.
   B. Approval of curriculums for the academic programs of the colleges.
   C. Exclusive responsibility over the admission of students to the academic program at the colleges.
   D. Continued employment of lecturers who taught part time at the university and completed their position at the colleges.
2. The college's responsibility:
   A. Payment of tuition of lecturers who do not work at the university.
   B. Transfer of payments to the university for payment of salaries to lecturers employed by the university.
   C. Collection of tuition from students and the State's part in funding tuition.
   D. Deduction of 15 % overheads to the university from the total payment to lecturers and tuition.

These operating principles also relied on the new approach by which the colleges, and most of all Ashkelon and Zefat, would function as a closed

256 Ibid. In a letter to the manager of one of the Extensions he wrote: "The opening of the program is stipulated upon finding a permanent budgetary solution that would not burden the university's budget" (1 July 1990).

economy, and therefore they are required to plan their steps wisely, including defining the scope of academic services offered by the university. The long term relationship was nearing its end, and the parties defined an interim period which was necessary in order to regulate the terms of termination of this system. The university prepared to complete all its financial obligations within a short period of time, mainly consisting of the obligation to continue to employ part time faculty members during the transition period. Upon completion of these obligations, it completed its separation from the tight relationship with the Ashkelon and Zefat Extensions, and to a significant extent also with the Jordan Valley. The university's position in its new relationship with its Extensions remained one of a supervising institution operating externally to the Extensions/Colleges. Despite Prof. Arad's strong belief in this path, the separation raised heavy doubts among the Managers of the Extensions, who saw the process as an existential risk to the future of the Extensions. Without the university's operative experience and the meager budget allocated by the Ministry of Education, the Managers of the Extensions could not see the light at the end of the tunnel. The general feeling was that of being abandoned by the mother institution, which is no longer interested in investing in the Extensions that have become a superfluous entity for the main campus.[257] Their apprehension was voiced on behalf of the managers by the manager of the Jordan Valley College in his letter to the Rector, in which he expressed his wish to moderate the sense of abandonment through the close support of the university's management in negotiations with government ministries so as to gain budgets for funding the BGS program. In his letter he noted:

> Regrettably the financial resources of the college would not enable significant development of the academic curriculum based on students' tuition alone. The position of the heads of the region's local authorities is that the matter must be solved with the support of the university and the central national institutions, in the absence of independent sources for each local and regional authority to subsidize the academic program.[258]

---

257 Interview with the Manager of the Zefat Extension/College Hebron Trabelci, 18 August 2009.

258 Jordan Valley College archive. Letter from the Manager Israel Elkabetz on behalf of all the colleges to Prof. Zvi Arad, 1 December 1991.

In his letter outlining the new operating principles, the Rector included words of encouragement and faith in the process, despite the managers' concerns:

> I am convinced that the arrangements detailed in my letter will lead to increased motivation and a real development of the Regional Colleges affiliated with the university. The colleges will also initiate steps to obtain funds from external sources such as government ministries and donations, and accordingly would be able to develop, with the university's assistance.[259]

Prof. Arad aimed to officially standardize the new relationship between the colleges and Bar Ilan University. The first step required a structural change within the university.

The Organizational Structure of the Colleges within the University

Within the university's organizational structure, Prof. Arad established an administration of colleges, headed by a Professor whose status parallels that of a Dean of Faculty, and in practice the administration functioned as one of the university's faculties. As in any other faculty, next to the dean, a Head of Colleges Administration was appointed, parallel to the Head of Faculty Administration. However, in order to distinguish the Colleges Administration from other faculties, it was decided that it would be known as the **Colleges System Administration**. Following the approval of the structural plan at the university's central committee, the Rector appointed Prof. Harvey Babkofh[260] who was the head of the Department of Psychology, as head of the Colleges System Administration. In a letter regarding the appointment, Prof. Arad outlined the position and the colleges' new organizational structure within the university, as shown in Figure 5:

259 Ashkelon College Archive, file 1991. Letter from the Rector, principles for operation of the Ashkelon and Zefat Colleges, 5 June 1991.

260 Ibid, Letter from the Rector to Prof. Babkofh, 19 September 1991. As is the procedure for all appointments of Deans at the university, the appointment was approved at the senate meeting held on 15 September 1991.

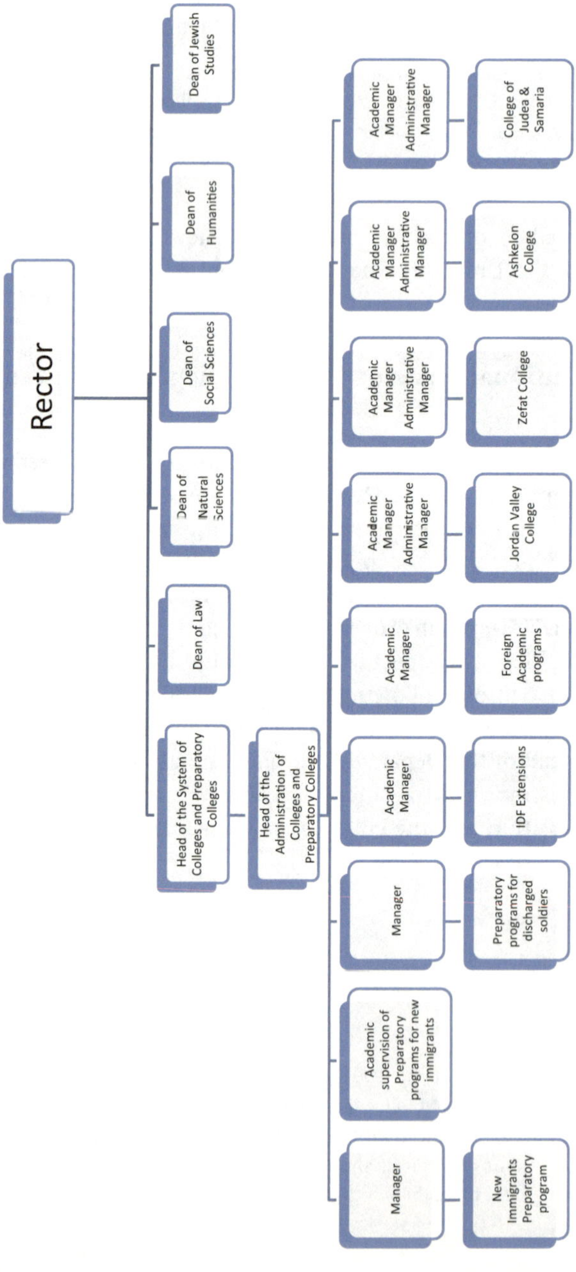

Fig. 5: Structure of the university's system of colleges

The purpose of the organizational structure was to supervise the university's activities at the Regional Colleges, at the Pre-Academic Preparatory Colleges and at other extra-campus activities which did not receive College status, such as operations within IDF bases. To deepen supervision of the academic level of the colleges under the university's auspices, and similarly to the practice at all faculties, a coordinating committee was appointment, whose members were the deans of faculties, and served as a high committee whose role was to approve annual curriculums at each college, and the academic faculty at the colleges – both those teaching at the university, and those recruited from the region.

To ensure implementation of the curriculum according to the university's guidelines, the organizational structure included the appointment of an Academic Manager at each college – either a Professor or Associate Professor. The appointment was made by the Senate, and the college covered the Academic Manager's full salary. The Academic Manager was the university's representative at the college, and was required to closely monitor the execution of its academic policies and decisions. He held academic responsibility for developing the college's academic programs and its presentation to the relevant parties at the university for their approval.

Prof. Arad's second initiative towards standardizing the university's relationship with the colleges was to draft new contractual agreements between the university and the Regional Colleges, and specifically with the colleges of Ashkelon and Zefat, which had been founded from their onset as Extensions and as an inseparable part of the university.

Contractual Agreements between the University and Zefat and Ashkelon Colleges

As opposed to the agreements signed between the university and the Zefat and Ashkelon Extensions in the beginning of the 1980s, those signed a decade later mark a new and different approach. The new agreements stipulate an official, contractual relationship between the Parties. The college was required to pay overheads for tasks which the university had taken care of for 25 years. To understand the significant turn in the university's approach towards the colleges, in the following paragraphs we will examine the university's behavior according to the same measures used to examine the contractual agreements of the 1980s. To recall, using the previous agreements between the Parties, we reviewed the relationship between Bar Ilan University and its Extensions, compared to that of other universities towards the colleges that enjtoyed their academic auspices.

1. **Initiative**
   1.1. **The 1980s agreement:** Bar Ilan University initiated the establishment of the Extensions. In the 1960s the university's founders invested extensive efforts in attempts to open Extensions located far from the main campus. In those years the Extensions had been an inseparable part of Bar Ilan's master-plan for developing a multi-campus university in Israel. Based on this measure, the university's initiative made it exclusively responsible for their operation and for covering their expenses. This responsibility was expressed in the university's direct and exclusive management.
   1.2. **The 1990s agreements:** The new agreements of the 1990s still retained the initiative in the hands of the university, although it now resulted from different motivations. The first aim of the university's management had been to fulfill its interests in needs. The financial burden and freezing of the Extensions' development in the 1980s led the university to perceive the Extensions as superfluous. They accumulated operational deficits due to a shortage of students and absence of PBC budgeting, and the university's management, being committed to advancing the university in line with customary academic criteria in the country's academic field, understood the accumulative financial damage in its continued operation of the Extensions under deficit.

Therefore, the purpose of the new agreements was first and foremost to release the university from a heavy financial burden. The road to achieving this goal involved separating the Extensions from the university's organizational structure and retaining its academic monopoly and reputation as a socially-minded institution, without financial responsibility. According to the new agreement, the university's exclusively academic responsibility may lead to a significant source of income in the following years. The previous advantages of Bar Ilan University's agreements with its Extensions compared to those of Ben Gurion and Haifa universities with the colleges under their auspices were no longer relevant, and there was no longer any difference between the status of those universities and that of Bar Ilan. The first few clauses of the agreement illustrate its similarities to those of all other universities:

> Whereas the college holds, inter alia, programs taught by faculty members from the institutions of higher education as part of the academic studies program; And whereas the university is willing to grant its academic auspices to studies in this study program, similarly to that offered to academic studies at Regional Colleges

by [other] universities in Israel, with the approval of the Council for Higher Education.[261]

2. **Time**
   2.1. **The 1980s agreement:** In comparing the auspices agreements of the University of Haifa and the Open University to those of Bar Ilan University and its Extensions during these years, we find a clear distinction in the position of each: While the University of Haifa and the Open University defined a limited duration for their agreements with the colleges, the agreement between Bar Ilan University and its Extensions was not limited in time. As explained, Bar Ilan's aims during those years were very different than those that led the other universities to their agreements with Regional Colleges. The limitation of the relationship within a predefined time frame had been one expression of the differences in the universities' positions.
   2.2. **The 1990s agreements:** The uniqueness of the agreement signed by Bar Ilan with its Extensions in the 1980s was made completely redundant in the new agreement. There was no longer any advantage or uniqueness compared to other universities which had granted their auspices in the 1980s. According to article 2.7 to the new agreement, the university has the right to unilaterally cancel the agreement at its exclusive discretion.

3. **Operations**
   3.1. The 1980s agreements: Contrary to the auspices agreements between the universities and Regional Colleges which left full operating responsibility in the hands of the Regional Colleges, Bar Ilan's agreements in those years left the operation entirely in the hands of the university. To fulfill this obligation the university appointed a Manager of the Extensions, who operated from his office at the university's main campus. Management was carried out remotely, and through weekly visits to the Extensions.
   3.2. The 1990s agreements: In the new agreements, the operating terms of Bar Ilan University's Extensions paralleled those of the Regional Colleges. Also in this measure we find no advantage to Bar Ilan's agreements with its Extensions. The colleges were managed on a completely local basis. This operational measure illustrates the university's relinquishing of all financial and managerial responsibility in the past, and consequently financial and managerial outcomes at present and in future.

261 Ibid, legal file 1991. Agreement draft dated 18 July 1991. The following words opened the agreement: This wording of the agreement will be used for each of the colleges, *mutatis mutandis*.

4. **Exclusivity**

4.1. **The 1980s agreements:** The agreements between Regional Colleges and the university granting them academic auspices focused solely on the academic aspect. The Regional Colleges offered other educational programs, some vocational and some enrichment studies. Bar Ilan University's Extensions, excluding the Jordan Valley Extension, did not offer any other programs and focused exclusively on academic studies and therefore were closely tied to the university from their establishment until the end of the 1980s.

4.2. **The 1990s agreements:** The preface clauses to the new agreement stipulated that the Ashkelon and Zefat Regional Colleges hold or may hold diverse programs which are unrelated to the university. The auspices agreement, based on which the relationship between the Parties is defined, covers the university's academic responsibility only, and does not apply to other programs held at the college. Entire clauses of the agreement between Bar Ilan University and its Extensions are identical to those between other universities and the colleges to which they grant their academic auspices:

> It is clarified that the academic auspices granted by the university to the college and accreditation of the courses studied at the college pertain only to courses included in the academic program for which academic supervision is enforced and for which the university has provided its written approval. It is clarified that studies in courses that are not part of the academic program supervised by the university, and all administrative activities without exception, are under the college's exclusive responsibility and the university does not and will have no obligation towards any activity, whether administrative or academic, carried out at the college, excluding its supervision responsibilities as stipulated in this agreement.[262]

Article 4.1 to the new agreement with the university expressed, more than any other, the change in the university's approach towards its Extensions and its ideological separation from their goals:

> The college will pay the university 15% overheads out of the total payments to the college's lecturers and the tuition paid by its students... In addition, and without derogating from the aforesaid in article 4.1 above, it is clarified that the college will cover any additional expense incurred by the university for any reason pertaining to the granting of its academic auspices and its supervision under this agreement (ibid).

262 Ibid, legal file 1991. Sections 2.5 and 2.6 to the agreement of 18 July 1991.

The Position of the CHE and the Ministry of Education

The managers of the colleges were opposed to many clauses in the agreement proposed by the university and refused to sign it despite the Rector's demands that they do so. However, their high level of dependence on the university resulted in a difficult dilemma: Should they risk their relationship with the university? For Ashkelon and Zefat, which only offered academic studies, a removal of the university's academic auspices meant an immediate threat to their very existence. The main question that troubled the managers of the colleges was whether to accept the university's conditions and to commit, at this early stage as an independent institution, to extensive financial expenses, which moreover endanger its very existence? Finally, left with no other choice, the managers of the colleges applied to the Manager of the Colleges Unit at the Ministry of Education, requesting him to act to prevent a rift in the relationship with the university, by reducing financial demands from the college and by officially supporting the colleges' refusal to sign the agreements. The Ministry of Education's position was that the agreement should not be signed if it includes payment of overheads and salaries to the university's lecturers completing their position at the college. This position was explained to the university's management in a number of telephone conversations as well as letters to the direct parties at the university dealing with the matter. In one of the letters the Manager of the Colleges Unit at the Ministry of Education wrote:

> The Ministry of Education budgets academic teaching hours for courses, whose academic nature has been approved by the Sub-Committee of the Council for Higher Education [. . .] The ministry does not cover overhead expenses, administrative and other costs, other than direct teaching expenses [. . .] Towards 1992, in view of the fact that two colleges are entering the regular budgeting system for the first time, a proposed curriculum must be presented to us [. . .] It should be noted that the colleges have only limited capability to pay for expensive teaching hours, considering the other general expenses of these courses.[263]

When the Rector's letter to Dr. Berreby, in which he described the new principles of behavior towards the colleges, did not provide a clear answer as to the question of overheads and payment to university lecturers completing their position at the colleges, the Manager of the Colleges Unit hastened to issued his response to this letter from Prof. Arad. In his response Dr. Berreby expressed his doubts as to the university's new policy towards its Extensions:

---

263 Association of Regional Colleges Archive, file 1991. Letter from Abraham Shenfeld to Dr. Berreby and Eli Gutman, 29 May 1991.

> It is unacceptable that the university should receive 15% overheads from the Ministry of Education's budgets and the tuition. The colleges are barely making ends meet and all their income is dedicated, according to the new arrangements, to paying its teachers and to its proper administrative management [. . .] While in parallel, with the burden passing on to the colleges, the university's burden has been alleviated. Moreover it is unacceptable that we should demand payment from the colleges for lecturers who are also employed at the university, based on the university's calculation. . . The expansion of the colleges' independence, development of local faculty, wage scale for teachers at colleges, close academic supervision by the universities and collaboration between all parties - the university, the Council for Higher Education and the Ministry of Education and Culture, are prerequisites for the development of the Regional Colleges which Bar Ilan University has nurtured so well over the years.[264]

The opposition against the university management's attempt to profit from the new situation required coordination between the CHE/PBC and the Ministry of Education, so as to make it difficult for the university to achieve its aims on two levels:

1. **The academic level – CHE/PBC:** Approval of the full undergraduate program was pending the CHE's decision and the implementation of the decision was in the hands of the PBC. According to all forecasts, both those of the university and of the managers of the colleges, the program's approval was key to the development of the colleges and to increasing their income, which indirectly would also result in enhancing the university's own income. Now, with the program having been submitted for the CHE/PBC's approval, the purpose of the coordination between the Ministry of Education and the PBC was to set rules which would be accepted by the Parties prior to the program's approval and implementation.
2. **The budgetary level under the Ministry of Education's authority:** On this level advance preparations were made in order to set restrictions for managing the colleges' budgets. It was stipulated that the purpose of the budget is to cover specific payments which do not include special payments to the university, such as administrative overheads and payments due to the university's lecturers completing their full time position at the college. This type of coordination was agreed upon between the PBC Chairperson Prof. Pazy and the Manager of the Colleges Unit Dr. Moshe Berreby towards a meeting with the Rector of Bar Ilan University scheduled for 31 October 1991. In their

264 Ibid. Letter from Abraham Shenfeld to the Rector, Prof. Zvi Arad, 1 July 1991, in response to the letters from the Rector to Dr. Berreby and to the PBC Chairperson Prof. Amnon Pazy, 12 March 1991.

coordination conversation the two expressed their decisive objection to the Rector's stipulation that the full undergraduate program would not be opened without the parties signing the agreement and the assurance of payments being made to the university as stipulated in the agreement:

> Under no circumstances should the matter of the BGS program be tied to the specific pressure of signing a long term agreement, which may lead the colleges to a commitment which they would not be able to meet [. . .] The PBC and the Ministry of Education should protect the colleges, which are the weaker party as opposed to the university.[265]

The university's pressure and the change in its approach to its Extensions contributed to the mutual agreement between the two men regarding the need for more fundamental and comprehensive arrangements which would be better suited to the great changes taking place in the higher education system. Bar Ilan University's initiative to prepare agreements regulating its relationship with the colleges urged the authorities' response. The PBC's Chairperson discussed the need for two stages of preliminaries: In the first stage procedures would be set in place to regulate the financial and academic relationship between the colleges and the universities granting their auspices, and these would regulate the relationship between Bar Ilan University and its Extensions and prevent undermining the colleges which have separated from the university but still depend on it to a large extent. After the system has been stabilized and the new institutions opened, the second stage would include the establishment of long term procedures aimed at leading colleges towards full independence, which would also include academic independence. In their conversation the initial outlines of the future plan were discussed:

> A meeting will be held between the PBC and the Ministry of Education, outlining an expanded plan for colleges - to include their relationships with the university, local teaching faculty, academic management of the colleges, students registration, and more. In addition, the financial terms of the agreement between the university and the college would be discussed, as well as the academic aspect. Clearly the university should not suffer losses, but it does not need to profit either [. . .] A permanent local teaching faculty should be discussed, including academic management, teaching committee, teachers admission committee, etc. [. . .], with an aim for colleges to become independent academic institutions and eventually Pazy [Prof. Amnon Pazy – PBC's Chairperson during the years 1991–1994] aims for the universities to ultimately leave the picture when the colleges become independent entities (ibid).

---

265 Ibid, file 1991. Record of phone conversation between the Manager of the Colleges Unit at the Ministry of Education and the PBC Chairperson, 27 August 1991.

Regulating the Relationship between Universities and the Colleges under Their Auspices

The urgent need that arose for regulating the relationship between the universities and colleges so as to protect the colleges attested to the fact that the Ministry of Education had been ill prepared: Its absorption of twelve Regional Colleges operating a university's academic program was not backed by a regulated plan, and they were not received with a practical operational system. essentially, the Ministry of Education did not have the necessary academic tools for supervising the academic programs,[266] as according to the CHE law these were the prerogative of the CHE's institutions only. Therefore, under the circumstances, the colleges found themselves in a complex and special situation: On the one hand, they could not be absorbed by the CHE as they were not academic institutions as defined by the law, and on the other hand they operated academic studies under the auspices of a university operating under the CHE law. The university was subjected to the CHE's supervision and the PBC's budgeting, while the college operating under its auspices was not recognized by the CHE/PBC as a teaching institution, and the relationship between it and these authorities was managed via the university. This situation led to double regulatory supervision of the colleges: on the one hand the CHE and its committees, mainly the Colleges Sub-Committee responsible for the academic aspects of their operation and for the university's activities within them, and on the other hand the Ministry of Education, which was responsible for defining the budgeting rules for their operation and for allocating these budgets.

The fact that the Ashkelon and Zefat Extensions were included in the list of colleges budgeted by the Ministry of Education and the pressure mounted on them and the Jordan Valley College by the university's Rector to sign the agreements with the university, emphasized the urgent need to form budgeting rules and define a budgetary framework for the colleges at the Ministry of Education. The heads of the Colleges Unit at the Ministry held a number of consultation meetings attended by the managers of the colleges to examine ways of coping with the many changes that occurred in higher education and define rules for a proper relationship between the universities and the colleges. During these meetings the policies of the authorities influencing the academic field were also examined, including the Ministry of Finance, the CHE/PBC

266 This was disclosed by the head of the Culture Administration at the Ministry of Education in meetings held at his office with the Managers of the Colleges. In retrospect, their absorption by the Ministry of Education was enabled as an interim stage until their identity and academic status would be ascertained, as their transition to the responsibility of the CHE/PBC was completed by the Ministry of Education eight years later.

and the Ministry of Education. In one of the first meetings, Abner Shalev, head of the Culture Administration, who was also responsible for the Colleges Unit, reported on the imminent change in the PBC's position regarding the colleges, which was moreover supported by the Ministry of Finance.[267] Contrary to the past, the PBC would work to promote the colleges' academic programs, thereby doubling their number of students in 1992/93. In coordination with the CHE/PBC, the Ministry of Education began forming a plan for determining budgeting rules and preparing for the colleges' future development. In preliminary documents issued by the Ministry of Education to the managers of the colleges, the ministry reported of the CHE's preparations for absorbing around 25,000 undergraduate students, some of whom would be admitted to the teachers' colleges, and others to the academic programs at colleges and schools of practical engineering operating under the auspices of the Technological Training Institute (operating under the Ministry of Labor). The CHE would encourage the Regional Colleges to hold all undergraduate studies at college campuses, so as to increase their attraction for young students.[268] Having developed initial procedures for budgeting the colleges at the Ministry of Education and the CHE, the Sub-Committee discussed ways to further promote Regional Colleges. The Ministry published a new document entitled "The Future Policy".[269] The first part of the document outlines initial attributes of the future action plan, while its second part stipulates the terms and scope of academic auspices and the obligations of the colleges operating under academic auspices of universities.

A. **The scope of the University's Auspices or Academic Supervision**
   1. Responsibilities towards students
      1.1. The university will define rules for admission of students to the academic program at the college.
      1.2. The university will define students' academic rights and obligations.
      1.3. The university will assure the continued education of college students at the university's campus if they choose to continue studying at the university.

267 Meeting held on 9 February 1992, attended by all managers of the colleges, heads of the Association of Regional Colleges and representatives of the Ministry of Education – Head of the Culture Administration and Manager of the Colleges Unit.

268 Association of Regional Colleges Archive, file 1991. Documents published by the Abraham Shenfeld, Manager of the Colleges Unit at the Ministry of Education, 29 October 1991 and 5 November 1991.

269 Ibid, file 1992. The document was developed at the Colleges Unit and distributed to the Regional Colleges on 24 June 1992.

1.4. At any stage of their studies, college students would be able to transfer to the university campus or combine studies at the two campuses.
1.5. Upon completing all academic requirements, college students will receive their degree from the university.

2. Commitment to maintain the level of studies
   2.1. The university's management will determine criteria for approving lecturers by the college's appointments committee.
   2.2. The university commits to propose lecturers for teaching at the college or to approve others suggested by the college's appointments committee and would promote their integration in the academic program, even if they are not part of the university's academic faculty.
   2.3. The university will ensure that the level of teaching at the college would be the same as the university's.
   2.4. Students completing their studies at the college will receive their degree from the university.
   2.5. As decisive proof of the level of teaching at the college, the university will admit college graduates to graduate degree studies according to the same admission criteria applicable to the university's students.

B. **Obligations of the Colleges**
1. To attract enough students to justify the opening of all courses offered at the college.
2. To be responsible for the employment of academic faculty members as per a letter of appointment as acceptable at the university, and to pay the lecturer's salary even if the course was not opened due to a shortage of students.
3. To appoint an academic coordinator or advisor who would work in close cooperation with the academic chairperson to be appointed by the university.
4. To cover all maintenance and good governance expenses entailed in the academic development of the college.

C. **The agreement and its scope**
1. The agreement between the Parties would be regulated by contracts, the contents of which would be approved by the CHE's Sub-Committee on Colleges and by the Colleges Unit at the Ministry of Education.
2. The college will compensate the university for all expenses incurred for its academic auspices. The extent of the compensation is subject to the Ministry of Education's approval.

D. **Ministry of Education's obligations**
   1. Assure a supplementary budget to the college's income from tuition, donations and special allowances from the ministry.
   2. The allowances will be defined by a professional body which will examine the operating costs and special expenses derived from the college's peripheral location.

E. **The PBC's obligations**
   1. To include in the universities' budget college students studying towards an undergraduate degree of the university. Colleges students will be considered university students for purposes of the university's budgeting by the PBC.
   2. Participation in the cost of employment of an academic coordinator for each college.
   3. Full funding of an academic chairperson for each college.
   4. Participation in the development of libraries at the colleges and their adjustment to the academic needs of undergraduate students.
   5. Participation in the preparation of a promotion program for local academic faculty members.

The PBC had also mobilized towards the implementation of the auspices model and determined policies and rules for budgeting its part in the university's academic activities at the colleges. The PBC's budgeting policy for the university was outlined in a letter from the PBC's CEO to the CEO of Bar Ilan University. The cornerstone of the policy was the assertion that the auspices agreements would pertain only to academic aspects and not to financial terms or other stipulations involving the university's commitment to hold academic studies at the college. To protect the colleges as the weaker party of the two, it was agreed that the PBC would budget the universities for expenses incurred due to granting their academic auspices and supervision. According to these guidelines, the PBC will compensate the university through fixed annual payments for each student attending the academic program of the college under the university's auspices. The payment calculation would be based on the scope of studies of each student, according to the F.T.E (Full Time Equivalent) index, with a full program amounting to 24 weekly hours. For each full time student studying at the academic program the university would receive ₪1,000 per year, in 1993 figures.

How the Introduction of Full Programs Influenced the Colleges in the Beginning of the 1990s

Until the beginning of the 1990s and the actual opening of full undergraduate programs, the programs taught at the university's Extensions were not very different than those offered by them in their earlier years: A cluster of courses in social sciences, which enabled students to accumulate academic credits, and in some departments most of year 1 obligations. My appointment as manager of the Ashkelon Extension and the appointment of Hebron Trabelci as manager of the Zefat Extension at the end of the 1980s and the change in the status of the Extensions did not mark a turning point in the scope of their activities, as can be seen in Fig. 8 and Tab. 33. The university was not eager to enhance the list of courses, fearing that we would not be able to bear the expected cost, and we were not quick to increase academic activities due to budgetary uncertainty and our inability to forecast the number of students and expected income. Consequently, the program did not change significantly during those years.

The change did not take place as quickly as expected by both the local management and the university, due to a difficulty which we had identified upon entering our positions and which had been well known to the Manager of the Extensions in the mid 1970s: the absence of a full curriculum in major departments and the need to make do with eclectic programs that over the years had prevented the further development of the Extensions. The number of students did not increase significantly, and until the beginning of the 1990s the Extensions were considered by students as a one of two year transitory stage. This format of studies affected the college's image and status in the following ways:

1. **Academic:** The operation of part time studies did not facilitate the establishment of a stable local academic faculty and lecturers were sent to the college from the university's departmental reservoir of lecturers. Most of these were faculty members who either needed to complete their monthly teaching hours to a full time position or had only just completed their graduate degree and were on their way to their PhD studies and there was no available position for them at the department. Many years of experience have shown that a young and promising lecturer with no permanent position at the university, which the department still wished to promote, was sent to teach at an Extension/College until a position would become available and he or she would then return to the department. In many cases the Extension lost lecturers who had integrated well in the local faculty and ultimately returned to their main department which controlled and supervised the faculty members employed at the Extension on its behalf.

The library and other academic facilities were also suited to partial studies, and therefore funds were not invested in the development of libraries or laboratories, and the college's entire academic facilities relied upon the university's own facilities. The fact that students transitioned to the university at early stages of their studies did not motivate the university to invest in the Extension, and this was also the position of the local management when the Extensions became Regional Colleges. The lack of academic facilities also affected the decision of department heads at the university to refrain from opening permanent study programs at the college, and so until the 1990s the Extensions were caught in an endless cycle of helplessness.

2. **Administrative/Budgetary:** The partial studies format significantly impacted colleges' financial capacity. The number of students each year could not be estimated in advance in view of the fact that the number of students that transitioned to the university campus at an early stage of their studies steadily grew as the identity of the students changed, with a growing number of young students arriving, who aimed to complete their studies within a reasonable time frame, and so more and more of them transitioned to the university as early as the end of year 1. This situation prevented an increase in the total number of students, even when in practice a growing number of students were admitted to year 1 at the college. The inability to present a growth in the number of students affected the attractiveness of the institution among potential candidates as well as for potential lecturers who aimed to establish themselves in a stable institution. This situation also led to planning difficulties towards a possible future academic independence. in the short term the institution's income from tuition was affected from its inability to grow and develop long term plans.
3. **Image:** Until the beginning of the 1990s students at the Extensions mainly came from among the adult population of the region. At Ashkelon, Zefat and the Jordan Valley, these were predominantly bank clerks who worked in the morning and studied in the evenings; IDF and Police officers from nearby bases and stations; nurses working at Poriya hospital in Tiberias, Zvi in Zefat and Barzilai at Ashkelon, who studied at the nursing school next to the Extension and completed their theoretical studies at the Extensions; and workers of local authorities who took evening academic courses as a long and slow process. Employees of the civil administration of the Gaza Strip located near Ashkelon all studied at the Ashkelon Extension. At Zefat these were IDF officers from the northern command, and at the Jordan Valley residents of the nearby Kibbutzim and Moshavim who could afford to take their time on the way to an academic degree. Generally, young adults recently released from military service did not choose to study at

> the Extensions. They preferred an academic institution offering full and diverse study programs so as to acquire a profession or academic education within a normal three to four year period. The implementation of a full and regulated program changed the image of the Extensions from institutions predominantly for adults, to ones that are relevant to younger populations of students, who from now on could find their place in them. Naturally, the change did not occur in one year, but the trend was clear, and it heralded things to come.

As expected, the new programs brought with them a development drive which the colleges had not seen from their formative days: the academic and budgetary difficulties that threatened their development were gradually alleviated, and hundreds of students from the region and even from farther away flocked to Bar Ilan's colleges. Moreover, the new situation led to a preference among young students to Bar Ilan's auspices colleges over other Regional Colleges, who had remained behind with only partial auspices programs. In the early 1990s Bar Ilan's colleges were the country's first Regional Colleges to offer a university's undergraduate studies as a full time, local program. The data presented in Figure 6 and Table 31 points to the onset of this changing trend.

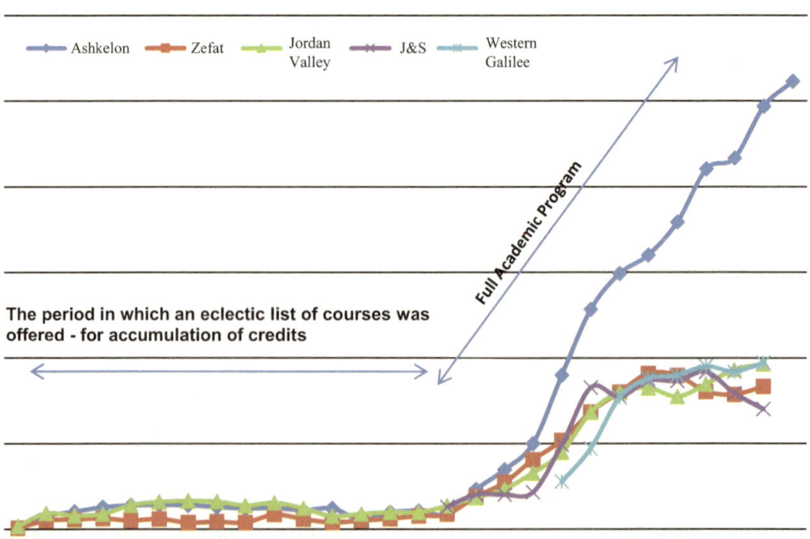

Fig. 6: Change in the number of students following introduction of Bachelor of General Studies (BGS) Program

Tab. 31: Students counts collected during the two periods

	Ashkelon	Zefat	Jordan Valley
1993/94	501	407	330
1992/93	349	275	237
1991/92	234	192	185
1990/91	90	89	137
1989/90	107	79	100
1988/89	100	63	100
1987/88	56	52	91
1986/87	122	41	77
1985/86	111	60	123
1984/85	124	87	156
1983/84	121	40	139
1982/83	130	45	162
1981/82	141	40	166
1980/81	142	61	160
1979/80	140	52	141
1978/79	129	64	90
1977/78	103	59	80
1976/77	79	52	94
1975/76	14	8	19

Source: The data in the figure and the table was collected from annual reports prepared by the Colleges Administration at Bar Ilan University, Ashkelon College, Zefat College and the Jordan Valley College. The numbers reported by the colleges until 1991/92 are not identical to those that follow this period as it is not possible to follow the number of students in the previous period, for two main reasons: (a) Students studied at the campus and the college; (b) the number of students reported until 1991/92 included "free listeners", who did participate in courses and attended examinations, but were not admitted to studies in the normal procedure and therefore were not recognized by the Ministry of Education or the CHE as students studying towards an academic degree, and thus the college and the university were not budgeted for these students.

The rise in the number of students and the implementation of an annual program led to revolutionary changes in the way the colleges were managed. Local capabilities were needed in order to plan a schedule; permanent academic faculty members were employed on an annual or multi-annual basis; the administrative and professional staff grew and from now on was also tasked with advising students in planning their studies, as is the custom in any other academic institution. More and more systems that had previously been operated remotely by the university, such as the registration process, professional advising and management of examinations, were now being operated directly by the college or as a mediating factor between the university and the students.

The operation of both administrative and academic systems required recruitment of administrative staff and the establishment of a suitable administration building. The three Extensions, now colleges, underwent a structural change, with many new employees recruited in order to be able to cope with the challenges posed by the changes and the new status. The administrative structure that developed at all the colleges was coordinated with the university and approved by it in all instances in which an administrative system operated at the college on behalf of the university, such as in the area of students advisors. The new organizational structure was managed through an Association or Non-profit organization, participated by representatives of the Jewish Agency, in cases in which the Agency raised funds for the college, such as in the case of the Jordan Valley. Figure 7 presents the organizational structure of Regional Colleges as presented by the Ministry of Education.

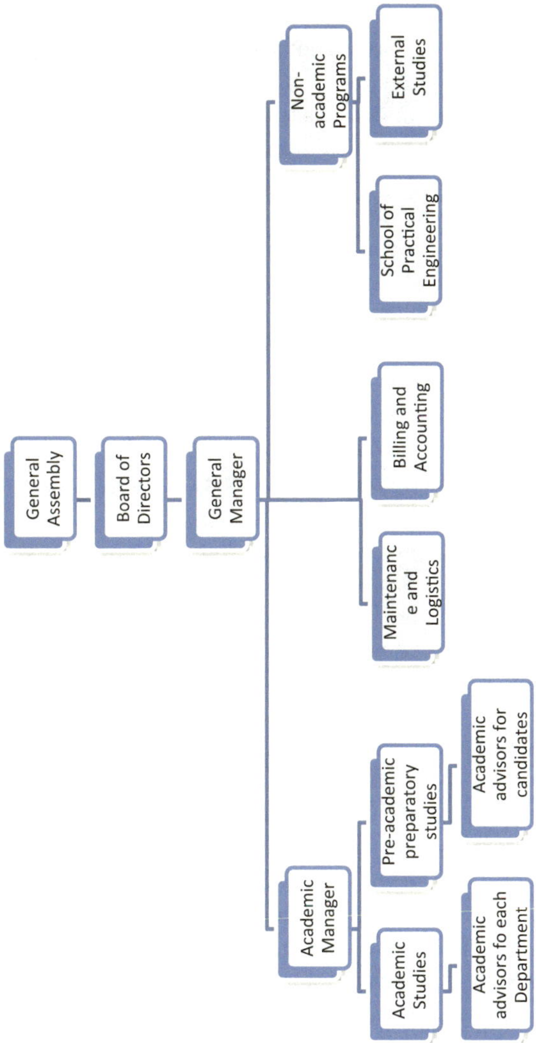

Fig. 7: Regional Colleges Structure as presented by the Ministry of Education

Conclusions

Towards the end of the 1980s, the growing demand for higher education forced the CHE to change its position on the question of accessibility to higher education. The CHE's policies and the strict positions of its members – the senior actors of Israel's academic field – changed somewhat because it was clear to all that it is no longer possible to ignore the demand for higher education and the social pressure of the periphery. Political changes towards the end of the 1970s and the ethnic awakening of the 1980s also contributed to the mounting pressures on the CHE which ultimately led to the change that would revolutionize Israel's academic system in the 1990s. The moderation of the CHE's position contributed to finding a solution, which while not being perfect, was certainly an improvement: An increased accessibility to higher education in the periphery through Regional Colleges dispersed throughout the country. This change of trend did not change the CHE's clear opposition to the existence of Bar Ilan University's Extensions, which it saw as part of the university, and therefore during that period conditions had still not ripened for the CHE's encouragement of Bar Ilan's social actions, even though the Chairperson of the CHE and other members reached the clear conclusion that academic auspices over colleges, such as the Extensions, is the best solution.

Bar Ilan's dilemma consisted of its need to choose between developing its main campus and improving its position as a research university comparable to other universities in the country, or continuing to invest in its religious and social ideas and ideals without State support. A solution to this dilemma was ultimately and unknowingly provided by the CHE, in its preference for the academic programs offered at Regional Colleges rather than at Extensions. With the appointment of NRP leader Zvulun Hammer as Minister of Education, the university's Rector Prof. Arad seized the opportunity which led him to the long awaited solution – the transfer of the Extensions to State budgeting and supervision as Regional Colleges and the university's separating from the financial burden of their operation. The budgetary separation left the university with only academic control.

The granting of academic auspices to the College of Judea & Samaria was enabled at a political era in which the country's appointed Minister of Education was among the founders of Gush Emunim.[270] The push to further establish the lives of the settlers in Judea and Samaria led the university to expand its social

270 Israeli Orthodox Jewish right-wing activist movement committed to establishing Jewish settlements in the West Bank, the Gaza Strip, and the Golan Heights.

and political mission to that region, as had been the aspiration of its founders. The university's Rector felt that he is able to fulfill his mission while also unburdening the university of the financial burden entailed in operating the Extensions, while continuing to fulfill the social targets dictated by the university's founders. Being highly familiar with the Extensions from his days as Chairperson of the Extensions Committee, Prof. Arad realized that budgetary disconnection is not enough in order to fulfill social tasks, and he acted to realize the dream of the university's first manager as well as its present ones – to hold full undergraduate programs at the Extensions under the university's auspices. He saw the establishment of studies at the Extensions not only a realization of social aims which had not been realized since their establishment, but also the continued path towards establishing the university's social status in the periphery. According to him, the Extensions' prosperity and the rise in their number of students would continue to contribute to the university's position as a social institution and would increase its total number of students and graduates without the university being burdened financially. Moreover, the university would gain an income from offering its academic auspices to the Extensions and would benefit from their numbers, which would be counted within the university's graduates. These changes resulted in the following organizational changes:

1. **The organizational structure of the Extensions:** The Extensions embarked upon an independent path, became Associations and managed their budgets independently. The official relationships between the university and its Extensions were regulated through agreements signed between the university and the managing Associations at Ashkelon and Zefat.
2. **Revolutionizing the Extensions' administration at the university:** A Colleges System Administration was established, headed by a Professor whose status parallels that of a Dean of Faculty, and a head of administrations. In addition, each department appointed an academic coordinator for each Extension.
3. **Full undergraduate program at the colleges:** The recommendations of the committee headed by Prof. Shlomo Yehuda, appointed to examine the feasibility of a full undergraduate program, were implemented within a short period of time, and as of 1999 undergraduate programs were introduced at Zefat, Ashkelon and the Jordan Valley. Bar Ilan's colleges were the first academic colleges of all Regional Colleges in the country to offer a full academic program granting a university's undergraduate degree. While the operation of studies had been completely transformed, still Bar Ilan's historical approach to this activity in the periphery granted it and its colleges clear advantages, as shall be seen in the following chapters.

Chapter 12 The Extensions as Academic Colleges and an Increased Accessibility to Higher Education

Preliminary Conceptualizations towards the Academization of Regional Colleges

As seen in the 1970s and 1980s, the CHE's principle position on the question of the expansion of the higher education system expressed a strictness that was not significantly moderated despite changes in the Western world and the first waves of immigration to Israel from the former USSR in 1989. Although discussions held at the CHE during those years led to the conclusion that higher education should be encouraged through academic programs at Regional Colleges and motivated an academization process among non-university institutions such as art and teaching colleges, this process did not include a structured plan for expanding the Higher Education System, but was more of a sporadic and limited academization process among institutions that achieved professional maturity. The limitations of this academization process can be seen in the CHE's decision to clearly distinguish between the academic degree granted by universities and that offered by non-university institutions. Based on this policy, an undergraduate degree preparing students for advanced research studies would be obtained only at universities, so as to avoid undermining the academic level of the Israeli student. However, in response to mounting pressures the CHE settled for approving undergraduate degrees in teaching and a number of other specific professional areas such as technology and music.[271] Despite such limited openness towards professional colleges to grant undergraduate degrees, the CHE's position towards Regional Colleges remained unchanged. These continued to teach programs offered by universities, did not offer complete academic curriculums and were offered no future horizons for granting undergraduate degrees. In the beginning of the 1990s Bar Ilan's Extensions operated as Regional Colleges, and

271 During the 1970's and 1980's many voices were heard at the CHE in favor of withstanding the pressure and the demand to open the gates of higher education. The tendency was to make do with a minimal change that would prevent degradation of the undergraduate degree, as mentioned earlier in the words of Supreme Court judge Moshe Landau.

their academic fates were tied to those of the Regional Colleges, except for the fact that they offered Bar Ilan University's full undergraduate program.

The CHE's decision not to certify non-university institutions to grant undergraduate degrees outside of a number of specific professions, increased the pressure on the general academic system, which in turn continued to lock its gates to many young candidates who wished to study academic areas other than teaching and technology.

The openness achieved in a number of professional institutions and Regional Colleges through their academic programs was simply not enough. A decision was needed for real change in the system's structure in order to create real and comprehensive accessibility to higher education. This position of the CHE can be noted in its decision of 1 January 1989:

> The existing universities…are able to absorb the excess demand for undergraduate studies in the foreseeable future, while ensuring a suitable academic level. The council is concerned to see trends of degradation in the value of the undergraduate degree, and therefore it does not see fit to established further institutions offering Bachelor of General Studies degree (BGS) programs. The council will continue its policy distinguishing between the academic degree granted by universities, which in principle paves the way to advanced degrees, and the academic degree granted by institutions of higher education that are non-universities […] The latter (degree) expresses the professional aspect of studies, such as "graduate of education", "graduate of technology". "Graduate of business administration", etc.[272]

This policy did not benefit the Regional Colleges, which were defined as multidisciplinary institutions. The academic program remained their main academic activity, and they were left with no academic horizon. Many discussions on the question of the status and authority of the Regional Colleges were held at the CHE over a period of two decades, with no practical solution in sight. This irresolute and conservative policy prevented young candidates from realizing their aims to study and acquire a general or professional academic degree, and many of them traveled abroad to study professions that were blocked to them in Israel including Medicine, Law and Business. Volansky (2005) noted a decline during this period in the proportion of year 1 students studying at institutions of higher education. In 1959, 45 % of all 12th grade graduates attended higher education, while in 1989 only 28 % despite the rise in the number of institutions of higher education in Israel following the academization of teachers' colleges. Of the total number

272 The Council for Higher Education principle decisions file, 1975–1990 (edited by: M. Assraf), 1992.

of students with a Bagrut high school diploma, the number of year 1 students at institutions of higher education declined from 89 % in 1979 to 58.5 % in 1989.

From a social class perspective, and as concluded by many studies showing a high correlation between the number of students at institutions of higher education among Ashkenazi Jews compared to those of Mizrachi descent, the CHE's policy during those years contributed to the further expansion of social gaps in the country.[273] The argument that the dominant Ashkenazi group has succeeded in perpetuating its hegemonic status by limiting access to prestigious institutions of higher education was discussed by Nahon (1987) and Shavit (1984), as well as others who reached similar conclusions (Shavit, Cohen, Stier & Bolotin, 2000). For instance, according to one study:

> Rather than transforming linearly during the 60's, 70's and 80's, class-based inequality in the acquisition of higher education showed continuous ups and downs [...] The inequality was influenced mainly by fluctuations in the number of university graduates of Ashkenazi descent. Inequality reached its lowest level not because of the progress of Mizrachim, but the decline in the number of holders of academic degrees among Ashkenazim.[274]

The State Comptroller's report reported on the condition of the Development Towns in the south of the country:

> There are significant (negative) gaps in nearly all measures between the southern Development Towns and national averages... The country's greatest Socioeconomic polarization can be found at the Beer-Sheva metropolitan area; alongside the Development Towns and the Bedouin settlements located at the bottom of the Socioeconomic ranking, are the towns of Omer, Meitar and Lehavim, ranked at the top echelon.[275]

The issue of social gaps in Israel led to the establishment of a parliamentary committee headed by Knesset Member Ran Cohen.[276] In December 2002, supported by research, it submitted a report reviewing the development of social gaps in Israel, finding significant gaps in education, from Primary to Post-Secondary. The committee's final conclusion in its chapter on education was:

---

273 The Horowitz Committee had discussed this matter in 1961.

274 Shavit, Cohen, Stier and Bolotin, 2000:400.

275 State Comptroller's report (1999), Report number 50 (b).

276 Meretz Party Knesset member 1984–2008, Minister of Industry and Commerce 1999–2000 and Chairperson of Meretz at the Knesset.

> In each stage of education we find a close relationship between financial status, parents' education and academic achievements. In the Jewish population, identical Socioeconomic background cancels achievement gaps between ethnic groups. The differences in achievements between Jews and Arabs are not canceled [...] Among university graduates the representation of non-Jews and Sephardic Jews is small, including those born in Israel.[277]

In the beginning of the 1990s the mounting pressures on the CHE led to its decision to once again examine ways to expand the Higher Education System and its accessibility to the various sectors. The council was faced with two central options:

1. Increase the capacity of the existing universities, mainly those that were still below optimal size, and add another research university or two while still maintaining the existing monolithic structure.
2. Adopt an extreme approach involving the transformation of Israel's Higher Education System into a binary system comprised of research universities and academic colleges that would focus on professional training and general higher education.[278]

The option to establish a further university was not supported by the CHE in the 1970s, 1980s or 1990s. Rather, it opted to increase the number of students studying at existing universities, a fact that had two main implications: The first was budgetary and the second the fear of undermining the level of research if the universities would be flooded by huge numbers of candidates which they would not be able to admit, and would have to dedicate senior faculty members, whose main purpose is research and teaching students of advanced degrees, to teach undergraduate students. Despite these considerations, the echoes of the CHE's historical policy that prevailed until the end of the 1980s and was expressed in the CHE's decision of 1 January 1989, led the CHE of the 1990s to reach a decision that combines the council's historical position with the emerging changes. Following a series of discussions also involving the Ministry of Finance and the Government, the CHE decided to expand the country's Higher Education System in two stages: The first combined a conservative approach with a revolutionary one. On the one hand, the system was expanded through non-university institutions, mostly colleges, and on the other hand the number of existing universities was expanded and the number of students in each was enhanced. According to the

277 Parliamentary investigation report on social gaps in Israel headed by Knesset member Ran Cohen, Jerusalem, December 2002: 38–42.

278 Pazy, 2005.

plan, most of the demand in the first stage (1991–1996) would be directed to the existing universities. The data from the two stages of the program showed a need to absorb 50,000 additional undergraduate student between the years 1991–2000. Thirty-two thousand would be admitted to universities and only 18,000 admitted to non-university institutions. For the first time since the establishment of the State, the country's Higher Education System transitioned to a binary model, as opposed to the monolithic academic system that had completely relied on research institutions and had been based on the model of the European-German research university.[279] A number of reasons led the CHE to decide to expand the country's academic system and to abandon its traditional position:

1. The increase in the number of students in the Higher Education System was mostly due to students interested in professional training and not necessarily in research, and therefore there was no reason to increase the capacity of research institutions beyond the optimal capacity of the newest ones, with the expansion aiming to achieve a higher level of professional training and the satisfaction of social needs.
2. Academically speaking, the PBC preferred a system that includes one institution type involved in research and a different type offering professional training, over a single institution that does both. Its concerns from a uniform system were due to an expected undermining of the level of research.
3. The costs entailed in increasing the number of students at research universities were high due to the need for increasing research budgets for these institutions. Conversely, increasing the number of students at colleges did not require a significant budget increase as there was no need to budget research components, meaning that a larger number of students could be admitted within a given budget.

In addition to these assumptions, the 1990s provided special reasons for the need to expand the country's academic system and increased the pressure on the CHE to address these needs:

---

279 Aliza Shenhar (2005) described the roots of the German model that formed the basis for the Hebrew University and the Technion, which is a foundation of the University of Berlin, founded by von Humboldt in 1810. Sarah Guri-Rosenblit (2005) also noted that in a 1996 study held in 14 countries on the questions of the perception of research and teaching among professors it was found that in Germany, Israel and Japan research is considered more important than teaching.

1. **The wave of immigration from the former Soviet Union:** According to the Central Bureau of Statistics, since the establishment of the State until 2008, about three million new immigrants (*Olim*) arrived in Israel ("*made Aliya*"), with about a third of them arriving between 1990 and 1999. Over 750,000 of them came from the former Soviet Union. About half a million Jews made *Aliyah* between 1989 and 1992,[280] of which about 350,000 came from the former Soviet Union. The following figure shows the significant changes in *Aliyah* trends in the beginning of the 1990s.

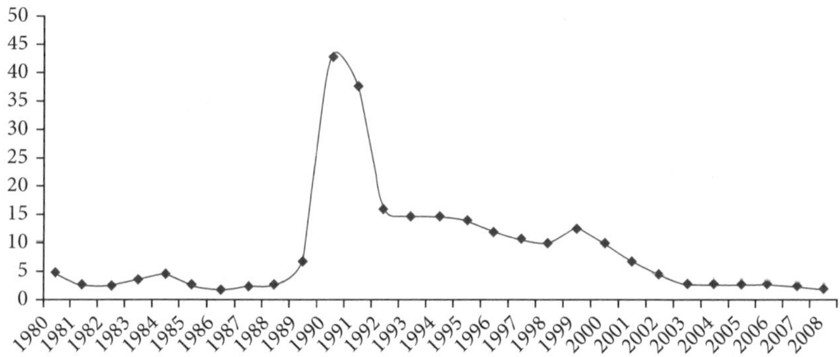

Fig. 8: New immigrants (Olim) by year of Aliyah per 1,000 persons in the population
Source: CBS Website: cbs.gov.il/hodaot 2009n. Date of entry: 1 August 2010.

The CHE and the Ministry of Finance estimated that the high rate of academics among the new immigrants from the former Soviet Union would lead to a high demand for academic studies, and therefore the government gave the PBC and the universities the green light to prepare for such demand. Although expectations for a huge flow of *Olim* to the country's institutions of higher education were not realized to the extent expected, preparations for such flows led in retrospect to the opening of the gates of higher education also to young native Israeli students.[281]

2. **Rise in the number of holders of Bagrut diploma:**

2.1. Rise in the number of 18 year olds – a significant rise was noted in the percentage of students eligible for a Bagrut high school matriculation diploma between

280 CBS Website: cbs.gov.il/hodaot2009n, Press release, 25 February 2009. Written by: Ayelet Cohen-Castro.

281 The PBC, Mendelzweig, R. (Editor). Annual report number 21, 1993–1994: 39.

1986 and 1996: In 1986 their number was about 28,100, reaching in 1996 approx. 47,600. The proportion of 18 year olds rose from 36.7 % to 46.9 %.

2.2. Rise in the number of students that completed pre-academic preparatory programs – the circle of academic studies candidates during these years saw a rise in the number of graduates of pre-academic preparatory programs: From about 6,000 in 1989 to about 10,800 in 1997. The 1990s wave of immigration added to the circle of candidates from among graduates of preparatory programs a further 2,700 students in 1990 and 1,607 in 1997.[282] These two figures together increased the potential number of students seeking acceptance to programs of higher education.

3. **Growing awareness to higher education:** Throughout the 1980s the demand for higher education amounted to 25,000 candidates. In 1991 alone the number of candidates reached 25,985, increasing in the following year to 27,816, with two thirds of the demand coming from new immigrants. However, nearly all of the growth in 1996 originated locally, reaching 32,924 candidates. The peak of demand was in 1984, with the average ratio between candidates and students being 1:2.3 for all fields of study. This year also marked the highest rise in the number of candidates rejected – about 35 % of all candidates. The growing absorption of students at universities and other institutions also increased the population's likelihood to submit candidacy to academic studies, and in fact the rate of rejections gradually lowered with growing capacities at institutions. The rate of rejections decreased to 19.3 % in 1996. The total number of candidates that year was 32,924, with 20,914 students admitted and commencing year 1. The average of candidates reached 1.6 in attractive areas such as medicine, law and business. The average number of candidates per student remained high, ranging from 3.2 in medicine to 2.1 in law.
4. **Legislative intervention:** From 1989 onwards, legislators intervened in order to change the CHE's official policy. This phenomenon reached its peak in the 1990s. A few of these attempts were successful, while others were not passed by the Knesset. Until 1993 two attempts were made to change the CHE's position: One attempt was successful and revolutionized the study of law, while another was blocked by the Colleges' managers.

   4.1. Legislation: The first precedent that led to a significant change in the CHE's response to social pressures was the amendment to the Bar Association Law of 1961, approved by the Knesset in 1989. For the first time in the

282 The PBC, Mendelzweig, R. (Editor). Annual report number 24, 1996–1997: 28–29.

history of the State, this precedent put an end to the hegemony of the universities, which until then had exclusive authority to decide, through the CHE and the Hebrew University, who can obtain a higher education in law: The amendment granted colleges that are not institutions of higher education the authority to offer a degree in law.[283]

4.2. Initiative for the establishment of a Council for Colleges: The exclusive control over the academization of colleges and their budgets led to threats of further legislation initiatives by a number of Knesset members in 1990.[284] The initiators of the amendment wished to establish, through legislation, a separate council for colleges which would be authorized to grant accreditations and certifications. Ultimately this proposal was not implemented, due to the CHE's subsequence agreement to change its policy. This willingness resulted mainly from concerns among CHE members that its exclusive position in the area would be undermined (Council for Higher Education bill, 1990). The heads of the Colleges also opposed the bill, although it was intended for the benefit of the Colleges, as they had been concerned that a separate council would lead to an academic distinction between the university degree and the one granted by colleges.

A highly important legislative change for the future of the colleges, that had revolutionized the system, was the 10th amendment to the CHE law that focused on colleges, on which I will further expand later, on the background for its legislation and the legislative change to which it led.

5. **The position of the Minister of Education and CHE Chairperson:** The Minister of Education and Culture Prof. Amnon Rubinstein was among the initiators of the amendment to the Bar Association Law of 1961, which was

---

283 According to the amendment, the law granted the Hebrew University, beyond the CHE's authority to define who has a higher education in law: (1) A graduate of a law faculty of an institution or of a college in Israel, recognized under the Council for Higher Education Law, of 1958, as an institution of higher education; (2) A law graduate of an institution abroad recognized (for the purposes of this provision) by the Hebrew University of Jerusalem, as an institution of higher education; or a person who has studied at such an institution and has passed examinations to an extent that, in the opinion of the Hebrew University of Jerusalem, he may suitably regarded as eligible for a degree in law.

284 For instance, the 1991 amendment to the Bar Association Law on the academic accreditation of institutions granting approval for law studies proposed by Knesset members Reuven Rivlin, Amnon Rubinstein, Avraham Burg, Mordechai Virshuvski, Eli Dayan and Yitzhak Levi.

passed by the Knesset in 1989. On every occasion he presented a clear position in favor of democratization of higher education. He rejected universities' allegations as if the opening of the system would lead to a decline in the level of higher education in Israel. As evidence he showed that the expansion of higher education in Western countries following World War II did not reduce society's academic level. His approach in favor of the system's expansion was based on the following assumptions:

5.1. The expansion of the primary and secondary education system will result in excess demand for higher education amounting to 30–35,000 thousand students.
5.2. More and more professions are becoming academic, including occupational therapy, accounting and nursing, with others expected to follow suit in future.
5.3. Social cohesion: Increasing the gap between the educated and non-educated classes possess risk to Israeli society. Society needs to reach the optimal situation of Western countries.[285]

The mounting social and public pressures during these years was expressed in a growing involvement of Knesset members who demanded to expand accessibility to higher education through legislation.[286] Such involvement undermined the PBC's monopoly over planning the country's higher education and therefore often led its decision makers to reach agreements and compromises so as to avoid legislation.

285 Rubinstein, 1995: 38–42. From a lecture in a conference organized by the Ministry of Education and the Association of Regional Colleges, 6 January 1994, at the Yezreel Valley College.

286 Towards the end of the 1990's a number of bills involving higher education were proposed to the Knesset, including: Meir Shitrit's bill for promoting higher education in Israel, 2000; Zvulun Orlev's bill on the Council for Higher Education (amended academic supervision of Extensions), 2001; and the bill by Knesset members Gideon Ezra, Ivet Liberman, Ran Cohen, Michael Nudelman and Yuri Stern for the amendment of the Council for Higher Education Law (promoting the establishment of Colleges and Extensions in frontier regions), 2000.

Chapter 13 The Program for Expanding the Academic System in the 1990s: In Practice

The program for expanding the academic system for 1991–2000 was officially approved by the government of Israel in 1994,[287] but was gradually implemented as of 1992. The program included a two-stage solution for addressing the growing demand for higher education: The first stage, 1991–1996 (based on the PBC's five-year budget), and the second stage, 1996–2000. Approx. 50,000 new students were planned to be admitted in the two stages. In the first stage about 24,000, of whom about 22,000 at the existing universities and only about 2,000 at colleges. In the second stage about 26,000, of whom only about 10,000 at universities, and 16,000 in colleges.

The First Stage, 1991–1996: Planning and Implementation

In this stage we can identify three combined steps initiated by PBC to increase the number of available undergraduate quotas:

1. **Increasing the number of students at Bar Ilan's colleges (previously – Extensions):**[288] The capacity of Bar Ilan's colleges was increased through the BGS program which was taught entirely at the local campus of each college, and the gradual approval of other specialized curriculums, in which the first two years are studied at the college and the third year partly at the college and partly at the university. So as to promote the national program, the PBC regulated the university's auspices for its academic programs at the colleges and stipulated a compensation formula for the university in return for its auspices, amounting to ₪1,000 for each full time student. Payment was transferred directly to the university from the PBC.[289]

---

287 Ashkelon College Archive, file 1994, Government decision number 3964, 28 September 1994.

288 Annual report number 21 of the Planning and Budgeting Committee, 1993–1994, pg. 45.

289 Ashkelon College Archive, CHE file No. 1/2000. Minutes of meeting held on 14 March 1996. Meeting attendees: representatives of the PBC, Ministry of Education and the university.

2. **Increasing the number of students at existing universities:** At first the PBC increased the quota of university students, with the main increase in student numbers being absorbed by the younger universities (or as named by Yogev (2000) – Target Universities): Bar Ilan University, the University of Haifa and Ben Gurion University. During these years the country's universities grew by approx. 29,500 students compared to the original plan of 22,000 students. In practice, about 20,000 students were admitted to the Target Universities, as follows:

   Ben Gurion University grew by 107 % – from about 5,900 to about 12,250 students.
   The University of Haifa grew by 85 % – from about 6,900 to about 12,800 students.
   Bar Ilan University grew by about 77 % – from about 9,300 to about 16,500 students, not including its colleges.

All other universities jointly absorbed the increase beyond the planned 20,000 students, and in total 9,500 students.[290]

3. **Increasing the number of students through new institutions:** The most significant change in the CHE's position had been the system's expansion through the academization of regional and technological colleges and the addition of a new academic college at the center of the country. Accordingly, the system transitioned from a monolithic model to a binary one relying mainly on two types of institutions: Research institutions, and Non-research institutions teaching undergraduate and graduate degrees.

The Academization Process and Selection of Colleges

The Regional Colleges to embark upon academic independence were selected from 11 Regional Colleges operating under the academic auspices of a university, including those under the auspices of Bar Ilan University. This process commenced with a regularization of the financial and academic relationship between the Regional Colleges and the universities granting their auspices, and predominantly between the historical Extensions and their founding university, Bar Ilan; and continued with defining criteria for the separation of the colleges from the university's auspices and their embarking upon a new path of

290 Report of the Planning and Budgeting Committee, number 27/26, 1998–1999, 1999–2000, Jerusalem 2001, pg. 102–103.

academic independence. This process included contractual agreements between institutions and was in essence procedural, consisting of a stabilizing and mapping stage for examining the necessity of the colleges in their regions, while the second stage consisted mainly of ranking the colleges pinpointed for independence by accrediting them as institutions of higher education as per the CHE Law and their inclusion in Israel's academic system.

The first expression of this new direction can be found in the following passage from the CHE's December 1992 Newsletter: "In the next few years the system will also be expanded through colleges offering undergraduate degrees, some based on today's existing Regional Colleges. The undergraduate colleges will focus mainly on teaching and will operate independently, with their own teaching faculty".[291]

Within the CHE's plans, the role of the Extensions at Ashkelon and Zefat, which had not been originally founded as Regional Colleges, was only recognized after the Ministry of Education had granted them the status of Regional Colleges. Accordingly, the CHE published a notice confirming this claim:

> The Regional Colleges at Zefat and Ashkelon operated in the past as Extensions of Bar Ilan University, and the Ministry of Education confirmed their becoming Regional Colleges [...] The Council for Higher Education also approved the request of Bar Ilan university to open a Bachelor of General Studies (BGS) Program [...] Offering a BGS program would open a wider range of courses and combinations for students at Regional Colleges, allowing them to complete most of their undergraduate studies at the college itself. The degree would be granted by Bar Ilan University.[292]

In conversations held in the beginning of the 1990s between the PBC and the Ministry of Education, after the Regional Colleges had been transferred under its responsibility, the defining lines were outlined between regulating the relationships between the colleges and the universities and the next stage leading to their academic independence. One of the conversations centered on the following topics:

> .... A treaty between the Council for Higher Education, the universities, the colleges and the Ministry of Education, regulating the matter of colleges. The aim is to achieve a stage of development for colleges operating according to fixed rules acceptable to all the above, and which would not be subject to individual agreements between a college and a university... The aim is for more independent colleges which would operate as academic institutions and eventually (according to Prof. Amnon Pazy), universities

291 Newsletter, The Council for Higher Education, Planning and Budgeting Committee, issue number 4, December 1992.

292 Ibid.

> would ultimately leave the picture and the colleges would become independent entities. Meanwhile, it is very important to ensure that students would be able to complete their three years of study at the college itself, under the university's auspices.[293]

At meetings held at the Ministry of Education between the heads of the Colleges Unit and the managers of the colleges, discussions were held on the direction to which the CHE and the Ministry of Education had been striving towards. Ministry officials emphasized the pressing need to establish new colleges and strengthen the existing ones, and later on grant academic independence to some of them.[294]

Criteria for Academic Independence

Following many meetings held by the heads of the Colleges Unit at the Ministry of Education with the managers of the colleges, on 24 June 1992 a draft CHE policy was presented, towards the independence of colleges. The document opens with a declaration that Regional Colleges are part of the country's Post-Secondary education system, and the academic programs offered at the colleges operating under the academic auspices of universities are an integral part of the higher education system. It was further determined that there is a social necessity to address growing demand for higher education in remote areas, and therefore both the Ministry of Education and the CHE agree to work together towards expanding the higher education system based on the following criteria:

A. Significant increase of the number of students at the Regional Colleges in the next few years.
B. Increasing the scope and diversifying the academic possibilities available to undergraduate students in these institutions.
C. Full three-year undergraduate programs at the colleges, under the academic responsibility of a university.

---

293 Association of Regional Colleges Archive, file 1991. Record of phone conversation between Abraham Sheinfeld, Manager of the Colleges Unit at the Ministry of Education and Amnon Pazy, PBC Chairperson, 27 August 1991. The question of the degree was no longer mentioned as an obstacle, and it was clear to all that there should be no discrimination based on the types of degrees studied at the different institutions.

294 It was clear to the Ministry of Education that this plan and the new openness expressed by the CHE would result later on in the transition of the colleges to the CHE/PBC's responsibility and budgeting.

D. Reinforcement of academic facilities at Regional Colleges towards granting a permit for opening independent undergraduate programs.
E. The colleges that would reach academic independence and be granted a permit to open an independent academic program would be budgeted by the PBC similarly to any other academic institution in Israel.

About a month following publication of the draft outline of the future policy, the CHE was presented with the plan developed by its Sub-Committee on colleges,[295] stipulating the rules for the colleges' independence. The document, prepared by the Chairperson of the committee Prof. Yaacov Rand, was submitted to the CHE plenum in two parts, the first describing the current situation at the colleges and the second focusing on the practical proceedings that would lead to their academic independence and the rules for determining their future positions. In the document Prof. Rand described the demographic trends which the committee had noted and the need to offer higher education in remote places and development towns. Following are the preliminary rules set forth by the committee for academic independence:

A. **Number of students:** A college wishing to embark upon the process of achieving academic independence must prove its stability in terms of demand and a critical mass of students in its academic program. Such information was required in order to prove the college's ability to attract students in its area of operation.
B. **Senior academic faculty:** To be free of the dictates of the university, each college embarking upon the path of academic independence had to prove the existence of a stable senior teaching faculty whose main work was a the colleges' academic program, and who does not belong to the senior faculty of the university granting its auspices to the college. Although this issue was not the center of the policy, over time it proved to have great practical importance for emerging academic institutions.

Having managed an Extension in which most lecturers came from Bar Ilan University, I should note that this dependence on the university had been to the detriment of the Extensions. The decisions of heads of departments at the

295 Archive of the Council for Higher Education, Colleges file. Report of the Sub-Committee on Colleges: "Academic programs at Regional Colleges – current situation and future policy proposal". 30 August 1992. The role of the Sub-Committee on Colleges was to examine applications of colleges to determine a supervision and approvals policy for their academic programs.

university did not always correspond with the best interests of the Extension, but usually of those of the department at the university. The department heads were not keen on sending their best teachers, and in many cases the ones who were sent to teach at the Extensions were those who were unsuccessful at the main campus but could not be dismissed. A further problem already noted was the young lecturers who were sent to teach at the Extensions and formed a potential reservoir towards the establishment of a permanent faculty at the college. However, the most successful of these were called back to the university immediately when a position became available there or at one of its research institutes. The situation of Bar Ilan's northern Extensions was even worse than that of Ashkelon due to their greater distance from the center, and consequently they found it difficult to recruit local academic faculty.

C. **Academic systems:** In view of the fact that the academic programs at the colleges were operated by the university granting its auspices, it also provided all academic services. The committee ruled that a college striving for academic independence should prove the existence of academic systems facilitating the provision of academic services, such as student consulting services, teaching committee, appointments committee, status committee, academic secretariat and various position holders as is common in academic institutions.
D. **Academic Facilities:** The college must prove the existence of suitable academic facilities such as libraries equipped for undergraduate needs, laboratories, classrooms and computers.
E. **System of rules:** As part of its independence process, the college will present its set of rules for academic Studies, that should include a statute for students, disciplinary rules, etc.

To establish the beginning of an academization process for colleges and achieve as many of the goals defined in the report, the committee raised operative proposals which would ensure the success of the process:

1. Urgently increase financial resources for developing academic facilities at the colleges, including libraries, laboratories and local faculty.
2. Vigorous operations by the budgeting authorities to double the number of students at colleges within three to five years.
3. Increase the number of students studying at least eight yearly hours (16 semester hours) at the academic program, with the aim of increasing the scope of operations of academic programs at the colleges.
4. Increase students' ability to complete their entire degree at the college, in coordination with the university granting its auspices.

5. Work to achieve mutual accreditation between universities for courses taught at colleges so as to encourage participation in the program.
6. Assist the college to develop suitable dormitories so as to enable intensive studies at the academic programs.

The Colleges Sub-Committee proposed the establishment of a committee that would specify the desired academic structure of colleges aiming for academic independence and lead the process so as to ensure the realization of all the aims listed in the report. It was proposed that the committee would include the Chairperson of the CHE's Colleges Sub-Committee, two representatives of the universities, a representative of the college and a representative of the Ministry of Education.[296]

In view of the fact that the process was predominantly academic, the Sub-Committee aimed to maintain the dominance of the universities so that the entire process would be promoted in line with the rules defined by the senior actors of the field. This position continued to maintain the dominance of universities until the end of the 1990s. However, the committee perceived the Ministry of Education, being the budgeting authority, as a partner to the entire process from its onset, and therefore proposed that the Culture Manager at the Ministry of Education establish a joint committee that would develop guidelines for granting budgetary allocations to the Regional Colleges as part of the process of preparing for academic independence.

The heads of the Colleges Unit welcomed the committee's report, and in a further managers' conference it was agreed that each College Manager who believes that the college he is heading is ready for academic independence would submit a proposal to the Colleges Unit by no later than 15 November 1992, so as to prepare for the submittal of a general plan for the CHE's review in the upcoming academic year.[297] However, despite the official proposal made by the Manager of the Colleges Unit, the factors that ultimately decided the identity of the colleges destined for independence included budgetary considerations,[298] geographic deployment, the existence of physical facilities and most of all the nature of the relationship between the college and the university granting its auspices. The good relationship between Bar Ilan University and the colleges under its auspices

---

296 Ibid.

297 Ibid, file 1992. Protocol of the managers' conference held on 23 September 1992.

298 Of the intent to propose three colleges in the first stage we learn from the remarks of the head of the Culture Administration at the Ministry of Education at a meeting with the colleges managers held on 9 February 1992.

was in this case to the detriment of the colleges, and the decision makers at the CHE and the Ministry of Education were not pressed to choose one of Bar Ilan's colleges as candidate for academic independence and the Ministry decided that they would continue to be Regional Colleges under the university's auspices. In coordination between the CHE/PBC and the Ministry of Education it was agreed that an academization process would be initiated at the following colleges: Three Regional Colleges – Sha'ar Hanegev College in the south, Tel Chai and Yezreel Valley in the north; a new college that would absorb excess demand at the center of the country – The Academic College of Tel Aviv-Yaffo; and three colleges teaching technological professions towards a B.Sc., which had previously taught practical engineering programs – Ort Bruada College in Karmiel in the north, the College of Engineering ("Afeka") in Tel Aviv, and the College of Engineering in Beer Sheva (currently the "Sami Shamoon College of Engineering").

Chapter 14 The Struggle for Academization at Bar Ilan's Colleges

Signs of opposition towards Bar Ilan University, prevalent in the 1950s and 1960s could be noted also in the 1990s. For the first time since the establishment of the State, an Israeli government was formed without religious parties, and particularly without the National Religious Party (NRP). Prof. Amnon Rubinstein from Meretz was appointed Minister of Education, and Bar Ilan University, which had taken advantage of Zvulun Hammer's time as Minister of Education to promote its Extensions towards the end of the 1980s, remained without ideological support at the Ministry of Education. The fact that none of the colleges under Bar Ilan's auspices were included in the Ministry's academization plans despite accounting for 40 % of all candidate colleges, was a surprise both to Bar Ilan and the colleges themselves. These feelings were all the more pronounced in view of Bar Ilan's long term operations in the periphery at a time in which none of the country's other universities had even considered reaching out to these regions. As one of the managers of the colleges under Bar Ilan's auspices, I met with the Minister of Education and asked for his position on this conundrum. His response was sharp and clear: The Ministry of Education and the CHE aim to assist colleges encountering development difficulties due to a bad relationship with the university granting them auspices, as opposed to Bar Ilan which dedicates its utmost for the development of its colleges. The Yezreel Valley and Tel Chai colleges which were under the auspices of the University of Haifa had a hard time developing their academic programs as the University of Haifa perceived them as competitors, and therefore the national authorities had no other recourse but to release them from their dependence on the university, to full independence. The Minister's response, however, was only partially true, as although the relationship between Sha'ar Hanegev College and Ben Gurion University had been a positive one, the college was still included in the academization program. Moreover, a new college was founded in Tel Aviv, in academic collaboration with Tel Aviv University, and it too immediately embarked upon the path to independence. As managers of Bar Ilan's colleges we felt the hostile atmosphere towards Bar Ilan, a fact that was further reinforced in interviews held with retiring PBC decision makers in 2009, as will be further detailed below.

After completing the first stage of increasing the number of students at the universities, the second stage commenced, consisting of the academization of colleges, which lasted through the years 1994–1999, as can be seen in Table 32.

Tab. 32: The first colleges that embarked upon academic independence

College	Academic auspices from	Year of permit	Year of accreditation	Type of degree
Yezreel Valley	University of Haifa	1994	1997	B.A
Tel Chai	University of Haifa	1994	1997	B.A
Sha'ar Hanegev	Ben Gurion University	1995	1997	B.A
Tel Aviv- Yaffo	Tel Aviv University (temporary auspices for the permitting stage)	1995	1996	B.A
Brauda	No auspices	1994	1995	B.Tech
Engineering in the Negev	No auspices	1995	1999	B.Tech
Engineering in Tel Aviv	No auspices	1995	1997	B.Tech

Data: Mendelzweig (1995; 1998).

The academization process included principles and rules for the recruitment and employment of academic faculty, administrative and academic structure and students tuition guidelines. To ensure the implementation of clause 15 to the CHE law, by which "A recognized institution is free to manage its academic and administrative matters" the CHE insisted on a complete separation in the institutions' operation. An institution that held non-academic studies such as vocational studies, advanced learning and practical engineering studies, was required to operate these through separate organizational systems. This led the Yezreel Valley and Tel Chai Colleges to stop offering their practical engineering program, that had been available for many years. Specialized engineering colleges were also required to separate from the establishment in which they had developed, while the Sha'ar Hanegev College, which did not embark upon a process of full independence, continued to offer two types of programs. The colleges included in the academization program remained under the Ministry of Education's budgeting and operations, until receiving the permit. With the granting of a permit to open independent departments and the accreditation received in 1998 as institutions of higher education, they transitioned to PBC budgeting.[299]

299 The CHE/PBC, annual report number 23, (1995–1996): 47–48.

The Alternative Academization of Bar Ilan's Colleges in the 1990s

Bar Ilan's Extensions at Ashkelon, Zefat, the Jordan Valley and the College of Judea & Samaria which operated under Bar Ilan's academic auspices, continued to be budgeted by the Ministry of Education as none of these institutions were included in the first stage of the colleges academization program. This obvious overlooking of Bar Ilan's Extensions worried the managers of the colleges, who knew that according to the terms of the academization program, PBC would give precedence to developing those colleges that had been selected for independence. Such precedence would be expressed in budgets for building and development, the allocation of donors and support funds to these colleges, as well as the PBC's direct supervision over them, without the Ministry of Education's mediation. The Regional Colleges remained the responsibility of the Ministry of Education, the practical implications of which being their integration in a multi-annual academic development program from which the multi-annual budgeting of the authorized body – PBC had also been derived. But the Ministry of Education's budgetary responsibility towards the other colleges meant an annual budget and the absence of supervision and responsibility by an authorized academic source. In practice the Colleges Unit administration at the Ministry of Education was unofficially academically guided by the PBC, and based on these guidelines it planned and managed the Regional Colleges budgets at the ministry. In view of this situation the managers of Bar Ilan's colleges approached the university's president and the head of the Colleges System Administration, detailing the expected detriment to be caused to the colleges because of the CHE's program, both academically and organizationally. The university's management, which had been unaware of the details of the CHE's program, was advised to prepare an alternative academization program to that of the independent colleges, emphasizing that the apparent discrimination in the CHE's program requires an urgent and different response by the university towards its colleges, as outright competition with the independent colleges may deal a final blow to the colleges under Bar Ilan's auspices, ultimately resulting in their demise. The biggest fear of the colleges managers stemmed from the PBC'S budgetary preference for independent colleges, which may in turn give them a clear advantage in recruiting academic faculty as well as in physical and academic development. In a letter to the university's management, the colleges managers proposed an action plan that would be based on the following principles:

1. **A redefinition of the college:** The previous chapter presented the Extensions' new status as Regional Colleges offering the university's academic program. Their budgetary independence was seen as progress, as indeed it was at the time, but the CHE's policy and the official separation from Bar Ilan after their becoming Regional Colleges left Bar Ilan's colleges in a situation in which potential candidates viewed it as lacking a well-established and supportive academic framework. We therefore proposed to officially include in the name of each college the fact that it operates under Bar Ilan University's academic auspices, believing that such a step would establish a clear affinity between the college and the university, thereby assisting the college's image and the expected competition with the independent colleges. Bar Ilan's colleges needed the academic prestige that the university was able to offer them. Our proposal was accepted, and the following was added to the official name of each college: "Under the academic auspices of Bar Ilan University".
2. **Budgetary support:** We requested the university's management to intervene with the Ministry of Education so as to compare the budgets of our colleges with those of Regional Colleges that were in the stages of academic independence. The main reasoning for this request relied on the assumption that Bar Ilan's colleges offer a full academic program requiring extensive financial resources in order to recruit academic faculty and develop academic and other physical facilities. The university's Rector at the time, Prof. Moshe Kave, acceded and approached the Minister of Education requesting to allocate a budget for Bar Ilan's colleges, that would be suited to their actual operations. In his letter to the Minister on 4 January 1994 Prof. Kave protested against the discrimination towards Bar Ilan's colleges and the fact that none of them were selected for embarking upon academic independence:

   > As Rector of Bar Ilan University I was very surprised to realize that none of the four Regional Colleges under Bar Ilan's auspices were included in this program, despite the fact that these four colleges are the only ones in which. . . full undergraduate programs are offered [. . .] The colleges did not receive the financial allocations necessary for these needs. Therefore, it would be appropriate to first promote all of these colleges and to allocate suitable amounts of money for the task.[300]

3. **Academic development:** The aims defined by the Ministry of Education for the development of each college were based first and foremost on increasing their number of students. The continued operation of general and uniform

300 Bar Ilan University Archive, Colleges Administration, file 1994. Letter from Prof. Kave to the Minister of Education Prof. Amnon Rubinstein, 4 January 1994.

programs at Bar Ilan's colleges may have undermined this aim and the competition with the independent colleges. Our assumption as managers relied on the CHE's policy encouraging the independent colleges to offer practical programs which would increase their attractiveness to young candidates. In order to cope with this assumption we had to be prepared to open diverse programs in specialized areas, rather than continuing to focus on the multi-disciplinary path. The university's management was asked to assist its colleges to develop specialized and new programs which were not offered at the university, such as nursing, Middle Eastern studies and optometry. This initiative was presented as an alternative for the academization of independent colleges.[301] The university's management was convinced of the importance of this process and began to act in a number of directions to fulfill our requests:

A. **Change of name and structure of the general degree:** A full BGS program was first introduced at Bar Ilan's colleges in the 1991/2 academic year. The purpose of the first year was to examine the attractiveness of the new program among young students at the colleges. After two years of operation conclusions were drawn, and we were able to convince the university that marketing the program under the non-attractive name of "General B.A" (Bachelor of General Studies, BGS) dissuades candidates who feared that potential employers would not be impressed, to say the least. Also in this case the Rector acceded to our request, which had been supported by the university's Colleges Administration, and approached the CHE's secretariat requesting it to approve the name change. The CHE's secretariat agreed that the name change would not attest to a change in its policy regarding Bar Ilan's colleges, and conceded to the Rector's request. In June 1993 the name of the degree was officially changed from General B.A to Multidisciplinary BA in Social Sciences or Humanities. The name change brought with it a new way of thinking at the university in terms of the structure of the degree and a diversification of the programs it offered. The program undertook a new form, characterized by a much broader structure consisting of two central study units and a complementary one that included all methodological studies and elective courses from various disciplines. As of the 1992/93 academic year, the structure of the degree was defined by main study units and a methodological one:

301 Ashkelon College Archive, file 1994. Letter from the managers of the colleges to Prof. Babkofh, 27 February 1994.

First unit		Second unit	
Elective courses	12 Weekly hours	Mandatory courses	6 Weekly hours
Seminar	2 Weekly hours	Elective courses	4 Weekly hours
Elective courses	6 Weekly hours		
Total	20 Weekly hours	Total	10 Weekly hours

Complementary (Methodological) unit			
Bibliography training	1 Weekly hour	Computer applications	2 Weekly hours
Statistics	3 Weekly hours	Interdisciplinary seminar	2 Weekly hours
Research methods	2 Weekly hours	Elective courses	8 Weekly hours
Total complementary unit: 18 Weekly hours			
Jewish Studies: 16 Weekly hours			
Total degree: 64 annual weekly hours = 128 semester hours			

Other departments at the university joined the interdisciplinary program, and the colleges increased their topics offered to students in this program. The general topics offered in the new program included society and criminology, society and life sciences, political science and communication, and others. Between 1992 and 1995 the university approved the opening of more than six multidisciplinary BA programs at Ashkelon, Zefat, Jordan Valley and Judea and Samaria.

B. **Inclusion of specialized programs:** Alongside the momentum propelled by the multidisciplinary BA program at the colleges, their managers aimed to also include professional programs, as offered by any academic institution. It was clear to us all that relying exclusively on the interdisciplinary program may in time lead to low ranking of the institution in the stratification measure (based on the Stratification approach), which is why we requested the university's approval to include specialized study areas. This request was also met affirmatively, and beginning in 1994/95, Social work and Education were added as specialized areas. All of these steps were fruitful, and as early as the period defined at the first stage in the CHE's program it was clear that a significant academic development is taking place at Bar Ilan's colleges, despite the preference given to other colleges in the process of independence. The following table presents academic activities between 1991 and 1996 at all Bar Ilan's colleges, compared to the independence colleges.

Tab. 33: List of undergraduate programs at Bar Ilan's Colleges in the first stage of the CHE's program for expanding the country's academic system

Study programs	Type of degree	Jordan Valley College	Zefat College	College of Judea & Samaria	Ashkelon College	Target population
Social Work	B.S.W	1989	1989	–	1989	Qualified Social Workers
Society and Economy	Multi-disciplinary B.A	1992	1993	1993	1993	General
Israel Studies	Multi-disciplinary B.A	1992	1993	–	1994	General
Society and Education	Multi-disciplinary B.A	1992	1993	1993	1993	General
Academization for teachers	B.A Education	1993	1993	1993	1993	Senior Teachers
Society and Criminology	Multi-disciplinary B.A	1995	1995	1994	1994	General
Society and life sciences	Multi-disciplinary B.A	1994	1994	1994	1993	Nursing
Geography and Life Sciences	Multi-disciplinary B.A	–	1994	–	1994	Environmental sanitation
Political science and communication	Multi-disciplinary B.A	1995	–	1996	1995	General
Society and Sociology	Multi-disciplinary B.A	1994	1995	1995	1994	General

(continued)

Tab. 33: Continued

Study programs	Type of degree	Jordan Valley College	Zefat College	College of Judea & Samaria	Ashkelon College	Target population
Society and Psychology	Multi-disciplinary B.A	–	–	–	1995	General
Society and Political Sciences	Multi-disciplinary B.A	1995	1993	1994	1993	General
General History and Middle East Studies	B.A History	–	1995	–	–	IDF Officers
Economics and Business Administration	B.A Economics and Business Administration	–	–	–	1995	General
Library and Information Studies	B.A Library and Information Studies (secondary)	–	–	–	1995	General
Total departments in multi-disciplinary programs		**8**	**8**	**7**	**10**	
Total specialization programs		**2**	**3**	**1**	**4**	
Total five year program		**10**	**11**	**8**	**14**	

Source: Ashkelon College Archive. Data collected from data files dated 1989–1997 and a report issued by the management of the Ashkelon College to the Anita Shapira Committee, 29 November, 1995.

The formal academization process of the independent colleges led to the opening of specialized multidisciplinary programs, albeit at a slower pace than had taken place at Bar Ilan's colleges. Table 34 lists the new programs included in the first part of the CHE's academization process.

Tab. 34: List of programs offered at independent colleges during the parallel period

Study programs	Type of degree	Yezreel Valley College	Tel Chai College	Tel Aviv-Yaffo College	Sapir College
Behavioral Sciences	Multi-disciplinary B.A	1996	–	1994	–
Education	B.A	–	1996	–	–
Social Sciences	Multi-disciplinary B.A	1996	1996	–	–
Communication	B.A	–	–	–	1995
Public Administration	B.A	–	–	–	1995
Industrial Management	B.A	–	–	–	1995
Social Work	B.S.W	–	1996	–	–
Computer Engineering	B.Sc	–	1996	1994	–
Biotechnology	B.Sc	–	1996	–	–
Society and Politics	B.A	–	–	1994	–
Economics and Management	B.A	1997	1996	1994	–
Total multi-disciplinary programs		2	1	1	0
Total specialized program		1	5	3	3
Total Departments		**3**	**6**	**4**	**3**

Data collected from Barshad and Biham (2000; 2001; 2003; 2005); Mendelzweig (1995; 1998).

A comparison between the academization of Bar Ilan's Colleges and that of the independent colleges points to the success of Bar Ilan's programs despite the clear preference of the CHE towards the independent colleges and the absence of special budgets allocated for the academization of Bar Ilan's colleges, as summarized in Table 35.

Tab. 35: Comparative date: Study programs at Bar Ilan's colleges and independent colleges in the beginning of the 1990s

Study programs	Colleges under Bar Ilan's academic auspices				Independent Colleges			
	Ashkelon	**Zefat**	**Jordan Valley**	**Judea and Samaria**	**Yezreel Valley**	**Tel Aviv Yafo**	**Tel Chai**	**Sha'ar Hanegev/ Sapir**
Multidisciplinary	10	8	8	7	2	1	1	0
Specialization program	4	3	2	1	1	3	5	3
Total:	**14**	**11**	**10**	**8**	**3**	**4**	**6**	**3**

The addition of multidisciplinary study programs as well as special programs for teachers and social workers did in fact make a difference: the scope of operations of the colleges gradually increased between 1991 and 1995. Figure 9 shows this growth trend by two measures indicative of scope of activity: Annual number of hours and number of courses at Bar Ilan's colleges.

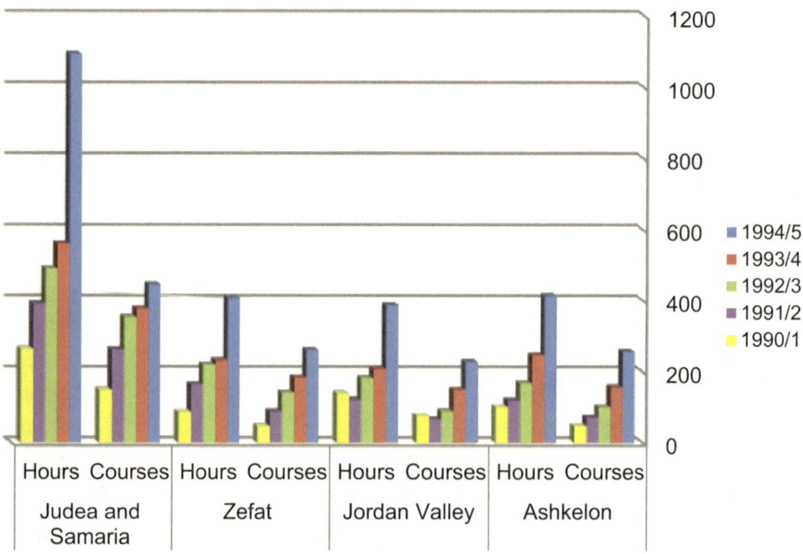

Fig. 9: Scope of Courses and Hours at Bar Ilan's Colleges (1991–1995)

The Second Stage in the CHE's Plan to Expand the Academic System, 1996–2000: Planning and Implementation

As noted above, the second stage in the expansion of the academic system was scheduled for 1996–2000. Contrary to the first stage of the program, the plan for the second stage covered most of the increase in the number of students at the independent academic colleges. Accordingly, the growth in the number of undergraduate students at the universities was blocked, with larger quotas allocated for advanced degrees. According to the plan, the academic colleges would absorb 20,000 students, according to the division shown in Table 36.

Tab. 36: Aims for the second stage of the CHE's program for expanding the academic system

Institution type	Number of students	Remarks
Academic Colleges	**planned for the five year period**	**B.A Studies**
Tel Aviv-Yafo College	4,000	
Tel Chai College	1,000	
Yesreel Valley College	3,000	
Sha'ar Hanegev	2,000	
Total:	**10,000**	
Technological Colleges		B.Tech undergraduate studies
Karmiel	2,000	
Beer Sheva	2,000	
Tel Aviv	2,000	
Total	**6,000**	
Academic Teachers Colleges	**4,000**	
Universities	10,000	For advanced degrees and undergraduate studies not available at colleges, such as: Medicine, Life Sciences and Exact Sciences, mainly Hard Science
Total each five year period	**30,000**	

Source: Pazy (2005).

Following the period defined as the second stage the planners realized that the Academic Colleges had also failed to meet their main aims in the second five year period:

1. Only about 10,000 students had been absorbed at the independent colleges, compared to the 20,000 planned.
2. None of the independent colleges came anywhere near the optimal size defined by the PBC of 4,000–5,000 students (Pazy, 2005).

According to the 1996–2000 five year plan, by 2000 and even afterwards there would be no need for additional academic institutions as the added universities and colleges should absorb the entire expected growth. Therefore, the planning in those years aimed to establish the final limits of Israel's academic system. However, despite the planning targets and growth forecasts, the program's planners were destined to encounter many surprises which significantly impacted the second stage of the program, and the face of the country's future higher education system. Three main factors influenced the continued expansion of the higher education system, which had not been allocated for in the 1990s plans:

1. **Accreditation of new colleges:** Political and public pressures on the CHE during the mid-1990s led to changes in planning and to the accreditation of five additional colleges as independent academic colleges, as opposed to the first master-plan. Pressures were asserted from a number of directions: Pressure from the Ministry of Finance on the CHE led to the accreditation of the Hadassah College in Jerusalem. The Ministry of Finance wished to recognize it as an independent college due to its relationship with the Global Hadassah Organization and the substantial donations received from the organization; other political and public pressures led to the accreditation of colleges in Jerusalem and the center; during the five year period 1996–2000 the CHE recognized the Holon Institute of Technology,[302] the College of Judea & Samaria, which in addition to operating under the auspices of Bar Ilan University, obtained a permit to offer an independent program;[303] the Hadassah Academic College in Jerusalem; the Jerusalem College of Engineering,[304] and the Ruppin Academic Center (formerly Ruppin College).[305] The accreditation of these colleges added approx. 6,000 student quotas to the system of budgeted institutions during the five year period. The increase in the publicly funded colleges amounted in the second stage to 15,875 students compared to the planned quota of 20,000. Only the inclusion of the new colleges had improved the performance of the academic colleges in the second phase of the master-plan.

---

302 Academic college for Engineering studies, Applied Mathematics and Design. Founded in 1969 through an initiative of the Municipality of Holon, and dedicated to training teachers of technology. In 1999 it was recognized as an independent academic institution and in 2006 changed its name to H.I.T: Holon Institute of Technology.

303 Ariel College was founded under the auspices of Bar Ilan University and focused on undergraduate programs. In 2013 it was accredited and recognized as Ariel University.

304 Academic College of Engineering Studies. Founded in 1999 and in 2013 changed its name to "Azrieli College of Engineering Jerusalem".

305 Founded in 1949 as the Ruppin College, named after Dr. Arthur Ruppin, one of the founding fathers of the agricultural settlement in the land of Israel and a prominent Sociologist. In 2001 the CHE recognized it as a budgeted public college accredited for undergraduate and graduate degrees in Social Sciences and Engineering.

2. **Amendment to the CHE law of 1958** (amendment number 10, also known as the Colleges amendment): Throughout the entire period scheduled for the expansion of Israel's academic system, meaning between 1991 and 2000, the CHE/PBC demanded that the planning would remain under their control, which included exclusive jurisdiction over determining the identity and official title of independent academic colleges. Answers to the questions whether a college would be defined as a Post-Secondary college or an institution of higher education and what would be the formal difference between it and Regional Colleges offering academic degree programs, remained exclusively in the hands of the CHE. The answers to these questions would have implications on the budgeting of the institution, its pace of development, and most of all would provide a solution to the vague status of Regional Colleges as institutions of higher education. The CHE's decisive position to retain final decision on all these questions forced many public representatives in the managements of Regional Colleges to initiate legislative interventions solidifying the official academic status of colleges in Israel. Knesset member Avraham Burg, who headed the Knesset Education Committee, dedicated himself to this task with the encouragement of the heads of Regional Councils and the managers of colleges in the north and south of the country.[306] Following initial discussions at the Knesset Education Committee, in which I participated together with the managers of the Yesreel Valley and Jordan Valley Colleges, an initial proposal was prepared for amending the CHE law. In view of the fact that the initiators of the amendment included public figures representing independent colleges, these initial proposals did not include Regional Colleges under a university's auspices, leaving them devoid of any protection and legal definition as an academic institution. According to one of the initial proposals to the amendment, article 1 to the law would be revised to define a college as an "academic or professional institution recognized under the law, which is not a university, is eligible to grant its graduates a recognized degree approve by the Council to one of its units".[307] Whereas the colleges under the auspices of universities did

306 Knesset member Burg supported the opening of the system and its accessibility to the entire population. In a conference organized on 6 January 1994 by the Ministry of Education and the Association of Regional Colleges, Knesset member Burg presented his view of the expansion process as a "Highway effect": The more the roads are expanded, the more cars use it. As the accessibility to undergraduate degrees grows, so does the demand for studies.

307 Yezreel Valley College archive. With his letter to the Yesreel Valley College on 23 December 1993, Knesset member Burg enclosed a bill that does not include the Regional Colleges – bill number 2261 dated 26 April 1994.

not offer their own degree, this definition left them outside the legal definition intended for academic colleges. At committee discussions and letters to its Chairperson we described the implications of the discrimination that may occur between the Regional Colleges and the independent ones which would grant their own degree. Knesset member Burg and others in the committee realized that in order to avoid legislative discrimination, the amendment must include all colleges offering academic studies, thereby expanding accessibility to higher education. Therefore the Chairperson of the committee decided to summon a number of College Managers to participate in the discussions as active partners in the amendment process, which lasted a number of months. Following a number of discussions it was decided that the definition would be amended to include Regional Colleges operating under a university's auspices. The amendment was approved by the Knesset, and contrary to the position of the CHE/PBC[308] it included a wider definition of an academic college, as shall be explained below.

The amendment to the law included an intervention in the planning and policy of higher education in Israel. The legislative principles showed a high level of intervention in the CHE/PBC's work, resulting from a lack of satisfaction from their position regarding the level of accessibility to higher education. The following legislative principles were stipulated in the committee's publications towards the amendment:

1. The education committee aims to enable higher education for all.
2. The committee believes that the structure of the Higher Education System is not suited to the needs of Israeli economy and society.
3. The higher education system is essentially a university system, and the burden of undergraduate studies hinders the ability of these institutions to focus on research.
4. The supply of Post-Secondary education transformed the system into one that is anti-equality and anti-integration.
5. The CHE does not consider the benefit of colleges, which in turn are required to operate in line with its guidelines and regulations which require them to

308 Extract of speech by Amnon Rubinstein in a conference organized by the U.S. Israel Education Foundation on 8 April 2003. He declared that the heads of the universities demanded that legislation would not be initiated on questions of higher education, and that he had responded that they had also been established through a legislative process. Ibid, pg. 37.

employ researches as lecturers, as do universities, although they do not have the tools to achieve such equality.

Following are the aims defined for the legislation:

1. Opening further higher education programs.
2. Enabling every graduate of the education system to acquire a higher education.
3. Reduce social and class gaps.
4. Increase the scope of technological and engineering studies.
5. Take measures to stop the waves of emigration from Israel to study abroad.
6. Facilitate admission to institutions of higher education.[309]

The clarifications enclosed with the bill included data from the Ministry of Education, by which the demand for higher education is expected to reach 40,000 applicants by the end of the decade, while a growing number of non-recognized institutions of Post-Secondary education are opened. The ministry's representatives at the committee argued that the academic level of these institutions should be evaluated and accordingly they should join the national mission to expand the existing academic system. The bill left the academic authority to recognize institutions in the hands of the CHE, but removed its authority to prevent a college that meets the rules to be called an "Academic College".[310] The amendment required the CHE to also recognize Regional Colleges as institutions of higher education, thereby preventing the existence of two types of colleges. The collaboration[311] and efforts of the colleges' managers and public figures were fruitful, and the Council for Higher Education Law of 1958 was officially amended as of 24 February 1995. The amendment also included the colleges under Bar Ilan

309 Yezreel Valley College archive, letter from Knesset member Burg to the College Manager, 23 December 1993. The letter included an addendum – 'Michlol', Legislation Principles, Chairperson of the Education and Culture Committee. Published on 24 December, 1993.

310 The Council for Higher Education Law Bill (amendment-colleges) of 1993. The proposal was sent in Burg's letter to Yoram Raz, manager of the Yesreel Valley College, 23 December 1993.

311 The Chairman of the committee shared all stages of the discussion towards the legislative change with a number of colleges managers. In its first stages, the bill did not include Bar Ilan University's colleges due to a misunderstanding regarding their precise definition. The intervention of three colleges managers – Ashkelon, Jordan Valley and Yesreeel Valley – led to their ultimate inclusion in the law.

University's auspices, dedicating article 1 to the law to them and to other colleges like them:

> "Academic college" – an institution requesting to use this title, and is one of the following: (1) An institution of higher education that is not a university, and has been recognized as per article 9 [. . .] (2) Offers at least one academic program under the auspices of a university.[312]

The explanations to the law attested to legislators' involvement not only in defining the status of colleges but also in research and social planning of the country's higher education system. it is safe to say with a high degree of certainty that amendment 10 to the CHE law forced the CHE to initiate a process of academization of further Regional Colleges in addition to those selected in the first stage. In the absence of a clear social policy at the CHE, the Education Committee saw itself as having been appointed to support the weaker social classes and residents of the periphery in increasing their accessibility to higher education. Although in the beginning of the 1990s the CHE/PBC had shown a certain openness and to a certain extent revised the Council's historic position, legislators realized that continuing to depend on the CHE's willingness for change would not suffice for initiating the transformation which the system required.

3. **Auspices colleges enhance their operations:** Contrary to the first stage in which a quota was defined also for the number of students studying at the academic programs at the colleges, the second stage froze the number of students attending universities, a step which also included the Regional Colleges under their auspices. The implications of this freezing threatened to deal a hard blow to Bar Ilan University, that had granted its auspices to about a third of the country's Regional Colleges.[313] But despite the planned freezing of quotas, Bar Ilan's colleges continued to grow, even adding new programs, mainly specialization ones, alongside the multidisciplinary program that had already been well established in the 1991–1995 five year plan. This increase in the number of students had been indirectly accepted by the PBC and resulted from the following factors, which will be discussed in greater detail in the following pages:

   3.1. Inclusion of the Western Galilee College as one of the colleges under Bar Ilan University's auspices.

   3.2. A rise in the number of students at the colleges in 1991–2000.

---

312 Council for Higher Education Law, 1958.

313 Association of Regional Colleges Archive, file 1995. Letter from Guri Zilca, CEO of the CHE/PBC, to Avikam Beller from the Ministry of Finance Budgets Department, 26 March 1995.

3.3. An increase in the number of hours available for students at colleges based on the F.T.E calculation, resulting from the change in the characteristics of students at the Colleges/Extensions.
3.4. An increase in the general scope of studies available at the colleges.

The Inclusion of the Western Galilee College under Bar Ilan University's Auspices

The Western Galilee College operated under the Ministry of Education's Colleges Unit as one of 12 Regional Colleges. The college, founded back in 1972, operated for a short period under the auspices of the University of Haifa, and in the beginning of the 1990s inaugurated an Open University learning center. Developments during those years positioned it at an inferior status to that of the other Regional Colleges. It offered an Open University degree program, which was not sufficiently attractive for young students and therefore its number of students significantly diminished. The program to expand the system and the growing demand for higher education forced its management to search for a university to grant it its academic auspices and operate study programs as had been done at other Regional Colleges. The College Manager, David Friedman, with whom I discussed the matter, had been impressed with Bar Ilan's favorable approach to its Extensions and their relative prosperity during those years and became convinced that the solution lies with Bar Ilan. He approached the CHE/PBC requesting to allow the college to examine a relationship with Bar Ilan University in the format encouraged by the Council itself – an academic program (not an Extension), under exclusively academic auspices.

The PBC's managers, realizing that this college could offer a solution for the growing demand in its region, were quick to embrace the initiative and the college management approached Bar Ilan, requesting it to grant it academic auspices. The university appointed a committee that visited the college and consequently recommended including it in the list of Regional Colleges under the university's auspices. The CHE's support of this initiative corresponded with the general atmosphere in the 1990s and the aim to address the growing demand for higher education, especially when dealing with a college operating in the heart of the periphery populated by underprivileged socioeconomic groups. The fact that it had been left without stable auspices also contributed to the decision to encourage the relationship between the college and Bar Ilan. The CHE/PBC could not allow themselves to ignore this request although it meant adding a further college to the university which was already academically responsible for four other colleges. Bar Ilan was the only university that considered granting its auspices, and had the required experience for this sort of operation. On 11 October 1994 the university's Rector informed the College Manager of the university's willingness to grant the college its academic auspices as of the 1995 academic year.[314] The CHE's Sub-Committee on colleges discussed the joint application by the Western Galilee College and Bar Ilan University and on 17 January 1995 decided to approve academic studies at the college under Bar Ilan University's academic auspices and responsibility. The approval was limited to year 1 and to the 1995 academic year only. The departments approved for this year were multidisciplinary B.A in social and life sciences, Society and Education and Society and Political Sciences.[315] The Western Galilee College joined the family of Bar Ilan colleges and began a gradual process of development. In the first year 279 students began studying towards Bar Ilan University's multidisciplinary degree.

The Rise in the Number of Students at the Colleges in 1991–2000

During this period, in which the Higher Education System expanded through independent colleges, Bar Ilan University was able to create convenient conditions for alternative academization at its colleges of auspices, resulting in the fact that their success proved to be no less prominent than that of the colleges selected for independence, and during the first period to the CHE's plan, even exceeded them. Table 37 and Figure 10 show changes that began in the period that preceded the operation of the full undergraduate degree program at the colleges, alongside other changes that took place during the period of the CHE's expansion plan: 1991–2000.

314 Bar Ilan University archive. F.T.E data file, 1995–1996, Colleges Administration.

315 Ashkelon College Archive, file 2000/1. Letter from Emanuel Cohen, Coordinator of the CHE's Colleges Sub-Committee to the head of the Colleges System Administration at the university and to the College Manager, 13 June 1995.

Tab. 37: Growth in the number of students at the four colleges operating under Bar Ilan University's academic auspices, 1990–2000 (as of 1995 the Western Galilee College was also added to this list)

	Ashkelon	Zefat	Jordan Valley	Judea and Samaria	Western Galilee
1989/90	107	79	100		
1990/1	90	89	137	130	
1991/2	234	192	185	204	
1992/3	349	275	237	203	
1993/4	501	407	330	217	
1994/5	899	519	451	494	279
1995/6	1,284	685	684	827	472
1996/7	1,493	800	798	773	769
1997/8	1,601	909	825	867	879
1998/9	1,795	898	775	866	899
1999/00	2,105	804	846	919	952

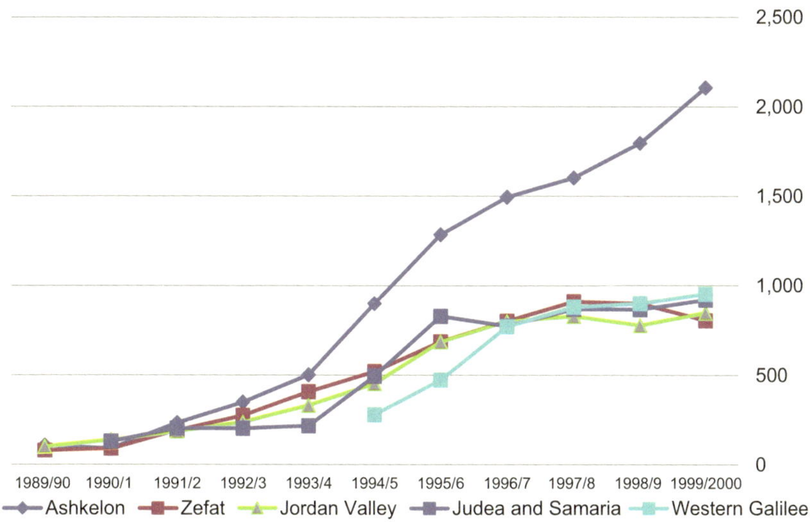

Fig. 10: Changes in the number of students in a decade (1991–2000)

Data from the Colleges Administration – Bar Ilan University, F.T.E data, 1994–1998 file.

According to the data summarized in Table 38, we note a clear transformation that took place at the colleges under Bar Ilan University's auspices. At the oldest Extension (Ashkelon) the number of students grew during the decade (1999–2000) from 90 to 2,105 students; at the Jordan Valley college the number of students that year grew from 137 to 846; at the Zefat from 89 to 804.

Tab. 38: Annual average growth

College	Number of students in 1991	Number of students in 2000	Average annual growth %
Ashkelon	90	2105	42.0 % +
Jordan Valley	137	846	22.4 % +
Zefat	89	804	27.7 % +
Judea and Samaria	130	919	24.3 % +
Western Galilee	279 * As of 1995	952	28.0 % +

Extent of Studies Based on the F.T.E (Full Time Equivalent) Index

The most indicative index on the change in the composition of target populations at Bar Ilan's colleges is the F.T.E calculation for each college. If in the 1970s and 1980s most students at the Extensions/Colleges were older student taking evening classes consisting of eclectic programs which included no more than six to eight weekly hours, the introduction of a full time academic curriculum in 1991/2 resulted in a transformation in the colleges' population and a proliferation of younger students. The number of hours studied by most students are equivalent to regular studies over a three-year program. The increase in F.T.E parameters points to the absorption of young students who came to the auspices colleges, thereby placing them in a single line with the independent colleges and other institutions offering a full time academic program. Table 39 presents the change in the number of students between 1994 and 1998 and the hours studied at each college.

Tab. 39: Rise in the number of students and F.T.E numbers in 1994–1998

	1993/4		1994/5		1995/6		1996/7		1997/8	
	Number of students	**F.T.E**	**Number of students**	**F.T.E**	**Number of students**	**F.T.E**	**Number of students**	**F.T.E**	**Number of students**	**F.T.E**
College of Judea & Samaria	218	250.3	491	622.5	789	937.1	767	902.1	846	951.1
Ashkelon College	495	320.8	900	700.1	1,211	1,017.5	1,485	1,364	1,583	1,447.6
Zefat College	392	325	499	501	656	617	739	715.6	792	785.8
Jordan Valley College	270	151.1	387	330.9	621	569	760	723	773	728.9
Western Galilee College			279	214.7	427	374.6	760	782.3	866	877.6

Data from the 1994–1998 F.T.E data file of Bar Ilan University's Colleges Administration. The 1994/5 data reported on 22 February 1994; the 1995/6 data reported on 1 August 1995; the 1996/7 data reported on 4 January 1996; the 1997/8 data reported on 17 March 1997; and the 1998/9 data reported on 29 April 1998.

Figure 11 presents the change in the two indices at all Bar Ilan Colleges.

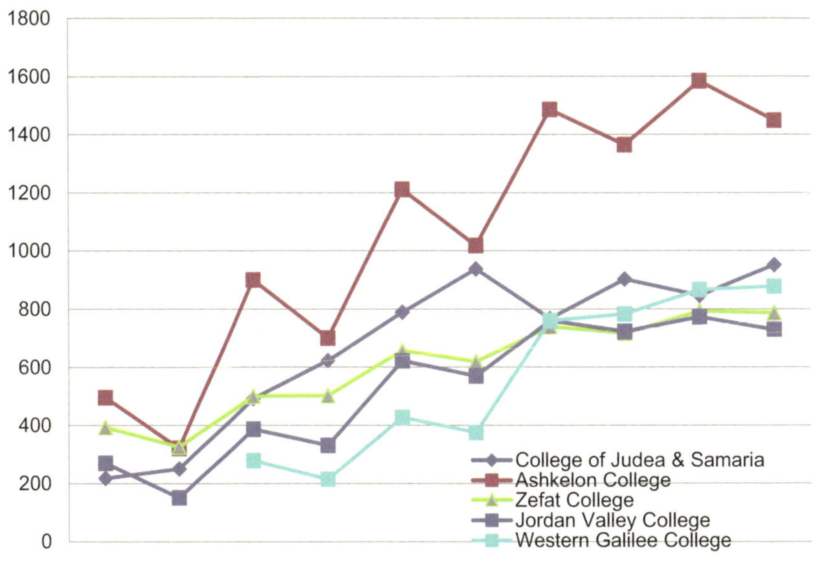

Fig. 11: F.T.E index, 1994–1998

Data from the Colleges Administration – Bar Ilan University, F.T.E data, 1994–1998 file.

Increase in the Scope of Studies at the Colleges

The previous indices show the increase in the hours studied by each student multiplied by the total number of students. The index pointing to the growth in scope of studies at the colleges during the examined period, meaning the first stage of the CHE's expansion program, consists of the number of hours available at each of Bar Ilan's colleges. Table 40 and Figure 12 illustrate the significant rise in the number of hours of study at each of the colleges, and the total number of courses offered each year.

Tab. 40: Scope of academic activities by courses and teaching hours at Bar Ilan's colleges

College	Parameters measuring scope of activity	1995/6	1999/00	Average annual change in %	Remarks
Ashkelon	Courses	398	883	22 %	
	Hours	654	1,315	19 %	
Jordan Valley	Courses	298	493	13.4 %	
	Hours	477	770	12.7 %	
Zefat	Courses	345	423	5.2 %	
	Hours	548	699	6.3 %	
Judea and Samaria	Courses	750	716	1.1 %-	The decline is a result of its independence
	Hours	1,182	912	6.2 %-	
Western Galilee	Courses	198	441	22.1 %	
	Hours	333	730	21.6 %	

Data from the 1994–1998 F.T.E data file of Bar Ilan University's Colleges Administration.

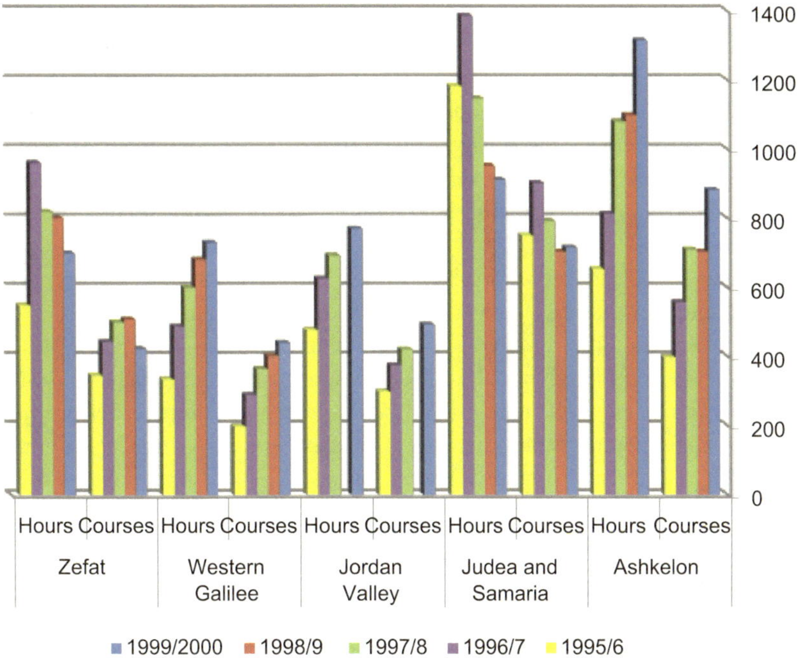

Fig. 12: Annual scope of academic activities hours at Bar Ilan's colleges

Tab. 41: List of study programs at Bar Ilan's colleges, 2000

Type of program	Ashkelon College	Zefat College	Jordan Valley College	College of Judea & Samaria	Western Galilee College
Multi-disciplinary program	11	13	15	12	7
Specialization program	5	3	2	1	0

Data from the 1995–2000 F.T.E data file of Bar Ilan University's Colleges Administration.

A further index pointing to the expansion of the scope of operations at Bar Ilan's colleges is the large number of departments offering full or nearly full academic programs in the second stage. As in the first stage to the system's expansion, also in the second stage Bar Ilan continued to develop multidisciplinary programs on behalf of the colleges. Alongside its multidisciplinary programs, Bar Ilan's management acted to obtain, in retrospect, approvals for specialization departments that had been studied at the Extensions before without the CHE's explicit approval due to their modest scope in their formative years. Through heavy pressure by the colleges and Bar Ilan, the Colleges Sub-Committee agreed to approve the university's specialization programs at the colleges. As stipulated by the committee, each of Bar Ilan's college would be able to offer a specialized study program provided that the university would commit to absorbing third year students at its main campus for six to eight weekly hours.[316] Upon obtaining the approval to offer these programs and expand available multidisciplinary ones, during 1996–2000 the number of departments at the colleges grew steadily, as shown in Table 41:

The specialization programs approved by the CHE's Sub-Committee included departments considered popular among young candidates, such as Business Administration, Psychology, Logistics, Criminology, and Computer Science which was offered for the first time at Ashkelon College,[317] and a few years later a number of similar programs were approved at the Jordan Valley and Zefat colleges as well.

The CHE/PBC's Response to the Alternative Academization of Bar Ilan's Colleges

The implementation of the plan for expanding the country's academic system in 1991–2000 focused the CHE/PBC's focus on the independent colleges while Regional Colleges remained under the general Ministry of Education budget without a proper development plan or well defined budgetary framework except for the ongoing budget derived from the ministry's diverse budgetary scope. The PBC's direct budgeting of independent colleges relied on a five year physical and academic development plan according to which the physical and academic development pace of each of the independent college was determined, alongside their integration in the general program for expanding the country's Higher Education System. Despite this discrimination Bar Ilan's colleges continued to develop in line with Bar Ilan's alternative academization program. All indices for assessing their scope of operation continued to point to a growth in the academic activities of these colleges.

316 Ashkelon College Archive, file 2000/1. The rules were presented in a letter from Ms. Michal Neumann's, Coordinator of the CHE's Sub-Committee, to the university's Rector, 7 January 1999.

317 Ibid, file 2000/2. As per letter from Ms. Michal Neumann, informing of the approval granted by the CHE's Colleges Sub-Committee for specialized degrees in Economics and Business Administration and in Library and Information Studies, first presented at the committee's meeting on 8 July 1996. The Departments of Psychology and Logistics were also approved at the committee's meeting on 20 July 1998.

However, the changes in the development indices of Bar Ilan's colleges did not integrate into the CHE/PBC's development plans, as the Council had failed to foresee such level of success. The non-inclusion of Bar Ilan's colleges in the colleges' academization plans in this decade seems surprising, as their clear success should have led to a national consideration of these institutions that continued to grow despite lack of planning. Moreover, the budget allocated for independent colleges so as to enable them to increase accessibility to higher education did not lead to the achievement of the targets defined for the first stage of the program. The total number of students in the four colleges that embarked upon academic independence was lower than the number of students at the colleges under Bar Ilan University's auspices. At the end of the first five year period (1995) there were 3,866 undergraduate students at Bar Ilan's colleges, and only 2,971 students at the four independent colleges that year, of which only 1,862 studied at the colleges' own academic undergraduate programs and the remaining 1,109 studied towards an undergraduate degree within the academic program under a university's auspices at those colleges. Moreover, the number of study programs offered by Bar Ilan's colleges exceeded those offered by the independent colleges, as presented above. Only by the end of the second five year period, in 2000, was there a notable growth in the number of undergraduate students at the independent colleges, while Bar Ilan's colleges continued with their development trend, as can be seen in Table 42.

Tab. 42: Students at Bar Ilan's colleges Vs. the independent colleges in 1995 and 2000

The	**1995**			**2000**		
independent colleges	**Auspices program**	**Independent program**	**Total**	**Auspices program**	**Independent program**	**Total**
Tel Aviv Yafo	–	925	925	–	2,168	2,168
Yesreel Valley College	100	745	845	–	1,996	1,996
Tel Chai College	161	192	353	20	950	970
Sapir	848	–	848	1,299	843	2,142
Total:	1,109	1,862	2,971	1,319	5,957	7,276
Bar Ilan's Colleges						
Ashkelon	1,261	–	1,261	2,060	–	2,060
Jordan Valley	650		650	804		804
Zefat	661		661	666		666
Judea and Samaria	823		823	896		896
Western Galilee	471		471	945		945
	3,866	–	3,866	5,371		5,371

Data on the independent colleges from: Barshad & Biham (2000; 2001; 2003; 2005): 51–53; Mendelzweig (1995; 1998): 52–53. The data on the colleges under Bar Ilan University's auspices from: The Colleges' Administration's F.T.E data files, 1994–1998.

The accelerated development of the auspices colleges and the continued growing demand for higher education forced the CHE/PBC to integrate them in the new 2001–2005 five year plan. The first response to developments at Bar Ilan's colleges since the formation of the program for expanding accessibility to higher education was expressed in the CHE's Colleges Sub-Committee's decision of 8 May 1995 to recommend that the CHE Chairperson and Minister of Education appoint an experts committee to examine the level and quality of the academic and administrative activities at the Regional Colleges and the validity of the approvals they have been granted.[318] In 1995 Bar Ilan's colleges consisted of about 40 % of all Regional Colleges, and it was clear to both Bar Ilan and to the managements of the colleges under its auspices that the committee would focus on them. The Minister's letter of appointment to committee members confirmed this evaluation: "The committee further requested that its first inspections would be held at the Ashkelon and Jordan Valley Regional Colleges".[319] Prof. Anita Shapira from Tel Aviv University was elected to chair the committee,[320] and its members included Prof. Ozer Shield from the University of Haifa[321] and Prof. Arik Cohen from the Hebrew University.[322]

The Shapira Committee and its Recommendations

As stated in the Committee's letter of appointment, the Ashkelon College was inspected first, being the largest institution with the most academic opportunities. Later on the university's and the colleges managements understood that the

318 Ibid, file 1995. Letter from the substitute secretary of the CHE to the Rector of Bar Ilan University and the manager of Ashkelon College, 10 July 1995.

319 Ibid, Shapira Committee file. The committee's letter of appointment, signed by Amnon Rubinstein, Minister of Education and Chairperson of the CHE, 22 June 1995.

320 Professor of the History of Israel at Tel Aviv University. Head of the Institute for the Study of Zionism in Israel. Awarded the Israel Prize in 2008 in Jewish history. Member of the CHE, 1987–1990. Dean of the Faculty of Humanities at Tel Aviv University, 1990–1995.

321 Professor of Psychology and Chief Scientist of the Ministry of Education, 1972–1976. Head of the School of Education at the University of Haifa. Rector of the university 1978–1990 and its president until 1993. Moved to Ariel and served as the first President of the Ariel University Center, currently the Ariel University. Served as member of the CHE and PBC and as Chairperson of the CHE Colleges Committee as of 2002 until his death in 2006.

322 Professor (Emeritus) of Sociology at Tel Aviv University. Social scientist and member of the Anita Shapira Committee that evaluated the status of Bar Ilan's Extensions.

committee had aimed, through the Ashkelon College, to assess the overall quality of Bar Ilan University's work at the colleges, and the scope of its academic auspices. Immediately upon commencement of its work, committee members realized that their evaluation of Ashkelon would serve as a model for the inspection of all other Regional Colleges and a prototype for examining the overall relationship between Bar Ilan University and the colleges under its auspices, and therefore there was no need to examine the other colleges, not even the Jordan Valley College which had been scheduled second in the committee's letter of appointment. The committee began its work by demanding Bar Ilan University's Rector Prof. Moshe Kave and the College CEO to present the committee with answers to 16 basic questions that included the wording of the auspices agreement, details of financial arrangements between the Parties, details of the academic structure, details of the programs offered at the colleges and their certification, and a list of faculty members and their terms of employment.[323] A year after the committee was appointed, and having visited Ashkelon College and Bar Ilan University, it submitted a draft report for the Rector's response in anticipation of the discussion at the CHE's Colleges Sub-Committee. The draft report pointed to the following findings:

1. In the report's introduction, the committee mentions that the management of the PBC did not present the national plan for expansion of the academic system and the Regional College's role in such plan, and therefore the committee had not attended to distinguish between the colleges that gained academic independence and the Regional Colleges that remained outside the five year plan of the 1991–2000 decade.
2. Despite barriers set by the CHE for opening study programs at the colleges, the Ashkelon College attempted to open study programs that are also in high demand in the center of the country, therefore also attracting candidates from the center.
3. The committee noted the university's close and multi-faceted supervision of the college, which included terms of admission, accreditation of academic courses and the academic faculty teaching at the college. For the first time ever, the committee's report gave official accreditation to Bar Ilan University's work at its Extensions/Colleges:

323 Ashkelon College Archive, Shapira Committee file. Prof. Anita Shapira's letter, 16 July 1995.

> The committee also positively notes Bar Ilan University's commitment to nurturing the chain of colleges affiliated to it in general, and the Ashkelon College in particular. The committee congratulates Bar Ilan University for its great success in nurturing the chain of colleges and especially the impressive rise in the number of students at the college in the past couple of years (Ibid).

4. However, the report does point to a number of difficulties in the auspices structure, as detailed below:
   - 4.1. The committee found that the vast majority of academic faculty members are not residents of the area but lecturers from the center of the country, many of whom belong to the university's faculty. According to committee members, this situation undermines the chances of establishing a local elite that would form the basis for the institution's academic faculty in future.
   - 4.2. As the college is not involved in research, there are concerns that the academic level of faculty members, who are not exposed to the latest research in their fields, would eventually diminish, a situation which could ultimately also undermine their level of teaching.
   - 4.3. Most of the study programs offered at the college are part of a multi-disciplinary program, with the main field of study mentioned. The committee has found that the university did not receive the CHE's approval to mention the main field of study (the major) in the multidisciplinary program. According to the committee's recommendation, the CHE must supervise the implementation of the decision to grant a multi-disciplinary degree without noting the main field of study, similarly to the general B.A program offered at Tel Aviv University.[324]
   - 4.4. The committee found that the specialization programs offered at the college do not correspond with the CHE's policy of nurturing unique professional programs at colleges, rather than theoretical ones. Also in

---

324 Prof. Shapira informed us that as the general B.A program at Tel Aviv University is successful, there is no reason to worry about the success of a general program at Ashkelon. The academic manager of the college and myself were surprised that the Chairperson of the committee compares between an institution permitted to only offer a general program and a university that offers all academic programs recognized in Israel, as well as a general one. This position points to the elitist approach that was typical of the senior actors of the country's academic field. Even when they become convinced of the need to open the system to new populations, they offer them non-prestigious programs, or in any event programs that would not resemble those reserved for the field's elite.

this regard the committee recommended retaining the CHE's policy, including reinforcement of professional programs.

As aforesaid, the committee made do with inspecting the Ashkelon Regional College, despite the instructions it had been given in its letter of appointment. Thus, with the submittal of its report on the Ashkelon College, the committee essentially concluded its role. The Shapira Committee recommendations continue to point to the existence of the same elitist approach that we have seen as of the 1950s until the 1990s. For many years this elitist group of academics refused to accept real change in the academic system and ignored parallel changes that had taken place in the western world. Even when they did show a certain openness, it had been limited to general and multi-disciplinary programs, rather than specialized ones, as explained by the Stratification theory. The prevention of specialization programs and the demand to make do with general and professional programs point to the country's academic elite's approach towards residents of the periphery – that these populations can make do with caregiving professions such as nursing, teaching, and others that are not at the top echelon of employment, and therefore do not contribute to social mobility as do other free and more prestigious professions.

The committee's report was submitted to the Colleges Sub-Committee, which commenced implementing its conclusions. Members of the Sub-Committee included Prof. Yaacov Rand from Bar Ilan University,[325] Prof. Shield from the University of Haifa and a representative of the Ministry of Education, Mr. Abraham Schienfeld. The chairperson of the committee at the time was Prof. Ozer Shield, who had also been a member of the Shapira Committee. The sub-committee's first conclusion was that new procedures need to be defined, the old ones refreshed, and the Regional Colleges entered into an operational framework that would make it easier for the Sub-Committee to supervise the work done at the colleges. Committee members realized that the university's direct supervision over its colleges is not enough, and that a mechanism is needed for direct supervision of the university and indirect supervision of the colleges despite the absence of a formal relationship between the Regional Colleges and the CHE/PBC. Indirect supervision over colleges was achieved through coordination with the budgeting authority, meaning the Colleges Division at the Ministry of Education, which had decided to only budget academic programs at colleges that had received the CHE's approval. This decision is an example of the CHE/PBC's indirect supervision of colleges which at the time were outside the PBC's

325 Prof. Emeritus of Education at Bar Ilan University, recipient of the Israel prize for Education in 2001.

budgetary framework. However, most of the Sub-Committee's efforts were dedicated to direct supervision of the university. The supervision of the university's operations at the colleges was achieved on two levels:

1. A renewed examination of the entire operation taking place at the colleges and its preparation for future inasmuch as it corresponded to the CHE"s plan at the colleges.
2. Approval of new activities at the colleges would be granted only as part of the CHE's general policy for colleges.

The CHE's Policy in Light of the Shapira Committee's Recommendations: A Renewed Examination of Bar Ilan Colleges

1. **Limiting the multidisciplinary BA diploma:** The Shapira Committee's recommendation to continue to encourage multidisciplinary degree programs at Ashkelon College turned out to be a mixed blessing: while the recommendation qualified the range of programs in that category, it also revoked the right to continue to specify the major field of study in the graduate's diploma. The committee concluded that Bar Ilan's approval to hold multidisciplinary BA studies did not include the right to specify the specific program studied, and in doing so the university deviated from the approval it had been granted. The committee further concluded that specifying the major field of study in the degree is misleading, as people may think that the degree includes a specialization in that area. The committee recommended making do with the existence of a multidisciplinary program that grants its graduates a diploma specifying the Faculty of studies without mentioning a major. For instance, a multidisciplinary diploma may be entitled: "Graduate of the Faculty of Social Sciences/Humanities" without specifying the specific major, contrary to the university's approach, which favored the following title: "Graduate of the multidisciplinary program: Economics/Criminology", etc. In his letter to Bar Ilan University the Chairperson of the CHE's Colleges Sub-Committee demanded that Bar Ilan immediately cease specifying the major field of study in its B.A diplomas. The Chairperson also specified the following limitations of the diploma: The degree will be general, without mentioning the major field of study, as had been the custom until them. As a gesture of goodwill in view of the expected decline in registrations to the program he proposed providing

graduates a Record of Studies document, in addition to the diploma, in which the courses studied would be specified.[326]

2. **Limiting specialized studies at the colleges' campuses:** In its conclusions regarding areas of specialization offered by the college, the Shapira committee emphasized that it does not recommended specialized studied at the colleges under the university's auspices. According to the recommendations, Regional Colleges should make do with general or professional studies addressing the social needs of the region in which the college operates. The implementation of this recommendation would have led to shutting down departments that had already been in operation at the colleges, under the university's auspices. The university's management argued that throughout the colleges' years of operation, there had been no requirement for any special approvals at the Extensions, and the fact that the university's own department in that area had been approved sufficed and left the decision in the hands of the university as to whether to offer the same department at the Extensions. As the colleges, being Extensions of the university, had gained such approval, the approval given to the university should be valid also for the colleges operating under the university's auspices.[327] The managements of the university and the colleges resisted the implementation of this recommendation, and following further negotiations the CHE's Sub-Committee tended to agree to grant a posteriori approval for all departments operating at the colleges, provided that the university submits a list of departments and a request for their fast-track approval. About six years following the establishment of a number of academic departments, the university and the colleges under its auspices presented their entire programs for the CHE's official approval. However, the approval eventually granted was limited and included only part of year at the college, with students required to complete six to eight weekly hours at the university campus. A further limitation of the approval was the Sub-Committee's decision to require the university to mention in graduates' diplomas that they had studied at the college, thereby creating a distinction between the degree studied at the university and the same degree at the college. As of 1997 students were required to complete their third year at the university campus.
3. **Limiting the opening of new departments:** The close supervision of the Colleges Sub-Committee during these years included a limitation to opening

326 Bar Ilan University Archive, Rector's office, CHE file. Letter from Prof. Ozer Shield to Prof. Yehuda Friedlander, the University's Rector, 7 May 1996.

327 Interview with Dr. Dov Levitan, 13 December 2007.

new departments, a practice which the university had done freely in the past. It was now no longer possible to open a new department and obtain a posteriori approval for it. Instead, the new regulations required full application of the rules for opening new departments, which included the requirement to employ local faculty members and to examine the department's necessity within the specific region of the college. The university's applications were evaluated based on the academic activity of other institutions operating in the same region. The limitation on opening further departments was implemented as of the university's request in 1996 to hold a multidisciplinary B.A program with a major in Economics and Criminology at the Western Galilee College. The launching of the multidisciplinary program in Economics at the Western Galilee College was stipulated upon the closing of a similar program offered as part of the still remaining programs under the auspices of the University of Haifa. The Criminology program was not approved either due to "a regional planning framework of budgeted studies".[328]

Another type of limitation was the prohibition to open programs at the colleges which do not have a parallel department at the university. for instance, the application to offer public communication studies at the Western Galilee College was not approved by the Sub-Committee, which argued that there is no parallel program at the university, even though the request was part of the multidisciplinary B.A program regarding which the Sub-Committee had ruled that the major field of study would not be mentioned on the diploma.

These decisions by the Sub-Committee[329] slowed Bar Ilan's Colleges' alternative academization process, on three levels:

1. **Undermining the image of the multidisciplinary degree:** The instruction not to specify the major field of study in the diploma undermined the attractiveness of the degree in the eyes of students and candidates, that gradually began to avoid this program.
2. **Undermining the possibility to hold studies in new areas of specialization:** Meeting the demand to recruit local faculty members whose main work is at the college was very challenging for Bar Ilan's colleges, which until then had been assisted by the university's teaching faculty. The demand to absorb local

328 Bar Ilan University Archive, Colleges Administration file, 1995. Letter from the Secretary of the Sub-Committee, 13 June 1995.

329 Archive of the Association of Regional Colleges in Israel, file 1999. Details of the limitations as stated in the letter from the Colleges Sub-Committee coordinator to the university's Rector, 7 January 1999.

faculty members required special preparations and an extensive transition period. In practice, the colleges did not meet this demand, and for the next three to four years they made do with the multidisciplinary degree, which despite the decline in its attractiveness was a central part of the academic activities at the colleges until 2005.

3. **Undermining the prestige of the specialized programs:** The CHE's demand to specify in the diplomas of students of the specialized programs that they had studied at the college, undermined the relative advantage which Bar Ilan's Colleges had presented to candidates – namely, the advantage of studying in a small institution where they would enjoy personal attention and ultimately gain a diploma of a large university. Specifying the place of study created a distinction between the diploma of a graduate of the college and that of a graduate of the same university. Moreover, the fact that the provision was applied in retrospect resulted in strong protests among students as well as legal suits by students' representatives against the university and the college.

These limitations on the university's operations at the colleges and the Sub-Committee's close supervision as of the mid 1990s led the managements of the university and the colleges to conclude that the CHE aims to directly undermine the university's expansion and its control of a large number of colleges, and for this reason the university's operations are being directly and indirectly restricted in various ways. The undermining of the colleges was in fact an indirect blow to the university itself, aimed at facilitating the development of independent colleges.[330] This can be noted from remarks by the colleges managers and specifically a memo prepared by the head of the university's Colleges Administration, Dr. Dov Levitan, towards a discussion held by the university's management on the CHE's new instructions and ways of coping with them. Based on conversations he had held with relevant persons, the head of the university's Colleges Administration reached the following conclusions:

1. The independent colleges have not met the aims stipulated in the first and second five-year plans, while the colleges under Bar Ilan's auspices have been successful in increasing their number of students and programs.

330 From the following interviews: Dr. Levitan, Head of Bar Ilan University's Colleges Administration, 13 December 2007; Prof. Harvey Babkofh, Head of the Colleges System Administration at Bar Ilan University (parallel to Dean of Faculty), 17 August 2009.

2. The independent degree offered by the independent colleges has still not gained a high level of prestige among young candidates, while the degrees offered by Bar Ilan at its colleges are university degrees held in high regard among students. The conclusion was clear: Students will continue to prefer a university degree and the accelerated development will continue, as will the struggle against the university and its colleges. As proof he notes the PBC's newly formed idea of stopping payments to the university for its auspices.
3. PBC's management does not wish to encourage students to attend Bar Ilan's colleges and instead aims to refer them to the independent colleges. The amendment to the CHE law (amendment number 10) which had been legislated against their better judgment, stipulates equal treatment to the colleges under Bar Ilan's auspices, and therefore they will try to deviate most of the students to the independent colleges so as to strengthen them at their expense.[331]
4. The heads of the CHE/PBC are suspicious towards Bar Ilan's "Academic imperialism", especially following the inclusion of the Western Galilee College in the list of colleges under the university's auspices. This and the growth in the number of students at all Bar Ilan's colleges created an extensive academic institution that controls the future of five other academic institutions and which competes with the CHE for accessibility to higher education in the periphery. Although the inclusion of the Western Galilee College was achieved with the CHE's approval, it was given as a last resort and for the sole purpose of supporting the only peripheral college that remained without academic auspices.

Dr. Levitan proposed acting on a number of levels to stop the discrimination against the university and the colleges under its auspices:

1. Request that the Rector hold a discussion with the heads of the CHE/PBC, the Minister of Education, the Chairperson of the Colleges Sub-Committee and the minister's advisor on higher education.
2. A request to increase the involvement of the Knesset's education committee in the situation.
3. A plea to the Supreme Court to expose the policy of discriminating between the independent colleges and the auspices colleges.
4. Exposing the problem in the media.

---

331 Bar Ilan University archive. Colleges Administration file, 1995. Letter from the head of the Colleges System Administration, 18 June 1995.

The recommendation to approach the CHE/PBC's decision makers had been accepted, and four days later the Rector Prof. Kave approached the Minister of Education Prof. Amnon Rubinstein, demanding to stop the budgetary discrimination and the practice of overlooking Bar Ilan's colleges in the CHE's plans. In his letter to the minister Prof. Kave reiterated the minister's promise that the fact that Bar Ilan's Colleges are absent from the CHE's plans does not necessarily mean that their status or budgeting would be undermined.[332] The head of the colleges system at the university also sent a similar letter to the chairperson of the Colleges Sub-Committee at the CHE, demanding accreditation of all programs that have been taught for years at the colleges, including those proposed at the new college under the university's auspices, the Western Galilee College. His concluded his letter by expressing a clear opposition to the mapping idea raised at the Sub-Committee regarding the Western Galilee College. He emphasized that the mapping of study programs is an attempt, albeit a forced one, to cause harm to Bar Ilan in order to promote other colleges.[333]

In parallel, the CHE continued to publish its plans which ignored the colleges under Bar Ilan's auspices:

A. A letter from the general manager of the CHE/PBC on 26 March 1995 outlined the CHE's planning forecasts, which did not include the colleges under Bar Ilan's auspices. The forecast that expected 20,000 new students in the year 2000 led to well a well-defined plan: 10,000 new students will be absorbed at the independent colleges, 6,000 at the independent technological colleges, and 4,000 at teacher-training colleges. According to this forecast the universities would not grow, and only if the plan would not succeed in increasing the number of students at the independent colleges, the surplus would be directed to universities and the colleges operating under their auspices:

> The universities would only grow in the advanced degrees (about 4,000 students), and only if necessary. In addition, the number of undergraduate students will grow if the entire increase cannot be directed to the colleges. The growth at the universities also includes the Regional Colleges that are academically adjacent to the universities and for which there will be no increase in the number of students beyond their number in 1995.[334]

---

332 Ibid, letter from the Rector to the Minister of Education, 22 June 1995.

333 Ibid, Memorandum dated 18 June 1995.

334 Association of Regional Colleges Archive, file 1995. Letter from Guri Zilca, CEO of the CHE/PBC, to Avikam Beller from the Ministry of Finance Budgets Department, 26 March 1995.

B. The CHE's July 1997 newsletter included the "five stages" plan, which also ignored the auspices colleges. The plan reviewed the development of Israel's Higher Education System and described its continued evolving over five development stages:

1. The seven universities. In 1997, a total of about 98,000 students attended the country's seven existing universities, of which about 5,700 at the Regional Colleges under the academic auspices of the universities. This stage reached its total capacity, meaning that future growth would be possible only in advanced degrees.
2. Specialized professional colleges such as the Shenkar School of Textile, the Bezalel Academy of Art and the Academy of Music.
3. The publicly funded colleges: Four general and three technological colleges.
4. Teacher-training colleges undergoing an academization process. These colleges will continue to grow.
5. Non-Publicly Funded colleges teaching highly demanded professions such as Law and Business. These will continue to develop as they release the CHE from the need to budget these professions in the national system.[335]

In conclusion, the struggle of Bar Ilan's Colleges in the 1990s illustrates the continued struggle of the senior actors of the field against Bar Ilan University and its independent initiatives to try and influence the image of academics in the periphery, in place of the CHE/PBC. In fact, this struggle was concluded only in the past decade, with the finalization of Bar Ilan's Colleges' academization program, and the severance of the university's official relationship with them.

The CHE's plan for expanding the academic system was initiated at a political period that was highly inconvenient for Bar Ilan. Initial ideas for the academization of the colleges were raised at the CHE at the start of the Tenure of Minister of Education Shulamit Aloni and were formed into a comprehensive program during the tenure of her successor, Prof. Amnon Rubinstein. This turning point in the Ministry of Education and the fact that for the first time in the history of the State of Israel a government had been formed without the religious camp, did not assist Bar Ilan in utilizing the changes in the system in favor of the colleges under its auspices, as it had been able to achieve in the days of Zevulun Hammer of the NRP as Minister of Education. Despite the fact that five Regional Colleges (about 40 % of all Regional Colleges in Israel) operated under

335 The Council for Higher Education Newsletter, Planning and Budgeting Committee, issue number 9, July 1997: 5–6.

the auspices of Bar Ilan University, none of them were included in the first phase of the national program for academization of colleges. Bar Ilan's Colleges, which had been largely overlooked, had to search for an alternative for the academization of their competitors and found a sympathetic ear in the university's management and a willingness to go forward in the struggle for academization. In retrospect, bar Ilan's experience in operating studies outside campus and its social approach were beneficial in its struggle for promoting higher education in the periphery. Based on the research material and my personal involvement in the process I can safely say that the success of Bar Ilan's Colleges can be credited to the university.

First, the CHE's practice of overlooking the university that had granted its auspices to five colleges encouraged the university to fight to prove the justness of its social path. The success of the academization of the other colleges threatened to destroy Bar Ilan's Colleges for lack of suitable budgets for academic development. The absence of a response by Bar Ilan would have led to its defeat in the struggle for its colleges.

Second, it is impossible to ignore the fact that the success of the colleges was expected to infuse significant funds to the university for its academic auspices. The higher education budget at the time was among the largest ever, and Bar Ilan wanted to ensure its share in the budgetary distribution to institutions in the periphery. But the CHE viewed the expansion of Bar Ilan's Colleges in the mid 1990s as a threat to its academization program, and in fact the data from Bar Ilan's Colleges pointed, as explained above, to a high success rate.

Third, their success emphasized the failure of other institutions and of the CHE's program in general, and the CHE preferred to take advantage of its authority so as to block such success. To prove this argument we have shown that only in 1995, thirty years following the establishment of the first Extension at Ashkelon in 1965, a committee was appointed to examine Bar Ilan's activities at the colleges. This committee, the Shapira Committee, comprised of representatives of competing universities, adopted an elitist approach that supported the CHE's historical position by which Bar Ilan's Colleges should not be permitted to teach specialized academic programs, not even those that were available at the time at independent colleges. The committee believed that studies should be permitted towards a General B.A (BGS) degree, or at the most professions such as teaching or nursing. Moreover, the committee appointed to examine the work of the auspices colleges in general, in practice only examined Bar Ilan's Colleges, and Ashkelon in particular, due to its proximity to the Sha'ar Hanegev – Sapir College which was included in the CHE's academization program. The Ashkelon College, which had led Bar Ilan's Colleges in its size and scope of its programs, posed a harsh competition to the Sha'ar Hanegev College and to the CHE's academization program. All evaluations made at the university and at Ashkelon college prior to the committee's arrival foretasted its actual outcome: The committee established to assess the Regional Colleges will not visit colleges operating under the auspices of other universities, and even worse, would arrive only at Ashkelon College due to its size, although its letter of appointment explicitly mentions the name of the second college to be evaluated after Ashkelon – The Jordan Valley College.

The committee's recommendations led to a wave of retroactive instructions, including a prohibition to continue to operate programs that had been offered at the colleges for years; a prohibition to note the major field of study in graduates' diplomas; the obligation to specify the place of study in specialized diplomas; a prohibition to open new programs and a prohibition to submit to the CHE's approval new specialized programs available in any similar institution in the country. The CHE, for its part, claimed that the reason for the retroactive application of its instructions was that Bar Ilan did not obtain approvals for such activities. Even if this argument is true, the application of provisions to activities that have existed for over 30 years points to the CHE's complete disregard of Bar Ilan's Extensions which had been in operation for many years, as well as to the Council's long struggle against the Extensions idea, therefore also making it unjustified for it to have acted as it had. The allegation as to the enforcement of a new order is highly surprising due to the timing of this new arrangement on the backdrop of the tendency to promote other colleges.

The implementation of some of the decisions undermined the image and credibility of the colleges and the university. Lawsuits were issued against the colleges and the university by students who felt deceived following the retroactive application of the instruction to refrain from mentioning the major field of study on the diploma and to obligate the university to specify the college name. The struggle against the CHE's instructions continued until some of them were revoked while others were differed or updated. However, this struggle and concerns regarding the formation of two types of colleges ultimately resulted in the colleges being embraced by the CHE in the beginning of 2000. This process will be discussed below.

Chapter 15 The Transition of Regional Colleges to PBC Funding

Although the initial program for expanding the country's academic system only included 3 of a total of 12 Regional Colleges, and despite the fact that the Program's basic assumption had been that the academic system reached its optimal number of academic institutions, eight years later (October 1998) the PBC agreed to include all Regional Colleges under its budgetary responsibility. This decision had many implications on the future of Regional Colleges in general and Bar Ilan's colleges in particular, and on the image of the country's academic system towards the new millennium. While the decision was essentially a technical one, consisting of the transfer of budgets from the Ministry of Education to the PBC, in practice it forced the integration of Regional Colleges within a larger academic system, with an even larger future expansion potential. This turning point was a result of a long process that began at the CHE in the 1970s and was fraught with high and low points in the Council's coping with the global phenomenon of the expansion of higher education. The peak of the process took place in the beginning of the 1990s, when a number of factors external to the CHE (described in the previous chapter), forced the council to provide answers to the growing demand for accessibility of higher education to new populations.

Since the approval of the master plan for colleges in 1992, the country's academic system became a binary one, replacing the monolithic system that had been prevalent until that period. A further change which the CHE had not foreseen and had become apparent in the 1990s was the failure of the new academic colleges to meet their performance targets for the years 1991–2000. On a backdrop of mounting public and political pressures on the CHE, Bar Ilan's Colleges continued to reap successes, even though they were not included in the CHE's academization program, and the Council was eventually left with no choice but to stop ignoring them. Moreover, the continued growing demand also forced the CHE/PBC to include the other Regional Colleges left outside its academization program, contrary to previous conclusions by which the system had reached its optimal number of institutions. Added to the above was the geographic deployment of the Regional Colleges and their contribution to the expansion of accessibility in the periphery. This allowed the CHE to bring academization to places located far from the country's main study centers without special investment while also serving to improve its public image which had long since been ingrained as alienated from the country's social periphery.[336]

In retrospect, steps taken by Bar Ilan's founders and their Extensions idea were ahead of their time and to a large extent reflected the global push to bring academy also to peripheral regions. The idea adopted from religious academic institutions in the United States was well suited to an immigrants society. The CHE's policy of encouraging the expansion of higher education through auspices had also positioned Bar Ilan in a better position: despite the CHE's disregard of Bar Ilan's colleges in its master plan for colleges, Bar Ilan continued with greater vigor to develop the academic side of the colleges under its auspices, and despite the CHE/PBC's struggle against the university, its colleges were more successful than those operating under the CHE's budget. Only when the CHE realized it was unable to stop this trend, as Bar Ilan's Colleges amounted to a significant part of the overall activity of colleges in the country, was the council forced to change its position and take Bar Ilan's Colleges under its wing, together with the other Regional Colleges – a decision that transformed the country's academic system beyond recognition. The decision to include them was preceded by extensive public lobbying and a variety of considerations among all parties involved:

1. **The Council for Higher Education (CHE):** While the Regional Colleges operated under the Ministry of Education's full responsibility and were included in its annual budget, supervision over the academic program at the colleges was indirectly implemented by the CHE's Colleges Sub-Committee. Contrary to the Division for Training Teaching Personnel at the Ministry of Education, upon its establishment the Colleges Unit operated under the Culture Division at the Ministry of Education and Culture, with its budget being organizationally linked to the budget of the country's theaters and cultural institutions. Thus, the budget for each college was determined based on the number of academic hours allocated for each institution, which was arbitrarily allocated according to the ministry's overall budgetary constraints. With the growing scope of operations at the colleges and the inclusion of Bar Ilan's Colleges towards the end of the 1980s, their allocation to the culture division at the Ministry became artificial and impractical. The Colleges Unit, charged with the task of supervising colleges, budgeting them and defining relevant procedures, was not allocated the necessary organizational tools to carry out its tasks. Work procedures were coordinated and defined in consultation with the CHE/PBC.

336 The CHE's image among the political system was discussed in the explanations to the proposals for amendments to the CHE law. See page 219–221.

Even in cases in which the Colleges Unit was assisted by external counsel, its dependence on PBC was still high.[337] Consequently, the CHE/PBC's involvement in the Regional Colleges gradually increased with the growing scope of academic activities at the colleges, as well as the number of students applying during the 1990s. Academic Departments at colleges were budgeted only following the approval of the CHE's Colleges Sub-Committee, and the budgeting rules for these departments as for others were coordinated with PBC based on tariffs for each field of study and on the number of students in each field. Therefore, as the CHE had set the academic rules for accreditation of programs to be budgeted at the colleges, and the PBC indirectly defined the budgeting method, it was only logical that the budgeting of academic programs at the colleges be transferred to the PBC's budgeting and professional supervision.

2. **The Ministry of Education:** Professor Ami Volansky, who for many years served as advisor to Ministers of Education on higher education policy and as the ministry's Deputy Director General for Policy Planning, notes in his book about higher education in Israel (2005) that the CHE's supervision on the colleges forced the Ministry to increase the budget allocated to colleges so as to improve their academic facilities for teaching purposes. An additional budget of ten million shekels was needed in order to maintain the existing academic programs at colleges. In the absence of such a budget, it was suggested to the Minister of Education at the time, Yitzhak Levi,[338] to transfer the colleges to the PBC's budget. This suggestion had been coordinated with the colleges' representatives, who welcomed it, viewing the transition to PBC budgeting as an important step on the path to academic independence. In the absence of resources and direct supervision, the Ministry of Education sealed the fate of the Regional Colleges at the ministry. The CHE's indirect supervision and the lack of suitable budgets within the Ministry of Education reduced the ministry's ability to impact the development of the colleges, and therefore their transition to the CHE was a necessary step. This of course was in contrast to the ministry's persistent holding on to the teacher-training colleges, and its long term opposition to their being transferred to the PBC/CHE, despite

337 The Ministry of Education was assisted by Eliyahu Israeli, former Deputy Director at the Ministry of Education. The budgeting method that he had developed for the Colleges Unit was also coordinated with PBC representatives.

338 Among the leaders of the National Religious Party (NRP) and its Chairperson as of 1998. Left the party towards the elections for the 16th Knesset and jointed the National Union party founded by former members of the NRP, Moledet and Herut parties.

the fact that the largest and most well established ones were in favor of such transition.

3. **The Regional Colleges:** The position of the Regional Colleges was presented at national forums by the Chairperson of the Association of Colleges, Moshe Nativ.[339] In all my discussions with representatives of the PBC, the Ministry of Finance and the Ministry of Education, they all reported the colleges unanimous position in favor of their transition to the CHE/PBC's supervision and budgeting. This uniform position of all colleges managers was a result of two factors: The first involved their public image and was based on the assumption that belonging to the national authority dedicated to budgeting and development of higher education in the country positions colleges in a single line with universities. The Ministry of Education, mainly dedicated to Primary and Secondary education, did not offer the colleges the aura they were seeking, i.e., an organizational positioning alongside the universities. The second factor was a professional one – the Colleges Unit did not offer professional manpower and failed to achieve a suitable organizational position at the Ministry of Education – although it had been upgraded to become an independent division – and was unable to provide a level of professional service suited to the colleges' needs.[340] PBC is considered a professional body possessing the specialized professional tools specifically created for budgeting higher education. Moreover, the absence of professional manpower at the Colleges Division and the lack of a budget suited to the wave of development of colleges in the 1990s often led to threats of strikes by colleges managers.[341] Demands to compare the conditions of Regional Colleges to the independent colleges under the CHE/

339 IDF Major-General and Commander of the IDF's Manpower Directorate in 1978–1983, Director General of the Jewish Agency in the beginning of the 1990's, member of the Tal Committee, President of the Council for a Beautiful Israel, Chairperson of the Amigur Board and Chairman of the Association of Colleges in 1997–2005.

340 Association of Colleges Archive, file 1997. In his letter to the CEO of the Ministry of Education on 10 February 1997, the Chairperson of the Association of Regional Colleges, Moshe Nativ, expressed the colleges' dissatisfaction from the functioning and authorities held by the Ministry of Education's Colleges Unit.

341 Ibid. Many letters sent to the Minister of Education, the Minister of Finance, the Minister of Foreign Affairs (David Levi), and the Chairperson of the Knesset's Education Committee, outline the discrimination of Regional Colleges as opposed to independent and teacher-training colleges budgeted by the Ministry of Education: Letter from the Chairperson of the Association of Colleges to the Chairperson of the Education Committee; letter from the Chairperson of the Association of Colleges to the Chairperson of the Forum of Regional Councils; letter

PBC's budgeting were left unanswered due to lack of budgets and the fact that these matters were considered low priority at the Ministry of Education. Of the entire group of Regional Colleges, the physical and academic development of the three colleges that embarked upon academic independence served as an example for the advantages of transitioning to the PBC's budgeting and proof of the justness of the Regional Colleges' clear position, that their place is with the CHE/PBC.

4. **The political system and the Ministry of Finance:** Demands to expand the Higher Education System were voiced more and more strongly at the Knesset as general demand for higher education grew, and it became apparent that the existing institutions are unable to meet the growing demand. The pressure to increase accessibility crossed partisan lines, and a range of legislation initiatives to increase accessibility to higher education were discussed towards the end of the 1990s. The first initiative, already mentioned above, was by Knesset members Silvan Shalom (the Likud party) and Hagai Merom (the Labor party and member of the Central Movement towards the end of the 1990s) to establish a separate council for Higher Education for colleges. From this proposal we can learn of the prevailing atmosphere at the Israeli parliament at the time:

> The Council for Higher Education has failed to read the map correctly [...] Instead of fulfilling its task efficiently and swiftly, it aimed to destroy the colleges while delaying their accreditation, time after time, and while regulating draconian accreditation rules... The Council for Higher Education, therefore, is an antithesis for pluralism in higher education, as it has become the gatekeeper of universities, rather than of higher education in Israel.[342]

In January 2000 Knesset member Meir Shitrit (Likud) presented a bill for encouraging higher education in Israel. According to the preface to the bill:

> The purpose of this law is to provide anyone interested a fair opportunity to acquire higher education... As the proportion of holders of a higher education in Israel grows, society would be able to meet with greater confidence the challenges of the future.[343]

---

from the Chairperson of Regional Councils to the Ministers of Finance, Education and Foreign affairs, all dated 28 October, 1997. A similar letter was sent to the Ministers on the same day from the Chairperson of the Council of Development Towns.

342 Education bill (terms of admission to institutions of higher education), 1994, bill number 379 c. Knesset website: http://www.knesset.gov.il/laws/heb/template.asp – Retrieved 30 January 2010.

343 Bill for encouraging higher education in Israel, 2000, bill number p/1246. Knesset website, ibid.

Following strong pressures by Knesset members, the Ministry of Finance began to formulate a position by which the solution for expanding accessibility to higher education is to increase the scope of colleges, rather than of universities. The idea to increase universities' capacity to absorb students required increasing PBC's budget to the universities according to tariffs based on research components, thereby increasing the per-student cost. Directing most of the demand towards the colleges, which had been defined in the five year plan as non-research teaching institutions, would achieve the same goal at lower costs than those expected at universities. Moreover, the deployment of colleges at northern and southern developing towns gave the CHE a relative advantage in the struggle for social equality. The colleges offered a solution for the main complaint voiced by Knesset members from the social lobby, namely that the CHE is not doing enough to expand accessibility in the periphery. The inclusion of the colleges in the list of institutions operating under the CHE increased the nation-wide deployment of academic institutions and as a result the number of students in the periphery increased to over 6,000 immediately upon transitioning the colleges to PBC funding.

At one of the meetings held at the Ministry of Finance in September 1997, in which the 2000–2005 five year plan was discussed, it was agreed that the Regional Colleges would be included in the multi-annual plan for 2005.[344] A year later it was decided that the Regional Colleges would join the CHE/PBC. The meeting was attended by representatives of all relevant bodies: The Ministry of Finance, PBC and the Regional Colleges. It was further agreed that the academic programs at the seven Regional Colleges – Eilat, Achva, Ashkelon, Hadera, Western Galilee, Jordan Valley and Zefat – Would be transferred to the PBC's budget as of 1 October 1998.[345]

344 Association of Regional Colleges Archive, file 1997. Minutes of meeting dated 14 September 1997. The meeting was held at the CHE and attended by the heads of the PBC, representatives of the Ministry of Finance and the Chairperson of the Association of Regional Colleges, Moshe Nativ.

345 Ibid, file 1989. Letter from Dr. Klein, Manager of the Colleges Division at the Ministry of Education, to the CEOs of the Regional Colleges, 19 July 1998.

The De facto Absorption of the Regional Colleges under the PBC

The absorption of the colleges within the CHE/PBC system (1998–2003) was a gradual process implemented in three stages. Each of the stages can be characterized based on the practical attitude of the absorbing authorities:

A. **Absorption and budgeting of the Regional Colleges:** The work of the heads of the PBC at this stage was characterized by a lack of planning or setting of aims for the integration of Regional Colleges in the country's general academic system. The absorption was considered a technical act which regulated colleges' budgetary framework. The transition of the colleges to PBC funding in the midst of the 1996–2000 five year plan did not facilitate a program that requires a designated budget early on in the planning stage, and therefore their absorption was subject to the Ministry of Education's budgetary dictates. The student quota defined by the Ministry of Education for each college determined their budget from the PBC in the first two years. As opposed to the independent colleges that enjoyed a budget which determined their physical and academic development process, the budget of Regional Colleges did not include physical or academic development clauses and they had to make do with an ongoing budget covering their approved student quota only. The first letters to the colleges from the heads of the PBC emphasize technical aspects and lack any organizational or planning considerations. For instance, the following was issued by the PBC's CEO to the managers of the Ashkelon Regional College:

> This transition does not in any way change the academic status of the programs that would remain under the universities' academic auspices. The 1998/99 academic year would be a transition year with the aim being to reach 1999/2000 with a clearer picture of the topics on the agenda and developed plans for future. The 1998/99 budget would be based on the assumption that the number of new students to be absorbed that year would be identical to the number absorbed in 1997/98.[346]

At this stage colleges were required to present technical information pertaining to their institution, such as documents of incorporation, manpower, and details regarding physical and academic facilities.[347] The absorption task focused on defining ongoing budgeting rules only, based on the principles by which PBC

---

346 Ashkelon College Archive, file 2000/1. Letter from Nissan Limor to the College Manager, 13 July 1998.

347 Ibid, Based on a letter from Amir Gat, 13 June1999.

budgets students admitted and studying at the college's academic program, and whose number in each college does not exceed the number defined by the Ministry of Education prior to the colleges' transition to the PBC. This stage lasted for about a year and a half, until 31 March 2000.

B. **Establishment of an academic corporation:** About eighteen months after their absorption, the PBC defined new rules for budgeting the academic programs at the colleges. This change was required under amendment number 10 to the CHE law, which granted colleges offering a degree of an Israeli university the right to be called an academic college. Based on the new rules, the current budgeting framework of Regional Colleges would end on 31 March 2000, and will be renewed only through a new corporation which will serve as an organizational framework for managing the academic programs only. Based on the PBC's rules, the new corporation would be established by the managers of the academic program at each Regional College, and it would be managed as an independent unit, unaffiliated to the Regional College. The Regional College would continue to exist as an institutions for non-academic studies, such as practical engineering studies and certificate programs. The aim of the new rules was to ensure the establishment of a new corporation that carries no financial liabilities that may hinder the management of the academic program. The new institution would ensure its independence of the local institution or any other public body other than the academic corporation. The reasoning behind this move by the heads of the PBC had been that the establishment of the Regional Colleges was in many cases an initiative of public activists at the Regional Councils in which the colleges operated, and therefore these institutions were highly dependent upon the local public system. For instance, most of the chairpersons of the Boards at Regional Colleges were heads of the local council or local politicians: Hanan Hassid, Chairperson of the Board of Achva College, was for many years head of the Beer Tuvia local council alongside his being Chairperson of the college Board. Shai Hermesh, Chairperson of the Board of the Sapir Academic College had for years served as head of the Sha'ar Hanegev Regional Council. At Bar Ilan's colleges, although not established by local political bodies, the local mayors served as Chairpersons of the Board: The Chairperson of the Board of Ashkelon College was Eli Dayan, Ashkelon's Mayor from the 1970s until the beginning of the 1990s. The next Chairperson of the Board of the college was the city's next Mayor, Benny Vaknin. The Mayors of Zefat, from Zeev Perl to Yossi Oz, also served as Chairpersons of the Board of the college. At the Jordan Valley College, the head of the Zemach local council had been Chairperson of the Board for many years.

This extensive involvement of local public figures and politicians in the management of the colleges was perceived as problematic by the heads of PBC and the policymakers at the CHE, who believed that the establishment of an independent academic institution requires independence from public figures and local political bodies. The guidelines presented to the colleges managers defined principles of incorporation as prerequisites for the PBC's continued support of the institution.[348] According to the first section, activities under the university's academic responsibility would be carried out under a new Association (rather than another type of corporation), whose statute would be similar to the one enclosed as addendum A. This statute would be based on the following principles:

1. The name of the new institution would include academic affinity to the university granting its auspices, but the term "auspices" was replaced by "academic responsibility". The full name given to the new corporation was therefore, "[name of college] College under the Academic Responsibility of [name of university]".
2. The new corporation would not engage in any other activity but academic studies.
3. The new corporation would not be entitled to budgets or contributions from any other source without the PBC's approval.
4. The statute of the corporation would ensure its non-dependence and full independence both from an administrative perspective and from a legal one.
5. The number of members in the corporation's institutions affiliated with interested parties such as local authorities and the university, will not exceed 20 % of all members in the corporation. Members of the corporation having conflicts of interests or being affiliated to another institution will not fill important positions in the new corporation, such as Chairperson of the General Assembly, Chairperson of the Board, or other administrative positions.

These guidelines created a further barrier between Bar Ilan's Colleges and their founding university, towards their final disconnection. From now onwards the membership of position holders at the university was banned from the institutions managing the colleges, and in any event university employees were included in the 20 % quota defined by the PBC for members coming from bodies suspected of conflicts of interests. The university's influence in its Extensions and colleges was gradually reduced to a purely academic one. The establishment of the "Academic

348 Ibid, file 2000/2. Detailed guidelines for all Regional Colleges were submitted in December 1999 in a guidelines document that included a proposed statute and request for PBC funding.

College" in 2001 was the next step of the process that began with the establishment of the Regional College in 1992, although back then the initiative was made by the university's Rector Prof. Arad. Concerns from the inability to influence the Extensions was expressed at the time by the Rector:

> As you know for the past 25 years there have been close ties between the Ashkelon Extension, currently college, and the university, through a full and fruitful collaboration during which the Extension/college gradually developed. In view of the above, the university's management objects to the fact that you did not see fit to first discuss with us the matter of the establishment of the said association, and the composition of its members.[349]

Even when the status of the Extension had already changed to Regional College in the beginning of the 1990s, the university's management protested as to the small number of its members in the Association that managed the Ashkelon and Zefat colleges, and ultimately it was able to maintain a high level of involvement. However, in 2000, with the establishment of the Academic College, its further involvement was prevented by the CHE and the road to complete severing of the ties had been paved, as we shall see from the CHE's third stage plans.

C. **Academic Independence:** This stage is characterized by a long term plan that regulated the position of Regional Colleges in the country's academic system in the new millennium. The plan was carried out in two steps: The first should be credited to legislators who acted to amend the CHE law (10th amendment). The amendment defined equal criteria for budgeting, as well as equal status for degrees granted by academic institutions in Israel. This led to further equality in the legal status of Regional Colleges and independent Academic Colleges (Volansky, 2005). In retrospect, the CHE/PBC's decision of the beginning of the 1990s to grant independence and academic accreditation only to three Regional Colleges of a total of 12 that existed at the time, seems after the legislation of the amendment to the law as completely arbitrary. The implementation of the amendment to the law forced the CHE to grant accreditation to Regional Colleges that offered an undergraduate program of one of the country's universities and to allow them to use the name stipulated in the CHE law: "Academic College".[350] To implement the provisions of the law, the Colleges Sub-Committee defined criteria for accrediting a college as an academic institution. Regional Colleges were required to present suitable physical and academic facilities and at least 700 students in at least three different

349 Ibid, Letter from the Rector to the College Manager, 11 March 1993.
350 Council for Higher Education Law, 1958, article 1, 1995 amendment.

academic programs.[351] The colleges that met the criteria underwent two statutory changes: (a) The establishment of a new corporation; (b) Change of the institution's name from Regional College under Academic Auspices or Academic Responsibility – to "The [name of institution] Academic College under the Academic Responsibility of [name of the responsible university]". Similarly to other colleges, Bar Ilan's Colleges – Ashkelon, Judea & Samaria, Western Galilee, Zefat and Jordan Valley – acted as required and presented to the CHE the necessary data and documentation required for accreditation. Within a short period of time the Ashkelon, Judea & Samaria and Jordan Valley Colleges were awarded their new status, joined two years later by the Zefat and Western Galilee Colleges.

The second step defined the country's academic system as of the beginning of the millennium until now: In the beginning of 2000 the PBC began examining ways to integrate the academic colleges that had been operating under the academic responsibility of universities into Israel's academic system and transforming them into independent colleges. The underlying assumption during the initial planning stages was that the model of academic responsibility by universities had reached the end of its life. The reasoning voices heard at the PBC in both public and internal discussions were the following:

1. **Third year studies at Bar Ilan's colleges:** When studies at Bar Ilan's Extensions had been accredited in the 1960s, they included only partial studies, excluding year 3. The final years of the undergraduate degree as well as advanced degrees had to be completed at the university's main campus. The extensive growth in the number of students at colleges towards the end of the 1990s led to the CHE's approval of full multidisciplinary programs at the colleges, and in the absence of close supervision by the council, the third year was included in disciplinary streams held at the colleges. Such full curriculum deviated from the CHE's guidelines, due to the council's concern that these students would not be exposed to sufficient academic facilities during their studies, thereby leading to an enhanced motivation at the CHE to put an end to the academic responsibility model.
2. **The model's irrelevance:** The academic responsibility model, or in its original form – the Extensions model – had been suited to small and partial scopes

351 Ashkelon College Archive, file 1/2000. The terms were presented in a letter from Ms. Michal Neumann, Coordinator of the CHE's Colleges Sub-Committee, 21 June 1999.

of study. The PBC believed that academic supervision on an Extension offering only a partial curriculum cannot be compared to academic supervision of an institution that offers a number of full time departments. This difficulty was further enhanced as efficient supervision was required for a large number of departments studied at different colleges, including Bar Ilan University's Extensions.

3. **Senior academic faculty:** The CHE's demand to establish a senior faculty whose main occupation is at the college was not implemented in the academic responsibility model when the majority of senior faculty members came from the main university campus, where they had been employed on a full or partial basis.
4. **Managerial inefficiency:** As the number of students at each colleges grew, so did the inefficiency of the academic services offered to students. in the beginning of 2001 a total of approx. 4,000 students attended Bar Ilan's colleges, but technical services such as admission, accreditation of previous studies, transitions between departments and appeals were held at the university, a fact that undermined the efficiency of both systems – the university's and the local one.
5. **Hostility towards Bar Ilan University:** The expansion in the scope of studies at Bar Ilan's colleges in the 1990s and the increase in the number of institutions under its supervision from three Extensions in the 1960s to five colleges in the 1990s created a hostile attitude towards Bar Ilan University. This attitude among CHE/PBC officials, that had been mentioned by the head of the Colleges Administration in his memorandum to the university's management, was confirmed by the retiring Chairperson of the PBC and Deputy Chairperson of the CHE from Bar Ilan University, Prof. Shlomo Grossman, and by Prof. Yehezkel Taler from the University of Haifa, in my interviews with them.[352] They noted the negative feelings towards Bar Ilan among certain PBC and CHE members, which resulted from the university's expansion ventures that had seemed to them as "academic imperialism" and Bar Ilan's wish to control a larger slicc of the country's academic budget.[353]

352 Prof. Shlomo Grossman (1938–2021) was a Biochemist, served as Dean of the Faculty of Natural Sciences, Deputy Rector of research at Bar Ilan university and Deputy Chairperson of the PBC during Prof. Lev Zion's Chair, and himself PBC Chairman following Prof. Lev Zion's retirement and until 2011. As of 2013 Prof. Grossman served as President of the Ashkelon Academic College.

353 Interview with Prof. Shlomo Grossman, PBC Chairperson, 27 October 2009; interview with Dr. Dov Levitan, Head of the Colleges Administration at Bar Ilan University, 13 December 2007; interview with Prof. Yehezkel Taler, 29 November 2009.

6. **Disregard and disrespect:** During visits by PBC representatives at Bar Ilan's Colleges, a few of the local managers voiced allegations of disrespect by heads of Departments at Bar Ilan towards the academic needs of the colleges, manifested mainly in sending junior lecturers or others who were unsuccessful at the university, to teach at the college. For some heads of Departments the colleges served as a type of "city of refuge" for permanent faculty members that for various reasons cannot be dismissed. These lecturers taught at the colleges a significant share of their teaching hours, up to a full time position. In addition to them, the university made it a practice to send inexperienced, junior lecturers to the colleges. The most promising of them, however, were sent for a limited period of time, until an opening became available at the university, while the less promising remained at the colleges.
7. **Multidisciplinary degree:** The accelerated development of the colleges operating under the academic auspices of Bar Ilan University during the 1990s should be accredited to the existence of a multidisciplinary program taught entirely at the college. However, this program, which is not a disciplinary program, became the colleges' main offering. During those years over 70 % of students at Bar Ilan's Colleges (excluding the Ashkelon Academic College) participated in this program. The CHE believed that these colleges are unlikely to succeed as independent academic institutions equipped to cope with the many changes and transformations in the higher education system of the new millennium, especially in view of the emerging success of the independent colleges. The success of the multidisciplinary program was met with scorn and disdain.[354] With this atmosphere and the sense among PBC members that the end of the responsibility model is near, the Chairperson of the PBC appointed a committee led by his deputy Chair at the time, Prof. Shlomo Grossman[355] to examine alternatives to the existing model. Alongside the committee's progress on the matter, the PBC's Chairperson made a number of further initiatives in this regard. In an article in the Economics quarterly (in Hebrew) he reiterated the social and academic reasoning leading to the conclusion that the model of academic responsibility has reached its end:

> The academic programs under a university's auspices at Regional Colleges contributed greatly to the advancement of local populations. This fact was expressed in the significant year by year growth in the number of students attending these institutions. This fast and

354 This had been the position of Prof. Yehezkel Taler, Deputy Chairperson of the CHE, in many conversations held between us throughout our joint work as well as in a dedicated interview held on 29 November 2009.

355 Interview dated 27 October 2009.

welcome growth in the number of students made it increasingly difficult for the university to implement the type of supervision required under its academic responsibility. Moreover, the university is unable to absorb such large numbers of students at the main campus for completing their third year of studies. Thus, the model of academic responsibility of a university over the academic program at colleges has reached its end, and these programs must separate from the university's responsibility.[356]

The Position of Bar Ilan University's Management

It was clear to the PBC's Chairperson that he must convince the university to renounce its continued academic auspices to the academic colleges (previously its Extensions). The university, which had already undergone an actual process of disconnecting from its historical Extensions when these transitioned to the Ministry of Education's budgeting and became Regional Colleges, was willing to agree to this final severing of ties with the colleges, for a number of reasons:

1. The multidisciplinary degree studies available at five colleges increased voices of opposition towards the university among CHE/PBC officials. The criticism focused on the level of lecturers sent to teach at the colleges, the terms of admission to the multidisciplinary programs, and most of all the belief that a college would not be able to develop by limiting itself to general, non-disciplinary programs. Such criticism did not add respect towards the university within the regulatory system.[357]
2. The university's level of achievements in research was low compared to other Israeli universities. It was ranked last in the country in terms of publications and the number of PhD students, alongside the University of Haifa and Ben Gurion.[358] Many of the university's faculty members believed that it should focus more on scientific research and less on its historical social and religious mission. One of the Deans of the university expressed this position as follows:

> It appears that in terms of academic prestige, the investment in the colleges was not worthwhile [. . .] The Hebrew University, for instance, invested its efforts and resources towards establishing research institutions. . . which made a significant contribution to the Hebrew University's image both among the Israeli public and in global academic circles. In contrast, Bar Ilan invested in the dissemination of higher education in the periphery. Ultimately, Bar Ilan paid a price for its positioning as a Target University affiliated with religious Zionism (Schwartz, 2006: 63–81).

356 Lev Zion, 2001: 91–102.

357 Interview with Prof. Taler, 29 November 2009.

358 Hershkowitz, 2007: 39–40: in 1990 there were 410 PhD students at Bar Ilan, compared to 1,620 in 2005.

Years later Prof. Dov Schwartz expressed his utmost respect to the university's Rector Prof. Yehuda Friedland who decided to establish an Appointments Committee that defined academic criteria for promoting faculty members. This turning point was, in his opinion, a revolution in the university's professionalization and quality level, and a clear expression of its embarking upon a new path (Schwartz, 2013). Prof. Kave, who until then had been the Rector of the university and later its President, prioritized the promotion of scientific research at the university. This goal, which had always been the focus of the CHE's major concerns, was regarded very positively, with the Chairperson of the CHE willing to assist in its promotion, at the expense of the university's social and religious mission at the colleges. This new support was expressed, for instance, in a significant increase in the university's quota of PhD students, which grew by more than 100 students. For the first time the university was granted the CHE's approval to open a Faculty of Engineering as well as additional fields in heavily research-based fields of exact sciences and it received further financial support to develop its research operations.[359]

Although Bar Ilan's case is quite different than the cases of Ben Gurion and Haifa universities which at that time had also disconnected their ties from the colleges under their auspices, the experience with the Sha'ar Hanegev-Sapir College had taught Bar Ilan's management that the agreement to disconnect does not necessarily have to result in immediate severing of all ties and that the transition period can extend through many years. The Sha'ar Hanegev-Sapir College had operated under the auspices of Ben Gurion University and in 1995 gained accreditation to operate as an independent institution. However, it continued to offer Ben Gurion University's programs even though it had become a large college in its own right and despite many decisions by the CHE. Even today the college continues to teach first year Engineering students towards their continued studies at Ben Gurion. While the university is not obligated to admit them and there is no official relationship between these students and the university, it is no coincidence that the programs and preparations towards engineering studies are held on behalf of Ben Gurion University.

Bar Ilan's management felt it is time to achieve scientific aims, even if this new prioritizing would come at the expense of the social and religious aims defined by the university's founders (there were those at the university who believed that a full disconnection is not expected soon). The dramatic changes that had

359 From interviews with Prof. Taler on 29 November 2009 and Prof. Grossman on 27 November 2009.

taken place in Israel and globally forced the university's management to differentiate itself in research and excellence from the dozens of institutions established throughout the country, as had been done by other institutions in the United States and Britain. Looking at a number of research indexes in recent years we find that indeed Bar Ilan is striving to chance its academic path.[360] I have used the following measures used by the PBC in determining the scope and level of research activities at each university:

1. The number of competitive research grants won
2. The number of grants won from other sources
3. PhD recipients and equivalent
4. Scientific publications

The measure of scientific publications is based on the number of publications by faculty members at each institution and their scientific impact, as measured by their impact factor (an index used for measuring the importance of scientific journals) of the journals in which the publications were made.[361] The number of PhD students at each institution was also examined. The findings point to the clear conclusion that Bar Ilan University is undergoing a process of change in all indexes. In recent years it has increasingly positioned itself as a research institution, whose primary activities are focused on science rather than social and religious activities as had been the case until the 1990s. Tables 43 and 44 summaize this changing trend.

360 On the dilemma between religious social university and research university, see the following latest publications: Schwartz: 52–15; Mevarech: 91–83; Iram: 127–119 – all the above in Iram, Friedlander and Ohayun, 2013.

361 The PBC, Barshad & Biham (editors), report number 30 (2002–2003).

Tab. 43: Number of PhD students at universities

Year/ Percentage of change	Total number of students	Hebrew University	Technion	Tel Aviv University	Bar Ilan University	University of Haifa	Ben Gurion University	Weizmann Institute
1989/90	3,910	1,420	520	850	**410**	90	170	450
Annual %		36.3 %	14 %	22 %	**11 %**	3 %	5 %	12 %
2005/06	9,835	2,700	880	2,120	**1,620**	845	990	680
Annual %		28 %	9 %	22 %	**17 %**	9 %	10 %	7 %
2007/08	10,300	2,700	910	2,090	**1,790**	990	1,120	700
Annual %		26.2 %	8.8 %	20.3 %	**17.4 %**	9.6 %	10.9 %	6.8 %
2009/10	10,567	2607	961	2,153	**1,851**	1,056	1,219	720
Annual %		24.7 %	9.1 %	20.4 %	**17.5 %**	10 %	11.5 %	6.8 %
2012/13	10,655	2,346	991	2,130	**1,877**	1,238	1,379	694
Annual %		22.0 %	9.3 %	20 %	**17.6 %**	11.6 %	13 %	6.5 %
2018/19	11,719	2,312	1,155	2,169	**2,192**	1,513	1,681	697
Annual %		19.7 %	9.8 %	18.5 %	**18.7 %**	12.9 %	14.3 %	6 %

Data processed from: CBS, Students in institutions of higher education by degree and institution type, table1: http://che.org.il/?page_id=6802, Retrieved 28 July 2011 2018/19 data from: CBS, Students at universities by degree and institution, table 2. Retrieved 10 March, 2020.

Tab. 44: Research measures in the budgeting model of Israeli Universities

Research measures	Budget year	Hebrew University	Technion	Tel Aviv University	Bar Ilan University	University of Haifa	Ben Gurion University	Weizmann Institute	Total Budgeting %
Research Component	2003/04	26.5 %	12.9 %	20.6 %	**8.7 %**	3.8 %	11.3 %	16.2 %	45 %
	2004/05	25.3 %	13.9 %	20.3 %	**9.7 %**	4.1 %	11.3 %	15.4 %	46 %
	2007/08	25.5 %	15.3 %	20.6 %	**10.0 %**	4.6 %	10.1 %	14.0 %	45 %
	2007/08	24.8 %	16.8 %	20.3 %	**9.7 %**	4.8 %	9.7 %	13.9 %	48.5 %
Of which: Competitive funds	2003/04	29.6 %	14.8 %	9.5 %	**4.7 %**	2.0 %	11.0 %	18.4 %	35 %
	2004/05	28.1 %	15.5 %	18.5 %	**4.8 %**	2.3 %	11.7 %	19.1 %	34.6 %
	2007/08	29.3 %	15.7 %	19.0 %	**5.0 %**	2.8 %	10.0 %	18.3 %	34.6 %
	2007/08	28.1 %	16.4 %	19.0 %	**5.5 %**	3.2 %	9.0 %	19.0 %	34.6 %
Scientific publications	2003/04	25.1 %	11.5 %	25.5 %	**9.6 %**	8.6 %	11.0 %	8.7 %	15 %
	2004/05	22.7 %	11.8 %	24.2 %	**12.0 %**	9.6 %	11.3 %	8.3 %	14.5 %
	2007/08	23.0 %	12.0 %	23.9 %	**12.0 %**	10.2 %	11.0 %	8.0 %	14.85
	2007/08	22.3 %	12.5 %	22.6 %	**11.7 %**	11.3 %	11.7 %	8.1 %	14.8 %

Source: Barshad & Biham (2006): Table 4.6; as above (2009): Table 4.6. 2012/13 data has been removed from the table.

A 10 year follow-up of the data years shows that this trend of Bar Ilan's continues – in 2019[362] 2,192 PhD students studied at Bar Ilan compared to 1,872 students in 2013, meaning a 1.1 % growth rate. In comparison, the Hebrew University and Tel Aviv University, defined as research universities, showed a moderate decline compared to 2013. Furthermore, the research component in Bar Ilan's budget continues to rise, reaching 10.6 % of its budget compared to 9.7 % in 2007/08. In the same year the research budget of the Hebrew University was 19.5 % and Tel Aviv's 15.4 %. Due to a change in the budgeting method, a breakdown of budgets for competitive research grants and scientific publications was not provided, and a comparison between these research components was only available for 2018/19. As of 2018, the new management of Bar Ilan University continues with the same trend defined by the university since 2010 – to be evaluated in the same way as all other universities in Israel and the world and be measured by research indices.

The Academic Responsibility Model: The End of the Road

Following a year in which he shared his intentions with all relevant parties including the managers of the colleges, Prof. Lev Zion (Chairperson of the PBC) presented to the CHE a decision proposal which essentially implied that the academic responsibility model has officially reached its end. The necessity of this decision resulted from the need to promote an alternative model which he requested to bring to the CHE's decision as soon as possible. At the CHE meeting of 6 March 2001 his proposal was accepted, and the academic responsibility model was officially terminated. The universities and colleges operating under academic responsibility of a university were required to prepare to complete the disconnecting process within four years:

> The format of studies at colleges under a university's academic responsibility had reached its end, and the colleges must disconnect from the universities no later than the 1995/96 academic year. 2005/06 will be the last academic year in which studies would be held at colleges under the academic responsibility of universities. The last academic year in which students would be admitted at colleges for studies under the academic responsibility of universities is 2003/04. . . To refute any doubt, the council requests to note the names of the colleges in questions, in which studies are held under the academic auspices of universities:
>
> A. Western Galilee Academic College - Under Bar Ilan University's academic responsibility

362 2019 data from: CHE, 2019 budget booklet, addendum 3: PBC's participation in the universities' budget, 2018–2019.

B. Zefat College - Under Bar Ilan University's academic responsibility
C. Jordan Valley Academic College - Under Bar Ilan University's academic responsibility
D. Judea and Samaria Academic College - Under Bar Ilan University's academic responsibility
E. Ashkelon Academic College - Under Bar Ilan University's academic responsibility
F. Sapir Academic College - Under Ben Gurion University's academic responsibility
G. Achva Academic College - Under Ben Gurion University's academic responsibility[363]

This decision paved the way for a new model by which academic colleges would operate under the CHE. We learned of the new ideas of the PBC's Chairperson, on which his program was based, from his letters to all relevant parties. In a letter to the Chairperson of the Association of Regional Colleges, whom he saw as a partner in determining the fate of the colleges, Prof. Lev Zion outlines his new ideas. He opens by listing the social advantages of the initiative and its contribution to Israeli society:

> Institutions of higher education are scattered throughout the country, as a deliberate policy of the PBC and the CHE, so as to support the distribution of the population. Colleges should serve their local population. As higher education further spreads to new population groups, some of which less affluent, the demand grows for study opportunities close to home. A student studying close to home not only saves on expenses but has better chances to find employment, and may integrate work with studies. If in the past students would have to relocate in order to study, today higher education comes to the students. The establishment of colleges, the raising of their academic level and expanding curriculums, tending towards applicative areas, would also attract students from the center. Therefore, this document pertains to the deployment of colleges in the south and the north.[364]

The Alternative Model

The committee, headed by Prof. Grossman, closely examined the academic programs offered at the colleges, visited them and learned from past experience in Israel and abroad, mostly in the United States.[365] Further to the committee's request, the Regional Colleges prepared a position paper on the topic of their integration in the country's higher education system. The first colleges established by Bar Ilan – Zefat, Ashkelon and the Jordan Valley, as well as the colleges under the university's responsibility – Judea and Samaria and Western Galilee, all

363 The CHE, principle decisions file, 2002–2007, March 2007. Decision dated 6 March 2001: 79–80. Nearly 12 years had passed from the decision until the disconnecting process was completed.

364 Association of Regional Colleges Archive, file 2000. Letter from Prof. Lev Zion to Moshe Nativ, 11 January 2000.

365 See footnote 208.

presented a unified position by which they prefer a combined operating model that would enable their students to choose between one of two programs college: An independent degree program, or a program offered by Bar Ilan University at the college, whose graduates would receive the university's diploma.[366]

A few months later the committee submitted its conclusions to the PBC Chairperson. During a conference for college managers held in Jerusalem on 6 June 2000 Prof. Lev Zion presented the "Academic complex" model.[367] And although he had decided to present a single model only, the discussion led to the presentation of additional possibilities which the committee had also examined. The PBC was presented with three options:

1. **Reducing the number of Regional Colleges in the country:** The location of some of the colleges in close geographic proximity, such as in the north and the south, raised the question whether colleges at such proximity can coexist and reach the critical number of students needed to justify their existence. Moreover, would they be able to form the senior academic faculty needed for holding independent academic departments? In the north, five colleges were located within a geographical radius of about 40 km, including Zefat, Tel Chai, the Jordan Valley, Yesreel Valley, and Western Galilee. In the south, within a small radius of about 20 km there were three colleges – Sapir, Ashkelon and Achva. The committee examined the minimal capacity of a college based on two measures: A critical mass of students and a critical mass of senior academic faculty.
2. **Academic independence for each college:** The experience accumulated as of the 1990s, with the Jordan Valley, Tel Chai and Sapir Colleges embarking upon academic independence, positioned the independence model as one of the alternatives examined by the committee.
3. **The establishment of a multi-campus institution – the 'Academic Complex':** The first option, consisting of closing down some of the existing colleges seemed to committee members difficult and unrealistic due to political and public opposition which each college could easily generate to its benefit.

366 Ashkelon College Archive, file 1998. Letter from the CEO and Academic Manager to Prof. Grossman, 1 November 1889, and letter from the Colleges Managers to the President of the University, 28 February 2000.

367 In response to the question raised by Prof. Shimon Sharvit, the academic manager of Ashkelon College, whether there are alternatives to the presented model, Prof. Lev Zion answered that the other alternative is to close colleges that are in too close a proximity to one another.

This option seemed unlikely also due to widespread public opinion that the expansion of the academic system is a pressing need, with many young adults striving to be admitted. The political structure by which elected officials in the central government depend on the support of elected officials in local government did not encourage the PBC to examine the possibility of closing down active colleges, although the option was raised during the planning stages.[368] The second option, to prepare all colleges for academic independence as had been done in the 1990s also seemed unrealistic due to the accumulated experience with independent colleges. On their path to independent these colleges had to pass some very bumpy roads including the risk of financial and academic collapse.

The option that gained the PBC Chairperson's preference was to establish an official multi-campus institution: An 'Academic complex'.[369] Prof. Lev Zion promoted his position in a number of parallel channels. In an article already mentioned previously, published in the Economics Quarterly Journal he wrote:

> The colleges under the academic responsibility of one of the universities were scheduled therefore to become independent colleges offering their own degrees, as had been done at Tel Chai, Yesreel Valley and Sapir. If this would happen, there would bc a total of ten colleges in the north and the south, which together don't amount to even one thousand students. Therefore, a number of alternatives are currently being examined, including a proposal for the establishment of a multi-campus institution which would incorporate four to six colleges jointly.

In a detailed document published by Prof. Lev Zion entitled "Planning the College System", he outlines his main guidelines for a strategic multi-annual plan for colleges:

> The proposal for planning the colleges system aims to create large institutions of higher education in place of a large number of small independent ones. We propose a new approach to institutions of higher education - an 'Academic complex' in which a number

368 At a conference for colleges managers organized by Prof. Lev Zion on 6 June 2000, in which he presented the complex, he also expressed his opinion that a number of colleges in close proximity to one another should be closed.

369 The initial and unformulated concept had been presented to the CHE at its meeting on 20 June 2000. The CHE Chairperson presented a document for discussion, that included a proposal to incorporate the colleges under a multi-campus institution – a "University College" – as stated in a letter from Prof. Yehezkel Taler, Deputy Chairperson of the CHE, to the managers of the colleges, on 20 July 2000. Ashkelon College Archive, CHE file 1/2000.

> of colleges would incorporate around an 'Academic center'. The 'Complex' would be the legal entity of the institution of higher education. The academic center of the complex would be located at a central location, within one of the colleges comprising the complex, with convenient access from all participating colleges. The center will include the offices of the President, the CEO and the administrative system including finance, human resources, etc. It will house the meetings of the managing bodies (Managing Board and Board of Trustees) as well as the academic council of the complex. Each college with suitable academic and organizational infrastructures will be granted the status of a faculty (similarly, for instance, to the Faculty of Agriculture in Rehovot, which is physically distanced from the Hebrew University of Jerusalem). The head of each college would be a Dean, and it will include all faculty-level institutions .[370]

The PBC Chairperson was led by a social consideration, that had been the focus of much criticism towards the PBC by many national agencies. The social pressure to expand accessibility to higher education came from many directions, as shall be outlined below. In any event, in his document Prof. Lev Zion first presents the academic advantages of the complex:

1. **Number of students:** An academic complex of three colleges or more, will include more students than any independent college anywhere.
2. **Academic faculty:** The academic faculty will be fully employed by the complex, with the likelihood of forming a full time local faculty being higher than at a small independent college. The complex would be able to offer lecturers a larger number of courses than a single independent college would. The presence of a large senior faculty would positively impact the ability of the larger institution to submit a request for graduate degree studies in the foreseeable future.
3. **Libraries:** The combination of existing libraries and their reinforcement through the complex, would ensure the pooling of resources into a larger and more comprehensive library than in any other independent alternative.
4. **Financial advantages:** The likelihood of courses with a small number of students in attendance at the complex is naught in comparison to an independent college operating courses through independent departments.
5. **Academic advantages:** During the process of academic Independence, the complex would be able to offer departments in which courses are taught by senior academic faculty members who are leaders in their fields, thereby increasing its likelihood of operating a larger number of departments than any independent college alone.

---

370 Ashkelon College Archive, file 2000/1. Letter from Prof. Lev Zion to College Managers, 11 January 2000.

Regional Colleges as Independent Colleges

In a letter to the colleges managers, PBC Chairperson Prof. Lev Zion presented the Academic Complex model as the only model up for discussion. It was clear to all that he had chosen it as the organizational model for the colleges' operations in the near future, and even beyond. He reiterated his planning approach:

> The proposal for planning the colleges system aims to create large institutions of higher education in place of a large number of small independent ones. We propose a new approach to institutions of higher education – an 'Academic complex' in which a number of colleges would incorporate around an Academic center. The 'Complex' would be the legal entity of the institution of higher education.[371]

The managers of the colleges opposed this model for a number of reasons:

1. The fact that the "Complex" model had been presented as the only available operating model without considering the opinions of the heads of the colleges themselves and without presenting other options or models, evoked anger and opposition among the managers of the colleges.
2. The "Complex" model would cancel the colleges' independence as distinct legal and local entities and would transform each of them into a faculty of the academic complex of the area. Even the colleges that had already achieve independent – Sapir in the south, Yesreel Valley and Tel Chai in the north – were expected to participate in this union, although being independent institutions they could not be forced to do so. For the large independent colleges such as Sapir and Yesreel Valley, such a unification could undermine their position as independent institutions. Smaller colleges, however, who were always coping with the danger of closing, might have seen such unification as a lifeboat and a chance to develop and proliferate. The question arose as to who would lead this new complex, both academically and administratively. Clearly, the voice of a small college in the complex could not be equal to that of a large one.
3. The public authorities of regions having a Regional College, saw the proposed model as the end of the local college which they had worked so hard to establish and nurture. The heads of the local councils wished to preserve the existing structure so as to continue to develop a large institution, which would leverage the area economically and culturally. The 'Complex' model revokes their control or influence on the development of their Regional College.

371 Ibid. Attached to the letter were explanatory remarks entitled "Planning the system of colleges".

To pressurize managers of the colleges to accept the proposed model, the PBC Chairperson instructed them during the first conference in which the model was presented, to refrain from submitting to the CHE Colleges Sub-Committee requests for accreditation of new departments, until the question of the operation of the colleges has been officially finalized. This instruction, which threatened the continued development of the colleges, and especially the smaller ones, increased the disillusionment and opposition to the 'Complex' model. During many meetings and discussion held by the heads of the colleges in various frameworks, it was agreed to act on a number of levels to prevent the acceptance of the model at the CHE:

1. **Dialectic dialogue with the PBC Chairperson**

Rejecting the model on the grounds of decisive opposition seemed to many an unwise move which may lead to a process that would block the colleges' development. The heads of the colleges decided to convene on a regional basis to form an agreed unification model and present it to the PBC Chairperson. At the south and north the heads of the institutions met to form a draft unification agreement. On 13 March 2000 a draft agreement was signed between the southern colleges – Ashkelon, Sapir and Achva – by which they would agree to the proposed unification, provided that it would upgrade them to the level of a non-research university which would be called the University of the South.[372]

In order to truly examine the possibility for unification, the forum of college managers decided to commission a comprehensive study to examine the advantages and shortfalls of the 'Complex' model. In June 2000 the Association received a comprehensive report prepared by Eliyahu Israeli, which focused on the southern colleges.[373] His conclusions were as follows:

1.1. A unification between colleges in the south as well as in the north must lead to an outcome that upgrades their status and to an organizational structure that would be called a university.

---

372 Ibid, file 2000/3. Minutes of meeting dated 19 March 2000, signed by the heads of the Achva, Ashkelon and Sapir colleges. At the north a unification seemed more likely than in the south, as these colleges had a smaller number of students than did Ashkelon and Sapir in the south (the largest of the northern colleges numbered at the time only about 1,300 students).

373 Association of Regional Colleges Archive, file 2000. "The University of the South – General guidelines for the establishment of a multi-campus and multi-disciplinary university in southern Israel". Eliyahu Israeli, Mashav – applicable research, planning and consulting for education, welfare and labor systems, Jerusalem.

1.2. Upon completion of the unification, a university would be established, with about 6,600 students. Within five years it would include about 10,500 students, as derived from the potential of students in the south.
1.3. The university would focus on teaching undergraduate and graduate degree courses and would not engage in research.
1.4. The university will offer most disciplines, including natural sciences and applied professions. Each of the campuses will aim to specialize in specific areas.
1.5. Faculty members will teach at all campuses, thereby increasing the likelihood of full time employment, which also makes it easier to recruit senior and stable faculty members.

The considerations in support of the establishment of such a university also relied on those presented by the PBC Chairperson in the 'Complex' model, meaning – academic and social considerations. The idea to upgrade the 'Complex' model to a non-research regional university model was aimed at exhibiting to the PBC Chairperson a true willingness to practically examine the possibility of unification between the colleges so as to address his wish to establish large institutions, while on the other hand elegantly rejecting the complex idea in the format proposed by the PBC Chairperson. The assumption of the heads of the colleges had been based on the foreseeable difficulties in obtaining the CHE's approval for the establishment of two more universities – one in the south and one in the north. The people comprising the CHE and the PBC, mostly members of the country's research universities, would not approve a proposal to establish a new university, a fact that would in turn prevent a direct confrontation with the PBC Chairperson.[374]

2. **Initiatives among the members of the Council for Higher Education**

Lobbying operations were initiated among the members of the CHE so as to organize opposition from within for the possibility that the 'Complex' model would be enforced upon the colleges. Each College Manager undertook to approach CHE members with whom they had personal ties, so as to present the colleges' position. These initiatives led to the colleges gaining the support of the deputy Chairperson of the CHE, Prof. Yehezkel Taler, and of CHE member Prof. Avi Ravitzki,[375] who were both opposed to the model's coercive nature. Prof. Taler,

374 From the following interviews with colleges managers: Hebron Trabelci, CEO of Zefat College – interview dated 18 August 2009; and an interview with Yoram Raz, CEO of the Yesreel Valley College, 17 August 2009.

375 Philosopher and researcher in the field of Jewish Studies. Professor at the Hebrew University of Jerusalem, among the founders of the Meimad left-wing religious Zionist political party and recipient of the 2001 Israel prize for Jewish thought.

who had also served as Chairperson of the Colleges Sub-Committee at the CHE, soon convened the heads of the colleges in an attempt to establish a unified front to oppose the 'Complex' model. Discussions with the colleges were held on two levels: The Sub-Committee headed by Prof. Taler summoned representatives of each college separately in order to understand its specific needs and positions, while the PBC management headed by Prof. Lev Zion summoned the colleges to promote the 'Complex' model.

3. Bar Ilan University

The colleges under Bar Ilan University's academic responsibility who were opposed to the 'Complex' model, approached the university's President, requesting his intervention in ensuring that the CHE does not approve the model. The main concerns of the colleges managers was the consequences of their having to disconnect from Bar Ilan, and as a result their graduates would not be eligible for the university's diploma. Moreover, the concern was that such a complex in the north or the south managed by a college that had already gained academic independence would result in practice in Bar Ilan's colleges replacing a prestigious university guardianship that had already proved its worth, with a less prestigious college guardianship which had yet to prove itself.

In a letter to the university's President, signed by the five managers of the colleges under Bar Ilan's academic responsibility, the managers called the university's management to intervene on their behalf at the CHE to reject the "Complex" model and encourage a combined model by which the colleges would grant their graduates an independent degree or a university degree, in two separate academic programs: One offered by Bar Ilan University at the college, and the other by the college itself, with students being able to choose which program to attend. This combined model assures a gradual process of achieving independence, with the university program offered at the college extending its prestige onto the college's new program. In view of the fact that the managers' letter reiterates the importance of the long term ongoing relationship with the university and the struggle to remain under the university's responsibility, contrary to the position of the budgeting institution, I have chosen to quote most of it below:

> You are aware that our clear position, as presented to you during the meeting participated by yourself and the Rector, is to support the continuation of the successful long term relationship with Bar Ilan University, with an aim to further strengthen, expand and develop these ties.
>
> The university and the colleges managements have reached understandings and agreements regarding their continued ties and their further reinforcement, to be achieved by a number of means, including offering study programs under the university's auspices

> with full academic curriculums towards an academic degree on behalf of the college (independently), as can be seen in the combined model that for many years had been in existence at the College of Judea & Samaria.
> We are in the midst of a public dispute and struggle over the future of the colleges and their continued affiliation with Bar Ilan University... It is unimaginable that the university's strong relationship with its colleges in the periphery, and this magnificent academic cultural operation, would be destroyed and cease to exist. Such a decision would negatively impact thousands of students in the north and south of the country.[376]

The Decision

Following months of discussions and disputes, during which the attempts of the PBC's Chairperson to approve the 'Complex' model proved unsuccessful, the efforts of the model's opponents led by Prof. Taler bore fruit, and at the CHE meeting held on 6 March 2001 a decision was reached to adopt the principles set forth in two documents presented to the council: One by Prof. Yehezkel Taler and the second by Prof. Nehemia Lev Zion. According to the decision, the colleges would be able to choose one of the following two alternatives:

A. To submit a request for accreditation as an independent institution of higher education.
B. That a group of colleges (accredited and others) would be able to apply for accreditation as a multi-campus institution of higher education.

Each of the two alternatives would include a gradual process leading to eventual independence from the academic responsibility of a university: The development of the college's own programs alongside programs under the academic responsibility of a university, together with a gradual reduction of the academic activities under the university's responsibility, until their eventual full termination.[377]

In view of this decision, Bar Ilan's Colleges were requested to refrain from issuing applications for accreditation of further university departments, and to prepare for the presentation of independent programs, whether under the independent alternative, or the multi-campus one, as decided by each college based on the model most suited to its needs.

---

376 Ashkelon College Archive, file 2000/1. Letter from the managers of Ashkelon, Zefat, Jordan Valley, Judea & Samaria and Western Galilee Colleges to the President of Bar Ilan University, 28 February 2000.

377 Ibid, file 2000/1. Letter from the Secretary of the CHE to the Rectors of Bar Ilan University and Ben Gurion University, 3 May 2001.

Due to disagreement as to the possibility that the unification of colleges according to the 'Complex' model would upgrade their status to the level of a non-research university, Bar Ilan's colleges found themselves faced with their only remaining alternative – academic independence.

Despite the many concerns from the expected change, especially in terms of students' reactions to the change in their diplomas, the three most senior Bar Ilan Colleges – Ashkelon, Zefat and Jordan Valley – chose to embark upon academic independence. The Ashkelon Academic College was the first to submit an application to open registration for undergraduate candidates at the Department of Social Work. Following an initial review of the program and the college's existing academic, physical and administrative facilities, it was decided that an academic review committee would be established towards the final accreditation of an independent department at the college. Later a similar application was issued by the Jordan Valley Academic College, and three years later the Zefat Academic College also made a similar application. Bar Ilan University accompanied the various stages of independence of the three colleges under its academic responsibility, offering a "safety net" for each of the independent programs submitted for accreditation by the CHE.[378] The purpose of this safety net was to enable the opening of the independent programs, with the university committing to admit students in the event that the CHE declares that one of the colleges had not met the academic requirements and is therefore not eligible for accreditation of the submitted department. Table 45 describes Bar Ilan's Colleges' gradual process of achieving academic independence, by departments.

378 As required by the CHE, every new institution applying for accreditation of a new department is required during the permitting stages to present the written commitment of an accredited institution to guarantee admittance of the new institution's students in the event that the new institution would not succeed in obtaining the CHE's accreditation for the new department. This 'safety net' accompanies the new institution until the Department's final accreditation.

Tab. 45: Independence of Bar Ilan's Colleges 2004–2007

College	Department	Type of degree	Date of recognition	Date of certification
Ashkelon	Social Work	B.S.W	3/2004	1/2007
	Social Work – career change	B.S.W	1/2008	1/2008
	Economics and Management	B.A	3/2004	6/2007
	Criminology	B.A	7/2005	11/2007
	Economics and Logistics	B.A	3/2006	3/2009
	Economics and Banking	B.A	3/2006	3/2009
	Computer Science	B.Sc.	4/2006	5/2009
	Psychology	B.A	2/2009	–
	Politics and Governance	B.A	3/2009	–
	Sociology and Anthropology	B.A	4/2008	–
Jordan Valley	Electrical and Electronics Engineering	B.Sc.	6/2004	6/2008
	Hotel Management & Tourism	B.A	7/2004	7/2007
	Information systems Engineering	B.Sc.	1/2005	10/2009
Zefat	Behavioral Sciences	B.A	6/2007	–
	Nursing	B.A	6/2007	–
	Social Work	B.S.W	12/2007	–

Data: Aharoni & Biham (2008); Barshad & Biham (2006).

In mid 2007 the Ashkelon and Jordan Valley Colleges were recognized as independent institutions of higher education under the CHE law and were declared independent colleges. The first independent departments were certified as required during that year. In 2014 the three oldest Bar Ilan colleges were still managing a duplicate academic curriculum: One independent, and one following the historic program with Bar Ilan University. Although a schedule was defined for completion of the transition period, in which the colleges also offer studies in Bar Ilan's programs, the academic colleges still offer two optional programs. For instance, Sapir College, which had been an independent institution for over 18 years, continued to offer Ben Gurion University's undergraduate program long after it had become fully academically independent.

An examination of the number of students at each of the independent programs shows that despite the many concerns of College Managers, the academic Independence process was a success, and moreover students were not deterred by the knowledge that these colleges would no longer issue university degrees in their independent programs, but college degrees. Table 46 presents the number of students enrolled at the programs offered by the three colleges that obtained academic independence, based on 2010/11 data.

Tab. 46: Number of students at Ashkelon, Jordan Valley and Zefat Colleges in 2004/05–2007/08

College	2004/05		2005/06		2007/08		2007/08	
	Bar Ilan's Program	Independent Program	Bar Ilan's Program	Independent Program	Bar Ilan's Program	Independent Program	Bar Ilan's Program	Independent Program
Ashkelon	2,747	192	2,647	473	2,396	884	2,275	1,017
Jordan Valley	1,011	58	1,044	115	1,195	169	1,305	197
Zefat	874	–	976	–	1,281	–	1,464	–
Total	4,632	250	4,667	588	4,872	1,053	5,044	1,214

Source: CHE website: che.org.il/skira-klalit.html. Retrieved 10 November, 2009.

Chapter 16 The Social Dimension in the Reasoning of the CHE/PBC and the Colleges

Since the opening of the gates of higher education and the transition to a binary system in the 1990s, the CHE has viewed the colleges as an instrument for reducing social gaps and promoting social equality. The geographic location of most former Regional Colleges meant that they hold most of the burden of this social mission, as institutions serving parts of the population for whom the gates of higher education had been blocked for many years. This national mission was joined in 2000 by Bar Ilan's colleges, which had been established in peripheral areas in the 1960s by idealist founders who wished to utilize higher education towards reducing social gaps in Israeli society. However, the committee appointed to planning higher education in Israel did not share this perception of colleges as a social instrument for reducing gaps in higher education, which had begun in the 1990s not following the CHE's regulated planning and social policy considerations, but rather due to constraints and public and political pressure during a number of periods beginning in the 1970s until the first decade of the new millennium. Similarly to the initial small scale academization process in the beginning of the 1990s being a result of constraints and public pressure, and therefore having been incorporated only at four general colleges and three technological ones, likewise in the beginning of the new millennium, the CHE was forced to adopt a more open social position which would lead to a higher level of accessibility. This new position contradicted the council's previous position by which the academic system had reached its optimal number of institutions. The plan for 1991–2000 had ignored ten Regional Colleges scattered throughout the country, which offered academic programs, including the original colleges under Bar Ilan's auspices. The decision to include them was a result of social and political pressures which in turn resulted in the establishment of a larger academic system and the inclusion of Regional Colleges in the national social mission. A number of events had a significant public impact which forced the CHE to adopt a more flexible social position than it had in 2000:

1. **The 1999 State Comptroller's report:** Although some of its findings were presented in previous chapters, it is worthwhile to mention this report again as it had led to a public outcry which forced the CHE to adopt a different social approach than had been expressed in its previous five-year plans. The report,

that had focused on the Development towns in the south, raised to public awareness difficult findings that required immediate government attention. The following table presents the main data reviewed by the report, pointing to low percentages of students in higher education from Development towns in the south compared to national averages in affluent towns, and even compared to Development towns whose situation had improved. The rate of continuing students was also substantially lower than in affluent towns. The most prominent gap was noted in the rate of holders of academic degrees in southern Development towns compared to affluent cities. Table 47 presents the gap according to a range of measures.

Tab. 47: Rates of higher education in southern Development towns compared to affluent towns

City/year	1992–1993 Percentage of	1995		Percentage of
	holders of Bagrut high school diploma among 17–18 year olds	Percentage of holders of academic degree	Percentage of holders of academic degree excluding new immigrants	students of academic degrees aged 20--29
National average	36 %	15.8 %	13.3 %	6 %
Average at Southern Development Towns	15 %–27 %	7.65 %	3.2 %	1 %–4 %
Ofakim		2.14 %		
Netivot				1 %
Sderot				1 %
Yeruham				4 %
Affluent cities:				
Ramat Hasharon		24.5 %		13 %
Givataim		19.6 %		14 %
Haifa		19.3 %		14 %
Jerusalem		19.1 %		
Tel Aviv		19.1 %		11 %
Development Towns with improved circumstances:	38 %–49 %			
Karmiel		12.05 %		
Yavne		10.29 %		

Data adapted from the 1999 State Comptroller's report, 50 (b): 71.

2. **Establishment of a Ministerial Committee and a Committee for Expanding Accessibility:** The report's difficult findings were dealt with by a special Ministerial Coordination Committee, which recommended that the government instruct the CHE to establish a committee that would examine ways to increase the number of students of higher education in the south. The government adopted the committee's recommendation with the following decision:

> The government requests the Council for Higher Education to examine, through a committee to be appointed by the Planning and Budgeting Committee, to be participated by representatives of the institutions and academic faculties in the south, the Ministries of Education, Finance, Labor and Welfare, the Negev Development Authority and the Local Authority in the south, which will discuss all matters pertaining to increasing the number of students from the southern region in higher education, to map the needs and determine principles for expanding areas of operation of colleges in the south.[379]

Despite the PBC's position as dedicated to planning higher education in Israel, a task which in 2000 should have automatically included also Development towns, the CHE, as in the 1990s, found itself responding to external pressures that led it to the development of a social-national approach and plan towards solving the problem of social gaps at Development towns. Further to the government decision, the PBC Chairperson appointed a committee to present a plan for expanding accessibility to higher education at Development towns in the south and north. The composition of the committee pointed to its social aims: Moti Avisror, Head of the Yeruham local council; Meir Sahar, Director General of the Negev Development Authority;[380] Yosef Farhi, Ministry of Labor representative; Jimmy Weinblatt, Ben Gurion University representative; Prof. Zeev Zachor, President of Sapir College; and Dr. Palti Stavi, Director General of the Association for Educational Advancement..[381] Having visited Development towns in the Negev and met with local educators, the committee submitted the first draft of its report for discussion at the Council. The draft raised the following points:

A. Due to the lack of motivation for academic studies among youths as a result of low image, psychological barriers and anxiety, the committee recommended

---

379 Association of Regional Colleges Archive, file 2000. Decision of the ministerial committee headed by Haim Ramon, 27 June 2000; Government decision number 58.

380 The authority was established following legislation in 1991 aimed at supporting the development of the Negev and especially coordinating between Government Ministries providing services to the region.

381 The Association was established in 1962 in order to reduce social gaps in education. It operates children homes and for many years also the pre-academic academies for soldiers who had completed their military service.

exposing the younger generation to institutions of higher education as early as junior high school, through visits to the institutions and lectures from faculty members. The committee also recommended that the Ministry of Education officially adopt the integration of academic studies in schools, towards the accumulation of academic credits.

B. The committee called the government to provide the necessary budgets to increase the number of students among youths in the south at the region's academic institutions through incentives such as significant discounts in tuition and scholarships.

C. The committee recommended the establishment of local information and support centers which would collect information on available educational opportunities and encourage local youths to apply to academic studies.

D. Opening of four-year academic programs for high school graduates not meeting university admittance terms, so that the first year would be dedicated to preparations for academic studies – through reinforcing knowledge in areas such as English and Math.

E. Expanding accessibility also to vocational training and preparation for academic studies through Community Colleges that would offer, for instance, practical engineering studies, hotel management, tourism, accounting and arts.

F. Considering the fact that a number of towns such as Ofakim and Netivot are populated by a predominantly Haredi (ultra orthodox Jewish) population, the committee recommended the establishment of programs suited to the life style of this sector, as had been done in Jerusalem and Bnei Brak – i.e., the establishment of separate centers for men and women, in which academic studies would be held under the auspices and operation of a university.

3. **Governmental dictates:** Following the draft report and its recommendations, the CHE now had to cope with further external intervention. In its meeting of 2 September 2001 the government decided to instruct the CHE to admit to the first year of undergraduate studies anyone with a Bagrut diploma. The government further decided to establish a team that would include representatives of the institutions of higher education to develop a detailed proposal on the matter.[382]

Further to the government's guidelines the CHE decided to collaborate with the Distressed Neighborhood Renewal Project, towards the implementation of a

382 Association of Regional Colleges Archive, file 2001. Government decision number 676 dated 2 September 2001.

national plan for accessibility to higher education in the periphery.[383] A preliminary work plan entitled "Expanding accessibility to Higher Education in the Northern and Southern Districts" was presented in a seminar for manpower development coordinators and for higher education coordinators in the north and the south, held on 26 January 2003. The plan's main targets included increasing the number of students at institutions of higher education among residents of the north and the south in all study programs: undergraduate studies, pre-academic preparatory programs and practical engineering studies. According to the plan, higher education coordinators will work within each town to increase awareness to higher education and will support candidates during the application process and during their studied. The meta goal of the plan was to increase the number of residents of the periphery holding an academic degree, raising it to national average.[384]

4. **Establishment of a parliamentary committee for examining ways of reducing social gaps:** Alongside hectic work on the question of accessibility to higher education, the Knesset published a report by its parliamentary investigation committee on social gaps in Israel headed by Knesset member Ran Cohen. The following was noted in the chapter on gaps in higher education:

> Among university graduates the representation of non-Jews and Sephardic Jews is small, including those born in Israel. The non-university Higher Education System (colleges) that began to develop in Israel by the end of the 1970's created a growth of 132% in the number of students in the past decade, 1990–2001. Also in these institutions we see underrepresentation of non-Jews and of Jews of eastern (Mizrachi) descent, but the relative representation of these two groups is larger than their representation at universities. Hence, these institutions contribute to reducing the gap between Jewish ethnic groups and between Jews and Arabs in Israel.[385]

---

383 The Distressed Neighborhoods Renewal Project was launched in 1978 by Menachem Begin's first government. The project focused on renewing distressed neighborhoods according to a list provided by government ministries. Renewal efforts included the physical renewal of bindings and construction of community centers, as well as social rehabilitation that included support funds for students from distressed neighborhoods and educational projects implemented through matching of funds from philanthropic foundations, private donors and government ministries.

384 Association of Regional Colleges Archive, file 2003. The plan was enclosed with a letter from the national commissioner of the higher education accessibility program, 8 January 2003.

385 The Knesset, Parliamentary investigation report on social gaps in Israel headed by Knesset member Ran Cohen, Jerusalem, December 2002, pg. 42.

In view of this extensive public work and after the Council had realized that it would not be enough to present a limited plan for enhancing the country's academic system, the newly appointed PBC Chairperson Prof. Shlomo Grossman presented a comprehensive position regarding the role of academic colleges in the country's higher education system. In a conference organized by the U.S. Israel Education Foundation,[386] Prof. Grossman presented the roles of the colleges according to the CHE/PBC:

> The purpose of establishing independent colleges in various areas of the country, including in the periphery, was to expand accessibility to higher education and assist in reducing Socioeconomic gaps. We have increased accessibility to higher education… our further goal is the social mission in peripheral areas - bringing higher education to students. Therefore, colleges were established in various areas of the country, north, south, and other areas. The aim is for graduates of those colleges to integrate in places of employment in the various sectors of the economy. In fact, some of them will and have integrated in place of employment in the same regions in which they have studied. This solves the problem of accessibility to populations for which studying or working far from home is not an option. It is possible to study close to home and obtain an education without traveling long distances (Grossman, 2004: 59–60).

The Colleges: A Means for Realizing Social Objectives

About three years following the decision to include Regional Colleges in the country's Higher Education System and grant them a permit for holding independent study programs, the CHE published data on the impact of these steps on the reduction of social gaps in higher education through colleges. The contribution of academic colleges to reducing social gaps can be measured on a number of levels:

1. **Increase in the number of students among Sephardic Jews (Mizrachim):** The follow up of changes among populations originating from Asia and Africa is difficult as the statistic data identify only those whose parents were born

386 Foundation establishing in 1956 by the Governments of Israel and the United States, that is responsible for organizing the Fulbright Program, initiated by Senator William Fulbright in 1946. The program aims to reinforce the foundations of peach in the world and the understanding between the United States of America and world nations. The foundation is also dedicated to organizing exchange programs for students and faculty members.

in Asia-Africa, and not those who are second generation in Israel to Asia-African descent or the children of mixed couples. And yet, data based on students' birth or whose fathers immigrated from Asia-Africa point to a process of change led by the academic colleges as of the mid 1980s: in three of the first colleges that embarked upon academic independence and at Bar Ilan's colleges, the number of students that had been either born in Asia-Africa or whose parents originated from there, exceeded their numbers at the universities at the time. During those years Israelis born in Asia-Africa or whose parents were born there amounted to 40.5 % of 18 year olds, but to only 24.2 % of all undergraduate degree graduates. As shown in Table 48, the proportion of the Asia-Africa group in universities in 1995/96 (excluding colleges) was only 25.7 %, while the proportion of the same population at independent and other colleges, including Bar Ilan's Extensions, was higher:

Tab. 48: Percentage of students whose parents were born in Asia-Africa, 1995/96

College name	Tel Chai College	Yesreel Valley College	Sapir	Brauda	Rest of the colleges, including Bar Ilan's Extensions	Universities
Percentage of students born in Asia-Africa	31.8 %	36.7 %	52.1 %	29.6 %	44.5 %	25.7 %

Source: Mendelzweig (1995; 1998): 39–40.

Figure 13 illustrates the gap between the proportion of students among this group at universities compared to colleges:

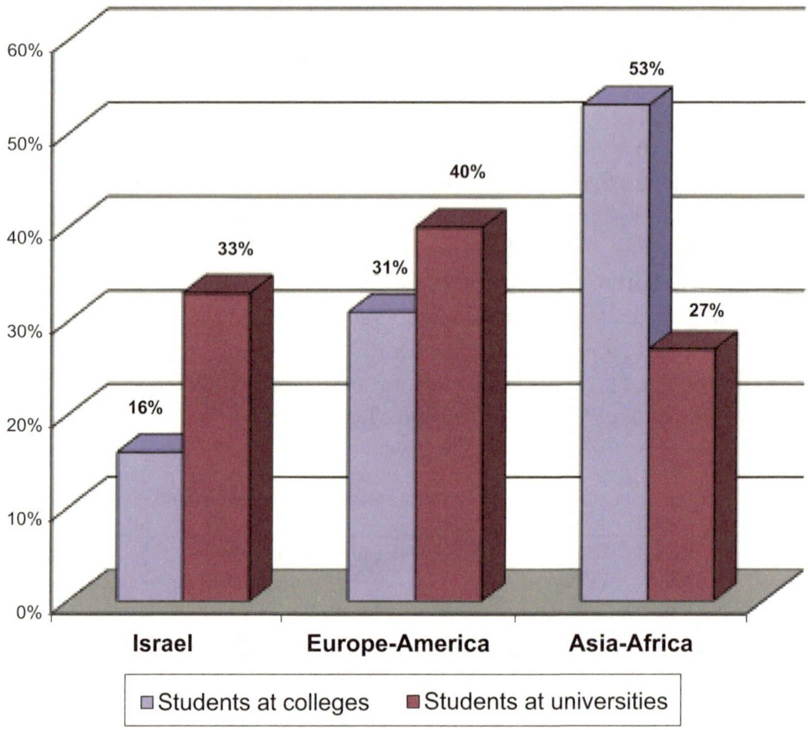

Fig. 13: Number of Undergraduate Students at Regional Colleges Compared to Universities By Ethnic Origin (Jews population), 1995/6

Source: Israeli (1997).

Table 49 shows that despite the difficulties in identifying Asian-African ethnic backgrounds as the years pass, it is still apparent that the proportion of this group among college students is higher than at universities.

Tab. 49: Undergraduate students at universities and academic colleges by religion, ethnic origin and budgeting source, 2003/04

Religion and ethnic origin	Universities	Academic Colleges		
		Total	Budgeting source	
			Public	Private
Absolut numbers (a)	78,561	51,086	32,233	18,853
Percentage	100	100	100	100
Jews and others	90.2	94.8	94.6	95.3
Of which: Jews	87.0	92.3	91.2	94.4
Arabs	9.8	5.2	5.5	4.7
Of which: Muslims–	6.3	3.5	3.8	2.9
Christians–	2.3	1.2	1.2	1.3
Druz–	1.2	0.5	0.5	0.5
Ethnicity (Jews and others) total:	100	100	100	100
Israel	41.6	39.3	36.5	45.0
Asia-Africa:	**22.4**	**28.6**	**28.6**	**28.5**
Born in Israel	20.7	26.7	26.5	26.9
Born outside Israel	1.7	1.9	2.1	1.6
Europe-America:	36.0	32.1	35.2	26.6
Born in Israel	19.2	17.4	16.8	18.7
Born outside Israel	16.9	14.7	18.0	7.9

Source: CBS (2006). Academic Colleges 2003/04, table i:19.

(a) Students whose religion is unknown were only included in the "total" line.

Data published by the CBS for 2008/09 points to the continuation of this trend: During this year 26.3 % students of Asia-Africa descent studied at academic colleges compared to only 19.8 % at universities.[387] In the 1990–2001 decade the system of academic colleges created a 132 % growth in the number of students among degree recipients from the non-Jewish groups.[388]

2. **Establishment of Colleges in the periphery:** A further indication for examining the success of peripheral academic colleges can be noted in their prevalence in their regions. The data in the following report points to the growth in

387 CBS, higher education in Israel, publication 1388, table i: 38.

388 The Knesset, Parliamentary investigation report on social gaps in Israel headed by Knesset member Ran Cohen, Jerusalem, December 2002, pg. 42.

the number of students and stability of peripheral colleges between 1995/96 and 2003/04. During these years we see an increase in the number of colleges with over 3,000 students. When I went back and examined the development of this trend, I found that in 2012/13 the number of colleges with over 3,000 students stabilized, reaching 10 colleges, as can be seen in Table 50.

Tab. 50: Changes in the number of colleges with over 1,000 students, 1995/96–2003/04

Students	Academic Colleges			
	1995/6	**1999/00**	**2003/04**	**2012/13**
Total	15	23	22	20
Up to 1,000	13	10	3	1
1,001–2,000	1	8	8	1
2,001–3,000	-	4	7	10
3,001–5,000	-	4	7	7
5,001–7,100	1	1	1	1

Source: CBS (2006). Academic Colleges 2003/04, table c: 15. 2012/13 data from: http://che.org.il/?page_id=6802, Retrieved 28 July 2014

As aforesaid, most of the increase in the number of undergraduate students occurred at colleges. For example, the average annual change in the number of students from 1989/90 to 1999/00 at universities was 2 % compared with 16.9 % at colleges. The annual average from 1999/00 to 2009/01 was 0.2 % at universities compared to 9.9 % at colleges. The pace of growth at colleges was slow in 2003/04–2009/10, with a 8.5 % annual average. Since the beginning of the past decade a deceleration is apparent in the pace of growth also at academic colleges, with the growth rate in 2012/13 being 3.1 % compared to 2011/12 (see my remarks on this matter in the introduction).

The ratio between the number of students at public colleges and those at private ones also shows a growth trend in the number of students at public colleges, which are the majority of college students. In 1999/00 we see a sharp rise in the number of students at public colleges from 17,422 students, amounting to 52.3 % of all college students, to 32,233 students which were 63 % of all colleges students.

3. **Ages of colleges students:** An important measure for assessing the social mission of colleges is the age of their students compared to those studying at universities and private colleges, as can be seen in Table 51:

Tab. 51: Undergraduate students at universities and academic colleges by age and budgeting source, 2003/04

Age	Universities	Academic Colleges		
		Total	Budgeting source	
			Public	Private
Total absolute numbers	78,561	51,086	32,233	18,863
Percentage	100	100	100	100
Up to 19 years of age	6.2	2.3	2.6	1.7
20–21	16.3	8.9	8.9	9.0
22–24	43.3	37.4	33.9	44.7
25–29	27.1	38.3	41.0	32.6
30–34	3.4	6.6	7.1	5.4
35+	3.8	6.5	6.6	6.5
Median age	23	25	25	23

Source: CBS (2006). Academic Colleges 2003/04, table h: 19.

According to the data, public colleges offer older students a "second chance", because of the accessibility of the college to their place of residence, and due to the extensive savings in travel costs entailed in studying outside ones' region. The 25–29 age group in public colleges amounts to over 40 % of all students, compared to only 27 % at universities and 32.6 % at private colleges. This trend can be also noted in the Israel Central Bureau of Statistics (CBS) data for the 2006/07 academic year: During that year the percentages of students in the 25–29 age group at academic colleges was 37.5 % compared to 32.4 % at universities. The 30–34 age group amounted to 8 % of the total number of students at colleges compared to only 4 % at universities. The median age at the colleges increased to 25.5 compared to 24.3 at universities.[389] When I continued to examine this trend onwards I found that the 2011/12 data point to its continuation: the 25–29 age group consisted of 40.4 % of all students at academic colleges compared to 36.2 % at universities, while the 30–34 age group amounted to 7.8 % of all students at academic colleges compared to 4.6 % at universities. Also in this year the median age remained 25.5.[390]

389 Ibid: 24.

390 CBS, Statistical Abstract of Israel 2013, table 8.56: 460.

4. **Absorption of immigrants:** Academic colleges play and important and central role also in the absorption of *Olim* (new immigrants) in general, and those from developing countries in particular. Table 52 summarizes data collected from the statistical leaflet published every year by the administration of *Olim* students, which shows the following picture:

Tab. 52: Percentage of immigrants studying at institutions of Higher and Post-Secondary Education

Institution	2007/08	2007/08	2008/09
Universities	43.0 %	41.0 %	38.0 %
Academic Colleges	36.3 %	39.3 %	43.4 %
Other institutions	20.7 %	19.7 %	18.6 %
	100 %	100 %	100 %

Source: Student administration Planning, Budgeting and Control Department (2019 publication). Overview of activities and statistical data (2007–2009). Jerusalem.

An examination of the absorption of special populations of *Olim*, such as from Ethiopia and Caucasia points to a larger absorption at Academic Colleges compared to universities, as can be seen in Table 53.

Tab. 53: Percentage of students at institutions of Higher and Post-Secondary Education among Olim from developing countries, 2007–2009

Country of	Universities		Colleges		Other institutions	
origin	2007/08	2008/09	2007/08	2008/09	2007/08	2008/09
Ethiopia	22.62 %	20.70 %	52.0 %	57.0 %	25.38 %	22.30 %
Caucasia	28.0 %	28.1 %	50.5 %	53.5 %	21.5 %	18.4 %

Source: Student administration Planning, Budgeting and Control Department (2019 publication). Overview of activities and statistical data (2007–2009), Jerusalem.

Researchers in the field of higher education who view the opening of colleges as a blessing for the system and for Israeli society, base their position on further numerical data pointing to changes that took place in the periphery and among the young generations in and outside these regions.

5. **Rejection of applications for academic studies:** In the first few years following the opening of the gates of higher education, a decline can be noted in the number of rejections of applications for academic studies, which then stabilized at 19 % in recent years.

1984/5	1988/9	1990/1	1996/7	1997/8
34.5 %	26 %	22.4 %	19.3 %	19 %

Source: Barshad & Biham (2009).

6. **Undergraduate Studies at Colleges:** The number of students for undergraduate degrees, which is the main focus of colleges, has shown constant growth in the two decades 1990–2007. The first decade (1990–2000) has seen an average annual growth of 24.7 % at academic colleges (not including academic colleges for teachers). Between 2000 and 2007 we see an annual growth of 8.7 %. The annual average of the two decades amounts to a total growth of 18.5 % at colleges compared to 2.9 % at universities.
7. **Graduate Studies at Colleges:** As of 1998/99 graduate studies were offered at academic colleges. Here too we see an increase in the number of colleges already teaching graduate studies compared to a decline at universities: In the 1990–2000 decade we see an increase of 6.5 % in graduate studies at universities. This upwards trend was moderated in 2000–2006, reaching 1.5 % compared to a decline of 3.2 % between 2006 and 2007. During the same period we see a growth of 11.1 % in graduate studies at academic colleges (not including the academic colleges for teachers) (CBS, publication 1333).
8. **Changes in the percentages of students by districts:** As of the opening of the gates of higher education, a significant change occurred in the number of students at districts having a small number of students. In areas in which there are academic colleges we see an increase in the number of students from these district. In the south, where we have Sapir College, Ashkelon College and the Beer Sheva Technological college, the number of students had multiplied. As shown in Table 54, in the north, not including Haifa, where there are the Zefat College, Brauda, Tel Chai, Yesreel Valley, Jordan Valley and Western Galilee, we see the number of students multiplied by three:

Tab. 54: Percentage of undergraduate students at institutions of higher education by area of residence, 1989–2008.

Year	1989/90	1994/95	1999/00	2004/05	2007/08	2007/08
Absolute number	55,250	86,320	126,900	155,900	163,530	168,000
Total %	100.0	100.0	100.0	100.0	100.0	100.0
Jerusalem	22.7	17.5	15.5	13.0	13.1	13.2
North	–	2.5	5.3	7.4	8.2	8.5
Haifa	21.7	22.0	17.9	16.4	15.4	15.2
Center	4.1	4.3	15.9	16.2	16.9	17.2
Tel Aviv	42.8	42.7	31.5	31.9	31.5	30.7
South	8.7	10.9	13.9	15.0	15.0	15.2

Source: Barshad & Biham (2009).

The writers of the report ascribe most of the changes in the distribution of students at the various districts to the deceleration in the growth in the number of students studying at universities compared to the substantial growth of their numbers at academic colleges. According to the report, in 1989/90 8.7 % of all undergraduate students were studying at the southern district, all of them at Ben Gurion University. In 2002/03 this district included approx. 15 % of the country's undergraduate students, over half of whom were studying at the colleges located within the district, including the Ashkelon College.

To examine whether the geographic deployment of institutions of higher education and their increased scope brought students from around the country to their gates, we will examine the proportion of students commencing their studies from an average cohort of 20–24 year olds. Table 55 presents the distribution of new students between 2002 and 2004:

Tab. 55: Number of students by districts and average percentages of their cohort

	2001/02		2003/04	
	Total year 1	% of average cohort	Total year 1	% of average cohort
National total	43,645	40.4	48,048	43.6
Jerusalem	3,570	26.2	3,674	26.1
North	6,914	35.7	7,588	39.0
Haifa	5,711	41.6	6,260	46.0
Center	10,895	45.7	12,427	50.4
Tel Aviv	7,971	44.1	8,399	48.9
South	6,796	42.9	7,626	45.8

Source: Aharoni & Biham (2008).

An analysis of the data shows that the southern district, that had lagged behind over the years, continued its six year growth trend. As mentioned, the disappointing figures in this district received special mention in the 1999 State Comptroller's report. According to the report, the proportion of holders of an academic degree among the Jewish population of Israel was 15.8 %, while the average proportion at the four southern Development towns was 7.65 %. This proportion is especially low in comparison to affluent cities such as Ramat Hasharon (24.5 %), Givataim (19.6 %), Haifa (19.3 %), Jerusalem (19.1 %), Tel Aviv (19.1 %), and even compared to improved Development towns such as Karmiel (12.05 %) and Yavne (10.29 %). The 2002–2004 data point to a significant change.

I found reinforcement for the approach that sees the expansion of the higher education system as contributing to the reduction of social gaps, in a paper by Prof. Yossi Shavit, relying on a comparative study between 15 countries from western and eastern Europe, Asia, the United States and Australia. The study examined accessibility to higher education in those countries in the 1980s and 1990s, and found that in all countries academic institutions underwent an accelerated expansion, most of which can be noted among second tier institutions – the public and private colleges, and less among research institutions. According to Shavit, since the publication of Raftery and Hout's theory in 1993, by which the higher classes take advantage of opportunities for professional advantage following the opening of the academic system, and despite its importance, real changes have taken place in higher education, which in turn reduced class inequality. According to Shavit, most of the system's expansion can be ascribed to colleges, for a number of main reasons:

1. The gates of the colleges are not as selective as those of research institutions and the number of students has grown substantially in all participating countries, including Israel.
2. The expansion of the academic system has also led to a privatization process, which if maintained at a reasonable level (up to 40 % of the higher education budget), contributes to the expansion of the system at higher and faster rates because private institutions accelerate the system's expansion better than do public colleges.
3. A further importance of the contribution of public colleges can be found in one of the conclusions to the findings of the study, by which when the higher education budget coming from private sources ranges between 25 % and 40 %, the level of inequality in higher education is considered low. In Israel and Australia the budget from private sources amounted to 25 % of the total higher education budget, and therefore the level of inequality found in these

countries was lower than found for instance in South Korea, where 80 % of the higher education budget comes from private sources. This fact, according to Shavit, reinforces the conclusion that public colleges contribute to accessibility for high education while maintaining a relatively low budget from private sources.[391]

391 D. Shchori, "The social importance of a 'sparse' undergraduate degree", Haaretz, 8 May 2005.

Chapter 17 Colleges as Means for Realizing Social Objectives: Updated Situation Report 2019

Two decades after the opening of the gates of higher education through colleges, the data points to the colleges having fulfilled their national role as defined by the CHE, and most of all addressing the demand for higher education that had been constantly growing as of the 1990s. The colleges generally and the public colleges in particular, lead to increased accessibility to higher education to new populations, or those that were not represented in it according to their appropriate proportion in the country's general population. The share of public colleges in fulfilling this goal is larger than that of all other institutions, as shall be shown below. To assess the contribution of colleges in general and that of public colleges in particular to furthering the accessibility of higher education, I have examined the following parameters:

a. The Positioning of Public Colleges and their Stability in the past two Decades
b. The number of Students in Colleges – Undergraduate & Graduate Degrees
c. The number of College Graduates after two decades
d. The colleges' part in absorbing special and peripheral populations

The Positioning and Stability of Public Colleges in the Past Two Decades

Public colleges are deployed throughout the country, from Tel Chai in the north to Beer Sheva in the south. Most colleges are located in the south and the north, specifically in the country's geographical periphery. This geographical positioning near the homes of many of the younger populations of the north and the south, is an important component of their decision to attend academic studies while avoiding the high expenses that accompany academic studies at the center, mostly consisting of travel and housing expenses. The physical proximity of colleges contributes to changing the general approach of young adults towards academia as both physically and mentally remote from their lives, and of academic institutions as alienated ivory towers. Thus, the fact that the colleges are located at close physical proximity to potential candidates is an important component in increasing the accessibility of academic studies also from a cognitive perspective and not only a geographical one. As the colleges acquire a stronger academic status, they become a natural academic home for the young adults of their regions.

Based on data accumulated until now, we can safely say that most hypotheses raised by researchers who perceived the opening of the gates of higher education through colleges as a recipe for lowering the overall academic level and for stratification of institutions, were mostly invalidated, although as I will show, it is difficult to point to a reduction of all types of gaps between center and periphery. Higher education is accessible today to large parts of the population who wish to gain an academic education. The data on all peripheral measures point to in increase in the number of students in the southern and northern districts, which had been very low until 1990. The number of students living in peripheral towns has also increased, a fact that points to the arrival of new populations, as well as to changes in the approach of the younger generations, who view the colleges in their regions as their natural academic homes.

An important point of attraction of colleges for these young adults is the range of programs offered by the colleges for both undergraduate and graduate degrees, and specifically the professional options such as nursing, accounting, social work and more. The offering is large and diverse: Programs in the arts, technology and additional areas such as economics, psychology, sociology and more.

Contrary to the Non-Publicly Funded colleges whose number was reduced from 16 to 12 in 2018, with two more currently undergoing processes of either closing down or merging, Public Colleges maintain their stability despite the long and tedious academization process they have endured. The reduction from 21 to 20 public colleges in 2015 resulted from Ariel Academic College becoming a university.

Alongside the stability of the public colleges, we also see a significant increase in their number of students. Compared to their establishment in 2000, when there were 10 public colleges with less than 1,000 students in each, in 2019 each of the colleges numbered 2,000–5,000 students. The number of colleges of education reached its peak in 2005: 26 colleges, which in 2019 were reduced to 21 colleges in total. This reduction is part of the CHE and the Ministry of Education's plan to reduce the number of colleges of education through unifications or mergers in order to enable efficient operation of institutions with at least 1,000 students. As some of the colleges of education there were less than 1,000 students in 2019, and these were instructed to unify or merge with larger academic institutions. The merger plan was approved by the CHE and is currently being enforced. Parts of it were implemented over the past five years (2015–2020): The Achva College of Education merged with the Achva Academic College and they became a single institution. The Kibbutzim College merged with the College of Technology and the Arts and they are now a single institution. Additional merger plans are currently being examined between colleges of education and other academic institutions.

Figure 14 presents the number of institutions in 1990–2018. In 2020 there were 11 Non-Publicly Funded institutions after a further college was closed in 2019 and another is currently being closed. At the time of writing this book, there are 60 colleges in total, of which 10 are Non-Publicly Funded.

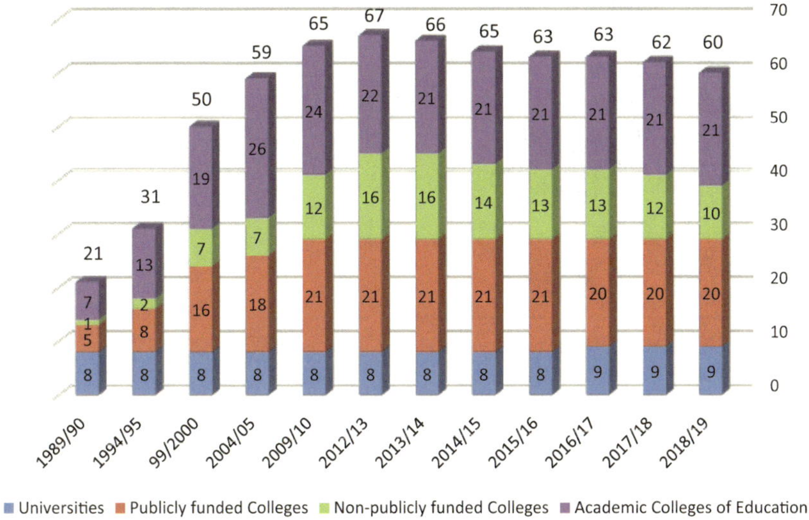

Fig. 14: Number of academic institutions in Israel, 1990–2018

Source: CHE website, Collection of data towards the 2018/19 academic year. Retrieved 21 March, 2020.

Number of Undergraduate and Graduate College Students

The trend we have noted in the first decade of colleges in Israel, continues. The number of undergraduate students at universities continues to decline, and in 2018/19 amounted to 74,106 students or 38.9 % of all undergraduate students, compared to 85 % in 1990. However, at colleges this figure shows a continuous growth curve, reaching 61 % of all undergraduate students in Israel in 2018/19. The CHE's decision to gradually sever the ties between the Extensions and the universities, at a time in which students studying at Extensions were counted as university students, strengthened this trend. This downwards trend continues despite Ariel College becoming a university and the subsequent allocations of its students to the universities count as of 2015. These trends are shown in Table 56:

Tab. 56: Undergraduate Students by Institution type, 1989/90–2018/19

	Total absolute numbers	Percentage	Universities	Academic Colleges including Colleges-Extensions	Non-Publicly Funded Colleges	Colleges of Education
1989/90	55,250	100 %	85.0	3.4	3.0	8.6
1994/5	86,320	100 %	72.8	9.5	5.9	11.7
1999/00	126,800	100 %	52.7	19.5	12.5	15.2
2004/05	155,900	100 %	44.8	27.1	13.7	14.4
2009/10	178,400	100 %	37.2	33.0	18.5	11.3
2014/15	191,691	100 %	33.8	34.0	19.4	12.8
2015/16	191,616	100 %	38.8	29.1	19.0	13.1
2016/17	191,241	100 %	38.7	29.5	18.4	13.4
2017/18	189,845	100 %	39.1	29.7	18.0	13.2
2018/19	290,996	100 %	38.9	30.2	18.1	12.7

Source: Central Bureau of Statistics Table 8: Students in institutions of higher education by degree, institution type and institution, 2018/19.

A downwards trend was noted in the Non-Publicly Funded colleges: Their number of undergraduate students declined in 2019 by 2,457 students compared to 2016. the publicly funded colleges still mark a moderated rise in their total number of students, with the decline noted between 2014/15 and 2015/16 resulting from Ariel College becoming a university. During the 2015/16 academic year, 9,580 undergraduate students were added to the total number of students at universities – all of them Ariel's students. 2018/19 has seen an increase in the number of new students in the entire academic system, following the decline of 2016/17–2017/18. Most of the increase was at public colleges.

In order to assess the general trend to be expected in the coming years, I have examined the number of students commencing undergraduate studies, as the entry of new students to the academic system points to a continued three-year trend (at least) following their entry. According to CBS data, the proportion of year 1 students at all institutions of higher education within an average age group, ranges between 47 % and 49 % as of 2009/10 to 2018/19. Table 57 shows that the trend has continued in recent years, and the number of college students is still on the rise.

Tab. 57: First year students at institutions of higher education by institution type

Total	Universities		Academic Colleges		Academic Teachers Colleges	
	Year 1	Annual change (percentage) 2009/10–2016/17	Year 1	Annual change (percentage) 2009/10–2016/17	Year 1	Annual change (percentage) 2009/10–2016/17
2009/10	22,982		26,384		5,084	
2012/13	22,767		30,677		5,844	
2013/14	21,943		28,823		6,241	
2014/15	21,200		29,951		6,596	
2015/16	23,557		28,097		7,205	
2016/17	22,141	0.5	27,844	0.8	7,956	5.7
2017/18	22,200		27,998		7,628	
2018/19	22,314		29,260		7,586	

Source: Central Bureau of Statistics Table 11: First year students at institutions of higher education by institution type.

As can be seen from the table, most new students in the system can be attributed to colleges, meaning that a continued growth in their numbers is also to be expected in the next three years. The number of students admitted to academic colleges in the past two years has grown both in comparison to universities and to colleges of education, in which a decline was noted in the number of new entrants in 2018/19. Moreover, the trend by which the number of students at colleges is increasing compared to other institutions, also points to students making colleges their first choice, rather than a second or third choice as could have been alleged in the first years of their operation.

Despite the increase in the number of undergraduate students in recent years, we also see a reduction in the overall number of graduate students. Only at the Non-Publicly Funded colleges and the academic colleges of education can we see a gradual increase in 2016/17. In 2018/19 we see a significant increase in public academic colleges and a continued growth trend in colleges of education. As can be seen in Table 58, the upwards trend in the Non-Publicly Funded colleges has not only stopped but declined by more than 6 %.

Tab. 58: Number of graduate students at colleges and universities 2013/14–2018/19

	Total	Total Univer sity	Percen tage	Academic Colleges						
	graduate students in all institutions	**students**	**of graduate students**	**Total Academic Colleges**	**General Academic Colleges**	**Percentage of graduate students**	**Non-Publicly Funded Colleges**	**Percentage of graduate students**	**Colleges of Education**	**Percentage of graduate students**
2013/14	54,738	38,855	71 %	15,883	3,432	6.2 %	7,788	14.2 %	4,663	12 %
2014/15	56,600	38,091	67.3 %	18,509	4,032	7.1 %	8,400	14.8 %	6,077	10.7 %
2015/16	58,303	38,778	66.5 %	19,525	3,452	6.0 %	9,525	16.3 %	6,548	11.2 %
2016/17	60,146	39,038	65 %	21,108	2,756	4.6 %	11,200	18.6 %	7,152	11.9 %
2018/19	61,014	38,148	62.5 %	22,866	4,623	7.6 %	10,466	17.2 %	7,777	12.7 %

Source: Central Bureau of Statistics Table 2: University students by institutions and degree 1989/90–2015/16 2018/19 data – CBS, table 8: Students in institutions of higher education by degree and institution type, 2018/19.

The data in the table point to a changing trend also in graduate studies, with the percentage of university students declining while increasing at colleges, similarly to the trend we have seen with undergraduate studies. The proportion of university students declined in the past five years from 71 % to 62.5 %, while at colleges it increased from 29 % five years ago, in 2013/14, to 37.5 % in 2018/19. As can be seen in Table 59, this figure has been showing a negative trend at universities for over a decade, and a clear and stable positive trend at colleges during the same period.

Tab. 59: Number of graduate students at universities and colleges and the annual change

	1999/00 1999/00	**2009/10 2009/10**	**2014/15 2016/17**	**2017/18 2017/18**	**2018/19 2018/19**	**Annual change percentage**	
						1999/00 2009/10	**2017/18 2018/19**
Total Graduate degree:	30,913	47,237	56,263	60,356	60,994	4.3	1.1
Universities	30,454	36,923	38,849	38,268	38,128	1.9	0.4
Colleges	459	8,198	11,674	14,463	15,089	33.4	4.3
Colleges of Education	–	2,116	5,740	7,625	7,777	--	2.0

Source: CBS, table 4.64 Students at Universities, Academic Colleges and Colleges of Education by degree, Statistical Abstract of Israel, 2019.

Based on the data we see that colleges have successfully increased the number of students attending the country's academic system and increased the accessibility of higher education to new populations. Universities lost their seniority in undergraduate studies, and the same trend can also be noted in graduate studies. The academic status of colleges had been solidified both in undergraduate and graduate studies. This solidification exceeds the CHE's plans, based on the fact that colleges were not scheduled to offer graduate studies according to the original plan accepted by the CHE for expanding accessibility to higher education. According to the plan, colleges had been entrusted with the task of absorbing the growing demand for undergraduate studies, with no option to offer graduate degrees, certainly not research degrees that include a thesis paper. The option for graduate studies at colleges was offered to students only two decades ago, and only at a small number of academic colleges. Less than a decade ago the first college graduate program with thesis had been approved. This approval was granted after many years of offering undergraduate degrees and graduate degrees without a thesis.

According to the academic system's expansion plan published by the CHE in 1994, colleges were defined as non-Research institutions, offering undergraduate studies only.[392] One of the goals of the plan was to train a reserve of students who

392 Government decision number 3964, 28 September, 1994.

would continue to advanced studies at the universities. As the years passed, it was clear that the CHE's limited plan did not stand the test of time. Moreover, the fact that the CHE defined the colleges as non-research institutions, leaving research exclusively in the hands of the universities, also did not stand the test of time. Academic teaching simply cannot exist without research and without keeping up to date with research being held in the field throughout the world, which is why colleges had to allocate resources to their academic faculties to do research and keep up to date.

This situation changed in 2012 when the first collective agreement was signed between the academic faculty at the colleges and the CHE. Under the new agreement, lecturers conducting research at colleges were allocated research and sabbatical budgets. Consequently, colleges began to engage in research, even though they are not eligible for direct research budgets as are universities. A further change in the CHE's plan took place following pressure by the colleges to be approved graduate studies with a thesis, as part of their natural development as academic institutions. The CHE's definition of colleges as non-research teaching institutions as had been the case in the CHE's first plan, is undergoing a continuous process of erosion, and their position in the academic field is continuously changing according to reality and the many parameters involved. Alongside these developments and following the expansion of colleges, a struggle ensued between universities and colleges over who would be students' choice, and a competition began between the institutions. The first outcome of this competition led to universities increasingly offering students a non-research graduate degree (without thesis), as opposed to their academic essence. According to CBS data, the number of students completing a graduate degree with thesis at universities is continuously declining. In 2008, a total of 3,833 students completed their graduate degree with thesis at all universities together, of a total of 11,759 graduates which are only 32.6 % of the total number of students that completed their graduate degree. This number declined over the years, stabilizing in 2017 at 3,844 graduates of 15,186 which are only 25.3 % of all graduate degree graduates at the universities. In 2016/17 the colleges presented 102 graduate degree graduates with a thesis, which were 5.7 % of the total number of graduate degree graduates in Israel.[393] This number is expected to grow as a result of approvals being granted to additional colleges for offering graduate programs with a thesis.

Number of College Graduates Following the First Two Decades of Their Operation

A further measure which may point to the accessibility of higher education in the two last decades through colleges is the total number of college graduates in both

393 CBS, Recipients of a graduate degree at universities and colleges, 2015/16.

degree levels. In fact, this measure examines the outputs of colleges compared to the more senior universities. In 1990, at which time only a small number of colleges had been certified to grant an undergraduate degree, only 400 students graduated from general colleges, and 655 more from colleges of education. That year universities had a total of 10,192 graduates. Within a period of 30 years the number of degree recipients multiplied by 5.2 compared to their number in 1990: At the Academic Colleges their number grew by 69.9 and at colleges of education by 16.5. Meanwhile, the number of graduates at universities increased by only 2.9. In 2000 there were 6,247 college graduates and 4,318 at the colleges of education and in total 10,604 graduates. At the universities there were 17,298 graduates that year. As of 2000 the numbers crossed and the total number of graduates at colleges exceeded that of universities. In 2009/10 – 2017/18 the total number of degree recipients grew by 30.1 %, especially at colleges of education, in which the number grew by 101.1 % (CBS, 2019). This general trend exists also for graduate degrees – until 2000 this degree was granted by universities only, and within a period of eight years (as of 2009/10), the relative proportion of graduate degree recipients at universities declined from 80.5 % in 2009/10 to 60.4 % in 2017/18, as can be seen in Table 60.

Tab. 60: Total number of graduates at universities and colleges (undergraduate and graduate degrees)

	1989/ 90	**1999/00**	**2009/10**	**2016/17**	**2017/ 18**	**Annual change percentage**		
						2017/ 18–2009/ 10	**2017/18– 2009/10**	**2017/ 18– 2016/17**
Total undergraduate degree graduates:	11,528	29,322	42,934	51,078	51,298	5.9	3.0	0.4
Universities	10,192	18,706	21,849	23,817	22,693	3.0	0.6	4.7
Colleges	400	6,243	16,072	20,329	27,964	16.4	4.4	2.3
Colleges of Education	655	4,373	5,013	6,932	7,801	10.0	7.6	12.5
Total Graduate degree recipients	2,790	7,528	15,649	23,443	25,261	8.8	8.3	7.8
universities	2,790	7,528	12,590	15,186	15,265	6.8	3.3	0.5
Colleges	–	–	2,709	5,466	7,012	–	17.2	28.3
Colleges of Education	–	–	350	2,791	2,984	–	42.9	6.9

Source: CBS, Higher education in Israel – Selected data on recipients of academic degrees in 2017/18 upon completion of the academic year. Table A: Degree recipients by institution type in selected academic years.

Note: The data include graduates of the Open University.

In the same report published by the CBS we see a prominent proportion of public colleges among recipients of undergraduate degrees. In 2017/18 the proportion of public colleges (not including colleges of education) was 23.4 %, while that of the Non-Publicly funded colleges was 17.2 % and of colleges of Education 15.2 %. As aforesaid, the proportion of university students among the total number of degree recipients is gradually declining. In 2017/18 60.4 % of degree recipients had studied at universities, and 27.8 % at colleges. The share of the publicly funded colleges that had begun offering graduate studies only in 2005, had been only 5.2 %, and at colleges of Education 11.8 %, while the share of the Non-Publicly funded colleges was 22.6 %.

A deeper examination of the efficiency of colleges' outcomes as new institutions focuses on the number of graduates that completed their studies within eight years after completing high school. The data examined by the CBS in 2017 following students that began studying towards their undergraduate degree in 2001–2003 and completed their studies within four types of durations: Standard duration, ranging from three to five years according to the program; three years following the standard time; two years following the standard time; and one year following the standard time. According to the data, 47.5 % of university students completed their studies at a standard duration. At the academic colleges, 51.4 % of students completed their studies at standard duration while at the colleges of education this figure was lower, at 39.1 %. When looking at the group of students that completed their studies three years following the standard duration, they consist of 78.1 % of university students and 72.3 % at colleges. This figure was lower at colleges of education, 60.9 %. Figure 15 presents 2017 data for the four groups.

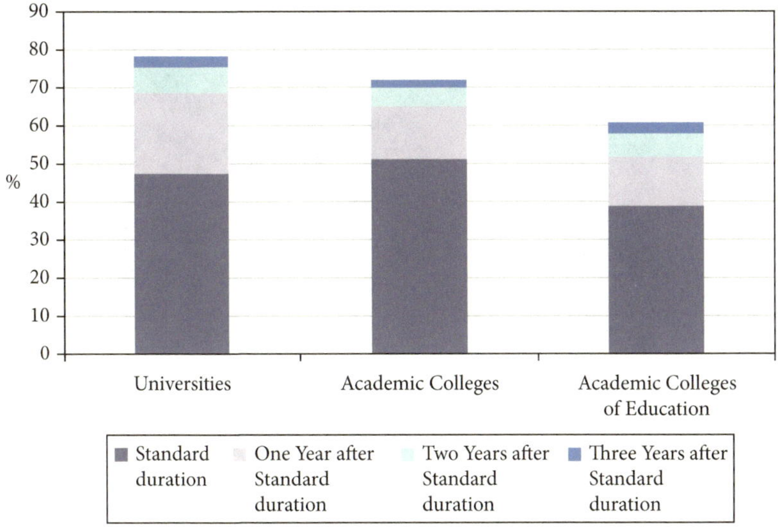

Fig. 15: Undergraduate students that completed their high school studies in 2001–2014 by Year of Graduation and Type of Institution

Note: The data does not include the Open University.

Source: CBS, Statistical Abstract of Israel 2017: 68.

2019 CBS publications point to an improvement in the number of students that completed their degree within the standard duration as well as the continued trend by which their percentage at colleges is higher than at universities. Students who began studying in 2011 and completed their undergraduate studies within a standard period of time amounted to 60.2 % at universities and 62.5 % at colleges. At the colleges of education 55.8 % of students completed their studies within a standard time. The percentage of students who completed their studies three years following the standard duration was 85.4 % at universities, 82.1 % at colleges and 75.8 % at colleges of education. Figure 16 presents 2018 percentages for each of the four groups.

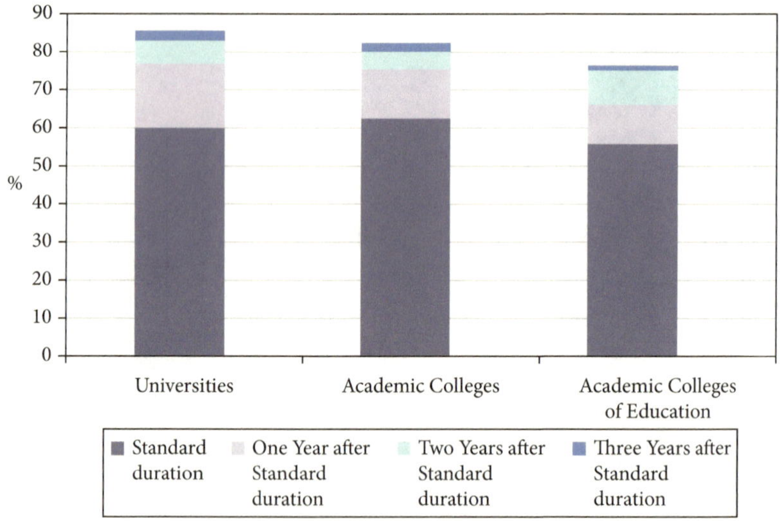

Fig. 16: Undergraduate students that completed their high school studies between 2011 and 2018 by Year of Graduation and Type of Institution

Source: CBS, Statistical Abstract of Israel 2019: 89. Note: The data does not include the Open University.

The 2017 and the 2019 data point to the colleges' success in terms of efficiency, exceeding even that of the senior universities. The assumption is that students at colleges tend to study professions, and less high duration programs such as medicine. However, there is no ignoring the success of colleges as available centers of study for populations interested in completing their studies within a short period of time and enter the work force relatively quickly.

The Colleges' Part in Absorbing Special and Peripheral Populations

The direct contribution of colleges in general and public colleges in particular to the national effort of increasing the accessibility of higher education, focuses on students from peripheral, less affluent towns. In fact, the first and foremost task of the colleges, defined in the CHE's plan for expansion of the academic system, had been the inclusion of new populations within the academic system, particularly ones from the social and geographic periphery; or in other words, the opening of the gates of academia to populations that had been otherwise excluded and did not take part in academic studies considering their proportion in the general population. Until the opening of the gates of academia in Israel, academic studies were mostly blocked to the following populations:

1. Residents of towns belonging to Socioeconomic clusters 1–4 and geographically remote towns, especially in the far south and north.
2. The Arab citizens of the State of Israel.
3. Israel's Haredi (ultra-orthodox Jewish) population.
4. The Ethiopian community of Israel.

I shall now examine the changes among these populations since the opening of the gates of academia by the colleges.

1. **Elevated accessibility to residents of the social and geographic periphery:** A general overview on the change in the proportion of students admitted to academic studies and those rejected between the two periods – prior to the expansion of the academic system (until 1994), and following the system's expansion (as of 1994 onwards), points to a general change of trend, from which we can also note the populations which did not participate in academic studies proportionally to their share in the population. The first general indication reinforcing the decision to open the gates of academia to new populations, can be found in the number of candidates that were admitted and studied at academic institutions compared to their previous numbers at universities. Prior to opening to gates of higher education, in 1980, 48.2 % of all applicants were admitted and studied at universities. Ten years later, in 1990, this number increased to 55.8 %. A further decade later, with the reinforcement of the colleges in 2000, the number further increased to 65.3 % and in 2015 reached 65.3 %. The expansion of the entire system began to show results in the growing demand for academic studies and the opening of the gates of the universities as a result of the growing competition with the new institutions over students and budgets.

The expansion of the entire Higher Education System as of the mid 1990s also affected the level of accessibility to higher education among populations in the country's periphery and among its disadvantaged populations. To assess this influence I examined the change in the number of students from peripheral towns and regions based on the CBS index and the change in the number of students by regions – south and north of Israel.

The CBS ranks towns by Socioeconomic clusters. I used this classification as a key for examining the ratio between the number of students from affluent towns and those from less affluent ones, as well as the differences between the number of students from peripheral towns and those coming from central locations, over the past two decades. The CBS classification was built based on a Socioeconomic rating ranging between 1 and 10, with 1 expressing a less affluent town which would normally be also geographically peripheral, and 10 expressing a central and affluent town. CBS 2017 publications refer to towns ranked 1–2 as highly peripheral, 3–4 as peripheral, 5 between periphery and center, 6–7 central and 8–10 very central.

Based on this classification, most of the country's Development towns are in the range of 1–5. Applying this index by regions, we can say that in general the south and north of the country are characterized by socially and economically weaker towns compared to the center of the country. Based on CBS 2015 distribution of towns in the north, over 60 % of local authorities are ranked in Socioeconomic clusters 1–4 (56 towns of 93 in the entire region). Only 15 local authorities (16.1 %) are ranked in Socioeconomic clusters 7–10. In the south, over 46 % of the local authorities are ranked in Socioeconomic clusters 1–4, and only 23 % in Socioeconomic clusters 7–10. Compared to the south and the north, in the central region, of 52 local authorities 35 (67.3 %) are ranked in Socioeconomic clusters 7–10.

Based on the above, when examining changes in the number of students based on CBS publications by regional distribution, we see a changing trend – a constant rise in the number of students from the country's social and geographical periphery during the period of operation of the colleges. As can be seen from the following table, the last publications towards the opening of the 2018/19 academic year points to a change in the number of students from the northern and southern regions.

Tab. 61: Undergraduate Students by institution district, 1989/90, 1999/00–2018/19

	1989/90	1999/00	2016/17	2017/18	2018/19
Total absolute numbers	55,250	126,900	191,915	189,845	190,650
Total percentages	100.0	100.0	100.0	100.0	100.0
Jerusalem	22.7	15.5	13.7	13.7	13.9
North	–	5.3	9.7	9.8	9.7
Haifa	21.7	17.9	13.4	12.4	12.1
Center	4.1	15.9	17.6	17.8	17.9
Tel Aviv	42.8	31.5	31.2	31.8	31.9
South	8.7	13.9	14.3	14.5	14.6

Source: CHE, Collection of data towards the opening of the academic year (2019–2020).

The percentage of students in the southern region increased between 1989/90 and 2017/18 by over 75 % and continued to rise in 2018/19. At the northern region, in which there were no students registered in 1989/90, we see an increase of 85 % in the proportion of students between 1999/00 and 2017/18. At these districts, where the number of students was significantly lower than in the central region, the number of students increased at the expense of the Tel Aviv and Jerusalem districts. This increase is an indication of the penetration of new populations who had previously been absent from the academic system or whose representation in it had been substantially lower than their proportion in the general population. However, the identities of populations within the southern and northern regions should be examined in order to assess the reduction of gaps between populations in the acquisition of higher education.

In 1991, the proportion of students from Socioeconomic clusters 1–4 reached 24.5 % in all institutions, while the proportion of students from Socioeconomic clusters 7–10 was 45.5 %. In 2008 the proportion of students from Socioeconomic clusters 1–4 was 24.8 %, while the proportion of students from Socioeconomic clusters 7–10 was 47.3 %. As of 2016 onwards, following 15 years of operation of academic colleges, we see an increase in the proportion of students from Socioeconomic clusters 1–4 which in 2018 reached 29.6 %, as can be seen in Table 62.

Tab. 62: Number of students by social clusters in 2019/20

Academic year/Social Cluster	**1–2**	**3–4**	**5–6**	**7–8**	**9–10**
2015/16	6.1 %	19.4 %	40.6 %	28.6 %	2.2 %
2016/17	7.5 %	20.7 %	25.5 %	40.7 %	2.7 %
2017/18	7.9 %	21.1 %	25.2 %	40.0 %	2.7 %
2018/19	8.3 %	21.3 %	24.6 %	40.0 %	2.7 %

Source: CHE website, Collection of data towards the opening of the academic year 2019/2020, page 8, Retrieved 22 March 2020.

Note: In 2016–2017 we see changes in Socioeconomic clusters 5–6 and 7–8 resulting from changes in the location of specific towns in these clusters.

Despite the rise in the proportion of students from towns pertaining to clusters ranked low, still the relative proportion of young adults from these towns (aged 18–30) is lower compared to their proportion in academic studies in 2014/15. There is a clear gap in the proportion of students from towns ranked low, as can be seen in Figure 17.

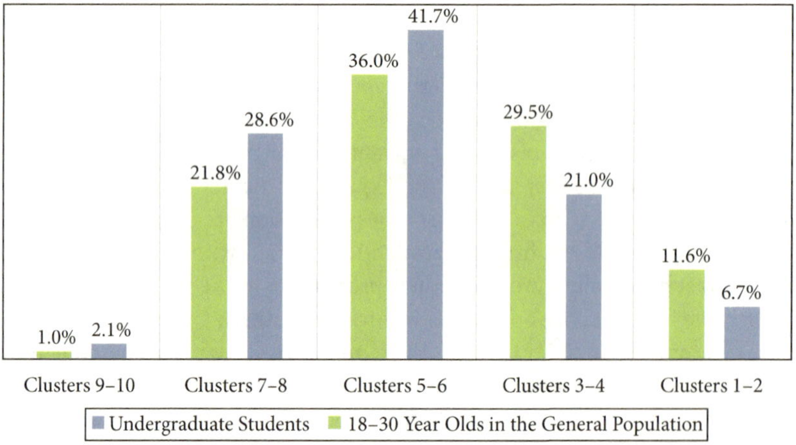

Fig. 17: Undergraduate students in 2014/15 compared to all 18–30 year olds in 2015 by Socioeconomic cluster

Source: Weinger (2016). The Knesset research and information center, Undergraduate students data, figure 3.

According to the data, the proportion of underground students in the low clusters (1–4) is smaller than the overall proportion of 18–30 year olds in those clusters in this age group in Israel. However, the proportion of students in clusters 5 and above is larger than that of 18–30 year olds in those clusters in this age group in Israel. When examining the distribution of these populations among the types of academic institutions, we find that a large part of the population attending publicly funded colleges comes from less affluent towns, while most students from affluent towns study at universities.

In 2014/15 the population of university students included 35 % of students from affluent towns ranked 7–10 while only 24 % of students were from towns ranked 1–4. At the publicly funded colleges, 22 % of students came from towns ranked 7–10, while 28 % of them came from towns ranked 1–4. At the Non-Publicly Funded colleges the composition of the population of students in both groups was similar to that of universities, as can be seen in Figure 18.

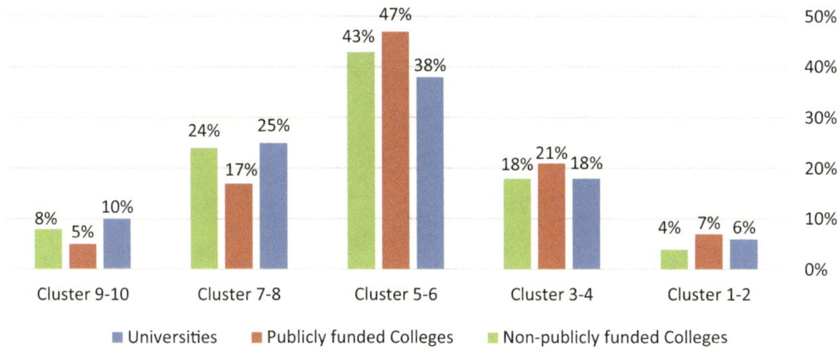

Fig. 18: Distribution of Students by Socioeconomic Clusters in High Schools, 2013/14
Source: The CHE, Israel's higher education system, 2015: 38.

As shown in Figure 19, three years later, the proportion of students from towns ranked 7–10 studying at universities rose to 49 % while that of students from towns ranked 1–4 reached 26.1 %, At the publicly funded colleges the proportion of students from towns ranked 7–10 reached 33.5 % while that of students from towns ranked 1–4 was 32.8 %. As can be noted from Figure 20, in 2017/18 we see a similar picture as in 2016/17.

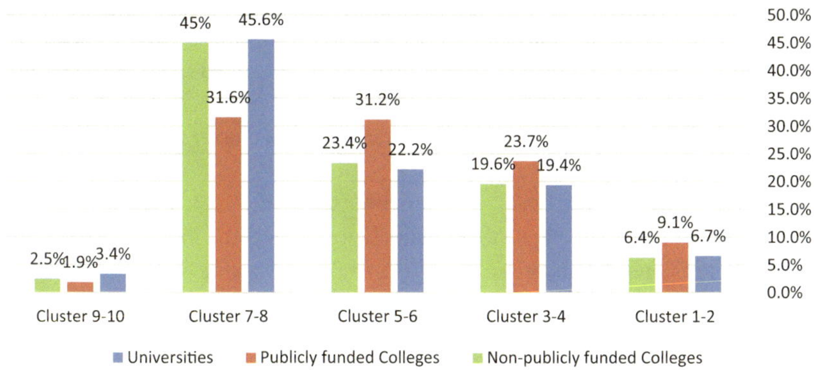

Fig. 19: Distribution of Students by Socioeconomic Clusters in High Schools, 2016/17
Source: The CHE, Israel's higher education system, 2018: 11

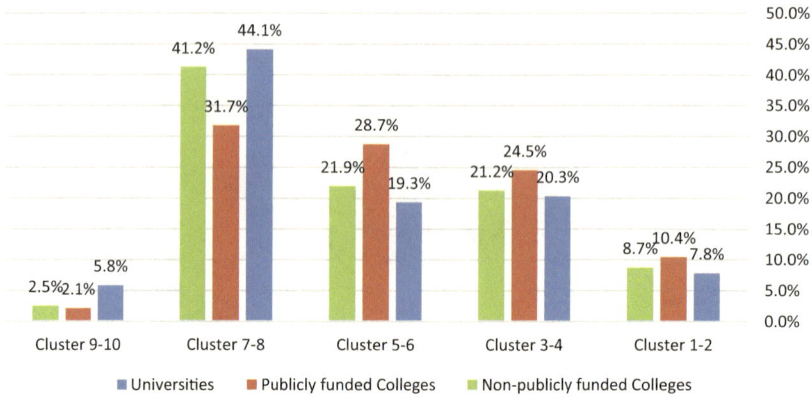

Fig. 20: Distribution of Students by Socioeconomic Clusters in High Schools, 2019/20

Source: The CHE, Israel's Higher Education System, 60 years of academic excellence: 24.

An overview of a decade of colleges in Israel in the number of students parameter leads to the conclusion that the number of students from peripheral towns has increased, both from a regional and a local perspective. The proportion of students from the southern and northern regions has been growing steadily since 1990, with a total increase of nearly 10 % in the north and nearly 6 % in the south. The proportion of students coming from Socioeconomic clusters 1–4 increased by about 5 % while that of students coming from clusters 7–10 remained unchanged. Considering the change that occurred during this period in the classification of a number of towns such as Sderot which was elevated from 4 to 5, the change in the number of students from clusters 1–4 is even more pronounced.

The data further shows that students pertaining to the higher clusters tend to study at universities, compared to students belonging to the lower and medium clusters. For instance, in 2016 50.6 % of students from clusters 9–10 were studying at universities, compared to 37.6 %–40.5 % of students from clusters 1–6. Students belonging to clusters 3–6 tended to study at publicly funded colleges, compared to students pertaining to other clusters in the same year. One of three students at publicly funded colleges belong to clusters 1–4 (32.7 %). The higher the Socioeconomic level of students, the more they tend to study at Non-Publicly funded colleges. 21.1 % of students pertaining to clusters 7–10 studied at Non-Publicly funded colleges. The lower their Socioeconomic ranking, the more students tend to study at colleges of education. 26.6 % of students pertaining to clusters 1–2 studied at colleges of education compared to 7.1 % of students in clusters 10–9.[394]

2. **Number of students among Israel's Arab citizens**: In 2018 Israel's Arab population (Christians and Muslims) numbers 1,878 million, or 20.9 % of the population. During that year the percentage of young adults in the relevant age group for academic studies, meaning ages 20–35, were 29.4 % of the total Arab population of Israel. Among this group, only 17 % studied at academic institutions in Israel in 2018, meaning that 12.4 % of the age group did not study in academia or studied in other countries with no data available. Nevertheless, CBS data of recent years point to a steady increase in the proportion of the relevant age group among the Arab population attending undergraduate studies.

The proportion of Arab students increased significantly between 2009/10 and 2018/19 in all degree levels: In undergraduate studies it increased from 13.1 % to 18.1 %, in graduate studies from 7.4 % to 14.6 % and in PhD studies we see an increase from 5.2 % to 7 % (CBS, 2019). The pace of growth of the Arab population in general and of the age group among undergraduate studies is described in Table 63.

Tab. 63: Pace of growth of Israel's Arab population and percentage of students in undergraduate studies

Year	Percentage of Arab citizens in Israel	Percentage among the relevant age group	Percentage of undergraduate students among the relevant age group
1999/00	18.5	24.8	10.1
2009/10	20.3	25.5	10.9
2017/18	20.9	29.4	17.1
2018/19	20.9	25.3	18.1

Source: CBS, Statistical Abstracts, years: 2000, 2010, 2008, 2018.

394 Weinger, A. (2016). The Knesset Research and Information Center, Data on Undergraduate students, segmented by field of study and Socioeconomic status, 30 March 2016.

The number of graduate and PhD students also shows a marked rise since 2009/10, as can be seen from the data published by the CBS, presented in Table 64.

Tab. 64: Percentage of Arab students among all students, by degree, 2009/10–2018/19

Degree/Year	Undergraduate	Graduate	PhD
2009/10	13.1	7.4	5.2
2010/11	13.5	8.0	4.9
2011/12	12.4	8.7	4.4
2012/13	12.8	9.0	4.8
2013/14	13.4	9.8	5.2
2014/15	14.3	10.2	5.6
2015/16	15.3	11.3	5.7
2016/17	16.3	13.0	6.2
2017/18	17.2	13.9	6.6
2018/19	18.1	14.6	7.0

Source: CBS, percentage of Arabs among students of academic degrees, 2009/10–2018/19

Among Arab students we see a similar phenomenon to that which we have seen among the Jewish population in peripheral towns – with more students studying at academic colleges and particularly at colleges of education. As can be noted from Table 65, most of the increase in undergraduate studies among Arab students was noted at the general academic colleges and the academic colleges of education.

Tab. 65: Percentage of Arab students in Israel compared to their relevant cohort

Year	Total Arab students	Attending university programs at colleges			Academic Colleges	Studying at academic colleges of education
		Total at Universities	Main campuses	University programs at colleges		
1999/00	10.1	9	8.1	16.6	6	20.9
2009/10	10.9	12.7	10.9	27	5.5	25.3
2017/18	17.1	15.8	15.7	31.2	16.2	24.1
2018/19	18.1	16.5	16.4	31.2	17.7	24.6

Source: CBS, Table 14 – Arab undergraduate students by institution types

An examination of the number of recipients of academic degrees among the population of Arab students also points to an improvement. The proportion of Arab students who received an undergraduate degree in 2017/18 was 13.7 %, compared to 11.9 % in 2016/17. The same positive trend can be also noted among graduate degree recipients: In 2017/18 13.3 % of all graduate degree recipients were Arab, compared to 9.9 % in 2016/17. In PhD studies we see an increase from 4 % in 2016/17 to 5.1 % in 2017/18. The percentage of Arabic students eligible for an undergraduate degree from an academic college was 12.9 % and 12.1 % at publicly funded colleges. In the graduate degree, 17.3 % studied at colleges compared to 9.1 % at universities. Most graduate Arab students received their degrees from colleges of education (25.7 %) and publicly funded colleges (19.4 %).

3. **Increasing accessibility to higher education among the Haredi (Jewish ultra-orthodox) population:** In 2015 the Haredi sector accounted for 11 % of Israel's population, and based on CBS forecasts this figure will rise to 20 % by 2040. CBS data point to a low rate of employment in this sector, especially among men. A review held by the CBS further to the State Comptroller's request shows that the employment and income gaps between Haredi and non-Haredi populations are significantly reduced when candidates from both sectors have an academic degree. In view of this data and with an aim to integrate the Haredi sector in the economy and in general society, the CHE and the Ministry of Finance signed multi-annual agreements for the allocation of 1.7 billion Shekels between 2012 and 2022 towards encouraging Haredi individuals to acquire an academic education. Accordingly, the CHE developed a two-phase program: The first phase includes a five year plan for 2011–2015 and the second a further five year plan for 2016–2022. The CHE's general program for integrating the Haredi population in higher education relies on a number of basic principles, the first of which consists of an acknowledgment of the unique characteristics of the Haredi population, their integration in studies while respecting their life style, an acknowledgment of the diversity existing within this sector and adjusting the solutions to its specific needs.

In fact, Haredi students took part in higher education even before the implementation of the CHE's five year plans. In 2000 Haredi students studied at existing institutions and in operational platforms initiated by the CHE. These platforms offered undergraduate studies by a number of institutions of higher education under one roof. In 2012 it was decided that the establishment of new platforms would no longer be encouraged, so as to create programs within existing campuses. These programs were called "Mahar Programs" (Frameworks for Ultra-Orthodox Students). The CHE's first five year plan for 2012–2016 included the establishment of 15 "Mahar" programs within existing institutions. One of the program aims was an annual growth of 19 % in the number of Haredi students by 2016. In 2010, prior to the implementation of the first phase, there were 5,500 undergraduate and graduate students in platform programs and Non-Publicly Funded institutions. This figure amounted to 2 % of all Jewish students in academia. The target for 2016 was 14,600 but in practice only 11,500 Haredi students studied that year, 79 % of the target and 4.2 % of all Jewish students.

A review of the number of Haredi students in 2000–2008 points to a continuous rise in the number of students from this sector, as presented in Figure 21:

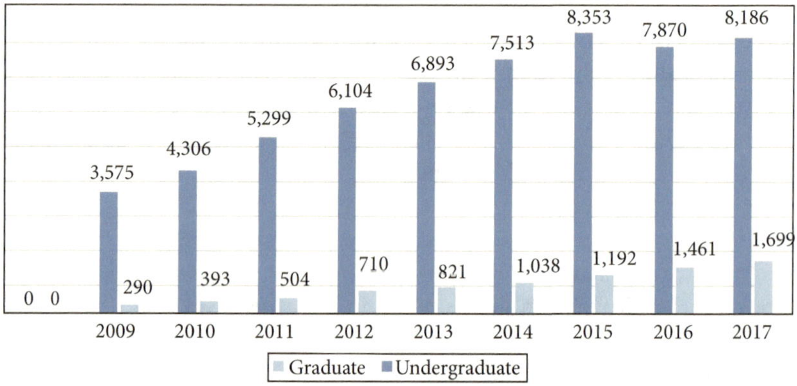

Fig. 21: Haredi Students studying towards an academic degree, 2009/10–2017/18

Note: The figure does not include Open 2009 University students.

Source: Avgar, I. (2018). Knesset Research and Information Center, Governmental support in the field of higher education for people coming from a Haredi background. Figure 6.

In 2018/19 the number of new Haredi students continued to grow, with a growth rate of 3.3 % compared to the previous year, reaching 12,000 students, including the Open University.

When analyzing the number of students by institutions we see that most undergraduate students from the Haredi sector study at colleges: In 2019 only 15.7 % of all undergraduate Haredi students studied at universities. Thirty percent of them studied at publicly funded colleges and 25.7 % at colleges of education, that are also budgeted. The proportion of Haredi students at the Non-Publicly funded colleges was identical to their proportion at universities. Nine years later, in 2017/18, the number of Haredi students at universities decreased to 14 % while their number at publicly funded colleges increased to 32.6 %. The colleges of education increased their share, reaching 29.8 % that year, and 23.5 % of Haredi students attended Non-Publicly funded colleges that year, as can be seen in Table 66.

Tab. 66: Number of undergraduate Haredi students by institution in 2009/2010–2017/18

Institution/ year	2009/ 10	2010/ 11	2011/ 12	2012/ 13	2013/ 14	2014/ 15	2015/ 16	2016/ 17	2017/ 18
Total	3,575	4,306	5,299	6,104	6,893	7,513	8,353	7,870	8,186
Undergraduate degrees									
Universities	562	650	761	819	1,046	1,011	1,124	1,130	1,153
Publicly Funded Colleges	1,073	1,160	1,402	1,557	1,941	2,245	2,538	2,724	2,668
Non-Publicly Funded Colleges	1,022	1,332	1,602	1,656	1,856	1,696	2,073	1,691	1,929
Colleges of Education	918	1,164	1,534	2,072	2,050	2,561	2,618	2,325	2,436

Source: Avgar, I. (2018). The Knesset Research and Information Center, Governmental support in the field of higher education for people coming from a Haredi background. Table 2.

Note: The data does not include the Open University.

The annual change between 2009/10 and 2015/16 was 15.2 % at all institutions. At the universities the percentage of changes was 12.2 % and at academic colleges 14.1 %. Of the above, at publicly funded colleges the percentage of change was 15.4 % and at Non-Publicly funded colleges 12.5 %. At the colleges of education the percentage of change was 19.1 % and 20.3 % for advanced studies.

The number of new entrants to academic studies from the Haredi sector in 2015/16–2017/18 points to a continued trend by which Haredi students choose to study at colleges, while their numbers at universities remain unchanged. The annual average of new entrants to academic studies at universities during those years was 10 % of all Haredi students. At the publicly funded colleges this average was 23 % and at the non-budgeted ones, 18.5 %. The colleges of education significantly increased their share among new entrants to academic studies, which reached 48 % during those years, as can be seen in Table 67:

Tab. 67: Number of year 1 undergraduate Haredi students by institution, 2015/16– 2017/18

Institution/Years	2015/16	2016/17	2017/18
Total number of new Haredi undergraduate students	3,477	3,078	3,108
Universities	381 10.9 %	312 10 %	295 9.5 %
Publicly Funded Colleges	803 23 %	793 25.7 %	626 20.1 %
Non-Publicly Funded Colleges	594 17 %	635 20.6 %	555 17.8 %
Colleges of Education	1,699 48.8 %	1,338 43.5 %	1,632 52.5 %

Source: Avgar, I. (2018). The Knesset Research and Information Center, Governmental support in the field of higher education for people coming from a Haredi background. Table 2.

Note: The data does not include the Open University.

The significant rise in the number of students at colleges of education expresses the large proportion of Haredi women in undergraduate studies – which accounted for over 68 % of all Haredi undergraduate students. Haredi women choose teaching more than other academic professions, as many studied in the past at teachers' training institutions within Haredi seminaries, and prefer to complete their training in the same field towards an undergraduate degree, so as to improve their salary level. The proportion of Haredi men in academic studies declined between 2012 and 2017 for two main reasons: The first is the cutting back of the scholarship program for men compared to the previous period, further to the CHE's decision of May 2017, which resulted from the overall increase in the number of Haredi studies. The second reason was opposition towards academic studies voiced by a number of prominent Hasidic Rabbinical leaders.

In graduate studies we also see a positive growth trend among Haredi students. Between the years 2009/10 and 2017/18 the number of Haredi graduate students multiplied by nearly 6, from 290 students in 2009/10 to 1,699 students in 2017/18. This number amounted to 2.2 % of all undergraduate degree recipients. Hence, over half of all Haredi graduate students studied at colleges, and 48 % at universities. This is true despite the fact that the universities have been offering graduate studies for many years and colleges have been doing so for only 15 years, and despite the fact that the range of graduate disciplines at universities is larger than the range available at colleges. It should be assumed that the number of graduate students at colleges would continue to grow as more and more areas of graduate studies become available. Table 68 presents the number of students by institution, showing that most graduate students at colleges can be found at colleges of education.

Tab. 68: Number of Haredi graduate students in 2009/10

	2009/10	**2010/11**	**2011/12**	**2012/13**	**2013/14**	**2014/15**	**2015/16**	**2016/17**	**2017/18**
Total Graduate degree	290	393	504	710	821	1,038	1,192	1,461	1,699
universities	192	241	328	408	503	585	673	748	829
Publicly Funded Colleges	45	55	24	52	64	54	48	46	64
Non-Publicly Funded Colleges	31	58	91	136	88	141	142	196	221
Colleges of Education	22	39	61	114	166	258	329	471	585

Source: Avgar, I. (2018). The Knesset Research and Information Center, Governmental support in the field of higher education for people coming from a Haredi background. Table 2.

Note: The data does not include the Open University.

While the demand for undergraduate and non-research graduate studies can be ascribed to Haredim wishing to integrate in the work force, the choice of graduate studies which include a thesis and PhD studies point to an interest in integrating in the academic world, and this may point to the first stages of a fundamental change in approaches towards academic life among the Haredi population. In 2014/15 the number of Haredi students who had completed a graduate degree with a theses was 10.3 % compared to 18.7 % among all Jewish graduate degree recipients and 0.7 % among all Jewish graduate degree recipients whose degree included at thesis.

The number of students advancing to PhD studies among Haredi students is persistently rising, reaching 63 students in 2018/19, which were 0.6 % of all PhD students in Israel that year. In 2009/10 only 28 Haredi students were studying towards a PhD, and this number rose steadily: In 2013/14 there were 49 Haredi PhD students and in 2015/16 there were 63, which were 0.6 % of all PhD students in Israel that year. The annual change between the years 2009/10 to 2015/16 was 14.5 %, with the overall annual change percentage being –0.1 %. Until 2014/15 20 Haredi students had completed their PhD, and this number is expected to grow considering the number of students registered as studying towards this degree in 2018/19.

4. **Students of Ethiopian descent studying at Institutions of higher education:** In 2019 the Ethiopian Jewish community of Israel numbered 151,800 residents, amounting to 1.7 % of the country's population. Over 60 % of the Ethiopian population reside in two main districts: The central district (including the Development town of Kiryat Malachi in which in 2018 Ethiopian residents amounted to 16.5 % of town's population), and the southern district with 25 %. The divorce rate among the Ethiopian population is higher than among the general Jewish population: 16 of every thousand marriages, compared to 9 of every thousand marriages in the general Jewish population. The percentage of single parent families among the Ethiopian population is twice as high as in the general population.

The percentage of 12th grade high school students attending Bagrut matriculation exams among the Ethiopian population in 2018 was 92.4 % compared to 95 % among the general Jewish population. The proportion of students eligible for a Bagrut diploma was 66.2 % compared to 80.2 % among the general Jewish population. The proportion of candidates meeting the minimal admission terms to universities ranges between 38 % in the general education system and 49 % in the religious system. These percentages mark a significant improvement compared to 2008 data: In that year, only 84.8 % of Ethiopian high school students attended Bagrut examinations, and the percentage of students eligible for a Bagrut diploma was 35.6 %; The proportion of candidates meeting the minimal admission terms to universities was only 20.8 %.[395]

Until 2011, the number of students of Ethiopian descent at institutions of higher education in Israel was lower than their proportion in the general population. In 2017 the CHE presented a multi-annual plan for increasing accessibility to higher education among the Ethiopian population, marking a target to be reached by 2022: Ethiopian students should account for 1.7 % of all students, which is their proportion in the general population. The plan proposed increased exposure to academia following military service as well as support throughout their studies towards undergraduate, graduate and PhD degrees, including pre-academic preparatory colleges, extra study hours and scholarships. Following the implementation of this plan, we see a rise in the number of students of Ethiopian origin: In 2011/12 2,372 Ethiopian students attended institutions of higher education, amounting to 0.92 % of all students. In 2017/18 3,291 Ethiopian students attended institutions of higher education, amounting to 1.27 % of all students in Israel. This number further grew in 2018/19 reaching 3,417 students which were 1.3 % of all students in Israel. Of these 2,989 Ethiopian students studied towards an undergraduate degree, which were 1.5 % of all students.

The distribution of the number of students by institution clearly points to colleges as the main focus of studies for the Ethiopian community, as can be seen in Table 69.

Tab. 69: Number of Ethiopian students by institution, 2017/18– 2018/19

Institution	**2017/18**		**2018/19**	
	Percentage of Ethiopian students	**Percentage of total students**	**Percentage of Ethiopian students**	**Percentage of total students**
Universities	28 %	38.1 %	28 %	38.1 %
Academic Colleges	58.3 %	46.3 %	57.8 %	47.5 %
Colleges of Education	13.6 %	14.7 %	14 %	14.4 %

Source: CBS, Press Release, The Ethiopian Population in Israel – Collection of data on the occasion of the Sigd holiday, 24 November 2019.

391 Ethiopian students studied towards a graduate degree, amounting to 0.6 % of all graduate students; 24 studied towards a PhD, which were 0.2 % of all students.

395 CBS, The Ethiopian Population in Israel – Collection of data on the occasion of the Sigd holiday, 2018, figure 7.

The Ashkelon Academic College: Case Study of an Extension with a Social-National Mission

The Ashkelon Academic College, Bar Ilan University's first Extension, whose founders had defined its religious and social aims upon its establishment, was included in 2001 in the CHE's national plan for expanding the academic system and increasing accessibility to higher education in the periphery. Upon its inclusion in the system of public academic colleges under the CHE's responsibility, in 2001 the CHE adopted the social aims defined by the founders of the Extension in 1965. The Ashkelon College, similarly to the Zefat College, joined the social-national task of expanding accessibility to higher education in the periphery.

To examine the realization of these social aims in the region by the Extensions/Colleges, I have chosen the Ashkelon College as a Case Study. I examined a number of variables pointing to changes in the educational data of the region's residents, in two time periods: Prior to the college joining the system of academic colleges under the CHE's responsibility, and after it had been recognized and certified as an academic institution in 2007. To obtain a comprehensive comparative picture, we will examine 1999 data, before the decision to include the Ashkelon College; 2005 data, which is the middle of the road in the new path; 2010, and updated data for 2020 following completion of the academic independence process. Following is the data examined for each of the time periods:

A. Number of students in each program
B. Number of students residents of a southern city
C. Number of students from among new immigrants
D. Number of older students
E. Number of college graduates residing in southern towns in one sampled year

A. **Number of students in each program (1999, 2005, 2010 and 2020)**

In order to examine the change in demand for higher education in the region and Ashkelon College's part in fulfilling its social role, I examined the number of students at the college during the relevant years and found a stable growth trend. This trend points to the realization of the college's national role as a center of attraction for local students providing the region's needs in the areas that have been taught at the institution from its establishment. Since achieving academic independence, additional fields have been added, which further enhanced the attractiveness of the college among the youths of the region. The number of students in each of the programs offered at the college has steadily increased since the college began to offer Bar Ilan's full undergraduate program, and then following its academic independence. The continuing rise in demand points to a general growing demand in the region as well as to the inclusion of new sectors of society in academic studies, including new immigrants and adult learners who require academic training for their professional promotion. This group includes police officers and other security services personnel and public service officials. The range of programs offered by the college during its alternative academization stage with Bar Ilan have proven as early as the beginning of the 1990s that there is a high demand for higher education in the region, the level of which did not decline when the college began offering its own degrees. The following data points to an upwards trend in demand for higher education at pre-academic preparatory colleges and practical engineering programs throughout the southern region – from Ashdod to the north of Ashkelon and Dimona and Beer Sheva to its south, even though a wide and diverse range of institutions of higher education had already been deployed throughout the region. The following table presents the number of students at all programs offered at Ashkelon College during the period that preceded its integration in the CHE's academic system (1992–2000), after it achieved academic independence (2000) and the latest 2019–2020 update.

Tab. 70: Number of students at each Program offered at the College (1999, 2005, 2010, 2020)

Study programs	Number of students in 1998/9	Number of students in 2004/5	Number of students in 2009/10	Average annual change	Number of students in 2019/20
Undergraduate Studies	1,798	2,929	3,426	7.5 %+	3,814
Graduate studies	–	–	–		108
Practical Engineering studies	103	330	493	40 %+	802
Pre-academic preparatory programs	317	506	493	4.6 %+	322
Total:	**2,223**	**3,765**	**4,406**	**8.2 %+**	**5,046**

Source: Programs follow-up section, Data from the college computer system, 1 March 2020.

The demand for academic studies grew in 1999–2010 at a stable annual rate of 5 % to 8 % following the substantial growth in the 1990s, which had ranged between 30 % and 40 % each year, thanks to Bar Ilan's alternative academization program. The cutting back of Bar Ilan's departments at the college in parallel to the accreditation of independent colleges contributed to the stabilization of the demand. The plans for independence at the Academic College had been expected to increase the number of students in parallel to the addition of new programs which were not offered under Bar Ilan University's auspices.

An examination of the number of students and the areas of study in 2020 verifies the forecast and the continued growth trend: As can be seen in Tab. 70, in 2020 we see a continued growth in the number of undergraduate students, the inclusion of research and non-research graduate programs, a rise in the number of students studying engineering professions, and new programs in new areas which had not been included in Bar Ilan's programs. The reduction in the number of students at preparatory colleges is a national trend that follows the alleviation in the terms of admission to undergraduate studies at many institutions, which in turn made the need to improve high school grades less necessary.

B. **Number of students residents of a southern city**

To assess the extent in which the Ashkelon Academic College can be seen as a center of attraction for young candidates in the region in which it operates, I examined the number of students at the college residing in the region and specifically the number of students coming from a number of large cities in the vicinity of Ashkelon.

According to regional data, the college clearly serves the youths of its region, as had been defined by its founders and by the architects of the CHE's program in 2001. Between 1999 and 2010 most college students were residents of the southern region – from Ashdod to Dimona, as described in the following table.

Tab. 71: Number of undergraduate students at the college, by districts (1999, 2005 and 2010)

	1999		**2005**		**2010**		**Average annual change**
The region	**Number of students**	**General percentage**	**Number of students**	**General percentage**	**Number of students**	**General Percentage**	
South	1,472	81.8	2,407	82.1	2,739	80	7.1+
Judea Mountains	54	3.0 %	141	4.8	198	5.7	22.1+
Center	240	13.3	351	12	447	13	7.1+
North	32	1.8	30	1.0	42	1.2	2.6+
Total:	**1,798**		**2,929**		**3,426**		

Source: Programs follow-up section, Data from the college computer system, 12 September 2010.

The slow but steady rise in the number of students from the center of the country (2020 data shown in Tab. 71 points to an even larger increase) is a result of new programs which were not available at the college in the past, and today are a source of attraction also for students from the center of the country. These programs include Banking studies, Logistics and Criminology as a major, Graduate studies, and more.

A renewed examination of the number of students by region following a decade of academic independence points to an ongoing general trend by which most students at the college are residents of the south and the vicinity of the college. Having said that, the percentage of students who came to study at the college from the center had increased, thereby lowering the number of students from the south, as a result of the offering of unique programs attracting students from the entire country, as described in Table 72.

Tab. 72: Number of undergraduate and graduate students at the college, by regions (2019/20)

Region	**Number of students 2019/20**	**General percentage of all students at the college**
South	2,758	70.3
Judea Mountains	465	11.8
Center	610	15.5
North	89	2.2
Total:	3,922	100

Source: Ashkelon Academic College, Students Administration, 2019/20.

When I segmented the number of students from the south by area of residence, I found that most students reside in southern cities ranked low on the CBS Socioeconomic rating, with most southern cities and local authorities ranked 5 and below. The high proportion of students from these cities studying at Ashkelon College points to its contribution to the region's social progress, based on the findings of the 1999 State Comptroller's report, summarized in Table 73, pointing to large and worrying gaps between southern cities and central ones in various areas including higher education.

Tab. 73: Number of students at Ashkelon College's academic program (1999, 2005 and 2010) residing at southern cities

City	Social cluster	1998/9 1999	2004/05 2005	2009/10 2010	Average annual change 1998/ 9–2009/10
Ashdod	5	327	634	766	11.2+
Ashkelon	5	761	877	881	1.2+
Kiryat Malachi	4	55	85	143	12.3+
Kiryat Gat	4	102	174	233	9.8+
Sderot	4	27	54	59	9.0+
Netivot	3	20	43	73	20.4+
Beer Sheva	5	59	184	195	17.7+
Dimona	4	5	25	31	38.6+
Yeruham	4	4	6	11	13.5+
Ofakim	4	30	32	65	8.9+
Arad	5	11	21	19	5.5+
Eilat	5	3	9	20	43.5+

Source: Programs follow-up section, college computer system, 12 September 2010.

A comparison of the overall number of students from six large cities in the south and their numbers at the Ashkelon Academic college also points to the college's substantial relative proportion of students from the same city, as can be seen in 2004/5 comparative data presented in Table 74.

Tab. 74: Percentage of Ashkelon College students, of the total number of academic students at selected southern cities in 2005

	Number of students in 2005			Of which at Ashkelon College	
City	Of which at universities	Students at colleges	Total	Number	Percentage of the city's total number of students
Ashkelon	1,374	971	2,345	877	37.5
Kiryat Malachi	154	136	290	85	29.3
Kiryat Gat	512	397	909	174	19.1
Ashdod	1,901	1,604	3,505	634	18.0
Sderot	145	314	459	59	11.7
Ofakim	138	164	302	32	10.6

Source: CBS, Demographic attributes of candidates, students and degree recipients at universities, 2003/04–2004/05, table 27 – Undergraduate students by institution and place of residence, 2004–2005. College data from the Programs follow-up section, college computer system, 12 September 2010.

According to 2005 CBS data, the largest number of students from the first four cities can be found at Ashkelon College. The number of students at Ashkelon College from these cities is higher than at any other institution of higher education in Israel. In unique programs – pre-academic preparatory programs and practical engineering studies, the proportion of students from southern cities is even higher than at undergraduate studies, and most of them come from Ashkelon, Ashdod and Kiryat Gat. The reason for this is that pre-academic preparatory programs and practical engineering programs are deployed in the area at higher numbers than institutions of higher education, and the general demand for studies at each of these institutions is lower than the demand for academic studies, as can be seen in Table 75.

Tab. 75: Number of students at pre-academic preparatory programs and practical engineering studies residing in the south (1999, 2005 and 2010)

	1999		**2005**		**2010**		**Average**
	Number of students	**General %**	**Number of students**	**General %**	**Number of students**	**General %**	**annual change**
Practical Engineering studies	98	95.1	330	90	487	94	**41.4**
Pre-academic preparatory programs	296	93.6	506	94	493	94	**13.8**

Source: Programs follow-up section, Ashkelon Academic College, college computer system, 12 September 2010.

2019/20 data continued to strengthen this trend by which the Ashkelon College mostly serves local residents, even though it has a growing number of students coming from outside the region. The rise in the number of students from central cities points to the college's further establishment as a national academic institution attracting students from the entire country. However, as can be seen from Table 76, most students still come from the southern region and the cities and towns located closest to campus.

Tab. 76: Number of undergraduate students in 2018 at Academic Colleges and at Ashkelon academic college – by selected southern towns

The city	Total Under-graduate students	Percentage of university students	Percentage of Open University students	Percentage of students at the academic colleges	Percentage of students at colleges of education	Number of students at Ashkelon College	Percentage of all students at Ashkelon College
Ashdod	4,990	23.7	16.2	52.8	7.2	510	10.2
Ashkelon	3,283	21.5	11.8	57.2	9.5	775	23.6
Kiryat Malachi	516	14.3	10.3	56	19.4	56	10.8
Kiryat Gat	1,257	20.4	15.8	52	11.8	191	15.2
Sderot	1,021	10.6	14.8	49.2	25.5	88	8.6
Netivot	7,66	13.3	12.1	43.1	31.5	78	10.2
Beer Sheva	6,231	29.8	20.0	39.7	10.6	340	5.5
Dimona	910	17.8	33.8	35.2	13.2	59	6.5
Yeruham	278	21.6	27.0	33.8	17.6	6	2.1
Ofakim	610	13.4	21.3	48.9	16.4	52	8.5
Arad	503	29.4	28.8	31	10.7	13	2.6
Eilat	1,359	42.5	20.7	20.8	16	18	13

Source: CBS, Table 2.32: Undergraduate students at institutions of higher education, 2017/18. Programs follow-up section, Ashkelon Academic College, 2017/18.

The number of undergraduate students at the college in 2018 declined compared to 2005 following the extensive growth in the population of the large cities of the region and the opening of new institutions in the area, including an Extension of the Sami Shamoon College in Ashdod and the Peres College in Rehovot. However, the relative share of the Ashkelon Academic College remained large. As already mentioned, 70 % of all students at the college in 2019/20 are residents of the region.

C. **Number of new immigrant (*Olim*) students**

As aforesaid, one of the factors that accelerated the expansion of the academic system is the large wave of immigration from Post-Soviet states in the beginning of the 1990s, which led to an increased demand for higher education and forced decision makers to increase the country's number of institutions of higher education. The absorption of *Aliyah* as a national mission has become one of the most important social tasks of the colleges. Jewish Agency data on new immigrants point to a similar trend to that which had been noted in recent years among native candidates: New immigrants prefer colleges, and their numbers at the universities is steadily declining in the past decade. The data on new immigrant students at Ashkelon College corresponds with this trend. The number of new immigrant students at Ashkelon College is gradually increasing, and its' share in absorbing immigration relatively to immigrants' proportion in institutions of higher education is high, as can be seen in the 1998/9 and 2004/05 data presented in Table 77.[396]

Tab. 77: Number of *Olim* (new immigrants) at the college in 1999, 2005, 2012 and 2013

Number of *Olim* at the institutions	**1999**	**2005**	**2012**	**2013**
Absolute numbers	10,379	8,958	6,594	5,753
Percentage	100 %	100 %	100	100
Of which: At universities	53.3 %	46 %	36 %	36 %
Regional/Academic Colleges	17.9 %	33.9 %	46.3 %	45.0
Technological Colleges	19.8 %	10.9 %	8.9 %	8.9
Teachers Colleges	5.1 %	5.7 %	7.3 %	7.8
Others	3.9 %	3.5 %	1.7	2.0
Of which: at Ashkelon Academic College	443	769	376	273
Percentage of students at the Ashkelon College of all *Olim* studying towards a degree	4.3 %	8.6 %	5.7 %	4.75

Source: Students Administration, Department of Planning, Budgeting and Control (2001); Overview of activities and statistical data (1999–2000); Overview of activities 2004–2005. Students Administration, Overview of activities and statistical data, 2011–2013, 2013–2012. The data on the number of students at Ashkelon College was taken from the Programs follow-up section, Ashkelon College.

In addition to its part in absorbing the large wave of immigration from Post-Soviet states, the college plays a special social role in the area of immigration – in the training of *Olim* from Ethiopia. This population of *Olim* required extensive pre-academic training, and the college, together with various absorption authorities, has contributed to their preparation for academic studies through special educational programs. As can be seen in Table 78, the college contributes substantially to the training of *Olim* from Post-Soviet states and Ethiopia considering its total number of students.

396 Due to a provision of the law by which students cannot be obligated to report their country of origin, I rely in the data bank of the students administration at the Ministry of Immigration and Absorption, and therefore the data only pertain to Olim who were directed to academic studies by the students administration. The students administration data pertain to the years 1998/9 – 2012/13 only.

Tab. 78: Number of Olim from Post-Soviet states and Ethiopia attending institutions of higher education and Ashkelon College in the years 1999, 2005, 2012 and 2013

Country of origin of new immigrants	1999	2005	2012	2013
New immigrants (*Olim*) from Post-Soviet states studying towards a degree at all institutions	6,962	4,830	1,615	1,315
Percentage	100 %	100 %	100 %	100 %
College students	390	570	771	627
Percentage of students at Ashkelon College	4.8 %	11.8 %	47.7 %	47.7 %
New immigrants (*Olim*) from Ethiopia studying towards a degree at all institutions	1,265	1,886	2,212	2,149
Percentage of students	100 %	100 %	100 %	100 %
College students	53	199	196	185
Percentage of students	4.2 %	10.5 %	8.8 %	8.6 %

Source: Students administration, Planning, Budgeting and Control Department (2001). Overview of activities and statistical data 1999–2000; Overview of activities 2004–2005. 2009/10 data from the Programs follow-up section, Ashkelon College.
Students Administration, Overview of activities and statistical data, 2011–2012, 2012–2013. The data on the number of students at Ashkelon College was taken from the Programs follow-up section, Ashkelon College.

The large rise in the number of students at the college from among *Olim* from Post-Soviet states results from the significant decline in the number of students defined as such, studying at institutions of higher education. The waves of immigration from these countries declined following the huge waves of the 1990s. The college's large proportion of students among *Olim* in 2012–2013 also results from the fact that together with the students administration at the Ministry of Immigration and Absorption, the college operates a pre-academic preparatory program for *Olim* in general, and from Post-Soviet states in particular. This fact also points to the colleges' fulfillment of its national and regional role.

D. **Percentage of older undergraduate students**

Further data attesting to the fulfillment of the college's social role in the region is the proportion of students aged 30 and above studying at the Ashkelon College, as can be noted in Table 79. The college offers this age group a second opportunity to acquire a higher education and more promising career opportunities.

Tab. 79: Distribution of students at the college by age (1998/9, 2004/05, 2007/08 and 2019/20) compared to universities

Age group	Percentage of students in 1998/9		Percentage of students in 2004/05		Percentage of students in 2007/08		Percentage of students in 2019/20	
	Universities	Ashkelon	Universities	Ashkelon	Universities	Ashkelon	Universities	Ashkelon
20–21	22.5	19.4	14.6	18.3	17.5	15.7	12.4	8.6
22–24	44.4	34.5	42.5	42.5	40.4	44.2	34.6	21.8
25–29	25.4	17.8	30.3	22.6	33.5	24.6	37.7	40.1
30–34	3.5	9.9	4	7	4.5	7.1	5.0	12.4
35+	**4.3**	**18.4**	**3.6**	**9.6**	**4**	**8.4**	**8.6**	**18.0**

Source: CBS, demographic attributes of candidates, students and recipients of degrees at universities, 2003/04–2004/05, table 22. 2007/08 data from: CBS, Higher education in Israel, table 14.2: 174. College data from the Programs follow-up section, college computer system, 12 September 2010.

Note: This table does not include 2009/10 data, as the universities' data had still not been published.

The data shows more than twice as many students from the 30+ age group at Ashkelon College compared to the same age group at universities. These students completed their studies at the college in recent years thanks to the successful completion of various projects for the encouragement of higher education in collaboration with work places such as banks, local authorities and government ministries. These projects were made possible following the CHE's decision to open pre-academic preparatory programs for candidates over 30 years of age with no Bagrut high school diploma. The reduction in the proportion of students over 35 years old at the college in the years 2004/05–2007/08 resulted from the utilization of most of the potential of older candidates in the region in special programs, and most of all the academization of teachers and nurses. The proportion of this age group is again increased in 2019/20 following introduction of new dedicated programs for the security forces, in which ages are higher than average. Based on students data published by the CBS[397] for 2017/18, the proportion of students at Ashkelon College aged 35 and above is identical to the average of this age group at academic colleges. However, in 2019/20 the proportion of this age group was substantially higher than this average – 18 % at Ashkelon College compared to 8.8 % at the academic colleges.

E. **Number of college graduates residing in southern towns**

An examination of the list of graduates shows that the college meets its social aim: About 65 % of all graduates in 2008 are residents of the south. In this year many graduates came from cities in the south ranked 5 and below in the Socioeconomic index. As can be seen in Table 80, the proportion of Ashkelon Academic College graduates of the total number of graduates residing in the south is higher compared to the proportion of graduates in all academic institutions in Israel, and at academic colleges in particular:

Tab. 80: Number of graduates at Ashkelon College compared to all graduates in Israel in 2008

	Total	Universities	Open University	Academic Colleges	Academic Colleges of Education	Ashkelon College Graduates
Total graduates in 2007/08	39,357	18,793	2,259	12,830	5,467	862
Southern district	12.1 %	13.4 %	6.5 %	11.3 %	12.1 %	18.1 %

Source: CBS, higher education in Israel, publication No 1388, table 20: 51.

397 CBS, table 4.66, Students at universities and academic colleges and at colleges of education by degree, age, population group and district of residence. Published 26 September 2019.

Only 80 graduates of the college in 2007/08, 9.3 % of all graduates that year, came from towns rated 7–10 in the Socioeconomic index. All other graduates came from towns ranked 1–4, the lowest rating. According to the Central Bureau of Statistics report for 2007/08, only 19.8 % of all graduates of universities reside in towns ranked 3–4 in the Socioeconomic index. The gap is further increased when looking at the number of university graduates from the 5–6 cluster: At Ashkelon College this percentage is 49.9 % compared to 25.5 % at universities and 29.6 % at the other academic colleges.

A similar analysis of the number of graduates at all academic institutions in Israel in 2018 points to an identical trend – that year 51,298 students completed their undergraduate studies at institutions of higher education in Israel. Of these, 21,693 graduated from universities, 20,804 from academic colleges, and 14,600 from colleges of education. One thousand ninety-three students graduated from Ashkelon Academic College that year, of whom 498 were residents of the south, 45.6 % of all graduates of the college.[398] When I examined the annual percentage of change among graduates of academic institutions residents of the south between 2009/10 and 2017/18 I found that the average annual change was 0.61 % com pared to 1.27 % between 2004/05 and 2009/10:

2004/05	2009/10	Annual change percentage	2016/17	2017/18	Annual change percentage
10.8	12.1	1.27	12.9	12.7	0.61

The percentage of graduates by institutions also points to the significant role of Ashkelon College in training the residents of the south: the percentage of graduates residents of the south at universities in 2017/18 was 11.1 %; the percentage of graduates residents of the south at academic colleges was 14.2 %; the percentage of graduates residents of the south at colleges of education was 13.6 %. The number of graduates residents of the south at Ashkelon College in 2009/10 was 878 and in 2017/18, 924, which are, as aforesaid, 45.6 % of all its graduates. The average annual change was 0.64 %.

398 CBS, table 4.74 Recipients of degrees from universities, academic colleges and academic colleges of education, by degree, gender, age and population group. Published 26 September 2019.

Most graduates of Ashkelon college this year, as in previous years, came from the large cities of the south:

City	Number of graduates
Ashkelon	228
Ashdod	133
Kiryat Gat	50
Beer Sheva	58
Kiryat Malachi	22
Netivot	18
Sderot	22

To conclude, the Ashkelon College, which was established as an Extension of Bar Ilan with an aim of fulfilling the university's religious-social mission, was selected based on the same social aims to fulfill a national-social role under the CHE, after the Council essentially opposed its existence for three decades. The social roles at the foundation of its establishment were adopted by the authorized national agency and are implemented by it. The social indexes examined point to the fact that the college fulfills an important role in increasing accessibility to higher education in this region of the country. As mentioned, the Ashkelon College is one of three Extensions and two Colleges of auspices that served as a model for the Regional Colleges that operated in Israel until their integration in the CHE's national academic system. The Ashkelon College, similarly to other Regional Colleges that operated under the CHE's auspices, enabled the CHE to immediately implement a dramatic change in the country's ability to address the growing demand for higher education, which reached its peak in the mid 1990s. Without the Regional Colleges, it is doubtful whether the CHE would have succeeded in such a short time to implement its mission of making higher education accessible to the public, as in all democratic western states.

Chapter 18 Higher Education in Israel in 2019: Social Gaps

Despite the data presented earlier in this book, pointing to the accessibility of higher education to new populations and peripheral regions, researchers still point to the existence of inequality in entering higher education and the job and science market.

The expansion of the academic system has attracted extensive interest among researchers in Israel and the world. Studies on the implications of this expansion point to the fact that it had indeed reduced social gaps in higher education, but that these still exist. Researchers distinguish between two dimensions of inequality: Vertical inequality and horizontal inequality. Vertical inequality is expressed in continued studies and the acquisition of degrees, while horizontal inequality is expressed in a number of levels: differences between types of diplomas on the same educational level, such as between diplomas from prestigious institutions and less prestigious ones; differences between areas of study; and differences between students who are their family's first generation in higher education, compared to those who are second generation and above.

It was found that parents' education is positively correlated to their children's income. The proportion of people with a higher income is higher among those whose father has an academic degree and relatively lower among those whose father has not completed high school (CBS, 2018). In addition it was found that 51 % of the 30 and above age group whose fathers are professionals, are also professionals. Accordingly, we see a lower proportion of professionals among employed persons whose father or mother were not professionals (Ibid.). Studies in the USA point to the existence of gaps in academic achievements between students from high income families to those with low incomes. In recent decades these gaps have increased (Reardon, 2011) and the same trend was also found in Israel (Dovrin, 2015; Ayalon & Yogev, 2005; Getz & Dar, 2007).

In a research report on the accessibility to higher education among young adults from Israel's social periphery, Feniger, Ayalon and Mcdossi (2013) point to the following finding: Despite the dramatic expansion of Israel's higher education system in the past two decades, there are still substantial and notable social gaps both in the vertical and horizontal dimensions of inequality. On the vertical dimension, young adults born to the long standing Jewish population, having similar backgrounds and achievements in their Bargut high school matriculation and Psychometric exam, still participate in higher education at higher proportions compared to young adults from the country's social periphery. This gap is even more pronounced in comparison to the Arab and Haredi sectors. Researchers found a further gap between students whose parents have a higher education and those who do no. It was found that the proportion of academics among 30+ year olds increases proportionally to their parents' education (CBS, 2018). On the horizontal dimension, gaps were found between dominant groups in Israeli society and those belonging to the country's social periphery. Immigrants from the former Soviet Union have a higher likelihood to attend academic studies in programs leading to higher incomes compared to young adults from a Mizrachi origin, Arabs, Jews of Ethiopian descent and even young adults from a mixed Ashkenazi-Mizrachi descent.

Further horizontal inequality can be found in the gaps showing higher income among university graduates compared to graduates of colleges (Shwed & Shavit, 2006). Moreover, Ayalon, Yogev and others have shown that the social profile of students of desired fields at colleges is similar to that of university students. Students from discriminated groups due to class, nationality or ethnic origin, utilize the expansion of the higher education system but take part in less prestigious programs (Ayalon & Yogev, 2005; Getz & Dar 2007). This means that the gaps are maintained also after studies have been completed. A further relevant study in this area addresses the situation in which employers faced with applicants coming from a wide variety of institutions adopt a quality ranking approach that not only examines graduates' field of study, but also the institution from which they graduated. Prestigious institutions are perceived by employers as not only teaching but also educating and better preparing for employment (Barzilay-Shacham & Yaish, 2015).

Inequality in Access to Higher Education among Young Adults from Established Areas and Those from Less Established Ones

Researchers have found that the number of students commencing their studies at institutions of higher education do not equally represent the different groups in Israeli society. Since the expansion of Israel's academic system, we see high rates of commencements of academic studies among Jews residing in towns belonging to the three highest clusters in the CBS' social-economic index, and low rates among Jews and Arabs residing in towns belonging to the lowest clusters (Feniger, Ayalon & Mcdossi, 2013).

According to these studies, the core of inequality is in the education system which is built as a pyramid – with the number of participants in each step diminishing towards the top. The top echelon, representing the proportion of university students, amount to only a third of the relevant age cohort. Even when the data point to an increase in the number of high school graduates eligible for a Bagrut matriculation diploma in less affluent towns, there is still a gap between those eligible for a Bagrut diploma allowing entry to academic studies, and one that does not (Ibid).

Such inequality has implications on earnings and consequently also on social mobility: Researchers have found a relationship between earning horizon and chosen major in high school. Students who have chosen to major in a scientific area were more likely to be accepted to higher education programs leading to a high income, such as engineering and the exact sciences, compared to students who majored in high school in the social sciences and education (Feniger, Ayalon and Mcdossi, 2013; Biggeri, Bini & Grilli, 2001; Davies & Guppy, 1997; Gerber & Schaefer, 2004). Thus, researchers believe that the geographical inequality in higher education begins in the local education system (Svirsky & Conor-Attias, 2017). The data affected by the education pyramid reinforce this approach, also according to the 2014/15 and 2018 data (Svirsky, Conor-Attias, & Liberman, 2018).

The key, therefore, to a more equal society, lies, according to these researchers, in the education system, and the change must begin in Primary and Secondary education. the expansion of higher education was achieved, according to this approach, in a way that reproduces the differential structure of opportunities that exists in the Primary and Secondary education system. This expansion did not lead to an increased level of equality in terms of the accessibility to higher education. While the Non-Publicly Funded Academic Colleges lowered barriers such as the Psychometric score as an admission requirement, still the relationship remained between financial ability and accessibility to higher education (Dagan-Buzaglo, 2007).

Vertical Inequality

Despite the rise in the number of students by district of residence, as presented in Tab. 61, in the past four years we see a deceleration in the number of students in general and in their numbers coming from the geographic and social periphery in particular, the main reason being a decline of about 4 % in the number of entrants into higher education among high school graduates between 2010 and 2011, compared to a 6 % increase among high school graduates in 2001–2010. The implications of this figure can be noted in the number of year 1 students attending institutions of higher education: The percentage of year 1 students in an average year reached its peak in 2012/13 at 49.4 %, declining to 47.8 % in 2015/16. In fact, as of 2013/14, the average proportion of year 1 students has gradually but constantly declined, stabilizing in recent years at about 47 %.

When examining the percentage of high school graduates continuing on to higher education and residing in towns ranked at a low Socioeconomic cluster, the figures are even lower than this average: The follow-up data published by the CBS in 2015/16, as can be seen in Table 81, point to gaps among high school graduates in the Jewish education system who continued to higher education within eight years, between affluent and less affluent towns: In the group of towns ranked 1–4 in the Socioeconomic index, only 34.2 % continued to higher education within eight years following their high school education; in the towns tanked 5–7, 50.6 % continued to higher education, and in towns ranked 8–10 (the highest Socioeconomic index), 65 % continued to higher education.

The proportion of high school graduates who began higher education in these towns has changed only marginally since the beginning of the transition in the country's higher education system, and has essentially remained nearly unchanged: In 1994 32.1 % continued to higher education from Socioeconomic clusters 1–4, 54.4 % from clusters 5–6, and over 64 % from clusters 7–10. Nineteen years later, in 2013, 34.2 % from clusters 1–4 continued to higher education, 50.6 % from clusters 5–7 and 65 % from clusters 8–10.

The above figures point to gaps being maintained between the number of new students entering higher education across Socioeconomic clusters. Moreover, assuming that at students' point of entry to higher education the situation is maintained for three and even four years of undergraduate studies, these gaps are expected to be maintained for at least three years. In fact, as can be seen in Table 81, the CBS' follow-up report for 2016/17 confirms this assumption.

The CBS' follow-up report also shows that until 2017/18 the gaps between the social groups were maintained, with the number of students in the Jewish education system residing in clusters 1–4 who continue to academic studies even somewhat declining from 34.2 % in the 2016/17 follow-up to 33.5 % in the 2017/18 follow-up. In the Arab system we see a slight increase in the same Socioeconomic clusters.

Tab. 81: Follow-up of students continuing to higher education in the Jewish and Arab education systems in selected years

Social cluster	2000/01	2004/05	2007/08
	Percentage of continuing students: Follow-up of high school graduates within eight years of high school graduation	**Percentage of continuing students: Follow-up of high school graduates within eight years of high school graduation**	**Percentage of continuing students: Follow-up of high school graduates within eight years of high school graduation (Follow-up until 2016/17)**
Jewish education system			
1–4	29.3	32.5	34.2
5–7	45.3	50.4	50.6
8–10	59.8	65.0	65.0
Did not continue	53.6	51.0	50.4
Arab education system			
1–4	22.1	27.0	27.6
5–7	30.0	33.3	33.8
8–10	16.7	46.7	41.5
Did not continue	75.1	69.7	69.2

Source: CBS, Statistical Abstract of Israel 2010, tables 8.43, 8.48. CBS, Statistical Abstract of Israel 2018, Chapter 4, Higher Education.

In a breakdown by social cluster and institution type we see that most students in these clusters studied in public colleges: In 2013/14 we see 28 % of students from social clusters 1–4 studying at publicly funded colleges, compared to only 24 % at universities. This gap is increased in 2017/18, with 33.4 % from these social clusters studying at the publicly funded colleges, and only 26.8 % at universities. At the Non-Publicly Funded colleges we see in 2013/14 22 % of students from clusters 1–4, and 26.8 % in 2017/18.

When looking at the proportion of students from affluent towns ranked 7–10 in the Socioeconomic index, we find that a majority of them study at universities and Non-Publicly Funded colleges: In 2013/14 35 % of students from these clusters studied at universities and 32 % at Non-Publicly Funded colleges. The proportion of students from these clusters increase in 2017/18 to 48.4 % at universities and 46.1 % at Non-Publicly Funded colleges. The proportion of these students at publicly funded colleges in 2013/14 was 22 % and in 2017/18 33.2 %.

Dropout Rates by Students' Place of Residence

A further index pointing to existing gaps between towns is the dropout index, which also points to the difficulty in closing the gaps between towns from different Socioeconomic clusters. While peripheral towns have accessibility to higher education through colleges, for a significant number of students admission to college does not assure graduation, because of existing gaps carried over from high school. The dropout rate among students from peripheral towns studying at colleges of education and teacher-training programs and at the Non-Publicly funded colleges is very high compared to university students and students of publicly funded colleges. The main reason for this is the type of students applying to each of these institutions: Students applying to universities and publicly funded colleges have relatively higher admission scores compared to those applying to colleges of education and Non-Publicly funded colleges, meaning that their ability to succeed in their studies is higher.

A study conducted in 2016 by the Knesset Research and Information Center (Weinger, 2016) points to the following conclusion: The lower their Socioeconomic ranking, the more students tend to study at colleges of education: 26.6 % from Socioeconomic clusters 1–4 attended a college of education, compared to 7.1 % from clusters 9–10.[399] CBS data also show that the higher the score in the psychometric exam, the lower a students' likelihood of dropping out compared to students who scored lower in the exam. In addition, the higher level of math studied at high school, the lower a student's likelihood of dropping out. These two factors are not part of the admission terms of colleges of Education and of Non-Publicly funded colleges. 2016 dropout data point to a high proportion of dropouts at colleges of education compared to universities and academic colleges as shown in Table 82.

Tab. 82: Undergraduate students at institutions of higher education who began studying in 2014/15 and did not continue in 2015/16

Total discontinuing	Universities	Academic Colleges	Colleges of Education
8.9 %	7.4 %	8.9 %	13.0 %
Of which are Jewish:	7.3 %	8.7 %	15.4 %
Of which are Haredi:	7.7 %	13.5 %	54.9 %

Source: Naftalovitz, A. (2018). CBS, Higher Education in Israel – a Regional Perspective, April 2018, Presentation during a CBS conference.

399 Weinger, A. (2016). The Knesset's Research and Information Center. Data on Undergraduate students, segmented by field of study and Socioeconomic status.

The above data also pertains to the time of termination of studies at the three types of institutions: Universities, academic colleges and colleges of education. 2019 CBS data point to a low proportion of students who completed their undergraduate studies at standard time (three to five years) at colleges of education compared to universities and academic colleges. A follow-up of students who began studying in 2001–2003 and completed their studies within a standard duration, points to a high proportion of graduates at the academic colleges (51.4 %), with 47.5 % at universities and 39.1 % at colleges of education. A follow-up of students who studied between the years 2011–2018 points to a similar improvement: The proportion of graduates continued to be high at the academic colleges (62.5 %), with 60.2 % at universities and 55.8 % at colleges of education.[400]

A further index that was found to influence dropout levels is parents' education. Based on CBS and OECD data,[401] parents' education does in fact influence dropout levels. One educated parent lowers dropout likelihoods, while both parents without an academic degree adversely impacts the likelihood of their children dropping out of academic studies (Ben David, 2017; Feniger, Ayalon & Mcdossi, 2013). Table 83 shows the gaps in dropout levels among students studying at universities and all types of colleges in the context of their parents' education.

Tab. 83: Percentage of dropouts by institution and parents' education in 2016/17

	Average for all institutions	**Universities**	**Publicly Funded Colleges**	**Non-Publicly Funded Colleges**	**Colleges of Education**	**Dropout percentage by parents' education**	
						No academic education for parents	**At least one parent with an academic education**
Dropout rate	8.7 %	7.4 %	8.0 %	8.8 %	13.7 %	9.6 %	7.3 %

Source: www.cbs.gov.il/kenes/kns_2_45_20.pdf Retrieved 23 July 2018.

An examination of the dropout rate in affluent and less affluent towns points to a clear correlation between the town's ranking and dropout levels: as can be seen in Table 84, the dropout level is low in towns ranked in clusters 6–10 and increases in clusters 1–5.

400 CBS, Statistical Abstract of Israel 2017, 2019.

401 OECD: Indicators. Education at a Glance (2014): chart A.1. p. 84

Tab. 84: Dropout average by Socioeconomic ranking of cities

Cities index	1	2	3	4	5	6	7	8	9	10
Dropout rate	18.7 %	10.0 %	10.2 %	11.0 %	8.5 %	7.7 %	7.0 %	6.9 %	6.9 %	5.5 %

Source: www.cbs.gov.il/kenes/kns_2_45_20.pdf, retrieved 23 July 2018.

In view of the fact that the percentage of academics at towns ranked 1–5 is lower than at towns ranked 6–10, the dropout index points to an increased gap between clusters. The national dropout average and the average by town reinforce this assumption. For instance, the percentage of dropouts at a town ranked 3–4 is twice as high as in at town ranked 10, and in a town ranked 1 it is more than three times as high as in a town ranked 10.

Qualitative Gaps in Horizontal Inequality

In the following section I will examine the qualitative gaps according to the indexes used by the OECD to measure higher education among its members countries. I will also compare these indexes between Israeli towns ranked in the Socioeconomic index at clusters 1–5 compared to those ranked 6–10.

Gaps in the Number of Research Students

The data presented in Table 59 based on CBS data points to growing gaps between the number of graduate students at universities to those at colleges. This will lead, in turn, to an increased gap between the total number of students studying towards a research graduate degree, and those studying towards a non-research degree. A clear manifestation of this gap can be noted in the number of students studying towards a non-research graduate degree both at universities and colleges. As mentioned above, in 2008 only 32.6 % of all graduate students at universities and colleges together were studying towards a research degree. A further figure pointing to this trend is the annual change in the number of graduate students between 2017/18 and 2018/19 which decreased to 1.1 % compared to the annual change between the years 1999/00 and 2009/10 which was 4.3 %. The number of PhD students is also declining: The annual change between the years 1999/00 and 2009/10 was 4.7 %, and between the years 2017/18 and 2018/19 it decreased to 3.6 %.[402]

402 CBS, table 4.64, Statistical Abstract, 2019: 1.

A further indication of a growing qualitative gap in Israel can be seen by comparing the data published by the OECD in 2017. Israel's advantage in undergraduate studies gradually declines when examining the advanced degrees: Israel's average in undergraduate studies in the below 30 age group was 41 % compared to a 36 % average at OECD countries for the same age group, and only 33 % in EU22 countries (The Schengen area).

This gap is gradually overcome when looking at advanced degrees: The average number of people under 35 years of age with a graduate degree in OECD countries is 15 % and 17 % in EU22 countries. In Israel the average for that age group is 18 %, with the average percentage of PhDs in Israel for that age group being 1.4 %, identical to OECD countries (1.5 % in EU22 countries). When canceling out the number of students in Israel who are foreign residents, the average becomes lower than EU22 countries and remains identical to the OECD average of 1.5 % compared to 2.0 % in EU22 countries.[403] When canceling out the foreign students, a further reason leading to the gap between PhD recipients in Israel compared to OECD countries is the fact that about half of PhD graduates in Israel between 2009/10 and 2015/16 were in the natural sciences and only 10 % during that period completed their degrees in Engineering and Architecture. Thus, in order to ensure that the number of PhD graduates grows in comparison to OECD countries, an parallel increase is needed in natural sciences disciplines.

Gaps in the Study of Leading Professions: On the National Level

A further qualitative gap can be in a quality review held by the OECD on its higher education indices in its member countries. The proportion of recipients of the undergraduate degree, which become candidates for the graduate degree, in STEM professions (Science, Technology, Engineering, and Mathematics) points to a gap in some of these professions between Israel and developed Western countries. In 2017 OECD publications it was found that STEM professions are in high demand among high achieving students. Graduates of these professions are employed more than graduates of other academic degrees and earn above the average of member countries. According to a follow-up study by an OECD work group on 2008 degree recipients, the income from work of undergraduate or graduate degree recipients is much higher than the income from work of people their age who do not have an academic degree. In Israel we see even larger gaps than those measured in OECD countries, especially among graduate degree recipients in

403 Table A3.3. First-time graduation rates, by tertiary level Education at a Glance (2015): OECD indicators.

engineering, architecture and construction – 249 % and in knowledge technologies and communication – 320 %.[404]

When examining the proportion of students in STEM professions in Israel, we see that Israel is not ranked as high as it is in the percentage of undergraduate degrees, and the percentage of academics in general. Table 85 describes gaps between Israel and selected Western countries in the classical sciences compared to Engineering and ICT (Information and Communications Technologies).

Tab. 85: Percentage of recipients of undergraduate degree in STEM professions in selected Western countries in 2015

Countries/Professions	Mathematical Science and Statistics	ICT Computer Sciences	Engineering professions
Germany	7 %	5 %	37 %
UK	17 %	4 %	7 %
Austria	9 %	4 %	14 %
France	9 %	4 %	8 %
Canada	11 %	2 %	7 %
United States	10 %	3 %	6 %
Australia	8 %	3 %	6 %
Israel	4 %	5 %	11 %

Source: www.cbs.gov.il/kenes/kns_2_45_05.pdf, 23 July 2018.

The above data point to gaps in research and technology based professions. When examining the number of undergraduate students in STEM professions in Israel, we see that the gap is maintained and even slightly declines, as can be seen in the above table. The OECD report shows that the gap is gradually closing in the engineering professions, and this fact is reinforced by the data published by the CHE towards the 2018/19 academic year. A CBS[405] review of this area points to the contribution of publicly funded colleges to the impressive growth in the number of engineering students in Israel: according to the data, in 1999/00 there were 11,802 students of Engineering and Architecture at universities. That year 8,179 students studied Engineering and Architecture at academic colleges, which were 41 % of all students of these professions in Israel. In 2015/16 the number of students studying Engineering and Architecture at universities increased to

404 CBS, Statistical Abstract of Israel 2017, table 4: 74.

405 Central Bureau of Statistics Table 2.2: Students at institutions of higher education, by degree, gender, field of study and institution type (not including Open University) – 2018/19 and OECD data in the organization's website.

18,623 and at colleges of engineering reached 15,437 which amounted to 45.3 % of all students studying these areas. In 2016/17 19,949 students studied Engineering and Architecture at universities, and 16,053 at colleges of Engineering, amounting to 45 % of all students studying these areas.

An examination of the number of new students who chose these professions points to the impressive contribution of colleges of engineering: The number of new students at colleges of engineering reached in 2016/17 a total of 3,902 which are 45.2 % of all students of these areas. At the universities that same year there were 8,638 students of Engineering and Architecture. The publicly funded colleges of engineering account to nearly half of all students of engineering, and even beyond that when considering two important facts:

a. Students of engineering and architecture at Ariel University were added to the university's count as of 2013/14. Without this addition the number of students at universities would have been lower than presented above until 2013/14.
b. CBS data for engineering professions at universities are combined with the data for students of architecture, while the number of students of engineering at the colleges is nearly entirely ascribed to engineering.

The Non-Publicly Funded colleges do not contribute to this area as they do not offer this type of studies. CBS data for 2015/16 point to a nearly uniform composition of students at these colleges, with 35 % of all students studying law and over 30 % studying business administration. Israel's situation in STEM professions is nothing like its situation in the area of engineering. Table 85 shows that Israel is in a relatively low position compared to developed Western countries, and is lagging behind in the proportion of students in these professions. Table 86 shows the decline in the proportion of students of these professions in Israel over two decades:

Tab. 86: Number of undergraduate students by STEM professions in Israeli institutions in selected years

	1996/7	2001/02	2007/08	2014/15	2016/17	2017/18
Total absolute numbers	101,230	137,540	163,300	191,690	191,915	189,845
Total percentages	100.0	100.0	100.0	100.0	100.0	100.0
Mathematics, Statistics and Computer Science	7.5	8.3	4.7	6.5	7.3	8.2
Physical science	1.6	1.8	1.8	1.8	1.4	1.4
Biological science	2.2	3.1	3.2	2.6	2.6	2.5
Engineering and Architecture	12.5	17.9	17.5	18.0	18.9	19.3

Source: CHE, Collection of data towards the opening of the academic year 2017/18, table number 3. For 2017–2018 data see note number 1.

The proportion of mathematics and technology within STEM professions increased in two decades by only 0.7 %, while physical science declined by 0.2 % and research-based biological science increased by only 0.3 % in the two decades in which Israel's academic system grew substantially. The reason for this deceleration and even decline in certain professions within these areas results from candidates perceiving these areas as intended for research and advanced degrees, rather than being a solution for those aiming to enter the work force and promote their social status within a relatively short period of time, as is the case with other academic professions. A further reason is the fact that most of these disciplines are not studied at colleges due to the absence of suitable research facilities and the belief that colleges are dedicated to academic teaching and to professions that can be easily applied in the work force.

Quality Gaps in the Study of Leading Professions between Established and Less Established Areas

As I have shown, despite extensive changes in the academic system and the growing numbers of students in the south and the north, gaps are maintained between affluent and less affluent cities, both in quantitative and in qualitative parameters. A Spearman's rank correlation was used to examine the relationship between the Socioeconomic index of a city and students' field of study in 2016/17. The results show a significant negative correlation between the Socioeconomic index and the study of education and teachers' training ($r = .757, p > .001$). Moreover, the results pointed to significant positive correlations between Socioeconomic index and other areas of study: A significant positive correlation between the Socioeconomic index and the study of Engineering and Architecture ($r = .679, p < .001$) and between it and the study of Physical science ($r = .527, p < .001$), Mathematics and Computer Science ($r = .43, p < .001$) and Biological science ($r = .177, p < .01$). At to other areas of study in the Natural and Exact Sciences, the results show that the higher a city's Socioeconomic index, the higher the frequency of students studying scientific and engineering professions. Table 87 presents the percentage of students of the examined areas of study at selected cities ranked high, medium and low in the Socioeconomic index.

Tab. 87: Percentage of undergraduate students in STEM professions and education at selected cities in 2017

City	Socio-economic rating	Education and teachers' training	Mathematics, Statistics and Computer Science	Physical science	Biological science	Engineering and Architecture
Ramat Hasharon	9	8.2	8.1	2.1	4.7	16.3
Gan Shmuel	8	10.5	10.1	1.8	5.4	18.1
Givataim	8	10.5	11.1	2.4	2.2	17.8
Modiin-Reut-Maccabim	8	11.2	8.6	2.7	3.0	19.5
Raanana	8	10.5	10.9	1.6	3.5	18.9
Shoham	8	11.3	12.5	1.7	2.8	22.4
Tel Aviv	8	9.4	8.5	3.0	2.1	28.0
Ramat Gan	7	10.5	9.0	1.8	3.0	19.7
Haifa	7	14.3	9.8	1.5	2.6	26.3
Ashdod	5	12.5	6.6	1.4	1.6	24.2
Beer Sheva	5	15.2	3.7	1.7	1.3	32.7
Jerusalem	4	23.8	6.2	1.6	3.0	14.0
Lod	4	21.2	6.3	1.5	3.1	12.6
Kiryat Malachi	4	31.9	3.6	0.2	1.3	15.2
Ramla	4	21.4	6.5	0.8	1.6	15.2
Sderot	4	30.6	3.6	0.5	0.4	13.7
Taibe	3	37.2	3.5	1.4	1.4	10.5
Tamra	3	27.4	4.7	1.4	2.7	8.9
Netivot	3	39.5	3.4	1.0	0.3	13.5
Um El Fahem	2	24.8	7.4	1.2	3.6	9.0
Bnei Brak	2	22.4	10.1	0.4	1.1	9.5

Source: CBS, table 2.35: Undergraduate students at institutions of higher education by field of study and city, 2017.

Following an examination of the general higher education data by Socioeconomic status I found further variables showing significant statistical correlations between the Socioeconomic index of the city and the examined variable. A significant positive correlation was found between the Socioeconomic index of the city and the percentage of students at universities ($r = .467$, $p < .001$). Hence, the higher the Socioeconomic index, the higher the percentage of students studying at universities. A similar positive correlation was found between Socioeconomic index and the percentage of students studying at Non-Publicly Funded colleges ($r = .258$, $p < .001$), meaning that the higher the Socioeconomic index, the higher the percentage of students studying at Non-Publicly Funded colleges. A significant negative correlation was found between the Socioeconomic index of the city and the percentage of students at publicly funded colleges (r = .231, p < .001), hence the higher the Socioeconomic index, the lower the percentage of students at publicly funded colleges. A similar correlation was found among students at institutions of education and teachers' training in general, and not only in the undergraduate degree, as presented above.

When examining the percentage of students at a city and their percentage at universities compared to their percentage at institutions of teachers' training in 2016/17, I found statistically significant correlations between affluent cities ranked 6–10 for university studies and less affluent cities ranked 1–5 for studies at teachers' training institutions. The same trend was identified in the context of the percentage of academics in these cities in 2015/16. Table 88 presents a number of variables selected from all variables examined in this context, together pointing to a clear trend.

Tab. 88: Education data at selected cities by Socioeconomic rating, 2017

City	Socio-economic index	Percentage of students at the city	Percentage of university students	Percentage of students at colleges of education	Percentage of holders of academic degree (2015/16)
Ramat Hasharon	9	10.2	51.5	4.2	40.9
Givataim	9	9.4	45.7	6.3	43.8
Gan Shmuel	8	11.8	72.1	6.4	44.8
Shoham	8	10.9	50.4	12.3	42.8
Raanana	8	10.7	53.5	5.9	32.9
Modiin	8	8.4	52.5	9.2	44.8
Tel Aviv	8	8.2	43.4	5.9	34.3
Haifa	7	6.0	52.8	13.8	28.0
Beer Sheva	5	5.6	37.6	16.3	19.1
Ashdod	5	5.2	28.0	10.5	15.5
Lod	4	3.3	25.7	13.0	11.5
Ramla	4	2.9	22.6	11.3	9.1
Jerusalem	4	2.9	37.2	22.6	12.6
Sderot	4		12.2	27.8	13.9
Kiryat Malachi	4		10.5	30.4	8.2
Tamra	3	4.0		17.5	10.7
Taibe	3	2.9	36.0	29.5	11.3
Netivot	3		8.5	55.4	11.0
Um El Fahem	2	2.3		18.3	8.9
Bnei Brak	2	0.9	20.6	38.7	4.6

Source: www.cbs.gov.il/kenes/kns_2_45_11.pdf Date 23 July 2018.

Data regarding percentage of academics in each city, from: CBS, Higher education data by city, 2015/16.

The results of the Spearman's rank correlation point to a strong significant positive correlation between a city's Socioeconomic index and its percentage of academics ($r = .895$, $p < .001$). The higher the Socioeconomic rating, the higher the percentage of academics at the city. Moreover, the results of the Spearman's rank correlation point to a significant negative correlation between a city's Socioeconomic index and its percentage of students of the humanities and social sciences ($r=.-431$, $p<.001$), meaning that the higher the Socioeconomic rating, the lower the proportion of students of humanities and social sciences. The results of the Spearman's rank correlation point to a significant positive correlation between a city's Socioeconomic index and its percentage of students of science and engineering ($r = .431$, $p < .001$) so that the higher the Socioeconomic rating, the higher proportion of students studying science and engineering.

Epilogue

During the 1950s, the founders of Bar Ilan University – the "Mizrachi" leaders in the USA, aimed to transform the image of emerging Israeli society. To do so they combined political and academic powers and adopted the principle of autonomy in education that had been accepted by the elites (politics of accommodation) during the Pre-State *Yishuv* period, and given national backing. A further model adopted by the "Mizrachi" was that of the Christian academic institutions in the USA. However, contrary to the success of these institutions in recruiting a supportive community, Bar Ilan's dependence on national budgets entailed its acceptance of national regulatory rules and a gradual submission to the dictates of senior members of the academic field – as described by Bourdieu in his Field (Champ) Theory. This submission was further enhanced with the establishment of the Council for Higher Education (CHE) further to the legislation of the CHE Law in 1958. The rules of the academic field restricted the founders' operations and limited their ability to undermine the order of the field through a paradigmatic strategy. The founders' initiative of spreading the religious-social operations of the Extensions through a multi-campus plan was rejected through legislative limitations. While the founders were successful in obtaining legislative authorization for the older Extensions, their enforced regulation marked the beginning of the surrender to procedure and led to a material transformation in their operative strategy. Continued operations through a paradigmatic subversive strategy gradually led to a change in the positions towards the Extensions and towards the university's priorities. The change in the founders' religious-social policy evolved gradually over four decades, and had been indirectly influenced by parallel national and global developments.

1. **Development of the main campus at the expense of the Extensions:** The development in the activities of the main campus in the 1970s also led to a change that resulted from increased dependence on PBC budgets: The enhanced operations required recruitment of additional academic faculty, and precedence was given to the main campus. The growing numbers of non-religious students at the main campus threatened the religious image of the university and forced its management to search for ways to cope with this threat, rather than making do with enrolling religious students at the Extensions. Management diverted its full attention to the main campus and in parallel activities at the Extensions gradually diminished until they ceased completely.

2. **The demand for higher education as a social policy change engine and its impact on the Extensions:** As of the mid 1980s the demand for higher education were a breath of fresh air for the Extensions, through national recognition of their social mission. CHE discussions during the 1970s and most of the 1980s were unsuccessful in bringing about change, and the controlling elitist approach continued to dictate the CHE's policies. As shown by Lissak and Horowitz (1990), the rise in social awareness of the power of the professional diploma for class mobility, as well as the political upheaval of 1977 which contributed to increasing governmental awareness to social problems, led to a transformation in the approach of the central government – represented by the Council for Higher Education (CHE) – towards local authorities and the periphery. The CHE had no other recourse but to grant limited recognition to senior institutions of art and teachers' training, while its policies towards general institutions of higher education remained strict and uncompromising. The continued rise in demand and the large waves of immigration from Post-Soviet states in the beginning of the 1990s led to heavy public pressures on the CHE, which included legislative steps. The CHE had no choice but to expand the academic system, in two stages: At first the CHE adopted and budgeted the academic programs developed at the Regional Colleges, and then formed a plan to change the structure of the academic system from monolithic to binary – meaning that in addition to the universities, the system now included academic colleges. This policy significantly influenced the Extensions, which admitted many students in the periphery. The recognition of academic programs at Regional Colleges under the auspices of other universities led to a shift in the CHE's tendency to ignore the Extensions. The CHE's recognition of the academic programs at Regional Colleges had been the key to the budgeting of the Extensions and the main reason for their disconnection from the university's budget, without needing to also disconnect from its religious-social missions. Bar Ilan University took advantage of this unique political situation and mounting public pressures to increase accessibility to higher education, and in 1990 the Ashkelon and Zefat Extensions were granted a status of a Regional College budgeted by the Ministry of Education. However, despite the financial separation, the university continued to provide academic auspices to the academic programs at the colleges, and continued to encourage the implementation of its social aims.
3. **The amendment to the CHE law (Colleges Law) and its academic impact on the Extensions:** Contrary to amendment number 3 to the CHE law which in 1972 prohibited the existence of Extensions, amendment 10 legislated in 1995 led the colleges (or Extensions) to their independent academic status. The amendment was initiated by the heads of the local authorities and managers

of the colleges through the social lobby at the Knesset. The fact that most Regional Colleges including Bar Ilan's Colleges were not included in the CHE's program for the expansion of the system resulted in political and public protest that forced the CHE to expand its plan to include all Regional Colleges. The change in the law led to a further recognition of Bar Ilan's Extensions as academic colleges. The third and last stage in the recognition of the Extensions/Colleges had been the academization of all academic colleges which gradually gained an independent status as academic institutions able to grant their own fully recognized undergraduate degree. This academization process rendered Bar Ilan's academic auspices redundant, and ultimately led to the final severance of its historical Extensions from the university.

4. **Global expansion of higher education and its impact on the change in Bar Ilan University's policy:** Following the financial hardships of the 1970s and 1980s, the recognition and budgeting of the Extensions in the 1990s and the removal of their financial burden from the university's budget, led to a gradual severing of the Extensions from the university. Allegedly, the financial alleviation should have resulted in Bar Ilan persisting in continuing its close ties with the Extensions, as it had done even in the most difficult years. However, a general change in the university's policy had taken place following the expansion of the academic system. The globalization of the academic field and the strive to prestige and academic status within the field, led Bar Ilan's management to change their priorities: A research orientation replaced an educational one, and the emphasizing of international academic aims replaced social and religious ones (Schwartz, 2006; Klein, 2006). The PBC encouraged this trend and compensated the university for agreeing to separate from the Extensions: The university was given the green light to open a Faculty of Engineering, its quota of students of advanced degrees, mostly PhD, was increased, as well as its budget for research facilities. In addition, the opening of a Faculty of Medicine at Zefat was also approved – an initiative that the university had aimed to achieve since the 1970s. In all research indices we see a clear trend of changing aims. The number of students of advanced degrees gradually and steadily grew over the years, with research budgets continuing to grow over the past two decades. These trends stand in contrast to Yogev's statements regarding stratification of the academic system. While international indices place Elite universities far from those of the Target ones, the trend in all other indices, such as the number of students and research budgets, point to a closing of gaps between Israel's Elite universities and Bar Ilan and Ben Gurion Universities.
5. **The Extensions – from a social-religious mission to a social-national one:** Although the social aims defined for the Extensions had not been achieved,

and although the necessary resources had not been invested for their existence as suitable academic institutions as stipulated by proponents of the Stratification approach, Bar Ilan's contribution to the country's periphery cannot be described as anything but decisive: First, the founders' initiative to operate at peripheral regions preceded the plans of the CHE and Ministry of Education, who failed to address the needs of the periphery, despite the social struggles of the 1970s. Second, the initiative was unparalleled in the alienated academic system of the 1950S and 1960s, and it led to the system's imminent diversification, as proposed by proponents of the Diversity approach. Third, the influence of the university's social initiative can be noted in a growing awareness of higher education, as measured in the growing number of students at the Extensions in the 1970s and 1980s. Researchers believe that this growing awareness had a significant cultural impact on the second generation of academics in the periphery (Cohen & Leon, 2008).

6. **Religious initiative and formation of a map of colleges in the periphery in 2001:** The social-religious ideal strongly resisted by the CHE until 1990 became the council's social ideal in 2001. Bar Ilan University's initiative had set the foundation for the establishment of independent academic colleges at Ashkelon and Zefat as of that year. There is no doubt that the founders' initiative and their decision to open Extensions in these cities determined the fate of academy in those regions and had a decisive impact on the distribution of colleges throughout the country. The data presented in this book leads us to the conclusion that without this initiative colleges would not have been established in these cities and it is doubtful whether many of the young adults residing in these areas and the many new immigrants absorbed in these regions would have gained access to any form of academic education.

This conclusion was indirectly ratified in the words of Prof. Nehemia Lev Zion, PBC Chairperson, in a discussion in August 2001 on the future of public colleges. Prof. Lev Zion presented to College Managers the "Academic complex" model as the only model up for discussion. In response to a question raised by the academic manager of Ashkelon College as to whether additional models for developing the colleges can be presented to the plenum, Prof. Lev Zion answered that he believes the best model would be to reduce the number of colleges, and that among the southern triangle of colleges – Ashkelon, Sapir and Achva – it would be highly advisable to close one or two; and in the north he would be happy to close one or two among Zefat, Tel Chai and the Jordan Valley. It is no coincidence that these threats were focused on two regions in which Bar Ilan University's three oldest colleges are located. At the time these institutions were still very much perceived as Bar Ilan's doing, and a part of what some people at the CHE would refer to as "academic imperialism".

7. **Bar Ilan's contribution to expanding accessibility to higher education in the periphery:** The original idea formulated by the university's founders led to its major impact on the country's academic map in 2010: Five of the 11 colleges scattered throughout the country operated under Bar Ilan's academic responsibility: Three of its early Extensions – Ashkelon Academic College, Zefat Academic College and Jordan Valley Academic College; and two colleges added in the 1980s and 1990s – the Academic College of Judea & Samaria and Western Galilee Academic College. In 2014, four of the five colleges were still operating independent programs alongside Bar Ilan's programs. The university's contribution can be noted in the academic establishment of these colleges and in their mentoring until they achieve full academic independence – a process that is still ongoing in some of these institutions.

Bar Ilan University's contribution is absent from many previous studies, including a prominent absence of in-depth discussions of its social mission and its devoted support of both the Judea & Samaria College and the Western Galilee College. Thus, the university's founders' religious initiative in the establishment of Extensions in the periphery in the 1960s has had a decisive impact on the map of colleges and academic institutions in Israel's northern and southern regions. As shown, there is no doubt that had the Extensions at Ashkelon and Zefat not been established, these cities would not have had academic colleges, if only due to the fact that four academic colleges are located at a very close proximity to these institutions – in the north and the south. The colleges fill an important social-national role in making higher education accessible to disadvantaged populations and contributing to the reduction of social gaps in Israel.

There is no doubt that Bar Ilan University's contribution to the establishment of the Judea & Samaria College (Ariel) as an academic institution, led the college in 2014 to become one of Israel's universities – the Ariel University. The community institution that had offered certificate programs in the early 1980s had become a college under the academic auspices of Bar Ilan University in the beginning of the 1990s and a university by 2014. Without Bar Ilan's academic support and auspices, this region would not have a university today.

While the senior actors of the country's academic field had distanced themselves from Bar Ilan and its religious-social approach (Ben Yosef, 1967; Gross, 2008; Klein, 1998, 2006), Bar Ilan University today is counted among the senior actors of the country's academic field and in recent years has even led this group, and its Extensions, which had suffered from this distancing for over 40 years, are now included among the country's recognized academic institutions. The social mission that Bar Ilan's founders had defined in 1965 for the Extensions was adopted in the CHE's 2000 plan for the expansion of the country's academic system, and the social-religious mission became a social-national one.

8. **The system's structural transformation and the absence of a clear classification into types of institutions and their roles:** The architects of change in the mid 1990s were led by the need to address the growing demand through academization of colleges and sending most of the demand for undergraduate studies their way. After two and a half decades we can safely say that the absence of a functional definition for each institution created a situation in which they each "grabbed as much as they could", within budgetary constraints. While the universities happily offer professional non-research degrees, the colleges strive to teach research-based degrees, even in the absence of suitable facilities. The result is a decline in the level of students for research degrees and areas of study that form the foundation for research such as physics, chemistry and biology. Encouraging these areas of study as well as additional research-based fields through distinct budgets, would have enabled universities to focus more on research while continuing to position themselves at the forefront of research and science in a way that corresponds with the huge growth of the academic system since the mid 1990s.

The uncontrolled expansion of the academic system undermines the quality of its results, both socially and nationally. The lack of supervision over the system's expansion and the resulting undermining of its quality, has led the CHE in 2020 to establish a joint team of experts representing all academic institutions, whose task is to examine the role of each institution so as to create a functional distinction and close supervision over the system's outputs.

9. **Change and reduction of social gaps:** The massification of higher education over the past two decades results from students striving to acquire professions that would lead to occupational promotion and higher pay. This expansion was enabled as higher education began to undertake professional roles resulting from the demands of modern economy, in addition to its more traditional roles. The result of this change can be noted in the relatively small number of students continuing to advanced degrees and research fields, despite the general increase in the number of students attending academic studies.

Despite the overall growth of the academic system, an examination of the percentage of entrants into higher education in 1994 within six years following high school graduation points to a proportion of 32.1 % among students residing in towns ranked 1–4 in the Socioeconomic index and 64 % in towns ranked 7–10. This ratio remained nearly unchanged between 2006 and 2016. During these years, the percentage of entrants into higher education among students residing in towns ranked 1–4 in the Socioeconomic index was about 34 % and in towns ranked 7–10 about 65 %. Thus, the gap between Socioeconomic clusters remains nearly the same as it had been before the colleges revolution of 1995. The key, therefore, to a more equal society, is to be found first and foremost in the education system, and the change must begin as early as Primary and Secondary education.

Increasing the number of students from less affluent towns creates, to a certain extent, an illusion that social gaps are reduced. However, our examination of particular areas of study points to a significant positive correlation between Socioeconomic cluster and the percentage of students at universities and at Non-Publicly Funded colleges. A significant negative correlation was found between Socioeconomic cluster and the percentage of students at teacher-training colleges and at publicly funded colleges. This phenomenon corresponds with the basic assumption of the Maximally Maintained Inequality (MMI) hypothesis: students from affluent towns were able to utilize opportunities for studying at universities and Non-Publicly Funded colleges, tending to select professions perceived as prestigious and leading to a high likelihood for social mobility, while candidates from weaker towns were less likely to utilize such opportunities. The higher percentage of students studying research-based professions taught at universities and characterized as leading to high mobility among populations residing at high ranking clusters, also points to the presence of a horizontal gap that is utilized more by this population and less so by populations from less affluent clusters.

Thus, in the absence of real change in the number of high school graduates eligible for a Bagrut matriculation diploma in peripheral towns, and assuming that a large wave of immigration is unlikely, the academic system has exhausted its available resources at the undergraduate level. The only option that would enable the system's continued expansion would be its ability to increase the number of new students from the country's social and geographic periphery and the Haredi and the Arab sectors who as I have shown are still heavily underrepresented compared to their part in Israel's general population.

10. **Horizontal and vertical gaps in social inequality in Israel:** The qualitative gaps measured in a number of parameters, such as professions leading to increased social mobility, have increased in cities ranked 1–5 in the Socioeconomic index in which less students choose STEM professions, engineering and ICT. In these cities the proportion of students of education and

teachers' training is very high, and normally the largest number of students in the city.

The dropout level index that points to the enhanced accessibility of higher education as well as to the inability to meet its requirements, points to growing dropout levels as the city ranks lower in the Socioeconomic index. The dropout proportion is generally higher than the national average when parents or at least one parent do not possess an academic degree. This finding points to difficulties in closing the gaps even when the second generation strives to change its social status.

11. **From micro to macro:** The expansion of the academic system does not correspond with the growth in advanced and research degrees, nor with the demand for STEM and ICT professions, which is why Israel is ranked lower than many advanced Western countries. The fact that universities, which account for the majority of research-based graduate degrees, are increasing their share of non-research graduate degrees, and that colleges are failing to fill this gap, means that the gap between graduates heading for research areas and those which do not will continue to grow in coming years. This, in turn, may lead to a shortage in the country's reserves of researchers at universities and research institutions. This situation does not exclude any university, including Jerusalem, Tel Aviv and the Technion which were defined by Yogev (2000) as research universities, as opposed to Bar Ilan, Haifa and Ben Gurion which were defined as Target Universities.

The expansion of the academic system in Israel, which began with the inclusion of Regional Colleges throughout the country, has led to an increased accessibility to higher education among many populations that had not been previously represented in it proportionally to their relative size in the general population. This expansion, similarly to that of any other system, requires a process of reorganization, as is always the case following a revolution. First, a clearer distinction is needed between types of institutions and their academic role. Second, the proportion of disadvantaged populations of the country's social and geographic periphery in the academic system needs to be enhanced, as well as that of students in professions that may potentially lead to change and social mobility. However, increasing the number of students is not the only solution. A qualitative change would contribute to the reduction of social gaps and would not undermine the ability of the academic system to cope with global challenges and the advancement of science and technology. Two and a half decades of development require a new way of thinking and the reduction of the number of institutions through joint ventures based on common areas of study.

References

Achdut, L., Gutman, E., Zussman, N., Lipiner, I., and Maayan, I. (2018). The wage premium on higher education: Universities and colleges. Jerusalem: Research Department, Bank of Israel.

Ackerman, V., Carmon, A., and Zuker, D. (Eds.). (1985). Education in an evolving society: The Israeli system. Tel Aviv: HaKibbutz HaMeuchad.

Adler, A., Lewin-Epstein, N., and Shavit, Y. (2003). Social stratification and Israel's development towns: A renewed discussion of old questions. Israeli Sociology, E(2): 394–365.

Aharoni, M., and Biham, A. (Eds.). (2008). Annual report of the planning and budgeting committee, number 33 (2005/2006). Jerusalem: The author.

Allen, C. M., and Allen, W. B. (2003). Habits of mind. USA: Transaction Publications.

Altbach, P. G. (2004). The costs and benefits of world-class universities. Academ, 90 (1): 1–5.

Avgar, I. (2018).Governmental support in the field of higher education for people coming from a Haredi background. The Knesset Research and Information Center (RIC).

Ayalon, H., and Yogev, A. (2005). Field of study and students' stratification in an expanded system of higher education: The case of Israel. European Sociological Review 21(3): 227–241.

Ayalon, H. (1994). Community characteristics and educational opportunities in Israel. Research in Social Stratification and Mobility, 14: 99–118.

Ayalon, H. (2004). Who studies where? A social and educational portrait of college and university students. In: The Roles of Colleges in expanding Israel's higher education system – Lessons learned from the American experience: Lectures presented in a Conference dated 8 April, 2003 (pp. 33–21). Tel Aviv: U.S. Israel Education Foundation.

Ayalon, H. (2006). Higher education. In: A. Ram, and N. Berkowitz (Eds.). (pp. 148–155). Beer Sheva: Ben Gurion University.

Ayalon, H. (2008). Who studies what? Where, why? Social implications of the expansion of diversification of Israel's higher education system. Israeli Sociology, J(1): 33–60.

Ayalon, H. (2018). The areas of study of first generation college students whose parents are financially established: A further look at horizontal stratification in Israel. Megamot, 53(1): 75–100.

Ayalon, H., and Addi-Raccah, A. (2008). From high school to higher education: Curriculary policy and participation in higher education in Israel. In Yogev, A. (Ed.). The Expantion of higher education in Israel (pp. 77–110). Tel Aviv: Ramot – Tel Aviv University.

Ayalon, H., Gamoran, A., Grodsky, E., and Yogev, A. (2000). Social Consequences of the Expansion of Higher Education: Comparison between Israel and the United States. Paper Presented at the Conference of the Research Committee on Social Stratification and Mobility of the International Sociological Association. Libourne France.

Bashaar Committee for Policies in the Higher Education System and Research Universities in Israel (2004). The status of higher education and research universities in Israel: Warning signs and policies. Bashaar – Academic Community for Israeli Society.

Bar Haim, E., Blank C., and Shavit, Y. (2009). Educational opportunity, employment, and income. Taub Center for Social Policy Studies in Israel, Policy Paper No. 09

Bar, M. (1972). Minister Haim Moshe Shapira and Bar Ilan University. Bar Ilan: Annual Book of Jewish studies and Humanities, I: 1–5.

Barshad, T., and Biham, A. (Eds.). (2000). Annual Report of the Planning and Budgeting Committee, Report number 25 (1997/1998). Jerusalem: The Planning and Budgeting Committee.

Barshad, T., and Biham, A. (Eds.). (2001). Annual Report of the Planning and Budgeting Committee: Report number 26/27: 1998/1999–1999/2000. Jerusalem: The Planning and Budgeting Committee.

Barshad, T., and Biham, A. (Eds.). (2003). Annual Report of the Planning and Budgeting Committee: Report number 28/29: 2000/2001–2001/2003. Jerusalem: The Planning and Budgeting Committee.

Barshad, T., and Biham, A. (Eds.). (2005). Annual Report of the Planning and Budgeting Committee: Report number 30 (2002/2003). Jerusalem: The Planning and Budgeting Committee.

Barshad, T., and Biham, A. (Eds.). (2006). Annual Report of the Planning and Budgeting Committee: Report number 31/32: 2003/2004–2004/2005. Jerusalem: The Planning and Budgeting Committee.

Barshad, T., and Biham, A. (Eds.). (2009). Annual Report of the Planning and Budgeting Committee: Report number 34/35: 2006/7–2007/8. Jerusalem: The Planning and Budgeting Committee.

Barzilay-Shacham, Y., and Yaish, M. (2015). Academic institution and graduates employment opportunities. Israeli Sociology: A Journal for the Study of Society in Israel, 16(2): 56–75.

Belbington, D. (1992). The secularization of British universities since the mid-nineteenth century. In: G. M. Marsden and B. J. Longgield (Eds.), The secularization of the academy (pp. 259 – 277). New York: Oxford University Press.

Ben David, D. (1985). Universities in Israel: Dilemmas of growth, diversification and administration. In: W. Acherman and A. Carmon (Eds.), Education in an evolving society: The Israeli system [A] (pp. 527–563). Tel Aviv: HaKibbutz HaMeuchad and Van Leer Institute.

Ben Haim, A., and Shavit, Y. (2018). Expansion, differentiation, and market structure in higher education. Megamot, 53(1): 101–124.

Ben David, D. (2017). An Overview of Israel's Education System and its Impact. Tel Aviv: Shoresh Institutution for Socioeconomic Research, Tel Aviv University.

Ben Sasson, H. H. (1967). Religion and society in the works of Ben-Zion Dinur and Yitzhak Baer. Molad, 21: 537–548.

Ben Yosef, A. (1967). The history of Bar Ilan University. Bar Ilan: Annual Book of Jewish Studies and Humanities, D-E: 11–33.

Ben Yosef, A. (1988). From vision to implementation – The establishment of Bar Ilan University. In: P. Churgin (Ed.), Vision and legacy: Selected works and writings of his life and legacy (pp. 26–33). Ramat Gan: Bar Ilan University.

Ben-David, J. (1972). Trend in American higher education. Chicago: University of Chicago Press.

Bernardi, F., and Ballarino, G. (2012). Participation, equality of opportunity and returns to tertiary education in contemporary Europe. European Societies: 1–21.

Bernstein, A. Z. (1988). The man and his literary legacy. In: P. Churgin (Ed.), Vision and legacy: Selected works and writings of his life and legacy (pp. 16–21). Ramat Gan: Bar Ilan University.

Biggeri, L., Bini, M., and Grilli, L. (2001). The transition from University to work: A multilevel approach to the analysis of the time to obtain the first job. Royal Statistical Society Journal, 164(2): 293–305.

Bolotin-Chachashvili, S., Shavit, Y., and Ayalon, H. (2002). The expansion of higher education and its implications on stratification in Israel: 1980–1996. Israeli Sociology, D(2): 317–347.

Bourdieu, P. (1984). Homo academicus. Paris: Editions De Minuit.

Bourdieu, P. (2005). Questions in sociology. Tel Aviv: Resling.

Brandes, O. (2007). The Kibbutz Ideology: A synthesis between colliding values. Doctoral Dissertation, Bar Ilan University.

Brandeis, O. (Ed.). (1996). The third jump: Changes and reforms in the educational system in the 1990s. Jerusalem: Ministry of Education, Culture and Sports.

Buber, M., Feiwel, B., and Weizmann, C. (1968). Jewish School of Higher Education. Jerusalem: Magnes, The Hebrew University.

Burg, A. (1995). Knesset member Avraham Burg. In: A. Shehan (Ed.), Models of regional colleges (pp. 27–29). Jerusalem: Ministry of Education, Culture and Sports. Colleges Division.

Burg, Y. (1972). Words spoken at national memorial services and public rallies. Bar Ilan: Annual Book of Jewish Studies and Humanities, j(A): 31–34.

CBS (2018). The Ethiopian population in Israel – Collection of data on the occasion of the Sigd holiday, figure 7. Central Bureau of Statistics, Jerusalem.

Churgin, P. (1967). Introductory remarks for Bar Ilan University student body annual publication. Bar Ilan: Annual Book of Jewish studies and Humanities, D-E: 9–11.

Churgin, P. (1967–1968). Introductory remarks. Bar Ilan: Annual Book of Jewish studies and Humanities, D-E: 5–7.

Churgin, P. (1988). Bridg to the Future: Speech at the university's cornerstone laying ceremony. In: P. Churgin (Ed.), Vision and legacy: Selected works and writings of his life and legacy (pp. 13–15). Ramat Gan: Bar Ilan University.

Cohen, A. (1998). The Tallit and the flag: Religious Zionism and the vision of the Torah State in the early years of the state. Jerusalem: Yad Izhak Ben-Zvi Institute.

Cohen, A. (2001). The Hebrew University of Jerusalem in the transition from *Yishuv* to state: First signs of the formation of a Credential Society in Israel. Zionism, 23: 297–329.

Cohen, A. (2002). The Hebrew University's curbing and expansion strategies in response to the establishment of The Hebrew University, 1953–1961. Iyunim Bitkumat Israel: A collection on the problems of Zionism, the *Yishuv* and the State of Israel, 12: 359–401.

Cohen, A. (2006). The Mountain and the Hill: The Hebrew University of Jerusalem in the pre-independence and beginning of Statehood eras. Tel Aviv: Am Oved.

Cohen, A., and Leon, N. (2008). On the question of the Mizrachi middle class in Israel. Alpaim, 32: 83–101.

Cohen, N. (2001). The universities there are still blooming. Academic: The Journal of the Committee of University Heads, 9: 5–9.

Collins, R. (1979). The Credential Society: An historical sociology of education and stratification. New York: Academic Press.

Council for Higher Education Law (1958). State of Israel.

Council for Higher Education Law (Amendment No. 3) (1971). State of Israel.

Dagan, M. (2013). Closing the gaps in the education system: An alternative approach. Dor Le Dor: Studies and Documentation in the History of Jewish Education. 45: 221–34.

Dagan-Buzaglo, N. (2007). The right for higher education in Israel, a legal and budgetary perpective. Tel Aviv: Adva Center.

Dahrendorf, R. (1995). LSE: A history of the London School of Economics and Political Science, 1895–1995. New York: Oxford University Press.

Dar, Y., and Getz, S. (2007). Learning ability, socioeconomic status and student placement for undergraduate studies in Israel. Higher Education 54: 41–60.

Davies, S., and Guppy, N. (1997). Fields of study, college selectivity, and student inequalities in higher education. Social Forces, 75(4): 1417–1438.

Denzin, N., and Lincoln, Y. (Eds.). (2000). Handbook of qualitative research. London: Saga.

Dobrin, N. (2015). Equal opportunities in education: Demographic and socio-economic barriers. Jerusalem: Central Bureau of Statistics.

Don Yechiya, E. (1989). Religious Institutions in the Political System: Israel's Religious Councils. Jerusalem: Jerusalem Center for Public Affairs.

Don Yechiya, E. (1990). Religion and Ethnicity in Israeli Politics: The religious parties and the 12th Knesset elections. State, Government and International Relations, 32: 11–54.

Don Yechiya, E. (2001). Political leadership in Religios Zionism: Rabbi Yehuda Leib Maimon, leader of "HaMizrachi". Bar Ilan: Bar Ilan, Year Book on Jewish Studies and Humanities, Bar Ilan University, 28–29: 123–160.

Don Yechiya, E. (2004). Leadership and policy in Religios Zionism – Haim Moshe Shapira, the NRP and the Six-Day War. In: A. Cohen, and Y. Harel (Eds.), Religious Zionism: The era of transition, a collection of essays in memory of Zvulun Hammer (pp. 135–170). Jerusalem: Bialik Institute.

Don Yechiya, E. (2008). Crisis and change in a New State: Education, religion, and politics in the struggle over the absorption of mass immigration. Jerusalem: Yad Izhak Ben-Zvi Institute.

Dore, R. (1976). The Diploma Disease: Education, qualification and development. London: George Allen & Unwin.

Dror, Y. (1996). The beginning of the Hebrew Technion in Haifa: 1902–1950; from a plan for a Jewish Institution for Higher Education, until the end of the prior of the Directorship of Shlomo Kaplanski. Iyunim Bitkumat Israel: A collection on the problems of Zionism, the *Yishuv* and the State of Israel, 6: 330–357.

Dror, Y. (1997). "The University School" between ה "Academia" and "Field": The development of the school of education at the University of Haifa, 1963–1982. Tel Aviv: Tel Aviv University.

Dror, Y. (2006). Past reforms in the Israeli education system: What can history teach us of the Dovrat Report. In: D. Inbar (Ed.), Towards an educational revolution? (pp. 35–59). Jerusalem: Van Leer Institute, HaKibbutz HaMeuchad.

Dror, Y. (2007). 'National Education' through mutually supportive devices. The Zionist Story. Jerusalem: Magnes, The Hebrew University.

Dror-Cohen, S. (2019). Collection of data from the 2018 Social Survey, Intergenerational mobility: Education, occupation and changes in the level of religiousness, published on 29 October 2019, Central Bureau of Statistics, Jerusalem.

Eisenstadt, S. N. (1973). Israeli society: Background, development & problems. Jerusalem: Magnes Press.

Eisenstadt, S. N. (2004). Changes in Israeli society. Tel Aviv: Ministry of Defence Publications.

Farnum, R. (1990). Prestige in the Ivy League: Democratization and discrimination at Penn and Columbia, 1890–1970. In: P. W. Kingston, and L. S. Lewis (Eds.), The high-status track: Studies of Elite Schools and stratification (pp. 75–103). Albany: State University of New York Press.

Feniger, Y., Ayalon, H., and Mcdossi, O. (2013). Accessibility to higher education among young adults from Israeli's social periphery. A Report submitted on March 2013 to the Gandyr Foundation, Herzliya, Israel.

Friedman, M. (1982). The NRP in transition – the background for its electoral decline. State, Government and International Relations, 19–20: 105–122.

Gal-Nur, Y. (2009). Higher education in Distress. Alpaim, a Multi-disciplinary Journal, 34: 130–147.

Gardner, H. (1995). Art, mind, and brain: A cognitive approach to creativity. Tel Aviv: Poalim Library.

Gerber, D. T., and Schaefer, D. R. (2004). Horizontal stratification of higher education in Russia: Trends, gender differences, and labor market outcomes. Sociology of Education, 77(1): 32–59.

Gleason, P). 1967(. American Catholic Higher Education: A historical perspective. In: R. Hassenger (Ed.), The shape of Catholic Higher Education (pp. 15–53). Chicago & London: The University of Chicago Press.

Goldberg, G. (2001). Zerach Warhaftig's contribution to Israeli Legislation. Bar Ilan: Annual Book of Jewish studies and Humanities, 28–29: 295–332.

Greeley, A. M. (1969). From backwater to mainstream: A profile of Catholic Higher Education. Washington: The Carnegie Foundation for the Advancement of Teaching.

Gross, N. (2008). The Hebrew University's Policy for maintaining its exclusive status: The Tel Aviv Extensions (1950–1970). Jerusalem: The Hebrew University.

Gross, Z. (2006). The educational role of Bar-Ilan University from the point of view of the conflict paradigm. In: D. Schwartz (Ed.), Bar-Ilan university: From concept to enterprise. [a]: Milestones in the History of Departments (pp. 85–106). Ramat Gan: Bar Ilan University.

Grossman, S. (2004). The role of the colleges in the higher education system – the PBC's position – CHE. In: The roles of colleges in expanding Israel's higher education system –lessons learned from the American experience: Lectures presented in a conference dated 8 April, 2003 (pp. 66–57). Tel Aviv: U.S. Israel Education Foundation.

Grossman, S. (Ed.). (2000). The 2001/02–2015/16 multi-annual plan for planning higher education in Israel. Jerusalem: The Council for Higher Education.

Guri-Roseblit, S. (1996). Trends in access to Israeli Higher Education, 1981–1996: From privilege to right. European Journal of Education, 19: 309–325.

Guri-Roseblit, S. (2005). Higher education in transition: Horizontal and vertical patterns of diversity. In: R. Nata (Ed.), New directions in higher education (pp. 23–46). New York: Nova Science Publishers.

Guri-Rosenblit, S. (1999). Changing boundaries in Israeli Higher Education. Mediterranean Journal of Educational Studies, 4: 91–114.

Guri-Rosenblit, S. (2005). Higher education in Transitional times: Horizontal and vertical patterns of internal diversification – professional advancement foundation. Panim: Quarterly for Society, Culture and Education, 34: 63–77.

Guri-Rosenblit, S. (2005). University: Its diverse ideological sources and manifestations. In: I. Gur Zeev (Ed.), End of Israeli Academia? (pp. 23 –68). Haifa: University of Haifa, Department of Education.

HaCohen, D. (2005). "The Historical Alliance" between Ideology and Politics. In: E. Don Yehiya (Ed.), Between tradition and innovation: Studies in Judaism, Zionism and the State of Israel: Yoshua Kaniel – in memoriam. Ramat Gan: Bar Ilan University.

Hans-Vaughn, D. (2004). The impact of parents education level on college students: An analysis using beginning post secondary students longitudinal study 1990–92/94. Journal of College Student Development 45: 483–500.

Hassenger. R. (1967). College and Catholics: An introduction, In: R. Hassenger (Ed.), The shape of Catholic Higher Education (pp. 3–13). Chicago & London: The University of Chicago Press.

Havighurst, R. V. (1989). Education, social mobility and social change in four societies. In: Shapira, R., and Peleg, R. (Eds.), The Sociology of education – a reader (pp. 187–203). Tel Aviv: Am Oved.

Hershkowitz, S. (2007). Research Universities in Israel's expanding higher education system. Jerusalem: The Council for Higher Education.

Horn, L., and Bobbitt, L. (2000). Mapping the road to college: First-generation students' math track, planning strategies, and context of support. Statistical Analysis Report. Postsecondary Education Descriptive Analysis Reports. U.S. Department of Education: National Center for Education Statistics.

Horowitz, D., and Lissak, M. (1990). Trouble in Utopia: The overburdened policy of Israel. Tel Aviv: Am Oved.

Hurtado, S. (1999). Students, colleges, and society: Considering the interconnections. In: P. G. Altbach, R. O. Berdahl, and P. J. Gumport (Eds.), American higher education in the twenty-first century: Social political, and economic challenges (pp. 298–322). Baltimore & London: Johns Hopkins.

Iram, Y. (1977). Theory and practice in Jewish Education: Alexander M. Pushkin's thought and work in the United States and in Israel. Tel Aviv: Cherikover.

Iram, Y. (2013). Religious Universities in the World: A comparative perspective. In: Y. Iram, Y. Friedlander, and S. Ohayun (Eds.), The role of a religious university (pp. 119–129). Ramat Gan: Bar Ilan University.

Iram, Y. (1996). Michlalot Ezoriyot – Regional Colleges in Israel: Challenges, promises, and prospects of an alternative model in higher education. In: R. Latiner Raby, and N. Tarrow (Eds.), Dimensions of the Community College: International, intercultural and multicultural perspective (pp. 291–301). New York: Garland Publishing Inc.

Israel. Central Bureau of Statistics (1981). University students, by degree, demographics and education. Statistical Abstract of Israel, 32: 637.

Israel. Central Bureau of Statistics (1986). University students, by degree, field of study, gender, age, population group and continent of birth. Statistical Abstract of Israel, 37: 596.

Israel. Central Bureau of Statistics (2002). Academic Colleges, 1995/6, 1999/00, 2000/01. Jerusalem: The author.

Israel. Central Bureau of Statistics (2002). Students of Universities and other Institutions of Higher education 2000/01. Jerusalem: The author.

Israel. Central Bureau of Statistics (2003). Academic Colleges, 1995/6, 1999/00, 2000/01. Jerusalem: The author.

Israel. Central Bureau of Statistics (2003). University students aged 20–29 by gender, age and continent of birth. Statistical Abstract of Israel, 54: 8.23.

Israel. Central Bureau of Statistics (2006). Academic Colleges 2003/04. Jerusalem: The author.

Israel. Central Bureau of Statistics (2006). Demographic attributes of candidates, students and recipients of degrees at universities, 2003/04–2004/05. Jerusalem: The author.

Israel. Central Bureau of Statistics (2007). Students of Universities and other Institutions of Higher education 2005/06. Jerusalem: The author.

Israel. Central Bureau of Statistics (2007). Higher education in Israel, 2007/08, publication No 1388, table 20: 51.

Israel. Central Bureau of Statistics (2008). Sixty years – a statistical perspective. Jerusalem: The author.

Israel. Central Bureau of Statistics (2008). Students at Institutions of Higher Education 2006/07. Jerusalem: The author.

Israel. Central Bureau of Statistics (2010). Higher Education in Israel 2007/08. Jerusalem: The author.

Israel. Central Bureau of Statistics (2010). Students at Universities, Academic Colleges and Academic Colleges of Education, by degree. Statistical Abstract of Israel, 61: 8.13.

Israel. Central Bureau of Statistics (2013). Students at Universities, Academic Colleges and Academic Colleges of Education, by degree. Statistical Abstract of Israel, 29 July, 2014.

Israel. Central Bureau of Statistics (2017). Higher Education 2016/17. Statistical 168. Retrieved 9 August 2020. https://old.cbs.gov.il/statistical/stat168_h.pdf

Israel. Central Bureau of Statistics (2018). Statistical Abstract of Israel, 4: 65–90.

Israel. Central Bureau of Statistics (2018). The Ethiopian population in Israel – collection of data on the occasion of the Sigd holiday. Central Bureau of Statistics, Jerusalem.

Israel. Central Bureau of Statistics (2019). Statistical Abstract of Israel, 4: 71–104.

Israel. Central Bureau of Statistics (24 February, 2010). Press Release: In: 2009 14,564 new immigrants (*Olim*) arrived in Israel – a 6% increase compared to previous years. Retrieved 1 August 2010.

Israel. Students administration, Planning, Budgeting and Control Department (2001). Overview of activities and statistical data (1999–2000). Jerusalem: The author.

Israel. Students administration, Planning, Budgeting and Control Department (2006). Overview of activities and statistical data (2004–2005). Jerusalem: The author.

Israel. Students administration, Planning, Budgeting and Control Department (2010). Overview of activities and statistical data (2007–2009). Jerusalem: The author.

Israel. The Council for Higher Education (1992). The Council for Higher Education principle decisions file, 1975–1990. Jerusalem: The author.

Israel. The Council for Higher Education (2007). The tenth Council for Higher Education, principle decisions file, 2002–2007. Jerusalem: The author.

Israel. The Council for Higher Education (2008). Table 4: Undergraduate students at the academic programs of the Regional Colleges 1992/3–2007/08. Retrieved 3 October 2010. http://www.che.org.il/download/files/Table%204.htm

Israel. The Council for Higher Education (3 October, 2010). Collection of data towards the opening of the academic year, 2010/11. Retrieved 3 October 2010. The Council for Higher Education, Jerusalem.

Israel. The Council for Higher Education Planning and Budgeting Committee (1992). Newsletter (The Council for Higher Education Planning and Budgeting Committee), 4: 1–8.

Israel. The Council for Higher Education Planning and Budgeting Committee: Report number 23, 1995–1996. Jerusalem.

Israel. The Council for Higher Education Planning and Budgeting Committee (1997). Higher education in Israel towards the third Millennium. Newsletter (The Council for Higher Education Planning and Budgeting Committee), 9: 5–6.

Israel. The Council for Higher Education. Collection of data towards the opening of the academic year (2019–2020). Retrieved 9 August 2020. https://che.org.il/wp-content/uploads/2019/10

Israel. The Knesset (1994). Education bill (terms of admission to institutions of higher education), 1994. Retrieved 15 May 2009.

Israel. The Knesset (2002). Parliamentary Investigation Committee on social gaps in Israel, led by Knesset member Ran Cohen. Retrieved 1 November, 2010. www.knesset.gov.il/committees/heb/docs/gap15-4.htm

Israel. The Shochat Committee to Examine the Higher Education System (2007). Report of the committee to examine the higher education system. Jerusalem: The author.

Israeli, A. (1997). Master plan: Regional colleges in Israel, development trends, characteristics and planning 1998–2003. Jerusalem: Mashov.

Israeli, A. (2000). Proposal – University Center – Galilee: General plan for the establishment of a multi-campus university center at the Northern District. Jerusalem: Mashov – applicable research, planning and consulting for education, welfare and labor systems.

Israeli, A. (2000). Proposal – University Center – South: General plan for the establishment of a multi-campus university center at the Southern District. Jerusalem: Mashov – applicable research, planning and consulting for education, welfare and labor systems.

James, M. J. (2013). The mission and purpose of college and universities sponsored by Christian Denominations in the USA. In: Y. Iram, Y. Friedlander, and S. Ohayon (Eds.), The role of a Religious University (pp. 7–30). Ramat Gan: Bar Ilan University.

Jones, D. R. (1988). The origins of Civic Universities. London: Routledge.

Katzburg, N. (1979). Introduction. Bar Ilan: Annual Book of Jewish studies and Humanities (pp. 16–17).

Katzburg, N. (1981). Bar Ilan University – twenty five year anniversary. Bar Ilan: Annual Book of Jewish studies and Humanities, 18–19: 5–9. Ramat Gan: Bar Ilan University.

Kave, M. (2001). The universities' challenge. Academia: The Journal of the Committee of University Heads, 9: 4.

Kirsch, A. (2010). Higher education policy in Israel – accessibility, quality and excellence with limited resources. Haifa: The Technion, Israel Institute of Technology.

Kirsch, A. (2014). The Higher Education System in Israel – issues, characteristics and unique aspects. Haifa: Shmuel Neeman Institute, The Technion.

Klein, M. (1998). Bar Ilan, academia, religion and politics. Jerusalem: Magnes Press.

Klein, M. (2004). Religion and Acedemia in Israel. In: A. Cohen, and Y. Harel (Eds.), Religious Zionism: The era of transition, a collection of essays in memory of Zvulun Hammer (pp. 201–253). Jerusalem: Bialik Institute.

Klein, M. (2006). Bar Ilan University's struggle for academic recognition. In: D. Schwartz (Ed.), Bar-Ilan university: From concept to enterprise [a]: Milestones in the History of Departments (pp. 61–23). Ramat Gan: Bar Ilan University.

Kortiokov, D. (2012). Higher education in Israel and OECD countries: A comparative perspective: Analysis of the OECD Report, Education at a Glance. Tel Aviv: The National Union of Israeli Students, Research & Policy Department

Kurzweil, B. (1967). In view of the spiritual confusion of our generation: His writings and critique. Ramat Gan: Kurzweil Institute at Bar Ilan University.

Lenski, G. E. (1996). Power and privilege. A Theory of Social Stratification. New York: McGraw Hill.

Lev Zion, N. (2001). Trends and challenges in planning Higher education in Israel. Economics Quarterly, 48(1): 91–102.

Levi, G. (2006). Education. In: A. Ram, and N. Berkowitz (Eds.), Inequality (pp. 181–188). Beer Sheva: Ben Gurion University.

Liff, H. (1988). Milestones in his life. In: P. Churgin (Ed.), Vision and legacy: Selected works and writings of his life and legacy (pp. 22–34). Ramat Gan: Bar Ilan University.

Lissak, M. (1996). "Critical" and "Institutional" Sociologists in Israel's academic community: Ideological struggles or a practical academic discourse? In: P. Ginosar, and A. Bareli (Eds.), Zionism – a contemporary polemic: Research and Ideological Approaches (pp. 60–98). Kiryat Sde Boker: The Ben Gurion Heritage Center.

Manzur, A. (23 March, 1975). Academization at Kibbutzim, a calling and not a mission. Haaretz Daily Newspaper, Tel Aviv.

Marsden, G. E. (1992). Introduction. In: G. M. Marsden, and B. J. Longgield (Eds.), The Secularization of the academy (pp. 3–7). New York: Oxford University Press.

Marsden, G. M., and Longfield, B. J. (1992). The Secularization of the academy. New York: Oxford University Press.

Marsden, G. M. (1994). The Soul of the American University: From protestant establishment to established non belief. New York: Oxford University Press.

Marsden, G. E. (1992a). The Soul of the American University: A historical overview. In: G. M. Marsden, and B. J. Longfield (Eds.), The Secularization of the academy (pp. 9–45). New York: Oxford University Press.

Meek, V. L., Goedegebuure, L., Kivinen, O., and Rinne, R. (1996). (Eds.). The Mockers and Mocked: Comparative perspectives on differentiation, convergence and diversity in higher education (pp. 206–236). New York: Pergamon for the IAU Press.

Meek, L. V., Goedegebure, L., Kivinen, O., and Rinne, R. (1996). Conclusion. In: Y. Melman (1 November, 1991). Haaretz: The Settlers' College.

Menachem G., Tamir, E., and Shavit. Y. (2008). The transformation of higher education in Israel in the 1990s. In: A. Yogev (Ed.), The expansion of higher education in Israel (pp. 25–53). Tel Aviv: Ramot– Tel Aviv University.

Mendelzweig, R. (Ed.). (1995). Annual Report of the Planning and Budgeting Committee: Report number 21 (1993/1994). Jerusalem: The Planning and Budgeting Committee.

Mendelzweig, R. (Ed.). (1998). Annual Report of the Planning and Budgeting Committee: Report number 24 (1996/1997). Jerusalem: The Planning and Budgeting Committee.

Mevarech, Z. (2006). The Educational metamorphosis of the concept of equality in Higher Education: Implications for Bar Ilan University. In: D. Schwartz (Ed.), Bar-Ilan university: From concept to enterprise [a]: Milestones in the History of Departments (pp. 126–107). Ramat Gan: Bar Ilan University.

Mevarech, Z. (2013). The Role of a religious university: Educational and practical aspects. In: Y. Iram, Y. Friedlander, and S. Ohayun (Eds.), The role of a religious university (pp. 83–94). Ramat Gan: Bar Ilan University.

Meyer, J. W., Ramirez, F. O., Rubinson, R., and Boli-Bennett, J. (1977). The World Education Revolution, 1950–1970. Sociology of Education, 50: 242–258.

Mizrachi, Y. (1994). History of the traditional college model and the Germanic university model in North America. Maof U'Maase at Achva College, 1: 11–26.

Morrison, T. (1998). Welcome to the World: Quality, higher education and change. Mauritius: Mauritius Institute of Education.

Nahon, Y. (1987). Patterns of expansion of Higher education and the structure of employment opportunities: The ethnic dimension. Jerusalem: Jerusalem Institute Israel Studies: Hed Artzi.

Neuberger, B. (1994). Government and politics [unit 6]: Religion, state and politics. Tel Aviv: The Open University.

Neuberger, B. (1997). Government and politics [units 7, 8]: Political parties in Israel. Tel Aviv: The Open University.

OECD: Education at a Glance (2012). Retrieved on 1 March 2020. https://www.oecd.org/education/highlights.pdf

OECD: Education at a Glance (2017). OECD indicators. Retrieved on 1 March 2020.

https://www.oecd-ilibrary.org/education/education-at-a-glance-2017_eag-2017-en

OECD: Education at a Glance (2019). OECD indicators. Executive summary, Retrieved on 1 March 2020.

http://www.oecd.org/education/education-at-a-glance 19991487.htm/?refcode=20190209ig

OECD: Indicators Education at a Glance (2014). Retrieved on 1 March 2020. http://www.oecd.org/education/Education-at-a-Glance-2014.pdf

Parsons, T. (1970). Equality and inequality in modern society, or social stratification revisited. In: E. O. Lauman (Ed.), Social Stratification. Indianapolis: Bobbs-Merrill.

Pazy, A. (2005). The colleges will continue to grow. Panim: Quarterly for Society, Culture and Education, 34: 73–83.

Rabinowitz, A. (2009). The University in a Global World: The new dilemmas of Higher education. New Directions, 20: 88–100.

Rackman, E. (1988). Introductory remarks. In: P. Churgin (Ed.), Vision and Legacy: Selected works and writings of his life and legacy (pp. 9–10). Ramat Gan: Bar Ilan University.

Racover, N. (1989). Hebrew Law in Knesset Legislation: Jewish sources integrated into Knesset discussions and the laws of the State of Israel. Jerusalem: The Jewish Legal Heritage.

Raftery, A., and Hout, M. (1993). Maximally maintained inequality: Expansion, reform and opportunity in Irish Education 1921–75. Sociology of Education, 66: 41–62.

Reardon, S. F. (2011). The widening socioeconomic status achievement gap: New evidence and possible explanations. In: R. J. Murnane, and G. J. Duncan (Eds.), Whither opportunity? Rising inequality and the uncertain life chances of low-income children. New York, NY: Russell Sage Foundation.

Reiss, P. J. (1967). The Catholic College: Some built-in tensions. In: R. Hassenger (Ed.), The shape of Catholic Higher Education (pp. 253–273). Chicago & London: The University of Chicago Press.

Rosen, G., and Razin, A. (2004). The race after the college: Local authorities in Israel competing over institutions of higher education. Jerusalem: Fliersheimer Institute of Policy Studies.

Rubinstein, A. (1995). Amnon Rubinstein, Minister of Education, Culture and Sports. In: A. Shehan (Ed.), Models of Regional Colleges (pp. 38–42). Jerusalem: Ministry of Education, Culture and Sports. Colleges Division.

Rubinstein, A. (2004). The dual role of colleges – institutions of teaching and foundations for future universities. In: The Roles of Colleges in expanding Israel's higher education system – lessons learned from the American experience: Lectures presented in a Conference dated 8 April, 2003 (pp. 35–39). Tel Aviv: U.S. Israel Education Foundation.

Schafferman, K. T. (2007). Inequality in Higher Education in Israel. Retrieved 13 April 2010. http://www.idi.org.il/Parliament/2007/Pages/2007_54/54_D/Parliament_Issue_54_d.aspx.

Schwartz, D. (2006). Bar Ilan, a number of aspects on the idea of the university and Religious Zionism. In: D. Schwartz (Ed.), Bar-Ilan university: From concept to enterprise [a]: Milestones in the History of Departments (pp. 81–63). Ramat Gan: Bar Ilan University.

Schwartz, D. (2013). A Religious University: Bar Ian's model. In: Y. Iram, Y. Friedlander, and S. Ohayun (Eds.), The role of a Religious University (pp. 15–52). Ramat Gan: Bar Ilan University.

Schweitzer, F. (2013). The role of the Religious University: A protestant perspective from Germany. In: Y. Iram, Y. Friedlander, and S. Ohayon (Eds.), The role of a Religious University (pp. 7–30). Ramat Gan: Bar Ilan University.

Shai, S., Dvir, E., Dahan, M., and Mironichev, N. (2002). Has disparity in education diminished? Jerusalem: Van Leer Institute.

Shalmon, Y. (1998/1999). Bar Ilan: Academics, religion and politics (a critique). Megamot 39: 590–597.

Shapira, A. (1997). The Labor Movement and the Hebrew University. In: S. Katz, and M. Heyd (Eds.), The history of the Hebrew University of Jerusalem: Roots and beginnings (pp. 675–689). Jerusalem: Magnes, The Hebrew University.

Shavit, Y. (1984). Tracking and Ethnicity in Israel secondary education. American Sociology Review, 49: 210–220.

Shavit, Y. (1990). Segregation, tracking, and the education attainment of minorities: Arabs and Oriental Jews in Israel. American Sociological Review, 55: 115–126.

Shavit, Y. (1992). Tracking and increasing rates of education among Arabs and Jews in Israel. In: A. Yogev (Ed.), The expansion of higher education in Israel (pp. 64–79). Tel Aviv: Tel Aviv University and Massada.

Shavit, Y., and Kraus, V. (1992). Changes to the educational stratification process on a yearly sequence. In: A. Yogev (Ed.), The expansion of higher education in Israel (pp. 17–28). Tel Aviv: Tel Aviv University and Massada.

Shavit, Y., Cohen, Y., Stier, H., and Bolotin, S. (2000). Ethnic inequality in University education in Israel. In: M. Mautner (Ed.), Distributive justice in Israel (pp. 391–410). Tel Aviv: Ramot.

Shchori, D. (8 May, 2005). The social importance of a 'sparse' undergraduate degree. Haaretz Daily Newspaper, Tel Aviv.

Shenhar-Elroy, A. (2005). Education without Barriers. Panim: Quarterly for Society, Culture and Education, 34: 94–99.

Sherman, N. (1996). Expansion of higher education in Israel and the Regional Colleges. Rehovot: The Center for Development Studies.

Sherman, N. (1996B). The College as a resource in the development of peripheral regions. Rehovot: The Center for Development Studies.

Shmida, M. (1987). Between equality and excellence: Reform in education and the comprehensive school. Ramat Gan: Bar Ilan University.

Shwed, U., and Shavit, Y. (2006). Occupational and economic Attainments of college and university Graduates in Israel. Tel Aviv: Tel Aviv University. Sociology of Education, 77(1): 32–59.

Soen, D. (2004). Center and periphery in education in Israel – Second opportunity for whom? Education and its surroundings: Kibbutzim Seminar Annual, 26: 153–166.

Stav, S. (2009). Development of higher education in Israel. A lecture presented at a discussion on the education committee program. Jerusalem: The Knesset. 11 May, 2009.

Supreme Court 131/81 Moshe Dover vs. The Council for Higher Education, verdict 35 (4), 263, 269–268 (1981).

Svirski, S., and Svirski, B. (1997). Higher education in Israel. Tel Aviv: Adva Center.

Svirski, S. (1990). Education in Israel: The district of separate programs. Tel Aviv: Brerot.

Svirski, S. (1995). Seeds of inequality. Tel Aviv: Brerot.

Svirsky, S., and Conor-Attias, A. (2010). Social Situational Report. Tel Aviv: Adva Center.

Svirsky, S., and Conor-Attias, A. (2017). Social Situational Report 2016. Tel Aviv: Adva Center.

Svirsky, S., Conor-Attias, A., and Abu Khala, H. (2010). Social Situational Report 2010. Tel Aviv: Adva Center.

Svirsky, S., Conor-Attias, A., and Liberman, A. (2018). Social Situational Report 2018. Tel Aviv: Adva Center.

Svirsky, S., Conor-Attias, A., and Ophir, A. (2013). Employees, Employers and the national income pie. Tel Aviv: Adva Center.

Teichler, U. (1988). Changing patterns of the higher education system: The experience of three decades. London: Jessica Kingsly.

The Council for Higher Education Law Bill (amendment-colleges) (1993), The Council for Higher Education, Tel Aviv.

The State Comptroller and Ombudsman (1990). Auspices over academic programs at Regional Colleges. Reports on the supervision at Institutions of Higher Education: 250–273.

The State Comptroller and Ombudsman (1999). Higher education in development towns. Annual Report number 50(b): 71–95.

Tippens, D. (2013). "So Glorious a Work": The evolving idea of the protestant University. In Iram, Y., Friedlander, Y. and Ohayon, S. (Eds.). The Role of a Religious University (pp. 7–30). Ramat Gan: Bar Ilan University.

Tonks, D. (1999). Access to higher education. 1991–1998: Using Geo demographics widening participation and life long learning, 1 (2). Retrieved 1 November, 2010. www.staffs.ac.uk/journal/volume5(1)rev-1.html

Traubman, T. (22 March, 2006). College students were not surprised: University graduates earn more. Haaretz. Retrieved 28 July, 2020. https://www.haaretz.co.il/misc/1.1092725

Trow, M. (2004). On mass higher education and institutional diversity. In: The roles of colleges in expanding Israel's higher education system –lessons learned from the American experience: Lectures presented in a Conference dated 8 April, 2003 (pp. 39–35). Tel Aviv: U.S. Israel Education Foundation.

Trow, M. (1970). Reflections on the transition from mass to universal higher education. Daedal US-Journal of American Academy, Winter: 1–24.

Trow, M. (1974). Problems in the transition from elite to mass higher education. In: Policies for higher education, from the general report on the conference further structures of post-secondary education (pp. 132–64). Paris: OECD.

Tzameret, Z. (1997). Across a narrow bridge – shaping the education system during the Great Aliyah, Kiryat Sde Boker: The Ben Gurion Heritage Center Vakant, L. (2002). On the sociological legacy of Pierre Bourdieu. Israeli Sociology, A Journal for the Study of Society in Israel, 4(2): 437–449.

Valimaa, J. (1999). Managing a diverse system of higher education. In: M. Henkel, and B. Little (Eds.), Changing relationships between higher education and the state (pp. 23–41). London and Philadelphia: Jessica Kingsley.

Volansky, I. (2005). Academia in a changing environment, Israel's Higher Education Policy, 1952–2004. Tel Aviv: Shmuel Neeman Institute for Advanced Scientific and Technology Studies.

Volansky, I. (2010). Reciprocity between higher education and periphery in Israel. In: Z. Tzameret, A. Halamish, and E. Meir-Glitzenstein (Eds.), Development towns in Israel (pp. 321–340). Jerusalem: Yad Izhak Ben-Zvi Institute.

Volansky, I. (2010B). Is there a discrepancy between improving the quality of higher education and its continued expansion and development? A presentation at a conference held at the Ashkelon Academic College.

Warhaftig, Z. (1988). An Israeli Constitution: Religion and the state. Jerusalem: Mesilot, The Global Hamizrachi – Hapoel Center.

Watson, D. (1999). Decoding dearing on diversity. In: M. Henkel, and B. Little (Eds.), Changing relationships between higher education and the state (pp. 37–325). London and Philadelphia: Jessica Kingsley.

Weinger, A. (2016). The Knesset's Research and Information Center. Data on undergraduate students, segmented by field of study and Socioeconomic status. Jerusalem: The Knesset.

Weitmann , S. (2002). Understanding Bourdieu's understanding. Israeli Sociology, A Journal for the Study of Israeli Society, 4(2): 411–425.

Yinon, Y. (2001). Zerach Warhaftig – A Rabbi and a Friend. Bar Ilan: Annual Book of Jewish studies and Humanities, 28–29: 9–12.

Yogev, A. (1992). Expansion of higher education in Israel and globally and its social implications. In: A. Yogev (Ed.), The expansion of higher education in Israel (pp. 7–16). Tel Aviv: Tel Aviv University, School of Education.

Yogev, A. (2000). Stratification of Universities in Israel and its implications of Higher Education Policies. Israeli Sociology, A Journal for the Study of Society in Israel. B (2): 481–498.

Yogev, A. (2008). The expansion of higher education and distributive justice in Israel. In: A. Yogev (Ed.), The expansion of higher education in Israel (pp. 7–23). Tel Aviv: Ramot– Tel Aviv University.

Yogev, A. (2008). The rope followed the bucket: The continuing stratification of university students. In: A. Yogev (Ed.), The expansion of higher education in Israel (pp. 143–163). Tel Aviv: Ramot– Tel Aviv University.

Yogev, A., and Shapira, R. (1992). Education, I.Q and the acquisition of Social Status: Ethnic aspects of Israel's development as a Credential Society. In: A. Yogev (Ed.), The expansion of higher education in Israel (pp. 29–53). Tel Aviv: Tel Aviv University, School of Education.

Yogev, A., Livne, A., Glosman, A., and Ayalon, H. (2008). Tracking in high school and institutional selection in Israel's higher education System. In: A. Yogev (Ed.), The expansion of higher education in Israel (pp. 55–76). Tel Aviv: Ramot – Tel Aviv University.

Zalikowski, D. (2013). Institutional history: The Judea & Samaria College at Ariel (2007–1982) – from College to University. Dor Ledor, 46: 203–235.

Zusman, N., Furman, A., Kaplan, T., and Romanov, D. (2006). Differences in the quality of higher education between universities and colleges: An examination through changes in the work force. Haifa: The Technion, Israel Institute of Technology.

Higher Education Archives

The Council for Higher Education

Report of the Sub-Committee on Colleges: "Academic programs at Regional Colleges – current situation and future policy proposal". 30 August 1992.

The committee on behalf of the Council for Higher Education for discussing Bar Ilan University's plans for a university campus at Zefat. 26 July 1971 (1971). Archive of the Council for Higher Education, pp. 1–17.

Decisions of the Council for Higher Education dated 7 November 1972 (1972). Archive of the Council for Higher Education, number 11(59): 2.

Meeting of the fourth Council, 1973. Archive of the Council for Higher Education, number 18(66): 1–3.

Meeting of the fourth Council – Decisions (1973). Archive of the Council for Higher Education, number 17(65): 1.

Meeting of the fourth Council – 8 November 1971 – Decisions (1971). Archive of the Council for Higher Education, number 1(49): 1

Meeting of the fourth Council (1974). Archive of the Council for Higher Education, number 27(75): 3–5.

Meeting of the fourth Council – Decisions (1975). Archive of the Council for Higher Education, number 28(76): 1.

Meeting of the Council for Higher Education – Decisions (1976). Archive of the Council for Higher Education, number 38(86): 2–9.

Meeting of the Council for Higher Education held in Jerusalem (1976). Archive of the Council for Higher Education, number 38(86): 2–3.

Meeting of the Council for Higher Education held in Jerusalem (1976). Archive of the Council for Higher Education, number 43(91), pp. 9–11.

Minutes of the Meeting of the fourth Council, 12 December, 1971 (1971). Archive of the Council for Higher Education, number 2(50): 2–4.

Minutes of the Meeting of the fourth Council (1974). Archive of the Council for Higher Education, number 23(71): 1–7.

Minutes of the Meeting of the fourth Council (1974). Archive of the Council for Higher Education, number 26(74): 3–11.

Minutes of the Meeting of the fourth Council (1975). Archive of the Council for Higher Education, number 28(76): 1–2.

Minutes of the Meeting of the fourth Council (1974). Archive of the Council for Higher Education, number 24(72): 1–5.

Minutes the Meeting of the fourth Council (1973). Archive of the Council for Higher Education, number 17(65): 1–2.

Minutes of the Meeting of the fourth Council, 25 January 1972 (1972). Archive of the Council for Higher Education, number 3(51): 2–3.

Minutes of the Meeting of the fourth Council (1973). Archive of the Council for Higher Education, number 16(64): 3–5.

Minutes of the Meeting of the third council (1971). Archive of the Council for Higher Education, number 18(46): 1–2.

Summary of the Council's decisions on the matter of colleges (1975). Archive of the Council for Higher Education: 1–4.

Planning of the colleges system in the south and northern regions, concluding remarks, 27 December, 2000. Archive of the Council for Higher Education: 1–7.

The Council for Higher Education/Bar Ilan University – Extensions File

Letter from Prof. A.M. Meir to the Manager of the Extensions at Bar Ilan University, 12 March 1978.

Letter from PBC Chairperson to the Rector, 31 March 1987.

Letter from the Secretary of the CHE to the Manager of the Center for Tertiary Education, 4 November 1975.

Letter from PBC Chairperson to the Rector, 31 March 1987.

Letter from Guri Zilca, CEO of the CHE/PBC to Ms. Nurith Zelig at the office of the Minister of Education and Culture, 22 October 1990.

Collection of data towards the opening of the academic year – 2013/2014. 10 October 2013

Letter from PBC Chairperson to the Chairperson of the Judea and Samaria CHE, 15 July 2012.

Structure of the system of Higher education in Israel and the Judea & Samaria University Center at Ariel. CHE, ref 6400 LC.

Archived Material, Institutions

Ashkelon College Archive

File number	Type of file	Document details
1968	Bar Ilan	Registration form for the 1968 academic year. Letter from Dr. Bar Ilan to the Secretary of the Jewish Federation of South Africa, 25 March, 1968.
1974	Municipality	Letter from the Mayor to the Rector, 26 December, 1974
1975	Municipality	Letter from Mordechai Peled to the Mayor, 5 November 1975. Letter from the Minister of Education to the Mayor of Ashkelon, 30 July, 1975. Letter from CHE Secretary Abraham Ben Yaacov to Mordechai Peled, Manager of the Tertiary Education Center at the Ministry of Education and Culture, 4 November 1975.
1976	Bar Ilan	Program Proposal for a University Extension at Ashkelon, 23 June 1976. Plan for A Bar Ilan University Extension and Teachers' College at Ashkelon, 10 September 1976.
1978	Bar Ilan	Letter from the Rector to the Chairperson of the CHE Colleges Sub-Committee Prof. A.M Meir, 8 January 1978.
1980	Bar Ilan	Letter from Dr. Berreby to the Education Department Manager at Ashkelon Municipality, 4 December 1985.
1983	Bar Ilan	Letter from Dr. Berreby to Moshe Yanai, 10 November 1983. Letter from the Extensions Manager to Moshe Yanai, 4 December, 1983. Letter from Dr. Haim Gaziel who replaced Dr. Berreby as Manager of the Extensions while Dr. Berreby was on sabbatical, to the Mayor of Ashkelon, 7 February 1983. Letter from the Chairperson of the Student Body to the Manager of the Department of Education, 31 March, 1983. Protocol of the Bar Ilan Extension Friends Association, 6 November, 1983.

File number	Type of file	Document details
1984	Bar Ilan	Draft agreement between the Ashkelon Municipality and Bar Ilan University, 13 November 1984.
		Agreement between the Ashkelon Municipality and Bar Ilan University, 1 February 1984.
		Letter from the Rector of the University to the Mayor of Ashkelon, 9 October 1984.
1985	Bar Ilan	Letter from the Chairperson of the CHE Colleges Sub-Committee to the Mayor of Ashkelon, 29 April, 1985.
		Letter from the Manager of the Training Division at the ministry of Labor to the Mayor of Ashkelon, 3 October 1985.
1989	Bar Ilan	Letter from the Rector to the faculty of the university and the Extensions, 11 October, 1989.
1990	Bar Ilan	Letter from the Rector to the Chairperson of the BGS Committee, 1 July 1990.
		Letter from the Rector to the Extensions Manager, 25 June 1990.
		Committee's report submitted for the BGS degree in June 1990.
		Letter from the Rector to the PBC Chairperson, 5 November, 1990. Application of the Mayor of Ashkelon to the CEO of the Ministry of Education Dr. Dan Sharon, 22 May 1990. Letter from the Mayor to the Minister of Education, 24 June 1990. Letter from the Rector to the Minister of Education, 23 September, 1990.
1991	Legal	Proposed Agreement between the College and the University, 18 July 1991. Operating principles for the Ahskelon and Zefat Colleges, 5 June 1991.
1991	Bar Ilan	Letter from the Rector to the Head of the Colleges Administration, 5 June 1991.
		Circular of the Ministry of Education, 30 April 1991. Letter from the Rector to Prof. Babkofh, 19 September 1991. Letter from the Rector to the College Manager, 11 March 1993.

File number	Type of file	Document details
1992	Bar Ilan	Letter from the Deputy Secretary of the CHE, 16 June 1992. Letter from the Rector to the College Manager, 25 June, 1992.
1993	Bar Ilan	Letter from the Rector to the College Manager, 11 March 1993.
1994	Bar Ilan	Letter from the Colleges Managers to the Head of the Colleges Administration at the University, 27 February 1994. Government Decision number 3964, 28 September, 1994.
1995	Ministry of Education	Letter from the Chairperson of the CHE to the Rector, 10 July 1995.
1995	Shapira Committee file	Letter of appointment for the Shapira Committee, 22 June 1995. Prof. Anita Shapira's letter, 16 July 1995.
1996	Ministry of Education	Report of the Sb-committee for examining academic studies, 23 June 1996.
1998	Ministry of Education	Letter from the CEO and the Academic Manager to Prof. Grosman, 1 November 1998 and letter from the Colleges Managers to the President of the University, 28 March 2000.
2000/1	CHE	Letter from the Coordinator of the CHE Sub-Committee to the Head of the Colleges Administration at the university, 13 June 1995. Rules for recognizing the colleges – letter from the coordinator of the CHE Sub-Committee to the Rector, 7 January 1999. Letter from Nissan Limor to the College Manager, 13 July 1998.
2000/1	CHE	Letter from Amir Gat, 13 June 1999. Conditions for completion of studies, as per letter from Ms. Michal Neumann – Coordinator of the CHE Colleges Sub-Committee, 21 June 1999. Minutes of Meeting dated 14 March 1996 Attended by representatives of the PBC, Ministry of Education and the University. Letter from Prof. Lev Zion to the College Managers, 11 January 2000. Letter from Prof. Yehezkel Taler, Deputy Chairperson of the CHE, to the Managers of the Colleges, 20 July 2000. Ashkelon College Archive, CHE file 1/2000. Letter from the CHE Secretary to the Rectors of Bar Ilan and Ben Gurion Universities, 3 May 2001.

File number	Type of file	Document details
		Letter from the managers of the colleges: Ashkelon, Zefat, Jordan Valley, Judea & Samaria, and Western Galilee to the President of the University, 28 February, 2000. Memorandum – Collaboration between Bar Ilan's Extension at Ashkelon and the Sha'ar Hanegev College,
2000/2	CHE	Letter from the Coordinator Colleges Sub-Committee at the CHE, detailing the Sub-Committee's decisions dated 8 July 1994 and 20 July 1998.
		Detailed guidelines for all Regional Colleges were submitted in December 1999 in a guidelines document that included a proposed statute and request for PBC funding.
		Prof. Lev Zion's letter to the Ashkelon College Management, including the "Plan of the Colleges Administration", dated 11 January 2000.
2000/3	CHE	Minutes of meeting dated 19 March 2000, signed by the heads of Achva, Ashkelon and Sapir colleges.

Bar Ilan University Archive

Container number	File number	Document details
1031	13	The Horwitz Committee Report, 27 February 1957
	8	The Corporation's articles of incorporation: Bar Ilan University, 5 August 1954, Addendum 1.
1458	209	Opening remarks by Prof. Churgin at the merger convention between "the Mizrachi" and "HaPoel HaMizrachi", 20 June, 1956.
	203	The management's message in anticipation of the university cornerstone laying ceremony, 7 August 1955.
	210	Protocol of the Higher Education Committee meeting held on 30 September 1956.
	206	University journal, 1967. University journal, 1970. University journal, 1968.

Container number	File number	Document details
1046	122	Students Information leaflet, 21 June, 1956. Bar Ilan University Association Statute, 29 September, 1968. Decisions of the Board of Trustees, 29 June 1971 Letter from the University's General Secretary and the Chairperson of the Finance Committee to the Minister of Education Aran, 28 November 1957.
753	285	Leaflet including responses to fifty questions about the Extensions, 1978–1979. Protocol of the Board meeting held on 30 January 1975 Daniv's letter to the CEO of the University, 2 April 1971. Letter from the Manager of the Extensions to the Rector, 6 April, 1970. Extensions Activity Report, 6 November, 1972 Letter from David Koliv to the Rector, 4 April, 1974 Letter from the Rector to the Mayor of Afula, 20 April 1972 Letter from the Rector to the Mayor of Netanya, 17 May 1972 Annual report from the Manager of the Extensions to the Board of the University, 17 May 1972. Review by the Manager of the Extensions 1972–1973 Letter from the Rector to the Secretary of the CHE, 4 March, 1974. Rector's notification to the Board, 20 January 1974. Letter from the Rector to the Mayors of Ashkelon, Zefat and the Head of the Jordan Valley Regional Council, 29 October 1974. Report of the Manager of the Extensions, 1974–1975. Estimate of expenses and income at the university's Extensions, 1975. Protocol of the Board meeting held on 30 January 1975 Remarks by Ministry Hazani at the Board meeting, 30 January, 1975. Statute of the Association for nurturing higher education in development areas.
753	285	Letter from the university CEO to the Minister of Education, 24 March, 1983 Letter from Prof. Levin to the CEO of the Ministry of Science, 1 December 1982 Zvi Slonim's letter to the CEO of the University, 6 December 1982. Protocol of the Public Council Committee for academic education in development towns, 29 December, 1982 Letter from the Rector to Knesset member Yigal Cohen-Orgad, 19 November, 1987.

Container number	File number	Document details
1088	338	Letter from Dr. Tuvia Bar Ilan to the management of "Hasharon" school in Raanana, 11 October, 1966. Protocol of the Board meeting held on 12 January 1967 Protocol of the Board meeting held on 21 February 1968 Protocol of the Board meeting held on 26 September 1968 Letter from the Manager of the Extensions to the Chairperson of the Board, 2 March 1966 Letter from the Manager of the Extensions to the Rector, 9 June, 1965. Letter from the Rector to the Extensions Manager, 24 July 1968. Report from the Extensions Manager's to the Senate, 4 January 1970 Protocol of the Board meeting held on 8 August, 1973 Protocol of the Board meeting held on 12 June, 1975
474	247	Letter from the university management to the Minister of Education, dated 24 January 1971. Periodical review by the Manager of the Extensions for 1972 Letter from the Secretary of the CHE to the Rector, 21 August 1972 Adv. Meron's letter to the Rector, 10 April 1972 Letter from the Rector to the CHE, 1 June, 1972Letter from the Rector to the Minister of Education, 10 April, 1972 Letter from the Manager of the Extensions to the Rector, 6 April, 1970
747	247	Report of the review Committee for university courses at Ashkelon, 1 January 1968 Dr. Bar Ilan's letter to the Rector, 21 July, 1968. Letter from committee members to the Chairperson of the Board minister Haim-Moshe Shapira, on 19 December 1967 The Jortner Committee Report 1971 Letter from the Manager of the Extensions to the President of the university, 12 February, 1968 Review from the Manager of the Extensions, 27 March, 1970 Letter from the Manager of the Extensions to the Rector, 21 July, 1968

Container number	File number	Document details
Manager of the Colleges	1994	Letter from Prof. Kave to the Minister of Education Prof. Amnon Rubinstein, 4 January 1994.
	1995	Letter from the Secretary of the Sub-Committee, 13 June 1995. Memorandum, 18 June 1995. Letter from the Rector to the Minister of Education, 22 June 1995.
	1996	Letter from Prof. Babkofh, 18 June 1995. Colleges Administration file, 1996. Memorandum, 18 June 1995. Letter from Prof. Ozer Shield to the Rector, 7 May 1996.
F.T.E data	1994–1998	Data for the 1993/4 academic year, based on report dated 22 February 1994 Data for the 1994/5 academic year, based on report dated 1 August 1995 Data for the 1995/6 academic year, based on report dated 4 January 1996 Data for the 1995/6–1996/7 Data for the 1996/7 academic year, based on report dated 17 March 1997 Data for the 1997/8 academic year, based on report dated 29 April 1998

Association of Regional Colleges Archive

File number	Document details
1991	Letter from the Manager of the Colleges Unit at the Ministry of Education to the University's Manager of Colleges, 29 May 1991.
	Letter from the Manager of the Colleges Unit at the Ministry of Education to the Rector, 1 July 1991.
	Record of phone conversation between the Manager of the Colleges Unit at the Ministry of Education and the PBC Chairperson, 27 August 1991
	Documents published by the Manager of the Colleges Unit at the Ministry of Education, 29 October 1991 and 5 November 1991
1992	Circular of the Ministry of Education to the colleges, 24 June 1992

File number	Document details
	Protocol of managers conference held on 23 September 1992
1995	Letter from Guri Zilca, CEO of the CHE/PBC, to Avikam Beller from the Ministry of Finance Budgets Department, 26 March 1995
1997	Plan submitted by Eli Israel: “Master plan – the Regional Colleges in Israel, Development trends, Characteristics and Planning”, 1998–2003.
1997	Letter from the Chairperson of the Association of Regional Colleges to the CEO of the Ministry of Education, 10 February, 1997 Letter from the Chairperson of the Association of Colleges to the Chairperson of the Education Committee, 28 October 1997 Letter from the Chairperson of the Association of Regional Colleges to the Chairperson of the Regional Council’s forums, 28 October, 1997 Letter from the Chairperson of the Regional Colleges to the Ministers of Finance, Education and Foreign Affairs, 28 October, 1997 A similar letter was sent to the ministers from the Chairperson of the development towns, 28 October, 1997
	Minutes of meeting dated 14 September 1997
1998	Letter from Dr. Klein, Manager of the Colleges Division at the Ministry of Education to the CEOs of Regional Colleges, 19 July 1998
1999	Details of the limitations as stated in the letter from the Colleges Sub-Committee coordinator to the Rector, 7 January 1999.
2000	Letter from Prof. Lev Zion to Moshe Nativ, 11 January 2000. Decision of the ministerial committee headed by Haim Ramon, 27 June 2000; Government decision number 58. Government decision number 676 dated 2 September 2001.

File number	Document details
2000	The University of the South – General guidelines for the establishment of a multi-campus and multi-disciplinary university in southern Israel. Eliyahu Israeli, Mashav – applicable research, planning and consulting for The education, welfare and labor systems. Jerusalem, 1999/2000. The study was submitted to the Association in June, 2000.
2003	Letter from the national commissioner of the higher education accessibility program, 8 January 2003.

Zefat Academic College Archive

Letter from the David Koliv to the Mayor of Zefat, 26 February, 1974.

Yesreel Valley Academic College Archive

The auspices agreement between the College and the University of Haifa, 23 January 1973
The auspices agreement between the College and the Open University, 26 March 1976
Addendum to the Agreement between the University of Haifa and Tel Chai College for the 1974/5 academic year
Letter from Knesset Member Burg to the Manager of the Yesreel Valley College, 23 December 1993, including bill proposal number 2261, 26 April 1994.

Jordan Valley Academic College Archive

Agreement between Bar Ilan University and the Jordan Valley Regional Council's Post-Secondary school, 12 August 1968
Regional conference on academic studies at Bar Ilan's Jordan Valley Extension – Trends and transitions required in adjusting to the needs of the region, Certificate dated 6 January 1988 and 27 January 1988, Baemek U'Barama College Journal, 73.
Letter from the Manager of the College to the Rector, 1 December, 1991

Archive of the Institute for the Study of Zionism in Israel

Religious Zionism Archive, division 025, file 15, date of certificate – 18 August 1954
Religious Zionism Archive, division 025, file 15, date of certificate – 23 August 1954

Interviews

Interviewee	Position	Period	Interview date
Prof. Shlomo Grossman	PBC Chairperson	1997–2003	27 October 2009
Prof. Yehezkel Taler	Member and Deputy PBC Chairperson	1994–2009	29 November 2009
Prof. Harvey Babkofh	Head of the Colleges System Administration at Bar Ilan University	1991–1998	17 August 2009
Prof. Zvi Arad	Rector and President of Bar Ilan University	1993–1989	18 December 2007
Dr. Moshe Berreby	Manager of the Extensions	1981–1991	13 December 2007
Dr. Dov Levitan	Head of the Bar Ilan University's Administration of Colleges	1991 onwards	13 December 2007
Yoram Raz	Head of the Yesreel Valley Academic College	1983 onwards	17 August 2009
Nachmi Paz	Head of the Academic College Sapir	1996–2015	8 July 2010
Hebron Trabelci	Head of the Zefat Academic College	1987–2009	18 August 2009
Moshe Yanai	Director of Education at the Municipality of Ashkelon	1986–2011	13 December 2007